Practice Theory

About NAEA

The National Art Education Association is the world's largest professional visual arts education association and a leader in educational research, policy, and practice for art education. NAEA's mission is to advance visual arts education to fulfill human potential and promote global understanding.

Membership includes elementary and secondary art teachers, middle school and high school students in the National Art Honor Society programs, artists, administrators, museum educators, arts council staff, university professors, and students from the United States and several foreign countries. It also includes publishers, manufacturers, and suppliers of art materials; parents; students; retired art educators; and others concerned about quality art education in our schools.

NAEA publishes *Art Education, Studies in Art Education*, and other professional papers on art education; holds an annual convention; conducts research; sponsors a teacher awards program; develops standards for student learning, school programs, and teacher preparation; and co-sponsors workshops, seminars, and institutes on art education. For further information, visit our website at www.arteducators.org.

© 2013 by National Art Education Association
901 Prince Street, Alexandria, Virginia 22314-3008

To order a copy of this book or obtain additional information, contact National Art Education Association: www.arteducators.org or 800-299-8321.

Order No. 321
ISBN 978-1-890160-57-9

Cover: Sonya Clark, *Synapse* (detail), 1998.
Photo credit: Tom McInvaille. Collection of Henry Drewal.

PRACTICE THEORY

Seeing the Power of Art Teacher Researchers

Melanie L. Buffington
and
Sara Wilson McKay,
Editors

Contents

NOTE: Headers on odd-numbered pages in Sections II-V reflect the chapter number and subsection title.

Acknowledgments

We would like to express our gratitude to the following people who assisted us in various ways throughout the process. First we thank NAEA, and specifically the Professional Materials Committee, for finding merit in our book proposal. Additionally, we thank all the respondents to our call who confirmed the need for and showed interest in this text. The NAEA Publications Staff patiently answered numerous questions and guided us through NAEA's publication process.

VCU's School of the Arts awarded us a Dean's Faculty Research Grant to cover editing and image expenses for which we are thankful. **Robert Sandkam** provided continual technical assistance throughout the process and offered us assurance that all the files were secure. **Yuki Hibben** and **Kristina Keogh**, the fantastic arts librarians at VCU, helped finding resources and purchasing library books for us to use. **Dr. Monika Markowitz**, in VCU's Office of Research, provided guidance for the IRB section.

In working with graduate students over the years, we are grateful for the provocations and ideas that prompted our interest in this topic. **Amy Bergh**, a current art teacher and Art Education graduate student at VCU, offered invaluable thoughts in the form of sidebars throughout seven chapters of the book. **Alana Greer**, a graduate student in Art Education at VCU, worked tirelessly as our research assistant for a year and handled much of the correspondence and the details of organizing so many authors and files. **Gerardo Perez**, a graduate student in Art Education at VCU, updated the graphic in Chapter 3.

We are grateful to **Dr. Pamela Taylor**, who served as our supportive department chair during this process and kindly read the manuscript to write the Foreword. Also we wish to recognize the ongoing support of our coworkers in the Art Education Department at VCU: **Sarah Branigan Fought, Marlena Brown, Dr. David Burton, Jan Johnston,** and **Dr. Nancy Lampert.**

We were fortunate to have **Dr. Enid Zimmerman** read and edit the chapters we wrote. As one of the editors of the groundbreaking 1997 research text from NAEA, Enid's ongoing mentorship and guidance mean a great deal to us.

We thank our families and friends for their love and support, especially Steven, Avery, and Ainsley. We also value each other as colleagues and friends and recognize the depth and importance that can come from collaborative efforts.

Foreword

PAMELA G. TAYLOR, PHD / RESEARCH DIRECTOR AND PROFESSOR, DEPARTMENT OF ART EDUCATION, VIRGINIA COMMONWEALTH UNIVERSITY, RICHMOND, VA

POWER… a provocative take on teacher research that distinguishes this book from many others. According to French philosopher, sociologist, and historian Michel Foucault (1980), power is deeply associated with everyday existence and takes many forms that both enable and control—beyond mere governmental or penal authorities. However strong or glaring the word and idea of "power" and its associations, editors Melanie Buffington and Sara Wilson McKay use it in this book to inspire and encourage while at the same time provoke teacher-guided and reflective research practices.

In keeping with Buffington and Wilson McKay's compelling use of metaphoric research connections throughout this book, I will share my personal approaches/links to research in this Foreword. I engage in academic research and writing practice in much the same way that I reverently set about making a work of art (as I am sure many others do, as well). I use the word "reverently" here because I believe strongly that artmaking at this point in my life should be pointed, if not poignantly meaningful—carrying with it a POWER to change those who view it. Indeed, with this chosen approach to the artmaking aspect of my profession comes a heady sense of purpose that requires a balance between a sense of wonder and a dedication toward grounded inspiration.

An artmaking idea, problem, impulse, area of attention, and/or important change or awareness may present itself to me in a variety of ways. Using what the editors of this book call a "lens of research," a scene from nature, a single blade of grass, or even a facial expression of someone I love (or not) often causes me to want to know more in order to see further. A news story about something I deeply care or am concerned about for personal or professional reasons may inspire me to look, ask questions, share, and discuss the topic/event/idea with others. In other words, before I ever consider making a piece of art I—in one way or another—work to know and understand that which is inspiring me. I have to do that. What I make cannot be meaningful to anyone nor world-changing without being supported through an honest, true, and inclusive investigation.

Granted, knowing and understanding are very different things. Although I use research to know, I believe that my understanding is greatly enhanced through my personal practice and connection. How does the news story affect those people and places I hold most dear? In addition to a precious shared memory, a moment of discovery, or just the wonder of nature, how does that scene or single blade of grass inform my view of the world, now and in the future? Typically, my understanding results from connective and practical research. I make marks on paper (tangible and virtual). I have boisterous discussions (silent and aloud). I plan and re-plan, crumple papers (deleted words, sentences, lines, and files), make experiments with marks and layers, and doodle through a form of mindful inquiry (Sullivan, 2005; Walker, 2009).

Like many artists, there are materials that I am typically drawn to use (pun intended). But, often just drawing is not enough. I have to look at other materials, techniques, indeed methodologies to use that are well-matched or appropriate for the project. Like editors Buffington and Wilson McKay's research metaphor of building a house in Chapter 5, the larger and important decisions related to structure and media must be considered before working on analytical details in research **and** artmaking. As a former secondary art teacher, I saw my share of highly detailed but disproportionate, skewed in perspective, and awkwardly gestured art projects. Although creative and inventive ways of breaking artistic conventions are often highly valued, an effective and meaningful artist—like a sound researcher—knows the rules before they toy with them.

That said, I can't overlook the power of artistic and research play, happy accidents, and slippages often associated with Freud and Lacan's theories of coded verbal signs of the unconscious (Fink, 2007). As driven and focused as I may be, it is often not until I step back that I become aware of deeper and more meaningful ideas and artistic ways of working. Similar to the idea that what I thought was going to happen in a research study gave way to something much more interesting and important, often my original intention for a work of art gives way to something better if I take time to step back and rejoice in just letting some things happen. Reflecting and understanding, as the editors of this book value, to authentically know our practices or ways of working is crucial for both artmaking and teacher research. Doing so with enough lightheartedness to allow a clearer view, embrace a differing stance, and/or just understanding more fully is an important practice for artist researchers.

After and/or during all these practices and ways of thinking, I draw, paint, glue, write, and/or type. When I feel stuck, in both my writing and my artmaking, I go back and think, "What is it that I want to say? What do I want my viewer/reader to do or think?" I may, for example, stop and write something like, "I want teachers to understand that **they** are really smart and powerful!" or "I want artists to know that they make powerful meaning **as a result** of their own research, training, media experiences, lives **and** intuitive play." Reminding myself of my basic intent as well as rethinking my key concepts keeps me from straying too far from the point—an annoying experience for both artists and researchers.

As mentioned earlier, I very much try not to attend to details until I feel the art work/research study is sufficiently grounded or structured. When it is time, I look very carefully, then look again. I read and re-read—always aloud. I refine areas in artwork with deeper values or intensities. I add headings and construct segues between paragraphs. Although often extremely messy, at this point I may block out or completely rework one or many areas of my art or writing as a result of this detailed reflective activity. Such intense (and cluttered) criticality is crucial to making meaning. As Graeme Sullivan (2005) so eloquently put it:

> …it is often from experiences that are both simple and complex, precise and uncertain, that the most insightful outcomes are revealed, and the most important questions arise. Thus it is not necessary to assume that theories are neat, practices are prescribed, all outcomes can be predicted, or that meanings can be measured. The messy resistance of new understanding relies on the rationality of intuition and the imagination of the intellect, and these are the kind of mindful processes used in art practice as research. (p. 226)

Such mindful processes do not stop once the artist/researcher puts down their proverbial paintbrush and pen. Indeed, exhibition, publication, and hopefully a long relationship with viewers, readers, other artists, and researchers adds layer upon layer of human and world significance to the art and research. I imagine this book to be one of those intensely used by teachers, graduate students, and professors—young and old. I'm sure that my copy will be tattered, torn, and heavily laden with highlights, dog-eared pages, and scribbled comments. I am honored to write this Foreword for this noteworthy book, edited by two shining stars in our art education profession. Melanie and Sara, thank you for all of your hard work. This book will make a difference!

REFERENCES

Fink, B. (2007). *(Jacques Lacan) Ecrits: The first complete edition in English*. New York, NY: Norton & Company.

Foucault, M. (1980). *Power/Knowledge: Selected interviews and other writings 1972-1977*. C. Gordon (Ed.). New York, NY: Pantheon.

Sullivan, G. (2005). *Art practice as research: Inquiry in the visual arts*. Thousand Oaks, CA: Sage.

Walker, S. (2009). Artmaking, subjectivity and signification. *Studies in Art Education, 51*(1), 77-89.

Introduction

MELANIE L. BUFFINGTON AND SARA WILSON MCKAY

GRADUATE STUDENTS IN EDUCATION: *I think that I've always done research in my teaching, but I did not call it research. Now, after this class, I make more notes about what I am doing when I change my curriculum, try something new for classroom management, or try something different in my teaching. (personal communication, December 12, 2007)*

Though the approach to research presented in this class might be helpful for people in universities, it just is not applicable to the world of public schooling. Teachers do not have the time, power, or ability to make changes in their classroom. Research just isn't the job of teachers, it never has been and it never will be. (personal communication, December 12, 2007)

Having a supportive environment at work can lead to many things. In our case, it led to discussions about art education graduate students' reactions to research and the practice of teaching that became the kernel of the idea for this book. Through casual conversations across the hall, over coffee, and in our offices, we shared ideas, hopes, and frustrations about graduate students conducting research. In reflecting upon our teaching and our work advising students, we came to believe that our expectations of students conducting research and their ideas about their roles in their schools did not align. As former public school teachers who now teach in an art education department at the university level, we see ourselves as both teachers and researchers. We felt a book expanding the views of research for art teachers could be useful to art education and for resisting the narrative of the powerless teacher. In our many visits to schools and interactions with teachers in our classes, we are reminded of times when we felt both powerful and powerless in the classroom. As university professors, we still have those moments.

We used to teach middle school and conducted informal research about our teaching. Now we teach at the university level and conduct both informal and formal research. We both believe strongly in the power of teachers and the power that exists in the relationship between teaching and research. But, in writing this book, we felt compelled to acknowledge ideas of the powerless teacher. Why is it that many teachers do not recognize their power?

The narrative of the powerless teacher is not new, as evidenced by the work of Banicky and Noble (2001) more than a decade ago. In their report, they looked at ideas behind the standards-based reform movement and realities of those who implemented reforms in the public schools in Delaware. They found a sense of powerlessness among teachers relating to many factors that were out of control as well as decrease in the number of decisions teachers could make, resulting in a "a culture of compliance" (p. 16). Further, they noted that teachers seemed to be resigned to their inability to make change. One teacher said, "Well, this is what the state has mandated. This is what you have, do it" (p. 18). Another teacher mentioned, "Teachers will do anything you tell them to do. Isn't that sad?" (p. 18). We believe that the increase in standardization at the state and national level as well as teacher attitudes may be contributing factors to the perception of powerlessness of teachers.

> When teachers are surrounded by other teachers complaining of their inability to do anything and their lack of power, it is easy to become "retired in place." It takes courage and determination to find ways to make changes and to not surrender to an environment of negativism. Teachers have to maintain positive attitudes and look for ways to creatively meet standards and expectations. There is always an easy way out but seldom does that benefit the student or the teacher.
>
> AMY BERGH[1]

When the Virginia Standards of Learning testing began I was astounded by the number of teachers, administrators, and parents who felt everyone should just teach to the test. Veteran teachers complained about all the things they would no longer be able to teach and how regulated everything would be. Although there are many who still feel very restricted by the state regulations, innovative teachers have found ways to move beyond the "standards" and have made learning fun and interesting for students. They teach for higher level thinking skills and not just how to pass a test. It is easy to blame and settle in teaching, to become a victim not an agent of change. Most teachers enter the field of education and researching to do what they do better, and that is why these activities offer such empowering experiences.

AMY BERGH

One of our hopes with this text is to work against this notion of powerlessness while making visible the power we believe teachers possess. We view teachers as powerful individuals who have the ability to effect change and meaningful educational reform. We write this book to help teachers recognize what they already do as intellectual work. Seeing research at the heart of teaching is a way to grow engaged educational practice. Said another way, we hope that this book works toward unearthing the relationship between what research is and why to conduct it. We believe this is a step toward teachers realizing their power and working toward educational reform.

Though there are excellent books about teachers as researchers (Burnaford, Fischer, & Hobson, 2001; Mills, 2007), excellent books about educational research (Creswell, 2007; Jaeger, 1997; Luttrell, 2010), and excellent books about art education research (Eisner & Day, 2004; Klein, 2012; LaPierre & Zimmerman, 1997; Sullivan, 2004, 2009), this book presents an additional approach to theories of research and realities of practical implementation from an art education perspective. It is also a book advocating teacher research as educational reform. Like Cuban (2003) we think that reform includes and should result in meaningful changes in classroom practice.

AUDIENCE

Though the main audience for this text is master's level students who are art educators as well as beginning researchers, this book also contains ideas for advanced researchers. We use the terms "teachers," "educators," "researchers," "teacher researchers," and "graduate students" throughout the book to refer to the multiple roles that many graduate students hold simultaneously. By including chapters on methodologies as well as example studies that take place in art education settings, we work to bridge the perception of a divide between theory and practice. Through this text, teachers and researchers can benefit from the rich knowledge of art teachers, university faculty members, and museum educators who may hold multiple roles. Further, we believe that educators can learn quite a bit from other educators, regardless of their discipline or the setting in which they teach. Though most of the examples and chapters in this text relate to art education in public school classroom settings, we intentionally include examples from other settings including senior citizen centers, preschools, museums, and international sites. Additionally, we chose pieces that reflect facets of education that may not be sufficiently addressed in other places including race, culture, sexual orientation, class, gender, nationality, among others.

We also wanted to ensure the inclusion of a voice from someone who lives the daily practice of a teacher researcher. Thus, we invited Amy Bergh, a graduate student from our program at Virginia Commonwealth University, to serve as a teacher commentator throughout this first section of the book.

Our current positions teaching preservice and in-service art teachers take us into a variety of schools in several local districts and give us an opportunity to see a wide range of teachers and schools and allow us to experience many school cultures. We view engaged teachers as powerful individuals who can and do conduct research on a regular basis in their continual improvement of their teaching practices. When teachers see what they do as working from a position of power, this may affect their research and teaching practices. We believe that our society does not routinely recognize teaching as a powerful profession.

Supporting teachers in coming to see their roles in the classroom as potentially being catalysts for change can help them understand the power of research and the powerful position that they hold. This increased awareness of their power and the ways that research improves teaching practices may lead to educational reform.

ORGANIZATION

This book is a collaboration of voices. Not only do our (Melanie and Sara's) voices converge on the subject of research from at least two different perspectives, but we also include a wide range of researchers who have various perspectives on how research occurs in art education. When we put out our call to the NAEA audience inviting submissions, we received many responses. We worked to include many of these voices as we felt it was important for this book to be as representative of the field as possible. Thus, this text is a collaboration of voices, telling tales of research, what works for some, what barriers others encountered, what

One advantage to teaching high school students is that they have a tendency to contact their teachers after graduating. Over the years I have been amazed at what the students remember about their high school art experiences. They are amusing when they ask for information about a project that they carried out years earlier and share stories about how something they "had" to do in high school greatly benefited them in college or with their job or family. These encounters cause me to repeatedly realize that I never really know what lasting impact I might have on the students I teach. These might not be major life-altering events, but to know that I influenced a student by making them feel more confident or helped them see the relevance of what they were doing makes me realize that what I do does indeed make a difference.

AMY BERGH

methodologies or methods work best for a particular study. Our hope is that all of these voices will help new researchers, teachers who may not have considered conducting research as a possibility for them, find a glimpse of themselves as a teacher-researcher in the contributions offered in this book.

When organizing this book, we were faced with a choice of creating the book by types of methodologies, or by issues. This research text is not just a "how to" book; it also is about helping teachers see the power of their practice and how this relates to research. Therefore, we chose to frame this entire text through a lens of teacher power that relates directly to issues facing art educators.

We consider this to be a partly edited book in which we co-wrote seven chapters, selected many others from among the submissions to a national call, and invited specific authors to contribute. The contributions range in length, but we included and grouped many to show important relationships in the varied topics. In this manner, the book shares the collective knowledge of various scholars in our field.

We organized the book around a variety of issues and goals that researchers may hold, rather than by quantitative and qualitative boundaries. The book is organized into five major sections: (I) Teaching, Research, and Power; (II) Knowing Our Practices; (III) Understanding People; (IV) Making Meaning; and (V) Changing Our Practices. We envision this book as a step in working toward more meaningful dialogue and interaction between faculty members, graduate students, and teachers in communities.

Through the chapters we wrote in the Teaching, Research, and Power section, we introduce the idea of teachers as powerful agents of change, the concept of paradigms and their relationship to research, and the process of identifying and clarifying meaningful problems in art education.

MELANIE: *As we collaborated to write chapters for this book, we were forced to rethink our habituated practices and beliefs. At times, our thoughts aligned smoothly and at other times, we found ourselves in the midst of significant quandaries about what it means to be a teacher or a researcher. Now, as we are in the final stages of editing, we literally cannot discern who wrote what portions and realize that we have rethought certain sections because the process of creating this book has changed our ideas and beliefs. We fully expect to continue growing in our ideas about teaching, research, and power and hope that the readers of this book will too.*

In the remaining sections, which include chapters and contributions written by many art educators, we organize the book around topics that teachers might want to know more about and address the underpinnings of why teachers engage in research. Accordingly, we grouped some methodologies that relate to various motivations for conducting research. Clearly, most methodologies can be used in a variety of ways. Each section introduction includes a variety of questions designed to encourage educators to embrace formalized research methodologies given their unique teaching scenarios and situational research questions. The methodology descriptions and exemplars provide ways to think about research for particular purposes, but are not intended to be limiting. We intentionally linked a methodological description with an example study to activate the ideas presented in the methodology description. Indeed, we view a variety of research methodologies as different tools that may be more appropriate for different research problems in the same way that hammers, screwdrivers, and pliers are all useful tools for different jobs. It is not that one tool is superior to another, but that it is a matter of finding a tool that will work well for the particular job to be done or finding a methodology that is appropriate and makes sense for the research project to be conducted.

Section II: Knowing Our Practices addresses specific methodologies including survey, quasi-experimental, and arts-based research. Through Section III: Understanding People, readers are introduced to methodologies that relate to research about people including ethnography, historical research, and portraiture. Section IV: Making Meaning explores theoretical research, case study, and narrative and autobiographical research. Through Section V, entitled Changing Our Practices, the contributors examine action research, participatory action research (PAR), tips and considerations for conducting meaningful research, and two complete research studies. The final chapter of the book offers many suggestions for being successful in a first research project, including some helpful technology tools, and discusses the powerful roles art teachers can play in shaping the field of art education through research.

Throughout the book, we utilize metaphors that work toward connecting research with everyday life with which teachers may be familiar. For instance, when creating a work of art, an artist makes conscious choices about many things including media, size, content, and style. All of these contribute toward the meaning of the work of art. Likewise, when planning a research study, a researcher must choose a topic to study, find a methodology that is appropriate, and develop a sound research question. All these factors are interrelated and all contribute to the meaning of the research study. As an artist makes decisions, experiments, refines, and reworks an artwork, a researcher also utilizes processes that are appropriate for conducting a particular research study.

REFERENCES

Banicky, L. A., & Noble, A. J. (2001). *Detours on the road to reform: When standards take a backseat to testing.* Retrieved from University of Delaware, Education Research & Development Center website: http://dspace.udel.edu:8080/dspace/handle/19716/2407

Burnaford, G., Fischer, J., & Hobson, D. (2001). *Teachers doing research: The power of action through inquiry.* Mahwah, NJ: Lawrence Erlbaum.

Creswell, J. (2007). *Educational research: Planning, conducting, and evaluating quantitative and qualitative research.* Upper Saddle River, NJ: Pearson Education.

Cuban, L. (2003). *Why is it so hard to get good schools?* New York, NY: Teachers College Press.

Eisner, E., & Day, M. (Eds.). (2004). *Handbook of research and policy in art education.* Reston, VA: National Art Education Association.

Jaeger, R. M. (1997). (Ed.). *Complementary methods for research in education.* Washington, DC: American Educational Research Association.

Klein, S. R. (2012). *Action research methods: Plain and simple.* New York, NY: Palgrave and MacMillan.

LaPierre, S. D., & Zimmerman, E. (Eds.). (1997). *Research methods and methodologies for art education.* Reston, VA: National Art Education Association.

Luttrell, W. (2010). (Ed.). *Qualitative educational research.* New York, NY: Routledge.

Mills, G. E. (2007). *Action research: A guide for the teacher researcher.* Upper Saddle River, NJ: Pearson Education.

Sullivan, G. (2004). *Art practice as research: Inquiry in the visual arts.* Thousand Oaks, CA: Sage.

Sullivan, G. (2009). *Art practice as research: Inquiry in the visual arts* (2nd ed.). Thousand Oaks, CA: Sage.

ENDNOTE

1   Amy has been teaching art at the secondary level since 1993 and in 2008 enrolled in the master's degree program in Art Education at Virginia Commonwealth University. She currently teaches at a high school with a schedule that changes every year and includes everything from Art Foundations, to AP Portfolio, to Art History. During her time at this school, she has helped increase the number of courses in the art program from 4 to 13 courses. As a child, Amy moved frequently with her family. By the time she began high school, she had already changed school nine times, lived in Germany, and traveled throughout Cold War Europe for 8½ years. Currently, Amy lives in Williamsburg, Virginia, with her retired art teacher husband Brian and three children Laura, Eleanor, and Theodore.

1 / T(Res)ea(r)cher

MELANIE L. BUFFINGTON AND SARA WILSON MCKAY

SARA: *In the course of one week in 2009, my daughters' two different schools hosted events for teachers to share their experiences with the school community. The first evening, a PTA meeting at an elementary school, included three teachers' reports about their recent travels to Spanish-speaking countries. These excursions, funded by the Parent Teachers Association (PTA), were designed to encourage and build a Spanish language culture in this school. The first teacher shared a few slides of her time in a school in Mexico as she learned to speak Spanish, culminating in her claim that it was not a good idea to take her spouse to witness her humiliation at not speaking a language well. With the aid of a PowerPoint, the second teacher described how her spouse and children accompanied her on her adventure in Costa Rica, reiterating over and over again how far they had to walk to receive their repetitive meal of rice and beans from their host family. The third teacher shared her love of Spain, wishing she had the technological savvy to share her pictures that evening, and repeatedly mentioning how beautiful Madrid was and how she had challenged herself to stay with a host family to further authenticate her Spanish experience. The evening was punctuated with a few misty-eyed moments when the teachers alluded to how their travels helped them remember how it feels to be a student learning new material, at times feeling very unsure of this new learning. The evening's program, a testament to a PTA's commitment to providing teachers experiences to grow and enhance their teaching, was a celebration of that investment with the teachers' words demonstrating a positive outcome of that investment.*

Later that same week, at my younger daughter's preschool, three teachers, who had just returned from presenting at the National Association for the Education of Young Children (NAEYC) conference, shared research from their classrooms that they had conducted the previous year. The research related to how young children respond to "wild spaces" (the unstructured outdoors). Important points throughout the presentation included an acknowledged intention by the teachers to spend time outside every day, despite the weather or other happenings within the school. The teachers contextualized their thinking and observations by reflecting what they noticed about the children in comparison with a book the teachers had read by Nabhan and Trimble (1994) titled The Geography of Childhood. *The teachers further compared and examined related practices of teachers around the world. One of the collaborating teachers reflected on gendered interactions of the children in the wild space outside their school walls. Another teacher closely attended to how children confronted risk when they were in new situations that the outdoor space provided. The actual delivery of the research was very well-planned and well-articulated, with teachers reading a fully developed paper while projecting carefully selected accompanying visual images. While it is tempting to understand this presentation as an uncommon activity of a small group of dedicated teachers, at the conclusion of this presentation, another group of teachers at this preschool presented their findings on what they learned about their students when the students wondered, predicted, and then explored what happened to the school at night. Clearly, this school supports a culture of research involving observation, documentation, and reflection that is not limited to just one or two teachers. The conversation that ensued after the presentations further extended the meaningfulness of the research as parents and other teachers responded to additional questions posed by the teachers.*

In reflecting on these two events, the first evening was indeed a nice communal sharing with its moral lesson in place—that is to say, by being a student in another country, the teachers recollected about being mindful of their own students' experiences. However, in light of the very professional, yet open, sharing of research in the second evening, the first evening pales in comparison. On the second evening, the commitment and professionalism with which each of the presenting teachers approached their teaching practice and the involvement of parents and community members in their questioning, demonstrated a full-on engagement by the teachers through a research lens.

Chapman (1982) suggested that, "Research is a process of being honest with ourselves and others. That is what makes it so challenging, demanding, and necessary, both to the conduct of our work and to the perception that others have of the work we do" (p. 112). If the Spanish travelers from the first evening had used a lens of research, how might their teaching practice change and how might the public perception of what a teacher does change?

The title of this chapter, "T(Res)ea(r)cher," shows our commitment to cultivating an enriched and integrated concept of the art teacher researcher. While this text is focused on art teaching and learning and its relationship to research, the opening examples of this chapter suggest a relationship of teaching and research that may apply to any teaching situation. By writing the words teacher and researcher in this overlapping fashion, we suggest that these roles do not coexist as alternating realities, nor that the roles produce a hybridity. Instead, the graphine T(Res)ea(r)cher is intended to make visible the shared components of both of these roles, present at all times in each of these capacities. As former K–12 teachers and now university professors, we believe that these roles mutually inform each other in significant ways. This chapter explicates how we see research and teaching as necessarily intertwined endeavors to achieve meaningfulness.

TEACHER RESEARCH

The idea that we can improve our teaching practice through research is not new and many educators have advocated this for years (Cochran-Smith & Lytle, 1993, 2009; Crosdaile, 2007; Erickson, 1986; Kincheloe, 2003). Known by many names, including reflective practice, action research, and teacher inquiry, the premise is that teacher research is "systematic and intentional inquiry carried out by teachers" (Cochran-Smith & Lytle, 1993, p. 7). This type of inquiry may take a variety of forms including studying classroom issues, teacher identity, school structure, and developing culturally relevant instruction (McGlinn Manfra, 2009). Within art education, Wanda May (1993) examined action research and explained how it contributes to the importance of continuing to learn about teaching:

> Learning to teach is a lifelong endeavor. Were we to know all there is to know about art, teaching, students, and ourselves upon initial certification, the remainder of our life's work would be incredibly predictable, unresponsive, and boring. Fortunately, neither life nor any profession is like this, and learning things that matter to us is never predictable or boring. Thus, I am operating on the assumption that most of us are not "burned out" or cynical about teaching and that teaching art matters to us a great deal. (p. 114)

Later, Zimmerman (2004) explored the idea that the knowledge base in our field related to art teacher education is still developing. Further, she emphasized how important it is for teachers to develop habits of reflective practice. We are writing this book from a similar mindset as May (1993) and Zimmerman (2004) and believe that research related to teaching practice is an important means to improve our practice as art educators.

> It is incredibly easy to get caught up in the daily events of life and teaching and think everything is as good as it can get. Reading about and conducting mini research within my classroom has totally reenergized my teaching.
>
> AMY BERGH

RELEVANCE OF RESEARCH TO ART EDUCATORS

When working with teachers conducting research projects, we have noticed many different attitudes toward research among our students, depending upon their previous experiences, attitudes toward their jobs, and view of their positions as being either powerful or powerless. These attitudes range from the recognition that research is an ongoing part of their practice to a significant amount of resistance to the concept and practice of research.

Based upon student comments, Buffington and Ishii (2008) developed a continuum of four stances that master's students in education took toward teacher research. Through their analysis of two classes of master's students, who were simultaneously teachers and graduate students enrolled in research classes, they developed a framework to understand the various lenses through which their students viewed research.

The four stances are recognition, reservation, reluctance, and resistance. The students who fell in the recognition category made comments indicating that they conducted inquiry on a regular basis in their classroom. However, many of them indicated that they did not previously consider this type of work research. In fact, learning about research in their graduate coursework helped them think about their daily practice of teaching in a more nuanced manner. The teachers in this category were the most interested and enthusiastic about their teaching practice and viewed research as an ongoing process that would help them make connections, throughout their careers, between the theoretical and practical aspects of their profession.

The students who had reservations about conducting research indicated their beliefs that they likely could not remain unbiased with regard to teaching their own students; they also expressed concerns about the act of reporting research that might have negative findings. The idea that their research might show a problem with their teaching, their students, or their school concerned them significantly. Though they were not opposed to research, they were concerned about the results of their research and how those results could be used or interpreted by others.

Students who indicated a reluctance to conduct research expressed the viewpoint that they were not sure that it would help their teaching, that it might take them away from their actual, immediate work with students, and it was likely they could learn just as much, if not more, by interacting with other teachers. These students seemed to view the concept of research as an additional burden on them that was not particularly likely to improve their teaching practices.

The fourth category, resistance, included the teachers who were, by far, most opposed to the concept of research as a component of teaching. The teachers in this category expressed their beliefs that research is not a part of teaching, teachers are powerless, and that teachers do not have abilities to make any meaningful changes. This group concerned us the most because they seemed to internalize a sense of learned powerlessness (Lieberman & Miller, 2005). If art teachers view their role in a school setting as being powerless and unable to affect meaningful change, they may be less likely to try new ideas and work toward their growth as professionals.

LEARNED POWERLESSNESS

An old joke goes, "What are the three best reasons to become a teacher?" The answer "June, July, and August" reinforces the perception that art teachers work fewer hours than others and that art teachers are not continually engaged in their profession. Unfortunately, many teachers, including those in preservice programs, fall easily into this trap of learned powerlessness (Lieberman & Miller, 2005), and seemingly, do not want to recognize the power that they do, in fact, have. Why does this happen?

We believe that art teacher education programs and the routine practice of public schooling do not do enough to encourage art teachers to see themselves and their profession as a site of power. Instead, there is often an anesthesia of complacency and rule-following behaviors. In much the same way that students who follow rules, perform adequately, and do not challenge traditional ideas are rewarded, so too are art teachers who work within a set of parameters that may not encourage new ideas and breaking traditions. Advocating a view of public education that is necessarily dynamic and responsive, we believe that art teachers can be powerful agents of change if they see and embrace the transformative power that they have in their classrooms. When art teachers believe they do not have any power or if they choose to ignore their strength, then they may succumb to the society-promoted view of art teaching as a fun and easy profession and as a way of getting paid for making cute art with children.

A TOUR GUIDE'S STORY OF UNRECOGNIZED POWER

MELANIE: *As a tour guide at a contemporary art center while in graduate school, I participated in numerous training sessions related to the exhibits. During these training sessions, the tour guides received volumes of information about the artwork, we listened to curators lecture about the works, we participated in sessions with the museum educators teaching us about how to talk about the artwork, and we often saw the artist lectures too. While observing other tour guides, I noticed that some repeated the information we received verbatim, but others did not. As I observed more and more tours led by different tour guides, I began to see the position as a powerful one and recognized how certain tour guides exercised their power by bringing in their own knowledge and experiences to enrich what the gallery provided to us. Though we were not paid, were not evaluated, and were not consulted, we had a significant amount of power in shaping the experiences of school groups at the museum. Over the years since this experience, I have reflected a great deal about how and where power circulates. Once I came to see my role as a tour guide as a powerful one, it changed how I approached the position.*

The situation of tour guides in museums may be analogous to many teachers in the classrooms. As the museum educators may develop tour materials in a museum, specialists often develop school curriculum at the national, state, and regional levels. However, it is the tour guides and teachers who often implement what others develop. In our society, we are more likely to recognize the power that the upper-level

Upon finding out that I had been accepted into VCU's Master's in Art Education program many of my coworkers offered congratulations and then asked what sort of artwork I would be making. They were totally shocked that there was a body of knowledge associated with art education not to mention doing research about teaching art.

AMY BERGH

positions carry as opposed to the power implicit in the implementation of curriculum. There is a significant amount of power where the proverbial "rubber hits the road," either in a classroom or a museum setting and it is art teachers or tour guides who often shape students' experiences far more than those who developed a curriculum for use at a particular level or in a specific setting. This power may not be recognized or embraced by the very people who have access to it. Instead, they may see a curriculum supervisor or head of a museum education department as powerful and view themselves as vehicles to implement what others have created.

A MENTAL PARADIGM SHIFT

To work toward this goal of art educators recognizing their power in more overt ways, we suggest a change similar to a paradigm shift (Kuhn, 1962) with regard to how many art teachers view themselves and their profession. A mental paradigm shift could entail helping more art teachers see their work as political, powerful, and socially and personally significant. This type of shift includes recognition of research as a powerful tool for assisting art teachers in continuing to progress as they develop in their profession.

A logical place for this shift to begin is in teacher education programs, and many have begun to include action research as part of their curriculum (Hahs-Vaughn & Yanowitz, 2009). If art teacher education programs were able to expand their course offerings and require more research-oriented coursework with rigorous standards, these programs might better be able to build a mindset of art teaching as intellectually engaged work. This mindset could sustain ongoing learning, artmaking, research, and growth during the course of a teaching career. Further, following the lead of Lassonde (2008), university faculty members could increase their efforts to engage with preservice art teachers, on a regular basis, as co-researchers engaged in collaborative projects. This type of modeling could help preservice art teachers find ways to use research throughout their teaching career.

> This co-researching would not only help the preservice art teacher but also ground research in practical applications adding credibility to university initiated research.
>
> AMY BERGH

Once preservice art teachers graduate and enter K-12 school environments, they often become part of another institutional context that may not value research and engaged teaching. School and district structures and policies may include a dictated scope and sequence or pacing guide that is so rigid that it takes many choices away from teachers. Further, the professional development that is meant to enhance teachers' classroom practice is often, "woefully inadequate" (Borko, 2004, p. 3). However, if preservice art teacher programs focused more on developing engaged professionals and schools allowed teachers to make meaningful decisions and changes, then there may be a significant change over time in art teaching. In this manner, the shifts may need to occur at two levels—within preservice art teacher education programs and within the institutional structures of the schools and museums in which they teach.

TEACHERS ARE POWERFUL

Most teachers see a range of attitudes and levels of engagement by fellow teachers. We can discuss qualitative differences between a burnt out teacher's motivations and those of a new teacher brimming with ideas and possibilities after successfully navigating student teaching. We can all think of those lifelong teachers who maintain a passion for their teaching practices even in their 25th year of teaching. We think education would benefit from more of these teachers, so what is the difference between the art teacher whose classroom is vibrant and buzzing and one who is clearly marking time and collecting a paycheck?

> In my undergraduate program the idea of teacher as researcher was never mentioned. If I had been exposed to at least a rudimentary introduction to research it would have empowered me with a voice within my teaching. Instead I followed the prescribed expectations of what art teachers were "supposed" to do.
>
> AMY BERGH

We suggest that research is key. While engaged art teachers may not immediately credit research as their driving force, there is no doubt that their classrooms are driven by curiosity and a desire to do more, be more, and know more about their craft for themselves and their students. Chapman (1982) suggests that, "Research activity thrives on curiosity and doubt. It invites us to question whether our beliefs are really as well founded as we usually assume they are" (p. 102). Engaged art teachers often see their teaching practice as a site for continual change and improvement. Likewise, they do not buy into an idea that external forces alone limit what their practice can be. Rather, these teachers often discover their power to resist the discourses that define "teacher" by a sole institutional role—often an image of teacher as a passive tool for delivering information to students. Engaged teachers resist this image, asserting their own power to be other than a limited vision of what many schools and much of society expect from those who assume the role of teacher.

In short, these art teachers exercise their power (instead of being victims of power-stripping institutions) by resisting a simplistic view of the teaching profession and question "how things work… at the level of those continuous and uninterrupted processes which subject our bodies, govern our gestures, dictate our behaviours, etc." (Foucault, 1976, p. 97). When teachers recognize their potential as agents in the "net-like organization of power" (Foucault, 1976, p. 98) and understand how power circulates in and through them, the power/knowledge connection becomes evident, with research as a vital tool for maintaining its vibrancy as a powerful achievement where theory and practice meet.

In a manner similar to the story about Melanie's experience as a tour guide recognizing her power, art teachers who see their power actively can resist a limited definition of their practice as merely information delivery through "ritualized routines" (Nuthall, 2005, p. 895). The ability to withstand the social pressure of limited ideas about what constitutes a teacher involves resisting anesthesia—the numbing qualities that perpetuate the status quo at many levels of our society (Wilson McKay, 2000). In the art classroom, this anesthesia can result in holiday art and rote technical exercises often marked only by formulaic teaching providing limited opportunities for students to make meaning. While there are administrators and parents who value engaged teachers and want classrooms to be dynamic spaces of change, there are also administrators who may hope for, and often reward, teachers who follow cooperatively with top-down mandates. In addition, there are some parents who may hold a negative view of teachers, reinforced by many popular culture images of teachers as disengaged from a reciprocal process of teaching and learning. As former K-12 teachers and now university professors, we have seen art teachers who have selected to limit their own power. Art teachers themselves may participate in self-fulfilling prophecies by seeking paths of least resistance for professional development and demonstrating a reluctance to entertain new ideas. The resulting passivity on the part of some teachers, who represent an anesthetized group of "professionals," may lead to their being disenfranchised and disengaged individuals who believe they have no power to challenge or change the status quo.

However, in resisting this anesthesia, other teachers who recognize their practice as always in process seek out means to conduct research in their classrooms. They recognize the power that resides in their ability to effect change, to vary their practice, and do so with intent to improve their teaching. Sometimes power itself is connoted negatively, as something to be avoided, especially when conceptualized as power over something else. Additionally, it is sometimes assumed to be totalizing, but this is not a conception of power that we advocate. As Foucault (1976) suggested, power is best understood as the circulation of social discourses, including the institutional and economic discourses that define what counts as knowledge and as being of value. To recognize the role of power in teaching, art teachers must achieve a level of comfort with the idea that all knowledge is partial and there are multiple ways of knowing. While art teachers can often be frustrated by an inability to influence those perceived to be "in charge," they can, however, thoughtfully exercise their power in the sphere where they have the ability to be reflective and conscious of their decisions and their impact—their classrooms. They can choose to shift their experience of art teaching from experience of learned powerlessness to an experience of powerful practice.

RESEARCH AS EXPERIENCE

To understand more fully this shift from experience to an experience, how would reframing Dewey's influential text Art as Experience (1934) as "research as experience" create new kinds of seeing? In his writing, Dewey's distinction between recognition and perception is a defining feature of what constitutes an experience. Recognition for Dewey (1934) is "perception arrested before it has had a chance to develop freely" (p. 52). He characterizes this experience of recognition by pointing out the habitual reliance on a stereotype or some other previously formed scheme of recognition that allows us to greet a person on the street without really seeing the person. In a classroom, this might look like an instance of a teacher presuming that all boys and all girls like and dislike similar things due to their gender, or that because it is a particular time of year, a teacher teaches a lesson that she or he always does at that time of year.

Bringing in new information that may conflict with what is already known requires mental work. In Dewey's terms, this requires a conscious commitment to struggle and to seeking what is partial or incomplete. If we live in a state of easy recognition, we no longer experience a fully embodied life. In short, we are anaesthetized. However, embodied perception uses conflicts between old and new

Another advantage to engaging in research is the credibility that is gained by individual teachers within their school systems. Administrators see them as educators actively engaged in improving what is happening not only within their classrooms but on a larger scale. When the need arises for major changes within the system researcher teachers find they suddenly have a voice and that others want to listen.

AMY BERGH

information to create resistance making us fully aware of our lived experiences. The cognitive dissonance between old and new information is the reflective moment when art teachers become alive, when superficial habits of classroom behaviors give way to reflective practice leading to passionate art teaching.

CRITICISM AND IMAGINATION

But how does this awareness occur? Enacting a critical attitude in encounters with teaching entails locating a historical and ideological situation from which the viewer perceives. Developing this awareness requires stripping away veils from one's eyes that manifest in habit and bias. By practicing theory, we become deliberately open to possibilities, or as Dewey (1934) puts it, we then are protected from influences of custom and inertia through "a deliberate openness to life itself" (p. 304). He goes on to argue for good criticism that develops a deeply realized perception, requiring ongoing perception and criticism. In other words, research is not only what you do to receive your master's degree, but rather is a means to a career-long way of practicing engaged art teaching.

> It's easy for an experienced teacher to dismiss things with a "that would never work in my school." It is especially difficult to admit that there is room for improvement; as if it is a sign of weakness or failure. When, in fact, admitting that you have room for and are working toward improvement shows great strength in your teaching.
>
> AMY BERGH

In our classrooms, we often develop habits, but when our habits become so strong that we conceive of them as impervious to rethinking, they eliminate our "power to vary" (Dewey, 1916, p. 49). Criticism can also be understood in contrast to habit: "Habituation is thus our adjustment to an environment which at the time we are not concerned with modifying" (p. 47). In contrast to habituation, criticism seeks difference with regard to experience, creating a non-static conception of experience, which yields possibilities to modify current situations. Pedagogically, criticism translates into education with the express purpose of challenging the status quo through an educational reform mindset tied to an ability to imagine something else than what is.

Dewey (1934) argues that imagination is what yields effective criticism in education, how this works requires exploration. He conceives of imagination as:

> possibilities that contrast with actual conditions…. A sense of possibilities that are unrealized and that might be realized are when they are put in contrast with actual conditions, the most penetrating "criticism" of the latter that can be made. It is by a sense of possibilities opening before us that we become aware of constrictions that hem us in and of burdens that oppress. (p. 346)

In short, if we do not imagine new possibilities for how things could be in our classrooms, we do not critique. The ability to imagine something else (the possible) is concomitant with the ability to be critical of the current situation (the actual).

If we truly believe education can be improved and that we can be better art teachers, imagination is vital. Dewey (1934) goes on to describe imagination, especially in an educational sense, as an "instrument of the good" (p. 346) because "the first intimations of wide and large redirections of desire and purpose are of necessity imaginative" (p. 348). As Dewey further explains, "Desires for something different, aversion to the given state of things caused by the blocking of successful activity, stimulates the imagination" (p. 348). As soon as the "vision of possibilities has been converted into a proclamation of facts that already exist and hardened into semi-political institutions" (as Dewey claims is historically the case, p. 348), imagination begins directing desire and thought in new ways. We view teachers conducting research as opportunities for art teachers to direct imagination in ways that align with engaged teaching. In short, imagination is an ability to remain critical in our perceptions, particularly as they pertain to education.

> Teacher researchers also need to recognize that not everything they try is going to turn out the way they expect it will and that is okay. If they are open to possibilities then they will see opportunities they did not expect and the experience will have been worth it.
>
> AMY BERGH

Thus, in considering research as experience from a Deweyan perspective, the ability to think critically about our current practice is important for resisting anesthesia—habituated status quo behavior. Research offers a tool through which routine practice can shift to engaged teaching. Crucial to this shift is our ability to discern things that need changing (criticism) and an ability to think of new ways to address those things (imagination). With these tools and an attitude of deliberate openness, art teachers can increase their understanding of their practice and their power to enact change based on these fuller perceptions. Research as reflective experience encourages art teachers to resist anesthetized practice.

UNEARTHING THE TACIT KNOWLEDGE OF TEACHERS

Art teachers can continually learn a great deal by observing students, trying new things in the classroom, and working with other teachers. In our teaching college students, engaged discussions with each other about our teaching, recording what we have changed in our teaching, written reflections about courses, and explorations of what we deem to be important in the classroom bring about significant improvements in our teaching effectiveness and in our interest in art education as a profession. Though these are all important and valuable ways to learn, we suggest that systematic research can offer even more opportunity for engagement. Like most teachers, much of what we have learned in our own teaching practice, we learned through trial and error. However, when we conduct specific research and focus on our teaching, we learn far more than if we attempt to remedy situations without a framework to assist us in our quest for innovation. As teachers at all levels, we all know things "in our bones" about teaching. Taking this type of tacit knowledge and working on a problem from a research perspective has, for us as university professors, yielded a deep and nuanced understanding of our teaching and problems that we encounter. For instance, when we take a general wondering about our teaching and formalize specific questions to research, we learn even more. This commitment to systematically collecting data and reflecting on it promotes deep engagement with the act of improving our teaching practices. According to Chapman (1982), "Research means—'searching again'—inquiring carefully into some matter of special concern. Although each of us may search for authentic knowledge through the private exercise of conscience, research is a more elaborate and public process" (p. 102). Due to differences between casually noting changes in a classroom and assuming a research orientation, we believe that the work involved in research has great potential, though no guarantee, to improve art teaching in ways that other methods may not.

LESSONS FROM REGGIO EMILIA

Circling back to the beginning of this chapter, the parent night related to the children in wild spaces occurred in a Reggio Emilia-inspired preschool. This philosophy of teaching and learning, one marked by an attitude of "everyone teaches, everyone learns," manifests an infusion of research and practice. In a sense one cannot be understood without the other. The director of this preschool, an accomplished lifelong educator who has worked in many educational contexts over the years, proclaimed her involvement with this preschool program as being the most intellectually stimulating experience of her career. Why is this? What can be learned from the philosophy of Reggio Emilia-inspired schools?

The highly acclaimed preschools of the Reggio Emilia region of Italy, built with community rejuvenation funds by parents in the community after the fall of fascism at the close of World War II, are founded upon a primary principle of the value of expression. Other facets of these preschools include intense documentation in attempts to make learning visible, collaborative reflective processing by teachers and the parental community, and intentionally building learning experiences on students' interests and teachers' intuitions. Many aspects of Reggio-Emilia preschools practices—the rich process of observing, documenting and analyzing what children are doing—constitute research (Edwards, Gandini, & Forman, 1998; Hendrick, 2004). In short, research is a way of teaching, a way of knowing, and a way of being in a Reggio-inspired school (Fraser & Gestwicki, 2002; Project Zero et al., 2003).

Such an orientation in art teaching lends itself to the ongoing nature of professional growth. Internalizing an attitude of openness and willingness, acknowledging the partial understanding of our practice, and a curiosity to know more deeply are skills that mark art teaching as an ongoing process aided through a research lens. Through sharing and documenting the intellectual work of teaching, via research, a power shift can occur in education. This shift is marked by what Dewey (1933) characterizes as disciplined, yet imaginative thinking. And this is no small feat for it involves avoiding "routine actions" and maximizing possibilities of our field of art education by identifying meaningful horizons for change (Dewey, 1933, p. 20).

These ideas of the latent power in art teachers doing research connect to an understanding of democratic education that involves a solid pursuit of social justice: "democratic educators seek not simply to lessen the harshness of social inequities in schools, but to change the conditions that create them" (Apple & Beane, 1995, p.11). It is with an eye toward this goal, that we propose the need for art teachers to develop their research eyes and minds and understand the theoretical frameworks from which they work and see.

REFERENCES

Apple, M. W., & Beane, J. A. (Eds.). (1995). *Democratic schools*. Alexandria, VA: Association for Supervision and Curriculum Development.

Borko, H. (2004). Professional development and teacher learning: Mapping the terrain. *Educational Researcher, 33*(8), 3-15.

Buffington, M. L., & Ishii, D. (2008, May). Becoming qualitative researchers: Teachers' struggles with the process. Paper presented at the Fourth International Congress of Qualitative Inquiry, Urbana-Champaign, IL.

Chapman, L. (1982). *Instant art, instant culture: The unspoken policy for American schools*. New York, NY: Teachers College Press.

Cochran-Smith, M., & Lytle, S. L. (1993). *Inside and outside: Teacher research and knowledge*. New York, NY: Teachers College Press.

Cochran-Smith, M., & Lytle, S. L. (2009). *Inquiry as stance: Practitioner research for the next generation*. New York, NY: Teachers College Press.

Croasdaile, S. (2007). What makes teachers reflect to improve their practice? Reflective practice in a social-organizational context. Paper presented at the Annual Meeting of the American Educational Research Association, Chicago, IL.

Dewey, J. (1916). *Democracy and education: An introduction to the philosophy of education*. New York, NY: The Free Press.

Dewey, J. (1933). *How we think: A restatement of the relation of reflective thinking to the educative process*. Lexington, MA: D.C. Heath.

Dewey, J. (1934). *Art as experience*. New York, NY: Perigee.

Edwards, C., Gandini, L., & Forman, G. (Eds.). (1998). *The hundred languages of children: The Reggio Emilia approach—Advanced reflections* (2nd ed.). Westport, CT: Ablex.

Erickson, F. (1986). Qualitative methods in research on teaching. In M.C. Wittrock (Ed.), *Handbook of research on teaching* (pp. 119-161). New York, NY: Macmillan.

Foucault, M. (1976). *Power/Knowledge: Selected interviews and other writings 1972-1977*. New York, NY: Pantheon.

Fraser, S., & Gestwicki, C. (2002). *Authentic childhood: Exploring Reggio Emilia in the classroom*. Albany, NY: Delmar.

Hahs-Vaughn, D. L., & Yanowitz, K. L. (2009). Who is conducting teacher research? *Journal of Educational Research, 102*(6), 414-424.

Hendrick, J. (2004). *Next steps toward teaching the Reggio way: Accepting the challenge to change*. Columbus, OH: Prentice Hall.

Kincheloe, J. L. (2003). *Teachers as researchers: Qualitative inquiry as a path to empowerment*. New York, NY: Routledge Falmer.

Kuhn, T. S. (1962). *The structure of scientific revolutions*. Chicago, IL: University of Chicago Press.

Lassonde, C. A. (2008). Looking "beneath the surface": Authenticating research and inquiry for undergraduate teacher candidates. *Teacher Education and Practice, 21*(1), 33-46.

Lieberman, A., & Miller, L. (2005). Teachers as leaders. *The Educational Forum, 69*, 151-162.

May, W. T. (1993). "Teachers-as-researchers" or action research: What is it, and what good is it for art education? *Studies in Art Education, 34*(2), 114-126.

McGlinn Manfra, M. (2009). Critical inquiry in the social studies classroom: Portraits of critical teacher research. *Theory and Research in Social Education, 37*(2), 156-192.

Nabhan, G. P., & Trimble, S. (1994). *The geography of childhood*. Boston, MA: Beacon Press.

Nuthall, G. (2005). The cultural myths and realities of classroom teaching and learning: A personal journey. *Teachers' College Record, 107*(5), 895-934.

Project Zero, Cambridgeport School, Cambridgeport Children's Center, Ezra H. Baker School, John Simpkins School (2003). *Making teaching visible: Documenting individual and group learning as professional development*. Cambridge, MA: Project Zero.

Wilson McKay, S. (2000). Resisting anaesthesia: Mapping the roles of vision in democratic art education. Unpublished doctoral dissertation. The Pennsylvania State University, University Park, PA.

Zimmerman, E. (2004). Introduction to teaching and teacher education. In E. W. Eisner & M. D. Day (Eds.), *Handbook of research and policy in art education*. (pp. 409-413). Reston, VA: National Art Education Association.

2 / How Theories Inform Teaching and Research

MELANIE L. BUFFINGTON AND SARA WILSON MCKAY

Having students learn about value as a property of color distinguished by light or dark is a common practice in many art classrooms, but how do art teachers structure this learning? One teacher might choose to teach value by having students draw a row of several small squares on a piece of paper and shade them, gradually changing the pressure on their pencils, to make a series of values. The goal of this exercise is to avoid obvious pencil lines, to have a smooth transition from lights to darks, and to teach students how to use pressure to create a variety of values. This may be extended to have students then apply their learning to shade a still life or other drawing with a range of different values. What have students learned in this scenario?

Another approach to the concept of teaching value comes from the work of Olivia Gude (2000). Working with a group of middle schoolers in Chicago, she led the students on an investigation of how color symbolism and value function in Thomas Cole's *The Voyage of Life* series, in *The Lion King* movie and book, and in other popular culture images. The project involved students learning to shade geometric solids with oil pastels to make the forms look three-dimensional. From there, the students and Gude moved on to continue their learning by investigating the question, "How does this culture value value?" (p. 48). They found that repeatedly, throughout *The Lion King* movie and book, light was associated with good and dark was associated with evil. The students and Gude experimented with changing the color associations and making the character of Simba dark and the hyenas light. They discussed how changing the color symbolism affected the meaning of the story. From there, the group moved on to creating large banners to hang in the school that they illustrated with cartoon characters. The students developed these characters based upon geometric solid figures that they shaded to make them appear three-dimensional. According to Gude (2000), "The banners include stories about racism and resisting racism based on interviews students conducted with adults in the community" (p. 48). These cartoon characters tell community stories and raise questions about the use of value in a variety of different local contexts and in society as well. What have students learned in this scenario?

CONNECTIONS AMONG TEACHING PRACTICES, THEORIES, RESEARCH, AND POWER

This chapter addresses how theory, research, and power relate to daily practices of art educators, as shown by the examples above. We begin with a brief discussion of what theory is and how it relates to practice. Then through discussion of teaching scenarios and theories underlying them, both informal and formal, we offer ideas about how theories operate within teaching and learning situations. Additionally, we introduce a range of different types of research.

WHAT IS THEORY AND WHY DOES IT MATTER?

Teachers have beliefs, either conscious or subconscious, that guide teaching practices. Teachers make choices daily about how to structure learning for students, and these choices reflect beliefs about how students learn and what knowledge base is needed for this learning. Taking time to reflect upon what students learn by engaging in various classroom activities and projects is a good first step to developing an awareness of the theories that influence teaching decisions. When teachers can see more about what informs their specific choices, they can assess what other choices could be made and decide which are effective ways to achieve desired goals. Research can lead to this kind of awareness and a position of increased power.

SARA AND MELANIE: *In writing this text, we became aware how often we used the pronoun "we" when referencing teachers. This brought to our attention that we consider ourselves to be teachers who also conduct research. As university professors, our jobs are divided into the categories of teaching, research, and service. In some ways these categories are artificial distinctions because these activities are intertwined. While writing and editing this book, we discussed the practice of teaching extensively and asked ourselves how teaching and research are related to each other and to the daily practice of art educators in other settings.*

Cultivating awareness of the underpinnings of teaching choices is an ongoing process because all teaching contexts, involving people, are dynamic, not static. Reflecting on the variability in all teaching interaction, Eisner and Day (2004) suggested, "Theory is a guide in human affairs, not a formula for action" (p. 4); formulaic teaching would be ineffective for students. Rather, in thinking of how theory guides teaching, theories are tools that our minds use to help us understand, explain, or predict, a certain conception that guides our inquiry. Formal theories are beliefs that have been substantiated through research. Informal theories derive from experience too, but generally, only from one person's or a small group of people's experiences. Conducting research may be one way for teachers to see what guides their teaching practice and offer additional perspectives on the theories that inform their teaching. To make a theory more generalizable to a wider population, research studies may be replicated over time. Also, the most effective curriculum frameworks and pedagogical strategies are built on theories.

We view teachers as powerful change agents. However, when teachers repeat past practices because they are familiar or comfortable with them, without thinking of underlying theories or values that they reinforce, they may unwittingly be working toward a goal with which they do not agree. As teachers plan units of instruction, it is useful to ask, "What will students learn from doing this?" and to think beyond technical skills. To move practices to a powerful position where meaningful changes in teaching and learning are possible, art teachers need to go beyond repeating their past secure practices. How often do any of us who teach think about *why* we do what we do in our classrooms? What is at stake if we do not consider the whys of our hows?

HOW THEORIES EMERGE AND EVOLVE OVER TIME

Many of us have heard the expression that "We teach as we were taught." Accepting this is not unlike a story told on National Public Radio. In this story, a man asked his wife why she always trimmed the ends off a pot roast before putting it in the pan. She replied that it was the way her mother had always done it. That question prompted the woman to ask her mother why she trimmed the roast in that way. Her mother replied that the size of roast that came from the butcher was too big for her pan. The daughter came to the realization that for years she had been wasting roast due to a custom she learned from her mother that was no longer relevant to her current situation. Similarly, might we be wasting class time or other resources if do not take the opportunity to think through the whys of our classroom decisions? Could we be unaware of a practice that we learned from a teacher or colleague that has limited relevance in our current situation? It is important, then, to consider how theories, formal and informal, drive our actions.

Within education, theories change over time, and there are numerous formal theories at work today regarding how humans learn and develop including Piaget's stage theory (Piaget, Gruber & Voneche, 1995), critical pedagogy (Apple, 2004; Freire, 2006; Giroux, 1997; hooks, 1994; Ladson-Billings, 1994), and multiple intelligences (Gardner, 1983), among others. Each theory puts forth different ideas about how humans learn, and our teaching practices are evidence of what theories we hold about human learning.

In daily life, many people use informal theories to help them understand their experiences in the world. For instance, a teacher may develop an informal working theory about why a certain child seems to be more creative than other children. This type of informal theory might be mainly based on the teacher's personal interactions and judgments of that child's artmaking process and products as related to the teacher's interactions with other children. This type of theory is likely not identified by the teacher as a conscious effort to theorize a situation.

However, theories are also formal and explicitly developed to understand significantly greater phenomena by studying larger groups of people. Whereas the teacher in the example above was trying to understand one child's creativity, others including Csíkszentmihályi (1991), Freedman (2010), Gude (2010), and Zimmerman (2009), develop theories about creativity and posit ideas that are meant to be applicable to a wide range of individuals. Although both types of theories, informal and formal, have merit

I have observed that the curriculum theories teachers utilize are the ones that they were exposed to in preservice studies. I thought the only option was DBAE. Preservice programs need to include clear instruction about the variety of curricular theories in art education and not just what the instructor favors or is in vogue. Art teachers also need to take the responsibility of keeping aware of the movements within art education so that they can make thoughtful decisions about what they find important in their art practice.

AMY BERGH

and help to understand experiences in the world, informal theories are typically limited in their applicability to new situations, while wider-ranging applicability is an important aspect of formal theories. We think teachers tend to be more aware of formal theories through their preservice and in-service training and may make intentional efforts to change their teaching practices to reflect theories. For instance, Howard Gardner (1983) advocates an educational theory of multiple intelligences, and many teachers overtly vary their instructional strategies to involve a range of intelligences in their teaching practices that are based on Gardner's theory. Thus, theories can be utilized to develop curriculum frameworks and instructional practices.

THEORY VERSUS PRACTICE: MYTHS PEOPLE BELIEVE IN

As discussed above, many things teachers do in practice are informed by theories, both formal and informal. However, the hands-on nature of artmaking could be considered by some to be outside the realm of theories and research. Chapman (1982) suggested that this belief might align with some art teachers' resistance to theory, which she thinks may, "contribute to the public impression that art, and the teaching of art, are not intellectually demanding" (p. 102). Some art educators' beliefs about theory and research are likely exacerbated in university art departments where deviating from a clear focus on making by taking theoretical classes or pursuing an art education degree can be viewed as a sign that students are not as serious about their artmaking as studio art majors. All of this belies the fact that theory and research are very much a part of artmaking. This point has been supported more fully in recent years by Graeme Sullivan (2004; 2009) in both editions of his important work *Art Practice as Research: Inquiry in the Visual Arts.*

As Sullivan (2004) explains, we make art informed by various theories about the world and our experiences of it. We also teach according to theories, though in art education we do not have a large number of well-developed formal theories directly relevant to art teaching and learning (Freedman, 2004).

For example, an elementary level art teacher may utilize templates and pre-cut shapes and forms as a basis for all her or his K-2 lessons. These projects may take the form of a teacher giving specific directions about where and how to attach, draw, collage, or paint various parts to create an artwork. Likely this teacher values having student art look similar and this value may come from the teacher's theoretical understanding of what art education is and should be at the K-2 level. Perhaps this teacher wants all students to feel successful, or perhaps the teacher learned this approach from previous teachers, or maybe is greatly influenced by "school art style" (Efland, 1976) as an informal theory base for art education.

In considering another example of theories at work in the classroom, as a result of an in-service education about Gardner's theory of multiple intelligences (Gardner, 1983), an art teacher might alter a familiar lesson plan to expand opportunities for exploring kinesthetic and musical intelligences in the course of a lesson. Within the scope of a lesson on Kehinde Wiley, students might study his 2005 series of paintings of VH-1 Hip Hop award winners. Instead of only looking at the images of these paintings, students might also listen to the award winners' songs and analyze the lyrics. A teacher could extend this by bringing in other aspects of Hip Hop culture including break dancing, graffiti, urban fashion, or even extend it to include contemporary poetry of Nikki Giovanni or other authors as prompts for visual expression. Whatever the reason driving instructional choices, a teacher's working theory of learning has a profound influence on her or his practice, her or his students, and these students' understandings of art and the world.

Thus, teachers clearly teach with theories of learning even though some educators may not be aware of the theories they hold; still others may view an opposition between theory and practice, rather than a symbiotic relationship between the two. Eagleton (1983) offers that, "Hostility to theory usually means opposition to other people's theories and an oblivion of one's own" (p. 7). Resistance to theory, when it occurs, may be attributed to "the fact that to admit the importance of theory is to make an open-ended commitment, to leave oneself in a position where there are always important things one doesn't know" (Culler, 1994, p. 14). A welcoming attitude toward theory then could be perceived as a threat to many teachers who embrace the belief that a teacher should convey certainty.

In this text, we understand theory and practice as interrelated concepts that mutually constitute each other (Colapietro, 1998; de Certeau, 1985; Dewey, 1957). Teachers who actively build awareness of how theory informs practice and how practice informs theory also build opportunities for growth and powerful actions in and beyond their classrooms. Educator and cultural critic bell hooks (1994) vehemently situates this idea another way claiming that splits between theory and practice, "deny the power

> This can also be seen in the K-12 classroom. Students often have a difficult time accepting the value of art activities that are not directly hands-on product-oriented. The value gained by directing students in thinking, talking, and writing about art can be challenging but extremely transformative to their lifelong art experience.
>
> AMY BERGH

of liberatory education for critical consciousness, thereby perpetuating conditions that reinforce our collective exploitation and repression" (p. 69). The shift then for some teachers to dwell in a possibility of change instead of simply adhering to what is given and comfortable may be unsettling. In coming to an awareness of theories and how they operate in teaching practices, teachers may see possibilities for using their power to bring about positive change through teaching.

RESEARCH AND POWER IN DAILY TEACHING PRACTICE

> There is something very liberating about the realization that you do not have to know it all and that your teaching can be constantly evolving. Having the attitude of "let me try this and see if it works better" can take a good idea and make it great. If there is a fear of failure then nothing new can ever be tried.
>
> AMY BERGH

Teachers conduct research daily. Though much of what teachers do may not be overtly recognized as research, it is. We define research as a form of inquiry designed to generate new knowledge. Thus, when a teacher tries a new lesson and reflects on its successes and challenges, she or he has conducted informal research. When a teacher tries multiple seating chart arrangements and finally arrives at one that works, she or he also has conducted informal research.

These examples represent types of scenarios art teachers may encounter in their daily practices. Coming to see daily practice as a research site and as a place for change is one way that teachers can increase their awareness of their power (Dana & Yendol-Hoppey, 2009). In gaining self-knowledge about what you value and what theories you employ in your practice, research, particularly based in practice, can be a way to broaden theories you consider, work with, and form on a daily basis. Again, this critical awareness can be a source of power.

MAPPING YOUR IDENTITY

SARA AND MELANIE: *In the book* Contemporary Issues in Art Education, *Kristin Congdon, Marilyn Stewart, and John Howell White (2002) introduce a strategy to help teachers recognize their underlying beliefs and how these may play out in their development of curriculum. In their chapter, they explain the importance of teachers coming to understand how their identities and values play out in their curricular choices. Through their two-step process, teachers first identify important aspects of their identity and then think through which aspects are most important. The goal is to build habits of reflective practice among teachers that lead to new insights into their teaching.*

There are multiple areas in which teachers' daily choices allow them to exercise their power. Among these are curricular choices teachers make, pedagogical strategies teachers use, and how teachers view themselves as powerful or powerless.

CURRICULAR CHOICES

Curriculum documents are political and based on the theories and values of those writing them. As relatively new residents of Virginia, we were surprised to learn that the state legislature appointed a panel in 1948 to investigate what was being taught in the history textbooks throughout the state. At this time, the legislators in Virginia, "viewed civil rights agitation as the work of communists and worried that subversive civil rights 'propaganda' could enter public schools" (Dean, 2009, p. 323). Further, the anti-civil rights legislators approved creation and dissemination of textbooks from the 1950s through the 1970s that were patently fabricated and described slavery in ways that made slavery appear as if the system met the slaves' needs (Dean, 2009). For instance, a seventh-grade textbook included the statement, "A feeling of strong affection existed between masters and slaves in a majority of Virginia homes" (Dean, 2009, p. 327). Further, the authors of this text went on to explain that, "Life among the Negroes of Virginia in slavery times was generally happy. The Negroes went about in a cheerful manner making a living themselves and for those for whom they worked" (Dean, 2009, p. 327). Thus, the authors created and perpetuated false histories about slavery that were circulated as fact through the required use of these textbooks in public schools and taught to children throughout Virginia. Children learned incorrect and fictitious accounts not just about the origins of and practices of slavery, but also about the Civil War, the Reconstruction period, Jim Crow era, and the Civil Rights era—spanning more than 350 years of Virginia history.

Thus racist views and fears of the legislators permeated the educational system and spread to children throughout Virginia through history books representing a deliberate effort to create a version of Virginia history that presented segregation, the system in place at the time these books were first written, in a favorable light. Though this may seem to be an extreme account and one that is not likely to be repeated at such a large scale, the 2010 Texas history and economics curriculum controversy highlights that political values and beliefs inherent in curriculum are likely to be ongoing areas of debate.

The elected board voted to accept a state curriculum that questions the Founding Fathers' belief in the separation of church and state, changes the word "capitalism" throughout the economics curriculum to "free-enterprise system," and removes Thomas Jefferson from a list of influential political philosophers (McKinley, 2010).

Teachers make choices daily about how we address art education curricula and related national standards. Certainly, teachers can address the National Visual Arts Standard #4 (Understanding the visual arts in relation to history and cultures) by teaching about 18th-century English painter Thomas Gainsborough and situating his work in its context of time and place. Alternatively, a teacher could address the same standard by teaching about contemporary British-Nigerian artist Yinka Shonibare. The complexity of his work and his understanding of nationality and ideas of shifting identity and duality can also be used to address this standard. Either choice in this case (or a choice to contrast and compare these two artists), but actually any curricular choice that a teacher might make, says something about the teacher's background, educational experiences, and values.

PEDAGOGICAL STRATEGIES

In addition to decisions about content, teachers make numerous choices daily about *how* to teach. Do teachers believe they hold all the knowledge and they are to deliver this fixed knowledge to students mostly through direct instruction? Do teachers see a need to help students make connections between past and current knowledge by building on students' interests? Do teachers work to set up situations where students teach each other and make connections between and among various ideas? Clearly, teachers communicate values and beliefs through how they structure their classroom activities.

In discussing her ethnographic study of successful teachers of African American students, Ladson-Billings (1994) articulates many aspects of their pedagogical strategies that foster student learning. For instance, in her analysis of the data, she found that teachers who utilized culturally relevant pedagogy actively worked to help "students make connections between their community, national, and global identities" (p. 34). Further, she noticed that teachers who utilize culturally relevant practices see their job as helping students unearth and recognize the knowledge that they have, rather than filling their students with teacher knowledge. These teachers may see teaching as "a reciprocal process" (p. 53) rather than as a form of depositing knowledge into their students. Thus, decisions that teachers in this study made about their teaching strategies reflected their beliefs about their students, their students' learning processes, and the role of the teacher in fostering student learning.

SARA AND MELANIE: *For further discussion about culturally relevant pedagogy, see Aparna Rae's example study in Chapter 39.*

For instance, a lecture is a method of delivering information efficiently; it is also a theoretical statement of a teacher's beliefs about how students learn if it is that teacher's main method of instruction. Teachers' pedagogical strategies reflect their theories and beliefs about student learning and the role of a teacher. There are strategies that teachers choose to employ in order to assist students in empowering themselves. There are also pedagogical strategies that reinforce the teacher's role as the head of the classroom. When thinking about teaching and possible areas to research, teachers need to consider all decisions that they make that construct teaching practice as it currently exists.

HOW TEACHERS SEE THEMSELVES

Whether art teachers view their role within their schools as part of a team of educators or as a planning period for other teachers, how they see themselves has a profound influence on the theories they hold and how they do their job. Referring back to Chapter 1, to the role of imagination for unearthing possibilities, when teachers imagine all that can be done with curriculum and pedagogical methods, they can come to more powerful position from which to work. By increasing what can be imagined as possible in teachers' roles, through awareness or "deliberate openness" (Dewey, 1934, p. 304), teachers can recognize themselves as influential, as integral team players and innovative change agents—powerful positions that resist a limited vision of what it means to teach.

Barrett (2003) argued that it is important for people to analyze underlying messages in visual culture they encounter to decide if they agree or disagree with the messages presented. Likewise, in this text, we argue that it is important for educators to analyze underlying messages that relate to what we teach, how we teach, and how we see ourselves. Research is one way that we can accomplish this and it will help us come to understand why we value certain ideas and choose to continue them in our classrooms. Though we may not be aware of the underlying reasons why we reject or value certain curriculum frameworks or pedagogical strategies, we can use this increasing awareness as a way to see possibilities for our classrooms. When we see that we have the power to vary our practice, to grow as teachers, to consciously challenge and improve upon the status quo, this is a position of power.

CONTINUUM OF RESEARCH

In a manner similar to theories, research exists as if along a continuum with informal research at one end and formal research at the other. One is not more valuable than the other; they both certainly have their purposes for art educators.

INFORMAL RESEARCH

Informal research is the kind teachers conduct in numerous ways while teaching each day. Teachers may conduct experiments to determine the best storage devices for clay works-in-progress. During a museum's teacher in-service, a museum educator may informally poll the art teachers about how often they teach about a female artist or a person of color. A high school teacher may try different strategies to introduce a unit, considering the resulting student learning.

THE MIDDLE GROUND

> Several years ago my entire school was divided into groups to find links to help support the math curriculum. Because the groups were forced and the participants were reluctant, the outcome was very poor. It is vitally important that group members are willing and see the value of what they are researching prior to beginning.
>
> AMY BERGH

Moving closer toward the formal end of the research spectrum, educators may participate in reflective practice groups where they, individually or as a group, focus on a particular aspect of the teaching/learning process. Reflective practice is an intentional focus on a particular aspect of one's teaching practice (Dana & Yendol-Hoppey, 2009), and often schools or districts create reflective practice groups to explore particular ideas collaboratively and to offer support in the inquiry process. Perhaps the group chooses to focus on math connections across the curriculum. A reflective practice group will need to collect data from teachers involved in a research project, analyze the data, and may make a commitment to report findings after a period of inquiry to the faculty.

FORMAL RESEARCH

Formal research typically involves a systematic plan that may be a requirement for a master's thesis or doctoral dissertation. School districts may also employ this kind of research as part of a grant or district's own research agenda. University faculty members, various granting agencies, and departments of education at the state and federal level routinely conduct formal research. Though formal research may take forms ranging from quasi-experimental to arts-based, there is a need to follow a methodology, achieve appropriate approvals (Institutional Review Board approval for research related to a university and district level approval for research in a school) and work within a research plan. Maybe a district art supervisor asks teachers to participate in a formalized district-wide art study about using backwards design, a method of designing curriculum by setting goals before choosing activities or content to teach (Wiggins & McTighe, 2005). Or a teacher may identify a research topic around mixed ability art classes with the intention of presenting findings at the state conference or conducting research as the basis for a master's thesis. These scenarios require formal research processes because of the intent to share findings with others and generalize or transfer findings to other situations. In this text, formal research will be the primary focus as the book is intended to offer support and guidance for masters' students conducting their first research study.

> **SARA AND MELANIE:** NOTE: *At this point, we are generally discussing a broad research topic. Later, in Chapter 3, we offer strategies about forming a specific meaningful research topic. In Chapters 4 and 5, we discuss ways to gradually refine a topic and develop a specific, manageable research question.*

DIFFERENCES AMONG TYPES OF RESEARCH

A particular issue could be addressed by informal, middle ground, or formal research. Thus, it is not the research topic that determines the type of research. For instance, a recent post on the Museum-Ed Discussion listserv (www.museum-ed.org) related to evaluating museum field trips. Certainly, a museum educator could conduct informal research by reflecting on a tour and thinking about which aspects were successful and which need to be changed. This issue could also be addressed through slightly more formalized research with the museum educator discussing with colleagues some of their experiences with tours and coming to an agreement among the group about successful strategies. To study this same issue in a formal manner and collect data from teachers, the museum educator could develop an online survey for teachers to complete that evaluates their field trip experiences. The museum educator could analyze the data from the survey by statistical means or by coding for important themes and use it in numerous ways: to make changes at the programmatic level, to develop new tour guide preparation sessions, to bring teachers into the tour development process, etc. Additionally, the museum educator could then share the results of the research in an informal way through sending a message to the listserv from which the question emerged. The museum educator could submit a journal article for publication or submit a conference proposal to present the results at the American Association of Museums (AAM) or various other local, state, or national conferences.

Though there is not an inherent relationship between the type of research and its dissemination, it is more likely that teachers share informal research verbally and within smaller geographic areas. Formal research is more commonly shared via journal publications and conference presentations. This distinction between types of research and means through which they are typically shared may be one way the power of certain ideas is reinforced through dissemination to communities outside a local area.

CONCLUSION

In this chapter we discussed connections between teachers' theories and how they make curricular and pedagogical choices. Additionally, we offered several examples of how teachers' lessons, teaching strategies, problem solving, and decision making are related to theory, research, and power. When teachers are aware of and see the choices they make as reflecting underlying theories, they may be able to vary their practice consciously to reinforce important ideas and ideals. Though the focus of this book is to prepare teachers to conduct formal research, we believe that teachers can begin with increasing their power to effect change through an awareness of informal research in their daily practice.

I agree that the implied power associated with formal research can feel very overwhelming to someone who is unfamiliar with the process of formal research. Prior to learning about conducting formal research I thought the only people who could conduct 'real' research were those working in higher education. I felt the professional journal articles rarely pertained to the classroom teacher and were not worth the effort and time to try and read. By learning about and recognizing research at different levels I have found a wealth of knowledge that I did not know existed.

AMY BERGH

REFERENCES

Apple, M. (2004). *Ideology and curriculum* (3rd ed.). New York, NY: Taylor & Francis Books.

Barrett, T. (2003). Interpreting visual culture. *Art Education, 56*(2), 6-12.

Chapman, L. (1982). *Instant art, instant culture: The unspoken policy for American schools.* New York, NY: Teachers College Press.

Colapietro, V. (1998). Natural processes *and* historical practices: Towards a postmodern cosmology of human semiosis. *Semiotica 119-1/2*, 105-155.

Congdon, K. G., Stewart, M., & White, J. H. (2002). Mapping identity for curriculum work. In Y. Gaudelius & P. Speirs (Eds.), *Contemporary issues in art education* (pp.108-118). Upper Saddle River, NJ: Prentice Hall.

Csíkszentmihályi, M. (1991). *Flow: The psychology of optimal experience.* New York, NY: Harper Perennial.

Culler, J. (1994). Introduction: What's the point? In M. Bal & I. E. Boer (Eds.), *The point of theory: Practices of cultural analysis* (pp. 13-17). New York, NY: The Continuum.

Dana, N. F., & Yendol-Hoppey, D. (2009). *The reflective educator's guide to classroom research: Learning to teach and teaching to learn through practitioner inquiry.* Thousand Oaks, CA: Corwin Press.

Dean, A. W. (2009). Who controls the past controls the future. *Virginia Magazine of History and Biography, 117* (4), 319-355.

de Certeau, M. (1985). *Heterologies: Discourse on the other.* (B. Massumi, Trans.). Minneapolis: University of Minnesota Press.

Dewey, J. (1934). *Art as experience.* New York, NY: Perigee Books.

Dewey, J. (1920/1957). *Reconstruction in philosophy.* Boston, MA: Beacon Press.

Eagleton, T. (1983). *Literary theory: An introduction.* Minneapolis: University of Minnesota Press.

Edwards, C. P., Gandini, L., & Forman, G. E. (Eds.). (1998). *The hundred languages of children: The Reggio Emilia approach—Advanced reflections.* Westport, CT: Ablex.

Efland, A. (1976). The school art style: A functional analysis. *Studies in Art Education, 17*(2), 37-44.

Eisner, E., & Day, M. (2004). *Handbook of research and policy in art education*. Reston, VA: National Art Education Association.

Fischer, J. C. (2001). Action research rationale and planning: Developing a framework for teacher inquiry. In G. Burnaford, J. Fischer, & D. Hobson (Eds.), *Teachers doing research: The power of action through inquiry* (p. 29-48). Mahwah, NJ: Lawrence Erlbaum.

Freedman, K. (2004). Editorial: Becoming a researcher in art education: Constructing theory based on research. *Studies in Art Education, 45*(4), 283-284.

Freedman, K. (2010). Rethinking creativity: A definition to support contemporary practice. *Art Education, 63*(2), 8-15.

Freire, P. (2006). *Pedagogy of the oppressed*, (M. B. Ramos, Trans.). New York, NY: Continuum. (Original work published 1970)

Gardner, H. (1983). *Frames of mind: The theory of multiple intelligences*. New York, NY: Basic Books.

Giroux, H. (1997). *Pedagogy and the politics of hope: Theory, culture, and schooling*. Boulder, CO: Westview.

Gude, O. (2000). Drawing color lines. *Art Education, 53*(1), 44-50.

Gude, O. (2010). Playing, creativity, possibility. *Art Education, 63*(2), 31-37.

hooks, b. (1994). *Teaching to transgress*. New York, NY: Routledge.

Ladson-Billings, G. (1994). *The dreamkeepers: Successful teachers of African American children*. San Francisco, CA: Jossey-Bass.

Mattil, E. L. (1966). *A seminar in art education for research and curriculum development*. University Park: The Pennsylvania State University: Cooperative Research Project V-002.

McKinley, J. C. (2010, March 12). Texas conservatives win curriculum change. *The New York Times*. Retrieved from www.nytimes.com

Piaget, J., Gruber, H. (Ed.), & Voneche, J. J. (Ed.) (1995). *The essential Piaget* (100th Anniversary Ed.). New York, NY: Jason Aronson.

Sullivan, G. (2004). *Art practice as research: Inquiry in the visual arts*. Thousand Oaks, CA: Sage.

Sullivan, G. (2009). *Art practice as research: Inquiry in the visual arts* (2nd ed.). Thousand Oaks, CA: Sage.

Wiggins, G., & McTighe, J. (2005). *Understanding by design*. Alexandria, VA: Association for Supervision and Curriculum Development.

Wilson, B. (1997). The second search: Metaphor, dimensions of meaning and research topics in art education. In S. D. LaPierre & E. Zimmerman (Eds.), *Research methods and methodologies for art education* (pp. 1-32). Reston, VA: National Art Education Association.

Zimmerman, E. (2009). Reconceptualizing the role of creativity in art education theory and practice. *Studies in Art Education, 50*(4), 382-399.

3 / Finding a Topic for Research and Understanding Institutional Constraints

MELANIE L. BUFFINGTON AND SARA WILSON MCKAY

MELANIE: *When I taught middle school, I incorporated a unit on storytelling that related to the work of Romare Bearden. Students wrote stories and visually depicted, through a collage, a scene from the story. In teaching this unit multiple times, I noticed that student projects and ideas seemed to largely break across gender. The majority of girls developed stories that related to themes of caring and helping in a personal manner—helping an older person plant a garden or rescuing a kitten. The majority of boys developed stories that related to a heroic act on a grand scale—throwing a game-winning touchdown or shooting down an attacking alien ship. As a feminist, I continually wondered why these stereotypical stories and images were so important to my students and if there was anything that I did to reinforce them or discourage their expressions in my teaching. This area of inquiry could have been the beginning of a formal research project.*

DETERMINING WHAT TO RESEARCH

In the context of the school day, immediate problem solving drives much of the informal research teachers do. However, a majority of this text focuses on research efforts at a more formal end of the research continuum, and these efforts create and provide opportunities for more conscious choice in determining research topics. Building on awareness of the many choices teachers make in their practice, as discussed in Chapter 2, we recommend paying attention to questions that exist in teaching practice, infused with personal theories about learning. Before honing in on an exact research question, we advocate starting with a general area of interest such as illustrated in the story above and gradually working toward a focus (Creswell, 2008). In what follows, we offer tools to identify general areas in art education about which research questions might be suitable for development. Looking at established maps of the field of art education and research agendas offered by NAEA as well as identifying sticking points in their own teaching practice, novice and experienced researchers can begin to see many possible areas of interest. Further, Creswell (2008) advocates that educational researchers identify a main area of research interest, review related literature, and then move to a more specific research problem. We recommend choosing a topic that relates to an intellectual curiosity and connects to classroom practice or another aspect of the researcher's life. When identifying a personal area of interest, it is advisable for researchers to also consider institutional constraints that will limit what they research. Savvy researchers usually consider what their institutions allow when they make initial decisions about their topic for inquiry.

GENERAL AREAS OF RESEARCH IN ART EDUCATION

In their investigation of the field of art teacher education, Galbraith and Grauer (2004) had to look into numerous bodies of literature, such as general teacher education and standards for teacher education programs, to access the wide range of published studies on art teacher education. This is an example of the challenge of undertaking research in our hybrid field where conceptions of both art and education constantly change.

Research in art education has a long history. Even before the important 1966 research seminar at Penn State, art educators actively pursued more and better ways to talk about research in our field (Mattil, 1966). The last 15 years include specific attempts to chart a course for research in art education that we address as a way of conceptualizing the field of art education and the realm of possibilities for research (Eisner & Day, 2004; Freedman, 2003; Hafeli, 2009; Thurber, 2004). Though there are many ways to identify a research topic in art education, we offer strategies to build on general topics that others have identified in our field followed by a means to identify a personal area of interest to help novice researchers begin the task of selecting a formal research topic.

WILSON'S WHEEL

In a representation of our field, Wilson (1997) developed a graphic of a wheel of concentric circles with the "possible content of art educational research" (p. 9) through which he identified twenty "dimensions of meaning," four different kinds of relationships to and with those meanings, and five "topical classifications to which research might be directed" (p. 8) [See Figure 1].

Wilson acknowledges that the wheel is certainly incomplete and that others will have their own views of the content of art education. However, reading the wheel through the various levels of concentric circles and along the "spokes" of the wheels helps envision a variety of research arenas. For example, combining results (item 7) with comparative relationships (item 2.2), a researcher could develop a study that looks at results of the amount of art instruction among different groups of students within the same school. Using a different combination of elements, a study could be built around the symbolic relationship (item 2.4) between the structure of student collages (item 1.9), and student conceptions of art (item 3.1). Spinning the wheel of the possible content in art education can generate innumerable ideas for interesting places as a start for conducting research within the field of art education.

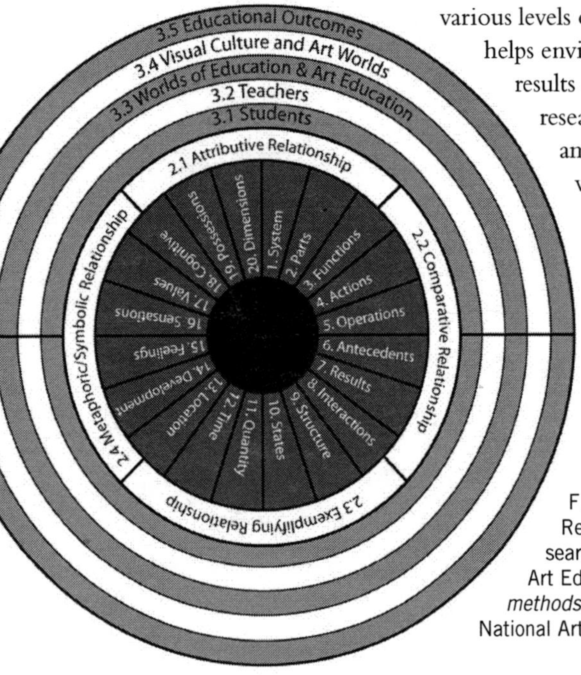

FIGURE 1. The Possible Content of Art Education Research. Reprinted with permission from Wilson, B. (1997). The second search: Metaphor, dimensions of meaning, and research topics in Art Education. In S.D. LaPierre and E. Zimmerman (Eds.). *Research methods and methodologies for art education* (pp. 1-32). Reston, VA: National Art Education Association. Graphic designed by Gerardo Perez.

Research Initiatives from NAEA Strategic Plan

COMMUNITY: The Research Commission contributes to a global network of knowledge about art education and supports diverse communities in using research to improve practice, advocacy, and policy.

SAMPLE QUESTIONS:
- What are some definitions of community within visual arts education?
- What are the attitudes and beliefs of art educators, museum educators, and their colleagues towards developing a professional community?
- What factors enable art educators to communicate effectively as members of a professional community?

ADVOCACY: The Research Commission advocates for a vibrant research culture that produces and disseminates research that informs art education practice, theory, and policy.

SAMPLE QUESTIONS:
- What are the factors that influence and shape parental and public opinion about the value of art education?

- What factors enable educational decision-makers and administrators to develop policies that validate and support the visual arts in education?
- How do museums become more accessible and comfortable for a wider audience in order to cultivate a life-long interest in museums?

LEARNING: The Research Commission helps members develop skills and understandings as researchers and use research to improve their professional practice.

SAMPLE QUESTIONS:
- How is student learning in art approached, accomplished, and measured when instruction is studio-oriented; focused on the study of visual and/or material culture; or is discipline-based; issues-based or integrated with other subject areas?
- How do the areas of curriculum, instruction, and assessment reflect the needs of preparing diverse teachers and students for a global and just society?
- What are some of the exemplary teaching and learning practices within art education?

NAEA RESEARCH PRIORITIES

Another source of ideas for research topics are the recent research recommendations developed through the National Art Education Association (NAEA). The current research agenda represents a culmination of various, specific research efforts over the last 10 years. Building on previous research reports, the NAEA released the *Research Needs Assessment* (2008). This document presents the results of a survey sponsored by NAEA that allowed members to express their opinions related to research and includes many possible topics for research in art education that address research needs specified by members of NAEA. Some researchers may find it preferable to work from an already identified need within the field because it has a direct relationship to their practice.

In 2012, NAEA formed a Research Commission as a part of the NAEA 2011-2014 Strategic Plan. The Commission has five goals relating to community, advocacy, learning, research and knowledge, and organizational vibrancy.

Much like Wilson's wheel, these categories represent a framework, though by no means an exhaustive one, sponsored by NAEA to support the research efforts throughout our field. Any of the above sources can help you select an area of research related to needs in our field as identified by prominent art educators.

PERSONAL AND SPECIFIC AREAS OF INTEREST: KNOTTY AREAS OF YOUR WORK

In addition to the possibility of working from a general overview of art education or a national research agenda, teachers can also identify potential areas of research interest directly related to their daily practice through a variety of inventory questions and reflective practices.

Reflective practice advocates Dana and Yendol-Hoppey (2009) refer to the process of locating a research area of interest as "finding a wondering" (p. 19). They suggest that teachers often ponder the expressions "I wonder…," "I think…," and "What if…?" based directly on their teaching practice (p. 20). Certainly, completion of these sentences would vary from teacher to teacher and resulting topics likely represent a high degree of engagement and passion on the part of the art teacher. Teachers in the preschools of Reggio Emilia refer to these kinds of ideas, the ones that come up repeatedly, as the "knotty problems" of our teaching and learning, "moments of cognitive disequilibrium, containing positive

It is very easy to become overwhelmed by the magnitude of possibilities and opportunities for research. To focus my energy and organize my thoughts, I keep a binder of items to work on. Everything from a unit that I felt the students should have gotten more out of, to how to better promote my program, websites to check out, information about art and artists and articles to read are kept in this binder. This is not a morgue for other people's lessons but a place for inspirations, thoughts,

/ CONT'D ON NEXT PAGE /

RESEARCH AND KNOWLEDGE: The Research Commission coordinates and facilitates programs, policies, and practices that demonstrate how teaching and learning visual arts in pK-16 classrooms, art museums, community programs, and other educational settings are strengthened through knowledge gained from research.

SAMPLE QUESTIONS:
- How can practitioners be more directly involved in the research process and become valued for their expertise and insights? What aspects of visual arts education research and knowledge are of most benefit to practitioners?
- How can research case studies be conducted and developed on the practices of exemplary teachers, students, administrators, policy makers, and other educators who work within diverse visual art education programs?
- How might a diversity of research approaches (e.g., experimental, qualitative, arts-based, ethnographic, historical, philosophical, action research, teacher as researcher) contribute to our understanding of visual arts education?

ORGANIZATIONAL VIBRANCY: The Research Commission utilizes systems and structures within the NAEA to promote a culture of research and leadership to advance the NAEA's mission and strategic plan.

SAMPLE QUESTIONS:
- What reasons do new teachers cite for joining NAEA?
- What factors influence an art teacher's decision to attend a state level art education conference?
- How could university pre-service art teacher preparation programs work more closely with NAEA to conduct research about NAEA and its dissemination of current scholarship?

(Retrieved from www.arteducators.org/researchcommission)

observations, and ideas. As I find additional materials for each issue I add them. I do not necessarily know immediately how to address my concerns or interest but I do recognize them as issues I could address. As time permits or need necessitates I at least have a starting place.

Trying to do research, after leaving the college environment, can be challenging. But I have found that as I talk to my fellow teachers, administrators, and school board personnel, many share common interests and are extremely willing to assist with finding information and sharing ideas. At times I find it amazing the number of articles and photocopies that I receive from a short conversation about a particular topic.

AMY BERGH

possibilities for regrouping, hypothesis testing, and intellectual comparison of ideas" (Edwards, Gandini, & Forman, 1998, p. 187). Being able to identify which areas of interest matter to you the most, as Melanie described at the beginning of this chapter, paying attention to how often sticking points come up in your daily practice and a willingness to address that knot as an opportunity to know more is an excellent way to identify a personal research topic.

Once a researcher comes to a general area of interest, such as multicultural education, it is helpful to start the research process of narrowing the topic by reviewing the literature (Creswell, 2008). Koroscik and Kowalchuk (1997) explore strategies specific to art education with regard to reading and interpreting literature in the form of journal articles. Researchers need to consult various fields, library databases, books, theses/dissertations, and so on, to acquire a comprehensive understanding of a particular topic. It is essential to look in a variety of places to find information on a topic because different fields may address the same topic in different ways.

For instance, in the case of multiculturalism, it was a trend in general education that then moved into the art education literature. Art educators advocating multicultural education often build upon the work of prominent authors from general education including Banks (2008) and Sleeter and Grant (2003). Digging further into general education would reveal studies of teachers' classrooms by Ladson-Billings (1994) and Au's (2009) edited text with a range of examples presented by teachers. After locating and reading numerous sources about a general topic, a researcher in art education might move on to investigate several of the prominent art education researchers who address multicultural art education, including the foundational work of Grigsby (1977) and the more recent work of Ballengee Morris and Stuhr (2001); Davenport (2000); Desai (2000, 2005); Eiserman (2009); Erickson and Young (2002); Knight (2006); Lai (2012); Lee (2012); Martinez (2012); Millman (2010); Powell (2012); Wasson, Stuhr, and Petrovich-Mwaniki (1990); and many others.

One of the best ways to access scholarly literature in art education is via searchable databases usually available through university libraries. Each database subscribes to different publications, so it is essential for a researcher to look in multiple databases to get a sense of the breadth of information on the topic. Some of the many databases that reference a range of research from art, education, and art education include ERIC, Art Full Text, ProQuest, Dissertations Abstracts, Wilson Web, and Art Bibliographies Modern. Numerous journals exist within art education that include relevant research: *Art Education, Canadian Review of Art Education: Research and Issues, International Journal of Education and the Arts, Journal of Aesthetic Education, Journal of Art and Design Education, Journal of Cultural Research in Art Education, Journal of Social Theory in Art Education, Studies in Art Education, Visual Arts Research, Visual Culture and Gender*, among others. Within general education, there are also many journals that publish art education related articles; some of these major education journals include *Educational Leadership, Educational Researcher, Harvard Educational Review, Review of Educational Research, Teachers College Record*. Another option is to search on the Web via Google Scholar. Searching Google Scholar brings up articles that are usually subject to some type of scholarly review process and include references. The NAEA website is also a good place to look for books on various art education topics. Because the books they publish are featured on their site with short descriptions, it is a helpful starting point to get a sense of which authors write on certain topics. One of our favorite ways of accessing literature on a specific topic is finding a good book on a topic of interest and, in addition to perusing that book or article's references, then doing some real-world browsing in the library by walking down the aisles and looking for related books in the same area of the library. While this is not an exhaustive way of identifying relevant literature, it is a useful way of seeing the kinds of literature that are available in the library, and occasionally stumbling upon something surprisingly useful.

SARA AND MELANIE: *Discerning quality and reliability among various articles on the same topic is a difficult task. One indicator of quality is if the journal is peer-reviewed or refereed. This means that when an author submits an article, the editor sends this article to several reviewers to read and critique. The reviewers offer comments and criticism on the article without knowing who wrote it. Typically, reviewers can recommend that an article be accepted as is, require minor revisions, require major revisions, or can reject the article for publication. Our field generally holds published articles that have gone through the peer-review process as more reliable than ones that have not.*

When conducting any search, it is important to try various search terms. In the above example of multicultural art education, a researcher would get different results from the searchable database if she or he entered the search term "multicultural art education" or "global art education" or "diversity and art education." Usually, locating the literature is the easier task. Deciding which literature is most reliable is a more challenging task. As researchers read articles, they scan the reference list of multiple articles and notice similarities and differences. When researchers find multiple articles citing the same author or article over and over, that is a sign indicating that author is particularly well known for publishing on that topic. The researcher then should find and read the article or book that multiple authors cite. Thus, in art education, it is crucial to search a range of databases and use a range of search terms to find sufficient literature on which to build an understanding of a topic.

As a researcher, it is critical to read and understand the work that has already been done on your topic. This builds your knowledge base and allows you to pursue the development of a study that will build upon the works of others and make a contribution to the field. Further, through this initial study of published literature, you may find a nuance to your topic that is especially interesting or that has not been sufficiently studied by others. Note that at this point, we suggest that the research area under consideration is still at the level of a general topic. In the following chapters, we offer suggestions for the gradual refinement from a general topic or area of interest to a research problem, statement of the problem, and a research question.

BALANCING THE PERSONAL WITH THE INSTITUTIONAL (OR MOVING FROM PERSONAL INTERESTS TO INSTITUTIONAL GUIDELINES)

Thus far in this chapter, the goal has been providing assistance in narrowing in on a personally meaningful topic of research. However, with a personal drive to conduct research, researchers need to strike a balance with institutional constraints that may govern what may be an appropriate and feasible topic for research. In what follows, we describe general parameters related to Institutional Review Boards (IRBs). It is essential that each researcher check with her or his IRB or other research review board to ensure that any proposed research project will meet the guidelines set forth by the governing body.

Institutional Constraints: Access, Time, and Practicalities

Simultaneous to your decision about the topic to research, you also need to consider what institutional constraints will contribute to your selection of research topic.

INSTITUTIONAL REVIEW BOARD (IRB)

Throughout this book and in your other classes, you will likely encounter references to an Institutional Review Board (IRB). IRBs often are termed research ethics committees or boards outside of the United States. An IRB is an official committee within a university that has responsibility to oversee all human subjects research affiliated with the university. This includes research conducted by graduate students earning a degree from that university regardless of the physical site of the research. The purpose of having this oversight is to ensure that all researchers follow ethical principles, regulations, and that the participants in every study are protected. Through the U.S. federal government, the Department of Health and Human Services (Office of Human Research Protections) and the Food and Drug Administration (FDA) regulate all research at universities that involves human subjects.

The legislation that governs IRBs in the U.S. began in 1974 and is entitled Title 45 CFR (Code of Federal Regulations) Part 46.

The FDA regulates research, which is primarily biomedical, involving investigational drugs, devices, and biologics and is likely not the kind of research you will be considering.

The system of federal oversight developed as a result of atrocities committed both internationally and within the US under the guise of research. Two of the most notorious violations of human rights relating to research include the Nazi medical studies and the Tuskegee syphilis study.

The Nazis conducted countless experiments on prisoners in concentration camps that resulted in death, disfigurement, and permanent disability. The supposed reason for these experiments was to help Nazi doctors improve their medical practices. The prisoners did not volunteer to participate, they did not have the right to decline to participate, and they were not informed of potential consequences. Not until the Nuremburg Code, which resulted from the Nuremburg War Crime Trials, was there a requirement for informed consent of persons participating in research.

(continued)

In the US, the Tuskegee syphilis study took place from 1932-1972 and was, "the longest nontherapeutic experiment on human beings in medical history" (Final Report, para. 5). One purpose of the research was to study the natural course of syphilis. This study intentionally recruited poor African American men to be the participants. Approximately half of the men had syphilis and the other half were the control group and did not have syphilis. The participants were not told the truth about their disease, the study, or their role in it; they were deceived many times. Even when penicillin was discovered to be a cure for syphilis, the doctors and nurses involved in this study withheld treatment from the participants. Further, they went to significant effort to ensure that the participants did not seek or receive treatment for this disease elsewhere. The compensation that the men received included free meals, free medical exams, and free burial insurance. Because the U.S. federal government supported this study, the egregious nature of how the human participants were treated continues to affect the medical system and research today.

While it is logical that there be safeguards like those implemented by IRBs to ensure such atrocities never happen again, there certainly are critics of IRB processes and procedures (Sanders & Ballengee Morris, 2008). Many critics are of the opinion that the federal regulations for human subject research are directed toward biomedical research and, as such, hamper social-behavioral research. Our field of art education may work with others in education to continually develop processes that better suit social science research. However, it is important to note that social-behavioral-educational research is not without its risks, and the IRB, as an objective body, is often in the best position to help a researcher identify and minimize risks that were not previously considered. Risks that are likely to occur with educational research include: a child feeling ostracized or ridiculed for participating or not participating in research; a child or parent feeling forced to participate in the research because the incentive is too good or the alternative is onerous; or a breach of confidential information about the student or family related to FERPA issues.

If you are a graduate student, you must apply for permission through your university's IRB to conduct your research if it involves human subjects. In many school districts you must also obtain official permission to conduct your research in a school setting even if you teach in the district. Though you may not be injecting your participants with any harmful drugs or placing them at physical risk, it is essential to follow the IRB-approved protocol and/or the school district protocol to ensure the physical, mental, and emotional well being of all your participants. Even though you do not foresee any possible harm to your participants, you are required to follow the IRB policies and procedures in place at your university. Unanticipated problems involving risk to subjects or others occur with astounding regularity in social-behavioral-educational research. Unanticipated problems may include a situation such as a child reporting abuse that must be acted on, but it is difficult to do this if identifying information is not collected. These types of unanticipated problems must be reported to the IRB so that measures can be adopted in the research to prevent recurrence.

As you think about designing your study, it is helpful to consider IRB regulations so that you can plan a feasible study for your timeframe. For instance, there are additional federal regulations for certain protected classes of human participants: children, pregnant women and fetuses, and prisoners. In addition, the IRB will require additional protections for other groups of vulnerable subjects such as cognitively impaired and financially deprived individuals. Designing a study that includes these groups of people will require a more extensive IRB review process and will likely take longer to get IRB approval. Thus, it is a wise decision to contact your university's or school district's IRB or research office to build an understanding of how the process works before you finalize your research plan. Grant agencies and many other funders may ask researchers for proof of IRB clearance before accepting a grant application from the researcher. Also, journals may require proof of IRB approval before publishing research articles. ■

REFERENCES

Final Report of the Tuskegee Syphilis Study Legacy Committee. (1996). www.hsl.virginia.edu/historical/medical_history/bad_blood/report.cfm

Sanders, J. H., & Ballengee Morris, C. (2008). Troubling the IRB: Institutional review boards' impact on art educators conducting social science research involving human subjects. *Studies in Art Education, 49*(4), 311-327.

ADDITIONAL RESOURCES

Banker, E. A., & Amdur, R. J. (2006). *Institutional review board: Management and function.* Sudbury, MA: Jones and Bartlett.

United States Department of Health & Human Services, Office for Human Research Protections (OHRP) IRB Guidebook. www.hhs.gov/ohrp/irb/irb_guidebook.htm

OTHER INSTITUTIONAL CONSTRAINTS BEYOND IRB

While satisfying IRB requirements at your institution is a primary responsibility in formal research, there are additional factors that can shape your study significantly. In your school or district there may be other gatekeepers that you must satisfy in order to conduct a study in your selected site.

Often it is helpful to conduct research within your own school to ease this process, but if your area of interest leads you away from your workplace, be aware of this choice, plan for it in terms of timeline and necessary approvals, and identify ways that your methodology selection and research question formation can help you achieve your research goals.

CONCLUSION

Research, no matter where it falls on the formal/informal continuum, contributes to the construction of a powerful art teacher as a change agent cognizant of her or his ability to shape teaching and learning experiences and not a teacher who is a victim of circumstances. The proposed ways of identifying areas of interest are a means to help teachers see connections to other fields and identify topics, either personal or related to the field in general, that interest them and could be the basis of a research project. As researchers make the initial decisions about their research topic, it is helpful to be aware of and plan for institutional constraints that make take the form of IRB review or school district policies.

> In my school system, school board approval is also required prior to beginning a study involving students or county personnel. Some of the other local school systems have so many researchers requesting to do research that they have someone in charge of approving and coordinating the studies so as not to overuse a particular population.
>
> AMY BERGH

REFERENCES

Au, W. (2009). *Rethinking multicultural education: Teaching for racial and cultural justice*. Milwaukee, WI: Rethinking Schools.

Ballengee Morris, C., & Stuhr, P. L. (2001). Multicultural art and visual culture in a changing world. *Art Education, 54*(4), 6-13.

Banks, J. A. (2008). *An introduction to multicultural education*. Boston, MA: Pearson.

Creswell, J. (2008). *Educational research: Planning, conducting, and evaluating quantitative and qualitative research*. Upper Saddle River, NJ: Pearson.

Dana, N. F., & Yendol-Hoppey, D. (2009). *The reflective educator's guide to classroom research: Learning to teach and teaching to learn through practitioner inquiry*. Thousand Oaks, CA: Corwin Press.

Davenport, M. (2000). Culture and education: Polishing the lenses. *Studies in Art Education, 41*(4), 361-375.

Desai, D. (2000). Imaging difference: The politics of representation in multicultural art education. *Studies in Art Education, 41*(2), 114-129.

Desai, D. (2005). Places to go: Challenges to multicultural art education in a global economy. *Studies in Art Education, 46*(4), 293-308.

Edwards, C. P., Gandini, L., & Forman, G. E. (Eds.). (1998). *The hundred languages of children: The Reggio Emilia approach—advanced reflections*. Westport, CT: Ablex.

Eiserman, J. (2009). They can still act Chinese and be Canadian at the same time: Reflections on multiculturalism and the Alberta art curriculum. *Canadian Review of Art Education: Research and Issues, 36*, 67-82.

Eisner, E., & Day, M. (Eds.). (2004). *Handbook of research and policy in art education*. Mahwah, NJ: Lawrence Erlbaum Associates.

Erickson, M., & Young, B. (2002). *Multicultural artworlds: Enduring, evolving, and overlapping traditions*. Reston, VA: National Art Education Association.

Freedman, K. (2003). Becoming a researcher in art education: Establishing research goals. *Studies in Art Education, 45*(1), 3-4.

Galbraith, L., & Grauer, K. (2004). State of the field: Demographics and art teacher education. In E. Eisner & M.D. Day (Eds.), *Handbook of research and policy in art education* (pp. 415-437). Mahwah, NJ: Lawrence Erlbaum Associates.

Grigsby, W. E. (1977). *Art and ethnics: Background for teaching youth in a pluralistic society*. Dubuque, IA: Wm. C. Brown.

Hafeli, M. (2009). Forget this article: On scholarly oblivion, institutional amnesia, and erasure of research history. *Studies in Art Education, 50*(4), 369-381.

Knight, W. (2006). Using contemporary art to challenge cultural values, beliefs, and assumptions. *Art Education, 59*(4), 39-45.

Koroscik, J. S., & Kowalchuk, E. (1997). Reading and interpreting research journal articles. In S. D. LaPierre & E. Zimmerman (Eds.), *Research methods and methodologies for art education* (pp. 75-102). Reston, VA: National Art Education Association.

Ladson-Billings, G. (1994). *The dreamkeepers: Successful teachers of African American children*. San Francisco, CA: Jossey-Bass.

Lai, A. (2012). Culturally responsive art education in a global era. *Art Education, 65*(5), 18-24.

Lee, N. (2012). Culturally responsive teaching for 21st century art education: Examining race in a studio art experience. *Art Education, 65*(5), 48-53.

Martinez, U. (2012). Culturally jammed: Culture jams as a form of culturally responsive teaching. *Art Education, 65*(5), 12-17.

Mattil, E. (1966). *A seminar in art education for research and curriculum development* (U.S. Office of Education Cooperative Research Project No. V-002). University Park: The Pennsylvania State University.

Millman, J. (2010). Writing and dialogue for cultural understanding: Multicultural art education in an art teacher certification program. *Art Education, 63*(3), 20-24.

NAEA (2008). 2008 NAEA research needs assessment. Retrieved from www.arteducators.org/research/2008_ResearchNeedsSurvey_Rpt.pdf

NAEA (2013). Research commission. Retrieved from www.arteducators.org/research/research-commission

Powell, L. S. (2012). 30 Americans: An inspiration for culturally responsive teaching. *Art Education, 65*(5), 33-41.

Sleeter, C. E., & Grant, C. A. (2003). *Making choices for multicultural education: Five approaches to race, class, and gender.* New York, NY: John Wiley & Sons.

Thurber, F. (2004). Teacher education as a field of study in art education: A comprehensive overview of methodology and methods used in research about art teacher education. In M. Day & E. Eisner (Eds.), *Handbook of research and policy in art education* (pp. 487-522). Mahwah, NJ: Lawrence Erlbaum Associates.

Wasson, R. F., Stuhr, P. L., & Petrovich-Mwaniki, L. (1990). Teaching art in the multicultural classroom: Six position statements. *Studies in Art Education, 31*(4), 234-246.

Wilson, B. (1997). The second search: Metaphor, dimensions of meaning, and research topics in art education. In S. D. La Pierre and E. Zimmerman (Eds.), *Research methods and methodologies for art education* (pp. 1-32). Reston, VA: National Art Education Association.

4 / Paradigms and Research

MELANIE L. BUFFINGTON AND SARA WILSON MCKAY

SARA: *When I was 17 years old and an exchange student, I was riding on a bus with a group of other tourists on the way to visit Canberra, Australia. On the bus ride from Sydney to Canberra, I heard a gentleman talking to his seatmate behind me. His words were absolutely tearing apart then U.S. President Ronald Reagan, declaring him a war-monger seeking power, not peace. Likely Reagan was in the news then because of his "Tear down this wall!" speech at the base of the Berlin Wall in June of 1987. I had grown up in a household where Reagan was revered, not criticized, and had never thought I should question whether U.S. involvement in other governments' affairs was proper or just. On that bus ride, I listened to the man behind me and kept thinking of things I wanted to say in return, like "As an American, I disagree with the way you are describing President Reagan." But instead, I stayed quiet and thought about his perspective and realized I had only really ever heard one perspective on Reagan's actions. Perhaps I needed more information and should consider what informs my views on things. Suddenly, a usually hidden paradigm of my life became visible and I was able to think more consciously about what informed my views.*

As you approach a topic of interest for your research, it is important to spend time thinking about your values related to knowledge (epistemology), truth (ontology), and research (methodology), because the theories that guide your teaching and worldview will likely also guide your research. In this chapter, we explain what paradigms are, how they relate to developing a research plan, and how this awareness can lead to changes in teaching and research practice.

SARA AND MELANIE: *Although scholars from a variety of disciplines at different universities use the terms* **paradigm** *and* **theoretical framework** *differently, there are some similarities between them. In writing this text, we had many discussions that led us to talk about paradigms as we do in this chapter. We will define what we mean by paradigm in the next section of this chapter, but for the purposes of this book, we are describing a* **theoretical or conceptual framework** *(these terms are used interchangeably in this text) as similar to the section of a thesis or dissertation in which researchers provide an in-depth discussion of the theories that underpin their research, a discussion of their point of reference related to concepts of truth and knowledge, and/or an explanation of the creation of their conceptual framework based on their inquiry. Throughout this chapter and the book, you will see references to paradigms and theoretical frameworks. If you are a graduate student, it is helpful to read recent theses from your department to get a sense of the general expectations of a theoretical framework section.*

We went to different universities for our graduate degrees and hold differing understandings of paradigms, conceptual frameworks, and theoretical frameworks. As we collaborated on this book, we struggled to develop a shared understanding of these concepts and this involved compromise based on our backgrounds, training, and work with students. We fully anticipate that our current understanding of all these evolving parts of research will be modified in the future. However you see these ideas relating to each other, thorough researchers are aware of the lenses they employ in their research process.

There are many factors that affect decision making when planning a research project and making initial decisions about a topic. Some of these may be practical factors. For instance, if you are an elementary school teacher, it will be far easier to conduct research in your own classroom or school instead of attempting to conduct a research project in another school. Other factors that influence decisions about topics are affected by the researcher's gender, race, sexual orientation, economic status, religion, ethnicity, language, geographic status, past experiences, and so on. For instance, see Chapter 27 by Amy Pfeiler-Wunder as an example of a study in which the author's socioeconomic status impacted her study. All of these aspects of who we are affect how we view the world, what we come to believe as truth, and what we

Learning about formal researchers' acknowledgment that my personal values and experiences influence my research surprised me. My impression was that all research was very sterile and void of any personal bias, or at least attempted to be. I have found that recognizing my personal values and experiences has not only influenced my research design but also provided insight into my daily teaching practice.

AMY BERGH

view as research or knowledge. Further, values that we bring to our research affect what we choose to research and what we want to accomplish through our research (Guba & Lincoln, 2011).

Earlier in your education, you probably developed an understanding about concepts of "truth" and "knowledge" as being fixed and rigid. However, in a theoretical sense, these terms are hotly contested, and various researchers use each of them differently to support their ideas. Different theories of truth and knowledge relate to the paradigms—ways we see the world—and to how we approach research.

For example, keeping students interested in the content of class is an issue that many teachers may encounter throughout their careers. In order to better understand this phenomenon, a teacher might decide to study student engagement and interest in art classes among high school students. One possible way to study this is to give a pre-test focusing on student interest levels to two groups of students before making any alterations to the curriculum. The teacher might then teach a unit emphasizing elements and principles to one group of students and contrast and compare it by teaching an issues-based curriculum to another group of students. These two groups of students would be assessed again after the completion of the unit to look for any changes in motivation or engagement as a result of learning from each differently focused curriculum.

Interviewing students about when they think they are learning the most in art class is another approach to this research problem. What topics engage them the most? What topics engage them the least? Why? Or maybe a teacher could take detailed notes about the level of engagement in her or his classroom on the lessons plans being used over a set period of time. Looking over the notes and comparing them with the actual curriculum, a teacher could draw some conclusions about what works well for engaging her or his students, present that information to the students, and then revisit the conclusions based on student input. Yet another way a teacher might approach student engagement in an art classroom could be to involve them in investigating local issues and inequities at their school. Conducting research in a particular class, a teacher and students might collect and analyze data together to understand why a particular situation exists, collaborate in developing ideas for ways to improve the situation, and engage in an art project with a specific and overt goal of working to improve this situation. This example of students' engagement with their art class suggests different ways that a research topic might be studied depending upon the paradigm of the researcher.

PARADIGMS

Unpacking your paradigm is essential to beginning your research. Where I initially felt within the paradigms is different from where I feel I am now as my understanding of research has evolved. I discovered that what I believed and what I did in the classroom did not always match. It forced me to examine what I truly felt was important and has forced me to strive for more consistency between my convictions and my actions.

AMY BERGH

Essentially, paradigms, what Creswell (2003) calls "knowledge claims" (p. 6), are worldviews that shape how we make decisions. Denzin and Lincoln (2005) regard a paradigm as

> an interpretive framework, a "basic set of beliefs that guides action" (Guba, 1990, p. 17). All research is interpretive; it is guided by the researcher's set of beliefs and feelings about the world and how it should be understood and studied. Some beliefs may be taken for granted, invisible, only assumed, whereas others are highly problematic and controversial. Each interpretive paradigm makes particular demands on the researcher, including the questions the researcher asks and the interpretations he or she brings to them. (p. 22)

An interesting aspect of paradigms is that though all people have them, many of us are not overtly aware of our paradigm(s) or how paradigms impact our lives. Usually we become aware of paradigms when something, often a college course, requires us to think about and unpack our own worldviews. In Sara's story at the beginning of the chapter, confronting a worldview much different from her own caused her to examine her own paradigm. Other times, we become aware of our paradigms because we encounter a situation that does not make sense to us. Paradigms relate to culture, socio-economic status, the time in which we live, and so on. Additionally, these theories contribute to framing how we see the world and interact with it. Thus, theories and paradigms are inter-related and inform each other.

Awareness of and understanding about paradigms helps researchers make informed decisions about a research plan. Paradigms affect how people conceive of truth and reality and, subsequently, they shape what researchers gravitate toward in structuring their research agenda. Thus, in the same manner that it is helpful to unpack curriculum to see how teachers transmit values to students, it is also helpful as researchers for us to unpack our own paradigms and become aware of them. This awareness can be a powerful place from which to work because it can lead to developing a strong research project that directly relates to improving one's own practice, to informing the field of art education, or to changing some inequities within art education or education in general.

PARADIGM DEFINITIONS

In this section, we introduce three paradigms: *positivism, constructivism*, and *critical theory*. There are certainly more paradigms at work within our field, but we chose to limit this discussion to three commonly used in educational research (Creswell, 2003; Guba & Lincoln, 2011). These three paradigms represent ways in which many art educators approach their lives and their work. They are not absolute, and it is certainly possible for an individual to either change paradigms over time or to simultaneously ascribe to aspects of multiple paradigms. Further, over time, the structure of a paradigm itself will change and shift (Kuhn, 1962) and boundaries among paradigms also will change and shift (Guba & Lincoln, 2011).

SARA AND MELANIE: *As Eisner and Day (2004) described theory as "a guide for human affairs," it may be fair to see significant overlap between theories, as discussed in Chapter 2, and paradigms. In writing this book, we recognize this overlap, but choose to bracket these terms in order to develop teachers' recognition of significant theories, both informal and formal, that may correspond to the informal and formal spectrum of research we described previously. Paradigms here make a solid transition into the pursuit of formal educational research. Understanding one's paradigm, a working worldview, can guide a researcher's selection of methodology and development of one's research question as well as data collection and analysis methods.*

The paradigm(s) to which researchers subscribe have a large impact on how they view truth and knowledge. Sometimes subtle differences between these two terms from different paradigmatic views are important when approaching a research project because how a researcher approaches a project and the type of research question that s/he asks will affect many decisions that a researcher makes throughout a project.

Positivism/Postpositivism. Positivism/Postpositivism is a paradigm that most closely relates to the scientific method. Within the positivist/postpositivist paradigm, researchers believe that they are able to discover an absolute Truth (capitalization intentional) or a likely truth about the focus area under study. Positivist approaches to research and teaching focus on the researcher or teacher remaining in a powerful and controlling role (Guba & Lincoln, 2011).

Art Education Research Informed by a Positivist/Postpositivist Paradigm

BURTON, D. (2001). A QUARTILE ANALYSIS OF THE "1997 NAEP VISUAL ARTS REPORT CARD." *Studies in Art Education, 43*(1), 35-44.

ABSTRACT: This article reports the results of a secondary analysis of the "1997 National Assessment of Educational Progress (NAEP) Visual Arts Report Card." In the original report the randomly selected sample of the eighth graders came from intact classrooms that were not art rooms. Therefore the sample was representative of eighth graders, but not of eighth graders taking art. The purpose of this study was to use quartile analysis of selected factors made directly from National Center for Education Statistics (NCES) data sets to compare the results of those who scored in the high and low quartiles. From a total of 548 comparisons made between the high and low quartiles, 36 factors presented a difference of 15% or more. Preliminary results suggest that a combination of factors contribute to art education progress and these relate to student attitude toward art, academic aptitude, self-initiated motivation, parental influence and teacher morale.

LAMPERT, N. (2006). CRITICAL THINKING DISPOSITIONS AS AN OUTCOME OF ART EDUCATION. *Studies in Art Education, 47*(3), 215-228.

ABSTRACT: This article discusses findings of a study that investigated the variance in critical thinking dispositions between arts and non-arts undergraduates. A consensus of findings in research literature on education and critical thinking indicates that an inquiry-based curriculum positively influences gains in critical thinking. Research shows, as well, that learning in the arts is largely inquiry-based. The synthesis of those findings and the results of this study indicate that exposure to learning in the arts positively influences students' disposition to think critically. The study reported in this article utilized quantitative data from the California Critical Thinking Disposition Inventory (CCTDI), a survey instrument. Data were collected from a sample of 141 undergraduates at a large, urban, public university on the U.S. east coast. The sample consisted of two discipline groups: arts and non-arts undergraduates; and two class rank groups; freshmen and juniors/seniors. As would be expected, when the class rank groups were compared, the juniors/seniors showed a significantly higher mean overall score on the CCTDI and were also found to have significantly higher scores on several of the subscales. Comparison of the two discipline groups showed no significant difference in overall mean CCTDI scores between arts and non-arts students, but the arts students were found to have significantly higher mean scores on several of the subscales within the research instrument: truth-seeking, maturity, and open-mindedness. These results suggest that learning in the arts builds strengths in several critical thinking dispositions and offers evidence that the arts do indeed enhance the disposition to think critically. ■

Positivist/postpositivist researchers believe that reality is discovered through carefully formulated experimental work by a neutral researcher. Through this paradigm, researchers design experiments and test hypotheses to determine cause and effect relationships and are focused on measuring and quantifying data (Flick, 1998). Usually, positivists plan out their entire research project before they begin any type of data collection or analysis; this is called an *a priori* research plan (Morse, 2003). Positivist/postpositivist researchers believe that their values do not influence the outcomes of their research (Guba & Lincoln, 2011). The humans involved in a research project often are referred to as "subjects" rather than "participants" in a positivist/postpositivist study. A researcher's role in this paradigm is to collect data from the subjects, analyze that data, and come to conclusions about the data. Because positivist/postpositivist researchers believe that their data analysis and findings are likely true, and because they hold the power in the study, they are unlikely to ask the subjects to review the data analysis and findings. The researcher believes that she or he is neutral and her or his interpretations of data are objective and fair. Working from this paradigm, experimental, quasi-experimental studies, and quantitative surveys (discussed in depth in Section II in this book) make a great deal of sense. Depending upon the stance of the researcher, historical research (discussed in Section III) may also be conducted from a positivist/postpositivist viewpoint.

In the student engagement example given here, the researcher uses pre- and post-tests to look for any changes in motivation or engagement as a result of each differently focused curriculum. Comparing results from these kinds of assessments assumes that most all else about the research situation stays the same except for the curricular change that the teacher/researcher controls and is indicative of a positivist/postpositivist paradigm.

Constructivism. Constructivism is one of many paradigms now accepted in the social sciences, and it is mainly concerned with understanding a phenomenon. Constructivist researchers plan the first steps of a study, and often review resulting information to determine the next phases; this is called emergent design (Gall, Gall, & Borg, 2003). This iterative process may be ongoing throughout the research project; frequently the next steps of a research project are influenced by results of the research and participants involved in the research. Constructivist researchers do not view themselves as objective and therefore being objective is not viewed as a problem. Instead, constructivists believe that it is important for researchers to understand their own values and that these values influence their research topics and ways studies are conducted. Constructivist researchers also may try to learn about and understand participants from the participants' points of view (Guba & Lincoln, 2011).

Constructivists believe that reality or truth is constructed and that numerous realities and truths can exist simultaneously (Guba & Lincoln, 2011). Truth(s) are socially constructed and change with time, place, and culture. For instance, if we consider the actions of Rosa Parks in 1955 and the ways that they were understood at that time, in the 1980s, and now, there are significant differences. In 1955, she was imprisoned for refusing to give her seat to a White passenger. As elementary school students in the 1980s, we learned that she was a tired old lady who finished a day of work and did not want to stand or move to the back of the bus. Now, Rosa Parks is described in heroic terms and her actions are depicted as strong, powerful, and intentionally defiant. What actually happened on that bus in 1955 has not changed, but societal understandings of that event and the way it is taught has changed and likely will continue to change over time. Thus, a constructivist would say that the truths surrounding Rosa Parks' refusal to give up her seat have changed over time; there are different truths depending upon the region and the culture of the people, and there are likely multiple truths still circulating about this event.

SARA AND MELANIE: *It is not surprising that a worldview that includes the idea of multiple versions of truth existing simultaneously developed in education too. Constructivist learning theory (Vygotsky, 1978) developed as a challenge in many ways to behaviorist efforts in education that reinforced predetermined outcomes instead of acknowledging that each student comes to learning able to contribute and construct knowledge in unique ways. Viewing students as active makers of knowledge, not just passive receptacles for fixed knowledge, is the cornerstone of constructivist learning. In Eliza Pitri's contribution at the end of this chapter she discusses how constructivist learning theory related to her constructivist approach to her research project.*

Art Education Studies From a Constructivist Paradigm

COLMAN, A. (2004). NET.ART AND NET.PEDAGOGY: INTRODUCING INTERNET ART TO THE DIGITAL ART CURRICULUM. *Studies in Art Education, 46*(1), 61-73.

ABSTRACT: This exploratory case study investigates pedagogical strategies meant to encourage secondary level students to think critically about their perceptions and use of the Internet. This process included guiding them in analyzing works of Internet art and introducing them to web authoring in order to create works of art that could be viewed on a web browser. Contrary to my original expectations, students were initially unable to translate their knowledge about the Internet and other art forms into an ability to purposefully explore Internet art. In this article, I describe and reflect upon the adjustments I made in my instructional methods to demystify Internet art for the students. These adjustments enabled them to engage in art criticism and studio production, describe Internet art's aesthetics, and articulate how their attitudes toward Internet art evolved.

STAIKIDIS, K. (2005). ARTISTIC MENTORSHIP WITH TWO MAYAN ARTISTS AS A SOURCE FOR CURRICULAR AND PEDAGOGICAL TRANSFORMATION IN HIGHER EDUCATION. *Electronic Magazine of Multicultural Education, 7*(2). Retrieved from www.eastern.edu/publications/emme/2005fall/staikidis.html

ABSTRACT: This study explores the possibilities for conducting research in Mayan artists' studios through painting mentorships. Mayan Tzutuhil and Kaqchikel ways of knowing are described as they inform the processes of painting, pedagogy, and mentorship in the studio as a site for research. Cross-cultural mentorship is discussed as a research strategy particularly useful to the field of art education. The transformation of curricula for preservice art educators at the college level based on Mayan teaching structures is explored. ∎

Epistemologically, constructivists believe that there are many types of knowledge, that knowledge changes and shifts over time, and knowledge is relative to individuals and to cultures (Guba & Lincoln, 2011). Knowledge can be gained through many different means including traditional education and reading highly respected texts, interactions with others, and self-awareness. However, because languages are symbolic, communication of knowledge among people is not inherently a simple process because people may have different understandings of truth and knowledge. In a constructivist research study, the human participants are often more than sources of data. In some instances, a researcher might involve participants in data collection and analysis. In other instances, researchers might ask participants to review findings of a study to ensure that the researchers' analysis was accurate. Thus, power in a constructivist study often is shared between the researcher and participants. Common methodologies used by constructivists in art education (and discussed in the latter sections of this book) include: action research, arts-based research, case study, ethnography, historical research, narrative research, portraiture, survey, and theoretical research.

To return to the earlier example about student engagement, interviews of students about their levels of engagement might be a way a constructivist would take up this research problem. If a teacher were to take notes about when students appeared most engaged in class, subsequently presenting her or his preliminary conclusions to the students, this may be another way a constructivist might conduct research revisiting the conclusions based on student input.

Critical Theory. Critical theorists are concerned with social change and issues of power. Their decisions about what to research and how to conduct research are motivated by their desire to work with their research participants to improve their lives. Like constructivists, critical theorists are interested in understanding the meaning making and worldview of those being researched. Critical theorists also believe that there are multiple realities. These realities are constructed by individuals, are subjective, and emphasize ways power affects realities (Sipe & Constable, 1996). Importantly, this construction is mediated by numerous factors including social status, political beliefs, economic status, ethnicity, gender, and religious affiliation, all of which may change over time. Critical theory researchers are overtly political and work to ameliorate a situation that oppresses people. Critical theorists try to understand the underlying social construct of knowledge and believe that power is closely tied to what is accepted as knowledge (Carspecken, 1999; Foucault, 1980). They realize that societies accept and reject certain ideas and this affects all members of a society, endorsing some knowledge and discrediting other knowledge. The methodologies of critical theorists are often participatory in nature and relate to constructing dialogues among a number of constituencies. In art education, participatory action research and arts-based research methodologies are frequently

When I first learned about critical theory I did not like the idea that I might be oppressed. I found the term highly offensive. As I studied critical theorists' beliefs I began to understand that oppressed could apply to practically anything that controls a person beyond his or her perceived ability to change a situation. One year the schedule at my school was changed so that we saw all eight classes every Monday and then a normal calendar the rest of the week. Mondays became a song-and-dance routine of constant disruptions, and my coworkers and I had to find ways to cope and teach our students.

AMY BERGH

used with critical theory research approaches. Depending upon the orientation of a researcher and a specific research project, other methodologies may also be used based on critical theory.

With regard to the student engagement research problem from earlier in the chapter, if a teacher chose to involve her or his students in investigating local issues and inequities at their school, s/he would likely be working from a critical theory perspective, especially if the intent is to change such inequities. A critical theory paradigm would lead a teacher to work with students to understand why a particular situation exists and collaborate to improve the situation.

Art Education Studies Informed by Critical Theory Paradigm

HUTZEL, K. (2007). RECONSTRUCTING A COMMUNITY, RECLAIMING A PLAYGROUND: A PARTICIPATORY ACTION RESEARCH STUDY. *Studies in Art Education, 48*(3), 299-315.

ABSTRACT: This article describes a participatory action research study that examined participant's perceptions of community and of the West End neighborhood in Cincinnati, Ohio, where the study took place. It is argued that oppressive situations have developed strong collective identities and social capital among residents, which can lead to the development of community art as a catalyst for social change and inform community-based art education. An asset-based community art curriculum was implemented and two murals were developed. Results from the study indicate that participants conceive of community, in general, as a safe, happy place that is clean and green, and the West End as a place with strong social bonds despite suffering from trash, violence, and drugs. Results also indicate that participants increasingly realized their own ability to affect change in their community to improve the landscape and promote a cleaner, greener place through art. Data reveal that the community art curriculum contributed to social change in the neighborhood by highlighting the role of neighborhood children and reclaiming a playground that had been associated with drugs and violence.

TAYLOR, P. G. (2002). SERVICE-LEARNING AS POSTMODERN ART AND PEDAGOGY. *Studies in Art Education, 43*(2), 124-140.

ABSTRACT: This article explores the idea that service-learning, when based on a postmodern art education pedagogy, is a work of art. The goal of service-learning is to deepen students' civic responsibility while providing opportunities for experiential knowledge in their academic study. While service-learning is meaningful and important across disciplinary boundaries, when it is combined with art education pedagogy there are explicit and implicit connections to the world of art and artmaking. Using Dominique Mazeud's Great Cleansing of the Rio Grande performance art ritual as an exemplar, one university art education service-learning program is described, reflected upon, and interpreted. Criteria are presented for the development of a postmodern service-learning art pedagogy as a transformative and socially reconstructive practice. These criteria are based upon the connection between the ritualistic nature of postmodern performance art and service-learning theories. The implications of this research extend the purposes of art education not only to include the power of the arts to educate, but to provide the service opportunities that transform and give us meaning in our lives. ∎

> At first I felt very drawn to a positivist idea that something was either true or not true and the nuances of examining data. But as I explored the ideas in critical theorist and constructivist paradigms I realized how important they are to the daily practice of teaching and studying real people in real situations.
>
> AMY BERGH

UNPACKING PARADIGMS

Because paradigms inform and shape what and how we research, the methodologies we choose to employ also are influenced by paradigms. While methodologies are not attached to specific paradigms, they may fit better with certain ones. Many researchers do not overtly state their paradigm in a journal article (though in a thesis, the theoretical framework section will likely indicate it), but a researcher's paradigm often can be inferred by reading between the lines about the goal of the research and how the researcher approaches those involved in the study either as subjects, participants, or co-researchers. As a new researcher, we encourage you to unpack your paradigm and write about it as a conceptual framework in order to frame your study and select your methodology in accordance with your values and thus, the paradigm that informs your work.

For example, new researchers might use Table 1, answering the questions at the top of the columns, to determine what paradigm(s) resonates most with them. Probably the most useful question is thinking about what the purpose of the research is—to predict, understand, or change. Careful researchers are sure to design a study that aligns with how they answer these questions. For example, a researcher working from a constructivist paradigm is unlikely to design a study to "prove" something; instead, a constructivist would likely interpret findings to contribute to a knowledge base. A researcher working from a critical theory paradigm is more likely to refer to people involved in a study as "participants" or "co-researchers," rather than as "subjects." However, a researcher working from a positivist/postpositivist paradigm may have "subjects." Aligning all parts of a research study, including terminology, is an important aspect of unpacking one's paradigm.

COMPARING PARADIGMS

Because paradigms can seem somewhat nebulous, it is useful to have means by which to compare them. Researchers frequently use the terms ontology, epistemology, and methodology as a way to understand paradigms. Sometimes researchers align specific methodologies as well with particular paradigms. We do not do that in this chart, because we believe that methodologies are not attached to specific paradigms even though some may work better with one or another paradigm.

SARA AND MELANIE: *Advanced researchers may push the boundaries of a methodology or paradigm and mix elements of them in non-traditional ways. This can result in innovative approaches to paradigms and research as well as new ways of conducting research. In general, we recommend that beginning researchers use an existing methodology for their first study. This is a discussion that each graduate student should have with her/his advisor early in the planning of the study. In Chapter 5 there are longer descriptions of methodologies.*

TABLE 1. PARADIGM CHART

PARADIGMS	WHAT IS TRUTH? (ONTOLOGY)	HOW IS KNOWLEDGE CONSTRUCTED? (EPISTEMOLOGY)	WHAT IS THE PURPOSE OF THE RESEARCH?
Positivism/ Positivism	Truth exists largely independent of cultures and people and it can be uncovered through careful research.	Knowledge has little or no cultural influence.	Researchers conduct research to predict or generalize.
Constructivism	People involved in various situations construct truth; multiple truths can exist simultaneously	Knowledge changes over time; it is constructed by people and may come through interactions with people.	Researchers conduct research to understand.
Critical Theory	Truth is shaped by social, political, economic, cultural, ethnic, race, religious and gender values.	Knowledge can be used as a political tool to oppress some and keep others in power.	Research has overtly political goals; researchers conduct research to work toward critique and transformation.

Ontology: What is Truth? Is truth something that is given to people? Do people discover truth? Do people make truth? How do we make sense of the possible existence of multiple truths? Ontology is a specific type of philosophy that relates to the nature of truth, being, existence, or reality in general, and the attempts to create some basic categories into which ideas about truth or reality can be organized. Depending upon a researcher's ontological perspective, there can be a range of understandings of truth: for example, one Truth (capitalization intentional to indicate the supremacy of a singular truth) or multiples truths that circulate simultaneously. A positivist/postpositivist typically believes that truth exists and that a careful researcher can discover it through systematic research processes. Constructivist researchers generally hold that people in certain places construct truths at certain times. These truths are most relevant in a local area and are geographically and temporally specific. Constructivists believe that truth is shaped by social, political, economic, ethnic, race, religious, and gender values (Guba & Lincoln, 2011). For instance, the Truth and Reconciliation commission that operated in post-apartheid South Africa, identified four different types of "truth" that circulated regarding the atrocities that were committed: factual or forensic truth, personal and narrative truth, social truth, and healing and restorative truth (Truth & Reconciliation Committee of South Africa Report, 1998). Critical theory researchers may question the existence of anything that can be labeled definitively as true, or believe that those in power create "truths" that they circulate among the general population in order to reinforce the position of those in power. A researcher's view of the concept of truth influences the design of her or his research study.

Most teachers tend to have set beliefs on what they do daily but they probably do not have studies or data other than experience to gauge these decisions. Many have probably always done these things automatically and could imagine no other way.

AMY BERGH

Epistemology: What is Knowledge? Epistemology is another branch of philosophy that relates to the central issue of knowledge and what is viewed as knowledge. From a broad view, epistemology encompasses questions like: What is knowledge? How do people acquire knowledge? Why do we know what we know? In different paradigms, ideas about knowledge are quite different. For instance, from the positivist/postpositivist paradigm, knowledge is basically objective and a researcher's values are not present in the results of the research. Research generates knowledge through carefully designed studies in which most decisions are made by the researcher before the study begins. In a constructivist paradigm, knowledge is viewed as socially constructed and people come to learn things through their interactions with others. Researchers working in a critical theory paradigm recognize knowledge as value-laden and connected to discourses of power. Critical theorists believe that those in power may use the creation of knowledge as a means to restrict or confine others.

REFERENCES

Berger, P. L., & Luckmann, T. (1966). *The social construction of reality*. Garden City, NY: Anchor.

Carspecken, P. F. (1999). *Four scenes for posing the question of meaning and other explorations in critical philosophy and critical methodology*. New York, NY: Peter Lang.

Creswell, J. W. (2003). *Research design: Qualitative, quantitative, and mixed methods approaches* (2nd ed.). Thousand Oaks, CA: Sage.

Denzin, N. K., & Lincoln, Y. S. (2005). The discipline and practice of qualitative research. In N. K. Denzin & Y. S. Lincoln (Eds.), *The Sage handbook of qualitative research* (3rd ed.) (pp. 1-41). Thousand Oaks, CA: Sage.

Eisner, E., & Day, M. (2004). *Handbook of research and policy in art education*. Reston, VA: National Art Education Association.

Flick, U. (1998). *An introduction to qualitative research: Theory method and applications*. London, England: Sage.

Foucault, M. (1980). *Power/Knowledge. Selected interviews and other writings 1972-1977* (C. Gordon, Ed.). New York, NY: Pantheon Books.

Gall, M., Gall, J., & Borg, W. (2003). *Educational research: An introduction* (7th ed.). Boston, MA: Pearson Education.

Guba, E. G., & Lincoln, Y. S. (2011). Paradigmatic controversies, contradictions, and emerging confluences revisited. In N. K. Denzin & Y. S. Lincoln (Eds.), *The Sage Handbook of qualitative research* (4th ed.) (pp. 97-128). Thousand Oaks, CA: Sage.

Kuhn, T. (1962). *The structure of scientific revolutions*. Chicago, IL: University of Chicago Press.

Lincoln, Y. S., & Guba, E. G. (1985). *Naturalistic inquiry*. Beverly Hills, CA: Sage.

Morse, J. M. (2003). The paradox of qualitative research design. *Qualitative Health Research, 13*(10), 1335-1336.

Sipe, L., & Constable, S. (1996). A chart of four contemporary research paradigms: Metaphors for the modes of inquiry. *Taboo: The Journal of Culture and Education, 1*, 153-163.

Truth & Reconciliation Committee of South Africa (1998, October). Concepts and principles. In Truth & Reconciliation Committee of South Africa Report (Volume 1, chapter 5, pp. 103-134). Retrieved from www.justice.gov.za/trc/report/index.htm

Vygotsky, L. (1978). *Mind in society: The development of higher psychological processes*. Cambridge, MA: Harvard University Press.

What's for Supper? Research Paradigms!

JULIE CROWDER, ERIN WALDNER, AND JAIMIE MERRELL / MASTER OF EDUCATION GRADUATES, VIRGINIA COMMONWEALTH UNIVERSITY

This section answers the question "What if research paradigms were supper?" Using three different approaches to the evening meal as a metaphor, we explore the characteristics of the positivist, constructivist, and critical theory research paradigms in depth. By addressing the three areas of methodology, epistemology, and ontology through the common cultural experience of sharing a meal, we seek to make the abstract criteria that define the three research paradigms more memorable and concrete.

The positivist believes there are correct methodologies, which are the key to discovering the facts of reality. The method of preparing dinner rarely changes. There is a specific routine of choosing a TV dinner from the freezer, opening the package, and placing it in the microwave for the amount of time specified on the box. By following this method exactly each time, the TV dinner will come out just the way he or she likes it every time, barring circumstances beyond the researcher's control. This type of consistency supports a world view where there is one reality. If

FIGURE 1. Supper—Positivist.

FIGURE 2. Supper—Constructivist.

A positivist supper could be a classic TV dinner. From the positivist perspective, there is only one type of dinner and if it isn't meat, potatoes, a cooked vegetable, and dessert, then it isn't dinner. This supper comes on a plate that separates the food items into clear categories and proportions. The raised plastic separating the food items prevents the danger of a green bean mistakenly rolling into the mashed potato area, confusing things. The positivist also appreciates that the portions are consistent, packaged by weight, and that the nutrition facts are written clearly on the box. This type of dinner appeals strongly to the positivist because, from his or her perspective, the nature of reality is singular and aspects of reality can be measured, categorized, and counted.

he or she happens to choose the chicken dinner rather than the Salisbury steak dinner, a different cooking time might be listed on the box; however the preparation methodology rarely varies significantly.

When the positivist looks at the box of his TV dinner, he makes a hypothesis about what his dinner will taste like based on the picture and based on similar TV dinners he has eaten in the past. Once purchased, the dinner procedure has been determined and no food item contained in the TV dinner will be altered or substituted. You might say that making a TV dinner is an a priori procedure.

A constructivist supper could be a potluck. In constructivism, reality is constructed through group interaction. A potluck

(continued)

only happens with a group of people working together. If Aunt Edna brings her signature pecan pie it will be a completely different experience than if she doesn't come and Douglas the vegan brings his TVP pilaf.

Constructivists believe that multiple realities can exist simultaneously and also come together to form new ideas. In a potluck, not only are there multiple foods, which may be unrelated to one another, but also within each category such as dessert or salad, there will be multiple interpretations. There will be a pasta salad, a mixed green salad, and a jell-o salad. There is no single definition of salad. The dessert table might hold pumpkin pie and tiramisu, or might shift to fresh fruit and yogurt. Reality is entirely dependent on the group.

In constructivism, understanding occurs symbolically. At a potluck you might tell me we are having sushi, but I might not know what your dish is unless I ask you. The group might discuss ahead of time what they are allergic to, or they might instead examine the food before eating it to determine if it smells like it contains nut products. Each item brought to the potluck tells a personal story about the individual who made that dish. Food is the language of a potluck.

FIGURE 3. Supper—Critical Theory.

Thus, a potluck is similar to a constructivist paradigm, which relies on building reality from the experiences of the participants. Just like the people at the potluck decide what food they want to share, participants of constructivist research decide what information to share. The people help determine the outcome of the inquiry.

A critical theory supper could be an organized event where a group has an opportunity to experience the unequal distribution of food in the world. The group might be randomly split into three groups representing the different realities of the world in terms of food and hunger. The participants of one small group would be given most of the food available. They might eat a full meal of rice, chicken, salad, and garlic bread, and could eat as much as they wanted. Another slightly larger group would be fed just enough food to barely quell their hunger: some rice and chicken or just a bowl of soup. All others would sit on the floor with a spoonful of rice for dinner, experiencing for possibly the first time what it feels like to be truly hungry.

A group discussion could follow the meal so that the participants can connect their symbolic experience to real issues. Similar to a critical theory approach to research, this supper has an agenda: to make participants become aware of the world's injustices and jump-start change. By experiencing an alternate point of view, the critical theory approach to dinner attempts to give people a desire to help change the current state of inequality. Participants in the critical theory approach to dinner may live in a society where most of people are able to eat and waste food. The illusion of an unlimited food supply is the dominant paradigm. In the Hunger Meal, participants are made aware of realities separate from their own and therefore of social changes that need to occur.

Just as there are multiple approaches to eating supper, there are multiple approaches to conducting research. Enlightened consumers of food or research are introspective enough to understand the lens through which they view their task, whether feeding the body or mind. ∎

CONCLUSION

It is not that one paradigm is better than another for conducting research. However, it is important that researchers are aware of their paradigms and work to craft a research project in which the various parts work well together. This is analogous to choosing an appropriate tool to conduct a home maintenance project. Though you could use the end of a screwdriver to pound a nail into the wall, it usually makes more sense to use a hammer. Understanding your personal paradigm(s) and developing your theoretical framework helps you choose a methodology (discussed in the next chapter) that not only makes sense for what you want to study, but also relates to your underlying values, beliefs about truth, and beliefs about knowledge. This is analogous to finding two pieces of a puzzle that fit together, with one piece being the researcher's paradigm and the other being the methodologies for the research study. Though it is sometimes possible to force two puzzle pieces together, there usually are pieces that fit better together than others.

SARA AND MELANIE: *The following section is an example of how a scholar, Eliza Pitri, explains her theoretical orientation toward socioconstructivist research. In Pitri's conceptualization of socioconstructivist research, she is addressing constructivism as a theory of learning which is distinct from, though related to, constructivism as a research paradigm. In her essay, she shows how constructivist student learning in the art classroom can also align with a constructivist research paradigm. Pitri advocates employing methodologies that yield a sense of situated context (attending to the social factors of a research site). Pitri's essay brings together ideas from the previous chapters as she discusses her beliefs about learning and her orientation toward socioconstructivist research.*

Approaches to Understanding Learning: Socioconstructivist Educational Research

ELIZA PITRI / ASSISTANT PROFESSOR, UNIVERSITY OF NICOSIA, CYPRESS

As teachers/researchers, we need to think about the beliefs we hold about how and in what ways students learn. Though we may not always be aware of it, we likely hold theories of learning that direct how we teach our students. When we make a conscious choice to study student learning, we need to be aware of the theories that we utilize in our teaching. One learning theory that provides teachers with insights on how students acquire knowledge is constructivism. Social constructivism as a learning theory emphasizes the importance on situating knowledge, which is an approach that affects teachers' choices of methods and strategies.

Further, constructivism as a learning theory maintains that individuals create or construct their own new understandings or knowledge through the interaction of what they already know and believe and the ideas, events, and activities with which they come in contact. Psychological or Piagetian constructivists regard that knowledge construction occurs as a result of working through dilemmas created by teachers for students who come to classrooms with ideas, beliefs, and opinions that need to be altered or modified. This approach assumes that development is an ingrained, natural, biological process that is the same for all individuals, regardless of gender, class, race, or the economic and sociocultural context in which learning and living take place. On the other hand, social or Vygotskian constructivism reflects a theory of human development that situates an individual within a social context and derives from social interactions within which cultural meanings are shared by a group and eventually internalized by the individual (Richardson, 1997).

Socioconstructivists assume a relativist ontology and a subjective epistemology emphasizing the fundamentally relational, social aspect of our existence. There are multiple realities and truths, local and specific in nature, which come into existence in and out of our engagement with them in our world (Crotty, 1998).

Knowledge and truth are created, not given or discovered by the mind; contextual, not absolute; mutable, not fixed. Learners do not transfer knowledge from a fixed and knowable external world into their memories but they construct meaning out of the events and phenomena they encounter in their lives. Knowledge is acquired through involvement with content instead of imitation or repetition (Kroll & LaBoskey, 1996).

Learning is situated, occurring in specific contexts with particular identifying features and purposes. Knowledge and skills are learned in the contexts that reflect how knowledge is obtained and applied in everyday situations. According to Stein (1998), to *situate* learning means to place thought and action in a specific place and time; to involve other learners, the environment, and the activities to create meaning; to locate in a particular setting the thinking and doing processes used by experts to accomplish knowledge and skill tasks. For example, students may be encouraged to express any concerns, questions, or interests on everyday issues, and teachers listen to them. These concerns lead to small group projects, which would include bibliographic and artistic study of an issue, artmaking based on individual and/or group decision making about tools and materials, peer and student-teacher discussions to evaluate artmaking and negotiate understandings, more art production and revision of previous artwork, combining different means of expression, solving problems related to the issue stated either by students or the teacher, more art production and revision of previous artwork, interviewing experts on the issue from the community, more art production and revision of artwork, transferring newly acquired knowledge to similar situations, and continuously documenting the learning process.

The methodologies typically employed in socioconstructivist research are naturalistic and consider the sociocultural context of phenomena. The researcher and the subject of study

(continued)

are interactively linked so that meaning making is "created" as the investigation proceeds (Guba & Lincoln, 1994). Methodological approaches come face to face with the social situations that reveal constructs and the taken-for-granted components of the world. Rather than sampling subjects to represent a population, researchers must focus on a local view and zoom in to a shot of the situated child. ∎

REFERENCES

Crotty, M. (1998). *The foundations of social research*. London, England: Sage.

Guba, E. G., & Lincoln, Y. S. (1994). Competing paradigms in qualitative research. In N. K. Denzin & Y. S. Lincoln (Eds.), *Handbook of qualitative research* (pp. 105-117). London, England: Sage.

Kroll, L. R., & LaBoskey, V. K. (1996). Practicing what we preach: Constructivism in a teacher education program. *Action in Teacher Education, 18*(2), 63-72.

Richardson, V. (1997). *Constructivist teacher education: Building new understandings*. Washington, DC: Falmer Press.

Stein, D. (1998). *Situated learning in adult education*. Urbana, IL: ERIC Clearinghouse on Elementary and Early Childhood Education. ED 418250.

5 / Refining a Topic, Making Methodological Decisions, and Crafting Good Research Questions

MELANIE L. BUFFINGTON AND **SARA WILSON MCKAY**

When building a new home, it is common to begin with a style in mind such as contemporary, mid-century modern, eco-friendly, or country. Other early considerations certainly include the budget, the size of the lot, and zoning requirements. Based upon these initial decisions and parameters, other decisions will follow including the floor plan, the overall size of the house, which compass direction the house will face, and plumbing and wiring systems. After these major decisions are made, then more detailed decisions follow—what style windows work best in each room, should the kitchen have French doors or sliding doors, which rooms should have tile floors? Though it may be possible to design an entire house around something as specific as a light switch, it is not advisable for obvious reasons as the whole project may never get out of the dark.

The analogy here is that research design is similar to organizing the many interrelated decisions of building a house. We recommend that teacher researchers make the larger and important decisions about paradigm and the methodology or methodologies to use before deciding which methods to use for data collection and analysis. Because this chapter focuses on how researchers put together all the parts in order to formulate a sound study, our comments here are directed toward masters' students, who are also teachers, conducting research with the guidance of an academic advisor. We want to stress how important it is for those in formal graduate programs to work closely with their advisors during the crucial process of designing their study.

SARA AND MELANIE: *In general, it is usually more successful for art teacher researchers conducting their first study to use one existing methodology as they learn about a particular research process. After gaining some experience with research design, data collection, data analysis, and building theory, researchers often combine elements of various methodologies, develop a new methodology, or adapt existing methodologies to work well with a particular problem.*

Typically, researchers choose their methodology or methodologies, while carefully considering their paradigm(s). After generating a research question or questions and planning the study, a researcher may decide on specific methods that will be used to collect data. However, it is important to remember, as with the house building analogy, that the decisions that go into the process of designing research are interrelated: "the choice of approach, ranging from the broad assumptions that are brought to a project to the more practical decisions made about how to collect and analyze data" (Creswell, 2003, p. 13) will create limits and guidelines for the overall study design.

In this chapter, we introduce various research methodologies used in art education research and situate these methodologies within a qualitative/quantitative framework. Jane Cera, a contributor to this chapter, offers insights about differences between methodologies and methods. The chapter then moves to suggestions for narrowing from a topic to a research question, including ideas for developing strong research questions, with guidance offered by contributor Lisa Hochtritt.

METHODOLOGY: WHAT PRINCIPLES AND PROCEDURES GUIDE RESEARCH?

Researchers work within guidelines to conduct research. Creswell (2003) described these guidelines as "strategies of inquiry" and explained that they "provide specific direction for procedures in a research design" (p.13). These strategies of inquiry also are called methodologies. Kumar (2005) described methodologies and their functions as analogous to planning a trip. "Just as there are posts along the way to your travel destination, so there are practical steps through which you must pass in your research journey in order to find answers to your research questions" (Kumar, 2005, p. 16). While a new researcher may deviate from a recommended path or linger at particular points on the journey, in general, it is advisable for new travelers to follow guidelines set forth in a travel guide. As decisions along the journey ultimately impact the quality of the trip, so too do the choices researcher make about research affect the quality of the finished study.

> At each operational step in the research process you are required to choose from a multiplicity of methods, procedures and models of research methodology which will help you to best achieve your objectives. This is where your knowledge base of research methodology plays a crucial role. (Kumar, 2005, p. 16)

Knowing the guidelines of a selected methodology can aid the development and implementation of a research study significantly.

Essentially, a methodology is a guide for research that can be flexible within some parameters. A methodology is an approach to research that involves some type of philosophical underpinnings; methodologies change over time and researchers can develop new methodologies or blend existing methodologies together to suit specific studies.

METHODOLOGIES FREQUENTLY USED IN ART EDUCATION

There are numerous methodologies in general research as well as a wide range of methodologies used in art education research. Commonly used methodologies in art education addressed in the edited portion of this book include: action research, arts-based research, case study, ethnography, historical research, narrative/autobiographical research, portraiture, quasi-experimental research, survey (qualitative and quantitative), and theoretical inquiry.

- **Action research** usually involves the study and enhancement of one's own practice. Also referred to somewhat interchangeably as "reflective teaching, teacher-as-researcher, teaching as inquiry and critical praxis" (May, 1997, p. 224). An art teacher researcher could employ action research study how utilizing a different classroom management strategy, based upon positive rewards, might improve student behavior.
- **Arts-based research** is the systematic use of the artistic process to understand and examine a research interest (McNiff, 1998). This methodology goes beyond artistic products as sources of data to include art process as a means for question generation, study design, data collection methods, data analysis, and reporting of findings. One possible arts-based study might be a teacher and a group of students focusing on the students' artmaking processes and ways of generating ideas for their artworks.
- **Case study** involves the in-depth observation and description of an individual (person, group, district, school, etc.) or limited set of individuals (Koroscik & Kowalchuk, 1997). This may include single-case, multiple-case, or cross-site analyses (Thurber, 2004). A researcher could study the teachers' strategies at an arts-infused interdisciplinary elementary school as a specific case.
- **Ethnographic research** involves the investigation of the cultural systems of a particular group or people (Koroscik & Kowalchuk, 1997). A museum educator employing ethnographic research might study the shared culture that develops among tour guides who lead school tours at that museum.

- **Historical research** is the systematic collection, evaluation, synthesis and interpretation of data related to past events including the "shaping of findings into credible patterns of interpretation" (Thurber, 2004, p. 499). For example, a researcher might study the emergence of a citywide program of summer arts classes in the 1960s that was developed by a parks and recreation system. The goal of this study might be to better understand the political and social factors involved in the emergence and continuation of this program.
- **Narrative/autobiographical research** involves telling the stories of the everyday experiences of teachers, students, artists, or other research participants within social, cultural, institutional, and linguistic narratives. In identifying the tensions among and within stories, researchers analyze and interpret data in a rich way (Clandinin & Murphy, 2009). One possible study might be investigating a school that is not meeting its annual yearly progress goals despite repeated interventions. By analyzing the narratives of teachers, administrators, and parents, the researcher may gain understanding of the factors that affect the school.
- **Portraiture research** is an-depth representation of a particular person or situation that results in a written portrait of the subject in question. The resulting written studies tend to be highly descriptive and offer insights into the nuances of the person or situation. One possibility for a researcher could be conducting a portraiture study of a particularly effective art teacher in the district.
- **Quasi-experimental research** involves the study of cause and effect relationships; controls for or manipulates independent variables to predict changes or to study outcomes (Koroscik & Kowalchuk, 1997). A teacher might implement a new curriculum in one class and compare the results of that class to the other classes that used a more traditional curriculum.
- **Survey research** usually relates to the description or characteristics of a large group of people from a smaller representative sample collected at a particular point in time (Koroscik & Kowalchuk, 1997). Surveys may be quantitative in structure using Likert scales or other close-ended questions or they may be qualitative using open-ended questions. A researcher might survey all the art teachers in her or his state to learn how they utilize multicultural art education practices in their classrooms.
- **Theoretical research** involves the analysis of key features of a concept with a purpose of adding to or articulating relevant complex connections within the field (Koroscik & Kowalchuk, 1997; Thurber, 2004). Research using this methodology can generate new theory or investigate an existing theory for its soundness (Thurber, 2004). A researcher might do an in-depth analysis of an existing theory and develop a rationale for how aspects of the theory could be used to build a curriculum structure for an art program.

As beginning researchers learn more about methodologies, it is useful to talk with a research mentor or university advisor about various methodologies and to read recent theses or dissertations that have used different methodologies. Understanding how others have used a methodology can help a research project significantly. In becoming aware of the nuances of a methodology, researchers can plan for and navigate potential obstacles. This process is a little like reading several guidebooks on the same travel itinerary to learn where previous travelers have run into complications or point out an added bonus that is worth the extra effort to see. By carefully reading literature on a specific methodology, which is effectively a travel guide through the research journey, researchers can increase the quality of their studies and hopefully maximize the benefits of each decision they make in designing a study.

SARA AND MELANIE:

METHODS: WHAT TOOLS DO RESEARCHERS USE TO COLLECT AND ANALYZE DATA? *Though the terms* methodology *and* methods *may be used interchangeably at times, they are fundamentally different. Whereas a methodology is a larger approach to research with specific guidelines involving the structure and process of conducting a study, methods are the specific means of collecting or analyzing data. Thus, a methodology may be case study, action research, or quasi-experimental research, but the methods may consist of interviews, questionnaires, pre- and post-tests, among others (see the Methods section in Chapter 6).*

SARA AND MELANIE:

MIXED METHODS & RELIABILITY: *Advanced researchers may conduct mixed methods research and utilize a range of methods of data collection and analysis, possibly involving both quantitative and qualitative approaches. For instance, a researcher might begin a study with a quantitative survey to gather demographics and characteristics of a large group of art teachers. From the survey, the researcher could then identify a smaller group of participants who agreed to participate in qualitative follow-up interviews. Large grants, especially for the federal government, may require quantitative data and may specify parameters that govern how a research study can be conducted, and researchers may employ mixed methods design in these cases. Employing multiple methods is one way to triangulate data collection and analysis. Using data collected by different methods and analyzing it in multiple ways is likely to increase the reliability of a study's findings.*

Reliability and validity are terms that are most generally associated with quantitative studies. Qualitative researchers utilize different terms including credibility, transferability, and dependability to represent similar ideas (Denzin & Lincoln, 2005). Though different researchers have nuanced understandings of these terms, they generally refer to the notion of reliability as published results of a study that are a good representation of the people being studied and what actually occurred during the course of the research. While validity in quantitative work typically refers to the degree to which the research measures what it was intended to measure and if the results can be trusted (Guba & Lincoln, 2011), in qualitative work, there are many types of validity including contextual validity (Saukko, 2005), catalytic validity (Kincheloe & McLaren, 2005), dialogic validity (Saukko, 2005), among others.

These terms as defined from a quantitative perspective may not apply to a qualitative research paradigm, but qualitative researchers find usefulness in considering the terms differently, "Reliability and validity are conceptualized as trustworthiness, rigor and quality in qualitative paradigm" (Golafshani, 2003, p. 604). While replicability in the results may not be a concern of qualitative researchers, examining the design of the study and the carefulness of the researcher's methods will increase the credibility and transferability, and aid in the evaluation, of the findings of a qualitative study. For a useful in-depth discussion of reliability, validity and triangulation in quantitative and qualitative studies, please see: www.nova.edu/ssss/QR/QR8-4/golafshani.pdf

When discussing qualitative research I find I must spend time explaining it because our society is more familiar with quantitative research. I have found those with a strong quantitative background seem to want hard numerical data where qualitative data can be a lot more subjective. I find myself explaining that qualitative research tends to be more site and situation specific—that while it potentially has implications for other situations, it is specifically about what is happening in a particular location, to a particular group at a particular time. In my teaching, qualitative research is of great value because it directly relates to realities of my situation. It is extremely helpful to me in gaining a rich understanding of a particular issue that I face within my teaching. Just like quantitative research there are particular steps that must be carried out in qualitative research.

AMY BERGH

QUANTITATIVE AND QUALITATIVE RESEARCH

At times, methodologies may be categorized as quantitative or qualitative. Quantitative methodologies aim to quantify specific variations identified in a study—structured in ways to measure *quantities*. Qualitative methodologies focus on describing phenomena and how phenomena vary—attending to specific *qualities* of the researched phenomenon.

In the previous chapter about paradigms, we discussed how ontology and epistemology inform a researcher's worldview. Additionally, those underlying beliefs inform what a researcher believes can be known through research and which methodology would best achieve a researcher's goals.

Quantitative Research. In general, researchers who favor quantitative methodologies assume an objective stance and assume that social reality is relatively constant across time and settings (Gall, Gall, & Borg, 2003). Additionally, these researchers employ predetermined research designs that may involve validated assessment instruments, such as standardized test formats, and various numerical data for statistical analysis (Creswell, 2003). Quantitative research emphasizes measurement or clarification of variables, often through a large sample size. Accordingly, quantitative research strives for reliability and objectivity (often considered to be value-free) as it explains the "prevalence, incidence, extent, nature of issues, opinions, and attitudes" while also "discover[ing] regularities and formulat[ing] theories" (Kumar, 2005, p. 18). Thus, in quantitative work, computational tabulations allow findings to demonstrate the magnitude and strength of a relationship(s).

Qualitative Research. In contrast, qualitative researchers assume that social reality is constructed and assume that it is continuously constructed in local situations (Gall et al., 2003), largely focusing on what Eisner (1998) deemed the "particular" of a research site (p. 12). Typically, research designs in this vein are flexible or emergent (Gall et al., 2003; Kumar, 2005). Qualitative researchers seek to understand a situation or phenomenon in-depth, and because knowledge generated is situated in a specific context, it does not claim to be value-free or to be generalizable.

Methodology is Not Method

JANE CERA / ASSISTANT PROFESSOR OF ART EDUCATION, INDIANA UNIVERSITY SOUTH BEND

I t is not uncommon to see the terms method and methodology conflated and misconstrued. It is important for researchers to understand the distinction between these two terms. Methodology is grounded in the researchers' philosophical approach to research and in their beliefs surrounding the nature of knowledge. Methodology guides the selection of methods. It is helpful to think of methodology as the *why* behind what a researcher does. Similarly, methods can be distinguished as *how* the researcher goes about collecting and analyzing data.

Feminist philosopher Sandra Harding (1987) discussed methodology as the theory of knowledge and the interpretive framework that guides research. In contrast, she distinguished method as the technique used to gather data. Researchers must deal substantively with the methodological, paradigmatic, or theoretical questions that frame their orientations to research before deciding upon the methods or techniques to be employed in gathering data.

In order to begin to examine some of these questions, it is helpful to view research in education through the lens of larger developments in theory on research in general. The contrast between a modern or postmodern view of science is particularly relevant, given the past emphasis on the scientific paradigm of research.

SARA AND MELANIE: *While we find this examination of research assumptions helpful in terms of understanding methodologies, we caution readers against inherently making a simplistic modernist and postmodernist assessment of all methodologies because they can be employed in different ways. Cera's thoughts are very useful as a means to explore another way of understanding methodologies philosophically.*

Modernist assumptions regarding scientific knowledge have had a tremendous impact on research. The assumption of the existence of universal knowledge or truth led scientists to develop methodologies aimed at discovering the one right answer: an answer that supposedly could be predicted, tested, replicated, and eventually explained as objective knowledge. An emphasis on measurement and the use of quantitative data dominated modernist methodological paradigms.

Postmodern theory attacks the views of knowledge as objective, true, and testable. Postmodern scientific thinking changed the nature of scientific investigation and opinion concerning reliability of scientific data. Researchers in quantum physics discovered that there was an interaction between the researcher and the experiment itself. The researcher had a direct effect on the findings (Wheatley, 1992). The idea of scientific objectivity thus became discredited.

Disappearance of the notion of objectivity for many researchers has led to proliferation of a variety of research paradigms. Postmodern theorists believe there are many right answers, all profoundly influenced by the circumstances, environment, socio-cultural contexts, and perspectives of those involved. Discourses spawned from postmodern theory emphasize the impact of complexity, multiple perspectives, context, and cultural diversity on the production of knowledge and have become central concerns in educational research.

Many types of methodologies exist to allow researchers to examine their questions: survey, historical, correlational, case-study, experimental, longitudinal, arts based, narrative, and action research, to name but a few. What is important is to realize that researchers choose methods, to best answer the research question that was built from their philosophical orientation to methodology.

Let us imagine a study revolving around a central topic in education: student learning.

One researcher believes philosophically in the existence of universal truths that can be discovered. That is, she believes she can discover what type of instructional technique will lead to better learning. Another researcher believes that student learning is widely dependent on the individuals involved, and on the environments in which they live and learn. The first researcher decides to use a quasi-experimental methodology and quantitative methods including a pre- and post-test. She constructs an experiment designed to measure the effectiveness of different types of instruction. The success of students on a particular task will be measured after they have been instructed via one of two techniques. The results will be analyzed, the two groups compared, and a determination made as to the more successful technique. The second researcher decides to conduct a qualitative narrative inquiry study and interviews students and teachers while

(continued)

observing classroom activity in many different types of schools and in many different areas of the country. This researcher looks for patterns that distinguish some groups of learners from others and draws conclusions based on these differences.

In this simplified example, note the differences between methodologies. One researcher holds more modernist views, the other, more postmodern. Their selection of methodology and methods is influenced by their basic beliefs about the nature of knowledge and research. The modernist researcher believes that objective answers can be discovered and measured, and hence chooses the methodology of quasi-experimental design. She could just as easily have chosen to analyze existing student achievement test scores and correlated them to the instructional technique used by the teacher. Still, her choice was based on her methodological orientation of looking at data to determine a single, generalizable answer to her research question. The postmodern researcher believes that individuals hold different answers that are right for them, and uses methods of observation and interview to examine a research question. This researcher could have chosen different methods as well. Perhaps a survey could be used to gather some of the same information as the observations. This researcher would still examine the survey results from the methodological orientation of looking for multiple possibilities in multiple contexts.

Researchers frame their methodology by reflecting upon personal philosophy. One's beliefs about the nature of knowledge and research form the basis of one's methodological orientation. Once this foundation exists, researchers can determine the best methods by which to collect and analyze their data in order to answer their research question. ■

REFERENCES

Harding, S. (1987). Feminism and methodology. Bloomington, IN: University Press.

Lather, P. (1992). Critical frames in educational research: Feminist and post-structural perspectives. Theory into Practice, 21(2), 87-99.

Wheatley, M. (1992). Leadership and the new science: Learning about organization from an orderly universe. San Francisco, CA: Berrett-Koehler.

NARROWING FROM A RESEARCH TOPIC TO A RESEARCH QUESTION

Creswell (2008) suggests that researchers gradually work from a general topic to a specific area of interest. We echo his suggestion and offered ideas in Chapter 3 for possible ways of finding a topic within art education. Once a teacher researcher identifies a potential **topic**, reviewing the literature about the topic is essential. After narrowing to a topic, it is important to clarify further and identify a **research problem**. Continuing with the example from Chapter 3 on multicultural art education (topic), a teacher researcher would need to further refine this to come to a manageable research problem. A research problem could be "the lack of resources specific to art education to foster multicultural, or culturally-relevant, teaching practices." Any topic could lead to a range of research problems; this is where the researcher brings in her or his interests, theories, and paradigms to determine the direction of the study. The next step that Creswell (2008) advocates is writing a **purpose statement**. In this short statement, the researcher clearly articulates the reason for conducting the research. With the multicultural art education example, a purpose statement might be, "To study what art teachers need in terms of curriculum resources to increase their teaching of culturally-relevant units." After clarifying to the point of a purpose statement, the researcher goes on to develop a specific research question(s). Many advisors will ask graduate students to write multiple iterations of their research problem, purpose statement, and research question(s). This clarity is crucial because the research question(s) drive the development of the plan for the research study.

RESEARCH QUESTIONS: METHODOLOGY MATTERS

After narrowing a topic to a research problem and further to a purpose statement, a researcher can begin to formulate a specific research question or multiple questions. It will be important, however, throughout this formulation process to consider the paradigm (and the methodology/ies) that resonates with the researcher's underlying beliefs. In Chapter 3, we explored ways of using pre-existing maps of the field and knotty areas of your teaching practice to identify a personal area of interest. Having passion for a particular research topic is a vital component in developing a sound research design, but a researcher also needs to consider how personal beliefs about research will inform methodology selection and question formation. For example, researchers who use quantitative methodologies tend to have questions that have yes/no answers that can be discerned from the data collected. Researchers who use qualitative methodologies have questions that typically aim to describe some area of interest or phenomenon. Regardless of the type of research, researchers carefully formulate research questions and employ a methodology with corresponding data collection and analysis methods, to elicit data that attempts to answer the research questions.

Quantitative Research Questions. If a researcher's approach to a study is quantitative, the researcher will likely deal with a hypothesis, a prediction about the relationship among variables, or a yes/no question. All researchers need to formulate questions or hypotheses in ways that are consistent with the methodology they mean to employ. Research questions in quantitative studies are fixed throughout the research period so it is important to phrase them carefully. Some examples of recent quantitative research questions in published studies include:

- Within the context of a descriptive study of the elementary art teachers in Florida who teach in multi-age classrooms, Broome asked, "Who are the art teachers in multi-age classrooms and what instructional practices do they use with their multi-age art classes?" (Broome, 2009, p. 173).
- In a study of Dutch teenagers comparing a group that participated in a special arts course and a group that did not participate, researchers investigated if, "the secondary students enrolled in CKV [a course on culture and the arts] participate more frequently in cultural activities and [is] their cultural attendance of more complexity?" (Damen, Nagel, & Haanstra, 2010, p. 149).

Qualitative Research Questions. Usually in qualitative research, researchers begin with a central question and then advanced researchers may develop associated sub-questions, generally not more than three to five (Creswell, 2003). Again, reviewing the literature of the intended methodology will help ensure rigor in a study beginning with the formulation of research questions because different methodologies offer guideposts for exploring topics differently. For example, an ethnographic study might "seek to understand," a case study might "explore a process," and a narrative research study might "report the stories" (Creswell, 2003, pp. 106-107). Some examples of recent qualitative research questions include:

- "How can Internet art be integrated into a secondary-level digital arts curriculum and taught to enable students to view the Internet more critically?" (Colman, 2004, p. 64).
- "How do art educative processes contribute to the transmission, maintenance, and evolution of artisan production in this particular context [a Zapotec weaver in Oaxaca, Mexico]?" (Davenport, 2007, p. 8).

Regardless of the methodology that a researcher employs, "powerful research questions emerge from 'felt difficulties'" (Dana & Yendol-Hoppey, 2009, p. 21), that teachers can identify. In the same way that teaching is more powerful when teachers ask students open-ended questions that relate to their lives, research is more meaningful when researchers ask meaningful questions, whose answers they do not know (Dana & Yendol-Hoppey, 2009) or cannot anticipate in advance of their inquiry. In the contribution that follows, contributor Lisa Hochtritt describes how crafting a sound research question reinforces many of these ideas and provides more specificity about this process.

As someone new to research I personally have a hard time narrowing my question. I try and include too much. I have learned that a more specific question is far more manageable. I think one of the pitfalls of new researchers is the feeling that they are not asking a big enough or important enough question. But as I examine other researchers' questions they narrow them down to a salient question in order to focus on what they want to learn.

AMY BERGH

Questioning What to Research

LISA HOCHTRITT / VISITING PROFESSOR, SCHOOL OF THE ART INSTITUTE OF CHICAGO (SAIC)

Creating research questions can be a collaborative and enjoyable process. The act of researching gives you an opportunity to look deeply into an issue and spend time reflecting on why it is so. The biggest mistake most beginning researchers make is to take on too much, making the topic of research too large. Narrowing your inquiry is key to a manageable research study so that it will produce useful results.

Deciding what to research can be difficult. This is a project you will be working on for a long time so you need to be very interested in the topic. First, start by reflecting on something you **notice** and then something you **wonder** about. Sullivan (2009, para. 6) calls it a "quizzical itch"—what do you want to know more about? For example, when I was a high school visual arts teacher I noticed that students readily congregated in the art room after school, and I wondered what encouraged them to make art outside of class. This idea led me to conduct a qualitative research study with young people who were involved in art forms that were not necessarily encouraged in classrooms, such as manga, graffiti art, and writing and performing rap music.

When I work with my own graduate students who are conducting research in their classrooms, I first ask them to write a paragraph about something they are interested in finding out more about. From the paragraph, students then complete a short literature review to see who else is writing in this area and what questions these authors explored in their studies. When we move to designing the research question, we make it a deconstructive and reconstructive exercise. We look at multiple research questions we think "work" then break them down into parts of speech or descriptors. The students then share their paragraphs with the class, and we collaboratively come up with research questions using a fill-in-the-blanks exercise. This is similar to a mad lib activity where key words are replaced with blanks and underneath the blanks are parts of speech or specified descriptors.

For example, a deconstructed research question might look like Figure 1.

Graduate students' (or teacher researchers') related qualitative research questions might then be:

- What are the outcomes when high school students create their own art lessons around the idea of defiance? Figure 2.
- Or, In what ways do third graders respond when they use visual literacy exercises to deconstruct Disney imagery? Figure 3.

A quantitative question that seeks to compare the relationship between two variables might be:

- Does participation in the arts increase student achievement in high school upper level math courses? Figure 4.

FIG 1	What		[when]		
		Verb and/or Noun	Who/Participants	Do what?	About what?

FIG 2	What	are the outcomes	[when] high school students	create their own art lessons?	around the idea of defiance?
		Verb and/or Noun	Who/Participants	Do what?	About what?

FIG 3	In what ways do		third graders respond	[when] they use visual literacy exercises	to deconstruct Disney imagery?
		Verb and/or Noun	Who/Participants	Do what?	About what?

FIG 4	Does	participation in the arts	increase student achievement	in high school upper level math courses?
		Verb and/or Noun	Do what?	Who/Participants? About what?

By referring back to initial research questions uncovered in the field, students can then collaboratively deconstruct them using the mad lib style. These fun and good-humored exercises generate many research questions and ideas from which the students can then choose which ones they might pursue in a research study.

Keeping the research question open-ended is essential for qualitative research. You definitely do not want a question that can be answered with a "yes" or a "no," unless you are conducting a quantitative study. In qualitative research, close-ended questions will not encourage you to delve deeply into your topic and will stop you before you understand the nuanced responses of your results. However, they are useful for hypothesis testing or for experimental or quasi-experimental research. As you work to identify your focused research question(s), you will, of course, also be considering which methodologies may be appropriate for the type of research you will be conducting.

Educational researchers and teachers, interested in delving further into an issue they have noticed or wondered about in their classrooms, frequently do not set out to prove something, but rather to better understand a situation or to improve practice. Spending reflective energy to pursue something you care about deeply is a meaningful activity that can illuminate next steps in your teaching and learning inquiries. ■

REFERENCE

Sullivan, G. (2009). *Art practice as research*. Retrieved from http://artpracticeasresearch.com

> You may find that the methodology needed to answer a question is different from how you initially identified your research interest. I found this to be the case and had to decide if I wanted to continue with the direction my research was going or change course entirely to align more closely with the paradigm I felt more attached to.
>
> AMY BERGH

CONSIDERING THE RELATIONSHIP BETWEEN METHODOLOGIES AND RESEARCH QUESTIONS

In the next sections of this book, we address how methodology (or methodologies) and research question(s) relate to each other and inform each other. Perhaps a clothing metaphor will help underscore the importance of this aspect of the research process. There are more appropriate types of clothing for going different places or doing different jobs. It makes sense to wear a bathing suit at the pool, but would probably elicit many funny looks if worn to grocery shop. Clothing is not inherently good or bad, but the reaction a wearer gets depends upon the context and its typical use. If the bathing suit is akin to case study methodology, it makes sense to wear that (use it) to understand how the art teacher in an otherwise low performing school helps students excel in art as evidenced by high acceptance rates for his or her students to the Governor's School for Creative Arts. But case study would not be an appropriate methodology if the researcher wanted to answer the question: What percent of students in x district choose art at the middle school level? That would be a mismatch of methodology and research question, and survey methodology would be a better fit with this question. Again, digging deeply into a methodology of interest (from reading the methodology chapters and exemplars in the second half of this book and reading further what specialists in particular methodologies have written) can assist a new researcher in designing and conducting a sound research study and increase the overall rigor of the study.

CONCLUSION

In this chapter, we discussed the distinctions between qualitative and quantitative research, explored the importance that methodology plays in building a sound research study, and discussed formulating high quality research questions by moving gradually from a topic to a research problem to a purpose statement to a narrowly focused research question or hypothesis. In the next chapter, we discuss additional steps in the research design process and introduce a range of methods for collecting and analyzing data.

REFERENCES

Broome, J. L. (2009). A descriptive study of multi-age art education in Florida. *Studies in Art Education, 50*(2), 167-183.

Clandinin, D. J., & Murphy, M. S. (2009). Relational ontological commitments in narrative research. *Educational Researcher, 38*(8), 598-602.

Colman, A. (2004). Net.art and Net.pedagogy: Introducing Internet art to the digital art curriculum. *Studies in Art Education, 46*(1), 61-73.

Creswell, J. W. (2003). *Research design: Qualitative, quantitative, and mixed methods approaches* (2nd ed.). Thousand Oaks, CA: Sage.

Creswell, J. W. (2008). *Educational research: Planning, conducting, and evaluating quantitative and qualitative research* (3rd ed.). Thousand Oaks, CA: Sage.

Damen, M. L., Nagel, I., & Haanstra, F. (2010). Short-term effects of compulsory multidisciplinary secondary school arts education on cultural participation in the Netherlands. *Studies in Art Education, 51*(2), 147-161.

Dana, N. F., & Yendol-Hoppey, D. (2009). *The reflective educator's guide to classroom research: Learning to teach and teaching to learn through practitioner inquiry* (2nd ed.). Thousand Oaks, CA: Corwin Press.

Davenport, M. G. (2007). Between tradition and tourism: Educational strategies of a Zapotec artisan. *International Journal of Education & the Arts, 8*(11). Retrieved from www.ijea.org/v8n11/

Denzin, N. K., & Lincoln, Y. S. (2005). The discipline and practice of qualitative research. In N. K. Denzin & Y. S. Lincoln (Eds.), *The Sage handbook of qualitative research* (pp. 1-32). Thousand Oaks, CA: Sage.

Eisner, E. (1998). *The enlightened eye: Qualitative inquiry and the enhancement of educational practice.* Upper Saddle River, NJ: Prentice Hall.

Gall, M. D., Gall, J. P., & Borg, W. R. (2003). *Educational research: An introduction* (7th ed.). Boston, MA: Pearson Education.

Golafshani, N. (2003). Understanding reliability and validity in qualitative research. *The Qualitative Report, 8*(4), 597-607. Retrieved from www.nova.edu/ssss/QR/QR8-4/golafshani.pdf

Guba, E. G., & Lincoln, Y. S. (2011). Paradigmatic controversies, contradictions, and emerging confluences revisited. In N. K. Denzin & Y. S. Lincoln (Eds.), *The Sage handbook of qualitative research* (4th ed.) (pp. 97-128). Thousand Oaks, CA: Sage.

Kincheloe, J. L., & McLaren, P. (2005). Rethinking critical theory and qualitative research. In N. K. Denzin & Y. S. Lincoln (Eds.), *The Sage handbook of qualitative research* (pp. 303-342). Thousand Oaks, CA: Sage.

Koroscik, J. S., & Kowalchuk, E. (1997). Reading and interpreting research journal articles. In S. LaPierre & E. Zimmerman (Eds.), *Research methods and methodologies for art education*, (pp. 75-102). Reston, VA: National Art Education Association.

Kumar, R. (2005). *Research methodology: A step-by-step guide for beginners* (rev. ed.). Thousand Oaks, CA: Sage.

May, W. T. (1997). Action research: Pt. 1. "Teachers-as-researchers." In S. LaPierre & E. Zimmerman (Eds.), *Research methods and methodologies for art education* (pp. 223-240). Reston, VA: National Art Education Association.

McNiff, S. (1998). *Art-based research.* London, England: Jessica Kingsley.

Saukko, P. (2005). Methodologies for cultural studies: An integrative approach. In N. K. Denzin & Y. S. Lincoln (Eds.), *The Sage handbook of qualitative research* (pp. 343-356). Thousand Oaks, CA: Sage.

Thurber, F. (2004). Teacher education as a field of study in art education: A comprehensive overview of methodology and methods used in research about art teacher education. In M. Day & E. Eisner (Eds.), *Handbook of research and policy in art education* (pp. 487-522). Mahwah, NJ: Lawrence Erlbaum Associates.

SARA AND MELANIE: *This short section with the work of two contributors is intended to give readers a glimpse into many of the decisions that researchers make as they plan and implement a study. Thinking through the various means of data collection and analysis as well as the plan for the research study before beginning the study is of paramount importance. In the section that follows this, there are many descriptions of data collection and analysis intended to help with planning a study.*

Phases of Managing a Case Study Research Project: Practical Considerations

JAE-YOUNG LEE / ASSISTANT PROFESSOR, KOREA NATIONAL UNIVERSITY OF EDUCATION

This section explores the value of dividing a research project into phases. Doing so makes the research process manageable and allows the findings of early data analysis to affect the development of subsequent phases of the research.

My case study research was designed to investigate how a small group of sixth-grade students understand their favorite popular images and consider the influences of the images on their sense of self. My teaching and research experiences helped me develop the curriculum for this research, which aimed to understand students' critical consciousness and empowerment. My research question was: *In what ways do students understand and respond to a curriculum designed to engage aspects of visual culture theory to develop students' critical consciousness and empowerment, and to respond and adapt to students' needs and interests?* This case study was inspired by a need to translate theory into practice because of the gap that exists between theory and reality. In order to do this, however, I realized I needed to think of my research in phases to develop a manageable flow for the study.

After the initial curriculum design, I conducted a pilot study in which I taught the visual culture-based curriculum. By collecting data and conducting intensive data analysis, I identified the need for a curriculum and instructional strategies that responded to and adapted to students' emergent needs, interests, and issues.

Because of the results of the pilot study, I revised the initial curriculum and developed a 10-session responsive curriculum with instructional methods that facilitated meaningful reflection for the sixth graders. To obtain a better understanding of their reflections, I needed to examine further how to integrate qualitative research components, in-depth interviews and constant data analysis into practice throughout the instruction conducted in an after school art class organized specifically for this research. Therefore, I developed the following four phases for the case study research project.

PHASE 1: INSTRUCTION (FOUR CLASS SESSIONS)

As the instructor, I provided four sessions of instruction involving self-portrait projects for students to consider their notions of "self." The projects were intended to encourage students to create two self-portraits that depicted themselves naturally in relation to the popular images they liked. Considering their relationship to these popular images, the students expressed various things such as accomplishment, desire, belongings, preferences, personality, appearance, etc.

PHASE 2: IN-DEPTH INTERVIEWS

By conducting two in-depth interviews with the students about their self-portraits and analyzing the collected data, this phase yielded an understanding of the influences and social issues derived from the images. These interviews were necessary to allow me, as the instructor, to differentiate further instruction in phase 3. I asked the students why they created their self-portraits and how these portraits represented them. By delving into the feelings, nuances, and consistency of the students' explanations, I recognized students' favorite popular images and the impact these images made on them in terms of the stereotypes and biases that sustain many ongoing social issues in our society.

PHASE 3: DIFFERENTIATED INSTRUCTION (SIX CLASS SESSIONS)

Based on what I found in phase 2, each student had three more artmaking projects. Students worked individually with their favorite images and the social issues. Each project and individual conversation engaged in during the instruction aimed to encourage the students' reflection on the images and self. To facilitate this, the first project asked students to depict visually the typically invisible problems of using the images in our society in terms of the kinds of knowledge, thoughts, values, and attitudes the students perceived from the images. The second project asked the students to deconstruct images by manipulating them and adding images of the students' superhero(ine) to highlight the inequality and injustice in our society. During the final project, students created an image of a better society in their minds by putting

(continued)

their favorite images into the contexts they experienced in daily life, and by considering how to enhance social justice and equity.

PHASE 4: IN-DEPTH INTERVIEWS AND WRITTEN PORTRAITS
I conducted three more in-depth interviews and applied intensive data analysis to create individual written portraits of the students. This fourth phase examined the effects of the curriculum implementation in terms of developing students' critical consciousness and empowerment.

From this case study, I found various social issues identified by students and the effects of a responsive instructional approach that sought to engage the students by structuring this study in these phases. By designing this research to focus on individual students' reflection of self and the influences made by the images they considered personally meaningful, I determined that the critical consciousness and empowerment of various types of students relate to their intellectual, emotional, and even moral responses to examining these influences critically. ■

Girls' Engagement in the Choice-Based Art Class

DIANE B. JAQUITH / VISUAL ART TEACHER, FRANKLIN ELEMENTARY SCHOOL, NEWTON, MA

In choice-based art education, where student autonomy is the goal of instruction, many variables influence learner engagement. Choices of content and media provide strong intrinsic motivation for most, but not all learners. This action research study examines girls' artistic behaviors for the purpose of improving achievement for those with low engagement. The descriptive research study involved 86 girls in a K-5 suburban elementary school and was conducted by the art teacher. Girls were assigned to cohorts representing high, average, and low engagement based on their performance in the art classroom during the first term. The high engagement cohort (HEC) consisted of learners who were extremely attentive to their work. Girls in the average engagement cohort (AEC) usually focused on their work. Students in the low engagement cohort (LEC) required frequent teacher interventions to remain on-task.

DATA COLLECTION
Data were collected using three sources: an observation checklist, student chart, and progress report comments. Simple systems enabled the teacher to collect data during class. A checklist documented artistic behaviors including inquiry, innovation, media use, reflection, time management, and social interactions over a 6-week period for each class. Students assisted with the second form of data collection. Each week, they placed color stickers onto a chart to record their choices of media. Third, classroom teachers' narrative comments on first-term progress reports were collected for every participant.

DATA ANALYSIS
Using a data analysis matrix (Sagor, 2000, p. 128), artistic behavior information was entered on separate grids for each participant (See Figure 1). Patterns were noted for cohort groups based on frequency of repetition. Media choices were tallied and averaged by cohort, using student sticker charts, for the entire first semester. This information was entered into a grade-level matrix for comparison. Progress report comments were sorted and tallied, by cohort, based on categories including reading, writing, math, creativity/higher order skills, and social skills.

FINDINGS
From the data analysis of artistic behaviors, trends were noted for each cohort. HEC participants prefer to work alone and persevere through failures, frequently taking risks. These innovators interact playfully with materials, revising and extending their original ideas. AEC girls also enjoy play and like to collaborate. Though their skills are strong, their artistic process is rarely unique. LEC participants rarely play with materials or take risks, abandon artwork when challenged, and frequently seek teacher support and affirmation. Choices of media revealed few differences among all

SOURCES OF GIRLS' ENGAGEMENT IN AND OUT OF ART CLASS

	PERSEVERANCE	CREATIVITY	RISK-TAKING	MAKING MEANING	PARTICIPATION
Instructional time	Focuses attention			Listens, applies concepts to work (if applicable)	Asks questions, comments
Studio time	Intrinsic motivators (curiosity, interests); extrinsic motivators (expectations, peer pressure); autonomy	Problem finding and solving, innovation, divergent thinking, plays with materials and techniques	Challenges self with new media, techniques, ideas; comfortable with ambiguity; repeats ideas with new direction; defers v. abandons work	Pauses to reflect, asks "What if;" relates work to previous work; self-assesses progress	Works independently or collaboratively; seeks support from peers and teacher; collaborative assessment
Clean up	Stores work in safe place				Takes responsibility
Sharing time			Discusses work with peers	Verbalizes intent, considers audience	Demonstrates interest in others' work
Classroom	Makes connections with curricula	Innovation and problem solving	Challenges self	Integrates class curricula with artwork	Asks questions, comments, seeks support
Outside school	Prepares for art class with plans, sketches, collections	Incorporates outside interests and experiences into artwork	Applies knowledge and skills to work	Artwork has personal relevancy	Shares artwork with family

FIGURE 1. A data matrix showing patterns for analysis of contributing factors in learner engagement during art class and outside of school time.

three cohorts. Two findings are notable: HEC girls in grades 2-4 specialized in fewer media, on average, versus their peers. Also, fourth-grade HEC participants chose digital media twice as often as their peers. Classroom progress reports revealed performance trends for the three cohort groups. AEC participants are generally working at grade level in all areas, while half of HEC and most LEC participants showed inconsistent performance across the curriculum. Most teacher comments pertaining to creativity and problem solving in the classroom addressed HEC participants, who are most innovative in art class.

IMPLICATIONS

As a result of this action research, the following strategies have been implemented to improve learner engagement:

- Facilitate opportunities for play with varied media, including digital technology for older students

- Understand why students abandon artwork (perceived failure, lack of interest, diversion)
- Highlight failures as new beginnings
- Model problem-solving techniques

Action research provides rich data to inform practice. The complexities of teaching while conducting research limited both the timing and duration of this study. Training students to self-monitor and student teacher support will facilitate future action research studies. ∎

REFERENCE

Sagor, R. (2000). *Guiding school improvement with action research.* Alexandria, VA: Association for Supervision and Curriculum Development.

6 / What Now? Planning a Study and Choosing Research Methods

MELANIE L. BUFFINGTON AND SARA WILSON MCKAY

MELANIE: *When I first started baking as a child, my mother always told me to read through the entire recipe first, check that I had enough of all the ingredients, and then start mixing up the cookie dough. Inevitably, I would not always go through all the planning phases and would discover, after adding several ingredients, that there was not enough flour or eggs or something else crucial for the recipe. This led to a scolding from my mother—combined with either an emergency trip to the grocery store, an attempt at a substitution that was, at best, marginally successful, or a baking project that had to be refrigerated until there was time later to go purchase the missing ingredients. None of these outcomes was as good as when I actually listened to my mother, read the complete recipe, and checked all the ingredients before beginning.*

This chapter has two distinct parts. The first part addresses planning the stages of a study, and the second part includes several short sections written by art educators that relate to methods of collecting and analyzing data.

Part I: Planning a Research Study

EARLY CONSIDERATIONS

> Reading studies that use similar data collection methods would also be extremely helpful in trying to understand the intricacies of your study.
>
> AMY BERGH

One reason why Lee's study of preschool and Jaquith's study of girls in elementary school (in the previous chapter) were successful is that the researchers carefully planned the various phases of the study before implementing them. As in the baking story above, before beginning a study, it is crucial to think through an entire research study and make decisions about a research plan in which the parts all work well together. While many qualitative researchers utilize emergent design and make decisions based upon early data analysis, these are not rushed or random decisions. As a chef may make reasoned substitutions or alter a recipe for a purpose, so too may a researcher change course based upon early findings. This means that your research plan relates to your paradigm and methodology, and it allows you to appropriately answer your research question. As you move from a research question to developing a study, it is important to discuss your intended question and emerging ideas for data collection and analysis with someone who is experienced conducting research or your research advisor.

It is also important that you develop an awareness of all factors that are coming together at this point in planning a study, including but not limited to: the theories that underpin how you think about teaching and learning; your paradigm(s); practical considerations of your research setting be it a classroom, school, community center, or museum setting, etc.; the topic you are researching; the methodology or methodologies; and the question(s) you developed and are addressing.

PUTTING THE PIECES OF A RESEARCH STUDY TOGETHER

There are two main ways that researchers approach the design of their study: *a priori* or emergent design. *A priori* (Latin meaning "prior to") design is common among quantitative studies. An *a priori* study design involves making virtually all decisions about the study before undertaking the collection of data. The researcher creates a plan and then follows it exactly. This predetermined structure in the design of the study is important to ensure that the same procedures are followed throughout all settings and stages of the research.

For instance, in a quasi-experimental study in which an art teacher wants to compare two different curricular approaches to teaching about contemporary artists, one oriented toward DBAE and another oriented toward social justice, it would be important that the assessment instruments used to measure student learning be the same for both groups and be determined before the study begins. In an *a priori* study design, the researcher cannot subsequently change the format of an assessment instrument to reflect situations that the researcher could not have anticipated before the study commenced.

In contrast to *a priori* design, emergent design is more common among qualitative studies. A researcher using an emergent design approach usually begins with a plan. However, as data are collected, they are also analyzed. The researcher uses these early findings to plan the next step of the study. Thus, the design is not haphazard; rather, the results of the early phases of data collection and analysis inform the later phases of the study.

In both types of design, *a priori* and emergent, the researcher creates a plan before beginning the research. The level of detail and possibility of adjusting the plan are different for these two types of designs. A researcher working to pull together the various parts of a research plan must consider several factors related to the methodology and the research question(s) including the participants, the location of the research, the methods of data collection, and the methods of data analysis.

PARTICIPANTS

A researcher needs to clearly think through how s/he plans to involve people in the study and what that will entail on the part of the participants (Creswell, 2008). For instance, conducting a case study of a teacher and his or her classroom setting will involve a considerable amount of time with one individual and likely will involve multiple interviews and observations with the teacher. Conducting a survey of art museum educators also involves participants, but their level of involvement will likely be of short duration. When making decisions about involving participants, it is important to be realistic and recognize that it is unusual to secure 100% participation from any group of people and that attrition from research studies is common. This does not mean that you should avoid involving people in your study, but you need to ensure that their participation is not onerous or too time consuming. Think through what you will do if a participant withdraws from the study overtly (as is their right at any time during a study), or how you will handle the situation if participants complete some, but not all, phases of the study.

Additionally, consider your research question(s) and the role of participants in your study while asking yourself several questions related to their involvement. What do you expect to learn from (or with) the participants? What is the optimum number of participants for your study? How will you gain access to these potential participants? How will their involvement help you answer the research questions? About how much time will their participation require? How will their participation benefit them? In general, people are more likely to agree to participate if their participation is relatively short term, they see the importance of the research, and they can see some relevance of the research in their own lives.

RESEARCH SITE

In addition to considering the people who will participate in the study, securing a research site is another essential early consideration. Even if you conduct research at your school, you still must follow official policies to acquire proper approvals. Many, if not most, school systems have a formal review process that researchers must go through to obtain official permission to conduct a study involving students or teachers in the district or to use a school facility as a research site (Creswell, 2008). This school or district level approval process is in addition to the IRB process (see section about Institutional Review Boards [IRB] in Chapter 3) that a university will require. Depending upon the district, this approval may take anywhere from a few weeks to several months or more.

A qualitative method of data collection may stress out those who like to have everything neatly planned prior to beginning any project. However the flexibility to make adjustments as situations evolve is incredibly helpful when conducting research in the teaching environment. Emergent design requires a little faith that all the parts will fall into place. There is so much that can happen in the classroom that is unforeseeable both good and bad that can greatly affect your study. It makes sense to be able to use these events as learning opportunities instead of having them viewed as a potential problem.

AMY BERGH

DATA COLLECTION

As you consider your research participants and research site, planning methods that you will use to collect data is important. Different types of data make more sense depending upon your methodology and the analysis that you plan to conduct. In quantitative studies, data usually take the form of numbers that are analyzed by various computational means. In qualitative studies, data are more likely to be texts (including videos, images, and audio recordings) that need to be interpreted and analyzed in different ways. Detailed later in this chapter, are numerous methods for collecting data including interviews, focus groups, and observations, among others.

SARA AND MELANIE: *Many researchers believe that it is important to triangulate their data collection and analysis; in research, triangulation refers to using multiple methods to collect and/or analyze data. This may involve collecting data through observations and interviews and/or multiple methods of data collection and analysis or having multiple researchers analyze the data (Maxwell, 2010; Patton, 2002).*

The plan for collecting data needs to clearly relate to the methodology and the research question(s). For instance, if you are conducting a quantitative survey, your questions should largely result in data that can be analyzed mathematically. Thus, phrasing the questions on the survey so that they will produce quantifiable data is important. "Yes/no" questions or Likert-style questions are likely to work well. When conducting a qualitative case study and using interviews as a method of data collection, phrasing the interview questions to yield data that can be coded for themes is crucial. Open-ended questions are likely to work well in eliciting data appropriate for a qualitative analysis. As you plan your data collection methods, remember that more data is not inherently better than less data; the quality of data is more important than the quantity of data.

DATA ANALYSIS

Concurrent with planning your data collection, you also need to consider the methods that you will utilize to analyze the data that you collect. There are many different ways to analyze both quantitative and qualitative data. The type of data analysis a researcher chooses needs to be appropriate for the methodology, the research question, and the type of data collected. Typically, quantitative data are analyzed using mathematical formulas to arrive answers to a research question. For instance, in the case of the quantitative survey question, "How many years have you been teaching art?" with the response categories of 0-3 years, 4-7 years, 8-11 years, 12-15 years, 16-19 years, 20-23 years, 24-27 years, 28-31 years, 32 years or more, a researcher might tabulate all the answers to each survey question and then determine the percent of the respondents who answered the question within each response category. There are numerous statistical calculations relevant to quantitative research including ANOVA, ANCOVA, and t-tests. Ryan Shin (Chapters 10-11) introduces some of these statistical processes and points toward additional resources.

SARA AND MELANIE: *In our work preparing this text, we realized that authors in art education are not always explicit about the processes they use for data analysis. We believe our field would benefit from additional attention directed toward disclosing methods of data analysis in research publications. This would help us, as a field, understand how researchers in art education come to conclusions. Making the process of data analysis more visible also might help new researchers navigate the processes they chose to use in their inquiries.*

I agree whole-heartedly that analyzing data is about the scariest thing to a new researcher. If more researchers explained this portion of their research more thoroughly, in language the average art teacher and graduate student could understand, it would be a great help.

AMY BERGH

SARA AND MELANIE: *In the current era of data-driven decision-making, pressure on educators to receive grants, and the importance of communicating what we do to those outside our field, conclusions that we draw need to be clearly explained by the data collected and the means by which it was analyzed. Tied into this, we believe that our field might benefit from a sustained discussion relating to the questions, "What does rigorous data analysis in art education research look like?" "What does rigorous statistical analysis look like?" "What does rigorous qualitative analysis look like?"*

I have sat in so many meetings that began with "the data show...." People tend to give just about anything that has data more credibility regardless of the topic and findings. If art educators want more credibility, within the educational system and society, than it behooves us to collect and present more data and how it was analyzed.

AMY BERGH

In qualitative research, data analysis is varied and may involve multiple methods. A common approach to analyzing qualitative data includes coding the data (Charmaz, 2005; Patton, 2002; Ryan & Bernard, 2000). In general terms, coding data begins with sustained interaction with the data that likely takes the form of thoroughly reading (or watching in the case of video data or looking closely if the data are artworks) all of the data multiple times. As a researcher engages with the data, she or he becomes increasingly familiar with it and will likely start to see similarities or differences among the data. Through multiple iterations of coding, the researcher progressively builds codes that are inter-related and finds themes that emerge form the data. The process of coding enables a researcher to better understand the data and to then draw conclusions from the data.

Another approach to data analysis is to employ grounded theory. At the basis of grounded theory is the premise that instead of using research to verify an existing theory, the researcher builds the theory from her or his data—essentially, the researcher builds theory from the ground up (Charmaz, 2005; Glaser & Strauss, 1967; Strauss & Corbin, 1998). Because a researcher's intent is not to prove or disprove a theory, but rather to build a theory, this is likely to lead to theories related to the daily experiences or practices of the participants. Thus, a grounded theory study produces a distinct shift in the role of theory and its relationship to the participants in the research project. In order to build an initial emerging theory into a substantiated formal theory, a researcher likely needs to conduct a number of related studies over time in order, usually with a larger number of participants who may differ on certain dimensions related to the study, to make meaningful claims.

GENERALIZABILITY AND TRANSFERABILITY

As the process of data analysis unfolds, researchers develop conclusions from their findings. When working through this process, researchers often work toward either generalizability or transferability. *Generalizability* is related to *quantitative* research methodologies and refers to a process by which a researcher draws conclusions from a population studied and asserts that the study can be replicated and that the conclusions from the study relate to others with similar characteristics (Greenwood & Levin, 2005). For instance, if a researcher conducted a survey of the elementary art educators who are members of National Art Education Association (NAEA), it is unlikely that the researcher would have a 100% response rate. However, if the researcher has an acceptable response rate, the findings from those who responded to the survey could reasonably be generalized to an entire population of elementary art educators who are members of NAEA. It would not be reasonable to generalize the results of a study to a different population such as middle school drama teachers. Usually, a researcher makes assertions about generalization of a study based upon the data analysis; thus, the power resides within the researcher to make these projections about how findings relate to other similar populations or circumstances.

In qualitative studies, generalizability is not the goal. Instead, *qualitative* researchers work toward *transferability* (Denzin & Lincoln, 2000). Because qualitative studies do not seek to find absolute "truths," generalizability does not make sense within the guidelines of qualitative methodologies. Transferability

The idea of coding data sounded very intimidating to me each time I thought about it. Then one evening in a research class Melanie shared with us a project she had been working on. She tracked different ideas within her data using color-coded sticky notes. Suddenly the idea of coding seemed very feasible. Each time we read something and mark common issues we are essentially doing basic coding. As we find additional related issues we add to it. Although there are certainly elaborate and sophisticated ways to track data, having a basic understanding and being able to practice is greatly helpful.

AMY BERGH

refers to implications of the findings for others that may be in similar settings or circumstances (Patton, 2002). Qualitative researchers work toward transferability through thick description (rich and extensive details concerning methodology and context) (Geertz, 1973) of their research participants and setting, significant details about the data collection and analysis process, and inclusion of examples of representative data. Presenting a significant level of detail allows readers of a research study to decide which aspects of the study and its findings can be reasonably transferred to their situation. Thus, the power with transferability resides with the reader of the research to make decisions about the relevance of findings for other settings, rather than in the researcher.

REFERENCES

Charmaz, K. (2005). Grounded theory in the 21st century: Applications for advancing social justice studies. In. N. K. Denzin & Y. S. Lincoln (Eds.), *The Sage handbook of qualitative research* (pp. 507-536). Thousand Oaks, CA: Sage.

Creswell, J. W. (2008). *Educational research: Planning, conducting, and evaluating quantitative and qualitative research*. Upper Saddle River, NJ: Pearson.

Denzin, N. K., & Lincoln, Y. S. (2000). The discipline and practice of qualitative research. In N. K. Denzin & Y. S. Lincoln (Eds.), *Handbook of qualitative research* (pp. 1-28). Thousand Oaks, CA: Sage.

Geertz, C. (1973). *The interpretation of cultures*. New York, NY: Basic Books.

Glaser, B. G., & Strauss, A. L. (1967). *The discovery of grounded theory*. Chicago, IL: Aldine.

Greenwood, D. J., & Levin, M. (2005). Reform of the social sciences, and of universities through action research. In. N. K. Denzin & Y. S. Lincoln (Eds.), *The Sage handbook of qualitative research* (pp. 43-64). Thousand Oaks, CA: Sage.

Maxwell, J. A. (2010). How might you be wrong? In W. Lutrell (Ed.), *Qualitative educational research: Readings in reflexive methodology and transformative practice*. (pp. 279-287). London, England: Routledge.

Patton, M. Q. (2002). *Qualitative research and evaluation methods*. Thousand Oaks, CA: Sage.

Ryan, G. W., & Bernard, H. R. (2000). Data management and analysis methods. In N. K. Denzin & Y. S. Lincoln (Eds.), *Handbook of qualitative research* (pp. 769-802). Thousand Oaks, CA: Sage.

Strauss, A., & Corbin, J. (1998). *Basics of qualitative research: Grounded theory procedures and techniques* (2nd ed.). Thousand Oaks, CA: Sage.

Part II: Methods of Data Collection and Analysis

The second half of this chapter includes short contributions written by different art educators that relate to specific methods of data collection and analysis. All of these methods have advantages and disadvantages and allow a researcher to collect different types of data that help answer different research questions. As you think through the design of your study, recognize how various methods of data collection may make sense for your study. Many of the contributions in this section are instructive, explaining the steps you need to take in order to employ a specific data collection method (see Greer, Nolte, and Rayala) or data analysis method (see Cera and Willis). We acknowledge that the methods of data collection and analysis presented here are not comprehensive. There are certainly other methods utilized within art education, and readers should be open to learning about and using additional methods as appropriate to a particular research study.

Additional essays in this section provide examples of how researchers in art education have approached their specific research interests in terms of data collection and analysis (see McClure and Kundu and Yang). In these cases, the processes of data collection and analysis are intricately intertwined and informed by the research topic. We include these examples to show the ways some art education researchers conduct research studies using data collection and analysis methods that best inform the research questions they are exploring.

Observations

ALANA GREER / MASTER'S OF ART EDUCATION GRADUATE,
VIRGINIA COMMONWEALTH UNIVERSITY

As teachers we constantly observe in our classrooms—assessing situations, checking for student understanding, monitoring behavior, reading students' levels of engagement. When formalized and documented, observation can serve as a research method for gathering both quantitative and qualitative data across methodologies. Observation involves gathering information first-hand at a specified location of research (Adler & Clark, 2008). Observation is often paired with other forms of data collection such as interviews, questionnaires, documents, and audiovisual materials (Angrosino, 2005; Creswell, 2008).

With observation, the researcher's role varies depending upon the selected methodology, research questions, access to the site, and rapport with the participants.

As a participant observer, researchers actually take part in the activities being observed while also recording information about the experience (Adler & Clark, 2008; Creswell, 2008). A teacher conducting a research project in her own class might take the role of a participant observer. In contrast, if an outside researcher were to come into a class to observe, she would likely begin her research as a nonparticipant observer—recording information on-site though not involved in the activities being observed (Adler & Clark, 2008; Creswell, 2008). Again, individual researchers must decide how involved they will become with their participants and assess how this interaction aides, hinders, or alters their research goals.

Data collected through observation commonly takes the form of field notes, drawings, diagrams, photographs, or coding on a pre-determined instrument (Creswell, 2008). Adler and Clark (2008) also recognized the extensive use of mental notes, especially by those researchers who are also participants. In quantitative behavioral observations, researchers use a pre-determined instrument such as a checklist or scoring sheet to record data when observing specific behaviors (Creswell, 2008). These "controlled (or systematic) observations" (Adler & Clark, 2008, p. 309) require consistent use of standardized procedures by trained observers (Creswell, 2008). Qualitative observations are also facilitated by determining observational protocol prior to beginning data collection so that observations remain consistent over time (Creswell, 2008). This protocol may take the form of a structured sheet for field notes that includes sections to note the date, the chronology of events, a description of the setting, a description or portrait of the participant(s), quotes, and so on (Creswell, 2008). Field notes may also be divided into a column for observations while leaving a column for later reflections (Creswell, 2008).

The detail and volume of observations will vary according to access to the site and the goal of the research. Creswell (2008) suggested a slow entry into the group of participants to make general observations of the setting before taking extensive notes. This movement from broad to specific observations presumes multiple opportunities to visit and observe the site (Creswell, 2008). It is advantageous for a researcher to spend time in the research setting observing in a general sense before collecting data with the specific intention of analyzing it. Frequently, it takes time to understand the dynamics of a setting and to develop a means for recording observation notes.

Rubizzi (2001), an educator from a preschool in Reggio Emilia, Italy where they practice observation and documentation on a daily basis, emphasized providing thorough detail of the setting and context in addition to noting dialogue and action, capturing the interaction between participants, and even noting times of inactivity. This idea, called "thick description," comes from the work of Geertz (1973). Whereas thin description is a simple notation of participants' actions, thick description include details regarding participant attitude and motivation as well as a possible meaning behind their actions (Adler & Clark, 2008). When the period of observation ends, researchers should withdraw slowly from the site, thanking participants, letting them know how the data will be used, and providing later access to the analyzed data (Creswell, 2008).

An advantage of observation is that the researcher is able to experience the research setting and activities. First-hand observation is particularly useful when working with participants who may have difficulty verbalizing their thoughts and ideas (Adler & Clark, 2008). Disadvantages to observation include researcher bias (validity), limited generalizability, and gaining access to sites (Adler & Clark, 2008). Also, participants' behavior may be altered due to the presence of the researcher (Adler & Clark, 2008). ∎

REFERENCES

Adler, E. S., & Clark, R. (2008). *How it's done: An invitation to social research.* Belmont, CA: Thomson/Wadsworth.

Angrosino, M. V. (2005). Recontextualizing oberservation: Ethnography, pedagogy, and the prospects for a progressive political agenda. In N. K. Denzin & Y. S. Lincoln (Eds.), *The SAGE handbook of qualitative research* (3rd ed.) (pp. 729-745). Thousand Oaks, CA: Sage.

Creswell, J. W. (2008). *Educational research: Planning, conducting, and evaluating quantitative and qualitative research.* Columbus, OH: Prentice Hall.

Geertz, C. (1973). Thick description: Toward an interpretive theory of culture. In C. Geertz, *The interpretation of cultures: Selected essays* (pp. 3-30). New York, NY: Basic Books.

Rubizzi, L. (2001). Documenting the documenter. In C. Giudici, C. Rinaldi & M. Krechevsky (Eds.), *Making learning visible: Children as individual and group learners* (pp. 94-115). Cambridge, MA: Project Zero.

Interviews

SAMANTHA NOLTE / DOCTORAL STUDENT IN ART EDUCATION,
THE PENNSYLVANIA STATE UNIVERSITY

Interviews are a common data collection format during research and are typically conducted over the phone or in person (Denzin & Lincoln, 2000). Interviews can be one-on-one or in a small group. Small groups allow for interactions between participants as well as the interviewer. Researchers should record interviews with a video or an audio recording device (Creswell, 2007). This ensures that it can be transcribed, reviewed, and interpreted later, when there is adequate time to consider how what was said contributes to answering the research question of the study (Creswell, 2007; Silverman, 2000). Interviews are useful when the researcher is seeking a person's perceptions about something or a person's internal experience of something (Silverman, 2000).

A structured interview format involves pre-determined questions with set wording in a set order. Often, combinations of closed-ended (answer choices are presented) and open-ended questions (answer in your own words) are used with this format (Adler & Clark, 2008). Structured interviews are used with quantitative methodologies and are excellent when the researcher needs to interview many people (Adler & Clark, 2008). During the interview, the pre-determined protocol is followed exactly (Adler & Clark, 2008; Denzin & Lincoln 2000).

The major advantage to a structured interview is consistency. Everyone received the same questions and answer options (Adler & Clark, 2008). Coding (finding patterns) and interpretation is easier with structured interviews than in other formats (Adler & Clark 2008). The major disadvantage is that there is little "wiggle-room" whereby unexpected answers and occurrences are more difficult to clarify or follow-up on. Structured interviews are the least flexible format option and rely heavily on the interviewer (Adler & Clark, 2008). But as the protocol is so explicit it can be easy to train an interviewer, which would be necessary if a large number of participants need to be interviewed in a short period of time (Denzin & Lincoln, 2000).

When considering a qualitative research methodology, using an unstructured or semi-structured interview may be more suitable (Adler & Clark, 2008; Denzin & Lincoln, 2000; Wolcott, 1988). Both of these options allow for more social interaction to occur (Adler & Clark, 2008; Denzin & Lincoln, 2000). What differentiates a qualitative interview from its quantitative counterpart is that the interviewer also acts as the research tool—using his or her knowledge of tone, inflection, and body language to better interpret and respond to what is said (Adler & Clark, 2008; Wolcott, 1988).

An unstructured interview is informal (Denzin & Lincoln, 2000). The interviewer begins with a general topic or prompt that is not too specific (Denzin & Lincoln, 2000). The interviewee responds to a prompt in a free-flowing dialogue, but the interviewer can ask for clarification or other questions as a result of what was said (Adler & Clark, 2008). Further unexpected but useful information may be volunteered. A major advantage of this format is its easy conversational tone (Denzin & Lincoln, 2000).

Unstructured interviews can be easily tailored to the needs of the interviewee. The disadvantage of this interview format arises from the uniqueness of each encounter that makes comparisons difficult. Unstructured interviews are the most flexible format and rely heavily on the interviewee to talk and narrate. The interviewer is there to listen, prompt, and facilitate the conversation. The interviewer must be highly skilled at listening and observing (Adler & Clark, 2008).

A semi-structured interview contains qualities of the other two formats. Like a structured interview, questions can be pre-determined and a guide for the interview can be created, thus allowing for general consistency between interviews (Adler & Clark, 2008). Still, an unstructured interview can maximize on the uniqueness of each encounter allowing the researcher to follow up on unexpected answers and tangents (Adler & Clark, 2008; Denzin & Lincoln, 2000). The major advantage of this format is its combination of flexibility and consistency, while the major disadvantage arises when several interviewers with varying abilities and interview skills are working on the study (Adler & Clark, 2008).

Whatever interview format the researcher chooses, interviews are a direct way to obtain information in a study. ∎

REFERENCES

Adler, E. S., & Clark, R. (2008). *How it's done: An invitation to social research* (3rd ed.). Belmont, CA: Thompson and Wadsworth.

Creswell, J. W. (2007). *Qualitative inquiry and research design: Choosing among five approaches* (2nd ed.). Thousand Oaks, CA: Sage.

Denzin, N.K., & Lincoln, Y.S. (Eds.) (2000). *Handbook of qualitative research* (2nd ed.). Thousand Oaks, CA: Sage.

Silverman, D. (2000). *Doing qualitative research: A practical handbook.* Thousand Oaks, CA: Sage.

Wolcott, H. F. (1988). Ethnographic research in education. In R. M. (Ed.), *Complementary methods for research in education* (pp. 327-353). Washington, DC: American Educational Research Association.

Focus Groups

ALANA GREER / MASTER'S OF ART EDUCATION GRADUATE,
VIRGINIA COMMONWEALTH UNIVERSITY

You may have heard of focus groups in relation to new product development and consumer reviews, but focus group interviews are also useful methods of collecting data when conducting educational research. Essentially, focus groups are facilitated discussions among a small group of people who share a similar trait. Focus groups provide researchers with insight into participants' feelings, reactions, and concerns regarding a particular issue (Flores & Alonso, 1995).

Ideally, focus groups should consist of three to twelve members (Adler & Clark, 2008) who share specific common traits related to the research topic (Krueger & Casey, 2000) but have not previously met (Adler & Clark, 2008; Flores & Alonso, 1995). Focus groups operate under the belief that people with similar concerns will open up and share their thoughts on the issue with other like-minded people. However, participants with prior relationships may prove reluctant to be open and honest during discussion (Flores, 1995). The commonality among group members may range from broad to narrow depending on the goal of the research (Krueger & Casey, 2000). In order to gather relevant data, researchers must carefully consider the composition of the focus group. For example, focus groups consisting of "teenage athletes," "female teenage athletes," "first-year high school athletes," or "teenage baseball players" would yield highly different results. Always review your specific research questions and group member characteristics when creating focus groups in order to obtain the most relevant and useable results. At least three focus groups of similar participants should be questioned in order to get a sense of emerging themes in that specific demographic (Krueger & Casey, 2000).

Since the goal of focus groups is to promote group discussion, the researcher functions as a moderator rather than an interviewer (Adler & Clark, 2008; Creswell, 2008; Flores, & Alonso, 1995). Focus group discussions are much easier to facilitate when the questions to be asked have been carefully thought-out and prepared. Krueger (2000) suggests that a sequence of questions that gradually become more specifically relevant to the study can help participants better formulate their opinions within a broader context and hopefully provide more reflective responses. Good focus group questions are open-ended, easily understood, and invite conversation. Shorter questions help to avoid confusion and will hopefully generate responses that relate directly back to the specifics of the question (Krueger & Casey, 2000).

The following example is a poor question: "Art teachers are not always considered essential members of the school faculty, because art is not included as a subject in standardized tests. How do you feel about this situation?" This question is too long, includes confusing negatives, and does not provide clear direction for the focus group members. The question could be reworked into a series of questions to be asked throughout the focus group interview, including: "As an art teacher, do you feel like an essential member of the school faculty? Why or why not? In what ways do standardized tests affect your role as an art teacher? Should art be included as a subject in standardized tests?"

Focus group discussions should be recorded and then transcribed for analysis. It is essential to have a high quality microphone attached to a recording device that is capable of picking up sound from throughout the entire room. This is something that the researcher needs to test ahead of time as it is not possible to re-create a focus group if the sound quality is too poor to transcribe. Extra batteries and an extension cord may also assist in problem-solving related to the technological aspects of recording. Further, it is advisable in any type of interview to have the researcher state at the beginning of the conversation that the conversation is being recorded and ask all the participants if that is acceptable to them. This recorded consent is in addition to IRB consent forms, not in place of it. To aid in transcribing the data, it is also helpful to have each participant state her/his name at the beginning of the recording giving the researcher a way to identify the speakers during the transcription process. The moderator should function as the data analyst, as she/he experienced the atmosphere as well as participants' facial expressions and body language (Flores & Alonso, 1995). While the moderator may take notes during the discussion, Creswell (2008) warned that some researchers may find the situation too hectic to write accurate documentation.

Potential problems of focus groups include members who dominate the conversation and members who are too timid to engage in discussion (Adler & Clark, 2008; Creswell, 2008). However, both of those obstacles could provide interesting insights into group dynamics and individual expression (Adler & Clark, 2008). Another concern is the confidentiality of member opinions expressed during the discussion (Adler & Clark, 2008).

Focus groups can prove beneficial when used in combination with other research methods. For example, they can provide

(continued)

interesting insight when compared to one-on-one interviews with the same group members (Adler & Clark, 2008). Morgan (1997) discusses how focus groups can also function as a preliminary step to quantitative studies, such as survey research, in order to better develop questions. Focus groups can put "a human face" on qualitative data already gathered (Morgan, 1997) and can reveal issues that questionnaires neglect (Adler & Clark, 2008). ■

REFERENCES

Adler, E. S., & Clark, R. (2008). *How it's done: An invitation to social research.* Belmont, CA: Thomson/Wadsworth.

Creswell, J. W. (2008). *Educational research: Planning, conducting, and evaluating quantitative and qualitative research.* Columbus, OH: Prentice Hall.

Flores, J. G., & Alonso, C. G. (1995). Using focus groups in educational research: Exploring teacher's perspectives on educational change. *Evaluation Review, 19*(1), 84-101. doi: 10.1177/0193841X9501900104

Krueger, R. A., & Casey, M. A. (2000). *Focus groups: A practical guide for applied research.* Thousand Oaks, CA: Sage.

Morgan, D. L. (1997). *Focus groups as qualitative research.* Thousand Oaks, CA: Sage.

Drawing as a Research Tool

MARTIN RAYALA / CHIEF ACADEMIC OFFICER, DESIGN-LAB SCHOOLS

Among the various methods for gathering research data, (interviews, observation, surveys, double-blind experiments, etc.), consider the value of drawing as a research tool. Researchers have effectively used drawing as a way to help observe, analyze, document, interpret and present research data for centuries (Barrow, 2008). Sketchbooks and journals kept by researchers in a variety of fields reveal their use of drawings along with other data (Lewis, 1997).

Making drawings as a way of collecting data (as argued here) is related to, but not the same as, analyzing drawings or interpreting visual images (Rose, 2006). In this instance, I am referring to drawings made by a researcher rather than drawings made by others that are analyzed by a researcher. Drawings made in the field as part of data gathering (pictorial ethnography) are an extension of visual anthropology and visual sociology traditions and have been used over time as research data (Rayala, 1983). Scientists from many fields have long created drawings, maps, diagrams, photographs, videos and other visual records as primary data in field and laboratory research.

Images in general have proven to be as useful as written transcripts or quantitative data in many research contexts including biology and chemistry (Frankel, 2002). Anthropologist Margaret Mead was an early pioneer in the use of photography and film as research tools, which later became a field known as "visual anthropology" (Mead, 1951). Drawing as a research tool owes a debt to this groundbreaking work with photography and film because visual means of communication in general have not always been accepted as appropriately "scholarly." Without the work of pioneers in scientific visualization it would be much more difficult to convince researchers of the scholarly value of drawing as a research methodology.

Much attention has been paid to the methods and procedures for using photos and films as research data (Collier, 1967) but there has not been as much systematic analysis of the value of drawings made by researchers in the field or lab. Research drawings include sketches, thumbnails, tracings, maps, diagrams, floor plans, site plans, charts, scientific illustrations, schematics, and any number of ways we generate, document and analyze visual data. The aesthetic or artistic qualities of the drawings are not as important as the discoveries that take place during the drawing process. Developing strong observational skills is more important than developing artistic ability.

There are several advantages for researchers who make their own drawings as part of their data collection and analysis process. In the initial stages of a research project, drawing on site is a good way to break the ice because drawing (1) helps provide a reassuring rationale for the presence of the researcher and (2) is intrinsically interesting to others. Outsiders (the researcher) entering a field observation setting may be regarded with suspicion because people wonder why they are there. Are they spies or potential robbers? The act of drawing is seen as benign, putting people at ease, and often can elicit contact and conversations not unlike the effect of going to a park with a puppy or a baby.

When a researcher is engaged in drawing it provides the time to settle in, observe and think about the work at hand in a way that simple observation or photography often do not. Making a drawing is one way to really "see" what is to be seen. Important details, nuances, subtleties, and hidden information that might have been missed often reveal themselves during the process of drawing. It is not uncommon for researchers to later find useful information in their drawings that they were not even conscious of putting there at the time.

Like any research method, one can expect to need a little training in how to do drawings for research appropriately. Few of us, for example, were born with a talent for statistical analysis—we had to learn how to do it. The same is true of research drawing; it can be learned with some effort. The ability to observe carefully and think visually is more important in research drawing than the ability to draw well.

There are many examples where an image conveys important information and ideas more clearly, accurately and effectively than words or numbers. James Watson and Francis Crick won the Nobel Prize for an image they created showing the double-helix structure of DNA (Watson, 1968). In the early 1950s, many scientists, including Linus Pauling and Rosalind Franklin, had all the necessary details of the composition of DNA but could not figure out how all the components fit together. Watson and Crick created the image of the double-helix that provided the missing piece. Their picture was the solution to one of the greatest mysteries of the 20th century (Watson, 1968).

Researchers should include drawing as part of their research toolbox for those times in which it is the most appropriate means to capture the necessary data. Once having gathered the data, researchers continue to make drawings to help analyze, clarify, and present their findings (Tufte, 1997). Archaeologist have found, for example, that making a drawing of an artifact can reveal insights and details that they had glossed over at first (Topper, 1996). Pangaea, the supercontinent that existed before the component continents were separated into their current configuration about 250 million years ago, was discovered as a result of prolonged analysis of existing drawings of the continents (Wegener, 1969).

As concepts of art education expand to include not only fine art but visual culture, design, and visual communication, it is easier to see how the use of drawing as a research tool takes on greater relevance. Designers, for example, use drawing as a way to research any design challenge (Cross, 2007). For designers, drawing is a way to do research, to gather information, generate ideas, and think about problems (Lawson, 2005).

As design fields like architecture and product design are introduced into art classes, students and teachers begin doing floor plans, elevations, and architectural renderings (Zell, 2008). Students research products by making exploded view drawings and concept sketches. These are all methods of research using drawings.

In the traditions of visual anthropology and visual sociology, art education researchers might gather and analyze data by doing research drawings of classroom floor plans or the layout of a museum (Zell, 2008). Researchers might do drawings of how children group themselves on playgrounds or in a cooperative learning environment.

Developing drawing as a research tool is a way that art educators can make a significant contribution to the growth of knowledge and understanding across disciplines. Developing the capacity to use drawing as a research tool is a unique gift art educators can give to all scholarship. ∎

REFERENCES

Barrow, J. (2008). *Cosmic imagery: Key images in the history of science.* New York, NY: W.W. Norton.

Collier, J. (1967). *Visual anthropology: Photography as a research method.* Albuquerque: University of New Mexico Press.

Cross, N. (2007). *Designerly ways of knowing.* Basel, Switzerland: Birkhauser Verlag.

Frankel, F. (2002). *Envisioning science: The design and craft of the science image.* Cambridge, MA: MIT Press.

Lawson, B. (2005). *How designers think.* Oxford, England: Elsevier.

Lewis, M. (1997). *The journals of Lewis and Clark (Lewis and Clark expedition).* New York, NY: Mariner Books.

Mead, M. (1951). *Growth and culture: A photographic study of Balinese childhood.* London, England: G.P. Putnam's Sons.

Rayala, M. (1983). *Pictorial ethnography: Drawing as a research tool* (Unpublished dissertation). Eugene: University of Oregon.

Rose, G. (2006). *Visual methodologies: An introduction to the interpretation of visual methods.* New York, NY: Sage.

Topper, D. (1996). Towards an epistemology of scientific illustration. In B. S. Baigrie (Ed.), *Picturing knowledge* (pp. 215-249). Toronto, Canada: University of Toronto Press.

Tufte, E. (1997). *Visual explanations: Images and quantities, evidence and narrative.* Cheshire, CT: Graphics Press.

Watson, G. (1968). *The double helix: A personal account of the discovery of the structure of DNA.* New York, NY: Touchstone.

Wegener, A. (1969). *The origins of continents and oceans.* London, England: Methuen.

Zell, M. (2008). *Architectural drawing course: Tools and techniques for 2D and 3D representation.* London, England: Barrons.

Children as Theorists: Potentials of Pedagogical Documentation as an Approach to Research

MARISSA MCCLURE / VISITING ASSISTANT PROFESSOR OF ART EDUCATION, PENN STATE UNIVERSITY

Pedagogical documentation is a catalyst for research and teaching. Educators working with young children (ages 0-6) in the small Italian city of Reggio Emilia developed approaches to pedagogical documentation to better understand the processes of learning and teaching. By documenting pedagogy, they sought to 'make visible' processes of learning that often seem to be invisible, or hidden within children's and adults' minds and memories. Documentation became an integral component of project-based curriculum, in which educators and children negotiate curricular outcomes. Educators in Reggio Emilia view project-based curriculum as a form of research and theorizing undertaken by children in collaboration with adults.

The term *documentation* can describe a number of approaches to documenting pedagogy. Pedagogy may include children's individual learning and learning in social groups, educators' preparations for teaching and learning with children, and the shared social and intellectual contexts of these endeavors. Documentation, however, is not a form of documentary (i.e. a method to document truth) but an approach to understanding subjective, nuanced, and phenomenological experience. In this way, it shares affiliations with phenomenological research, ethnography and microethnography, and arts-based research. An

FIGURE 1. Part of a documentation wall in the entrance alcove to the classroom. Digital photographs changed frequently. We used them to understand the relationships between overlapping long- and short-term projects in the classroom, in collaboration with children's memories and recorded conversations and to share with visitors the research we undertook in the classroom.

FIGURE 2. A digital video still of three-year-old children drawing plans to construct a "hiding space" in the classroom. We (myself, my co-teacher, and the children) later referred to both the drawings and the girls' conversations to construct/install the space and to understanding how "hiding" (a private place) functioned within the social space of the "classroom." At least two parallel research trajectories emerged: Adults' interest in the social meaning of "hiding spaces" and children's process of understanding design and installation.

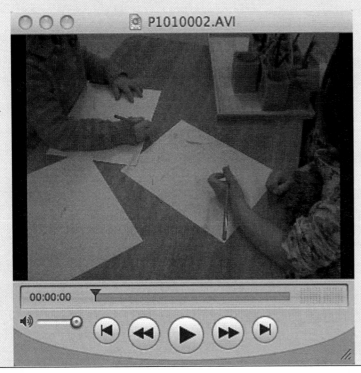

Designing a Hiding Space

Several of the three-year-old girls requested a hiding space at the beginning of the year. We talked about how to make it logistically possible (a big problem/project for us). The girls gave us drawings full of charming scribbles that had little architectural application. Until recently, when they sat together and submitted a plausible design (kind of like a tent that envelopes the children sitting within it). It's amazing how those small things that seem like they could be projects in September gain a new life and momentum in April. We'll work to make it a go...stay tuned!

POSTED BY MARISSA MCCLURE AT 3:32 PM
LABELS: DOCUMENTATION, PROJECTS

educator engaged with documentation may begin with questions such as: What does learning look like? What are the relationships between educators and learners? How might I use what I have learned about learning to develop approaches to pedagogy? How might children participate in teaching and research?

In Reggio Emilia, and increasingly in Reggio-inspired contexts throughout the world, documentation is a process through which educators, children, and families more fully understand the experiences of learning and teaching. It provides a visible, auditory, and olfactory memory—sometimes spanning years—of the experiences of individual and small groups of children and teachers within classroom relationships. Educators use insights they develop during the process of documenting to shape curriculum design and further research inquiry. For example, in project-based work, an educator may not begin with a curricular end in mind. Rather, he or she would project multiple pathways that children might take in their own investigations. These insights contribute to ongoing theory-building about how children learn in individual and group contexts (Project Zero & Reggio Children, 2001). Documentation is also a tool for advocacy as it is exhibited in well-designed installations in schools and galleries to 'make visible' what happens in schools and what children experience when they are in relationship with educators and what adults (and other children) experience when they engage with learners (Figure 1). Educators and children review documentation together to determine the directions in which a curriculum may travel (Figure 2).

Educators review documentation together to better understand what directions might be most meaningful to children and what pedagogical approaches are most appropriate for the goals that they and children wish to set and achieve. In this way, educators position themselves as researchers through documentation. They utilize their own hypotheses in developing curricular pathways. Complementarily, documentation positions children as researchers and theorists, who test their own sets of hypotheses as they move more deeply into project-based work. Educators in Reggio Emilia describe this process as *progettazione,* which roughly translates to "planning" or "design."

As a qualitative research approach related to sociocultural (e.g. Buckingham, 2009; Walkerdine, 2009) and social constructivist methods of researching children's experiences, documentation subverts three inter-related premises often associated with research about young children. First, documentation is site-specific and subjective. Through it, educators map the experiences of relatively small, stable, relational groups who are affected deeply by the intellectual, social, and physical environments in which they teach and learn. In documentation, children are not objects of study but protagonists of learning and teaching who encounter

and describe their worlds using multiple symbol systems. Documentation seems most closely affiliated with sociological approaches to understanding children. It fits within James, Jenks, and Prout's (1997, 1998) description of the new social studies of childhood, and within it, children are positioned as agents situated within social spaces. Educators in Reggio Emilia espouse postmodern social theory (Rinaldi, 2006) in their interpretations of how children are situated within predominant power relations.

Second, because children are involved in the research process as subjects, documentation is both a decolonizing approach (Smith, 1999) and a form of research with children (Freeman & Mathison, 2009; Mitchell & Reid-Walsh, 2002). In documentation, both teachers and children may pose research questions, collect and interpret data, and present their findings. The documented trajectories of negotiated curriculum, then, become research (Figure 3). Research findings, or meanings, take two complementary paths; one that propels curriculum and one that contributes to an augmented understanding of teaching and learning.

FIGURE 3. A screen capture of the blog we used with the children. In this entry, we described the origins of the idea of the "hiding space." We began to use the blog with the children in order to have an easily-accessible/searchable archive available for the documentation we compiled throughout the school year and to support our school's LEED (Leadership in Environmental and Energy Design) certification by reducing paper used for printing data.

Third, documentation is political. It is rooted in a construction of children as competent and interactionist. In this view, children have the right to be considered as whole persons, not as

(continued)

incomplete persons lacking adulthood. In this way, documentation eschews the construction of childhood that was predominate in developmental psychology in the 20th century; one in which children were in the process of "becoming" adult. It challenges "tribal" views of childhood (Freeman & Mathison, 2009; James, Jenks, & Prout, 1998) in which children are seen as culturally independent of adults. Rather, documentation concerns itself with the moments of learning that occur in layered interactions between adult and child culture.

Data collection processes in documentation may include a variety of qualitative and emergent approaches including but not limited to photography, video, audio recording, field notes, and increasingly, digital media (Figures 2 & 3). Educators/researchers and children may choose the tools that best suit their investigations. But, because documentation is not premeditated but proactive, data collection approaches may change throughout the course of an experience or project. Unlike traditional approaches to research, documentation does not necessarily have a definite beginning and ending, but is an ongoing approach to understand intersubjective educational relationships. Documentation often endures as long as the relationships themselves (i.e. complete school years, a child's many years in one preschool, educators' decades of work together). It is a spiral process in which insights are made richer through revisitation and reflection. In documentation, individual educators may generate questions; groups of teachers may generate questions; children may generate questions, or a combination of these circumstances may apply. Data collection can then include teachers' documentation of children's work as well as children's documentation of their own work, conflicts, understandings, and questions. These queries may take parallel or complementary courses or may not necessarily intersect.

Data analysis in documentation complements data collection approaches and includes textual, discursive, and narrative analysis of children's conversation, theories, and stories; interpretations of the social contexts of children's making with art media; interpretations of adults' interpretations and experiences; and ethnographic analysis of patterns and themes that emerge in particular learning experiences and relationships. Findings may take the shape of research papers, narrative accounts, video productions, and installations, among other traditional and emergent arts-based forms (Figures 1 & 3).

The profound influence of Reggio-Inspired documentation world-wide may be rooted in the pooled power of a collection of situated examinations, or microethnographies. Further analysis is needed to understand the particular social conditions that surround each approach to documentation and the implications and potentials of using an approach developed as a response to a particular set of social and historic conditions in varied contexts. ∎

REFERENCES

Buckingham, D. (2009). New media, new childhoods? Children's changing cultural environment in the age of digital technology. In M. Kehily (Ed.), *An introduction to childhood studies* (2nd ed.) (pp. 124-140). New York, NY: Open University Press.

Freeman, M., & Mathison, S. (2009). *Researching children's experiences.* New York, NY: Guilford Press.

James, A., Jenks, C., & Prout, A. (1997). *Construction and reconstructing childhood: Contemporary issues in the sociological study of childhood.* London, England: Falmer Press.

James, A., Jenks, C., & Prout, A. (1998). *Theorizing childhood.* Cambridge, England: Polity Press.

Mitchell, C. & Reid-Walsh, J. (2002). *Researching children's popular culture: The cultural spaces of childhood.* London, England: Routledge.

Project Zero & Reggio Children (2001). *Making learning visible: Children as individual and group learners.* Reggio Emilia, Italy: Reggio Children.

Rinaldi, C. (2006). *In dialogue with Reggio Emilia: Listening, researching, and learning.* London, England: Routledge.

Smith, L. (1999). *Decolonizing methodologies: Research and indigenous peoples.* London, England: Zed.

Walkerdine, V. (2009). Developmental psychology and the study of childhood. In M. Kehily (Ed.), *An introduction to childhood studies* (2nd ed.) (pp. 112-123). New York, NY: Open University Press.

Journaling, Coding, and Member Checking Methods

JANE CERA / ASSISTANT PROFESSOR OF ART EDUCATION, INDIANA UNIVERSITY SOUTH BEND

Researchers often employ an array of techniques to gather and analyze data, rather than relying exclusively on one method. As a feminist, I privilege personal experience in research and value the voices of other participants. These forms of data have not always been considered important. Hence, when I constructed a case study of my own professional experience and practice, I used journaling, coding, and member-checking conversations as some of my methods. Journaling incorporates personal experience, recollection, and reflection. Coding is a technique of data analysis by which to identify trends in the data as well as areas where more information is needed, and thus also helps guide further data collection. Member-checking conversations, as opposed to participant interviews, help position the participants' self-identification as being of central importance, rather than the researchers' interpretation of others' voices. These methods can be used together or in combination with other methods of data collection and analysis. This section will address each of these methods more in depth.

JOURNALING

There is a well-established tradition of feminist research based on personal experience, evidenced in early work by Dinnerstein (1976), Griffin (1978), and Burgos-Debray (1984). Dinnerstein's (1976) study provided an example of using personal experience in research. She described her research as coming from deep within herself and from her personal experiences. Griffin (1978) dealt with both the use of personal experiences, and with what she termed *associative writing* as a method. She discovered she could use writing to stimulate her memory and could also use her intuition. Rigoberta Menchu, as translated by Burgos-Debray (1984), helped readers understand that telling one's own story is a way by which one might come to understand one's own power.

Journaling requires reflection. Usually, writing is the medium through which one conveys thoughts in a journal but graphic journals can be just as powerful. Researchers can use journaling as a technique to gather data about their personal experiences. Donmoyer (1990) discussed the immense knowledge base that professionals construct based on their experiences in the classroom. He described this knowledge as experience-based, instinctual knowledge that was under the surface of conscious thought for most practitioners. Journaling is one method by which researchers can begin to surface their own knowledge. It

may be helpful to construct some questions or writing prompts designed to begin to identify major points or events relative to the study in question. Scheduling a recurring time to journal can provide opportunity for further reflection. It is also helpful to remain open to unexpected opportunities to add observations to the journal throughout the day. Researchers should consider whether an electronic, hand-written or other physical form for the journal suits their purposes best.

CODING

Once the researcher records several entries (or has some other body of data to analyze, such as interview transcripts, for example) coding can begin. Spradley (1979) discussed the importance of analyzing data during the process of data collection in order to identify areas from which to collect more data. There are many ways to conduct coding and researchers should proceed in the manner that seems to best suit their intellectual style and preferences. The idea is to begin by identifying major recurring topics. Some researchers color code topics as they read through the journal or other text. Marking passages with letters, numbers, or symbols to code the topics, and using index cards or electronic cutting and pasting are other possible ways to proceed. Once the researcher identifies major themes, or domains s/he looks for further subdivisions within each. As these domains and subdomains are labeled, one can visually identify trends in the data. Researchers examine the domains for where the most emphasis seems to be placed and look for areas that need to be rounded out more fully. Journal writing can continue, or other data collection methods can be employed, to gather more information for these topics.

In my study, I sought to identify how my own professional development progressed. I started journaling by asking myself what seemed to stand out as the major turning points or events in my professional life. The journal entries were then color-coded by topic. Two of the recurring domains included: my work with the teachers' association and my work with other arts educators in my school system. As each color-coded section of text was cut apart and sorted, further subdivisions became evident. For example, my teachers' association work revolved around the themes of my initial contact with the vice president, my various experiences on association committees, and running for election to association office. After completing the coding, I returned to the research

(continued)

questions I initially proposed in order to determine which categories seemed to address each question, and to identify areas where I needed more information. I decided that an observation of a teacher's association meeting was in order. I also realized that many of my colleagues were mentors who became influential in my development and that I needed to gain information from them. I realized they were also members of the study, and I wanted to check on how their observations and recollections of events might differ from my own. Although the methods of journaling, and member checking, are not inherently linked, the coding of my writings provided a natural impetus for further investigation. It became clear to me through the coding that I needed to gather data from others in addition to my journal recollections.

MEMBER CHECKING

Member checking is a technique that researchers use to gain information on the perceptions of others involved. Although one could conduct member checking through a variety of means, I choose to engage in a conversation with my colleagues as the member checking method in my study.

Reinharz (1992) commented on the use of conversation as a means of gathering and displaying data:

> Reading conversations makes me very sensitive to the way single-authored writing (and published interviews) smooth out controversy and silence voices. Conversations are harder to read because the reader has to take part, and work out differences; in single-voiced writing, readers can simply sit back and "listen" to the voice of authority. (p. 231)

Reinharz points out an important difference to note between the methods of interview and conversation. Researchers generally structure interviews much more than conversations and interviews are subject to more intervention by the researcher. Researchers often publish interview results without the transcript, or quote from the transcript. Researchers *conduct* interviews, and thus often determine the direction of the dialog. When researchers *participate in* conversations, less can be predetermined and participants are freer to discuss what is important to them about the topic. Transcripts of recorded conversations are open to interpretation by the reader. I decided to carry out a member-checking conversation with my colleagues and presented the transcript of the entire conversation as further data in the study.

According to Spradley (1979), "Within a short time after beginning to collect data, analysis begins" (p. 94). During a journal writing exercise, writing on one topic may suggest connections to other topics. Coding will further identify areas for collection, and whether the researcher employs one or many methods, eventually data collection must cease and meaning making begins. As the researcher begins to perceive patterns in the data analysis, a member-checking method may provide validation or further enlightenment as s/he continues to synthesize meaning. It is important for researchers to clearly elucidate their particular theoretical stance relative to the synthesis of their findings. For example, in my case my feminist orientation led me to explore critical theory as the lens through which to interpret my findings. For purposes of this discussion, it is enough to state that a major emphasis in critical theory is on how the dynamics of power affect individuals and situations. Critical theory provided the structure upon which I was able to build meaning. I distilled my interest in critical theory into questions and used each question to examine the data in the study. For example, the question "How might teacher leaders work to emancipate other teachers?" led me to refer to the data in the journals and in the member-checking transcript in order to generate an answer to the research question and synthesize meaning. ■

REFERENCES

Burgos-Debray, E. (Ed.) (1984). *I, Rigoberta Menchu an Indian woman in Guatemala*. New York, NY: Verso.

Dinnerstein, D. (1976). *The mermaid and the minotaur: Sexual arrangements and the human malaise*. New York, NY: Harper and Row.

Donmoyer, R. (1990). Generalizability and the single case study. In E. Eisner & A. Peskin (Eds.), *Qualitative inquiry in education: The continuing debate* (pp. 175-200). New York, NY: Teachers College Press.

Griffin, S. (1978). *Woman and nature: The roaring inside her*. New York, NY: Harper and Row.

Spradley, J. (1979). *The ethnographic interview*. New York, NY: Harcourt Brace.

Reinharz, S. (1992). *Feminist methods in social research*. New York, NY: Oxford University Press.

Content Analysis of Student Reflective Journals: How Student Perceptions Change

STEVE WILLIS / PROFESSOR OF ART EDUCATION, MISSOURI STATE UNIVERSITY

The purpose of this piece is to discuss content analysis of reflective journals and how I used content analysis to better understand the experiences of a group of pre-service teachers and the changes in their perceptions of others. First, I will provide contextual background of the setting, then discuss the process of data collection, and conclude with an analysis of the data from multiple sources suggested by Gay (1996) by examining how qualitative analysis can be designed to excavate *qualities* not found with other methods.

THE SETTING

All Art Education students at Missouri State University (MSU) must spend two semesters, 20 hours each, involved in Citizenship and Service Learning (CASL). To offer a CASL designation for the art education courses I teach, it is my responsibility to ensure that (1) students are actively engaged, beyond observation, with a community partner; (2) their experiences are integrated within the course curriculum; and (3), they produce reflective and analytical narrations of their experiences.

Gaining an understanding of the reflective nature of their journal entries using qualitative research is insightful for the students and me alike. I believe that reflective journals are essential in the educational process. I draw heavily from Dewey (1934) when he referred to the *action* of learning, the necessary *reflection* on that action, and ultimately, the *reaction* to the original learning.

The Art Education students discussed in this section taught incarcerated adults at the Greene County Justice Center (GCJC), a correctional facility that houses adults awaiting trial or transfer to a federal prison. While at the GCJC, the preservice teachers instructed the adult prisoners in visual art education. Materials were limited (crayons, colored pencils, tempera paint, papier maché), and the prisoners could work only with art materials while under the supervision of the preservice teachers. Prisoners could not take art materials to individual pods or cells. Both the male and female prisoners were consistently thankful for the preservice teachers' instruction and engagement as evidenced by the two of the many notes received (see Figures 1 & 2).

THE PROCESS

While engaged in CASL, students submitted four multi-page reflections in the categories of *Expected* (what is anticipated), *Actual* (what was in fact witnessed), and *Reflective* (how it is important to self and situation). Having students record information for review and reflection is an important aspect of educational practice. Specifically, in reference to student journals, Anderson and Milbrandt (2005) suggest that when students collect information, "A premise of this activity is that how knowledge is gained is part of the knowledge itself—that how we find out is inseparable from what we find out" (p. 177). Over the years, CASL reflections consistently showed a change of perceptional awareness through constructed knowledge. However, understand-

(continued)

FIGURE 1. A note written to the preservice teachers from one of the partici-pants. Note transcription: "I really appreciated the Ladies coming in for the Art class and having cool ideas for us. I believe along with the ideas, hands on projects and good tunes, are great stress relievers and lets us mentally go elsewhere for the moment. Thanks so much! You girls are great!"

FIGURE 2. A note written to the preservice teachers from one of the partici-pants. Note transcription: "I really liked the class it helped get my mind off all the stuff I have going on right now The Ladys was great Thank you so much"

ing the reflections is complicated because of the density of experiences and differences of students' insights (action), stylistic differences of reporting (reflection), and levels of understanding (reaction). Through the CASL experiences, their formative entries developed depth and analysis, and the summative self-reflection captured some of the perceptions (see Figure 4).

The question: *How did student perception of learners change as a result of the CASL experience at the GCJC?* may appear simple, but it is complicated because it reveals levels of personal and societal influences relevant to the students and their teaching practices. An excerpt from this November 6th, 2007, GCJC journal entry reported stereotypes such as this:

I judge people and I admit it. I do change my opinions once I know that person. Working in the jail has really made me realize this. When I first came to the jail I expected the women to be rude, butch, horrible, and bad people. Once I got to know them I realized this judgment was all wrong. Now I know them and know that they are nice people that just made a bad decision.

As a result, these experiences and reflections influenced teaching practices through a broader understanding of cultural dynamics, socioeconomic differences, and [limited] educational experiences the incarcerated adults had experienced. For example, the curriculum needed to be presented at a basic level because chronological age and artistic knowledge varied greatly. At the same time, in recognition of the social dynamic, classroom management required attention to address secondary students' needs. But beyond curriculum, management, and pedagogy, what I consider most important is the understanding of the individual and community, and from that understanding, teaching the individual.

THE ANALYSIS
Analysis and comparison of students' first journal entries with their intermediate and final summative entries revealed the growth, maturation, confidence, and empowerment of the preservice students. But, how is this determined beyond opinion, and how can it be used as a referential point for qualitative research?

To gain a thorough understanding of the students' CASL experiences, more information was necessary. The first data collection strategy was to assemble information from verbal presentations that each student offered four times to the class. To do this, I took notes on student comments from their presentations for points to discuss more thoroughly with the class and to support my intuitive insights. This type of data collection requires careful attention to words, but just as important are the students' verbal tonality and body language, which also transmit valuable information. Careful attention to these aspects of their presentations adds the necessary balance to gain meaningful insights.

In addition to the more formal journal entries provided to me, each student submitted four entries in Blackboard, an online discussion group, which served as the second device for collecting data. Not surprisingly, students' digital conversations revealed information that was not included in the verbal classroom conversation or the formal papers. I have come to realize that some students are more comfortable with digital conversations that they may see as an opportunity to think through the conversation carefully. As well, some indicate that they prefer this format to avoid confrontational situations. Regardless of the reasoning, the digital conversations provided both breadth and depth not evidenced in other methods.

A contextualized word selection (Figure 3) was the third mechanism I employed to gain deeper insights into the journal entries. This evolved through classroom discussions in which spontaneity and intuition are more evident, and the combination of the comfort and distance provided by multiple digital conversations, as well as the formal reflective journal entries.

Words that appear consistently and frequently determine the word selection for a frequency report. The selection directs the grouping of words, and by grouping words, generalities can be deduced. This is important for an open-ended data review. When investigating more specific areas, researchers select more specific words. Table 1 presents words and word groups that were filtered from the written journal entries. The word frequency

FIGURE 3

WORD FREQUENCY DISTRIBUTION MATRIX									
38 pages				**20,517 words**			**journals (2004-2007)**		
Response	Skill Skills Skilled	Help Helpful Helping	Anxiety Anxious Nervous Afraid Scared	Teach Teacher Teaching	Learn Learner Learning	Student/s	Ability Disability	Experience	Bad
1	15	36	12	45	47	136	3	36	15

Difference Different	Management	Behavior	Good/great	Idea	Challenge
29	6	7	34/8	18	3

FIGURE 4

SELECTED STUDENT REFLECTIONS OF SITUATION AND SELF

	REFLECTIVE OF SITUATION	REFLECTIVE OF SELF
Response	We got some amazing responses.	Overall, I loved my time spent at the jail…
Skill	There were so many different skill levels in the room.	Each individual needed special attention according to skill level.
Help	The prisoners really told what was in their heart and I do believe that it helped them…	…the journal entries were because the teacher gets to know the student…
Anxiety	A lot of my expectations were similar to the first group, although I had a lot less anxiety.	…I had learned a lot about myself and the prisoners…
Teach	I expected to be teaching art to a group of scruffy men with bad attitudes while guards stood watch in the room.	I've found myself excited to go to the jail each time; I'm always thinking about what I could bring that they would enjoy creating, and I've stopped thinking of them as inmates and started thinking of them as my students.
Learn	I learned to dislike the behavior and not the student.	…I feel like I have learned a lot that I will be able to use in the classroom.
Student	They loved painting the gourds and each made really beautiful cards for the cancer patients. One student said, "It's so nice of you girls to do this for the patients!" I replied, "We're not the ones decorating the pumpkins and making the cards for them, you are!" He seemed almost shocked, and was able to realize that he was doing a really great thing by simply participating in the activity.	…and I ended up talking to a few of the students about our class. One student said, "Have we ever thanked you guys for comin' here? We really appreciate it." Then, I spoke to another student who told me that he loves the time he has in our class, and that it's the only thing he looks forward to all week. He says people in the jail look at him and every other inmate as prisoners already, not as real people. He told me that we are the only people that do not treat him like that. It was an amazing day for me, because we were able to get a lot out of them, and they got a lot out of us.
Adapt	No comments	No comments
Ability	Since we have been going to the jail twice each week for about an hour, I expect their artistic ability to begin increasing.	…when you mentioned that the prisoners would have the ability of a fourth grader, I wasn't expecting much. All-in-all, I felt like I was teaching a high school class, not a fourth grade class.
Disability	No comments	No comments
Experience	This is definitely a learning experience. I'm learning what works and what doesn't and how to teach to a diverse group.	I think the women truly are getting a lot out of the experience, and because of their cooperation and enthusiasm, I think we are learning a lot about teaching.
Good/great	After they realized that it felt good to simply draw and create, they relaxed and enjoyed themselves. As a result, they came up with more creative, thoughtful pieces of art.	I am really glad that I chose to do this project at the Justice Center. It has been a great experience for me both as a person and as a future teacher. I like that we have to come with the lessons and present them, it is really good practice for when we teach.
Bad	When I decided to do my community service hours at the jail, I was expecting a stressful, unmanageable group of inmates. Although I think it is an unfair stereotype, it's easy to categorize inmates as bad people and expect them to live up to that socialized concept.	These people are just like everyone else, except that they have done something bad and illegal, but that doesn't make them any less of a person, everyone makes mistakes. This project has really made an impact on me and changed the way I think of inmates.
Challenge	When they saw that they could create an interesting composition, they felt compelled to continue, do more and challenge themselves.	I thought that most of them would be glad to make and talk about art but I figure there would be one or two that would not want to be there and they would be a challenge.
Idea	It kind of took them awhile to get them going, but it really helped if someone was talking to sit down next to them and sort of make them focus on getting an idea. A lot of the students jumped to the occasion.	…when individuals give up drawing their development is virtually arrested at that level." Never has this idea been more apparent to me than during my visit to the jail.
Different	It is extremely hard, I think, to mesh our singular styles with prisoners who are on all different levels with diverse interests.	I'm not really sure how to relate these experiences to class. There is one woman who is very intelligent and different than the others. She has always been very good at the artwork and writings. I can't imagine why she is in jail, she's so smart and well rounded, it is just weird that she's in jail. I think she could possibly be gifted, because of the way she thinks about things, she's just different.
Management	the inmates are so well behaved.	the only thing I regret about my teaching experience at the jail is that I'm not learning any classroom management skills.
Behavior	Before we had our class with the men, I was extremely nervous. Although Michelle told us the men were all in the class because they wanted to be, and because of good behavior, I was still unsure of how they would act.	By doing this, we created an atmosphere that is too casual for a classroom. We didn't think anything of it, until we were talking casually during a class and one of the students took the opportunity to insult us. We told him that what he said was wrong and that he shouldn't do that again.

was determined from 38 pages composing 20,517 words in seven journals from 2004 through 2007. A search mechanism in Microsoft Office identified the words selected. Word selections were determined mostly by student verbal and textual usage as well as faculty input. Word frequency itself is not interpretive, but it leads to dense and contextual interpretation.

With the inherent limitation of being constructed only from text, what is not evidenced in the frequency matrix is that *Anxiety/Anxious/Nervous/Afraid/Scared* appears minor by the 12 notations from the text, but classroom conversations indicated prominence and the primary concern of the preservice teachers. This prominence and concern would not have been revealed without a triangulation of variable sources, data collection methods, and interpretive awareness. Figure 3 captures representative comments of the complexity excavated through reflective vignettes, but it is important to recognize that these are limited selections from the students' 38 pages.

Using qualitative methods results in an analysis that Stake (1995) describes as building "... on ordinary ways of getting acquainted with things" (p 49). In many ways, this study amplified ordinary verbal and textual conversations, but through magnified attention, they became extraordinary.

Figures 3 and 4 are abbreviated reports of a complicated issue of perception, which came from ordinary class discussions with casual remarks from a natural setting. These seemingly casual comments were the catalyst of this research, which led to curricular changes within my classroom construct. These changes placed more emphasis on student empowerment, focused on student-to-student teaching, and individualized instruction and dialogic pedagogy. Additionally, I deemphasized reliance on standardized curriculum and theoretical management strategies.

CASL's reflective and analytical activities are valuable and vital components in the classroom and provide a platform for investigative, narrative, and reflective thought. Through their interpretation, students had the opportunity to create meaning, and Barrett (2003), though referring to the interpretation of art, indicates: "To interpret is to make something meaningful for ourselves and then, usually, to tell another what we think" (p. 202). Interpretation of data is both difficult and rewarding because one insight frequently leads to another.

CONCLUSION

As culture is dense with layers of meanings, so the query *How did student perception of learners change?* revealed the density of faceted perceptions with both students and me. In this instance, casual comments catalyzed this research, and the resulting interpretations exposed the layers of students' changing perceptions. My findings allowed for the reconstruction of the course format by considering student empowerment as a guide for course conversations. Additionally, the course struck a balance between reading professional literature and the day-to-day activities of the CASL experiences. The students accepted the responsibility of being teachers, and in this, taught each other valuable, shared experiences of their struggles and successes.

With any query, the selection of one topic automatically eliminates others, and biases influence every researcher's decisions. For example, in the word frequency matrix (Table 1), selection included some words and ignored others. If multiple researchers would have evaluated the same CASL data, there may have been dissimilar conclusions because of differing emphasis of the researcher. Multiple researchers working within the same paradigm may produce a more complex report. Qualitative research provides both a broad overview of a situation as well as capturing specific moments of nuance and subtlety. ∎

REFERENCES

Anderson, T., & Milbrandt, M. K. (2005). *Art for life: Authentic instruction in art*. New York, NY: McGraw-Hill Higher Education.

Barrett, T. (2003). *Interpreting art: reflecting, wondering, and responding*. New York, NY: McGraw-Hill Higher Education.

Dewey, J. (1934). *Art as experience*. New York, NY: Perigee Books.

Gay, L. R. (1996) *Educational research: Competencies for analysis and application* (5th ed.). Saddle River, NJ: Prentice-Hall.

Stake, R. E. (1995). *The art of case study research*. Thousand Oaks, CA: Sage.

TeachArt Wiki and Narratives of Knowing

RINA KUNDU / ASSISTANT PROFESSOR, UNIVERSITY OF WISCONSIN, MILWAUKEE
GUEY-MEEI YANG / ASSOCIATE PROFESSOR, EASTERN MICHIGAN UNIVERSITY

As teacher-researchers, how do current Web technologies change the ways we think about our practice? In what follows, we use our study of *TeachArt Wiki,* which investigates how people build knowledge together, to discuss online data collection and analysis.

We believe that learning is social and that the new social tools of Web 2.0 allow groups of people to participate as a collective in creating and disseminating knowledge. A wiki is a Web 2.0 technology where anyone can write or edit anything at anytime. The "writing" capability of a wiki permits readers to revise the work of authors, collapsing the boundary between authors and readers (Kangas, 2008). Furthermore, a wiki's open access and "history" function, which documents editorial changes, make participants' writing and editing processes and products available for others to preview and engage with anytime, anywhere. Because of the social learning potential of wikis, we created *TeachArt Wiki* and studied its effects.

In our study, more than 100 students in art history, art education, and museum education classes at two universities created understandings about non-Western art and cultural issues by researching artworks, writing about them, and creating lesson plans on the wiki. Because students were negotiating meanings as they edited and extended each other's work, our research question was, "How do students engaged in the co-construction, deconstruction, and reconstruction of art knowledge in a non-hierarchical social learning community of a wiki make meanings about objects, themselves, and others?" All *TeachArt Wiki* entries shared a simple structure, which consisted of two components. The first component included information about an artist and her/his artwork. The second component was the addition of art lessons. In general, students researched and wrote content, and then revised their work as they received feedback from the instructor and their peers.

We used narrative inquiry as a methodology to understand the students' production of knowledge because the wiki consists of user-generated materials involving many authors and editors. Narrative analysis is well-suited for this project because the representation and dissemination of art is placed in the control of those participating in the meaning-making process. In this case, it was a way to understand how students hand down experiences, understandings, traditions, and values about art to others through the description, analysis, and interpretation of art, as well as the development of lesson plans. Narrative analysis focuses on the meaning making process of the storyteller, his or her actions in constructing meaning, and how stories change through social interactions, with peers and instructors.

We sorted the *TeachArt Wiki* entries into six categories described by Labov and Waletzky (1997), focusing on orientation, complicated action, evaluation, and resolution. We then analyzed them by considering how storytellers were positioned; where they directed others to head as an endpoint to the story told about an object; how they used a supporting cast of characters, such as the contextual information provided about the artist, his or her milieu, and the culture in which the work was made; and how they sequenced and re-sequenced events discussed through writing and editing to show how they revealed some events in the life of the object versus others. For example, in our analysis, we found that many students told particular stories about the identity or role of the artist and his or her craft. One of the dominant stories told is that of a "cultural agent" where emphasis is given to the artist's role in conveying his or her socio-cultural values through shared and individual symbols. Students noted that artists not only employed visual signs and icons from traditions found in their society but also expanded upon them to speak to the contemporary world. Another dominant story told is that of the "heroic narrative" where prominence is given to the artist's individual agency to construct innovation in art. These different narrative structures provide insight into how people come to understand art and the type of actions they take as a result—how they disseminate knowledge. Students' narratives involved making sense of non-Western art, how they valued it, and finding connections between art and life.

New Internet technologies give us different tools for collecting and analyzing data. Because the Internet has made it easy to disseminate information, more people are documenting themselves, leaving "digital traces" of their communications behind (Welser, Smith, Fisher & Gleave, 2008). These digital traces make capturing data online convenient. In our case, the wiki technology provided a simple way to collect complex data online that include all student wiki entries (texts, images, and videos), revisions (when and what changes were made in the wiki), and written comments to another student, using its built-in tools. Digital traces of what students have written previously can be compared with what they are currently writing, allowing us to see

(continued)

how narratives are shaped through social interaction within the wiki community. For example, we found that entries changed in relationship to other entries written for the same object, one student building upon the ideas of another. The social environment of the wiki is thus embedded in relational contexts, and so we continued to look for relationships within this bounded population, particularly communication amongst individuals working on the same entry and the approaches students took to edit the work of others and construct their own.

On the other hand, new Web technologies create various challenges. First, the issues of confidentiality, authorship, and concern with IRB approval and informed consent become more complex in online environments (Fielding, Lee, & Blank, 2008). For example, in our research, the issue of confidentiality was compounded with that of authorship. Some students saw the *TeachArt Wiki* as a publication and displayed their names. While editing, other participants deleted these students' names, thus challenging the issue of identity and ownership over knowledge. Second, because most of the data collected online are texts, it may pose a challenge to reading "non-textual" communication (Fielding et al., 2008). Although all research stories are partial, the absence of visual or tonal clues of human interactions may limit researchers' abilities to construct complexity. Therefore, we felt it was important to triangulate the *TeachArt Wiki* text data with observations of class discussions and interviews to gauge beliefs and feelings about participating in the online environment and to understand the students' narrative constructions. ■

REFERENCES

Chase, S. E. (2005). Narrative inquiry: Multiple lenses, approaches, voices. In N. K. Denzin & Y. S. Lincoln (Eds.), *The Sage handbook of qualitative research* (pp. 651–680). Thousand Oaks, CA: Sage.

Fielding, N., Lee, R. M., & Blank, G. (Eds.). (2008). *Sage handbook of online research methods.* Los Angeles, CA: Sage.

Kangas, D. (2008). Wikis: Revising our theories on writing, authority, and expert. *Language Arts Journal of Michigan, 24*(1), 22–27.

Labov, W., & Waletzky, J. (1997). Narrative analysis: Oral versions of personal experience. *Journal of Narrative and Life History, 7,* 3–38.

Welser, H. T., Smith, M., Fisher, D., & Gleave, E. (2008). Distilling digital traces: Computational social science approaches to studying the internet. In N. Fielding, R. M. Lee and G. Grant (Eds.), *Handbook of online research methods* (pp. 116–140). London, England: Sage.

SECTION II: KNOWING OUR PRACTICES
Introduction

MELANIE L. BUFFINGTON AND **SARA WILSON MCKAY**

How Do We Know Our Practices?

MUSINGS AND WONDERINGS FROM THE FIELD

What are the effects on high school students taking a ceramics course when the teacher's style shifts from skill-based to idea-based? What can students and their teacher learn from exploring their artmaking processes together? How do art teachers differentiate instruction for Gifted & Talented students? Who is teaching art? What are the effects on middle schoolers of teaching contemporary art and visual culture versus an emphasis on 'Old Masters' and traditional European works of art? What relationships are there between the demographics of elementary art teachers and their likelihood of working collaboratively with classroom teachers? In what ways is artmaking a research practice? How do I show my principal and school board that my students are learning?

In this section, authors introduce three methodologies: *Survey research, quasi-experimental research,* and *arts-based research.* Art educators often use these methodologies, seemingly quite different, to generate knowledge about practices that are common in our field.

OVERVIEW OF METHODOLOGIES

- **Survey research** usually focuses on gathering and interpreting information about the ideas or characteristics of a large group of people. Researchers identify a clear group to study; this group could be wide-ranging and might include students, parents, community members, teachers, or members of a professional organization.
- **Quasi-experimental research** is used to determine if a particular intervention or program has the predicted effects on the participants. Other teachers or administrators may use the results of quasi-experimental research to change their practice or to plan future curriculum initiatives.
- **Arts-based research** employs the processes of artists as a way of knowing. Arts-based research may involve the study of an artist and her/his working practices; it may use artistic processes and products as sources of data and data analysis; it may also be used as a form of social action.

SURVEY RESEARCH

7/ Survey Research

JEFFREY L. BROOME / ASSISTANT PROFESSOR OF ART EDUCATION AT
FLORIDA STATE UNIVERSITY

ABSTRACT: *The first section of this chapter describes the use of survey research methodology suitable for the needs of art teacher researchers. Survey research is most appropriate for exploring research questions that can be answered by collecting responses from large groups of people who can self-report descriptive information about themselves, their practices, and their opinions. This chapter introduces appropriate approaches for generating research questions suited for survey research, and how such instruments can be designed for use in either quantitative or qualitative studies. Suggestions and options for writing surveys, selecting participants, administering surveys, and enhancing response rates are also discussed. The chapter also provides resources to aid in the analysis of collected survey data and draw attention to existing examples of survey research in art education.*

There is something to be said for the often-heard cliché, "*You'll never know unless you ask.*" In spite of all the complex academic talk about research methodology and theories, perhaps the most effective way to obtain information from research participants remains simply to ask people questions. Survey research continues to represent one of the most frequently used strategies for getting such real-world answers from live participants.

Even though most of us have completed some sort of survey questionnaire at different points in our lives, that is not to say we all understand all the options involved in conducting effective academic survey research. In general, survey methodology can be characterized by the collection of data from large groups of people who self-report information about themselves, usually by responding to written questionnaires or a scripted bank of interview questions (Hutchinson, 2004; Rea & Parker, 2005). This chapter provides an overview of survey methodology suitable for art teacher researchers, as well as introductory discussions on generating applicable research questions, constructing and administering a questionnaire, and analyzing survey data. In a single chapter it will be impossible for me to address all the considerations involved in conducting such research, as entire volumes have been devoted to the subject of survey methodology. Instead, my approach is to offer examples and information most relevant to beginning art teacher researchers, and to direct the readers' attention to additional resources for addressing complexities that are beyond the scope of a single chapter.

WHEN TO USE SURVEY RESEARCH

When beginning a research study, it is not so much a matter of deciding which research methodology you would like to use, but rather a matter of determining which methodology is best suited to answer the questions that guide your investigation. If you are seeking data that comes directly from questions posed to real people, then you might turn your attention to methods such as qualitative interviews or survey research. Generally, qualitative interviews are more useful when seeking in-depth information from a small number of participants, whereas survey research is more useful in obtaining aggregates of information from a larger number of participants (Babbie, 2004). Beyond seeking data on a broad scale, survey research is commonly used to collect descriptive information on the characteristics, practices, or opinions of a chosen population (Hutchinson, 2004).

Because the information collected from survey research tends to be either descriptive in nature or to express the perceptions of respondents, surveys are best used to answer guiding research questions that reflect these same goals. Following recommendations offered by Cox and Cox (2008), I have written and adapted some sample guiding research questions below that may be suitable for survey research methodology for art teacher researchers.

- Who are the art teachers in the X School District who volunteer to supervise art education student teachers without compensation and why do they do so?
- How effective are the distance learning art education classes at X University, according to instructors and students involved in such courses?
- Do elementary and secondary art teachers working in public schools in the State of X differ in their views regarding the importance of including visual culture art education objectives within their curricula?

AN EXAMPLE IN ART EDUCATION

To review the information presented so far, I suggest examining a study conducted by three art education professors whose goal was to determine the nature, scope, and peer-determined rankings of all graduate art education programs in the United States and Canada (Anderson, Eisner, & McRorie, 1998). As the professors reviewed the literature on the subject of graduate programs at that time, they were able to identify 248 institutions of higher education that publicly claimed to have such art education programs in operation. With this many potential participants, it simply was not reasonable to sit down and attempt to conduct, transcribe, and analyze qualitative interviews with real people working at all of the identified colleges and universities.

Moving beyond feasibility, the three professors might have next considered the nature of their research problem in order to determine which remaining research methods were most suitable for answering their guiding questions. In this case, their goals were descriptive (to describe the scope and foci of graduate art education programs) and they sought to collect the perceptions of others (in order to peer-rank such programs). It is important to note that these goals could be achieved through gathering self-reported data from representatives of the identified graduate programs in art education. In this case, survey research offered the best method for achieving the goals.

PLANNING AND ADMINISTERING A SURVEY

There are many factors to consider when planning survey research, including (1) selecting a group of potential participants, (2) the content and format of your survey, and (3) strategies for enhancing the return of completed surveys. For the purposes of this chapter, I will first explore the selection of survey participants, as such a selection can directly impact the content and phrasing of questions on a survey.

SELECTING SURVEY PARTICIPANTS

The selection of survey participants should always begin with guiding research questions in mind. If you are interested in finding out about students' and teachers' opinions toward distance learning art education classes at a particular university, it obviously is not necessary to send surveys to all the art education students and instructors at the university, but instead, only to those directly involved with such coursework. Secondly, the selection of potential survey participants may directly depend on the type of research that you are conducting.

Participants in quantitative studies. The goals of many quantitative studies are to collect data in the form of inferential statistics that can be generalized to larger populations (Fraenkel & Wallen, 2003). A hypothetical example might include a research study that sought to collect information on the integrated use of visual arts education and its perceived importance to all teachers of all disciplines at all grade levels in a large urban school district. It is unlikely that a researcher could ever effectively reach all members of such a large population, let alone compel them all to return a survey. Instead, quantitative researchers often survey smaller samples of a large population with the intention of generalizing the findings of the smaller group to the larger whole. In order to determine just how many people represent enough of a sample to stand for a larger population, beginning researchers can consult major professors, existing studies of similar content, and relevant sources on collecting and analyzing inferential statistics (Hutchinson, 2004; Rea & Parker, 2005).

In order to avoid even an unintentional bias in selecting a sample of participants, quantitative researchers often prefer to randomly choose research subjects from a larger population. The logistics of this process, known as randomized sampling, have been discussed in other sources (Babbie, 2004; Rea & Parker, 2005).

Participants in qualitative studies. Researchers conducting qualitative investigations, on the other hand, are rarely concerned with using inferential statistics to make generalizations to larger populations. Instead, qualitative studies tend to be field-focused and involve the detailed description of the interaction of humans with each other and their environment on a day-to-day basis (Eisner, 1998). Because data collected from survey research can be helpful in providing self-reported descriptions of people's actions and opinions, some qualitative researchers will mix survey research with qualitative fieldwork for descriptive, rather than inferential, purposes (Schutz, Chambless, & DeCuir, 2004).

Because of this emphasis on describing the qualities of specific experiences, qualitative researchers are more likely to use criterion-based sampling, or choosing survey participants based on predetermined factors, rather than through random selection (LeCompte & Preissle, 1993). There are a variety of methods for making such selections based on specific criteria, including quota sampling, comprehensive sampling, and network or snowball sampling (Babbie, 2004; LeCompte & Preissle, 1993).

I used criterion-based sampling in my own research when I sent a survey to a select group of purposefully identified elementary art educators who were involved in teaching mixed-age and mixed-grade level classes within public schools in Florida (Broome, 2009). The random sampling techniques used in quantitative research were not appropriate for my study because my goal was to qualitatively describe the practices and opinions of a specific set of art teachers under unique circumstances, and not to generalize findings to all art teachers in Florida. Instead of administering my survey to a random sample of all art educators in the state, I used the presence of mixed-age elementary art programs that purposefully combined two or more grade levels in the same classroom (Kasten & Clarke, 1993) as the initial criteria for narrowing my survey population. Next, I eliminated any remaining art teachers who worked with mixed-age groups in private school settings as a way not to diminish the concerns of those working with multi-age groups in public schools where mandated standardized testing tied to age-specific grade level promotion and retention cannot be bypassed. In the end, the specific criteria that I used in my sampling methods for identifying potential survey participants were appropriate for reaching my goal of describing a unique set of art educators. This goal could not have been achieved through randomized sampling and my methods would not have been suitable for making formal inferences to larger populations as would be expected in most quantitative studies.

WRITING THE SURVEY

Writing a survey can be a complicated process, but becomes much easier with guiding questions and intended participants already in mind. For instance, there is no reason to include any survey items that do not directly relate to your guiding questions or the background of your participants. Furthermore, knowing the characteristics of your participants helps you to phrase questions in an appropriate manner. You would likely use different terminology in questioning middle school students than you would professional art educators.

Even with a basic focus in mind, creating a survey entirely from scratch can be overwhelming. Weisberg, Krosnick, and Bowen (1996) suggest referring to existing standard survey questions when planning a project of your own, and I advise you to examine published surveys that relate to your interests in terms of content or the types of guiding questions you hope to answer. You can find these surveys by conducting an Internet search of literature in educational databases (Fraenkel & Wallen, 2003). Most librarians can provide you with information about databases that are appropriate for conducting searches on your given topic, and I suggest that you include the term, "survey research," among the descriptors that you use when searching these databases. Many of these published surveys have undergone a rigorous validation process in order to ensure or improve each instrument's capacity for dependably and accurately collecting information related to its intended measure (Cox & Cox, 2008). If you find an applicable report that publishes the findings of survey research but does not include a copy of the actual survey itself, do not hesitate to contact the author(s) directly to ask for a copy of the questionnaire. Critically referring to existing resources that are similar in nature and altering these resources in ways that are necessary and appropriate for your own research goals can serve as a useful starting point.

It is also useful to look for individual survey items that generally seek to answer the same types of questions that guide your research. For instance, if your goal is to variably measure the attitudes of survey respondents, then it may be wise to use an established scale for obtaining such information rather than developing one of your own (Hutchinson, 2004). An example of such an existing scale used to measure opinions is known as a Likert scale (Rea & Parker, 2005). Likert scales offer respondents a continuum of options for representing their attitudes toward predetermined statements. Some typical options offered by Likert scales include (1) strongly agree, (2) agree, (3) neutral, (4) disagree, (5) strongly disagree. There are many other existing scales commonly used in survey research including the Guttman, Thurstone, and Bogardus scales (Babbie, 2004). The trick is to find an existing scale that is most suited for collecting the type of information needed to answer your guiding research questions.

As you begin to assemble your own survey, it is wise to remember that written questionnaires should be aesthetically pleasing and the items asked should be reasonably few in number (Fraenkel & Wallen, 2003). While there is no universal limit to the number of questions allowed on a survey (Hutchinson, 2004; Weisberg, Krosnick, & Bowen, 1996), the suitability, effects, and factors that contribute to the length of surveys have been discussed. Overly-long surveys may discourage potential respondents from completing a questionnaire, and educated professionals with vested interest in a topic appear the most likely to follow through on finishing longer surveys (Hutchinson, 2004). While both free-response and forced-choice items (such as multiple choice) may be included, answers to these different types of questions will require different sorts of time commitments in completion and in analysis. When considering the number of items on a survey, however, designers should not exclude questions that seek descriptive background information from respondents. Such items can help to provide an overall context and informational foundation about survey participants.

Pretesting your survey prior to its actual administration offers one way to obtain feedback on the length of initial survey drafts and also to check on its overall clarity (Fraenkel & Wallen, 2003). Consulting available experts in survey research and individuals with similar backgrounds to your intended participants is advisable during this pretesting process. When I was developing my survey for the teachers of mixed-age art classes in Florida (Broome, 2009), I sent a draft of my survey to an education professor and his class of 22 doctoral students who were studying survey research. Revisions were made after periodic meetings with the professor and again after a group meeting that included the entire class. This revised version of the survey was then pretested and discussed with a group of art educators to check for content concerns within the discipline for which it was designed. Although not every teacher researcher will have easy access to professors

Constructing Surveys

DAVID BURTON / PROFESSOR, ART EDUCATION, VIRGINIA COMMONWEALTH UNIVERSITY

GENERAL PRINCIPLES

Keep it simple. What information do you really want? What questions do you need to ask in order to answer your research questions? While other survey questions might be interesting, if they do not help you answer your research questions, drop them.

Keep it clear. Phrase the questions clearly and succinctly. Attend to the choice of words. Avoid jargon, such as "artsy-craftsy" unless you specifically define it in your cover letter. Jargon has baggage; the respondent is likely to exercise a bias—for or against—jargon-laden terms. Avoid compound questions that have two or more parts or items.

Keep it objective. Allow for a full range of responses. Avoid intentional or unintentional bias. Do not introduce leading questions, such as "Don't you agree that…"

Keep it short. People are unlikely to answer lengthy surveys. A good length is 10-20 questions. Demographic questions might add 5-10 more questions.

Provide a cover letter that includes a rationale, clear instructions, definitions of terms, and a thank you. The rationale politely invites the respondent to participate in your survey. It states the purpose of the survey, why the data gathered by the survey is important, and how it will be used. Respondents are often hesitant to reply if they do not know the intent of the researcher or do not understand how the data will be used. Assure confidentiality. Provide clear instructions on how to take the survey. Include definitions of important or unusual terms used in the survey. At the end of the cover letter and again at the end of the survey, thank the respondents effusively and reiterate their important contribution.

and groups of doctoral students studying survey research, it is still advisable to pretest your survey instrument with people who have similar characteristics to your eventual participants (Babbie, 2004).

OPTIONS FOR ADMINISTERING THE SURVEY

Currently, there are many existing options for disseminating surveys including mailed surveys, phone or face-to-face interviews, and surveys completed through the Internet (Rea & Parker, 2005). Each method appears to have its advantages and disadvantages, but ultimately researchers should choose the format that best meets the needs their participants and that fits within their established budgets.

Mailed surveys are relatively anonymous and inexpensive to administer (Rea & Parker, 2005). Participants may appreciate the ability to visually study options on, say, a Likert scale, but it is more difficult for a researcher to follow-up on open-ended answers when a response is unclear. Phone or face-to-face interviews used in survey research involve lists of scripted questions similar or identical to those on written questionnaires, but are instead administered orally by a researcher or group of trained assistants (Fraenkel & Wallen, 2003). While the interview approach allows the researcher to ask for clarification when answers are unclear, the process is often costly (whether in travel expenses, telephone bills, or hiring research assistants to conduct the interviews) and can be collectively quite time consuming to complete, transcribe, and analyze (Rea & Parker, 2005).

Surveys conducted through the Internet may be appealing to researchers, especially as more online survey providers are including built-in database programs that can store responses in ways that assist in the early stages of data analyses (Cox & Cox, 2008; Hutchinson, 2004). In terms of cost-effectiveness and time management in collection and early analysis, it may seem as if the use of Internet surveys should be the preferred method of data collection for all survey researchers. However, just because technology makes data collection easier on a researcher, it does not mean it is most effective in eliciting responses from participants. Dillman (2007) has detailed numerous reasons why online survey research can be potentially problematic including inherent limitations posed by populations that may not have the means to receive such surveys, the possibility for some participants to reply more than once, and several variables that may lead to a reduction in response rates. Still others see much potential in the use of online surveys and claim that additional research is needed to make fair comparisons between surveys administered through the Internet and through more traditional means (Babbie, 2004; Hutchinson, 2004).

DEMOGRAPHICS

All surveys should include at least a few demographic questions. Demographic data allow you to form a general profile of the respondents and allow you to relate the data from your survey to data from other surveys if the demographic profiles are similar.

Demographic questions should be very simple and quantitative. "What is the total number of years you have been teaching?" 0-5, 6-10, 11-15, 16-20, 21-25, 26 or more.

Traditionally, demographic questions are placed at the end of the survey because they are routine and boring. If they are the first questions in the survey, the respondent may not be motivated even to begin answering. Put your "sexy" questions at the beginning of the survey.

FORMAT

Format the questions to fit the data. Quantitative data are easier to analyze but of little use if the nature of the questions is qualitative. For example, if you want to understand teachers' attitudes, a qualitative question would make more sense. Alternatively, if you want to know the average class size, a quantitative question would make more sense.

Make the structure of the question clear to understand, objective, and easy to answer. The ideal question is a yes/no question (although they rarely provide the depth of insight you wish).

The options in multiple choice questions should be mutually exclusive. For example, the question "How many years have you been teaching? 0-5, 5-10, 10-15, 15 or more" is unclear. If you had been teaching 5 years, which option would apply? The correct options would be 0-5, 6-10, 11-15, 16-20, 21-25, 26 or more.

Likert Scales allow respondents to make relative (or quasi-subjective) judgments. They can be quantified by the researcher later. A Likert Scale is usually broken into five to seven segments that together constitute an obvious scale or range. A subjective question, such as "What is the general morale among teachers at your school?" lends itself to a Likert Scale (see Figure 1).

VERY NEGATIVE		NEUTRAL			VERY POSITIVE	
1	2	3	4	5	6	7

FIGURE 1. Example of a Likert Scale for answering the subjective question: *What is the general morale among teachers at your school?*

(continued)

The decision of whether or not to use online surveys might be best made by your knowledge of your intended participants (Cox & Cox, 2008). If I knew that a group of selected research subjects actively participated in a common electronic mailing list, I would not hesitate to use an Internet-based survey. However, due to a number of factors, I would not presume that even potential participants with regular access to computers would necessarily be more likely to respond to an Internet survey than to a mailed questionnaire.

ENHANCING RESPONSE RATES

A great deal of planning is also involved in finding ways to encourage research subjects to actually return completed surveys. In the case of written questionnaires, Fraenkel and Wallen (2003) suggest the inclusion of a brief, polite, personalized cover letter that explains the purposes of the survey, why the findings may be important, how the respondents' identities will be protected, and gratitude for their participation. Other suggestions for enhancing response rates include the provision of (1) small incentives or raffles for those who return surveys, (2) addressed, stamped, return envelopes, (3) periodic polite reminders to initially nonresponsive participants (Fraenkel & Wallen, 2003), and (4) clear due dates (Rea & Parker, 2005). Opinions on acceptable response rates seem to vary, except to say that the highest return rates possible are desired. I would advise a beginning teacher researcher to consult with his or her major professor to determine an acceptable response rate when planning a new survey research project. In the event that the suggestions above still lead to an unacceptable response rate, readers can consult additional measures suggested by Rea and Parker (2005) to further encourage additional responses.

ANALYSIS

There are numerous ways to analyze survey data, and to discuss them all in a single chapter is not possible. But, if you have been consistent in keeping your guiding questions in mind and have designed a survey that addresses these overarching issues, then you should have also already identified whether your analysis will involve calculating descriptive or inferential statistics, correlated data, factor analysis, coded responses, or any other number of ways of making relevant meaning from results (Babbie, 2004; Sonquist & Dunkelberg, 1977). If you are only just beginning to question how you will analyze your data after your surveys have been disseminated, then you may have already put yourself in a position where your research questions may not be answerable with the data that you are collecting.

Provide an escape option or back door for multiple choice questions, such as N/A (not applicable), or "Other," with a blank space for comments.

Content analysis can be applied to open-ended questions. The key words can be determined before beginning the word analysis or, if using grounded theory, the codes may emerge from the data. Provide two or three lines for short answers. Avoid "essay" questions.

PILOT-TESTING QUESTIONS

If your survey is intended for teachers, give it to a small group of non-teachers first to test the questions for clarity and readability. Do they understand the questions (even if they can't answer them)? Ask them what they think the questions mean, not just what the words say. If they do not understand the questions, probably teachers will not either.

Next, give your survey to a small group of the target population. Are their responses consistent among the group? Are they what you expected with regard to your research question? If not, you need to revise your questions and pilot-test them again.

TARGET POPULATIONS

There are two types of target populations: *parametric* and *non-parametric*. When you survey a parametric population, you survey every member of that designated population. For example, you could easily survey ALL the elementary art teachers in your school district. Surveying an entire population is obviously most desirable—everyone in the target population is exposed to the survey whether they respond or not. If you are persistent in your follow-up efforts with non-responders, you can increase the response rate.

A non-parametric population is just a sample of a larger (parametric) population. For example, it is not feasible to survey all the elementary art teachers in the United States, but you can select a representative percentage, or sample, to survey.

If you select the non-parametric target group randomly, it is statistically likely that the relatively small number will accurately reflect the same views or data as the total (parametric) population. Various methods exist for choosing people randomly including purchasing lists through NAEA or Educational Directories, Inc. of Mt. Prospect, IL.

While it is important for beginning researchers to understand which types of analysis they should be using and why these analyses provide answers to their guiding research questions, it is rarely necessary for researchers to do the calculations themselves. With advances in user-friendly technology, easily accessible software, and just some simple training, even beginning researchers can enter data into computer programs such as Microsoft Excel and obtain instant results for interpretation. Some large graduate programs in education even offer courses on using computer programs, such as the Statistical Package for Social Science (*SPSS*), for the purpose of analyzing research data. In such cases, you can learn how to use computer technology to analyze your survey results and receive college credit simultaneously. With knowledge of Microsoft Excel, *SPSS*, or similar programs, a simple set of descriptive quantitative statistics obtained from forced-choice survey items can be directly entered into such computer programs and can be immediately translated into averages, percentages, frequency tables, histograms, or other forms of graphic representation.

The data collected from free-response items, however, will require careful content analysis and coding before any results can be produced (Babbie, 2004). During this coding process, researchers sort through their data and assign summative phrases, or codes, to regularly occurring themes in respondents' answers to specific questions. By clustering answers to specific questions in categories of like-themes, researchers can still present findings from open-ended questions as descriptive statistics represented by averages, percentages, graphs, or charts, if it is desirable. However, unlike responses to forced-choice questions, the researcher will also have the option of pulling representative quotes from individual surveys for use in presenting qualitative findings.

CONCLUSIONS

Survey research continues to be a frequently used methodology in both quantitative and qualitative research studies. Perhaps because so many of us have completed questionnaires at some point or another, beginning researchers do not always understand the enormous amount of time and intricate decisions that are involved in planning survey research studies. In this chapter I presented a basic introduction to the use of survey methodology along with examples from research in art education and my own experiences that I hope have proved useful to beginning art teacher researchers. If you find that your research interests are best explored through obtaining real answers provided by real people, then survey research methods may figure prominently in your future academic pursuits.

For a large population, such as U.S. elementary art teachers, you ideally want at least 400 responses to obtain reliable statistics. According to Fink (1995) as the sample size increases, the variability of responses decreases. Thus, once a researcher gets 400 responses, the statistical differences among responses decreases significantly. Beyond 400, the responses tend to be quite similar and that makes 400 a sufficient number from which to generalize. However, only a fraction will respond to your survey, so you may need to send it to at least 4000 people in order to get 400 responses. Although achieving a response rate of 400 is ideal for a large population, it is not always possible because the size of the population may be smaller. Recent studies in our field utilize the survey methodology but do not always have a sample size of 400 or more. For instance, Broome (2009) had a sample of 36 respondents from a whole population of 69. Milbrandt and Klein (2008) conducted an electronic survey that had 100 responses out of a population of 422 subscribers to a listserv. The greater the response rate, the more representative the results of the survey will be of the entire population.

If responses are low or slow, survey researchers frequently send out a second or third wave of the same survey to the same people. This strategy boosts the number of responses. Depending upon IRB requirements and the availability of funding, a researcher may want to consider offering an incentive to participants for completing a survey. ∎

REFERENCES

Broome, J. L. (2009). A descriptive study of multi-age art education in Florida. *Studies in Art Education, 50*(2), 167-183.

Fink, A. (1995). *How to sample in surveys.* Thousand Oaks, CA: Sage.

Milbrandt, M. K., & Klein, S. R. (2008). Survey of art teacher educators. *Studies in Art Education, 49*(4), 343-357.

REFERENCES

Anderson, T., Eisner, E., & McRorie, S. (1998). A survey of graduate study in art education. *Studies in Art Education, 40*(1), 8-25.

Babbie, E. (2004). *The practice of social research* (10th ed.). Belmont, CA: Thomson Wadsworth.

Broome, J. L. (2009). A descriptive study of multi-age art education in Florida. *Studies in Art Education, 50*(2), 167-183.

Cox, J., & Cox, K. B. (2008). *Your opinion, please!: How to build the best questionnaires in the field of education* (2nd ed.). Thousand Oaks, CA: Corwin.

Dillman, D. A. (2007). *Mail and internet surveys: The tailored design method* (2nd ed.). Hoboken, NJ: John Wiley and Sons.

Eisner, E. W. (1998). *The enlightened eye: Qualitative inquiry and the enhancement of educational practice.* Upper Saddle River, NJ: Prentice Hall.

Fraenkel, J. R., & Wallen, N. E. (2003). *How to design and evaluate research in education* (5th ed.). New York, NY: McGraw Hill.

Hutchinson, S. R. (2004). Survey research. In K. deMarrais & S. D. Lapan (Eds.), *Foundations for research: Methods of inquiry in education and the social sciences* (pp. 283-301). Mahwah, NJ: Lawrence Erlbaum.

Kasten, W. C., & Clarke, B. K. (1993). *The multi-age classroom: A family of learners.* Katonah, NY: Richard C. Owen.

LeCompte, M. D., & Preissle, J. (1993). *Ethnography and qualitative design in educational research* (2nd ed.). San Diego, CA: Academic Press.

Rea, L. M., & Parker, R. A. (2005). *Designing and conducting survey research: A comprehensive guide* (3rd ed.). San Francisco, CA: Josey-Bass.

Schutz, P. A., Chambless, C. B., & DeCuir, J. T. (2004). Multimethods research. In K. deMarrais & S. D. Lapan (Eds.), *Foundations for research: Methods of inquiry in education and the social sciences* (pp. 267-281). Mahwah, NJ: Lawrence Erlbaum.

Sonquist, J. A., & Dunkelberg, W. C. (1977). *Survey and opinion research: Procedures for processing and analysis.* Englewood Cliffs, NJ: Prentice-Hall.

Weisberg, H. F., Krosnick, J. A., & Bowen, B. D. (1996). *An introduction to survey research, polling, and data analysis* (3rd ed.). Thousand Oaks, CA: Sage.

JEFFREY L. BROOME is Assistant Professor of Art Education at Florida State University. His teaching and research interests include explorations into multi-age art education, cultural diversity, classroom management, and interdisciplinary approaches to art education. He presents regularly at national and state conferences, and has presented at international symposia and on thematic instruction at school district workshops. His manuscripts have been accepted for publication in such academic journals as *Studies in Art Education*, the *Journal of Multiage Education*, *Art Education Australia*, and the *Journal for the Multiage Association of Queensland*, *Art Education*, the *Journal of Art for Life*, and as a *National Art Education Association Advisory*. He worked for 8 years as a public school art teacher in Florida and earned recognition from his colleagues in the Hillsborough County School District with a Teacher of the Year Award. Throughout his career he has worked with K-12 students in variety of contexts, including public schools and nonprofit community arts organizations.

8 / Cooperative Art Education: Practices and a Rationale for Art Curricula

BRYNA BOBICK / ASSISTANT PROFESSOR OF ART EDUCATION AT THE UNIVERSITY OF MEMPHIS

ABSTRACT: *The purpose of this study is to investigate how elementary art teachers conduct cooperative art activities in their classrooms and why they consider these activities important. The study included the content areas of the cooperative art activities, the ways in which these activities were facilitated, and the barriers and facilitations elementary art teachers encountered when teaching cooperative art activities. The researcher used a qualitative survey methodology to conduct a study of cooperative art activities being taught in preK-5 schools in Georgia. A survey of 135 elementary art teachers focused on cooperative art activities, teachers' attitudes towards the activities, and how activities are included in art education curriculum.*

This research study involved a survey with elementary art teachers in Georgia. My research question was "What are elementary art teachers' attitudes toward cooperative art experiences and to what extent do they include these experiences in the curriculum they teach?" I designed the survey to determine how elementary art teachers conduct cooperative art activities—activities that involve small mixed-ability groups working together to achieve a goal—in their classrooms and why they consider these experiences important. The survey described, analyzed, and evaluated the role cooperative art education plays in their art education curricula.

In this study, I investigated cooperative art education in elementary art rooms through art teachers' attitudes and experiences. The study investigates the content of the cooperative art instruction, the ways in which these activities are facilitated, and the barriers elementary art teachers have encountered when teaching cooperative art lessons. The survey focused on cooperative art instruction, teachers' attitudes toward the lessons, and how the instruction is included in the art education curricula.

LITERATURE REVIEW

Cooperative learning involves groups of students working together to achieve a goal. It involves every class member and allows students in a large class to voice their point of view as a member of a team. When teachers introduce cooperative learning to their class, they must establish new classroom practices and help the students learn to interact with their classmates to complete an assignment. In order for cooperative learning to benefit students, the assignment should be challenging, have a common goal, and allow the students to interact. Students should understand the benefits of working together and each student should be

fully engaged in the assignment (Gillies & Ashman, 2003). According to Bellanca and Fogarty (1991), cooperative groups include two to five students of different ability, skill, motivation, or gender who work to achieve a single learning goal. In a cooperative classroom, a teacher uses a variety of structures and teaching strategies.

Johnson, Johnson, and Holubec (1993) wrote that cooperative learning may not look the same in all learning situations. Some learning situations involve formal cooperative learning, others informal cooperative learning, or cooperative based groups. For the purpose of this research, I am defining cooperative learning as a teaching strategy in which students work together to achieve a learning goal including formal or informal practices. Such approaches allow students to learn in a social environment and involve every class member. Students work with their peers to create a group response to an assignment.

METHODOLOGY

Qualitative research is a term for inquiry in a real-world setting (Ritchie & Lewis, 2003) that "helps us to understand and explain the meaning of social phenomena with as little disruption of the natural setting as possible" (Merriam, 1998, p. 5). Overall, qualitative research is concerned with understanding the actions, decisions, beliefs, or values of people within their social worlds. According to Tuckman (1999), certain data collection methods have been associated with qualitative research. They include interviews, group discussions, observations, narratives, and surveys. Eisner (1994) pointed out that all knowledge, including that gained through qualitative research, is referenced in qualities, and there are many ways to represent and understand the world.

There is a consensus that qualitative research is a naturalistic, interpretative approach concerned with understanding the meanings that people attach to actions, decisions, beliefs, or values within their social worlds (Gay & Airasian, 2003; Tuckman, 1999; Wiersma, 1995). The purpose of this qualitative survey was to describe the characteristics of cooperative art activities and teachers' attitudes towards cooperative learning in elementary art rooms. Each respondent had a different educational background and unique experiences with cooperative art education. The survey research allowed me to understand elementary art teachers' attitudes, beliefs, and teaching practices involving cooperative art education. In using the surveys, I relied on the honesty and accuracy of the participants' self-reporting.

PARTICIPANTS

I conducted a study of cooperative art activities being taught in preK-5 schools, which involved survey research. After providing the president of the Georgia Art Education Association (GAEA) a brief outline about the research study, I received permission from the president of the GAEA to use the membership list to disseminate this survey. The GAEA mailing list contained 400 names in the elementary category that included a cross-section of educators who taught in various size elementary schools. This list also represented art educators from across the state of Georgia.

DATA COLLECTION

Because the contact information from the GAEA was mailing addresses, not e-mail addresses, I chose to conduct a mail survey. Before preparing the final form of the survey, the items were pilot tested with a professor of art education and a group of graduate students in the field of art education. The pretest of the survey questions revealed deficiencies, misunderstandings, and inadequate questions. Thus, I revised the questions.

After I finalized the survey questions, I assigned each of the elementary art teachers a number and I wrote the number on a self-addressed stamped envelope. This allowed me to monitor which art teachers returned the survey, even those who did not include their name or address. Overall, 400 surveys were mailed and 135 were returned.

I included 20 questions in the survey; 5 were open-ended. Though this survey included some demographic and close-ended questions, this chapter focuses on the 5 open-ended questions[1] that I analyzed with qualitative methods.

ANALYSIS OF SURVEYS

Marshall and Rossman (2006) discussed that typical analysis of data can fall into a variety of phases. Using their suggestions, I broke the analysis of the surveys into the following phases: (1) organizing the data; (2) immersion in the data; (3) generating categories and themes; (4) coding the data, and (5) offering interpretations through notes and memos. Each phase of the

data analysis required data reduction, this made the collected data from the surveys more manageable. The data reduction allowed me to transfer the raw data into a more useful form.

The mailing produced 135 responses, which represents a 33.75% response rate. The total number of responses varied from question to question because of item non-response. As the completed surveys arrived in the mail, I scanned each survey to see the number of questions that the teacher answered and if it included any examples of cooperative art activities. These procedures served as the initial guide for categories and potential coding schemes.

From the survey data, I found myself confronted with a large amount of information on cooperative art activities conducted in elementary art classrooms. At this point, I became immersed in the data. I read and reread the survey data and became familiar with teachers' responses. Seven of the returned surveys were blank, and I chose to discard them. Thus, I carefully analyzed responses from 128 surveys.

The open-ended questions, numbers 15-19 (see the list at the end of this chapter), allowed each participant the opportunity to express ideas and feelings and include additional information that would not have been available with the selected-response items. Through responding to the open-ended questions, elementary teachers revealed their attitudes toward cooperative art education. The purpose of each open-ended question was to gather specific information about cooperative art lessons. I created Microsoft Word documents for each of the five open-ended questions and as specific themes emerged from each question, I added the data to the theme. These themes included the relationship of academic subjects to cooperative learning, barriers to cooperative art education, the omission of lessons, and summarization of a cooperative art activity.

Miles and Huberman (1994), suggested several ways to record data and ways to generate themes and categories including one technique of developing data recording charts. I created a color-coded system for each of the Microsoft Word data-recording charts. This allowed me the opportunity to reflect on the responses and to generate categories and themes. As I coded the data, a greater understanding of the role cooperative art education played in elementary art classrooms emerged (see Figure 1).

After coding the surveys, I explained the color-coded charts and the Word documents to two peer reviewers, doctoral students in education. Each peer reviewer coded all the surveys, reviewed the Word documents, and the data were checked for intercoder reliability. Intercoder reliability (similar to inter-rater reliability) refers to independent reviewers evaluating how the data were coded (Tuckman, 1999). The peer reviewers and I discussed the results, I took into account their interpretations, and I used their interpretations in the presentation of the survey results.

Total Number of Responses	No Barriers	Lack of Time	Storage	Scheduling	Ownership	Student Attitude	Other
109	25	24	98	109	10	24	9

FIGURE 1. Example of a coded data analysis chart based on the answers to Survey Question 15: *Did you encounter any barriers when you taught cooperative learning activities?*

DISCUSSION OF FINDINGS

Based on the survey's findings, elementary art teachers included cooperative learning in art education for a variety of reasons. When elementary art educators have a personal interest in cooperative learning, it is included in their curricula. In addition, cooperative learning is a practical way to accomplish a specific art activity with elementary students.

RELATIONSHIP OF ACADEMIC SUBJECTS TO COOPERATIVE LEARNING

The open-ended survey questions revealed a variety of information. When asked if cooperative learning was related to other academic subjects, 88% of the respondents indicated they relate cooperative learning to an academic subject. The following five categories emerged from the written responses: science, math, social studies, language arts, and other—including technology, music, theater arts, and community. The respondents report they use cooperative learning to reinforce topics covered in the regular classroom.

BARRIERS

In addition, 23% respondents did not encounter any barriers when teaching a cooperative learning activity, while the remaining 77% encountered barriers including lack of time, scheduling, ownership, student attitude, and other. Based on the written comments, the barriers should be addressed before attempting future cooperative art activities.

Time. For example, one participant explained that cooperative learning activities require additional work for the teacher and careful planning. In her situation, the particular cooperative learning activity involved ceramics. She had to "stay additional hours after school to prepare the materials and make sure the group ceramic project was ready to fire in the kiln." Time constraints were described as contributing to the unsuccessful way cooperative learning occurred in another respondent's classroom. She taught her students for only 30 minutes each week. She stated "The 30-minute classes were not conducive for cooperative learning experiences."

Student attitude. In addition, another participant wrote about unsuccessfully pairing students to work together. This led to "the problem of disagreement on certain issues, and the group of students being too rowdy during class." Also, one respondent pointed out "that large size groups of students did not work well, but three to four students seem to be ideal for cooperative learning groups."

SUCCESS OF COOPERATIVE LEARNING

Nearly all the teachers (114) responded to the survey question that addressed whether elementary art teachers find cooperative learning in an elementary art education curriculum to be successful and useful. After reading each response, I created three categories (i.e., successful, somewhat, not successful). Based on the survey data, 81% found cooperative learning to be successful, 11% found it somewhat successful, and 8% did not find it successful and useful. A few of the written comments are shared here:

- "Cooperative art activities provided an opportunity for students to experience helping and caring through art education."
- "The cooperative work helped to teach them empathy and have the opportunity to experience community."
- "Cooperative learning allowed students to learn compassion for others and interact with members of the community."
- "These experiences relate to their lives beyond the art room."

INTEGRATION OF COOPERATIVE LEARNING INTO THE CURRICULUM

Based on the responses, the majority of survey participants were able to integrate cooperative learning into their existing curriculum. Only one respondent indicated that s/he needed to omit an individual lesson in order to include a lesson utilizing cooperative learning strategies. When analyzing the responses to the question about how cooperative learning is included in the curriculum, a theme that emerged from the comments was the idea of including cooperative learning in the overall design of the visual arts curriculum. One respondent indicated that the curriculum is wide open and art teachers can use their knowledge of the arts to relate it to anything and everything, including cooperative learning.

EXAMPLES OF COOPERATIVE LEARNING

The final survey question allowed the respondents the opportunity to summarize a successful cooperative learning lesson and 80% of the respondents did so. An analysis of the comments reinforced the idea that teachers use cooperative art education in a variety of ways with a variety of media in elementary art classrooms in Georgia. Elementary art teachers presented various activities that crossed grade levels and subject areas. Some utilized cooperative learning experiences with pairs of students, while others included an entire grade level. The responses indicate cooperative art education can be implemented on a limited budget. One response mentioned a drawing lesson that used markers and drawing paper, underscoring ways an art teacher can introduce cooperative learning to elementary students that can be completed in one or two class periods, and not spend a large portion of the art budget on one activity.

CONCLUSION

These particular elementary art teachers generally accepted the concept of cooperative learning within the visual art program and across the curriculum. They subscribed to an integrated approach by including cooperative learning activities in various ways. Along with art studio activities, cooperative learning incorporated art history, aesthetics, and art criticism. In addition, the activities related to academic subjects and provided opportunities for art teachers to reinforce topics being taught in the regular education classrooms.

For many of the survey respondents, their personal interest in cooperative learning was pivotal in it being included in their art education curriculum. While other respondents wanted to promote positive social skills and a sense of community in the art classroom, very few taught any cooperative learning activity primarily due to requests from their school administrators. The written comments and the summarized lessons suggest that the art teachers shared common ideas and approaches to cooperative learning, but their lessons met the particular needs of their students. These elementary art teachers draw attention to the lack of class time and scheduling conflicts as problems with teaching cooperative learning. In any classroom situation, it is difficult for an art teacher to include instruction through cooperative learning when they teach students on such a limited basis. Further research into successful cooperative learning strategies in the art classroom could help our field mitigate these instructional obstacles.

AUTHOR NOTE

The author would like to thank the editors for their assistance with this chapter and the Georgia Art Education Association for the survey list.

REFERENCES

Bellanca, J., & Fogarty, R. (1991). *Blueprints for thinking in the cooperative classroom*. Palatine, IL: Skylight.

Eisner, E. (1994). *The educational imagination: On the design and evaluation of school programs* (3rd ed.). New York, NY: Macmillan College.

Gay, L. R., & Airasian, P. (2003). *Educational research: Competencies for analysis and application*. Columbus, OH: Merrill Prentice Hall.

Gillies, R. M., & Ashman, A. F. (2003). *Co-operative learning: The social and intellectual outcomes of learning in groups*. New York, NY: Routledge Falmer.

Johnson, D. W., Johnson, R. T., & Holubec, E. J. (1993). *Circles of learning: Cooperative in the classroom*. Edina, MN: Interaction Book Company.

Marshall, C., & Rossman, G. B. (2006) *Designing qualitative research*. Thousand Oaks, CA: Sage.

Merriam, S. B. (1998). *Qualitative research and case study applications in education*. San Francisco, CA: Jossey-Bass.

Miles, M. B., & Huberman, A. M. (1994). *A qualitative data analysis: A sourcebook of new methods*. Thousand Oaks, CA: Sage.

Ritchie, J., & Lewis, J. (2003). *Qualitative research practice: A guide for social science students and researchers*. London, England: Sage.

Tuckman, B. W. (1999). *Conducting educational research*. Belmont, CA: Wadsworth Group/Thomson Learning.

Wiersma, W. (1995). *Research methods in education: An introduction*. Needham Heights, MA: Allyn and Bacon.

ENDNOTE

1 **Open-Ended Survey Questions:**

- Did you encounter any barriers when you taught cooperative learning activities? If yes, briefly explain.
- When teaching a cooperative learning activity, did it relate to any other academic subject? If yes, briefly explain.
- As an elementary art teacher, do you find cooperative learning in an elementary art education curriculum to be successful and useful? Why or Why not?
- When teaching cooperative learning, did you omit a specific art lesson from the curriculum? If yes, which lesson was omitted and why?
- Please summarize a cooperative learning activity you thought was successful and any additional comments.
- For the purpose of my research, I am defining *cooperative learning* as a teaching strategy in which students work together to achieve a learning goal; such approaches allow students to learn in a social environment and involve every class member. Each student works with his or her peers to create a group response to an assignment.

BRYNA BOBICK is an assistant professor of art education at the University of Memphis. She is a former elementary art teacher who graduated from the University of Georgia (BFA and EdD) and the University of West Georgia (MEd). Her research interests include demographic research of K-12 art specialists, museum education, and urban art education.

9 / Utilizing a Survey as a Means to Evaluate a Program

DAVID WEBSTER

ABSTRACT: *This chapter is an example of the method in which a survey can be utilized as a quantitative research instrument. The purpose of this research study was to undertake a formative evaluation of the certification track in art program at a mid-sized midwestern university through an investigation into how well art teachers thought they were prepared for their teaching positions as a result of their participation in the program. To research this issue in objective terms, a questionnaire survey was presented to the entire population of graduates from the program over a 5-year period. The intention was to measure their reactions to particular response categories, in order to analyze, compare, and cross-reference their responses. This made it possible to identify, determine, and categorize common themes and general patterns of responses. The analysis of the collected data provided the empirical evidence necessary to recognize problematic areas in the program's structure and organization, and to warrant changes deemed important for it to become more successful in achieving its organizers' goals. The topics addressed in this chapter include formative evaluation, the structure of a certification in art program, the creation and implementation of a survey, data analysis, and recommendations for program improvement.*

The U.S. Department of Education's National Center for Educational Statistics' report [NCES] (1999) reported that only one in five teachers felt well prepared to work in a modern classroom. With regard to art teacher preparation, Day (1997) claimed that too many of the nation's colleges and universities allow their candidates to graduate without strong professional preparation. He argued that art teacher preparation programs must change and improve to meet the changing issues and expectations of art education. In the 1990s, arguments were made that gaps in art teacher preparation need to be addressed and that the preparation of teachers should become central to art education research (Davis, 1990; Day, 1997; Mason, 1997; Zimmerman, 1997).

Regarding teacher preparation program evaluation, reform, and improvement, Ayres (1988) claimed that institutions need to determine how successful they have been in preparing students, and that empirical evidence is useful for making changes to any particular recognized problem. Collecting such evidence cannot be accomplished without including and considering the cooperation, views, and opinions of teachers (Day, 1997; Fullan & Hargreaves, 1996). With these concerns in mind, the purpose of this research study was to undertake a formative evaluation of the art teacher certification track at a mid-sized midwestern university. The study involved a survey that investigated how well art teachers thought they were prepared for their teaching positions as a result of their undergraduate teacher preparation. Ayres (1988) suggested the collection of follow-up data is best undertaken during the first 5 years after graduation,

as generally after that period the data will be of little use because the program's effects upon the teachers generally will have been superseded by other factors and influences. Following this suggestion, the focus of analysis for this research study was on the entire population of 31 teachers who graduated from the program between 1999 and 2003, and who were currently employed within the state teaching art at various grade levels, K–12.

METHODOLOGY

To understand how well the graduates of this program felt they were prepared to teach, the researcher used a survey as an instrument for data collection. The focus of the survey was to obtain an understanding of individual participants' perceptions and experiences of the teacher preparation program. As Patton (1990) indicated, gaining an understanding of participants' concepts, thoughts, understandings, attitudes, and beliefs about a program can assist in gathering the empirical evidence necessary to analyze and evaluate its effectiveness.

SURVEY DESIGN

Conway (2002) conducted a similar study that attempted to evaluate a music teacher preparation program, examining the perceptions of beginning teachers with regard to what they considered to be the most and least valuable parts of their teacher preparation and what suggestions they had for the program. Using Conway's study as a model for this study, the researcher chose to determine the teachers' overall opinions as to how well the program prepared them. Additionally,

1. How well did the program adequately prepare you for your position as an art teacher?

   Very Poorly   Poorly   Reasonably Well   Well   Very Well

2. What were the most beneficial aspects of the program that helped prepare you to teach art?

   Art Education   Studio Art   Art History   Professional Education   Student Teaching   Liberal Arts Core
   Why?

3. What were the least beneficial aspects of the program that helped prepare you to teach art?

   Art Education   Studio Art   Art History   Professional Education   Student Teaching   Liberal Arts Core
   Why?

4. What were the biggest problems you faced when you first started teaching?

5. What suggestions would you make to improve the program?

FIGURE 1. List of the survey questions.

the researcher presented the teachers with questions that would assist in understanding which of the six program areas[1] they considered to be the most and least beneficial, and to provide an opportunity for them to give open-ended feedback to explain the reasons for their choices (see Figure 1). An additional area of the survey included questions about the biggest problems the teachers faced when they first started teaching. The researcher analyzed and cross-referenced the responses to determine common themes regarding specific issues or concerns that the program could address. A final question provided an opportunity for the teachers to offer suggestions to make the Art Education teacher preparation program more successful. See Figure 1 for a full list of the survey questions.

Although 31 students graduated from the program during the selected time frame, contact information was available through the university's alumni office for 28. For an immediacy of response, the researcher sent the survey to 25 teachers via e-mail. Because the researcher could not obtain e-mail addresses for the remaining three teachers, they received hard copies of the questionnaires by regular mail. After 3 days, the researcher sent follow-up e-mails to the e-mail non-respondents, and 7 days later sent hard copies to those who had still not responded. Two weeks later hard copy reminders were sent to all non-respondents. Ultimately, 13 teachers completed and returned the survey questionnaire. The goal was to survey the entire population of program graduates during the specified time frame, a parametric population. This response rate impacts the generalizability of the findings to the entire population.

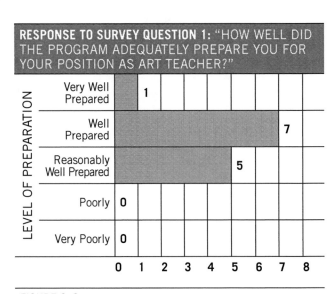

FIGURE 2. Survey response.

SUMMARY OF SURVEY FINDINGS

Content analysis, comparison, and cross-reference of survey results revealed general patterns and themes (Eisner, 1998; Patton, 1990). The teachers' responses to Question 1 indicated that none of them thought the program prepared them very poorly or poorly for their teaching positions, only one felt very well prepared, while five felt reasonably well prepared, and seven felt well prepared (see Figure 2).

In response to questions 2 and 3, some teachers selected one area of study as being most or least beneficial, while others selected more than one. Art Education was regarded as the most beneficial area of the program, as it included

SARA AND MELANIE: *The point that Webster raises here about teachers indicating their Liberal Arts Core classes and classroom evaluation courses were not relevant to art or teaching is interesting. This point could lead to further study related to whether art teacher preparation programs should include general education courses from a range of disciplines or whether education degrees should be limited to only courses in the content area and pedagogy. Another approach could be a study that looks at the success teachers have in implementing a meaningful integrated curriculum as related to the courses included in their undergraduate preparation. Also, a researcher could investigate how or to what degree art education majors are able to make high level knowledge transfers that may be required to make meaning from varied coursework and find applications for their teaching practice.*

experiences in teaching art to children, planning and writing lesson plans, and observing experienced art teachers in their the classrooms. Studio Art was the second most beneficial area, as it provided opportunities to explore and experience different media and learning new artmaking techniques.

The area identified as the least beneficial was Professional Education, as many thought that much of the course content was not relevant to the practice of teaching art, and that classroom management issues were not addressed adequately. In particular, many identified a classroom evaluation instruments course as being of least benefit, as it failed to address assessment methods and procedures specific to art, such as portfolio assessment, rubric design, formative assessment, or methods for grading performance. The second largest area considered of least value was the Liberal Arts Core, which a number of respondents indicated was not relevant to art or teaching.

Finally, overall, the biggest problems the teachers faced during their first years of teaching were classroom discipline and curriculum planning.

Eight overarching themes emerged from the teachers' suggestions for improving the program, which could be seen to relate, in part, to those the National Art Education Association (1999) identified as skills art teacher candidates should possess, and also to those Day (1997) identified as significant components of many art education programs. These suggestions for improvements relate to the themes of (1) art knowledge, (2) curriculum development, (3) meaningful art assessment, (4) classroom management, (5) pedagogical strategies, (6) professional development, (7) clinical experience, and (8) preservice course requirements.

The data indicated that, overall, the teachers thought the most beneficial aspects of the program were their experiences in the art education and studio art courses, thus resulting in the suggestion that increased studio art courses would lead to more in-depth art knowledge. The second theme, related to curriculum planning and development, concerned identifying strategies for integrating art into an interdisciplinary school curriculum as well as developing and structuring cohesive art curricula. The third theme related to developing knowledge of strategies and methods for creating meaningful and appropriate criteria and procedures for art assessment. Classroom discipline proved to be the biggest problem faced by the teachers during their first year

of teaching, and suggestions were made to address this issue further during the program. The fifth theme addressed pedagogical knowledge, instruction, and teaching methods—in particular gaining further knowledge about various instructional strategies and procedures conducive to student learning. The sixth theme related to professional development and suggestions included inviting experienced teachers or principals to discuss contemporary issues in education. The seventh theme correlated with the desire to extend opportunities for further clinical experience, both in the form of classroom observations and student teaching experiences.

The final theme concerned the structure of the program, in terms of course requirements. One issue was with the quality and/or quantity of the Professional Education and, to a lesser extent, the Liberal Arts Core courses. Suggestions were made that these courses could be reduced in number and more Studio Art and Art Education methods courses added, in order to develop content and pedagogical knowledge that relate specifically to teaching art. Overall, the respondents indicated that the content, structure, teaching methods, and learning strategies presented in the Professional Education and Liberal Arts Core courses failed to make relevant connections with the Studio Art and Art Education courses. Rather, the courses were presented as separate entities and survey respondents felt that efforts should be made to develop more interdisciplinary continuity and consistency among courses.

APPLICATION OF INFORMATION GAINED FROM THE SURVEY

From the information acquired from the survey, the researcher determined that a number of issues and concerns about the program need to be addressed so that the program provides education and training that will assist preservice candidates in becoming more effective and efficient art teachers. Gaining an understanding of the teachers' thoughts about their experiences in the program provided an opportunity for the program planners to develop an awareness of how successful their efforts have been, and in gathering the empirical evidence necessary to determine, recommend, and justify specific aspects of program reform.

Based on the teachers' responses to the survey, recommendations made to the program planners included adding more Studio Art and Art Education courses and reducing the number of Professional Education course requirements. Further, the researcher recommended the content of the Art Education courses should include more information regarding interdisciplinary and cohesive curriculum planning; assessment in art education; classroom management procedures; extending opportunities for classroom observations and student teaching; and inviting knowledgeable experts to discuss various contemporary educational issues.

Overall, the least valuable aspects of the program were considered to be the Professional Education courses, as they failed to make relevant connections with the Studio Art and Art Education courses. As the specific needs of the preservice art teachers differ from those of general education candidates, it is likely that the Professional Education faculty were unaware of their unique needs. Therefore, one recommendation is that Art Education and College of Education faculty discuss the content of the Professional Education courses to determine interdisciplinary methods for making it more related, relevant, and meaningful to preservice art teachers.

REFERENCES

Ayres, J. B. (1988). Teacher education follow-up evaluation: How to do it. In W. J. Gephart & J. B. Ayres (Eds.), *Teacher education evaluation* (pp. 85-111). Boston, MA: Kluwer Academic.

Conway, C. (Spring 2002). Perceptions of beginning teachers, their mentors, and administrators. *Journal of Research in Music Education, 50*(1), 20-36.

Davis, J. D. (1990). Teacher education in the visual arts. In R. Houston (Ed.), *Handbook of research on teacher education* (pp. 746-757). New York, NY: Macmillan.

Day, M. D. (1997). Preparing teachers of art for the year 2000 and beyond. In M. Day (Ed), *Preparing teachers of art* (pp. 3-26). Reston, VA: National Art Education Association.

Eisner, E. W. (1998). *The enlightened eye: Qualitative inquiry and the enhancement of educational practice.* Upper Saddle River, NJ: Prentice Hall.

Fullan, M., & Hargreaves, A. (1996). *What's worth fighting for in your school?* New York, NY: Teachers College Press.

Galbraith, L. P. (1997). What are teachers taught? An analysis of curriculum components for art teacher preparation programs. In M. D. Day (Ed.), *Preparing teachers of art* (pp. 45-72). Reston, VA: National Art Education Association.

Mason, T. (1997). Assisted performance and teacher education in an urban school. *Action in Teacher Education, 17*(4), 83-87.

National Art Education Association. (1999). *Standards for art teacher preparation.* Reston, VA: Author.

National Center for Educational Statistics. (1999). *Teacher quality: A report on the preparation and qualifications of public school teachers.* Washington, DC: U.S. Department of Education.

Patton, M. Q. (1990). *Qualitative evaluation and research methods.* Newbury Park, CA: Sage.

Sevigny, M. J. (1987). Discipline-based art education and teacher education. *The Journal of Aesthetic Education, 21*(2), 95-128.

Willis-Fisher, L. (1993, Winter). Aesthetics, art criticism, art history, and art production in art teacher preparation programs. *National Art Educational Association Advisory.* Reston, VA: National Art Education Association.

Zimmerman, E. (1997). Whence come we? Whither go we? Demographic analysis of art teacher preparation programs in the United States. In M. D. Day (Ed.), *Preparing teachers of art* (pp. 27-44). Reston, VA: National Art Education Association.

ENDNOTE

1   The structure and content of the program was similar to many other certifications in art programs offered throughout the nation, as it consists of six distinct areas: Art Education, Studio Art, Art History, Professional Education, Student Teaching, and Liberal Arts Core (Galbraith, 1997; Sevigny, 1987; Willis Fisher, 1993).

DAVID WEBSTER'S research interest lies in the areas of preservice art teacher preparation. He believes it is important to determine the adequacy of preservice programs in the light of contemporary and evolving significant art educational trends, issues, philosophies, and practices. During recent decades, art education has undergone significant changes in approaches to curriculum planning and instruction, and art teacher preparation programs need to be structured to meet these changing concerns and expectations. As future art teachers are expected to bring knowledge of current theories and practices to the profession, they hold a central position to the future of the field of art education. Therefore, their preparation to effectively and efficiently meet these requirements should be considered of the utmost importance. Webster believes that research into preservice preparation can assist program planners to reflect upon and evaluate the adequacy of their programs, in order to determine, consider, and bring about any changes deemed necessary.

QUASI-EXPERIMENTAL RESEARCH

10 / Quasi-Experimental Research Design: Conducting Research in the Art Classroom

RYAN SHIN / ASSOCIATE PROFESSOR, SCHOOL OF ART AT THE UNIVERSITY OF ARIZONA

ABSTRACT: *In this chapter I describe the nature and process of quasi-experimental research in educational settings. First, I explore the reasons why art education researchers and practitioners might design and conduct this type of research in the art classroom. In so doing, I discuss several important concepts necessary to understand the logic of quasi-experimental research and provide some examples of previously performed research in this field. Drawing from this foundation, I then describe a typical research design project, explaining the importance of formulating a primary research question, selecting a research design from among several possible quasi-experimental designs, and collecting and interpreting data. At the end, I suggest possible future research topics and examples involving quasi-experimental designs in art education, revealing the strength of this design in providing some hard data for assessing and promoting the value of art education.*

The purpose of experimental research in educational settings, whether true or quasi-experimental, is to establish cause-and-effect relationships between what is taught and applied, and its outcome as the result of experiment. An example of experimental research is to identify if a new teaching method or strategy, which is called a "treatment" or "intervention," has a positive effect on student learning as evidenced by test scores. Researchers often involve two or more groups of subjects to see if a treatment clearly improves students' abilities and skills in an educational setting. This is the main reason we conduct research involving true or quasi-experimental design: to improve educational qualities and to provide effective instruction or preventive treatment.

The purpose of quasi-experimental design is similar to that of experimental research design. As *quasi* in Latin means "likeness," or resembling something, quasi-experimental design shares a similarity to true experimental design in almost every aspect of research logic and process. The primary exception is that it lacks the randomization of assignment of subjects, which is to say that all participants are pre-determined to be part of a given group and are not randomly sorted into groups by the researcher. For example, in a school setting, all of the students registered for a specific course are pre-determined to be a part of that group. This makes quasi-experimental design perfect for application within an academic context where random assignment is impractical and sometimes impossible because student schedules are not flexible enough to create a new research group by assigning them randomly. Additionally, school structures inhibit designing a purely experimental environment that eliminates any extraneous factors that might affect the research results. Therefore, educational researchers often use intact groups in school settings. Some classes, grades, schools or even districts are often selected to participate in quasi-experimental research. When educational researchers discuss their study outcomes and their generalizations to the entire population, they need to consider the effects of using a methodology that does not involve random sampling and how this influences the data analysis and interpretation. I will discuss some factors that affect analysis and interpretation later in this chapter when I discuss the concept of validity in research.

In conducting research, two concepts—which I first learned about in a graduate research methodology class—are critical. An understanding of them helps readers figure out quickly the purpose and intent of most experimental research. These two concepts are *independent variables* and *dependent variables*. The independent variable in educational research is a variable that affects the dependent variable under study (Fraenkel & Wallen, 1996), such as a teaching method, strategy, or program. Researchers are interested in studying the change or improvement an independent variable can bring.

The dependent variable, often called the *outcome variable*, is directly related to the intended change. A researcher is looking for a change in such variables as cognitive abilities, knowledge acquisition, manipulative skills, and psychological levels. Because the goal of any research project is to examine the effects of independent variables on dependent variables, it is important to note that a dependent variable must be measurable and quantifiable in order to help researchers see if there is a significant change as the result of the research experiment.

A brief literature review of true or quasi-experimental research in art education helps us understand these concepts and the potential of this research methodology. The following table presents an overview of what kinds of research questions have been addressed employing quasi-experimental designs in the past in this field, focusing on independent and dependent variables. My review does not include all past studies. However, it highlights some examples that I believe help readers develop a good picture of what has been done with quasi-experimental designs. In the table provided here, I list independent variables in the first column and dependent variables in the second column. Readers should be able to figure out what researchers tried to do by identifying the cause-and-effect relationship between them.

INDEPENDENT (EXPERIMENTAL) VARIABLES	DEPENDENT (OUTCOME) VARIABLES	AUTHOR(S)
Exposure to arts education	Students' critical thinking dispositions	Lampert (2006)
Two dimensional stimuli and three-dimensional stereoptic stimuli	Students' spatial representation in drawings	McGraw (2004)
Two instructional approaches: Intrinsic and instrumental	Student artistic production, knowledge of art, and preferences	Brewer (2002)
Descriptive drawing as a means to promote understanding of scientific concepts and explanations	Science concepts learning	Edens & Potter (2001)
Critical and historical inquiry combined with studio experience	Students' ability to understand or appreciate historical art works.	Short (1998)
Two approaches: child-centered vs. discipline-based	Students' self-concepts, art attitudes, art knowledge, and the aesthetic sense.	Brewer (1991)
Two- and three-dimensional visual referents	Representational human figure drawing	Dowell (1990)
Philosophical inquiry	Verbal reasoning ability and defining art	Russell (1988)
Students' sense of agency or self-determination as a motivational force in art learning.	Self-concepts and attitudes toward art	King (1983)
Three art teaching approaches: Studio, art history, and critical appreciative	Aesthetic sensitivity	Fitzner (1980)
Teaching formal elements, structure, and details of the modeled human figure	Clay modeling skills	Grossman (1980)
Art and aesthetic awareness activities	Understanding of art concepts	Stahl & Webster (1978)
Art criticism instruction	Art attitude	Mittler (1972)
Perception training lessons	Students' perception of paintings	Wilson (1966)

FIGURE 1. An overview of quasi-experimental studies in art education.

As seen in the table, researchers in art education have long been interested in making changes to dependent variables, such as improving the students' cognitive and perception skills, helping them to learn art content effectively, and having an effect on their attitudes and dispositions. In order to make such intended changes, they have experimented with various teaching approaches or strategies, and often combined two or three approaches at once. These independent variables are what researchers select or manipulate in terms of time and amount. At the end of this chapter, I will provide some examples of future research agendas that feature independent and dependent variables, involving quasi-experimental designs related to current trends in art education.

A BRIEF OVERVIEW OF LOGIC AND PROCESS IN QUASI-EXPERIMENTAL DESIGNS

I noted that establishing and examining the cause-and-effect relationship is the essence of quasi-experimental research. One of the most important questions that must be answered here is how a researcher develops a research question in quasi-experimental research. Choosing an appropriate research question is critical to any study and its outcomes. Rather than repeating a previously listed example from the table in Figure 1, I have developed my own research question related to the current interest in and promotion of visual culture education. Although many have argued for the inherent value of this paradigm and its effect on student learning from philosophical, social, and critical theory perspectives (Duncum, 2002; Freedman, 2003a; Garoian & Gaudelius, 2004; Tavin, 2003; Taylor, 2007; Taylor & Ballengee-Morris, 2003), there have been few experimental or quasi-experimental research projects that have attempted to employ empirical data for the purpose of promoting the importance of visual culture education. Personally, I agree with and am in favor of the value and benefit of teaching visual culture in K-12 schools (Duncum, 2006; Freedman, 2003a; Taylor, 2007). However, one must still determine what the ultimate impact or result of teaching with this new approach would be. I have often wondered whether a curriculum focusing on visual culture actually increases the value of art education in the minds of students and parents. In the example I develop more fully here, I was interested in seeing the effect of a visual culture-based curriculum, in which students' main activities are equally balanced between criticism and studio production (Duncum, 2003; Freedman 2003b), as opposed to an approach that only focuses on criticism.

My next job was to create a specific research question or hypothesis: Can a studio-focused visual culture curriculum have a positive influence on the value perception of art education among students and parents? Another important aspect in this stage was to consider how to assess value judgment in relationship to art education. Does an instrument—such as a questionnaire for conducting a survey of value judgments relevant to art education in school—currently exist that I could use for this purpose?

After undertaking a literature review of the previous studies named in the table above, I found that no such tool was available. So I set out to design my own survey instrument, involving several key areas in

Quasi-Experimental Methods

NANCY LAMPERT / ASSISTANT PROFESSOR, VIRGINIA COMMONWEALTH UNIVERSITY

In education, the term *quasi-experimental research* refers to an experimental study that does not use random samples of students. Instead, a researcher might study two or more intact classrooms of students assigned to the classes by the school; or a single group of children who volunteered for an after-school program.

All experimental or quasi-experimental studies in educational settings are difficult to do because many variables cannot be controlled by the researcher. As we all know, people and learning environments are full of variations. Researchers need to be prepared to accept that many unforeseen variables may impact the expected outcomes of a study.

In many quasi-experimental research studies, the researcher introduces a variable to the group of subjects and then observes or tests the group to determine if the variable changed the group. The variable the researcher introduces is called an *intervention*, or *treatment*. If the researcher studies two groups, one that receives the treatment and one that does not—the group that does not receive the treatment is the control.

The variable that is introduced to the treatment group is called the independent variable. Researchers observe or test groups to see if the treatment, or independent variable, affected the dependent variable in the study. The dependent variable is the change or effect the researcher speculates will occur from the treatment.

For example, I conducted a quasi-experimental study with a pre-test/post-test design. It was a 12 week study of one group of elementary school children. I wanted to learn what effect art lessons that required problem solving had on the children's critical thinking abilities. At the beginning of the study, I used an educational test (also called a testing instrument) to measure the dependent variable, the critical thinking ability of the children. After 12 weeks of art lessons (the treatment), I administered the

order to assess value judgment. These key areas, using a Likert scale with 5-point levels (1 being "strongly disagree"; 5 being "strongly agree"), included satisfaction, value, usefulness, and support, from which I was able to formulate several more specific questions, or sub-categories, under each category. For example, a question related to value is, "Are art classes in school very important for my child's intellectual (or emotional) development?" Another sample question would be, "Should art education be valued as much as math or science education?" The 5 point-scale, registering the individual's relative disagreement or agreement with a stated question, can be created for the comparison of involved groups as well as statistical analysis. Because I already formed my research question with the independent variable (a studio-focused visual culture curriculum) and the dependant variable (the value of art education in school), the next step was to choose a research design.

RESEARCH DESIGNS

There are several options in choosing a research design for any quasi-experimental research. In this section, I introduce the three most popular quasi-experimental designs: non-equivalent control group design, time series design, and multiple time series design, which is the combination of the time series design with the non-equivalent control group design (Fife-Schaw, 2006). Among them, **non-equivalent control group design** is widely used in educational research for its practicality and favorability when comparing the treatment and control groups. This design involves a pre-test and a post-test for both the treatment and control group. When applied to the visual culture curriculum study, a treatment group will participate in classes from the visual culture curriculum, and a control group would participate in the traditional art curriculum. Both groups would take the art education value survey as the pre-test and post-test.

When choosing this research design, be aware that you will need to have two groups of samples: The two groups could be selected from the same grade level and teacher; or you might select one group each from two different schools. However, the researcher making the latter choice will need to consider whether both schools function under similar contexts in terms of student instructional time, location (urban or suburban), student population characteristics, parents' socio-economic status, and teacher experience. This process requires careful interpretation when considering these extraneous variables.

Time series designs take only one sample group and involve testing or measuring dependent variable(s) several times in sequence, over a longer time period. The advantage of this design is that it helps

test again. To determine if the difference in the average test scores of the children before and after the treatment was statistically significant, I performed a statistical analysis called a *t* test. As shown in Figure 1, the analysis showed a statistically significant increase ($p = .020$) in the children's average critical thinking skills score over the course of the 12-week program (Lampert, 2008).

To locate educational tests that might be used in quasi-experimental research, the *Mental Measurements Yearbooks* are valuable resources. They are available though most academic library databases. The *Mental Measurements Yearbooks* have information about who publishes tests and they also include reviews which discuss the reliability and validity of tests (Geisinger, Spies, Carlson, & Plake, 2007). You can also contact authors of research articles to inquire if they will share with you how you might obtain the testing instrument used in the author's research. ■

REFERENCES

Geisinger, K., Spies, R., Carlson, J., & Plake, B. (2007). *The seventeenth mental measurements yearbook*. Lincoln, NE: Buros Institute of Mental Measurements, University of Nebraska Press.

Lampert, N. (2008). Enhancing critical thinking with art education. In A. Albanel & X. Darcos (Eds.), *Evaluating the Impact of Arts and Cultural Education: A European and International Research Symposium* (pp. 103-117). Paris, France: Centre Pompidou.

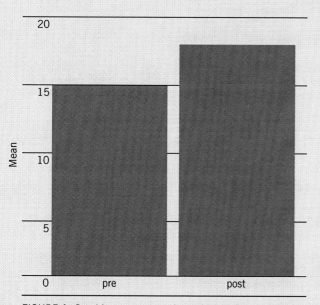

FIGURE 1. Graphic mean comparison of the pre-post test scores.

researchers see if there is a significant change before and after the treatment. A good example of time series design is to see what effect a visual culture curriculum has on students' art enrollment where art is elective. As seen in the graph, the researcher might observe visual arts enrollment over two separate 5-year periods: 5 years before the introduction of a visual culture curriculum in a given school; and another 5 years after implementing the curriculum (see Figure 2). Time series designs can be used to see if a newly introduced program or policy has the desired effect on art enrollment as predicted by teachers or administrators. Since this design involves multiple observations (or tests) and is administered over an extended time period, it is more difficult to run the same instrument repeatedly: such as art attitude, motivation, and specific cognitive skills. So choosing a dependent variable that does not rely heavily on testing effects is more appropriate for this design, using such data as student behavior observation, yearly administered standardized tests, or, as in this case, art enrollment numbers.

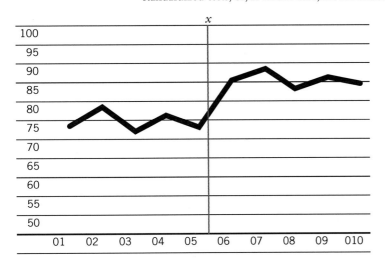

FIGURE 2. An example of time series design. In this graph, the vertical line "X" indicates the first year the visual culture curriculum was implemented. The "O" before each number (1-10) along the horizontal axis stands for the observation period: the five year period before the new curriculum was implemented (1-5), and another five year period following implementation (6-10). The vertical axis represents student enrollment numbers.

Multiple time series designs simply add a control group to the time series design to see if the change in the treatment group is truly the result of a given experiment. Thus, it attempts to take into account some extraneous factors that might inadvertently affect the research. For example, the addition of the control group helps us see whether or not the improvement of the experimental group is the result of the maturation of subjects, or perhaps simply demonstrates the effect of taking the same test multiple times. It adds credibility to this design, ruling out other possible explanations that the positive effects of the experiment result from unknown extraneous factors. If I were to use this design in the aforementioned study example documenting the effect of implementing a new visual culture curriculum, I could then involve a control group by adding a second school without the visual culture curriculum to the study to see if there is any change in the art student enrollment between the two schools.

The three basic designs described here are the most popular in designing and implementing quasi-experimental educational research. However, they are just a few of the possible variations of quasi-experimental designs (Fife-Schaw, 2006). For example, a researcher might extend the non-equivalent control group design, by adding two different levels of visual culture curriculum: one group in a school where art is required, another where art is elective, with a third group of students as the control group. I encourage readers to explore various applications of the three quasi-experimental designs described here and to study other quasi-experimental designs outlined in Sahdish, Cook, and Campbell (2001)'s text, *Experimental and Quasi-experimental Designs for Generalized Causal Inference.*

INCREASING RESEARCH QUALITY: INTERNAL AND EXTERNAL VALIDITY

I have explained several quasi-experimental research designs. Now I would like to move on to the issue of validity because I believe that this helps one figure out and better understand the two kinds of validities I will explain in this section: internal validity and external validity. For a good research design, both are important and cannot be ignored. *Internal validity* addresses the question of accuracy with regard to the final results of a research project. How can we trust what we have presumably found out? Are positive changes in the dependent variables necessarily the direct outcome of the pre-determined independent variable of the experiment, or might they also be the result of some extraneous factors? A researcher wants to be able to answer these questions and to eliminate the influences of any other factors that might allow for any conflicting explanations or interpretations of the collected data. Good quasi-experimental research depends on one's ability to define and control the variables and clearly reflects the researcher's confidence in claiming the causal relationship between the treatment and its effect.

A researcher is also interested in the extent to which what is found in the study can be generalized or applied to other people or settings. If I conduct an experiment involving a sample drawn from a particular population, I am ultimately seeking to discover if the result of the study can be applied to the population as a whole. This is called *external validity*: the capacity for research related to a small sample group to be applied to a larger, more general group of individuals. The validity of any quasi-experimental research project depends on how researchers ensure both internal and external validities by controlling possible threats or variables that might invalidate the project's findings.

Here I will introduce some possible threats to validities related to quasi-experimental design. First, I discuss internal validity. Campbell and Stanley (1966) listed eight threats to internal validity in their classical research textbook, *Experimental and Quasi-experimental Designs for Research*: history, maturation, testing, instrumentation, statistical regression, selection, mortality, and selection interactions. I will explain each using my example of the visual culture curriculum.

- *History*: Unique experiences of students during the study might affect the outcome. In my example, a well-known Pop artist's visit to the school may affect the attitudes and value judgment of art, leading to a high score on the post-test.
- *Maturation*: Change due to the natural passing of time. Students' loss of interest in art in the preadolescent period might affect the test result in a long-term research project.
- *Testing*: The effect of testing. Pre-test experience often affects a posttest score. Running the same test twice might affect some of the student participants because students may remember the test content, and this directly affects the post-test.
- *Instrumentation*: Change of a measurement method during the experiment period. Allowing more time for the test, or administering the instrument during different times of the day or week, may affect the test result.
- *Selection*: Effects on the test score from selecting different groups of participants in the beginning of the research. Choosing two schools that differ in parents' socio-economic status might affect how parents ultimately respond to the study result.
- *Mortality*: The loss of participants in the study. A significant number of students moving or transferring into or out of the school might affect the study outcome.
- *Statistical regression*: The effect of selecting subjects who score extremely low or high on their pretest scores. If a selected group performs extremely high or low on the pre-test, their score on the post-test regresses towards the mean of the population under study. For example, this can occur when a group who values art highly is selected to participate in the visual culture curriculum, and this interest is reflected in the pre-test. However, there is no room to grow, so the post-test result may be closer to the average of the whole population.
- *Selection interactions*: One group of subjects selected for the study responds differently to one of more of the threats: such as history, maturation, or instrumentation. A group of students who are growing up relatively faster than the other group can affect the post-test score.

In order to minimize these threats to internal validity, a researcher must always consider these threats before beginning the quasi-experimental study and carefully analyze them after conducting research. An awareness of these factors helps us avoid common short-comings of experimental research. To increase internal validity and avoid misinterpretation of study outcomes, Fraenkel and Wallen (1996) suggest that a researcher choose an appropriate design, standardize the experiment conditions, and obtain more information on subjects and extraneous events in the course of the study.

External validity, on the other hand, might also concern itself with the question of whether or not an improvement on the test score in the experimental group can also be applied to the population. In quasi-experimental designs where random sampling is not practical and feasible, an alternative method for increasing external validity with regard to generalization is necessary. One way to do this is to replicate the study using different groups of participants in different settings. So, if the result of repeated studies is similar among settings, a researcher could have confidence when more generally applying his/her findings (Fraenkel & Wallen, 1996).

DATA ANALYSIS AND INTERPRETATION

After completing an experiment, the researcher will have data from the pre-test and post-test. These numbers will be used to establish the outcome or effect of the experiment. Statistical software, such as *SPSS* (Statistical Package for the Social Sciences), is popularly used in comparing the mean scores of the treatment and control groups. There are many available manuals that describe how to enter data and run the program to calculate the significance of the difference between both groups. Statistically, researchers compare the difference between the mean scores of both groups for significance. Typically, a t-test is used to compare two groups, and the Analysis of Variance (ANOVA) is used for more than two groups (See the accompanying exemplar chapter for details on the t-test and ANOVA). The t-test produces a t-score that can be converted into a P value (which stands for the probability of observing an event); and the ANOVA produces an F-score that also can be converted into a P-value. If this P-value is less than .05, a researcher can have confidence in saying that the treatment produced a significant difference, thereby confirming its effectiveness. Then, a researcher can accept a research hypothesis. Otherwise, researchers will need to reject the original hypothesis as invalid.

Even though there might be a statistically significant difference between involved groups (i.e., the treatment and control groups), the researcher will need to consider the previously explained internal and external validity factors in interpreting and discussing these results. This also means that the researcher should avoid drawing absolute conclusions on the effectiveness or ineffectiveness of the new program or treatment because the possibility exists that the study outcomes were affected by some extraneous variables that might negate or jeopardize their validity. A careful discussion of the internal and external validity, along with the consideration of previous studies that have dealt with the same research question(s), will need to be provided before definitive statements or conclusions can be made.

SUGGESTIONS FOR USING QUASI-EXPERIMENTAL RESEARCH IN ART EDUCATION

In this final section, I explore possible research ideas and examples involving quasi-experimental designs in art education. I list them according to the two basic research designs, non-equivalent control group designs and time series designs. Multiple time series designs are not included here because they are essentially extensions of the time series model.

Research agendas using non-equivalent control group designs:

- Effects of new teaching methods on teaching cognitive abilities or technical skills in art. For example, how can Edwards' (1993) ideas about "drawing on the right-side of the brain" improve students' drawing skills compared to other teaching methods in drawing?
- Improving creativity, problem-solving skills, or critical thinking skills through art education.
- Effects of an art program on improving self-concept, esteem, or efficacy.
- Change of attitudes and beliefs through an art program related to special topics, such as multiculturalism, gender-equity, diversity, and technology.
- Effects of multiple museum visits on student achievement in school subjects.
- Research agendas using time series designs:
- The impact of the No Child Left Behind (NCLB) Act on school art programs.
- Impact of a new policy on school art class enrollment, student attitude, and administrator's perception in the art.
- Effects of museum educational programs on the increase of the student visitor numbers.
- The impact of visual arts programs on incidences of school violence.
- Effect of an art therapy program on prevention of student dropout or behavioral change of students with disabilities.

CONCLUSION

I have seen a significant decrease in true or quasi-experimental research in schools, museums, and community settings over the past decade. Recently, few journals have reported studies involving this research design in schools in the field of art education, which may indicate obstacles posed by the cumbersome IRB review as well as the influence of qualitative methodologies' strengths in providing rich materials for art education discourse. This observed lack of studies contrasts with the 1980s when there was much theoretical discussion of Discipline-Based Art Education (DBAE), and when a significant number of researchers conducted quasi-experimental studies in art education, looking for the effects of teaching studio art, aesthetics, art criticism, and art history, as well as the impact of DBAE on cognitive and psychological development (Brewer, 1991; Fitzner, 1980; Russell,1988; Short, 1998). However, with the current emphasis on theoretical exploration of postmodernism and visual culture education, I think that art educators may have come to question the merit of conducting quasi-experimental studies in these areas. The primary reason I chose a visual culture art curriculum as an example in explaining quasi-experimental design was to show that experimental studies are still useful and offer a powerful means to provide some empirical data for policy makers and school administrators interested in assessing and promoting the value of art education. I hope that art education professors and pK-12 practitioners develop more quasi-experimental research projects appropriate and useful to the current scholarship and discourse in art education.

REFERENCES

Brewer, T. M. (1991). An examination of two approaches to ceramic instruction in elementary education. *Studies in Art Education, 32*(4), 196-206.

Brewer, T. M. (2002). An examination of intrinsic and instrumental instruction in art education. *Studies in Art Education, 43*(4), 354-372.

Campbell, D. T., & Stanley, J. C. (1966). *Experimental and quasi-experimental designs for research.* Chicago, IL: Rand McNally.

Dowell, M. L. (1990). Effects of visual referents upon representational drawing of the human figure. *Studies in Art Education, 31*(2), 78-85.

Duncum, P. (2002). Clarifying visual culture art education. *Art Education, 55*(3), 6-11.

Duncum, P. (2003). Visual culture and studio practice? *International Journal of Art Education, 1*(3), 45-66.

Duncum, P. (2006). *Visual culture in the art class: Case studies.* Reston, VA: National Art Education Association.

Edens, K. M., & Potter, E. F. (2001). Promoting conceptual understanding through pictorial representation. *Studies in Art Education, 42*(3), 214-233.

Edwards, B. (1993). *Drawing on the right side of the brain: A course in enhancing creativity and artistic confidence.* Los Angeles, CA: Jeremy P. Tarcher/Perigee.

Fife-Schaw, C. (2006). Quasi-experimental designs. In G. M. Breakwell, S. Hammond, & C. Fife-Schaw (Eds.), *Research methods in psychology* (pp. 85-98). Thousand Oaks, CA: Sage.

Fitzner, D. H. (1980). The effects of combined art teaching approaches on the development of aesthetic sensitivity among selected elderly adults. *Studies in Art Education, 21*(2), 28-37.

Fraenkel, J. R., & Wallen, N. E. (1996). *How to design and evaluate research in education.* New York, NY: McGraw-Hill.

Freedman, K. (2003a). *Teaching visual culture: Curriculum, aesthetics and the social life of art.* New York, NY: Teachers College Press.

Freedman, K. (2003b). The importance of student artistic production to teaching visual culture. *Art Education, 56*(2), 38-43.

Garoian, C. R., & Gaudelius, Y. M. (2004). The spectacle of visual culture. *Studies in Art Education, 45*(4), 298-312.

Grossman, E. (1980). Effects of instructional experience in clay modeling skills on modeled human figure representation in preschool children. *Studies in Art Education, 22*(1), 51-59.

King, A. (1983). Agency, achievement, and self-concept of young adolescent art students. *Studies in Art Education, 24*(3), 187-194.

Lampert, N. (2006). Critical thinking dispositions as an outcome of art education. *Studies in Art Education, 47*(3), 215-28.

McGraw, T. M. (2004). The effects of two-dimensional stimuli and three-dimensional stereoptic stimuli on spatial representation in drawings. *Studies in Art Education, 45*(2), 153-169.

Mittler, G. (1972). Efforts to secure congruent and incongruent modifications of attitude toward works of art. *Studies in Art Education, 13*(2), 58-70.

Russell, R. L. (1988). Children's philosophical inquiry into defining art: A quasi-experimental study of aesthetics in the elementary classroom. *Studies in Art Education, 29*(3), 282-291.

Sahdish, W. R., Cook, T. D., & Campbell, D. T. (2001). *Experimental and quasi-experimental designs for generalized causal inference.* Belmont, CA: Wadsworth.

Short, G. (1998). The high school studio curriculum and art understanding: An examination. *Studies in Art Education, 40*(1), 46-65.

Stahl, R. J., & Webster, N. C. (1978). Validating a model for art and aesthetic awareness activities: Results of an experimental study. *Studies in Art Education, 19*(2), 19-33.

Tavin, K. (2003). Wresting with angels, searching for ghosts: Toward a critical pedagogy of visual culture. *Studies in Art Education, 44*(3), 197-213.

Taylor, P. G. (2007). Press pause: Critically contextualizing music video in visual culture and art education. *Studies in Art Education, 48*(3), 230-246.

Taylor, P. G., & Ballengee Morris, C. (2003). Using visual culture to put a contemporary "fizz" on the study of Pop Art. *Art Education, 56*(2), 20-24.

Wilson, B. G. (1966). An experimental study designed to alter fifth and sixth grade students' perception of paintings. *Studies in Art Education, 8*(1), 33-42.

RYAN SHIN is Associate Professor in the School of Art at the University of Arizona. He received his PhD in Art Education from Florida State University in 2002, taught at the University of Wisconsin at La Crosse from 2002 to 2007. His research interests include Asian folk art; Asian visual culture; minority visual culture; digital media and visual culture education; cross-cultural approach to understandings of art and visual culture; and quantitative research methods. His articles have appeared in *Studies in Art Education, Art Education, Visual Arts Research, Journal of Cross-Cultural Research in Art Education,* and *NAEA Advisory.* He also has authored numerous book chapters, and has presented his work at national and international conferences.

11 / A Quasi-Experimental Research Design: Can Art Critique Improve Students' Critical Thinking Skills?

RYAN SHIN / ASSOCIATE PROFESSOR, SCHOOL OF ART AT THE UNIVERSITY OF ARIZONA

ABSTRACT: *In this chapter, I describe a quasi-experimental research project I designed and conducted to assess whether or not teaching art critique improves students' critical thinking skills in a high school art classroom. This will provide an example of how art educators can use a quasi-experimental research methodology to provide supporting data related to this inquiry. First, I will describe the purpose of this study, then report on how I formulated a research question and developed a hypothesis to answer it. Next, I will explain why I chose this particular research design from among several possible quasi-experimental designs. I then provide a detailed description of the adoption and development of instrument of testing critical thinking skills, my research setting, followed by the procedure of my study. Finally, I will share the outcomes of the study and provide an interpretation of its corresponding results.*

PURPOSE OF THE STUDY

Almost 30 years ago, Feldman and Woods (1981) noticed the relationship between art criticism and critical thinking, and argued for the importance of teaching art critique that involves complex cognitive skills such as "hypothesis testing," "creative problem solving," and "deductive and inductive reasoning (p. 79)," which are essential components that students are expected to learn in the art classroom. More recently, Duke (2000) contends that interacting with art could teach students to be "independent observers capable of making informed choices and reasonable judgments about art" (p.17).

Many authors in the field of art education agree that teaching critical thinking skills to students is a vital educational goal (Anderson, 1990; Buffington, 2007; Feldman, 1994). Many others have claimed that involving students in the visual arts through reasoning, interpreting, and making judgments about artworks, as well as discussion and writing activities on aesthetic issues, can help students acquire critical thinking skills (Perkins, 1994; Perkins & Salomon, 1989; Risatti, 1987).

However, there have been very few empirical studies examining the effects of instruction in the area of art critique on critical thinking skills, and researchers have yet to demonstrate a linear and positive relationship between the two. Lampert (2006) agrees with me and notes that few empirical studies have been conducted to test the theory that higher exposure to art critique and aesthetic inquiry fosters critical thinking skills and disposition. Therefore, my main goal in this study is to identify if involving students in art critiques will improve their critical thinking skills. More specifically, I want to know if training in the area of art critiques has a positive impact on an individual's critical thinking skills, showing improved test scores of critical thinking skills.

RESEARCH QUESTION

I have formulated a research question based upon a critical literature review of this field along with my personal interests in examining the connection between art critique and critical thinking skills. My question is: Can students who are involved in art critique lessons significantly improve their critical thinking ability? This also can be stated as a *hypothesis*: Students who receive training in art critique demonstrate a marked improvement in their critical thinking ability when compared to those who receive no such training.

The next thing I did was to translate my research question, or hypothesis, into a null hypothesis. The null hypothesis is made to test the research question (or hypothesis) and is an essential step in inferential statistics, which is then used to make inferences about a given population from a representative sample group. That is, inferential statistics help a researcher determine if a sample group's (e.g., an eighth-grade class involved in a research project) improvement on an art skill, by means of a particular teaching strategy, can be generalized to include all eighth graders in the region or nation. A null hypothesis is typically stated in the following manner: "There is no difference between the test scores of one group of students receiving method A and the other group with method B." (Fraenkel & Wallen, 1996). In this study I was interested to see if students who were exposed to art critique lessons could measurably improve their critical thinking skills scores and, in so doing, reject the null hypothesis, which would mean a positive result with regard to my research questions.

Null hypothesis: There is no significant difference between the critical thinking ability of the treatment group (those who participated in art critique lessons) and the control group (those who received no similar art critique lessons from the researcher).

Only two groups of students participated in my study. However, this model can be extended to involve various age groups, genders, socio-economic classes, or ethnic groups. Further study could, for example, compare the achievement of students' critical thinking skills according to these variables. A researcher can create research questions to see if there is a difference in critical thinking skills between genders, ages, and socio-economic classes by simply adding more sample populations. Another variation would be to examine if students who are exposed to both visual arts and math classes show a higher level of critical thinking skills than students who are involved with math classes only.

Before moving on to a more in-depth explanation of my research, I will provide definitions of terms that are stated in observable and measurable expressions in quasi-experimental research. This should help eliminate any confusion and difficulties in planning and conducting subsequent or repeated studies on this topic (Fraenkel & Wallen, 1996).

To define critical thinking skills, I relied on Ennis (1987) who described critical thinking as, "reasonable reflective thinking that is focused on deciding what to believe or do" (p. 10). Four main sections in critical thinking skills include induction, credibility judgment, deduction, and assumption, which are tested by multiple-choice items in the Cornell Critical Thinking Skills Test. For the purpose of this study, I utilized Anderson's (1991) description of art critique as, "A direct personal encounter with a specific work of art resulting in linguistic analysis and/or interpretation of the work" (p. 18).

RESEARCH DESIGN

In choosing a research design, I considered sampling. If I were able to assign samples randomly, I could use a true experimental design. However, assigning each subject randomly to a group was not practical in my research setting because I could not create a well-controlled laboratory setting, a non-natural environment, which might affect the experiment result. Rather, quasi-experimental design is feasible in public schools in which student schedules are not

GROUP	PRETEST	TREATMENT	POSTTEST
Treatment Group	O	X	O
Control Group	O		O

FIGURE 1. The non-equivalent control group design. In this table, X symbolizes the treatment (participating in art critique lessons), and the Os indicate the measurement of the two groups' critical thinking skills.

flexible enough to coordinate the students who consented to participate in my research. That is, I was not able to randomize the school sample in the region because it was not practical or possible. As a best alternative, I employed a quasi-experimental design comprising the non-equivalent control group design (See the accompanying methodology chapter for details on various quasi-experimental research designs). This study involved one control and one experimental (treatment) group of students: that is, two art classes in the same high school. Both groups were given the pretests at the beginning of the study and posttests at the end of the treatment period. However, the students in the control group did not participate in the research classes (see Figure 1).

RESEARCH SITE ACCESS

Before I began this study, I had to gain entry to a research site as an outsider. First, I contacted an art teacher who was willing to offer her classes as research classes. Then she also gained an informal permission from her school principal. The principal asked me to gain permission from a research review board at the school district. It took more than 2 months for the board to complete the review of my application. From this process I learned that anyone who wants to conduct a research project involving a public school student population should contact the school district office in advance for the procedure of approval. Additionally, as a graduate student, I needed to gain permission from the Office for Human Research Protections of Florida State University, where a human subject committee reviews all research proposals involving human participants. As regulated by the U.S. Department of Health and Human Services, my proposal was reviewed by the committee. It was accepted, and I could proceed to the data collection phase. The last step was to get consent from participants and their parents, who were asked to sign a consent form approved by the Human Subject Committee. Since my research was integrated into the school curriculum, all students agreed to participate, and their parents also consented for the research.

SAMPLE

The study was conducted during the 2001 fall semester at Lincoln High School in Tallahassee, Florida. Participants consisted of students who took the same art class, Digital Design, which met daily for 50-minute sessions. The sample in the two art classes consisted of 36 students in grades 9-12. Students in both classes met in a computer lab with about 24 Macs, and worked on digital art projects—such as cartoons, comics, animation, and optical illusion—using computer applications.

The student population that participated in the two sample classes also closely resembles the characteristics of the overall school student population in that it represented the racial balance of Leon County, a North Florida community whose population consists of 70% Whites, 25% African Americans, and 5% others. The free- or reduced lunch rate is about 13% of the school population and is comparable to the 25% average of Florida public schools. Figure 2 shows the demographic of the sample population.

GROUP		FREQUENCY	PERCENT (%)
Treatment	Male	8	44.4
	Female	10	55.6
Control	Male	10	44.4
	Female	8	55.6

FIGURE 2.
Sample Population
Demographics.

INSTRUMENTATION

One of the most important aspects of conducting this quasi-experimental research was to assess students' critical thinking skills. In this section, I share how I reviewed and adapted an instrument from available assessment tools in order to test students' critical thinking skills.

My interests in critical thinking skills led me to look at available tests for my research. Since critical thinking skills, or higher level thinking skills, are emphasized as educational goals in schools, some researchers have been interested in developing an instrument to test these skills. My literature review and web search helped me find ten instruments that claim to measure critical thinking. Most of the instruments are multiple-choice tests. The one exception is the Ennis-Weir Critical Thinking Essay Test (Ennis & Weir, 1985), an essay instrument to assess students' abilities to think critically about everyday issues. A few of the other widely used tests in educational studies are the Watson-Glaser Critical Thinking Appraisal, Cornell Critical Thinking Test, Test of Enquiry Skills, and The California Critical Thinking Skills Test. Each has been designed for its own population characteristics of different ages and abilities.

There are three available instruments that can be used for high school students: (1) the Cornell Critical Thinking Tests (CCTT); (2) the Enquiry Skills Test; and (3) the Ennis-Weir Critical Thinking Essay Test. The Enquiry Skills Test was not selected because it includes heavy science and social studies content not relevant to art critique. I also did not select the Ennis-Weir Critical Thinking Essay Test because it cannot be retaken as the posttest. That left the CCTT, which was ideally suited for my purpose and easily administered. I purchased forty copies from The Critical Thinking Company for my research.

The CCTT was used as an indicator of the individual student's critical thinking ability. It consists of two general critical tests: *Level X* and *Level Z*. *Level X* is designed for students in grades 4-14; *Level Z* for advanced and gifted high school students, college students, and other adults. *Level X* consists of 71 multiple-choice items, and *Level Z* 52 items. Both are intended to be taken in a 50-minute period. This study employed *Level X* because most of subjects were non-gifted high school students. The test is divided into four sections: Part I – Induction, judging whether a fact supports a hypothesis; Part II – Credibility, judging credibility of observation reports; Part III – Deduction, deciding what follows; and Part IV – Assumption Identification, judging what is assumed in an argument.

PROCEDURES

Comparing the critical thinking test results of both groups, after teaching art critique lessons only to the treatment group, was the main activity of this study. The study was performed over an 8-week period, with the first week and last week saved for taking the CCTT tests, which I administered. Therefore, the treatment group was taught 2 hours per week for 6 weeks by the researcher during the regular class period. The control group met for their regular computer art class, working on computer art projects. Main activities for the treatment group were to study art vocabulary words, learn how to critique artworks, and practice description, interpretation, and evaluation of artworks. Students were invited to work with an art criticism model of my own design, which was developed to help them use their metacognitive consciousness in critique, applying Terry Barrett's art criticism principles. (For further information, see Shin, 2005.)

RESULTS

The main objective of this quasi-experimental research project was to see if there was a difference in the pre-test and post-test critical thinking skills scores of the two groups. The t-test and the Analysis of Variance (ANOVA) are two popular statistical techniques used to compare group differences. The t-test, a statistical test using a t-score, is used to compare if there is a significant difference between the two groups' mean scores; the ANOVA is used to compare test scores of two or more groups. In the ANOVA test, the researcher looks for the P value, which is computed by using *SPSS* (Statistical Package for the Social Sciences). The P value is then used to identify whether a significant difference exists between two or more groups. For example, if a researcher wants to test which two new teaching methods are most effective, this involves three groups: one group for method A, another for method B, and the third group just for comparison. Using the ANOVA, the researcher can compare any significant differences that exist among groups.

In this research, I actually used a third statistical technique, called the Analysis of Covariance (ANCOVA), which is similar to the ANOVA in that it produces a P value. However, I found it to be preferable to the ANOVA because it also allows the researcher to control initial pre-test differences between two groups. For example, if one group produces a very high pretest mean score and the other a very low score, the ANCOVA can be used to accommodate the difference in pre-tests between the two groups.

The ANCOVA result indicated no significant difference between the treatment and control groups on the four subsections of the CCTT-LX pre- and posttests: Induction (F = .921, p = .346); Credibility (F = .146, p = .705); Deduction (F = 3.799, p = .057); and Assumption Identification (F = 1.460, p = .237). The general rule is, if a P value is greater than 0.05, it indicates that the study's null hypothesis was sustained and the main hypothesis was not accepted. In this case, the null hypothesis was clearly sustained since all four P values were greater than .05. Therefore, my data suggested that there was no significant difference between the critical thinking skills of the two groups. This result was unexpected because most researchers, including myself, would have expected the data to confirm that a new teaching method—in this case, the teaching of specific art criticism skills—was effective in improving the critical thinking abilities of the treatment group to a greater extent than those of the control group. However, my data were inconclusive in this regard, so I had to accept the end result.

DISCUSSION

The results of this study show no significant statistical difference between the treatment and control group on critical thinking skills. This indicates that the students' exposure to art critique did not make a significant contribution to the improvement of critical thinking skills. This result contradicts the claim that exposing students to art criticism will help them exercise and improve their critical thinking skills (Anderson, 1990; Buffington, 2007; Duke, 2000; Feldman, 1994).

Here, I offer a couple of reasons for the lack of a significant positive increase in critical thinking scores. One is due to the lack of time students were exposed to the art critiquing instruction. The short research period might not have allowed enough time for students to develop critical thinking skills. Recently, DeSantis and Housen (2007) have reported that it requires significant time for students to develop critical thinking skills through art instruction. In their research, which examined the effects of Visual Thinking Strategies on students' critical thinking, they did not find differences until the third year of students' museum visits, even though they claimed it only through interview data and essay tests.

Therefore, further research adopting standardized critical thinking skills tests with various art teaching strategies are needed.

The other reason is that the control group of students (those who did not participate directly in the research classes) were also art students who might have been formally or informally involved with critique sessions in their previous and current art classes. This could have effectively diminished the gap between the control and treatment group. This explanation is consistent with Lampert's (2006) report that high art exposure can enhance students' disposition to think critically. This might result in no statistically significant difference between the two groups. Therefore, further studies involving non-art students as well as art students will need to be performed to see the effect of art critique with regard to critical thinking.

Additionally, it should also be noted that the study focused on general critical thinking skills claimed by the CCTT developers. Recently, some educators have claimed that critical thinking skills need to be defined and tested within distinct disciplines (Renaud & Murray, 2008). This raises another issue of studying art-specific critical thinking skills. What are subject-specific critical thinking skills in art education, and how do we measure them? These questions provide an agenda for future research.

CONCLUSION

Critical thinking skills are widely believed to correlate to art criticism. However, this study could not provide empirical evidence of the effects of art critique on the development of critical thinking skills, despite the consensus of many art educators (Duke, 2000; Perkins, 1994; Perkins & Salomon, 1989; Risatti, 1987). This might be due to a lack of students' exposure time to art critique, the interference of students' previous art experience, or other extraneous variables. Longitudinal research with students with various backgrounds and abilities, as well as other areas of art instruction beyond art criticism, may provide further, more rich evidence in this critical area.

REFERENCES

Anderson, T. (1990). Attaining critical appreciation through art. *Studies in Art Education, 31*(3), 132-140.

Anderson, T. (1991). The content of art criticism. *Art Education, 44*(1), 17-24.

Buffington, M. (2007). Contemporary approach to critical thinking and the world wide web. *Art Education, 60*(1), 18-24.

DeSantis, K., & Housen, A. (2007). *Aesthetic development and creative and critical thinking skills study.* Retrieved from www.vtshome.org/pages/major-findings#4

Duke, L. L. (2000). Mind building and arts education. In R. Smith (Ed.), *Readings in discipline-based art education: A literature of educational reform* (pp. 15-19). Reston, VA: National Art Education Association.

Ennis, R. H. (1987). A taxonomy of critical thinking dispositions and abilities. In J. Baron & R. Sternberg (Eds.), *Teaching thinking skills: Theory and practice* (pp. 9-26). New York: W.H. Freeman.

Ennis, R., & Weir, E. (1985). *The Ennis-Weir critical thinking essay test.* Pacific Grove, CA: Midwest.

Feldman, E. B. (1994). *Practical art criticism.* Englewood Cliffs, NJ: Prentice-Hall.

Feldman, E. B., & Woods, D. (1981). Art criticism and reading. *Journal of Aesthetic Education, 15*(4), 75-95.

Fraenkel, J. R., & Wallen, N. E. (1996). *How to design and evaluate research in education.* New York, NY: McGraw-Hill.

Lampert, N. (2006). Critical thinking dispositions as an outcome of art education. *Studies in Art Education, 47*(3), 215-228.

Perkins, D. N. (1994). *The intelligent eye: Learning to think by looking at art* (Occasional Paper 4). Retrieved from ERIC database (ED375069).

Perkins, D. N., & Salomon, G. (1989). Art cognitive skills context-bound? *Educational Researcher, 18*(1), 16-25.

Renaud, R. D., & Murray, H. G. (2008). A comparison of a subject-specific and a general measure of critical thinking. *Thinking Skills and Creativity, 3*(2), 85-93.

Risatti, H. (1987). Art criticism in discipline-based art education. *Journal of Aesthetic Education, 21*(2), 217-225.

Shin, S. (2005). A metacognitive art criticism module accessed by high school students using an interactive CD-ROM, the Internet, and virtual chatting. *Visual Arts Research, 30*(1), 63-75.

RYAN SHIN is Associate Professor in the School of Art at the University of Arizona. He received his PhD in Art Education from Florida State University in 2002, taught at the University of Wisconsin at La Crosse from 2002 to 2007. His research interests include Asian folk art; Asian visual culture; minority visual culture; digital media and visual culture education; cross-cultural approach to understandings of art and visual culture; and quantitative research methods. His articles have appeared in *Studies in Art Education, Art Education, Visual Arts Research, Journal of Cross-Cultural Research in Art Education,* and *NAEA Advisory.* He also has authored numerous book chapters, and has presented his work at national and international conferences.

ARTS-BASED RESEARCH

12 / A/r/tography

RITA L. IRWIN / PROFESSOR OF ART EDUCATION, AND ASSOCIATE DEAN OF TEACHER EDUCATION, UNIVERSITY OF BRITISH COLUMBIA

ABSTRACT: *This chapter describes a/r/tography as a practice-based methodology emphasizing the practices of artists, researchers and educators. Moreover, a/r/tography is inherently a relational form of inquiry that pursues meaning making, understanding and the creation of knowledge. After describing a/r/tography briefly, the chapter discusses how to develop research questions and how to use living inquiry as a basis for a/r/tography. Living inquiry is essential for a/r/tography as it is an embodied encounter constituted through artistic and textual* **understandings** *and* **experiences** *as well as artistic and textual* **representations***. The chapter ends with a section on presenting a/r/tographic studies and provides a short example for the benefit of the reader.*

DESCRIPTION OF ARTS-BASED RESEARCH

According to Thomas Barone and Elliot Eisner, arts-based educational research (ABER) is inquiry that enhances our understanding of human activities through artistic means (see Barone & Eisner, 2006, p. 95). Depending upon the art form chosen, the aesthetic qualities, processes and products will vary significantly and therefore the design of the project will also vary (see also Knowles & Cole, 2008). ABER is inherently different from many other forms of educational research. Traditional forms of research search for knowledge that is certain, valid, and reliable with the findings being used to explain and predict outcomes. ABER, on the other hand, is not about certainty but rather the "enhancement of perspectives" (Barone & Eisner, 2006, p. 96). Through the arts, heightened perception about events, conditions and encounters allows those involved in and/or viewing the project to come to new understandings that may lead to the improvement of educational policy or practice. Arts-based research (ABR) is essentially the same but without the intention of influencing educational matters. Certainty is not the goal for ABER and ABR, but enlarging one's understanding is. Related to ABER is practice-based research (see Candy, 2006; Sullivan, 2005). While ABER uses the arts to examine educative events, practice-based research (PBR) uses the practices of those pursuing the inquiry (e.g. the practices of artists and educators). Moreover, most ABER advocates stress the representation of findings while PBR's focus is on the understandings derived from the processes *and* the products of the inquiry.

A/r/tography is a form of inquiry within practice-based research that includes the practices of the artist (musician, poet, dancer, etc), the educator (teacher/learner) and the researcher. It is here that a/r/tography has strong linkages with action research. Over the last two or three decades, action research has been wide spread in education. It has taken on many forms within the quantitative to qualitative traditions. A/r/tography borrows from a particular perspective that sees action research as a living practice (Sumara & Carson, 1997). From this viewpoint, inquiry-laden practices are not merely added to one's life but are one's life so that "who one is becomes completely caught up in what one knows and does" (p. xvii). In this way, the practices of educators and the practices of artists become sites for inquiry. Furthermore, as inquirers they are researchers. Research is no longer perceived from a traditional scientific perspective, but rather from an alternative point of view where research is conceived of as "re-search" and is a living practice intimately connected to the arts and education.

RESEARCH QUESTIONS

A/r/tography is living inquiry, an embodied encounter constituted through artistic and textual *understandings and experiences* as well as artistic and textual *representations*. In this sense the subject and the form of the research are in a constant state of becoming (Springgay, Irwin, Leggo, & Gouzouasis, 2008). Thus, while a/r/tographic projects may begin with one or more research questions, the act of living inquiry assumes these questions will evolve during the project. A/r/tographers are able to create artifacts and written texts that portray the understandings gained from their original questions; however, they also pay attention to the evolution of inquiry-led questions. It is here that the a/r/tographic project often becomes a transformative act of inquiry. Research questions are steeped in the practices of artists, educators or artist-educators and therefore have the potential to influence that practice in and through time. As with action research, a/r/tography often has an interventionist nature that aims to benefit the lives of the participants. A/r/tographers focus their efforts on the improvement of practice, understanding practice from a different perspective, and/or the use of their practice to influence the experiences of others. Given some of my recent research here are some sample research questions: (1) How does a particular programming model influence teachers' conceptions of integrating the arts across the curriculum? (2) What changes occur in students' knowledge generation through an arts-based form of inquiry? (3) What artistic products might be created through a community-engaged process examining the immigrant experience in the City of Richmond as a geographically and culturally hybrid place?

LIVING INQUIRY

For some researchers the idea of artistic artifacts being data and the inquiry process being data analysis is difficult to accept. The reason for this is that data is often understood as verifiable, organized and/or symbolic information. A/r/tographers prefer to think about the practices of artists and educators as occasions for creating knowledge. The process of inquiry becomes as important as, sometimes more important than, the representation of the perceived understandings. Artists engage in artistic inquiry that helps them explore issues, themes or ideas that inspire their curiosity and aesthetic sensibilities. Educators engage in educational inquiry that helps them explore issues, themes and ideas that inspire their learning, and learning to learn. These processes form the basis for living inquiry. It is living inquiry because it is about being attentive to life in and through time, relating what may not appear to be related, knowing that there are always connections to be explored. A/r/tographers may use social science-based qualitative forms of data collection (surveys, document collection, interviews, participant-observation, etc) and are often interested in personal stories, mementos, and photographs. As with any form of qualitative research there is the possibility of collecting a tremendous amount of data. Here is where ethnographic strategies may be employed for some data collection and analysis. Searching for prominent themes across data is important. However, a/r/tography also recognizes that perceptions should be explored.

Artists understand the power of the image, sound, performance, and word, not separate or illustrative of one another but interconnected to create additional meanings. Exploring ideas, issues, and themes artistically offers ways to make meaning, personally and collectively. Thus, using art and text, practice and theory, allows for interconnections, a form of conversation as relational. So while a/r/tographers may use social science forms of data collection and analysis, they also employ their own form of artistic inquiry and educational inquiry. A/r/tographers are constantly engaged with ideas, data, and artistic processes as ways to create new understandings through knowledge creation. Moreover, a/r/tography resists being stabilized by particular forms of data collection and analysis, or artistic processes and products, in favor of being responsive to contemporary practices. It is essential for a/r/tographers to be familiar with work of contemporary artists and educators, and consider how those practices might influence their perceptions, their ways of pursuing inquiry, and their ways of creating knowledge.

Simply stated, a/r/tographers' work is reflective, recursive, reflexive, and responsive. Reflective, as they rethink and review that which has gone before and what may happen; recursive, as they allow their practices to spiral through an evolution of ideas; reflexive, as they interrogate their own biases, assumptions, and beliefs; and responsive, as they take responsibility for acting ethically with their participants and colleagues. With these notions in mind they engage in their own form of artistic and educational activities as a way of collecting information, analyzing ideas and creating new forms of knowledge.

Although the intentions are the same regardless of artist or educator identities, the forms, processes, engagements, documentation, interpretation, and representation may be different (albeit connected). Accessing this diverse array of data, information, and knowledge creation, may seem confusing. This is because the rhizomatic nature of a/r/tography is constantly making connections. If we imagine a detailed street map and identify our way from point A to point B, following a straight line would be efficient but would likely miss many important contextual details if we did not allow ourselves to deviate from the straight line on occasion. Allowing oneself to take in more information along the way, by diverging from the original route and exploring other paths, may seem like an unfocused journey, but ironically it may be even more focused by grasping the particularities of the place. Choosing connections offers us an enlarged understanding of the original route. Moreover, although point B may have been the original destination, the region of point B may become the focus. Instead of moving from point A to point B, we explore the context of the in-between space and therefore move to appreciating the complexity yet particularities of that space. This is a metaphoric rendition of the rhizomatic nature of a/r/tography. It illustrates that making connections is inherently a relational activity.

EXAMPLE STUDY

During a recent study (for more detail see: Irwin, Bickel, Triggs, Springgay, Beer, Grauer, Xiong, & Sameshina, 2009; Sameshima et al., 2009; Triggs & Irwin, 2008) working with an immigrant community one of the original research questions asked: What artistic products might be created as we examined the immigrant experience in a specific city? We worked with eight multigenerational immigrant families over a 4-year period of time. We collected visual artifacts from the families while we also took photographs of events and gatherings we shared as part of the project. We also collected regular interviews, field notes, and our own regular reflections. The a/r/tographers guiding the study represented artist-educator-researchers working in Faculties of Education or Fine Arts: Some had international reputations as artists, while others had international reputations as scholars. Thus, the results of the study included scholarly and visual interpretations. Each year an exhibition of the art created during the year was shared either in a formal gallery space or a community center. Although university-based artists took leadership roles with the art, all of the participants and a/r/tographers were invited to participate in the conceptualization and creation to the degree in which they were comfortable. Thus, each artwork included various levels of involvement from participants and a/r/tographers.

The city in which the study took place is named Richmond, which, when translated into Mandarin (a dominant immigrant group) means Richgate—a place of opportunity. Exploring the notion of gates, although not originally part of the study, might have seemed like a deviation but instead provided a fertile base to explore ideas such as border epistemologies, arrivals and departures, thresholds, and beginnings and endings. This inspired artistic products, theoretical engagements and educational pursuits. A reader might wonder how pursuing deviations like this may happen when institutional research boards (IRB) expect specificity. Over time, I have learned to ask for more forms of data collection than I may use, for recognition of the research participants' right to work with a/r/tographers as co-inquirers, and if necessary, to submit addenda for further review if the study deviates substantially. It is important that IRBs understand that a/r/tography is a relational form of inquiry that pursues meaning making, understanding and the creation of knowledge. Relational concerns underpin all aspects of a/r/tography.

In the following gate image, the viewer is introduced to Gabriele Ailey's family. Gabriele was born in Poland after her family was driven from Estonia. At 9 days of age, Gabriele was carried by her grandparents as they escaped with very few belongings into Germany where transitional settlements existed. They soon moved to Canada to settle in northern Alberta where they homesteaded land. Her mother died shortly thereafter and the ensuing years were difficult. Despite their challenges, the family learned a new language and adjusted to the new culture. Later, Gabriele became an art educator and soon met her husband, an airline pilot. His family's experience was very different, having been born in Canada into a stable family environment. Gabriele recounts her history through a visual narrative in Gabriele's gate (see Figure 1). It illustrates the few belongings her family brought from Estonia, the letters family members sent over the years, and the tracing of journeys, homes, and family members. The "gate" structure further illustrates the threshold of change, the monumental effects of change, the power of the family unit, and how an art educator chose to use her story as a way to help EAL learners (English as an Additional Language) in her elementary school. It is also linked to other immigrant stories as the image portrays another gate hanging behind Gabriele's gate, allowing viewers the possibility of walking through the visual narratives of each family. The exhibition should provoke new understandings of the power of the particular within immigrant stories while evoking for each of us a deeper understanding of how we each visualize our life stories.

As a/r/tographers we intervened in a silent immigrant community by telling untold stories and portraying the diverse immigrant nature of the City of Richgate. Through a number of exhibitions using different thematic orientations, the project lead to an overall understanding of how the City of Richgate was actually a City of Richgates where a city center was reconceptualized as a network of city centers. Moreover, as the final visual project was situated in many places around the city, we pursued the power of public pedagogy to engage with evocative and provocative visual images to involve citizens of the city as they reimagined what the city as home meant to them.

FIGURE 1. Gabriele recounts her history through a visual narrative. Gabriele's Gate: Beer, R., Gu.,X., Irwin, R., Grauer, K., Springgay, S., Bickel, B. (2005). *Richgate Exhibition*, installation photograph. Art Gallery of South West China University, Chongqing, China.

The project was inherently a relational activity that pursued relational aesthetics, relational peda-gogy, and relational inquiry, and constitutes the conditions for living inquiry. Relational aesthetics (see Bourriaud, 2002) is about the relationship between the a/r/tographer and the art form, between visual ideas (or musical ideas, dramatic ideas, etc.) and interpretations, and between artifacts and viewers. Understanding how artists, educators and researchers, as well as others viewing the work, create meaning is of great interest to a/r/tographers. A/r/tographers are constantly concerned with how their interven-tions are impacting others and themselves.

Within these conditions is the need to investigate the concepts that penetrate living inquiry. For a/r/tographers, concepts are flexible and intersubjective locations in which analysis can occur. Whereas the conditions for a/r/tography are interested in relationality, the concepts are interested in the renderings of that relationality. While specific renderings have been identified that may help an a/r/tographer engage conceptually with the research project, a/r/tographers need to re-evaluate what renderings are suitable for their project. The first set of published renderings included living inquiry, contiguity, openings, metaphor/metonymy, reverberations and excess (for elaboration see Springgay, Irwin, & Wilson Kind, 2005). They represent possibilities for engagement and may be useful as starting points. Consider these brief defini-tions as an entryway into one's data analysis or artistic processes. Living inquiry has been addressed earlier and is a way of being and becoming in the world. Contiguity is the relationship between *and* alongside identities, art *and* graphy, theory *and* practice. Openings reside in these in-between spaces ("*and*") and suggest (metaphorically) there may be cracks, ruptures, tears, or cuts in what we perceive. Openings help us to see beyond the taken-for-granted. Using metaphor/metonymy a/r/tographers can make what we sense understandable and accessible to others. Reverberations portray the movement between many connections. It represents the tension and impulse to connect, to construct, and to co-labor. Finally, excess is a prompt for us to look to what others have cast aside, ignored, dismissed. It is a rich place to study. By artistically or educationally engaging with these concepts or renderings, pathways to meaning making are nurtured. A/r/tographers are encouraged to consider other concepts or renderings that may be different or in addition to these. Ultimately, attending to the conditions (relationality) and the concepts (render-ings) within a/r/tography is bringing a conceptual framework to the methodology. From this conceptual framing, a/r/tographers are then able to identify how their work should be evaluated. For instance, how well did the a/r/tographer use metaphor as an artistic strategy for ongoing inquiry and creating a compel-ling and evocative representation of the new understandings? Another way of perceiving evaluation is to draw from Barone and Eisner's criteria for forming judgments (see Barone & Eisner, 2006, p. 102) by considering generativity (ability to promote new questions), incisiveness (ability to focus on salient/significant issues and questions), and generalizabilty (relevance to related matters). While their criteria are situated within ABER, a/r/tographers may gain from considering these concepts as additional ways to judge their work and the work of other a/r/tographers.

PRESENTING A/R/TOGRAPHIC STUDIES

While traditional forms of research generally follow a template for the dissemination of research findings, no such template exists for a/r/tographers. There is no right or wrong way of portraying an a/r/tographic project, nor is there a checklist for judging the work. However, there are ways of engaging with the work that should compel readers and viewers to a new level of understanding. Often this means pursuing an artistic engagement throughout the inquiry that ultimately leads to an artistic representation. A/r/tographers want to portray their projects in ways that resonate with the inquiry itself as well as the new understandings. They want the readers and viewers to understand something in a new and compelling way and to make a difference to the community they serve.

A/r/tography occupies an intellectual and imaginative space for inquiry. With the advent of pervasive technology and its emphasis on the visual and sensory comes an opportunity for arts educators to embrace their practices and to share their inquiries with their communities. In so doing, a/r/tography will help fill a pedagogical void in local communities and an imaginative void in schools or other learning environments. Treated as an academic intention, a/r/tography broadens the horizon of possibilities for artists and educators interested in ongoing living inquiry.

At one time a/r/tography was portrayed as an autobiographical inquiry among art educators (Irwin & de Cosson, 2004), and since then autobiographical *and* socio-cultural implications have been explored across the arts (Springgay et al., 2008). Despite the artistic and educative potential, arts based educational research, practice based research and a/r/tography still need to be embraced by many. Lone arts educators, practicing without the support of a community of like-minded people, remain isolated and often misunderstood in their academic and professional communities. A/r/tographers will need to explore how they can manage the demands of being an artist, researcher *and* teacher within their professional contexts. A/r/tographers will also need to study how interventions may transform particular contexts, how viewers may perceive their work differently in several situations, and how they themselves may be changed through their ongoing living practices.

REFERENCES

Barone, T., & Eisner, E. W. (2006). Arts based educational research. In J. L. Given, G. Camilli & P. B. Elmore (Eds.), *Handbook of complementary methods in educational research* (pp. 95-106). New York, NY: Routledge.

Bourriaud, N. (2002). *Relational aesthetics*. Paris, France: Les presses du réel.

Candy, L. (2006). *Practice based research: A guide*. Retrieved from: www.creativityandcognition.com/resources/PBR%20Guide-1.1-2006.pdf

Irwin, R. L., Bickel, B., Triggs, V., Springgay, S., Beer, R., Grauer, K., Xiong, G., & Sameshima, P. (2009). The City of Richgate: A/r/tographic cartography as public pedagogy. *International Journal of Art and Design Education, 28*(1), 61-70.

Irwin, R. L., & de Cosson, A. (Eds.). (2004). *A/r/tography: Rendering self through arts-based living inquiry*. Vancouver, BC: Pacific Educational Press.

Knowles, G., & Cole, A. (Eds.) (2008). *International handbook of the arts in qualitative social science research*. Thousand Oaks, CA: Sage.

Sameshima, P., Irwin, R. L., Beer, R., Grauer, K., Gu, X., Bickel, B., & Ricketts, K. (2009). Rendering embodied heteroglossic spaces. *Journal of Arts and Communities, 1*(2), 129-146.

Sinner, A., Leggo, C., Irwin, R. L., Gouzouasis, P., & Grauer, K. (2006). Arts-based Educational Research Dissertations: Reviewing the practices of new scholars. *Canadian Journal of Education, 29*(4), 1223-1270. Retrieved from www.csse.ca/CJE/Articles/FullText/CJE29-4/CJE-4-Sinneretal.pdf

Springgay, S., Irwin, R. L., Leggo, C., & Gouzouasis, P. (Eds.) (2008). *Being with a/r/tography*. Rotterdam, The Netherlands: Sense.

Springgay, S., Irwin, R. L., & Wilson Kind, S. (2005). A/r/tography as living inquiry through art and text. *Qualitative Inquiry, 11*(6), 897-912.

Sullivan, G. (2005). *Art practice as research: Inquiry in the visual arts*. Thousand Oaks, CA: Sage.

Sumara, D. J., & Carson, T. R. (Eds.). (1997). *Action research as living practice*. New York, NY: Peter Lang.

Triggs, V., & Irwin, R. L. with Beers, R., Grauer, K., Xiong, G., Springgay, S., & Bickel, B. (2008). Educational arts research as aesthetic politics. *Working Papers in Art & Design 5*. Retrieved from http://sitem.herts.ac.uk/artdes_research/papers/wpades/vol5/vtriabs.html

RITA L. IRWIN is Professor of Art Education, and Associate Dean of Teacher Education, at the University of British Columbia, Vancouver, BC, Canada. She is also the current President of the International Society for Education through Art. Rita publishes widely, exhibits, and has secured a range of research grants to support her work. Recent books include *Curriculum in a New Key: The Collected Works of Ted T. Aoki* (co-edited with William F. Pinar), *Revisions: Readings in Canadian Art Teacher Education* (co-edited with Kit Grauer and Mike Emme), and *Being with A/r/tography* (co-edited with Stephanie Springgay, Carl Leggo, and Peter Gouzouasis). She is a prolific writer with numerous refereed journal articles, authored and edited books, art exhibitions, and professional publications. Rita is an artist, researcher, and teacher deeply committed to the arts and education.

Collages and Poetry and a Play:
An Arts-Based Research Journey

LISA KAY / ASSISTANT PROFESSOR, TYLER SCHOOL OF ART,
TEMPLE UNIVERSITY

Artmaking by its very nature is a creative process through which a researcher can examine and clarify multiple relationships, patterns, and meanings during the research process. I offer and describe four examples of arts-based research methods from my research study investigating how students and teachers in alternative high schools characterize art education to illustrate this process: (1) collage as an organizing metaphor; (2) poetry as data gathering/data analysis, (3) "bead collage" as an in-depth interview method; and (4) a play to report research findings. The data collected in this study included visual field notes, textual (word) field notes, interview transcripts, play, artwork, and poems.

COLLAGE AS AN ORGANIZING METAPHOR

Before selecting my research sites, I visited four art teachers in four different alternative educational environments. Throughout that day I kept encountering "torn" paper everywhere (torn newspaper, napkins, paper towels, students making torn paper self-portraits), so I created a visual field note of my experiences (Figure 1) and wrote about "torn" representing the students in these sites. *Torn* became an organizing metaphor for my thinking and the title of the play describing my findings.

POETRY AS DATA GATHERING/DATA ANALYSIS

Researchers can reflect on visual art using poetry as well. Poems *TORN 1* and *TORN 2* were written as a data-gathering strategy after creating art about a site visit (Figures 2 & 3). After, and sometimes during, field visits I created artwork about my observations and my responses to what I experienced. I created 12 x 18-inch drawings and collages that I cut it into 4 x 6-inch cards and wrote field notes on the backs of these cards. Other times I

TORN 1

ripped, a (part)
torn to pieces
not whole not complete
torn
in parts
torn between two things

FIGURE 2. *TORN 1,* a poem written while reflecting on visual art created after a site visit.

TORN 2

troubled,
in trouble,
traumatized,
the'other',
the outsider,
relationships,
normal?

FIGURE 3. *TORN 2,* a poem written while reflecting on visual art created after a site visit.

---

created poems in response to my reflective artwork as a method to understand the data.

I returned to *TORN 1* during the data analysis phase and wrote a third poem, *TORN 3* (Figure 4) because writing poetry helps make sense of data in a non-discursive manner (Kay, 2008; Leavy, 2009; Richardson, 1992). In poetic form I played with the words/metaphors associated with the words *torn* and *form* and in the collage process, which I used in my visual memos, I reflected on how something torn can be made whole. I discovered that I needed to move from *torn* to *whole*, much like the art teachers in my study were moving their students beyond *torn* to something holistic.

Using metaphors of the word *torn* helped clarify the essential questions in this research study: What teaching and learning occur in art education classrooms with adolescent students at-risk in alternative high schools? What is the art teacher's role in this type of setting? What are the goals of the art teacher? What are the goals of the students?

FROM T.O.R.N. TO TRANS FORM

ripped,
a (part)
torn to pieces
not whole
torn
not complete
torn
in parts
torn between two things
to take shape
to form
in[form]
de[form]
re[form]
con[form]
[form]ation
[form]ative
[form]fiting
[form]ulating
per[form]
trans[form]
art education
transformation

FIGURE 4. *TORN 3,* a poem written during data analysis.

FIGURE 1. *Torn,* visual field note.

FIGURE 5. Bead collage created by an interview participant.

"BEAD COLLAGE" AS AN IN-DEPTH INTERVIEW METHOD

As a part of the interview process, I asked my participants to select beads to facilitate the construction of knowledge and reflection of meaning. The art teachers selected a bead, held it, reflected on their students, their teaching philosophy, and/or the research experience and as they related their personal stories, the construction of knowledge continued. Each participant chose and arranged beads into a three-dimensional metaphorical representation of her experience and talked about her bead selections and their application to her pedagogy and practice. This bead process helped the art teachers articulate their thoughts and ideas in a tactile way Kay, 2013. Interview transcripts and photographs of finished bead collages (Figure 5) served as a method of data collection.

A PLAY TO REPORT RESEARCH FINDINGS

As students changed classes and their art teachers prepared for their next class, I visualized actors quickly moving props and sets and assuming stage positions and decided to write my findings in narrative form as a play (Figure 6). This dramatic format like ethnodrama, which presents research findings as a dramatic script (Leavy, 2009), represented the participants' stories naturalistically and realistically, using their multiple voices and words. The inclusion of the narrator/researcher's voice offers both description and interpretation of the data like the play *Our Town*, in which the narrator's voice is ever-present.

CONCLUSION

When making art, the artist/researcher searches, looks, examines, explores, organizes, arranges, sorts, and connects with the data as an ongoing form of inquiry. In this arts-based research process, artist/researchers can construct alternative readings of the data that shift beyond descriptions and realistic details to include visual images. As non-linear language, visual images, poetry, and dramatic narratives record and document observations, experiences, and responses to the research data in a concrete way that text alone does not. ■

ACT I

(It's warm outside and it's extremely warm in the art education classroom at Kozol. The heat is on in the building; the sun is generating more heat through the large windows. Examples of student artwork hang on the walls. A bulletin/ chalk board displays daily announcements and class/school information. Quotes that read "Artists create the world they imagine" and "An artist is a person who uses imagination and skill to communicate ideas in a visual form" frame the teacher's desk.)

NARRATOR: *Students enter the multi-grade/multi-level art classroom – some with MP3 players and headphones in place, tired and sleepy, most wearing huge, invisible backpacks – filled with their emotions, hardships, struggles, and their troubles. They may self-identify as losers, quitters, and/or addicts. There is minimal difference between students here and in other regular traditional schools. There is an art studio atmosphere in the class. Art supplies, for students' use, are organized in drawers, on open shelves, and in cabinets or storage closets. Students are simultaneously working at multiple levels on various assignments with different media. The teacher moves from student to student checking on their progress, demonstrating lesson(s), offering technical assistance, encouragement and/or support.*

SCENE 1: BEGINNING

LOUISE: *All right class, let's get started. Sign in and take your seats. Who's not here today? Who's finished with their projects and who needs my help?*

BEN: *I've been told I was artistically challenged.*

LOUISE: *By whom?*

BEN: *Everybody—my parents, my teachers, my friends.*

ADAM: *I'm an art hater!*

LOUISE: *Hater? That's really a strong statement.*

FIGURE 6. Excerpt from the play, *T...O...R...N...* (Kay, 2008, p. 84; Kay, 2010).

REFERENCES

Kay, L. (2008). *Art education pedagogy and practice with adolescent students at-risk in alternative high schools* (Unpublished doctoral dissertation). Northern Illinois University, Dekalb.

Kay, L. (2010). T...O...R...N... Research Findings as Performance Art. *Liminalities: A Performance Studies Journal, 6*(1), 1-40.

Kay, L. (2013). Bead collage: An arts-based research method. *International Journal of Education & the Arts, 14*(3). Retrieved from http://www.ijea.org/v14n3/

Leavy, P. (2009) *Method meets art: Arts-based research practice.* New York, NY: Guilford Press.

Richardson, L. (1992). The consequences of poetic representation: Writing the other, rewriting the self. In C. Ellis & M.G. Flaherty (Eds.), *Investigating subjectivity: Research on lived experience* (pp. 125 -137). Newbury Park, CA: Sage.

13 / Art-Based Methodology: Alternative Forms for Research on Educational Practice

MARY HAFELI / DEAN OF THE SCHOOL OF FINE AND PERFORMING ARTS, STATE UNIVERSITY OF NEW YORK

ABSTRACT: *This chapter provides an overview of art-based educational research methodology. It describes specific studio-based tools and non-traditional writing and presentation forms that can be used to examine what teachers do and what and how students learn in art education contexts such as classrooms, museums, and community settings. Examples of art making and writing approaches used throughout the research process— such as mapping, mixed-media collage, and portraiture—illustrate how studio ways of working can help identify a topic of investigation, gain new insights into related literature, formulate research questions, and carry out a study and present its findings. Challenges inherent in art-based educational research methodology, such as those related to interpretive openness and validity of findings, are highlighted as normative issues that continue to engage educational researchers who use art-based approaches.*

Inquiry into the practices of art teaching and learning has traditionally relied on numbers-based and words-based methodologies. Within and alongside these approaches, some researchers now engage arts practices to inform their work. The use of artmaking in the examination of educational practice and theory is one form of art-based educational research.

How can art-based research methods be used as tools for inquiry into the practice of art teaching and learning? In this chapter, I focus on studio-based approaches that stem from art production, and highlight the tools, processes, and presentation forms I have used in my own research and in teaching qualitative research methods courses. The chapter also presents non-traditional writing methods and forms for researchers who are interested in alternative text-based approaches, as they examine the immediacy of what teachers do and what and how students learn in art educational contexts such as classrooms, museums, and community settings. Though there are multiple approaches to and views about art-based research, the approach that I advocate in this chapter is to use art making throughout the research process to identify a topic of investigation, gain new insights into related literature, formulate questions, and carry out the study.[1]

Art-based researchers and those who write about its practices use various terms to describe the use of "art" or "the arts" in or as research (see, for example Cahnmann-Taylor & Siegesmund, 2008; Eisner, 1981, 1997, 2006; Knowles & Cole, 2008; Leavy, 2009; Sullivan, 2005, 2006). For the purposes of this chapter I use the term art-based (*art*-based, not *arts*-based) educational research to mean systematic, qualitative inquiry—focused on the study of issues and topics related to teaching and learning—that uses visual art production methods, visual art forms, and artistic ways of thinking and practice as a means to (1) generate research questions, (2) analyze and interpret information or data, and/or (3) communicate findings of the study.

As a set of methodologies—broad philosophical approaches and orientations that are more than a collection of specific research methods and tools—art-based educational research seeks to create and present new knowledge that, in Eisner's (2008) words, "is not expressible in ordinary discourse" (p. 7). However, there are several approaches to art-based research. For example, Knowles and Cole (2008) conceive of *arts-informed research* as "a way of redefining research form and representation and creating new understandings of process, spirit, purpose, subjectivities, emotion, responsiveness, and the ethical dimensions of inquiry" (p. 59). In Springgay, Irwin, and Kind's (2008) methodology of *A/R/Tography*, "The identities, roles, and understandings of the artist/researcher/teacher are intertwined in an approach to social science research that is dedicated to perceiving the world artistically and educationally" (p. 84). The emergence of qualitative research methodologies over 40 years ago,[2] as an alternative to quantitative research, offered narrative and unapologetically rich descriptive interpretation through words, in contrast to assumed objective analysis through numbers. Similarly, art-based educational research methodologies offer another angle from which to see, know, and question not only the supposed and named phenomena we study as art educational researchers interested in the particularities of art teaching and learning (for example, the art practices of students, the content, context, and methods of art instruction), but also ourselves as tacit subjects in the research process.

While some educational researchers choose a single methodology that aligns broadly with either a quantitative or qualitative approach (art-based educational research is considered here as a qualitative approach), many studies are grounded in methodologies that involve mixed methods. In mixed methods approaches, the researcher typically uses quantitative tools to collect certain kinds of information (for example, numerically scored surveys in which students give feedback about an instructional approach), and text-based qualitative methods to gather more detailed information (open-ended interviews that uncover nuanced reasons for students' survey responses). At various times within the research process, art-based methods can be useful "mixers" in blended methodologies—in forming questions, in gathering, analyzing, and interpreting data, and in the presentation of a study's findings at any point in the process. In what follows, I illustrate some applications of art-based methods in this context through examples from my own research practice.

CONCEPTUALIZING THE TERRAIN AND READING THE LITERATURE

"What are good topics for art-based educational research?" is a question that is understandably of great interest to beginning researchers in the field. But in its effort to delineate and particularize, this question may instead serve to prematurely limit possibilities for the use of art-based educational research methodologies and methods.[3] A more useful question at this stage may be: "How can studio methods help generate research questions for art education research?"

Art media, studio processes, and artistic ways of thinking can be helpful in the early stages of a study, when the researcher is deciding on a topic and developing related research questions. Just as qualitative researchers in general may broaden, narrow, and reformulate initial research questions as they read the literature and perhaps do some exploratory fieldwork, art-based educational researchers may arrive at a topic of inquiry and questions that are shaped and reshaped during the research process. For researchers who use art-based methods, ideas may both be imposed on and emerge from "source material"—the classroom, the students, and insights gained from personal practice as teacher and artist. Just as important, ideas also emerge through working with materials, both studio-based and text-based.[4]

One art-based analytical and presentational strategy that can be helpful in the question generating process is *visual mapping or imaging* of the conceptual framework. Visual mapping is a piece of artwork—a drawing, collage, digital image, or three-dimensional model—that relates the different areas, concerns, or issues that present themselves at a particular point in the research process.

For example, considering conceptual frameworks for research on teaching and learning, Eisner (1998) and Bruner (1996) have used the metaphor of the classroom as ecosystem to describe the complex interdependence through which teachers and students create learning in instructional settings. In Figure 1, I have begun to sketch an image that maps the classroom as an ecosystem under a microscope—a microcosm. In the center of the system is a goal or purpose shared by teachers and students. This goal, *authentic artistic engagement,* is the construct I am interested in studying as a researcher.[5]

Moving outward from the goal/construct are three major influences—*teacher, students,* and *physical/ social environment.* The lines connecting these influences display arrows on either end; this indicates not a one-way directional movement, such as teacher-to-student, but a reciprocal relationship (teacher-to-student and student-to-teacher). This is the case among all three major influences. Each of the items that surround the major influences—such as the teacher's philosophy of teaching and mandates for instruction, the students' experiences and narratives—both further play into the "ecology of the art class" image and affect the goal of authentic artistic engagement. These related items appear near where they may seem to be most connected at a given time (the teacher, the students). But in reality elements of art teaching and learning, and their position in relation to one another, are dynamic, not static. They shift and merge, and grow and diminish in prominence as one part of the ecosystem is affected and thus affects the entire

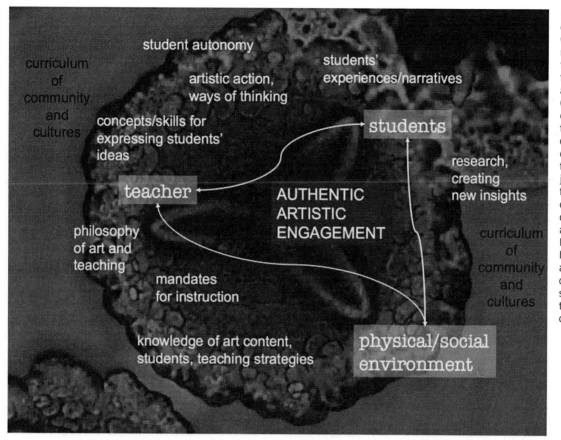

FIGURE 1. The ecology of the art class. Conceptual framework maps can take many forms. Colors, shapes, typefaces, images, and physical materials (paint, collage, ink, etc.) all can be used to identify groupings of concepts into categories. In addition to linear connections, juxtaposition, layering, transparency, scale, and contrast can indicate different relationships among concepts. Maps can also show hierarchies, as well as sets and subsets of ideas (themes and subthemes) through these same coding devices.

system itself. It would take the medium of video animation to more accurately portray the movement and activity of these influences on the teaching and learning microcosm as I have imagined it here.

This kind of image mapping is always in flux. Based upon my experience creating this image map, I came to develop research questions worth pursuing within the ecology of the art class focused on *authentic artistic engagement*. The questions include:

> What theories and philosophies about art, teaching, and learning lend themselves to the study of authentic artistic engagement? In what ways is students' authentic artistic engagement promoted and/ or hindered by particular:
> - curriculum content?
> - instructional strategies?
> - classroom environments?
> - styles, manners, and sensibilities of the teacher?
> - classroom rules and management strategies?
> - levels of student decision-making?

Visual mapping of the conceptual framework, saved as in-process "snapshots" as the framework evolves in successive iterations, can also function as a map of the research process itself—and of my own development as I become more and more immersed in the study and data.[6]

LITERATURE REVIEW

Visual mapping also can be a useful strategy for synthesizing key ideas found in the review of existing research related to one's topic of inquiry. As in mapping conceptual frameworks, key concepts—this time gleaned from the work of other researchers—can be arranged to show relationships between and among those ideas and findings. This kind of mapping also allows the researcher to play with a variety of compositional strategies for organizing or "arranging" findings from the related literature in a subsequent written synthesis.

However, a second way in which art practice can be an analytical and presentational tool in educational research is through *material responses to key ideas* in readings from the literature. In addition to summarizing and annotating readings through traditional forms of writing, art-based educational researchers use studio methods and tools, and a variety of techniques and processes, to further interpret and re-present the literature. Media and approaches that lend themselves to multi-sensory "readings" of

FIGURE 2. Art-based responses to Eisner's (2004) *The Arts and the Creation of Mind* (Artwork by Amber Carky, 2008). In re-presenting ideas from the literature through making artwork, art-based educational researchers move beyond mere illustration of texts to synthesizing and transporting ideas contained in them into new interpretive realms. For Amber, this involved a slowing down of the "reading" process—through identifying salient ideas within the text and purposefully choosing materials, methods, and forms with which to consider those ideas. Ultimately, Amber learned not only that materials actively mediate one's experience and internalization of the ideas of others but also that the visual products of her analyses are not simply a *re*formulation but a physical and tangible *trans*formation of others' ideas. Transforming through studio processes ideas originally presented as written text can provide an art-based researcher with new insights as well as new research questions to pursue.

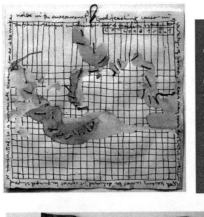

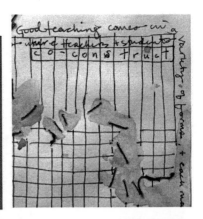

...good teaching cannot be "delivered." Teaching, like knowledge, cannot be shipped, pumped, or transmitted....In a sense all that teachers can do is make noises in the environment. (p. 47)

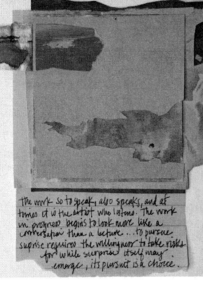

The individual takes his or her lead from the work. The work, so to speak, also speaks, and at times it is the artist who listens. The work in progress begins to look more like a conversation than a lecture . . . to pursue surprise requires the willingness to take risks, for while surprise itself may emerge, its pursuit is a choice. (pp. 78-79)

and material responses to the literature can create a reflective space in which new ideas and questions related to the study may emerge, allowing the researcher to "see" the author's ideas in a new light. In Figure 2, for example, mixed media works by Amber Carky, a graduate student in a course I taught, combine collage materials and handwritten text in a response to self-identified key passages from her reading of Eisner's (2004) *The Arts and the Creation of Mind*. In the pieces at the top, Carky's overtly visible methods of attaching disparate elements in the *constructing* of the artwork—through sewing, for example—invite a parallel way of thinking about Eisner's thoughts on constructivist approaches to teaching and learning. Her methods of construction and their visual effect and semiotic meanings become essential, and materially conceptual, elements in themselves. Her selection of the scroll as an alternative presentational form (lower right) both echoes and visually re-presents Eisner's thoughts about teaching as an "endless gesture" that "never ends until we do" (p. 56). While Carky's material interpretations focus on layered visual depictions of ideas from a single text, key ideas from multiple texts also can be extracted and re-presented using studio-based methods.

ANALYZING/INTERPRETING/RE-PRESENTING DATA

Another art-based analytical and presentational tool is a *textual collage*. This can be a useful strategy for synthesizing the work of other researchers found in the existing literature related to one's research topic

By having things in the studio, and if there's enough of them, it raises the level to which they might tap me on the shoulder and go, "Psst. Did you notice that I've been sitting next to so and so? And when you were out of the room, I spoke to so and so." I need that.
Richard Wentworth

There are a lot of tricks you have to keep playing on yourself to keep at it because every time you hit a problem you want to walk away.
Janet Fish

I don't come to this work through books. I don't make this work in response to other people's theory. And I don't think about what the piece means and then make it. Jessica Stockholder

There's an organic aspect in much of my work that maybe has to do with keeping the rules really open. There's this hand held, hand made aspect....It's not something that I'm really trying to go after— it's sort of a by product I think. Tim Hawkinson

Then I started to think, "What about making meaningless gestures that mean nothing?"....People read all kinds of things into my paintings that make me say, "Huh? What you think you're seeing is not what I intended to be there." Susan Rothenberg

It seems I have learned to bear the anxiety of uncertainty. Now I accept that one can't know ahead of time what is on the other side.
Anne Truitt

We don't make mistakes here, we just have happy accidents. Bob Ross

I put my trust in the materials that confront me, because they put me in touch with the unknown. It's then that I begin to work...when I don't have the comfort of sureness and certainty.
Robert Rauschenberg

I think you have to learn by procedure. Half of the most interesting things in the world are the result of spilling the water and turning around. Moments of recognition.
Richard Wentworth

There is no such thing as good painting about nothing.
Mark Rothko

Painting is the way I speak....when I started to paint I was creating a visual language through which I could say anything I wanted.
Joan Snyder

I started using patterns, but I shouldn't have....It broke the ideas I had in my head. I should have stayed with my own ideas.
Nettie Young

When you work with ideas....the form the work takes also depends on the material that is available to me. Sometimes it's the other way around, I have an idea first and then search for the material with which it can best be realized.
Mona Hatoum

And for an artist, it just seems to me it's not so important to have that level of technical perfection. It's important to also have a flow and have things be able to germinate and not get caught in the trap of perfection—because that can be a real trap for anybody who makes things.
Martin Puryear

How do ideas survive in culture?.... how do ideas stay around long enough to have a conversation?
Mel Chin

What kinds of problems, and what kinds of meanings, happen in the paint? Or as one historian puts it, what is thinking in a painting, as opposed to thinking about painting? These are important questions, and they are very hard to answer using the language of art history.
James Elkins

When I started, I thought, 'Oh, it won't change a thing.' But then I realized I could empower people with it. I think the best that can happen is that you open up a dialogue.
Sue Coe

I love Minimalist work, but....I need texture, surface, and different kinds of materials.
Patricia McKenna

I don't start with a color order, but find the colors as I go.
Helen Frankenthaler

I just take my cues from putting the color down and seeing how it works.
Elizabeth Murray

FIGURE 3. Collage of artists' perceptions of studio practice (in Hafeli, 2009b). These quotes were selectively chosen from interview texts found in the literature to highlight artists' perceptions of their own studio thinking and practice, in an effort to incorporate these dimensions as criteria in a larger discussion of "authentic" tools and practices for assessing student artwork (see Hafeli, 2009b). In exploring the question "How do artists describe their thinking and processes as they make artwork?" the purpose of this particular textual collage is to highlight the dispositions, attitudes, and thinking processes reported by the artists: for example, dealing with uncertainty and ambiguity, forestalling closure, forming meaning if so desired, inventing one's own questions and imagining solutions, and recognizing and capitalizing on unanticipated "surprises" in the studio process. The organizing form of the collage, a spiral, simultaneously (1) suggests that our understanding of studio thinking and practice is not linear but layered and evolving, and (2) shows, through clusters of thematically related quotes, that there is not always agreement among artists about the importance of such things as meaning, intention, and craftsmanship. By making this collage, I learned that how the researcher visually juxtaposes and presents data can purposefully reveal both consensus and discord in the findings. In the larger context of assessing student learning, of which this data analysis was a part, this collage makes clear that artists' perceptions about studio thinking and practice are not all of a kind, and we need to account for these divergent approaches to studio thinking as we form criteria for the evaluation of student artwork.

and questions, as well as aid in analyzing, interpreting, and presenting data gathered directly by the researcher in the field. I will now present two examples of textual collages created to help analyze data from different studies I have undertaken. In both, collage is used as a visual strategy to juxtapose similar and divergent voices or "takes" on a single topic.

The first textual collage, shown in Figure 3, depicts a visual "conversation," a pieced-together "debate" among more than 20 artists.[7] This collage purposefully juxtaposes direct quotes from various artists, for the viewer's own analysis and comparison. As such, it is another form of data to be analyzed. Part of the intrigue of a good collage—what draws one in to look (or, in this case, listen) closely and then linger—relies on tension in the conversation, and debate among its disparate, sometimes dissonant, voices or elements. Dissonance (in some places) and consensus (in others) contained in the visual-textual dialogue are "made sense of" by the viewer/reader, as well as by the researcher in a written analysis. In Figure 3, artists' individual

Your painting must:

--Include at least two people

--You must be one of the people

People should be the main focus of your painting

Do not include words—your ideas, thoughts should be visually represented

You will use things like color, exaggeration, distortion, and/or point of view to emphasize the mood of your piece

Well, you had to make them look like they were doing some kind of action. You had to express through body language and not words . . . you had to describe the mood.

It had to be like, just two people reacting to each other. . . . She just wanted us to show, like, different types of things, and different, like, ways to look at it, I think.

It had to be more than two people. You had to be one of the persons.

It had to have two people. I had a lot. And I had to be in there.

We were supposed to, like, draw a picture from different, like, angles, I think.

Well, we were supposed to pick, like, a thing you wanted to do for a painting, like something that really expressed you. It had to have at least to people in it and one of the people had to be you.

FIGURE 4.
Individual students' interpretations of the teacher's "given" lesson (seventh grade) (adapted from Hafeli, 2000). As part of a larger study (see Hafeli, 2000), this textual collage addresses the question "How do students understand the teacher's assumed 'given' of a studio assignment?" Here, the teacher's "must-dos" for a painting assignment (top), which were discussed in class, posted on the board, and distributed in a handout, are "received" and "retold" rather differently by individual students (bottom) who, in my interviews with them, idiosyncratically zeroed in on particular aspects of the assignment.

perceptions of studio thinking, their idiosyncratic conceptions of creative production, *and the tenor and tone of their voices*, are made visually distinct by the use of a variety of type faces and styles.[8]

The textual collage approach for analyzing and presenting data can be applied to any topic an art teacher may be interested in examining, from general questions—such as "How do artists describe their processes as they make artwork?" or "What are students' perceptions of a good teacher?"—to one that deals with a specific classroom issue, such as "How do individual students interpret the goals and guidelines of my assignments?" The textual collage in Figure 4 addresses the latter question. It is adapted from a study on the relationship between students' and teachers' goals and intentions for, and judgments about, student artwork created in art class. Figure 4 contains field data gathered from curriculum documents related to a seventh-grade painting assignment and student interviews about the project. The collage's composition purposefully juxtaposes the teacher's "official" guidelines for the assignment with students' individual understandings of those guidelines, and reveals that students do not always interpret assignments in a uniform fashion. Similar to Figure 3, the act of visually juxtaposing similar and dissonant views and understandings in a text-based collage calls attention to similarities and differences in perceptions among dialogue participants.

Another strategy for analyzing, interpreting, and re-presenting data is one that was discussed earlier in this chapter, *visual mapping*. In Figure 5, a mapping strategy similar to that used in Figure 1 illustrates the anatomy of a high school student's thinking about the process of creating a single artwork, a kinetic wood sculpture of an angel. Using direct quotes from thematically coded interview transcripts, Figure 5 illustrates how an individual student's art ideas are forged through a consideration of personal, family, and cultural narratives, formal issues, responses to and actions on the materials at hand, and, finally, the directives of the lesson itself. While this map is a visual form of data analysis (not unlike a chart or table of coded data chunks), it goes beyond aggregating coded interview excerpts into larger themes. It creates a grounded theoretical model highlighting relationships between the artist's work, the artist's background, the "given" lesson, and the sources for ideas and meaning in the artwork. In this way, the visual mapping moves from data analysis (the coded interview transcripts) to interpretation of findings (a model for how the coded data themes relate to one another in addressing the research question).

ARRIVING AT AND PRESENTING FINDINGS

So far in this chapter, I have described and illustrated several art-based educational research methods that can be used throughout the research process—(1) visual mapping, (2) materials-based interpretation of key ideas in the research, and (3) textual collage. Some of the examples feature written text formatted in art-based ways, such as the piecing and juxtaposition of similar and disparate elements in collage and the use of metaphorical imagery as a conceptual and visual organizing framework for research.

The final art-based method presented here is that of *portraiture*. While text-based "portraits" are frequently used as presentation forms in qualitative research (see Lawrence-Lightfoot & Davis, 2002), art-based educational researchers can use studio media and methods to create artworks that represent, for example, "the uniqueness of each research participant" (Jongeward, 2009, p. 239). Although portraiture can be integrated at any time in the process (as is the case for the other strategies presented throughout this chapter), it is particularly useful when creating a visual synthesis of the study's emerging findings.

Figures 6 and 7, on pages 118 and 119, are examples of visual portraiture approaches I have used in previous qualitative studies. In Figure 6, a study of a high school painting class (Hafeli, 2008) is presented through a portrait of "Sondra," a fictitious student in the class. Figure 6 shows excerpts from my creation

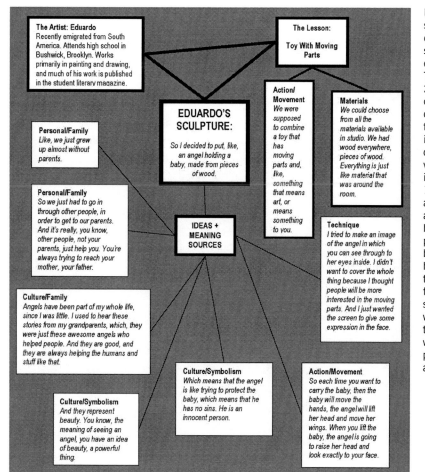

The Artist: Eduardo
Recently emigrated from South America. Attends high school in Bushwick, Brooklyn. Works primarily in painting and drawing, and much of his work is published in the student literary magazine.

The Lesson:
Toy With Moving Parts

EDUARDO'S SCULPTURE:
So I decided to put, like, an angel holding a baby, made from pieces of wood.

Action/ Movement
We were supposed to combine a toy that has moving parts and, like, something that means art, or means something to you.

Materials
We could choose from all the materials available in studio. We had wood everywhere, pieces of wood. Everything is just like material that was around the room.

Personal/Family
Like, we just grew up almost without parents.

Personal/Family
So we just had to go in through other people, in order to get to our parents. And it's really, you know, other people, not your parents, just help you. You're always trying to reach your mother, your father.

IDEAS + MEANING SOURCES

Technique
I tried to make an image of the angel in which you can see through to her eyes inside. I didn't want to cover the whole thing because I thought people will be more interested in the moving parts. And I just wanted the screen to give some expression in the face.

Culture/Family
Angels have been part of my whole life, since I was little. I used to hear these stories from my grandparents, which, they were just these awesome angels who helped people. And they are good, and they are always helping the humans and stuff like that.

Culture/Symbolism
Which means that the angel is like trying to protect the baby, which means that he has no sins. He is an innocent person.

Action/Movement
So each time you want to carry the baby, then the baby will move the hands, the angel will lift her head and move her wings. When you lift the baby, the angel is going to raise her head and look exactly to your face.

Culture/Symbolism
And they represent beauty. You know, the meaning of seeing an angel, you have an idea of beauty, a powerful thing.

FIGURE 5. High school student's conceptualization of studio work in an art class (in Hafeli, 2002). The study (Hafeli, 2002) is based on the question "In what ways do adolescents describe the sources for and influences on the content of their artwork?" This visual map is based on an interview with Eduardo, 17. His sculpture and the meaning he associated with it were heavily influenced by his personal life experiences, being separated from his parents, and by traditional narratives from his culture. The sculpture's moving parts were designed to stage the kidnapping of a baby, with the angel cast as protector and the viewer as kidnapper.

of Sondra's sketchbook, which portrays Sondra and her experiences as she documents the completion of a class assignment. The fictitious sketchbook-as-portrait—though based directly on classroom observation notes, sketches, and interviews with the students and their teacher—tells the story of students' attitudes, as narrated and visualized by Sondra, toward incorporating contemporary art themes into their own work. Rather than simply reporting the actual students' statements—from a researcher's perspective and in a traditional journal article format—I wanted (1) a student to tell the story in her own voice, and (2) to invent a visual format that would mirror the content and findings of the study.

Figure 7 exemplifies another type of portrait, this one of Eduardo, the high school student discussed previously. Figure 7 shows details from a mixed media painting in progress—it incorporates field texts such as coded interview transcripts and other research artifacts related to Eduardo's conception of his creative and ideational processes as an artist. The work contains images of angels, which figure prominently in Eduardo's work, and a wood construction—reminiscent of the additive methods Eduardo used in his angel sculpture—that is attached to and extends out from the surface of the painting. The color palette—various tints and tones of blue, red, green, orange, and yellow, plus white and gray—reflects the colors I originally used to code the data during the initial analysis.

In working on this piece, after completing a focused, traditional qualitative analysis of the data years ago, I now wish to create a more comprehensive and materials-based portrait of the artist and his ideas, one that includes both his own words and my analysis of them (with the inclusion of collaged coded transcripts). In engaging studio processes of painting and construction, similar to my creation of Sondra's journal, I am coming to understand Eduardo as a young artist who was heavily influenced by his personal experiences and culture and full of specific intentions and meanings for his work. In shifting from written text to the "text" of materials, I am in turn expanding my understanding of myself as researcher and as artist, also full of evolving intentions and meanings for my work.

FIGURE 6. Portrait in the form of a fictitious sketchbook (in Hafeli, 2008). In crafting this research as a portrait of a student, by means of the contents of her sketchbook, I hoped to optimize the verisimilitude, or believability, of the study's findings. The spiral bound sketchbook is an actual object: attached to the cover is the introduction to the article (top left) which explains the topic of the study and the presentation format, the top right and bottom left pages are excerpts from the sketchbook, and at bottom left is the outer back cover of the sketchbook, to which is clipped the reference list for the article. More than anything, this method of working—in journal format, with studio materials, and creating a "character's" anecdotal commentary—gave me a heightened sense of "getting inside the heads" of the study participants. The invention of Sondra as synthesis and reporter of the findings, and her sketchbook as their mode of presentation, were invaluable in creating a compelling and accessible research narrative.

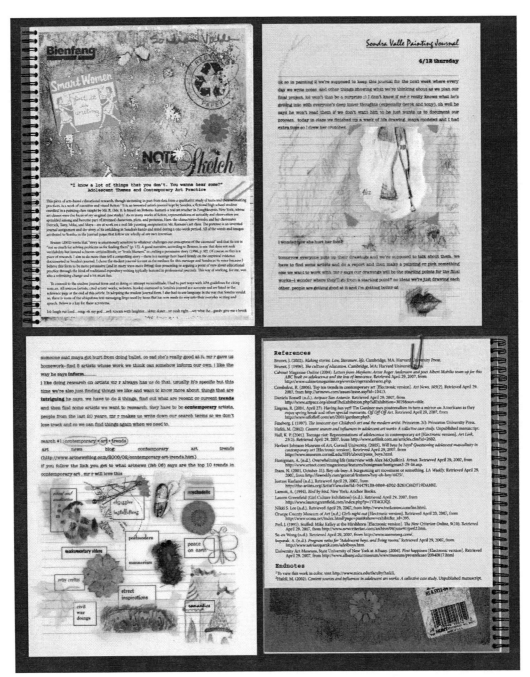

By engaging studio portraiture as an approach to data analysis and the presentation of research findings, the researcher has the opportunity to (1) more intimately understand, or "walk inside the shoes" of, the people whose perceptions form the basis of the study, (2) re-visit and gain new insights about data that may have been previously analyzed through traditional writing forms, and (3) formulate and present findings about research participants and phenomena that cannot be understood through other forms of presentation. In Figures 6 and 7, experimenting with studio materials and creating these portraits has taught me that the more lenses I can use to analyze and interpret the data and the more varied the materials and methods through which I can experience the data and present findings, the richer my study may become.

Art-based educational research methods afford opportunities for new ways of "seeing" data and arriving at "findings." Artistic ways of thinking and practice allow us to view all aspects of the inquiry process—research questions and contexts, key concepts from the related literature, field data collection

FIGURE 7. Eduardo portrait (details). These three details of the painting in progress show portions of Eduardo's interview transcripts and images of the types of angels he referred to in his narrative (top left), a close up of one interview transcript with selective, key ideas prominently displayed and surrounding, contextual elements partly or wholly obscured with ink and paint (top right), and transcripts with original analytical notes and color coding as a ground for painted areas (bottom).

and analysis, and presentation of findings—from fresh perspectives and in new lights. However, with these new ways of "seeing" come interesting questions and conundrums regarding issues of subjectivity, validity, and interpretation. For example, in A/R/Tography, "complication" is an intentional characteristic: "Rather than reassuring a reader/viewer with an easily shared idea or a commonly held belief, a/r/tography recognizes that meaning making can be disturbing, unexpected, and hesitant" (Springgay, Irwin, & Kind, 2008, p. 84). Useful and challenging questions continue to be asked about the validity of art-based educational research, precisely because of the interpretive openness and intentional ambiguity that often accompanies compelling art works and, by extension, art-based educational research (Hafeli, 2009a; O'Donoghue, 2009). As art-based educational research continues to grow and mature in its methods and methodologies, and in its presentation models and dissemination forms, the door is open for new voices and visions to engage these issues.

REFERENCES

Baldacchino, J. (2009). Opening the picture: On the political responsibility of arts-based research: A review essay. *International Journal of Education and the Arts, 10*(Review 3), 1-15.

Barone, T. (2006). Arts-based educational research then, now and later. *Studies in Art Education, 48*(1), 4-8.

Bruner, J. (1996). *The culture of education.* Cambridge, MA: Harvard University Press.

Butler-Kisber, L. (2008). Collage as inquiry. In J. Knowles & A. Cole (Eds.), *Handbook of the arts in qualitative research* (pp. 265-276). Thousand Oaks, CA: Sage.

Cahnmann-Taylor, M., & Siegesmund, R. (2008). *Arts-based research in education: Foundations for practice.* London, England: Routledge.

Davis, D., & Butler-Kisber, L. (1999). Arts-based representation in qualitative research: Collage as a contextualizing analytical strategy. Paper presented at the annual meeting of the American Educational Research Association. Montreal, Quebec, Canada. *Resources in Education, 34*(11), 1-10. Retrieved from ERIC database. (ED 431 790)

de Ville, N., & Foster S. (Eds.). (1994). *The artist in the academy: Issues in fine art education and the wider cultural context.* Southampton, England: John Hansard Gallery, University of Southampton.

Eisner, E. (1981). On the differences between scientific and artistic approaches to qualitative research. *Review of Educational Research, 13*, 1-9.

Eisner, E. (1997). The promise and perils of alternative forms of data representation. *Educational Researcher, 26*(6), 4-10.

Eisner. E. (1998). *The kind of schools we need: Personal essays.* New York, NY: Heinemann.

Eisner, E. (2004). *The arts and the creation of mind.* Cambridge, MA: Yale University Press.

Eisner, E. (2006). Does arts-based research have a future? *Studies in Art Education, 48*(1), 9-18.

Eisner, E. (2008). Art and knowledge. In J. Knowles & A. Cole (Eds.), *Handbook of the arts in qualitative research* (pp. 3-12). Thousand Oaks, CA: Sage.

Elkins, J. (2002). *Stories of art.* London, England: Routledge.

Ely, M., Vinz, R., Downing, M., & Anzul, M. (1997). *On writing qualitative research: Living by words.* London, England: Falmer Press.

Freeland, C. (2002). *But is it art? An introduction to art theory.* Oxford, England: Oxford University Press.

Glaser, B., & Strauss, A. (1967). *The discovery of grounded theory: Strategies for qualitative research.* Piscataway, NJ: Aldine Transaction.

Hafeli, M. (2000). Negotiating "fit" in student artwork: Classroom conversations. *Studies in Art Education, 41*(2), 130-145.

Hafeli, M. (2002). Angels, wings, and Hester Prynne: The place of content in teaching adolescent artists. *Studies in Art Education, 41*(1), 28-46.

Hafeli, M. (2008). "I know a lot of things that you don't, you wanna hear some?" Adolescent themes and contemporary art practice. *Art Education, 61*(2), 59-69.

Hafeli, M. (2009a, April). *Doing art-based educational research (2009 Manuel Barkan Memorial Award Lecture).* Paper presented at the meeting of the National Art Education Association, Minneapolis, MN.

Hafeli, M. (2009b). What happened to authenticity? "Assessing Students' Progress and Achievements in Art" revisited. In R. Sabol & M. Manifold (Eds.), *Through the prism: Looking into the spectrum of writing by Enid Zimmerman* (pp. 215-230). Reston, VA: National Art Education Association.

Harrison, C., & Wood, P. (Eds.). (2002). *Art in theory 1900-2000: An anthology of changing ideas* (2nd ed.). Malden, MA: Wiley-Blackwell.

Harrison, C., Wood, P., & Gaiger, J. (Eds.). (1991). *Art in theory 1645-1815: An anthology of changing ideas.* Malden, MA: Wiley-Blackwell.

Harrison, C., Wood, P., & Gaiger, J. (Eds.). (1998). *Art in theory 1815-1900: An anthology of changing ideas.* Malden, MA: Wiley-Blackwell.

James, P. (2000). Working toward meaning. *Studies in Art Education, 41*(2), 146-163.

Jongeward, C. (2009). Visual portraits: Integrating artistic process into qualitative research. In P. Leavy, *Method meets art: Arts-based research practice* (pp. 239-251). New York, NY: Guilford Press.

Knowles, J., & Cole, A. (2008). Arts informed research. In J. Knowles & A. Cole (Eds.), *Handbook of the arts in qualitative research* (pp. 55-70). Thousand Oaks, CA: Sage.

König, K. (1994). The Franfurt Städelschule. In N. de Ville and S. Foster (Eds.), *The artist in the academy: Issues in fine art education and the wider cultural context* (pp. 137-150). Southampton, England: John Hansard Gallery, University of Southampton.

Lawrence-Lightfoot, S., & Davis, H. (2002). *The art and science of portraiture.* San Francisco, CA: Jossey-Bass.

Leavy, P. (2009). *Method meets art: Arts-based research practice.* New York, NY: Guilford Press.

O'Donoghue, D. (2009). Are we asking the wrong questions in arts-based research? *Studies in Art Education, 50*(3), 354-368.

Plagens, P. (2002). How art has changed a lot. *American Art, 16*(1), 8-10.

Sabol, R., & Manifold, M. (Eds.). (2009). *Through the prism: Looking into the spectrum of writing by Enid Zimmerman.* Reston, VA: National Art Education Association.

Springgay, S., Irwin, R., & Kind, S. (2008). A/r/tographers and living inquiry. In J. Knowles & A. Cole (Eds.), *Handbook of the arts in qualitative research* (pp. 83-92). Thousand Oaks, CA: Sage.

Sullivan, G. (2005). *Art practice as research: Inquiry in the visual arts.* Thousand Oaks, CA: Sage.

Sullivan, G. (2006). Research acts in art practice. *Studies in Art Education, 48*(1), 19-35.

Walker, S. (1996). Designing studio instruction: Why have students make artwork? *Art Education, 49*(5), 11-17.

Walker, S. (2001). *Teaching meaning in artmaking.* Worcester, MA: Davis.

Wypijewski, J. (Ed.). (1998). *Painting by numbers: Komar and Melamid's scientific guide to art.* Berkeley: University of California Press.

ENDNOTES

1   I am an artist, educator, and researcher who critically examines the everyday, real life worlds of art teaching and learning and of studio practice. Any research methodologies and tools that stand to deepen my understanding of these topics are integral to my work and, therefore, fair game for use in the research process. Some writers on art-based research and studio methodology, such as Baldacchino (2009) and Sullivan (2006), caution against their integrative use in the social sciences in general and qualitative research in particular. Twenty years ago, similar arguments for "art not forsaking art" were made in other higher education interdisciplinary contexts (deVille & Foster, 1994, p. 77). These writers might categorize the mixed-methods approaches described in this chapter (integration of studio practice in "traditional" qualitative research) as "decorative research rather than critical inquiry" and "locked within the constraints of the social science research" (Sullivan, 2006, p. 24). While art-based research should not be immune to critique, I do not subscribe to the either-or, all-or-nothing polarities that politicize some of these stances. Mixed and blended research methodologies and methods involving the arts, like other types of interdisciplinary inquiry, have the potential to achieve collectively what their individual parts or disciplines, on their own, cannot. This rationale is obvious in blurred and blended methodological approaches exemplified in contemporary art (Wypijewski, 1998) and much art school instruction (intermedia arts), it continues to permeate other writing on art-based educational research (Barone [2006], Eisner [2006], Leavy [2009]), and it informs the work presented in this chapter.

2   See, for example, Glaser and Strauss (1967).

3   A parallel question for artists is "What are good topics for art?" The futility of attempting a definitive answer in this context has been well documented throughout the history of art and its contemporary practices (Freeland, 2002; Harrison & Wood, 2002; Harrison, Wood, & Gaiger, 1991, 1998; König, 1994; Plagens, 2002).

4   One approach I use myself and with students is to make a piece of self-directed artwork and document through written description and analysis (1) the processes of choosing and working with materials, (2) the forming of intentions/ideas and shifting directions in response to the work in process, (3) perceived problems, challenges, and attempted solutions, and (4) degree of satisfaction with and meanings attributed to the finished artwork. When we compare the individual outcomes of this activity across the group we are invariably surprised to find that there are extremely divergent responses within each part of the assignment and that these differences form certain patterns of results. For example, some love being free from the constraints of externally imposed guidelines while others are frustrated or stymied by the lack of teacher expectations. Some choose to try a new medium while others opt for a material with which they are familiar. Some view the exercise as a safe environment for risk taking and don't mind if the visual result is not viewed (by themselves or the group) as satisfactory while others feel the need to show a certain level of mastery. We do the same activity again, but this time with a set medium (teacher-assigned) and several "must-dos" (also teacher-assigned); then, we compare our responses to the utility, or perceived frivolity, of the imposed constraints. In the process of purposeful "mucking around" with materials ourselves, documenting the process, and comparing the results within these two scenarios, a number of potential research questions arise around the varieties of ways in which artists—and young people in art classes—approach the making of artwork and the degree to which teachers may or may not acknowledge these divergent responses in their teaching and curriculum design.

5   *Construct*, used here as a noun, is meant not as a theoretical abstraction but rather as a concrete idea that encompasses multiple parts, a number of which can become areas of focus in the qualitative study. My definition for the construct *authentic artistic engagement* is articulated in Hafeli (2000, 2002, 2009b) and is similar in sensibility to others' writing on meaning in student artwork (James, 2000; Walker, 1996, 2001).

6   For parallel and multiple examples of how art historians individually envision, depict, and map various movements in art throughout time and place, see Elkins (2002) *Stories of Art*.

7   I created the collage in Table 3 for a chapter on assessment of student learning in art—"What Happened to Authenticity? 'Assessing Students' Progress and Achievements in Art' Revisited," in Sabol and Manifold (2009) *Through the prism: Looking into the spectrum of writing by Enid Zimmerman*.

8   A textual analysis of the views about "what art is," as process expressed by the artists in Table 3, is presented in Hafeli (2009b). For an excellent resource on other alternative art-text crossover approaches in qualitative research, see Ely, Vinz, Downing, and Anzul (1997). For an extensive discussion about the role of collage in art-based educational research, see Butler-Kisber (2008) and Davis and Butler-Kisber (1999).

MARY HAFELI is Dean of the School of Fine and Performing Arts at the State University of New York, New Paltz. Her research examines the ideas, ways of thinking, decisions, and judgments that characterize the active practices of artists, both adults and children, as they make artwork. Her publications trace the sources of young artists' studio ideas and their relation both to what is taught in art class and to practices of contemporary artists. Her work also analyzes the pedagogical conditions that promote students' development of independent artistic judgment, and compares professional artists' descriptions of their studio processes to the ways in which students' art works are evaluated by their teachers. Research awards include the Manuel Barkan Award (2009) from the National Art Education Association (NAEA), Mary Rouse Award from the NAEA Women's Caucus (2006), and the Marilyn Zurmuehlen Award (2005) from the NAEA Seminar for Research in Art Education. Currently a member of the NAEA Research Commission and *Studies in Art Education* Editorial Board, she has served on the editorial board for *Art Education* (2002-2006) and as Chair of the NAEA Research Task Force on Student Learning (1999-2002). She received a BFA in studio art from the University of Michigan, and EdM and EdD degrees from Teachers College, Columbia University.

Visual and Verbal Methods in Studying Educational Identities and Practices

ANNIINA SUOMINEN GUYAS / ASSOCIATE PROFESSOR OF ART EDUCATION, COLLEGE OF VISUAL ARTS, THEATRE AND DANCE, FLORIDA STATE UNIVERSITY

The following section explores visual/verbal data collection, analysis, and representation methods as a way of teachers' study of self and practice. I will explore three methods of working with visual and/or written materials, provide explanations of theoretical frameworks, share examples from previous research projects (method-in-use), and make suggestions for their use. First, I explore *visual inventories* as a method of visually mapping and analyzing one's private and professional contexts. Second, I explain *photo-writing*, a narrative or poetic writing method that helps the researcher tap into the complexity of meanings embedded in visual representations. Finally, I introduce *memory work*, a method of studying personal memories as they relate to wider socio-cultural discourses.

My research, teaching philosophy, educational experience, epistemology, and beliefs about research methodologies, all inform my work. These intertwining, guiding concepts of research work and evolve in response to the needs of the project and the researcher, or other participant/contextual needs. I promote the continued development of methods of data collection and analysis that best respond to the largely visual/material data and information of our field, methods that are essential for understanding human experience as well. The methods discussed here are examples of this philosophy. I use ideas and methods of understanding, documenting, and analyzing visual and material data from other fields such as visual sociology, ethnography, anthropology, geography, cultural studies, and art and then modify these practices to best fit each study I conduct.

VISUAL INVENTORIES

This method, a visual mapping or inventories of one's work or private context, is based on critical visual ethnography and visual anthropology, visual sociology, and inspired by various texts concerning visual methodologies as well as artists and photographers conducting ethnographic inventories of domestic spaces (Chaplin, 1994; Clifford & Marcus, 1986; Collier & Collier, 1986; Grimshaw & Ravetz, 2005; Pink, 2001; Prosser, 1996; Rogoff, 2000; Rose, 2001; Stanczak, 2007). The forms of knowledge that have strongly directed the development of these methods are multi-layered: bodily-knowledge, tacit-knowledge, craftsmanship-knowledge, as well as intuition. My feelings and emotions also impact the direction these methods take.

Visual inventories as a method evolved during my doctoral research (Suominen, 2003). The method entails a visual listing and/or spatial mapping of objects and possessions focusing on the relationships between objects as well as the suggested absences and gaps within the photographed contexts. Studying my immigration experiences I conducted semi-systematic inventories of my belongings to evaluate the status and nature of my adjustment to my new environment. I photographically mapped all my dorm room possessions and compared these to the photos I took of others' dorm rooms. These images functioned as a source of data to explore how various subjectivities were expressed and symbolism assigned onto material possessions in limited spaces. It was evident in the photographs that while the provided physical spaces and furniture of the rooms were the same, objects and non-objects, such as bedding, posters, photographs, scented candles, food items, technology, lightning, music, and temperature of the room were used to represent personal taste and cultural, social, gender, and academic affiliations.

Although I have always used photography in my research, other artistic methods could be used for similar purposes. Both students and educators could perform visual inventories of personal or educational spaces or map other visual/material signifiers. For example, studying the placement of personal items or artist reproductions in a workspace could begin or support an action research project.

PHOTO-WRITING

The method of photo-writing suggests that spontaneous or reflective writing practices are conducted in relation to the acquired or created visual materials with the intention to further one's understanding of the data by verbalizing it. While I prefer to work with a camera, the following method could again be applied to other forms of artistic expression. This method encourages teachers and scholars to explore information available through their artistic creation without the pressure and limitations of structured analytical patterns typical of learned art criticism. In short, the method entails creative writing practices as a reaction or in relationship to photographs taken by the investigator, or artworks constructed by the participants, or pre-existing materials. Regardless of the form or format the writing takes, it is conducted based on visual stimulation. I have applied poetic writing, word listing, and narrative writing to further engage with my photographs. I often "live with" the photographs for a while placing them where they can be seen often for a kind of meditation period. When I feel ready to explore and verbalize the meanings embedded in my photographs I write informal poems or narratives. Sometimes these become part of the final artistic presentation of the study or of a written article; often they are modified and rewritten after the initial "reactionary" writing process.

I understand this method as a meditative creative process, an important bridge between the visual/artistic data collection processes and the critical essay writing and concept development. Replacing, or in addition to conducting, content and context analysis of the collected visual data I suggest that analysis of any research materials would benefit from different forms of creative writing. For example, one could photograph all the visuals posted on the classroom walls to study how a teacher's pedagogical views are materialized in the use of wall space. The investigator could then proceed by creating thematic categories or groupings of the content (e.g. portrayed female artists, classroom rules, diversity), and/or write narratives, memory accounts, or poems based on the studied materials. Good examples of holistic inquiry involving artistic practices and writing can be found in a/r/tography (see Irwin & de Cosson, 2004; Springgay, Irwin, Leggo, & Gouzouasis, 2007).

MEMORY WORK

"Memory work" (Kuhn, 1995; 2000) as a method is a critical analysis and recollection of past events and experiences in contemporary contexts. The method includes narration of past events evoked by personal memories and/or memorabilia or public documents of cultural significance. While the visual and verbal documents are often personally significant to the inquirer, these are analyzed recognizing and in relation to the wider socio-political contexts. The purpose of memory work as a method is to unravel "the connections between memory, its traces, and the stories we tell about the past" (Kuhn, 1995, p. 3) and to analyze the connection between private and public memories as they become embodied in various documents or narrated orally (Clare & Johnson, 2000; Haug, 2000; Treacher, 2000). This method is often used for its potential to unearth silenced and untold stories as fragments of autobiography are written or verbalized for the purpose of research.

In my research, memory work as a method emerged as I was reading and writing stories relating to representations of gender in my family. Utilizing this method I performed various photo writings and analytical readings of a single image; paired previously disconnected family photos to form new connections; analyzed family photographs through the lens of assumed different generational perspectives and by using multiple voices; interviewed family members formally and informally; wrote letters to a character assumed by a family member in a photographic portrait created by myself; and analyzed family narratives in light of private collections of public documents, such as birth records, collections of obituaries, and funeral poetry.

The method helps me theorize and contextualize how gendered subjectivities, the socially learned contextual gender roles, influence my epistemology. In a sense the memory work method could be applied to any project in which the past is studied in conjunction with the present/future and in which private and public memories or experiences are understood as inherently interconnected. To explore how one's educational and artistic experiences have impacted current practices and epistemology one could begin the study by narrating memories evoked by artwork created in the past. These narratives would then be analyzed in relation to past pedagogical movements, educational philosophies, personal autobiography, dominant cultural movements and subcultures (as appropriate), and policy. What defines memory work method is the constant interplay between, and relational nature of, private and public discourses. ∎

REFERENCES

Chaplin, E. (1994). *Sociology and visual presentation.* New York, NY: Routledge.

Clare, M., & Johnson, R. (2000). Method in our madness: Identity and power in a memory work method. In S. Radstone (Ed.), *Memory and methodology* (pp. 179-196). New York, NY: Berg.

Clifford, J., & Marcus, G. (Eds.). (1986). *Writing culture.* Los Angeles: University of California Press.

Collier, J., Jr., & Collier, M. (1986). *Visual anthropology: Photography as a research method.* Albuquerque: University of New Mexico Press.

Grimshaw, A., & Ravetz, A. (2005). *Visualizing anthropology.* Bristol, England: Intellect Books.

Haug, F. (2000). Memory work: The key to women's anxiety. In S. Radstone (Ed.), *Memory and methodology* (pp. 179-196). New York, NY: Berg.

Irwin, R., & De Cosson, A. (Eds.). (2004) *A/R/Tography: Rendering self through arts-based living inquiry.* Vancouver, Canada: Pacific Educational Press, University of British Columbia.

Kuhn, A. (1995). *Family Secrets: Acts of memory and imagination.* New York, NY: Verso.

Kuhn, A. (2000). A journey through memory. In S. Radstone (Ed.), *Memory and methodology* (pp. 179-196). New York, NY: Berg.

Pink, S. (2001). *Doing visual ethnography: Images, media, and representation in research.* Thousand Oaks, CA: Sage.

Prosser, J. (1996). *Image-based research: A source book for qualitative researchers.* Falmer, CO: Routledge.

Rogoff, I. (2000). *Terrra infirma: Geography's visual culture.* New York, NY: Routledge.

Rose, G. (2001). *Visual methodologies: An introduction to the interpretation of visual materials.* Thousand Oaks, CA: Sage.

Springgay, S., Irwin, R., Leggo. C., & Gouzouasis, P. (Eds.). (2007). *Being with a/r/tography.* Rotterdam, The Netherlands: Sense.

Suominen, A. (2003). *Writing with photographs, reconstructing self: An arts-based autoethnographic inquiry* (Doctoral thesis). Retrieved from Ohio Link Electronic Theses & Dissertations Service. (Document No. OSU1061236352)

Stanczak, G. (2007). *Visual research methods: Image, society, and representation.* Thousand Oaks, CA: Sage.

Treacher, A. (2000). Children: Memories, fantasies and narrative: From dilemma to complexity. In S. Radstone (Ed.), *Memory and methodology* (pp. 179-196). New York, NY: Berg.

14 / Body Critical: Child-Centered Poly-Media[1] Research and the Fotonovela

MICHAEL J. EMME / ASSOCIATE PROFESSOR OF ART EDUCATION, UNIVERSITY OF VICTORIA AND **ANNA KIROVA** / PROFESSOR OF EARLY CHILDHOOD EDUCATION, UNIVERSITY OF ALBERTA

ABSTRACT: *Like the school life itself, research in schools that aims to discover and describe childhood experience involves people and power. In this chapter, a variety of arts-based approaches to data gathering, interpretation and dissemination employing the layered complexity of polymedia in the form of fotonovela are described. By collaborating with children through these arts-based methods, we playfully opened the control of their process and purpose as researchers. The range of findings about immigrant children's experience of their first day, school routines, bullying, and playground culture grow out of a photography club and end in student created fotonovelas designed by those students to guide and warn the next new kids who will come to their school.*

Classrooms, hallways, washrooms, cafeterias and playgrounds are each places of power that children work to understand so that they can find the safety, companionship and opportunity that are the adult promises behind public education. "Schools are usually strictly hierarchical institutions, where power relations are regarded as crucial to the proper functioning of the learning and teaching community" (Burke & Grosvenor, 2008, p. 162). Although educational philosophy and pedagogy have undertaken significant changes over the last century, schools remain essentially the same—classrooms, corridors, timetables, bells, and playgrounds.

Children are sensitive to space, and designed or built environments are significant factors in their educational journey. In childhood, walking through the door into a classroom for the first time is an exhilarating risk. The space, full of smells, heat, and sounds, that others seem to take for granted, is strangely intense for the new student. The choice or necessity of submitting to any new environment is generally accompanied by a hyper-awareness of one's body. In a school situation, while the new child's movements may feel awkward, slow and exaggerated, the teacher and classmates all appear to move with confidence. The language, equipment, activities, rules and rituals are not the child's yet, so she/he pays close attention to gestures, strains to decipher words, and engages all of her/his senses searching for clues in all of the complexity about what to do, when and with whom.

Although, as John Holt (1995) described it, the spaces, places, textures and smells that hold meaning to the young child are mostly forgotten or lost to the adult, as childhood memories, some remain vivid into adulthood. They are especially powerful for immigrant children whose first experiences of school may coincide with experiences of living in a new country and hearing a new language. The following is an adult recollection of such an experience:

> I was so overwhelmed all the time. Everything was so new. Just to know where the door to my classroom was required so much energy. There was so much to figure out. My teacher had no idea what to do to help me. She did not realize that she should take me around the school and show me where things were and how to get from place to place. It all seemed so obvious to her and to the other children. Of course how could she have known what life was like in Fiji. I was left to navigate my own system. I was left to figure out my own way. I would count how many steps it was from the classroom door to outside. Then I would have to figure out what to do to get back. What I did most recesses was worry about how to get back to the door to my classroom. I was afraid to go too far out. All the doors looked the same. There was no way for me to differentiate. Every door could have been my door. I came to realize early on that it was important to be at the right door. I could not play at recess until I got the whole door thing figured out. (Dachyshyn, 2004, p. 12)

Reflecting on concepts about simultaneity and the geography of power proposed by Edward Soja (1989), for new students, their first experience of a classroom and school can make it seem that all of the space is taken up with bodies, gestures, language, games and tasks that may feel inaccessible, leaving that new child feeling powerless. We wondered how participation in an arts-based collaborative study could empower children to become researchers of their own school experiences as they live them?

CREATIVE OPENINGS FOR COLLABORATIVE RESEARCH

This chapter describes an arts-based research project conducted in collaboration with a small group of students in an inner-city elementary school in Western Canada. All of the children involved are members of immigrant or refugee families where English is not the first language in the home. Because most of the children's families arrived in Canada within one year prior to the beginning of the study, the research setting was their first experience of school in English and in Canada. Framed by a discussion of more recent directions in critical theory (Santos, 2001), this chapter will explore the need to playfully overlay memory and presence in research conducted in collaboration with this small group of children, giving particular focus to the experience of power relations as they move between home and school, between countries and cultures, and among peer groups. Informed, also, through a phenomenological understanding of play as experience and meaning (Kirova & Emme, 2010), researchers joined these elementary school students in playfully exploring their school and relationships. Beginning with photography, collaborative arts-based research (Emme, Kirova, Kamau, & Kosanovich, 2006) led to performance and creation that generated fotonovelas as shared research designed to bridge the gap between "data" and "fiction" to tell artful, embodied stories of arrival, loneliness, misunderstandings and connection.

PHOTO CLUB: DROPPING-IN BETWEEN THE CLASSROOM AND THE PLAYGROUND

The study began with play.[2] For the first photo club session, we invited all 14 children in a grade 4/5 class to join a photography club that was held during lunch recess. Only two of the children chose not to be involved in those first playful moments that provided the opportunity to take a digital camera around the school during recess to collect snapshots. After about 15 minutes the children returned and learned how to plug the memory card from the camera into a printer to generate small thumbnail prints. Enthusiasm about the camera was followed by enthusiasm about the prints. Some children cut out and exchanged their pictures. Others put them in scrapbooks, and still others dropped the pages of pictures on the floor in their haste to run outside to get in on the last minutes of recess. For some children in the class, that was the full experience. Eight of the children chose to return to the next photo club session and remained members of the club for almost 2 school years. To help these children develop a sense of purposeful use of the cameras, we invited them to think of themselves as reporters.

Indicating some innate awareness about photography as a means to interact, as described by Sharples (2003), the children took photographs of each other to craft Photo-ID badges. One of the first tasks of the "reporters" was to take photographs of places in the school building that they found confusing. It is important to note here that the school in which the study took place was built in 1912 and thus reflected the views of learning environments of that time rather than of the 21st century. In its reconstruction in 2004, rather than removing the old school, a decision was made to acknowledge the importance of the past and incorporate it in the present. The thoughtful, artful amalgamation of architectural elements from different historical eras in the school attracted the attention of two British educational historians who wrote the following about it:

> Within the reception area is a pronounced display of educational technology from the past: an original slate mounted on the wall, the original terrazzo flooring and old photographs and artifacts.... The stairwells have kept the original stairs and banisters (the risers came from the Carnegie street mill in Pittsburg[h] in 1911), but the stairway now features ceramic tiles on the walls. (Burke & Grosvenor, 2008, p. 156)

However, this meeting of past and present in the school building created a sense of confusion in some of the young photographers. For example, a photo of the hallway with the artifacts and photographs of the wall was described by the child who took the photo as a "museum" (see Figure 1) The stairwells were seen as confusing because "you don't know which floor you are on," (see Figure 2) and the entire school was perceived as a "castle"—a metaphor for undeniable power.

FIGURE 1 (LEFT). Student photograph: The school "history wall" and bodies-in-motion. Two different ways photography represents time. (PhotoShop alteration by researcher—as per ethics requirement.)

FIGURE 2 (RIGHT). Student photograph: School stairwell. A child's exploration of, point-of view, lens perspective and abstraction. (PhotoShop alteration by researcher—as per ethics requirement.)

CHILD-RESEARCHERS' SEARCH FOR PATTERNS, THEMES, AND MEANINGFUL STORIES

It seemed to us that the children really enjoyed "being on a photo-journalistic mission" and we asked them what other aspects of the school they might enjoy exploring and documenting. A decision to take pictures on the playground, as their next assignment, was unanimous. The children collectively generated a list of "things that happen on the playground" that they used for a photographic "treasure hunt." This search for specific images struck a balance between play and investigation, reflected in many other studies involving kids and cameras (Hubbard, 1991; Kids with Cameras, n. d.).

Given the limited number of cameras and our goal to help children become collaborators while "on assignment," the children were paired and asked to focus on the list of activities and situations they generated prior to their fieldwork. In talking with kids about what it might be like to be a reporter with a camera, we asked the students to imagine the kinds of things they might see in a walk around the school. These included: kids rules/adults rules, playing/reading, leading/following, alone/together, listening/ talking, etc. Based on their extended ideas, we created a checklist that became a bit of a treasure hunt. While the first few minutes of the reporters' work on the playground was predominantly about taking pictures of their friends, the rest of time was spent looking for moments that they could document in relation to the list they carried to the playground. Without dividing the responsibilities between the partners in the pair prior to the fieldwork, most of the children agreed that the one who is not holding the camera at the moment would "look for things that the photographer will shoot." Once an image was shot and a box checked, the pairs of kids traded roles and carried on in search of their next discovery.

In collaboration with the children, we examined this second set of images for their clarity and for their pertinence to the themes on the list of playground activities. We asked the children to use color-coding to indicate which of the images they took and printed belonged to which theme by placing a colored dot next to the image. This simple selection process helped the children discover that an image can have, and it usually does have more than one meaning. The question, "Which of the possible stories would you like to tell?" was guiding children's thinking about meanings embedded in possibilities. From there, the natural development of the process of learning to tell a story was to choose a single image from each child's collection and place it in the center of a three-frame storyboard (See Figure 3). With this we invited the children to use drawing, writing or photography to describe what happened before or after the selected image. A more traditional interview session with each child who created these first

FIGURE 3. Student collage storyboard: Sequential artmaking as child-researcher's data analysis. (PhotoShop alteration by researcher—as per ethics requirement.)

storyboards followed in order to clarify meanings of both images and words (Kirova & Emme, 2008).

THE POWER OF PLAY IN RESEARCH

From the trajectory of this first cycle in the research, the dance-like ebb and flow between child-directed and researcher input is evident. There is a significant correlation between the sometimes playful negotiations by a small group of children with several researchers, and Soja's thoughts about the disorientation created by contemporary architecture (Soja, 1989). As researchers, our broad interest was in the embodied ways that immigrant children both successfully and unsuccessfully engaged with school life. We were also interested to discover if child-directed photo-storytelling and creative play could be integrated into the young participants' experience. Much of what we did with our young research-partners was guided by their interests, enthusiasms and concerns.

While Soja is interested in a geographer's reading of the fragmentation that many see as a consequence of late capitalism, children, and particularly immigrant and refugee children across generations, have responded to their daily experience of disorientation by playing (Kirova, 2010). As we have discussed elsewhere (Kirova & Emme, 2009) children's play is an effective, embodied strategy for understanding that involves the collective creation of new worlds through a combination of invention and analogy built, in part, from pieces gathered in the new world of adults which is largely beyond the children's control.

FIGURE 4 (TOP LEFT). Student photograph: Investigating the school as a place full of significant objects.

FIGURE 5 (TOP RIGHT). Student photograph: Initial camera play included kids photographing each other photographing (meta-photography) which created an awareness of point-of-view.

FIGURE 6 (BOTTOM). Student-generated playground photograph: Initial camera experiences were just about play as a way of developing relationships between researchers and students.

All images have PhotoShop alteration by researcher—as per ethics requirement.

Between the children's playful first uses of the camera (See Figures 4–6) and the narrative possibilities when their images were sequenced with words to function as a storyboard, several competing conventions that were familiar to many of the children converged. Written language and the telling of both fictional and "realistic" stories were a daily experience of children's work in school. The body language of the playground, the informal learning of games and territories, and the formation and collapse of friendship alliances all constituted another, more self-directed aspect of child-life in the school day.

STORYBOARDS AS THE SYNTAX FOR MULTILINGUAL STORYTELLING

For many, the storyboards were also familiar in their echoing of the visual sequencing, dialogue and thought balloons and the text box commentary from comic book conventions. These conventions, described by artist commentators such as Will Eisner (1985) and Scott McCloud (1994) encourage each storyteller to decide how much to rely on each of the media forms of written language, drawing, body language, photography, and sequencing. We argue that in the multi-lingual, multi-cultural context of this (and many other) classrooms, a storytelling form that can be effective on so many different levels becomes an opportunity for each child to follow their competence and share their ideas most effectively with students and teachers sensitive to the many ways that communication can happen. Nakazawa (2005), a developmental psychologist, and McClay (2000), a contemporary literacy expert, find growing evidence of competency in reading poly-media texts among the young. We think children who frequently approach disorientation playfully may find meaning from making art in a comic book form.

In discussing their first storyboards, the children and researchers came to a shared interest in telling stories to others. We chose a new photo-game that involved role-playing. In teams, children photographed themselves acting the part of the principal, the school nurse, older kids in the junior high playground, and as their own teacher. This role-play introduced elements of performance, direction, body awareness, and commentary on social structure. Alsop's notion of poly-media (2007) describes a convergence of individuals who bring their skills and cultural visions to a collaborative process of creativity. Because the digital technologies encouraged images to be used in a variety of ways, much of our shared process with the children involved discovering the many possible stories and perspectives in a single narrative moment. This blending and negotiation of power and purposes resonates with theorists (Habersmith, 2005, Petrescu, 2007, Soja, 1989) who have argued for a shift away from metaphors of history and linearity in explaining power relationships to geography and metaphors of space and simultaneity.

FOTONOVELAS AS A CREATIVE-COLLABORATIVE RESEARCH PROCESS

The children's common experience of being new to the school and their growing comfort working collectively on story telling and image-making projects created a transition to the performance of remembered experiences that could be photographed and then crafted into comic book form based on the *fotonovela*. Though their 60-plus year history as a form of popular literature in Mexico is largely about adult audiences, the combination of photographic panels, comic book sequencing and simple dialogue make fotonovelas a good fit for younger audiences (Emme, Kirova, & Cambre, 2006). At the center of all research focused on people are relationships. One of the advantages of an arts-based approach to research is that you can allow those relationships to remain complex and dynamic. As an artist, you can enter a situation with a very light grasp on what will constitute "success" because your practice has made you responsive to people, materials and moments as a means of discovering purpose. Defining objectives after, rather than before, is part of the rigor of being an artist. In the context of this study, we had to frame our work in formal terms when negotiating with granting agencies, the University, and the school district just to get the resources to begin. Once that permission was given, our decision was that it was more important to be responsive to the kids' interests, directions, and needs than it was to carry agendas into their day. Many months of relationship building and open play with cameras in the "drop-in" context of the photo club helped us find a place in the kids' creative lives. This loosely structured time helped us to recognize how the children would guide the research in terms of both methods and questions, and eventually lead to a number of themes, including creative inquiries into: "First Day," "Lunchtime," "Getting into Basketball," and "Bullying."

The first fotonovelas the children created with our help were brief stories about the children's memories of their first day in a Canadian school. The idea of developing these came from the individual interviews with the children about their experiences at school when they first came to Canada. Although the interviews were conducted in children's first languages with the help of bilingual research assistants, as researchers we felt that the children remembered a lot more about their experiences of the first day in school than they could verbally express (Kirova & Emme, 2006). Based on the importance of this particular experience indicated by all children, and children's demonstrated interest in role-playing, we decided to offer them an opportunity to act this moment out in the form of tableau.

BODY CRITICISM: TABLEAU AS A SPACE BETWEEN EXPERIENCE AND REPRESENTATION

As a performative art form, tableau is a non-language-dependent medium that "transcends the customary limits of discursive language, making coherent the knowledge and the understanding that students may not be able, at first, to express in spoken language but that, once embodied in movement, can be translated into spoken and written language" (Salvio, 1990, p. 272). A further description of tableau as a still-image in structuring drama work clarifies that in the process, either "groups devise an image using their own bodies to crystallize a moment, idea, or theme, or an individual acts as sculptor to a group" (Neelands, 1998, p. 19).

The process we used involved the children identifying characters (teacher, principal, parent, "mean kid," "future friend") that they and the researchers should play. Many students took turns physically entering (or because of their memories, being escorted) through the doorway of the classroom for the first time. Using a digital camera connected to a laptop[3] so that the viewfinder was large enough for many eyes at once, these moments were photographed. This unique approach to working with a single camera combines a collaborative self-portrait process (Emme, 2003) and participatory theatre (Conrad & Campbell, 2008) to support children working through an embodied recollection of an important moment that can be represented in a tableaux photograph (Pauli, 2006).

GETTING PERSONAL: STUDENTS' DEVELOPMENT OF FIRST DAY STORYBOARDS AND TABLEAU

Like their images of things that happen on the playground, each student took this first photograph depicting the central moment of entering their new classroom and placed it at the center of a 3-frame storyboard (See Figure 7). This time, with the group as a creative resource, each student directed the production of their personal "before" and "after" moments as tableau photographs. Once the three images for each student were in hand, each used comic book thought and speech bubbles to recall what they heard and to suggest what they imagined others were thinking at that critical moment. The children's unsolicited use of comic book conventions in their earlier playground storyboards served as an invitation to the adult researchers to encourage that approach with these, more reflective stories.

FIGURE 7. Student "First Day" stories. Collective tableaux based on individual student's stories of entering a Canadian classroom for the first time. (PhotoShop alteration by researcher—as per ethics requirement.)

FIGURE 8. Student tableau: Based on student research about food at home and in the school, this single page is part of an 8-page book developed by the students to represent choices and procedures the next new kids should know to navigate their first trip to the cafeteria. (PhotoShop alteration by researcher—as per ethics requirement.)

STUDENTS' CREATIVE PROCESS AS COLLABORATIVE RESEARCH PROCESSES

From this, our conversations and brainstorming with the children led to thinking about stories that they could create for other new students who would come to the school. Themes were proposed such as getting involved in games, dealing with bullying and how lunch (a free program available to all students) worked from a kid's point of view. Each theme touched on issues of power, expectations, fitting in, and keeping safe that were daily experiences in school. The students developed processes of image-based researching, storyboard interpretation, representation through tableaux performance, collective composition and sequencing of events in constructing the fotonovela, and individual reflection through the addition of dialogue and thought bubbles.

LUNCHTIME ROUTINES: STORIES FROM OLD-NEW KIDS TO NEW-NEW KIDS

In the case of the story about the cafeteria, an initial documentary process combined pictures of the actual cafeteria, line-ups and people with an opportunity to take the cameras home and photograph "home food." This second step opened up conversations where differences in diet and even the aesthetics of food were discussed. Not surprisingly, the schools ban on "junk food" was also a focus of the kids' attention. A collective story about food was storyboarded and performed in tableau. When the children had the opportunity to add text to their copy of the visual story they were able to highlight what they found fun and frustrating about the experience. Interestingly, when we worked on creating a single text that could be shared with "next new students" (Figure 8) the group self-edited their frustrations about food and lines so that the story read more like instructions about getting served lunch (Kirova, Mohamed, & Emme, 2006).

For many children school is the first opportunity to experience regulation both as a structure (i.e. the various forms of institutional coordination), and as a process (i.e. the way in which "the rules of the game" are constructed) (Dupriez & Maroy, 2003). These experiences may be confusing because, even though school is "a locus of discipline, control and power," some manifestations of the above are more obvious and clear cut than others (Simpson, 2000, p. 60). Furthermore, as Schimmel (2003) points out, there is a fundamental conflict between the formal or official curriculum taught through lectures, texts, and tests and the informal or hidden curriculum taught through school rules, punishments, procedures,

and norms. The lunchtime fotonovela developed by the children provided a guide to the newcomer to the school to navigate the cafeteria rules and procedures.

NEW EYES: THE POWERFUL POSSIBILITIES OF UNBINDING POLYMEDIA TEXTS

By now it should be clear that the fotonovela form as a polymedia text allows critical and creative input into meaning from young researcher-participants all through the information gathering, analysis and presentation stages. We have published elsewhere (Kirova & Emme, 2008) on another fotonovela project, "Getting into Basketball" where these same students explored the challenges of a newcomer who was excluded from a basketball game at recess. What is important here, with our focus on contemporary critical theory, is the choice to invite a number of kids from another classroom, who were not directly involved with the story development to write their own text balloons for the basketball story. With the student creators' support, this new group of kids were given the visual layout of that fotonovela with all of the student author's words removed. These visually rich, but textually blank stories were then given to a new group of kids who were invited to write their own text balloons based on their visual reading of the body language and visual sequencing that had been so carefully developed by the initial group of young researchers. One of the most insidiously powerful structures in the classroom is the array of bound publications and products that frame meaning and success through binding, packaging and seeming inaccessible production values (Apple & Christian-Smith, 1991). By unbinding our own research data and giving some control of it to our student researchers, and asking them to give some of it to other students, we accessed additional stories and meanings and also modeled a strategy of critical play with classroom texts that could be applied to any resource in the school. Thus, this strategy introduced further complexity to the layers of power relations in both the research process and the many perspectives this familiar playground narrative generated.

COMPLEX COLLABORATIONS: COMBINING FOTONOVELA RESEARCH WITH OTHER CLASSROOM AGENDAS

The fotonovelas described briefly were completed during the first year of the photo club. While we continued to offer the photo club at the school on a bi-weekly basis, and continued to explore different topics with the children that interested them (i.e., dress at home and school which resulted in publishing a

FIGURE 9. Student tableau: Student's personal bullying experiences. Performed, photographed, designed and written by students in the context of a counselor-guided bullying response strategies workshop. (PhotoShop alteration by researcher—as per ethics requirement.)

"fashion magazine" about the school dress), we were also invited to combine this research process with the work of a counselor who was guiding a class through investigating choices to avoid bullying. The process was dynamic and the students engaged with the idea of identifying situations, performing them, and visually organizing their stories.

When it came to collectively adding text, though, it was interesting to see how "in class" with the counselor differed from the "photo club" process. This more teacher-directed research purpose resulted in text that was more focused on external rather than reflective narrative. Because the counselor's curriculum involved teaching a set of escalating response strategies a child could use if they found themselves in a bullying situation, the children's stories strongly mirrored those planned structures (see Figure 9). Where there was resistance, or childrens' views that did not reflect the proscribed narratives, they chose to act them out in the tableau rehearsals, but did not incorporate them into the final fotonovelas. This suggests that their poly-media approach, wherein students shape the experience, in fotonovela research is sensitive to the power relations between student and teacher when it is used in a school setting.

CONCLUSION

As poly-media forms, the children's fotonovelas accommodated each child's physicality and body language, unique voices and perspectives while resulting in shared creative works. Not only could blended and distinctive stories be negotiated (and re-negotiated), but accessible newer technologies made it possible for the fotonovelas, as arts-based research, to be shared and altered by young readers not party to the initial research process. Returning to Soja's (1989) reconsideration of critical theory from a geographical perspective, it is possible to think of what we are calling the "fotonovela method" as having a complex architecture. Combining the multiple modes of communication and the possibility of layers of construction and re-construction with children's play as research not only allowed for the children's participation in the research findings to be expressive, adaptable and available, but encouraged the extension and expansion of the creative community to others who could have a hand in continuing the poly-media research process.

As represented by the work of both child and adult researchers in this chapter, fotonovela research combines the possibility of an overwhelming richness of data combining both images and text, thus allowing for multiple voices to emerge which in turn encourage multiple interpretations. These multiple possibilities raise challenging questions about authority and validity that are at the heart of debates around the emergence of arts-based research (O'Donoghue, 2009). Literature that focuses on narrative and auto-ethnographic approaches certainly speak to some of this (Irwin & de Cosson, 2004). Our own research with children suggests a social semiotic approach to understanding image manipulation as a resource to meaning (Emme & Kirova, 2005). Like current interest in social theory on play as both representation and as an "an attitude characterized by a readiness to improvise in the face of an everchanging world" (Malaby, 2008, p. 2) this group of children used fotonovela to playfully research and represent a new world.

REFERENCES

Alsop, R. (2007). *Compositional processes in developing poly-media performance works.* Retrieved from http://people.smartchat.net. au/~rogeralsop/Compositional_Processes_R_Alsop.doc

Apple, M. W., & Christian-Smith, E. (Eds.). (1991). *The politics of the text-book.* New York, NY: Routledge.

Burke, C., & Grosvenor, I. (2008). *Schools.* London, England: Reaktion Books.

Conrad, D., & Campbell, G. (2008). Participatory research—An empowering methodology with marginalized populations. In P. Liamputtong & J. Rumbold (Eds.), *Knowing differently: Arts-based & collaborative research methods* (pp. 247-263). New York, NY: Nova Science.

Dashychyn, D. (2004). *Children dwelling in the absence of home.* Unpublished manuscript, University of Alberta, Edmonton, Alberta, Canada.

Dupriez, V., & Maroy, C. (2003). Regulation in school system: A theoretical analysis of the structural framework of the school system in French-speaking Belgium. *Journal of Education Policy, 18*(4), 375-392.

Eisner, W. (1985). *Comics and sequential art.* New York, NY: Poorhouse Press.

Emme, M. (2003). Critical self-portraits. *Photoed, 8*(2), 32-35.

Emme, M., & Kirova, A. (2005). Photoshop semiotics: Research in the age of digital manipulation. *Visual Arts Research, 31*(1), 145-153.

Emme, M., Kirova, A., & Cambre, C. (2006). Fotonovela and collaborative storytelling: Researching the spaces between image, text and body. *Exposure, 39*(2), 45-51.

Emme, M., Kirova, A., Kamau, O., & Kosanovich, S. (2006). Ensemble research: A means for immigrant children to explore peer relationships through fotonovela. *Alberta Journal of Educational Research in Education, 52*(3) 160-181.

Habersmith, J. (2005). *Queer time and place: Transgender bodies, subcultural lives.* New York: New York University Press.

Holt, J. (1995). *How children learn.* New York, NY: Da Capo Press.

Hubbard, J. (1991). *Shooting back.* New York, NY: Chronicle.

Irwin, R. L., & de Cosson, A. (Eds.). (2004). *A/r/tography: Rendering self through arts based living inquiry.* Vancouver, BC: Pacific Educational Press.

Kids with Cameras. (n.d.). Retrieved from www.kids-with-cameras.org/home/

Kirova, A. (2010). Children's representations of cultural scripts in play: Facilitating transition from home to preschool in an inter-cultural early learning program for refugee children. *Diaspora, Indigenous, and Minority Education: An International Journal, 4*(2), 1-18.

Kirova, A., & Emme, M. (2006). Using photography as a means of phenomenological seeing: "Doing phenomenology" with immigrant children. *Indo-Pacific Journal of Phenomenology Special Edition: Methodology, 6*(1). Retrieved from www.ipjp.org

Kirova, A., & Emme, M. (2008). Fotonovela as a research tool in image-based participatory research with immigrant children. *International Journal for Qualitative Methodologies, 7*(2), 35-57.

Kirova, A., & Emme, M. (2009). Immigrant children's bodily engagement in accessing their lived experiences of immigration: Creating poly-media descriptive texts. *Phenomenology & Practice, 3*(1), 59-79. Retrieved from www.phandpr.org/index.php/pandp

Kirova, A., Mohamed, F., & Emme, M. (2006). Learning the ropes, resisting the rules: Immigrant children's representation of the lunchtime routine through fotonovela. *Journal of the Canadian Association for Curriculum Studies.* Retrieved from www.csse.ca/CACS/JCACS/V4N1/jcacs_V4N1.html

Malaby, T. (2008). Anthropology and play: The contours and playful experience [Abstract]. *Social Science Research Network.* Retrieved from http://ssrn.com/abstract=1315542

McClay, J. (2000). "Wait a second": Negotiating complex narratives in "Black and White." *Children's Literature in Education, 31*(2), 91-106.

McCloud, S. (1994). *Understanding comics: The invisible art.* New York, NY: Harper Paperbacks.

Nakazawa, J. (2005) Development of manga (comic book) literacy in children. In D. Schwalb, J. Nakazawa & B. Shwalb (Eds.), *Applied developmental psychology: Theory, practice and research from Japan* (pp. 23-42). Greenwich, CN: Information Age.

Neelands, J. (Ed.). (1998). Structuring drama work: A handbook of available forms in theatre and drama. Cambridge, England: Cambridge University Press.

O'Donoghue, D. (2009). Are we asking the wrong questions in arts-based research? *Studies in Art Education, 50*(4), 352-368.

Pauli, L. (Ed.). (2006). *Acting the part: Photography as theatre.* London, England: Merrell.

Petrescu, D. (2007). Altering practices: Feminist politics and poetics of space. London, England: Routledge.

Salvio, P. M. (1990). The world, the text, and the reader. In A. A. Lunsford, H. Moglen & J. Slevin (Eds.), *The right to literacy* (pp. 269-275). New York, NY: Modern Language Association.

Santos, M. (2001). Memory and narrative in social theory: The contributions of Jacques Derrida and Walter Benjamin. *Time & Society, 10*(2-3), 163-189.

Schimmel, D. (2003). Collaborative rule-making and citizenship education: An antidote to the undemocratic hidden curriculum. *American Secondary Education, 31*(3), 16-35.

Sharples, M. (2003) Children as photographers: An analysis of children's photographic behaviour and intentions at three age levels. *Visual Communication, 2*(3), 303-330.

Simpson, B. (2000). Regulation and resistance: Children's embodiment during the primary-secondary school transition. In A. Prout (Ed.), *The body, childhood, and society* (pp. 60-77). London, England: Macmillan.

Soja, E. (1989). *Postmodern geographies: The reassertion of space in critical social theory.* London, England: Verso.

ENDNOTES

1   "Poly-Media" is a term… chosen to create a distinction from "Multi-Media." As described by Alsop (2007) poly-media artmaking is considered as a collaborative system in which all collaborators, such as composers, video artists, choreographers, actors, and writers contribute to the final product by interacting collaboratively throughout the development process to the eventual presentation of the work. The potential for all of these creators and processes to retain distinctive and even contradictory elements is one reason why this system is distinct from a "multi-media" approach where the different aspects may be developed independently and then marshaled towards the end of the development process.

2   The playful first moment of this research was actually preceded by nearly a year of negotiations among the researchers, the University, several school boards and provincial officers tasked with enforcing very recently passed freedom of information and privacy legislation. With much work, the shared enthusiasm of the researchers, supporting principal and classroom teacher calmed the various institutions that were torn between interest in the research purpose and approach and a self-imposed conservatism about taking risk in the face of untested ethics and privacy legislation. You will note that all of the images have been Photoshopped using the same, "cut-out" filter. The capacity to do this was actually one of the ways we assured concerned administrators that we would be able to allow the kids some playful freedom with the cameras while ensuring some anonymity in using their images.

3   Canon digital point-and-shoot cameras are particularly useful in the classroom as they have a function called "remote capture." When the camera is connected to a computer and the software opened, the viewfinder is live on the computer screen and all camera functions (including manual exposure settings) can be controlled from the computer. Hit the spacebar to snap and the image is saved directly to the computer. If the computer is connected to a data projector, the whole class can look through the projection of a single camera viewfinder at once.

MICHAEL J. EMME, an Associate Professor of Art Education at the University of Victoria in British Columbia, is an exhibiting artist, educational researcher and studio instructor. His research centers around the ways that "lens media" and digital technology can support collaborative-creative inquiry. Emme has co-created comic books, gallery art, installations, and performance works with elementary students, educators, and fine arts graduate students in Canada and the USA. He has also taught at the University of Alberta, Central Washington University and the Nova Scotia College of Art and Design. Dr. Emme has published extensively in art and education journals and served as editor of the *Journal of Social Theory and Art Education*. He currently edits *The Canadian Art Teacher*. He was honored as the state post-secondary art educator of the year in Washington in 1999, and the provincial post-secondary art educator of the year in British Columbia in 2009.

ANNA KIROVA is Professor of Early Childhood Education, Faculty of Education, University of Alberta. Her research focuses on the need for understanding the culturally and linguistically diverse children's experiences of loneliness and isolation at school, and the possibility such an understanding offers for culturally responsive pedagogy. Her wide-ranging repertoire of research methods includes hermeneutic phenomenology, arts-based methodologies, and community-based participatory action research aimed at gaining insights into human phenomena by including vulnerable populations in research that is both meaningful and empowering. Her current collaborative research in developing an intercultural early learning program for newcomer children in which children maintain their home language and culture while learning English has resulted in a number of documents providing guidance to early childhood educators in supporting young English language learners' bilingual and bicultural identities which has potential to lead to socially just institutional reform in schools and curriculum development and implementation.

SECTION III: UNDERSTANDING PEOPLE

Introduction

MELANIE L. BUFFINGTON AND **SARA WILSON MCKAY**

HOW DO WE UNDERSTAND PEOPLE INVOLVED WITH OUR PRACTICE?

MUSINGS AND WONDERINGS FROM THE FIELD

Why are teachers in my school doing the same art projects from when I was in school? How do trends in our field come and go, as evidenced by what is published in *Art Education*? At my previous school, the teacher climate was very supportive of arts across the curriculum, but here at this new school it is not. How can I better understand this new working environment? How is my school culture changing due to an influx of new students? What are the motivations of one graffiti artist's legal and illegal practices? When, how, and why was my state art education association formed and how has it changed over time?

Art education involves the study of artists, art teachers, art students, museum educators, administrators, policy makers, and others involved in the arts and education. In order to understand these people as individuals and groups, researchers may utilize a range of methodologies. Though other research methodologies relate well to understanding people, we find ethnography, historical research, and portraiture to be particularly useful for developing in-depth situated knowledge of people.

Researchers choose to conduct **ethnographic research** when they are interested in understanding a particular culture-sharing group. As art educator Vesta Daniel frequently says, culture is "the way we do things around here." Culture-sharing groups vary widely and could include a group of artists who share a common studio space, all the teachers at a school, a group of students, or a group of supportive parents.

Typically, researchers employ **historical research** to understand past events and people in relation to a contemporary situation. This methodology frequently relies heavily on the use of documents and may involve interviews or other methods of data collection to understand multiple perspectives on a past issue.

Portraiture is a methodology that usually involves looking closely at an individual, a group of individuals, or an event. The researcher writes in a highly descriptive manner that is attuned to the many nuances of a situation or person.

ETHNOGRAPHIC RESEARCH

15 / Ethnography

ALICE LAI / ASSOCIATE PROFESSOR OF THE ARTS AND EDUCATIONAL
STUDIES AT EMPIRE STATE COLLEGE

ABSTRACT: *This chapter describes the social research methodology known as ethnography. Ethnography has evolved from the study of non-Western society to the study of the researcher's own community. Eschewing a positivist approach, ethnography employs a naturalistic and exploratory approach to the study of culture and human groups. First-hand and immersive field experience distinguishes ethnography from other qualitative research methodology. The mainstays of ethnographic research methods include participant observation, interviewing, field notes, audio or visual documentation, artifact collection, and archival study. Six important features of educational ethnography are introduced: A study of a culture, multiple data collection methods and diverse forms of data, prolonged engagement in the field, researcher as instrument, high status of participant's own narratives in ethnographic writing, and cycle of theory building (Walford, 2008). These six features are illustrated with current ethnographic studies in art education in order to offer K-12 art teachers ideas for conducting ethnographic study.*

ETHNOGRAPHY AND ITS APPLICATION IN EDUCATIONAL RESEARCH

Rooted in 19th-century Western anthropology, ethnography is a descriptive account of a culture (Hammersley & Atkinson, 2007; Walford, 2008). Historically, missionaries and travelers who lived in a non-Western society for an extended period of time, often acquired language proficiency to converse with the local people, and observed and participated in their everyday life activities, produced ethnographic accounts. Such first-hand and immersive "field" experience allowed ethnographers to gain an intimate understanding of distinctive ways of life, cultural values, belief systems, and patterns of behavior. Traditionally, anthropologists relied on such missionaries' and travelers' accounts to develop comparative interpretations and theories of culture. Over time, anthropologists, such as Bronisaw Malinowski and Margaret Mead, began to carry out their own first-hand empirical investigations and systemize fieldwork methods, many of which are still applied by present-day researchers in various academic fields. Today, ethnography refers to forms of social research and research products related to the study of various types of cultures.

When studying the culture and people of Samoa in the 1920s, Margaret Mead (1969) instituted a fieldwork method known as participant observation. Around the same time, from the 1920s to the 1950s, the Chicago School of Sociology developed an approach to the study of human life and society that was similar to that of anthropological research (Hammersley & Atkinson, 2007; Walford, 2008). The Chicago School sociologists also applied participant observation along with other ethnographic fieldwork methods to study communities in Chicago's urban areas. As the location of fieldwork shifted from the unfamiliar to the familiar and the study subject from non-Western to Western, and later to researchers themselves (i.e., autoethnography), researchers increasingly applied ethnographic methodology to study their own surrounding community or workplace. This expansion of relevant locations also encouraged the adoption of the ethnographic research methodology in a broad range of academic fields, such as the arts, cultural studies, education, medicine, and so forth.

The American anthropologist George Spindler, regarded as a founder of the anthropology of education, began applying ethnography to the study of elementary schools in the early 1950s. In doing so, Spindler and Spindler (1987) maintained that researchers should study anthropology as a discipline, and they should acquire a profound understanding of cultural processes before doing ethnography. Researchers should utilize qualitative methods, field investigation, participant or nonparticipant observation, descriptive journalism, or other methods similar to those of anthropological research. Thus, to call a research study ethnographic entails "some model of social or cultural process in both the gathering and interpretation of data" (Spindler & Spindler, 1987, p. 1). Today, Spindler and Hammond (2006) still believe that "ethnography, a research tool devoted to looking at human interaction as cultural process rather than individual psychology, can shed light on educational processes framed by the complex, internationalized societies we live in today" (p. ix).

Contemporary emerging forms of ethnography include autoethnography (Ellis, 2004; Liao, 2008; Pine, 2008; Suominen, 2005) and virtual ethnography (Hines, 2000; Lai, 2002b; Scott & Morrison, 2006). An autoethnography is "an analytical personal account about the self as a part of a group or culture" (Pine, 2008, p. 264). Teachers can use autoethnography to analyze their own lives and relationships with others to uncover unexamined beliefs, values, and patterns of daily activities that affect their educational practices (see, for example, Suominen, 2005). Virtual ethnography can be used to explore disembodied, technology-mediated, classroom culture (see, for example, Lai, 2002a, 2002b).

Ethnography has gained increased popularity in art education (Desai, 2002). Art teachers and educators have conducted ethnographic case studies of certain aspects of the classroom or school culture (see, for example, Bresler, 1994, 1996; Guay, 2003; Hafeli, 2000; Lai, 2002a, 2002b; Russell, 2007; Thomson, Hall, & Russell, 2007). Art educators also applied ethnography to study artists, artworks, and the artmaking process. For instance, Desai (2002) examines the artistic practices carried out by the artist-as-ethnographer. Lai and Ball (2002) explore the practice of yard art in a rural community. Staikidis (2006) studies Mayan artmaking and teaching processes.

METHODOLOGICAL APPROACHES AND FEATURES OF EDUCATIONAL ETHNOGRAPHY

Hammersley and Atkinson (2007) argue that the study of culture and human groups through ethnography should employ a naturalistic, open-ended and exploratory approach, rather than a positivist, measurement, or hypotheses-driven approach. Ethnographers usually begin their study with pre-fieldwork motivated by the selection of a problem or curiosity toward some aspect of the lives of the people they study (Beach, 2005; Delamont, 2008; Hammersley & Atkinson, 2007). To gain a deep understanding of the culture and human group being studied, extensive fieldwork and prolonged engagement in everyday contexts are necessary. Fieldwork typically consists of participant observation, interviewing, field notes, audio or visual

---

SARA AND MELANIE: *In this short contribution, Prévost discusses how she personalizes ethnographic fieldwork in ways that make explicit her power as the researcher in the sites she examines. Intentionally working with an awareness of power relations, Prévost describes the theoretical mindset that accompanies her use of ethnography in the research she conducts.*

Fragmented Becoming: Ethnographical Method

NATASHA PRÉVOST / RESEARCHER AT THE CENTRE DE RECHERCHE ET DE DÉVELOPPEMENT EN ÉDUCATION (CRDE), UNIVERSITÉ DE MONCTON, NEW-BRUNSWICK, CANADA

In this section, I will first describe the Fragmented Becoming ethnographic method by defining the key concepts of the method such as becoming, power relation, experimentation, and minority. The method is an extension of my understanding of Deleuze and Guattari's work. What interests me is the process of establishing a positive and creative symmetrical power relation with my social surrounding and, more particularly, with the people participating intensely in research projects. The method does not have a set of pre-established rules. It works differently every time you meet someone new, at every renewed encounter. Its application is only possible if you entertain the desire to deconstruct dominant power relations. Secondly, I will give two examples of how I reflected on my relational process within ethnographic fieldwork as an application of the Fragmented Becoming method.

The Fragmented Becoming method refers to a moment in time, through ethnographical fieldwork research, when people exchange their life experiences and modify their perceptions and interpretations of it by doing so. The concept of "Becoming," following Deleuze and Guattari (1987), is to be in constant flux and movement. By doing so the individual is in her/his own ongoing production—s/he cannot be fixed in one identity. Becoming is a way to escape domination, in that the individual is different depending on how a series of elements (geographical location, socio-economic class, race, sex, gender, religious faith, and so forth) come together at each encounter.

I developed the Fragmented Becoming method in order to have new words and concepts more adequate to my fieldwork research that focuses on actively deconstructing power relations be-

documentation, artifact collection, and archival study. Ethnographic data therefore are collected from the fieldwork. In the process of conducting fieldwork, ethnographers gradually refine their research focus and eventually determine a specific set of research questions, specific sites for frequent observation, specific people with whom to conduct in-depth interviews, and specific data analysis strategies. As ethnographers continue to gather data, interpret what they see and hear, and engage in rigorous reflexivity, they also continue to develop theories or narratives to explain human behaviors and culture. According to Spindler (2006), the process of data analysis involves reading the data and writing about it repeatedly in order to find and clarify relations among a body of data. The researcher then can interpret the meanings and significance of patterns, social rules and human behaviors of the community being studied.

In the discussion that follows, I draw examples from art education to elaborate further on what Walford (2008) regards as six critical features of educational ethnography.

A STUDY OF A CULTURE

Generally, ethnographers can study a culture from either a "materialist" or an "ideational" perspective (Fetterman, 1998, p. 17). From a materialist perspective, ethnographers search for observable patterns of behavior, customs, and ways of life. From an ideational perspective, ethnographers search for the ideas, beliefs, and cultural knowledge shared by the people studied. In the context of K-12 practice, art teacher-researchers have utilized both perspectives to explore certain aspects of the culture of art classrooms and schools. By listening to classroom conversations (ideational) and observing interaction or changing behaviors between teachers and students (materialist), Bresler (1994, 1996) investigated the visual arts instruction in three elementary schools. Guay (2003) examined how art teachers, para-educators, and students with disabilities interact with each other and how the interaction impacts student learning. Hafeli (2000) and Russell (2007) explored how judgments about and meanings ascribed to student artworks are formed. Thomson, Hall, and Russell (2007) investigated the practice of displaying children's artwork on school walls and how the school's culture (e.g., conceptions of what constitutes good artwork, a good student, good teaching, and a good school) is shaped by the displays.

tween the researcher and the research colleagues. For example, the researcher can use the dominant idea that "well-educated" people are superior to people who did not go to school for long, by having an attitude of superiority toward the research participants-colleagues. This is an asymmetrical power relation and it reflects the dominant Western patriarchal White male order.

Therefore, the word research "colleague" is favored over the words "informants" and "research subjects" because of their implicit asymmetrical power connotation. The word "informant" clearly states that the individual is there to give information to someone collecting data. However, in ethnographic research, research colleagues and the researcher spend an amount of time together that goes beyond a unique interview session. Furthermore, from my research experience, people willing to participate in a research project address—when the researcher does not—what their participation will give them in return, such as exposure or changes within the community. Multiple times, I heard potential participants clearly affirming that they were tired of giving their time to academic researchers who never follow up afterwards to reveal what happened with the information they acquired from the research participants. The phrase "research subject" sounds to me like someone under scrutiny or subjected to the gaze of the research observer. In actuality, the research colleague is the one

sharing her/his life experience with the researcher. The researcher has very limited power over the research colleagues, if s/he wants to have a significant field experience.

By working on establishing a reciprocal and symmetrical power relation, the very process of the development of a relationship becomes central to analyzing the subjectivity of the people involved, including the researcher. The method is a mixture of creativity from the researcher and active participation from the research colleagues. An always renewed encounter is also grounds for using our intuition, empathy, and creativity, in order to break apart the dominant framework of power relation. The dominant framework perpetuates the asymmetrical power relation between researcher and research colleagues, where academic knowledge is only shared among a small intellectual elite and never returns in a useful form to the people who are at the source of the construction of this knowledge.

At the analysis level, the researcher employing the Fragmented Becoming method enters into a dialogue between the developing reciprocal and symmetrical relationship and the dominant institutionalized order of power relations. In the process, the researcher uncovers various boundaries, prejudices, and strategies of control between institutionalized power and minority groups and facilitates power relation critical deconstruction,

(continued)

MULTIPLE METHODS, DIVERSE FORMS OF DATA

Hammersley and Atkinson (2007) stress, "Cultures are complex and multi-faceted" (p. 8). Therefore, to study culture, ethnographers employ multiple methods and gather "whatever data are available to throw light on the issues that are the emerging focus of inquiry" (p. 3). Russell's (2007) study of children's artmaking and the meaning making process reflects this key feature. She conducted pre-fieldwork to familiarize herself with the participants and school history and environment. She then applied multiple fieldwork methods to collect data. Methods included field notes, participant observation, and interviews of participants (e.g., children, teacher, artists, parents, and related school personnel). Russell also employed visual ethnographic methods to maximize the data pool. She produced video or photo documentation of the interviews, children's artwork, conversations and interaction among participants, and classroom behavior of children, teachers and artists being studied. Data, therefore, consisted of field notes, interview transcripts, photographs, video recordings, and documents relating to national and school policy. As a result, Russell's (2007) data enabled her to generate ethnographic knowledge about "how the artists teach; how and if [their] ways of teaching differ from teachers' pedagogy, and the impact of artists' involvement on the development of arts pedagogy in schools more generally" (p. 44).

ENGAGEMENT

An ethnographic research project involves immersion in the community, the act of "hanging around" to witness everyday life and the effort of building up relationships with individuals in the community being studied (Hammersley & Atkinson, 2007). Committed to deep engagement, Russell (2007) undertook an 11-month fieldwork experience at Holly Tree primary school. Participant observation took place weekly. Pre-fieldwork and weekly visits allowed her to become a familiar face and gained her some rapport with the participants. Her relationships with individuals went beyond the children, teachers, and artists being studied to include parents and a range of school personnel. To fully acquire cultural knowledge shared by the participants and accurately interpret their patterns of behavior in the classroom, Russell (2007) also extended her fieldwork to include a study of school culture (also see Thomson, Hall, & Russell, 2007). Active engagement in the school allowed her to further identify visual documentation as a proper

opening possibilities to relate to each other in a different, positive and creative fashion. The term "minority" is used following Deleuze and Guattari's (1987) definition in which a minority is not defined by its numeral quantity but by its capacity to become different from the hegemonic dominant majority. The minority "women" might literally outnumber the White male heterosexual hegemonic dominant majority, but stay a minority because of their rejection of the ideals of the majority. What defines a minority is its creative potential of becoming, of resisting and escaping domination. The uncountable aspect of the minority is characterized by connections, that is the additive conjunction "and." For instance, the minority women include: White Western women and African American women and Chicana women and Asian women and middle-class and poor and heterosexual and lesbian and mother and Voodoo priestess and Catholic, and so forth. I will illustrate the method with two personal examples.

While conducting fieldwork research in Brazil with transvestites (2000-2001) and later on with children (2003-2005), I questioned the process of establishing a relationship with the people with whom I worked. I became more aware of the contradictions in my own identity as I looked for ways to build relationships with those with whom I was conducting research. On the one hand, being a woman, I consider myself as part of a minority.

On the other hand, I was born in North America. I am White and belong to the low-middle class that has access to higher education. This critical awareness of changing identities depending on with whom I was working and in which country I was, gave me many insights into identity fluidity and becoming. More important, I started a conscious process of identifying how asymmetrical power relations could be diminished in fieldwork research in order to increase one's power of acting. When I work with someone and later write about her or him, I always ask myself if I am rendering the individual's complexity.

When I worked with transvestites in Brazil, I was in my mid-twenties and spent most of my time with a group of transvestites who were my own age. In my master's thesis I used the term "friend" instead of "informant" when referring to the transvestites with whom I had worked. Many of them told me that I was their only female friend, and that in fact they had not thought it possible to have a female friend. How did it happen? First, I placed myself in a position of receptivity toward them. Second, I continually worked to keep my interaction with them as free from prejudices as possible. I profoundly liked who they were. My interest went beyond my research. The time I spent with them involved all sorts of activities, from organizing a birthday party for one, to accompanying them in their daily routine. Third, I was

data collection method. Moreover, eventually children acted confidently and naturally when she filmed their activities. In a nutshell, ethnographic engagement in the school setting entails visiting the school frequently, participating in school activities, and becoming acquainted with the people in the school and especially its culture and environment. Building up relationships with participants can earn their willingness for in-depth interviews and participation in visual documentations.

RESEARCHER AS INSTRUMENT

Because ethnography is a narrative account of an ethnographer's interpretation of a culture, the ethnographer becomes an instrument of data collection and analysis. However, the information gathered by the ethnographer is partial and subject to bias, especially when the ethnographer encounters unfamiliar belief systems and behaviors. Hence, Fetterman (1998) and Walford (2008) urge that ethnographers remain open-minded about events in the field and employ multiple methods and data to become aware of patterns across datasets. Ethnographers keep their bias and assumptions at bay by exercising constant reflexivity. This means ethnographers must frequently examine their own ideas and compare them to those of the participants. Ethnographers also must constantly ponder their role in the field, especially in terms of how it may affect data collection and analysis, how it may influence what they assume to be worthy of observation, how they choose whom to interview, and so on. For example, in my study of yard art (Lai & Ball, 2002), being aware that my academic training in art and art education may alienate local people who create or display yard art as a leisure activity, when interviewing them, I made sure to avoid using the word "art" or "craft." Instead, I asked informants about the words they used to refer to the items that they displayed on their yards. I later became aware that I had privileged certain types of yard art and creative processes over others. As I began analyzing photographs taken for the study, I realized that photographs showing hand-made or discarded objects outnumbered those of store-made decorative objects. My interview questions regarding the creative process often connected creativity to originality and the hand-made rather than the ability to select and arrange ready-made objects in interesting ways. Realizing my bias, I returned to the field to conduct additional visual documentation and interviews.

empathetic to their suffering from being marginalized and excluded and also to their ambivalent feelings toward their own way of life and gender identity. In return, they trusted me, they protected me, and they were proud to introduce me to their relatives. In this particular case, my specific background became accessory to them, in terms of our one-on-one interaction, but served to show to the dominant society that a transvestite could indeed walk in public with a female foreigner during the day. It was a way of deconstructing dominant ideas and prejudices attached to their marginality. This kind of relationship can be defined in my view as reciprocal with "sharing" and "exchanges" replacing power.

Still in Brazil, when I worked with children between the ages of 7 and 13 from different socio-economic classes, I encountered another problematic power relation. In their eyes, I was an adult, and the adult represents an authority figure. However, my French accent in Portuguese and my lack of vocabulary related to childhood served me well. The children thought of me as a strange "aunt" to whom it was necessary to patiently explain things that were common knowledge for any other adult in their life. This was the first breach I used to deconstruct the dominant society-established power relation between adults and children. Second, I designed my methodology to give full autonomy to the children. We worked out together how the research should be

conducted, which were the important themes to be developed, and what kind of activities could be done in order to collect data. When I visited their homes, they introduced me to their families as a friend they were going to show around. However, I thought it more respectful to refer to them as my "research colleagues" in my PhD thesis. Again, through conscious awareness of dominant power relations governing relationships with the children minority, I worked on finding creative solutions to deconstruct generational hierarchical power. The most important was to believe in children's autonomy in thinking and designing a research project concerning themselves.

The Fragmented Becoming method can be applied to any group, as long as the research goal is to think with the "research colleagues" outside the institutionalized dominant framework and that both sides work towards a symmetrical and reciprocal relationship. ∎

REFERENCE
Deleuze, G., & Guattari, F. (1987). *A thousand plateaus: Capitalism and schizophrenia* (B. Massumi, Trans.). Minneapolis: University of Minnesota Press.

PARTICIPANT ACCOUNTS HAVE HIGH STATUS

Walford (2008) offers three arguments concerning why ethnographers sometimes include a large portion of the participants' own narratives in their writing. First, as noted previously, ethnographers should remain open-minded, and they should welcome narratives different from their own, especially those of the participants. Second, ethnography aims to generate empirical experience of another culture. When making a particular statement about a culture under study, ethnographers present the participant narratives as evidence to support their arguments. Third, participant narratives are used to demonstrate cultural knowledge in the language of the native community. Unlike early anthropological work in which non-Western subjects were often seen as unable to speak for themselves, many current ethnographers are more aware of the power relationship between the researcher and the subject, and therefore, many ethnographers believe that subjects should be allowed to speak for themselves (Clifford & Marcus, 1986). For example, in the writing of the study of how judgments are formed about students' artworks at Clayton Middle School, Hafeli (2000) interwove direct quotes from interviews, student drawings, and her interpretation of the meaning of conversations with students and teachers.

CYCLE OF HYPOTHESIS AND THEORY BUILDING

Ethnography can be used to generate theory or provide a descriptive or explanatory account of culture. Either way, data analysis and theory building are essential. They involve "interpretation of the meanings, functions, and consequences of human actions and institutional practices, and how these are implicated in local, and perhaps also wider, contexts" (Hammersley & Atkinson, 2007, p. 3). Ethnographers perform close and comparative reading of the data, and simultaneously, develop a set of analytical categories that can be based on recurring ideas or episodes, unusual ideas or events, interesting narratives, or ideas that they find particularly relevant to their research questions. For example, using "compositional interpretation," "content analysis," and "discourse analysis" (p. 44), Russell (2007) analyzed photographs and video recordings by looking at the content, color, spatial organization, timing, dialog, instructional strategies, and interaction among children, teacher and artist. She discovered a pattern in that when a teacher misinterpreted a child's artwork, the child would alter his artwork or the meaning of his artwork to conform to the teacher's (mis)interpretation. In another example, by comparing video recordings of teacher-student conversations, interviews and student drawings, Hafeli (2000) noticed a recurring pattern which indicated that teacher and students had different interpretations about the assignment requirements for a project on expressive painting. Hafeli then analyzed a selected conversation between a student and teacher. She hypothesized that the student's drawing did not fully meet the assignment requirements because of the student's own perception of aesthetic codes, skills, and preference for a certain subject matter. According to Hafeli, these differing interpretations of assignments may contribute to a student's development of a sense of individuality or resistance to trying new skills.

THE WRITE-UP

Hammersley and Atkinson (2007) identify two typical styles of ethnographic writing. In *thematic writing*, researchers present significant ideas, patterns, phenomena, or problems based on the results of data analysis (see, for example, Bresler, 1994; Guay, 2003; and Hafeli, 2000). In *chronological writing*, ethnographers present an episode, experience, or history sequentially. The researcher chooses this style to highlight the importance of processes of "becoming" or the time importance of certain phenomena. The finished ethnographic writing can be a monograph, an academic thesis, a journal article, a pamphlet, or an autobiographical account of the research experience. Below are elements of a typical ethnographic-based academic thesis, adapted from Gregory (2005, p. xix):

- A personal, often autobiographical, introduction leading to the foreshadowed problem to be investigated.
- A discussion of any pilot study or pre-fieldwork illustrating further the nature of the problem and the subsidiary questions arising.
- A literature review of relevant studies and indication of the need for conducting the investigation.

- A discussion of the methodology and design of the study, stressing the ethnographic orientation, ethical concerns, and use of multiple ethnographic methods to collect a range of data.
- An analysis of recurring ideas and episodes from the data in order to formulate hypotheses or interpretation. This can be organized thematically or chronologically.
- A refinement of hypotheses and interpretations, and a discussion of how these develop and extend existing theories.
- A conclusion summarizing the findings and making suggestions for future research. The researcher's reflexivity if not explicitly discussed previously should be included here.

CONCLUSION

This chapter introduced the social research methodology known as ethnography, particularly within the study of art and art education. Ethnographic work depends fundamentally on first-hand, extended personal involvement in the lives of people and the culture being studied. The mainstays of ethnographic data collection methods include participant observation, interviews, field notes, audio or visual documentation, artifact collection, and archival study.

What makes educational ethnography a distinctive and rigorous method for the generation of knowledge about certain aspects of classroom or school culture, as Watson-Gegeo (1997) argue, is its long-term (e.g., over the entire period of a semester or an academic year), holistic (e.g., inclusion of the study of the classroom as well as the school setting, interview of students, teachers, parents, and other related school personnel), and intensive (e.g., emphasis of relationship building with the participants,) study of people and culture. Although ethnographic research may be a challenging task, it is well worth the effort; ethnographic research allows teachers to examine the practices, problems, and policies of art education in a holistic and complex way as they exist in the real world. Finally, teachers are also able to meaningfully develop hypotheses or solutions that are grounded in data collected from the field and of possible direct benefit to the people, classes, and schools being studied.

REFERENCES

Beach, D. (2005). From fieldwork to theory and representation in ethnography. In G. Troman, B. Jeffrey & G. Walford (Eds.), *Methodological issues and practices in ethnography* (pp. 1-17). San Diego, CA: Elsevier.

Bresler, L. (1994). Imitative, complementary, and expansive: The three roles of visual arts curricula. *Studies in Art Education, 35*(2), 90-104.

Bresler, L. (1996). Ethical issues in the conduct and communication of ethnographic classroom research. *Studies in Art Education, 37*(3), 133-144.

Clifford, J., & Marcus, G. (Eds.). (1986). *Writing culture: The poetics and politics of ethnography.* Berkeley: University of California Press.

Delamont, S. (2008). For lust of knowing—Observation in educational ethnography. In G. Walford (Ed.), *How to do educational ethnography* (pp. 39-56). London, England: The Tufnell Press.

Desai, D. (2002). The ethnographic move in contemporary art: What does it mean for art education? *Studies in Art Education, 43*(4), 307-323.

Ellis, C. (2004). *The ethnographic I: A methodological novel about autoethnography.* New York, NY: Altamira Press.

Fetterman, D. M. (1998). *Ethnography: Step by step* (2nd ed.). Thousand Oaks, CA: Sage.

Gregory, E. (2005). Introduction: Tracing the steps. In J. Conteh, E. Gregory, C. Kearney & A. Mor-Sommerfeld (Eds.), *On writing educational ethnographies: The art of collusion* (pp. ix-xxiv). Stoke on Trent, England: Trentham Books.

Guay, D. M. (2003). Paraeducators in art classrooms: Issues of culture, leadership, and special needs. *Studies in Art Education, 45*(1), 20-39.

Hafeli, M. (2000). Negotiating "fit" in student art work: Classroom conversations. *Studies in Art Education, 41*(2), 130-145.

Hammersley, M., & Atkinson, P. (2007). *Ethnography: Principles in practice* (3rd ed.). New York, NY: Routledge.

Hines, C. (2000). *Virtual ethnography.* London, England: Sage.

Lai, A. (2002a). From classrooms to chatrooms: Virtualizing art education. *Art Education, 55*(4), 33-39.

Lai, A. (2002b). *Virtualizing art education: An educational ethnographic case study of a distance art education course* (Unpublished doctoral dissertation). Ohio State University, Columbus.

Lai, A., & Ball, E. (2002). Home is where the art is: Exploring the places people live through art education. *Studies in Art Education, 44*(1), 47-65.

Liao, C. L. (2008). My metamorphic avatar journey. *Visual Cultural & Gender, 3*, 30-39.

Mead, M. (1969). *The social organization of Manu'a.* Honolulu, HI: Bishop Museum Press. (Original work published in 1930)

Pine, G. J. (2008). *Teacher action research: Building knowledge democracies.* Thousand Oaks, CA: Sage.

Russell, L. (2007). Visual methods in researching the arts and inclusion: Possibilities and dilemmas. *Ethnography and Education, 2*(1), 39-55.

Scott, D., & Morrison, M. (2006). *Key ideas in educational research.* London, England: Continuum Press.

Spindler, G. (2006). Living and writing ethnography: An exploration in self-adaptation and its consequences. In G. Spindler & L. Hammond (Eds.), *Innovations in educational ethnography: Theory, methods, and results* (pp. 65-82). Mahwah, NJ: Lawrence Erlbaum Associates.

Spindler, G., & Hammond, L. (2006). Preface. In G. Spindler & L. Hammond (Eds.), *Innovations in educational ethnography: Theory, methods, and results* (pp. ix-xx). Mahwah, NJ: Lawrence Erlbaum Associates.

Spindler, G., & Spindler, L. (1987). Issues and applications in ethnographic methods. In G. Spindler & L. Spindler (Eds.), *Interpretive ethnography of education: At home and abroad* (pp. 1-10). Mahwah, NJ: Lawrence Erlbaum Associates.

Staikidis, K. (2006). Personal and cultural narrative as inspiration: A painting and pedagogical collaboration with Mayan artists. *Studies in Art Education, 47*(2), 118-139.

Suominen, A. (2005). Stranger within. *The Journal of Social Theory in Art Education, 25,* 15-44.

Thomson, P., Hall, C., & Russell, L. (2007). If these walls could speak: Reading displays of primary children's work. *Ethnography and Education, 2*(3), 381-400.

Walford, G. (2008). The nature of educational ethnography. In G. Walford (Ed.), *How to do educational ethnography* (pp. 1-15). London, England: The Tufnell Press.

Watson-Gegeo, K.A. (1997). Classroom ethnography. In N. H. Hornberger & D. Corson (Eds.), *The encyclopedia of language and education. Volume 8: Research methods in language and education* (pp. 135-144). Norwell, MA: Kluwer Academic Press.

ALICE LAI is Associate Professor of the Arts and Educational Studies at Empire State College, State University of New York, where she also chairs an undergraduate program in the arts at the college's Center for Distance Learning. Her research spans the areas of critical multicultural art education, critical pedagogy, visual culture studies, and distance education. She authored and has been teaching online/blended courses such as Artistic Expression in a Multicultural America, Images of Women, and a methodology course in folklore studies: Documenting Community Arts and Traditions. In these courses, she implements ethnographic research methods (e.g., interview, participant/non-participant observation, and audio/visual documentation) to facilitate student's exploration of visual culture, folklore, and women's creativity and lived experience. She has served on the board of directors of New York Folklore Society. Her publications have appeared in *Studies in Art Education, Art Education, Pedagogy, Visual Arts Research,* and *Visual Culture and Gender.*

16 / A Study of Rastafarian Culture in Columbus, Ohio

IVY CHEVERS / ADJUNCT LEVEL II INSTRUCTOR, SINCLAIR COMMUNITY COLLEGE, DAYTON, OHIO

ABSTRACT: *This chapter is an exemplar of autoethnographic research. It discusses how research was conducted with the Rastafarian community in Columbus, Ohio, by a researcher affiliated with Rastafarian culture. The chapter gives a brief overview of Rastafarian culture, discusses the participants, location of research, and methods of data collection and analysis. It provides suggestions for K-12 teachers who are considering conducting research with groups or cultures in which they are participants.*

AUTOETHNOGRAPHY

Referred to as the "cultural study of one's own people" (Schwandt, 2001), autoethnography has evolved into a distinctive process of blending ethnographic research and reflexive writing. My interest in ethnography was stirred when I began graduate school at The Ohio State University. A former Peace Corps Volunteer gone "native," I had recently returned to Ohio after living in Jamaica for almost twenty years. In the department of comparative studies, I was exposed to the writings of scholars whose work is immersed in cultural anthropology (Frank, 1995; Gluck, 1991; Toelken, 1996). In art education I read scholars who employed arts-based qualitative research as a means of educational inquiry (Barone & Eisner, 1997). I was intrigued with their approaches to research, as well as the stories, characters, and plots they wove in their texts that examined educational policies.

My confidence in lending a reflexive voice to my research grew as I became invested in the autoethnographic literature of Ellis and Bochner (2002) and Reed-Danahay (2001). One of the main characteristics of an autoethnography is that the autoethnographer is a boundary-crosser, and the role can be characterized as having a dual identity (Reed-Danahay, 1997). After spending so many years in Jamaica, I did indeed feel like a boundary-crosser with a dual identity. As autoethnography has evolved, it has become a term to also signify research written by an ethnographer who has "insider" or "native" status (Tedlock, 2003). I questioned how I might apply my experiences with Jamaican Rastafarian culture and my interest in ethnography to topics in art education.

Rastafarian culture comprises rich material and visual cultural elements with historical roots in the African Diaspora. The increased interests of visual culture studies in art education help validate my choice to explore Rastafarian culture as a topic for research. Rastafarian culture has been adopted by people in Ghana, Australia, England, America, the Pacific, and the Caribbean. It has become an agent of social change among some indigenous people (Lipsitz, 1997; McNee, 2002; Moyer, 2005; Savishinsky, 1994; Van Dijk, 1998). However, there is a gap in literature regarding Rastafarian culture in the United States, especially in the midwest. Initially, I set out to question the cultural appropriation of Rastafarian culture in Columbus, Ohio, because that is where much of the literature written about *RastafarI* (a term denoting plural Rastafarian participants) outside of Jamaica begins (Lipsitz, 1997; McNee, 2002; Moyer, 2005; Savishinsky, 1994; Van Dijk, 1998). While Rastafarian culture, in general, maintains some authenticity in Jamaica, in a contemporary sense, it strives to negotiate the spaces between media representation and globalization. I was interested in investigating how Rastafarian culture is lived and experienced in Columbus.

SARA AND MELANIE: *Personal passions and art forms that we find important and relevant can often lead us to study a particular group of people. Careful examination of a group's cultural practices can lead to richer context and deeper understanding of a cultural group. Cultural groups go beyond race, class, gender, or national origin. Thus, cultures can also be composed of the teachers working at a high-performing school, artists with shared backgrounds, or a cohort of graduate students. Investigations of cultural practices, like this ethnographic study, can inform how we approach art in our classrooms.*

This is a qualitative study using ethnographic and autoethnographic approaches. Interviews and participant observations were the primary methods of data collection. Twelve people participated in the study. The study took approximately 1½ years to complete. I analyzed the data using a descriptive interpretation. In this chapter, I discuss autoethnography as a methodological approach to research. I give a brief synopsis of Rastafarian culture, discuss the participants and location of my study, and methods of data collection and analysis leading to my findings. I will also address the relevance of autoethnography to K-12 teachers.

BACKGROUND TO THE STUDY

Autoethnographic texts are characterized by the incorporation of elements of one's own life experience when writing about others through biography or ethnography (Denzin & Lincoln, 2003). Prior to traveling to Jamaica, during undergraduate school, I began to purchase reggae albums and grow my hair in dreadlocks. In Jamaica, I was drawn to Rastafarian culture, when I traveled there as a Peace Corps Volunteer. After 5 years as a volunteer, I returned to Ohio. Three years later, I went back to Jamaica where I resided for another 13 years. I became immersed in Jamaican culture and was drawn more closely to Rastafarian philosophy.

The history of the RastafarI movement is complex. Scholars of Rastafarian literature vary in their usage of spellings and terms related to RastafarI. Out of the Rastafarian movement, a language emerged that combines, Jamaican dialect with the movement's philosophical symbolism. The words "you" and "me" are rarely used in Rastafarian speech. Instead, the term "I and I" is used in conversation to signify a singular reference to the self or a plural reference with the self and others. The term *Rastafarianism* is generally avoided in favor of *Rastafarian, Rastafari* or *RastafarI*. For purposes of this chapter, I use *RastafarI* and *Rastafarian* interchangeably to denote both plural and singular references.

The Rastafarian movement emerged in Jamaica during the 1930s. The movement has been documented in Rex Nettleford's (1970) *Identity, Race and Protest in Jamaica*, Leonard Barrett's (1977) *The Rastafarians: Sounds of Cultural Dissonance*, Joseph Owens's (1976) *Dread: The Rastafarians of Jamaica*, and Ennis Edmonds' (2003) *Rastafari: From Outcasts to Culture Bearers*. RastafarI has been defined as a social movement, sect, cult, a way of life, and a philosophy (Yawney, 1995). RastafarI is embedded in the cultural fiber of a country with a strong history of resistance to colonialism. Ninety percent of Jamaicans are of African descent whose ancestors were sold into slavery, beginning with Spanish and then British colonialism (Barrett, 1977). In Jamaica, the Maroons (runaway slaves) created communities that fought and resisted slavery. In these communities, Africans were able to preserve cultural retentions relating to food, language, and religion, some of which still exist in Jamaica today.

The most fundamental belief of Rastafarian culture is that Haile Selassie, a former emperor of Ethiopia, is God. Haile Selassie was crowned King of Kings, Lord of Lords, Conquering Lion of the Tribe of Judah, on November 2, 1930. His name prior to the coronation was Tafari Mokonnen, Ras Tafari, from which the Rastafarian movement's name is derived. The coronation was well publicized. Heads of States from foreign countries and journalists and photographers from *Time* and *National Geographic* attended the coronation in Ethiopia. Some Jamaicans interpreted the coronation

as a biblical sign (Psalms 68:31 and Revelation 19:16) of Haile Selassie's divinity. These Jamaicans called themselves Rastafarians. Early Rastafarians came from the oppressed poor in Jamaica who were despised by the elite and ruling powers because they fought against British colonialism. They believed in Ethiopianism, which is derived from Pan-African and Back-to-Africa ideology. The notion of Ethiopianism is attached to biblical sentiments, as well as, to the solidarity that was formed among Africans in the Diaspora, when Italy launched wars against Ethiopia in 1896 and 1935. The country of Ethiopia is mentioned over 30 times in the Bible (for examples see, Genesis 2:13; Psalms 68:31; Psalms 87:4; and Acts 8:37). Italy's attacks on Ethiopia created emotional reactions that strengthened the bonds of pan-Africanism among descendents of Africans around the world (Harris, 1994, p. 24). Nowhere was this much greater than in Jamaica.

SOCIAL MOVEMENT THEORY, RASTAFARI, AND THE ARTS

Collective identity is the inclination of a social movement to form a group image that shapes the consciousness of individuals. RastafarI function as a group consistent with characteristics inherent in social movements as described by Kebede, Shriver, and Knottnerus (2000). They argue that, "Since the movement's inception, the Rastafarian collective identity has revolved around a number of core themes associated with language, music, rituals, and appearance" (p. 315). Eyerman and Jamison (1998) claim that it is the cultural effects of social movements that live on through songs, art, and literature in absence of the particular political platforms and struggles that brought them into being. Additionally, social movements are key agents of cultural transformation.

For example, reggae is a genre of music associated with Rastafarian culture. Many reggae musicians are Rastafarians and their lyrics reflect Rastafarian philosophy. Columbus, Ohio, has a vibrant local and international reggae music circuit. Live reggae music or DJs spinning the latest Jamaican reggae tunes can be heard on any given night in the city. Popular Jamaican Rastafarian reggae musicians tour Columbus at least seven times a year. "Chanting down Bablyon" are popular lyrics in reggae music that signify protesting against the "worldly state of affairs in which the struggle for power and possessions take precedence over the cultivation of human freedom and the concern for human dignity" in Rastafarian culture (Edmonds, 2003, p. 24). To Rastafarians, the word *Babylon* signifies institutionalized systems that support prejudice and inequity.

Rastafarian visual artists create images of a Black God in the person of Haile Selassie in their paintings and wood carvings. The colors of the Ethiopian flag, red, gold, and green are prominent at Rastafarian and reggae gatherings. Black, green, and red are also symbolic colors to Rastafarian culture. Red signifies the blood that Africans shed in the fight against oppression, green represents Africa, and black, the color of African skin.

PARTICIPANTS AND LOCATION OF RESEARCH

Jamaica is ranked as the leading Caribbean country that sends Black immigrants to the United States. In 2005, Columbus, Ohio, was listed as number 15 of a ranking of the top United States metropolitan areas for foreign-born Blacks residing in the United States (Kent, 2007). Additionally, Columbus has the second largest Somali population in the United States, next to Minneapolis. The surprisingly high numbers of continental Africans and Blacks of African descent in Columbus led me to investigate literature that historicizes relations between Columbus, the Caribbean, and the African Diaspora (Christian, 2004; Harris, 1982, 1994; Scott, 1978; Shack, 1974; Shepperson, 1960). The Ohio Historical Society archives also contained valuable documents from the early 1900s to support evidence of relations between Columbus, the Caribbean, and Africa.

Before I began the study, I completed application through the Institutional Review Board (IRB) for the study of human subjects at The Ohio State University. Participants read and signed a consent letter explaining the nature of the research and granting permission to use their names. One of the first sites I visited to gather data was a local reggae record shop, Roots Records. There, one of the employees informed me that the Rastafarian community in Columbus was planning a celebration on November 2, to commemorate the coronation of Haile Selassie. On the second of November, I attended the event and spoke with Rastafarians there about my research, and took the names and phone numbers of people I met. Throughout the next year, I developed a friendship with one of the women I met that day; sister Queen, a Rasta for over 20 years, who buys, sells and makes Rasta garments, jewelry, flags, and banners.

On another day, I went to the record shop again to introduce myself to the owner and ask him for an interview. Roots Records specializes in the sale of reggae music and collectibles. The owner, Carl Root, has promoted live reggae acts in the city for over 10 years. Carl introduced me to two people, whom I later interviewed, including Jennifer Cabrera, whose father, Hugo (deceased) was a major player in promoting reggae and Jamaican culture in Columbus during the 1970s and '80s. Through e-mail correspondence, Carl introduced me to Roger Steffens (2001) author of *The World of Reggae Featuring Bob Marley Treasures From Roger Steffens Archives*, co-founder of *Beat* Magazine, and chairman of the Reggae Grammy Committee. I made contact with two Rasta men I met in Jamaica, Basil Walters, a journalist for the *Jamaica Observer* newspaper, and Cedric Brooks, a musician who resides in New York. Their interviews and Roger's were done via telephone and e-mail correspondence. On a study abroad trip to Brazil I met Nelson Silva, a professor of visual arts in Brazil, whom I interviewed because he is well versed in African history and reggae and

Rasta discourse in his country. Nelson, Basil, Cedric, and Roger spoke to the appropriation of Rasta and reggae from a general sense. They provided me with data to compare and contrast the presence of Rastafarian culture in Columbus to various ethnic and geographic locales. Other participants included: Terry Bob, founding member of Columbus reggae group, The Ark Band; Tom Carroll, founder of SeefarI, a reggae band in Wilberforce, Ohio, a small town approximately 40 miles from Columbus; and Haile Israel, a Rasta musician, who travels extensively between Hawaii and Ohio. A graduate student introduced me to her friend, Matt Stinson, a Rasta man from Columbus, whom I later interviewed. Andrew Buck, an OSU classmate, Rasta man, and former Peace Corps volunteer in Uganda, also participated in the study.

METHODS OF DATA COLLECTION

I entered the role of a researcher, with that of an insider/outsider status. I spent approximately 1½ years in the field. Two of the participants, Queen and Carl, became primary sources for my research and provided me with countless hours of information that I collected through recorded open-ended interviews. Carl is heavily invested in the reggae business. Queen vends at reggae shows and participates in RastafarI and Afrocentric events throughout the midwest. During that time, I attended 13 live reggae concerts in Columbus, featuring major international reggae acts and one in Dayton, Ohio featuring local musicians. I attended events where Rastafarian holidays were celebrated, including the most important Rastafarian holy days, the coronation and birthday celebrations of Haile Selassie. In Brazil, I was invited by Professor Alex Ratt from the University de Federal in Goiânia to attend a reggae session. Alex is conducting research on reggae in Goiânia. My participation at events outside of Columbus helped me to understand factors in Columbus that are unique to the appropriation of Rasta and reggae in Columbus.

Open-ended interviews and participant observation were the primary methods of data collection. I wrote brief field notes at events and during interviews and took longer notes immediately after returning home from an interview or event. I took pictures with a digital camera and recorded events with a video camcorder and conducted interviews at coffee shops, in participants' homes or their places of business. Participants received a copy of the questions I prepared. The interviews were one to two hours and recorded on cassette tapes. Other sources of data included books, scholarly articles, newspapers, and archival records. I conducted a literature review in cultural, popular, and critical theory (Fiske, 1989a, 1989b; Fuery & Fuery, 2003; Giroux, 1992; Giroux, & Simon, 1993; How, 2003; Kellner, 1990; Storey, 1996) and in art education (Duncum, 1987; Freedman, 2003; Lanier, 1969; Smith-Shank, 1996, 2003; Tavin, 2005).

DATA ANALYSIS

The description of persons, places, and events is the cornerstone of qualitative research (Janesik, 2003). Rather than provide concrete findings in my research, employing autoethnography, I provided an interpretative account of the interviews I conducted and descriptive observations of events and places where Rastafarians gather in Columbus. The study provided an account of the historical influences that brought a Jamaican cultural phenomenon to Columbus, Ohio. It also provided insight into how this phenomenon is lived and experienced in Columbus. Geertz (1973) refers to this as "thick description" (p.10). The product of ethnography is the interpretation of data in written form. Prior to writing up the research, I listened to each interview at least two times. Next, each interview was transcribed verbatim. I read and re-read, each transcribed interview, checking for themes, categories, patterns, ideas, consistencies, and inconsistencies (DeWalt & DeWalt, 2002). I used a process of inductive analysis to analyze the data in my study. Inductive analysis "means that categories, themes and patterns come from the data" (Janesick, 2003, p. 63). As the themes, patterns, ideas, consistencies, and inconsistencies emerged, I used a system of tallying to keep track of my progress. Member checks were used to solicit additional feedback from participants. Member checks are used in qualitative research as method of corroborating or verifying findings or ensuring the validity of findings (Schwandt, 2001). Throughout the study, I wrote reflexive vignettes in *italics* to illustrate stories, observations and personal conversations, taken from my field notes. Some of the vignettes juxtaposed my lived experiences in Jamaica with my experiences of studying Rastafarian culture as a research topic.

For some of the participants in this study, RastafarI and reggae music provides a space for the teaching of Black culture and history. For others, RastafarI and reggae music provides sites where Africans in the Diaspora come together in Columbus to dance, socialize with each other, have a good time, network, and form business relations. These networking and business relations inform Diasporic communities of Africans in Columbus about issues and events of interest to their communities. For some participants in the study, RastafarI and reggae music provides a means to make a living by promoting the music, writing about the culture or creating, buying and selling RastafarI arts and crafts. My research, suggest that reggae music supporters and members of the Rastafarian community in Columbus are very much concerned with issues of social justice, race, and economic disparities.

CONCLUSIONS

Ethnography has been acknowledged as a viable research strategy for inquiry into educational practices (Barone & Eisner, 1997; Lightfoot, 1983; Wolcott, 1997). In my study, I observed informal educational practices at Rastafarian gatherings. At the Rastafarian holy day events I participated in, youths of RastafarI parents were present. At these events, parents made special efforts to set up activity tables for the youth. At times, I was asked to assist in providing artistic and educational activities, as well. I observed and learned that maintaining African cultural heritage and teaching African history are important objectives of RastafarI community members in Columbus just as it is with Rastafarians in Jamaica. I also observed that socially conscious reggae music lyrics provided for some newcomers to Rastafari in Columbus, a vehicle for learning African history and culture.

Autoethnography provided a methodology for me to investigate a cultural phenomenon, of which I am a participant. For K-12 classroom teachers, autoethnography offers many possibilities. One's own school culture could be the subject of a rich study. For example, the teacher at a high performing school in a high needs district might want to understand the culture that makes that a successful school. Or, teachers may study a micro-culture within their school. This might take the form of a drama teacher conducting research that investigates learning communities among drama students. Teachers of English Language Learners (ELL) might consider investigating the cultures and communities from which their students' original languages derive. In many respects, teachers who conduct educational research in their own schools begin with insider status. Autoethnography can provide a means for educators to identify and conduct research with learning communities to which they are personally connected.

In this study, autoethnography provided a method to investigate a Jamaican social movement in Columbus, Ohio, while engaging the reader in a personal account that disseminated knowledge of and described the complexities and issues relevant to Rastafarian culture.

REFERENCES

Barrett, L. (1977). *The Rastafarians: Sounds of cultural dissonance.* Boston, MA: Beacon.

Barone, T., & Eisner, E. (1997). Arts-based educational research. In R. Jaeger (Ed.), *Complementary methods for research in education* (pp. 73-98). Washington, DC: American Educational Research Association.

Christian, M. (2004). Marcus Garvey and the Universal Negro Improvement Association (UNIA): With special reference to the "lost" parade in Columbus, Ohio, September 25, 1923. *Western Journal of Black Studies, 28*(3), 424-434.

Denzin, N., & Lincoln, Y. (2003). The discipline and practice of qualitative research . In N. Denzin & Y. Lincoln (Eds.), *Strategies of qualitative inquiry* (pp. 1-45). Thousand Oaks, CA: Sage.

DeWalt, K., & DeWalt, B., (2002). *Participant observation: A guide for field-workers.* Walnut Creek, CA: Altamira Press.

Duncum, P. (1987). What, even Dallas. Popular culture with the art curriculum. *Studies in Art Education, 29*(1), 7-16.

Edmonds, E. (2003). *Rastafari: From outcasts to culture bearers.* Oxford, England: Oxford University Press.

Ellis, C., & Bochner, A. (Eds.). (2002). *Ethnographically speaking autoethnography, literature, and aesthetics.* Walnut Creek, CA: Altamira Press.

Eyerman, R., & Jamison, A. (1998). *Music and social movements mobilizing traditions in the twentieth century.* Cambridge, MA: University Press.

Fiske, J. (1989a). *Reading the popular.* Boston, MA: Unwin Hyman.

Fiske, J. (1989b). *Understanding popular culture.* Boston, MA: Unwin Hyman.

Frank, G. (1995). The ethnographic films of Barbara Myerhoff: Anthropololgy, feminism and the politics of Jewish identity. In R. Behar & D. Gordon (Eds.), *Women writing culture* (pp. 207-233). Berkeley: University of California Press.

Freedman, K. (2003). *Teaching visual culture: Curriculum, aesthetics and the social life of art.* New York, NY: Teachers College Press.

Fuery, P., & Fuery, K. (2003). *Visual cultures and critical theory.* London, England: Arnold.

Geertz, C. (1973). *The interpretation of cultures.* New York, NY: Basic Books.

Giroux, H. (1992). *Border crossings cultural workers and the politics of education.* New York, NY: Routledge.

Giroux, H., & Simon, R. (1993). *Popular culture schooling and everyday life.* New York, NY: Bergin & Garvey.

Gluck, S. (1991). Advocacy oral history: Palestinian women in resistance. In S. Gluck & D. Patai (Eds.), *Women's words: The feminist practice of oral history* (pp. 205-219). New York, NY: Routledge.

Harris, J. (Ed.). (1982). *Global dimensions of the African diaspora.* Washington, DC: Howard University Press.

Harris, J. (1994). *African-American reactions to war in Ethiopia 1936-1941.* Baton Rouge: Louisiana State University Press.

How, A. (2003). *Critical theory.* New York, NY: Palgrave MacMillan.

Janesick, V. (2003). The choreography of qualitative research design: Minuets, improvisations, and crystallizations. In N. Denzin & Y. Lincoln (Eds.), *Strategies of qualitative inquiry* (pp. 46-79). Thousand Oaks, CA: Sage.

Kebede, A., Shriver, T., & Knottnerus, J. (2000). Social movement endurance: Collective identity and the Rastafari. *Sociological Inquiry, 70*(3), 313-337.

Kellner, D. (1990). Critical theory and the crisis of social theory in sociological perspectives. *Critical Theory, 33*(1), 11-33.

Kent, M. (2007). Immigration and America's black population. *Population Bulletin, 62*(4). Retrieved from http://findarticles.com/p/articles/mi_qa3761/is_200712/ai_n24392730/?tag=content;col1

Lanier, V. (1969). The teaching of art as social revolution. *Phi Delta Kappan, 50*(6), 314-319.

Lightfoot, S. (1983). *The good high school.* New York, NY: Basic Books.

Lipsitz, G. (1997). *Dangerous crossroads popular music, postmodernism and the poetics of place.* London, England: Verso.

Moyer, E. (2005). Street-corner justice in the name of Jah: Imperatives for peace among Dar es Salaam street youth. *Africa Today, 51*(3), 31-58. Retrieved from www.ohiolink.edu

McNee, L. (2002). Back from Babylon: Popular musical culture of the diaspora. Youth culture and identity in Francophone West Africa. *Critical Studies, 19*(1), 213-228. Retrieved from www.ohiolink.edu

Nettleford, R. (1970). *Identity, race and protest in Jamaica.* Kingston, Jamaica: Collins and Sangster.

Owens, J. (1976). *Dread: The Rastafarians of Jamaica.* London, England: Heinemann.

Reed-Danahay, D. (2001). Autobiography, intimacy, and ethnography. In P. Atkinson (Ed.), *Handbook of ethnography* (pp. 407-425). London, England: Sage.

Reed-Danahay, D. (Ed). (1997). *Auto/Ethnography rewriting the self and the social.* New York, NY: Berg.

Richardson, L. (2000). Writing a method of inquiry. In N. K. Denzin & Y. S. Lincoln (Eds.), *Handbook of qualitative research* (pp. 516-529). Thousand Oaks, CA: Sage.

Savishinsky, N. (1994). Rastafari in the promised land: The spread of a Jamaican socioreligious movement among the youth of West Africa. *African Studies Review, 37*(3), 19-50. Retrieved from www.jstor.org

Schwandt, T. (2001). *Dictionary of qualitative inquiry.* Thousand Oaks, CA: Sage.

Scott, W. (1978). Black nationalism and the Italo-Ethiopian conflict 1934-1936. *The Journal of Negro History, 63*(2), 118-134.

Shack, W. (1974). Ethiopia and Afro-American: Some historical notes, 1920-1970. *Phylon, 35*(2), 142-155.

Shepperson, G. (1960). Notes on Negro American influences on the emergence of African nationalism. *The Journal of African History, 1*(2), 299-312.

Smith-Shank, D. (1996). Microethnography of a Grateful Dead event: American subculture aesthetics. *Journal of Multicultural and Cross-cultural Research in Art Education, 14*(1), 80-91.

Smith-Shank, D. (2003). Community celebrations as ritual signifiers. *Visual Arts Research, 28*(2), 57-63.

Steffens, R. (2001). *The world of reggae featuring Bob Marley treasures from Roger Steffens' reggae archives.* Beverly Hills, CA: Global Treasures.

Storey, (1996). *Cultural studies and the study of popular culture: Theories and methods.* Athens: University of Georgia Press.

Tavin, K. (2005). Hauntological shifts: Fear and loathing of popular (visual) culture. *Studies in Art Education, 46*(2), 101-117.

Tedlock, B. (2003). Ethnography and ethnographic representation. In N. Denzin & Y. Lincoln (Eds.), *Strategies of qualitative inquiry* (pp. 165-213). Thousand Oaks, CA: Sage.

Toelken, B. (1996). From entertainment to realization in Navajo fieldwork. In B. Jackson & E. Ives (Eds.), *Reflections on the fieldwork process* (pp. 1-17). Urbana: University of Illinois Press.

Wolcott, H. (1997). Ethnographic research in education. In R. Jaeger (Ed.), *Complementary methods for research in education* (pp. 327-398). Washington, DC: American Educational Research Association.

Van Dijk, F. (1998). Chanting down Babylon outernational: The rise of Rastafari in Europe, the Caribbean, and the Pacific. In N. Murrell, W. Spencer & A. McFarlane (Eds.), *Chanting down Babylon: The Rastafari reader* (pp. 199-216). Philadelphia, PA: Temple University Press.

Yawney, C. (1995). Tell out King Rasta doctrine around the whole world: Rastafari in global perspective. In A. Ruprecht & C. Taiana (Eds.), *The reordering of culture: Latin America, the Caribbean and Canada in the hood* (pp. 57-74). Ottawa, Canada: Carleton University Press.

IVY CHEVERS is a graduate of The Ohio State University in Columbus, Ohio. She holds a degree in art education with a minor in African and African American studies. Her research interests include the study of Rastafarian and reggae discourse in historical and popular culture contexts. In February 2009, she curated the Columbus Rastafarl exhibit at the King Arts Complex in Columbus, Ohio. Ivy's research interests also include the relationships between African-centered arts-based pedagogies and academic performance among students of color in K-12 learning communities. She is interested in understanding how educators incorporate the teaching and learning of multicultural and African-centered art practices and discussions in the K-12 curriculum.

HISTORICAL RESEARCH

17 / Accounts About Before From Now: Historical Research Methods

JOHN HOWELL WHITE / PROFESSOR OF ART EDUCATION AND CHAIR OF THE DEPARTMENT OF ART EDUCATION AND CRAFTS, KUTZTOWN UNIVERSITY

ABSTRACT: *This chapter provides an introduction for teachers to historical research methodologies in art education. Novice researchers interested in the possibility of studying the ideas, events, people, institutions, practices, objects, and laws on the local and national level will be provided with a framework for advancing their projects. To that end, I include a description of those activities often associated with historical research, such as some motivations for embarking on historical research, the uses of a historical study, kinds and origins of historical questions, places to find relevant information, and the importance of the historical narrative. Throughout the chapter, I provide examples from my own historical studies and references the historical studies of other art educators.*

> If the study of history does nothing more than teach us humility, skepticism, and awareness of ourselves, then it has done something useful... We should be wary of the grand claims in history's name or those we claim to have uncovered the truth once and for all. In the end, my own advice is to use it, enjoy it, but always handle history with care.
>
> —Margaret MacMillan (2009

WHY HISTORY?

As a teacher, you have likely often had responses in your professional life to which you ascribed values, "This policy is maddening" or "I love teaching about contemporary art." Generally, you rely upon your personal past to develop narratives about these subjects and your reactions to them. Your personal history is enmeshed in its own network of emotional responses, its subjects being contingent upon your life and your ability to recall information. Historical research provides a robust means to address these limitations. Historical research can serve as a tool to extend the reach of your limits of understanding.

The term "history" has roots that are related to inquiry, story, witnessing, and recording (Barzun & Graff, 1977). Consequently, to engage in historical research you will need to develop an empathetic imagination, a critical capacity for the recovery and organization of data, and a narrative voice that tells the story of your subject in ways that are both accurate and useful to your audiences (Barzun & Graff, 1977; Kaestle, 1997; Stankiewicz, 1997). To address the concern that knowledge of the world is informed and constrained by the perceptual context, situated within the biological and psychological, and the cultural context, situated in interpersonal relations, of the knower, contemporary historians wonder how their beliefs inform their views of the past. As a researcher, your views will have an effect upon the subjects you study, the methodologies you employ, and the narratives you develop (Iggers, 1997).

Historical imagination, your capacity for empathetic reactions to the conditions of the lives of others, provides a means to address both continuities and differences. While questions are a distinguishing feature of research and they serve to prompt, invigorate, and focus conclusions, it would be impoverished activity if the only motivation for research is "the question." People are drawn to the past though stories, objects, lived experiences, and yes, questions, all of which will impress themselves upon your research agenda.

Historical research also relies upon accurate information, which supplies the most durable link to past events. Your readers, including other historians, will look at the specific information, the reliability of your sources, the causal connections that you develop, your inferences you make related to personal, social, and ideational forces, and finally, the way that you tell your story. The history that you write is built upon accurate data.

The sustaining forces for your research will be a desire to resituate your subjects into the world of your readers or listeners. You will accomplish this through your historical narrative. Objectivist historians work to remove themselves from the story while pragmatic historians may insert themselves into the narrative through questions, first person voice, and sidebars. Historians ask us to consider: (1) the context of phenomena as they occurred; (2) the use phenomena have been put to as they move through time; and (3) the ways that today's conditions reprioritize the relative value of past phenomena.

USING HISTORIES

You may feel that art education's histories are only remotely related to your work. While you may not pay homage to the exploits of art educators on a regular basis, you are deeply enmeshed in forms of authority—classroom configurations, tools and materials, theories of teaching and learning, laws, standards, curricula and instruction—inherited from others. Historical research presents opportunities to look to other art education locations in time to see how teaching might be different.

Historical work can provide you with rewards that are intrinsically, instrumentally, and extrinsically valuable. The intrinsic value of historical research will come to you through your interest in: (1) the objects, people, and/ or systems that you are studying; (2) the tasks involved in carrying out your research; (3) the telling of the story to others through conversation, presentations, and papers; and (4) the theorizing or thinking you do as you reflect upon your data and findings. The instrumental value of historical research comes as it invigorates your practices outside of the research. Historical research can have an effect on: (1) your teaching; (2) your school's curriculum; (3) your classroom and school environment; (4) your relationships with other teachers; (5) advocacy initiatives directed toward parents, administrators, legislators; (6) your students; (7) the field of art education; and (8) your artwork.

Extrinsic rewards come when communities, like your professional field, express their faith in the value of your work. Fields, like individuals, develop through both the accumulation of experience and reflection on the validity of that experience. The histories of art education demonstrate that the field has always been a contested space as social forces, economic conditions, educational priorities, theories of learning, theories of art, charismatic leaders, and new technologies have altered the way teaching and learning takes place (Amburgy, 1990; Bolin, 1990; Bolin, Blandy, & Congdon, 2000; Collins & Sandell, 1984; Congdon, Blandy, & Bolin, 2001; Efland, 1990b; White, 2001). They can show us how the field can be captivated by social trends that affect the values that we hold.

ASKING QUESTIONS

People collect all kinds of things, objects, stories, ways of approaching things, affectations, small green things—you name it; people fixate. Collecting data alone does not constitute historical research. The detritus from the past, both from external artifacts, and internal habits and memories, will offer up both discontinuities and affinities, which as a researcher you will put into some kind of order. Questions, however, like any other collectable, are innumerable, so questioning per se is unhelpful. Rather, it is the active and resonant development of questions, which become increasingly more nuanced and robust, that guides the relevance of your research. A central well-developed research question will form the anchor of your study to save you from churning away in a sea of fascinating details.

Historical questions vary, but inevitably their answers come through the study of past practices, theories, and social networks, among other things. Often historical questions ask us to reposition ourselves. My work, which resulted in the study of the contributions of Pedro deLemos, *School Arts Magazine's* editor from 1919 to 1954, evolved through a series of different kinds of questions including theoretical, inductive, and improvisational.

THEORETICAL QUESTIONS

It is important to develop a theoretical question, which is flexible in its application to a wide range of phenomena. Theory or "Given my best guess, the world works like this" can provide focus and motivate your work. Theoretical questions imply possibilities for rethinking habits. Theories are often derived from other fields of study. Art historian Linda Nochlin's (1973) classic "Why have there been no great women artists?" builds upon feminist theory that interrogates that ways that gender is socially constructed. Her question rests within larger theories of natural rights and social justice. Her work in turn provoked a series of historical questions related to the art world, including the training of artists, the exchange value of artworks, and the legitimacy of judgments based upon transcendental notions of quality. This work, which uses theory to pry open cherished values, influenced the promotion of gender studies in art education. Nochlin's ideas influenced my own study of Pedro deLemos, the Latino editor of *School Arts Magazine* who used Native American images to re-image the field. Through Nochlin's work I could see that cultures are constructed through complex networks of largely unstated rules and that people can construct, perform and interrogate these rules through images and objects.

INDUCTIVE QUESTIONS

Often it is not theory that provokes the historical question but rather an object, image, event, story from the past, or even another history. Inductive questions emerge as your collections of associations and objects clash, as the object stares back at you daring you to try for a moment to put it to rest. I began my study by looking at old issues of *School Arts Magazine*. I asked "Why are there so many images of Native American related materials in this periodical during the late 1920s through the 1940s?" This was not the original reason that I was looking through these materials but rather the question that came forward out of my browsing.

IMPROVISATIONAL QUESTIONS

Improvisational questions are grounded in your familiarity with the material and your general willingness to be open to the flood of associations each of us prodigiously produces. Here, gaps are registered and not overlooked: a statement seems out of place; an artifact is slightly different; a pattern is broken; and a connection is developed. I noticed that before deLemos became *School Arts* editor (1919) his name appeared on the masthead (1916) as a member of the editorial board. Those board members, who were once drawn from the east, had been conspicuously and evenly distributed geographically. deLemos was the sole California representative. While Davis Press used the membership of its board to promote the magazine geographically, deLemos used *School Arts* to promote his western sensibilities, bringing Native American images to American public schools.

You may take up a familiar questioning style, but this will change as your research develops. Your questions come out of your lived experience, which most likely differs dramatically from the worlds of the people in your study or the approaches of other researchers. It is important that your questions are framed to be both critical, such as "How were Native American-focused lessons used to leverage a wider circulation of the magazine?" and empathetic, "What role did Native American-focused lessons play in the field's maturing conception of human rights and social justice?" You will often find that something that is remote and esoteric to you will be folk knowledge to others.

As a critical historian your role is to understand some of the forces through which your sources construct their reality. You will need to make judgments based upon (1) the information that you have collected, (2) the conflicting accounts of events, (3) the underlying values that influence the perspectives of your sources, and (4) events and ideas that contribute to a reinterpretation of the time and place that you are studying. For example, although it may be important to note that a source believed "x" to be the case, it does not follow that in fact their interpretation was reliable in light of other considerations.

HISTORY'S LABORATORIES

The world writ large is the historian's laboratory, although your primary concerns are the lives, institutions, and transactions of people. While there are multiple entry points to your research, reliable follow-through is much more restricted and requires work. Central to your methodology will be a consistent, robust, and specific means to catalogue your data. Software products enhance the manageability of this process, but inevitably, you will work back and forth between a data storage program, written notes, photographs, and other recorded material. You will need to record (1) where the data is housed, (2) where and who it came from (possibly the same place), and (3) the kinds of information found within and associated with it. To avoid confusion, plan your system from the beginning knowing that you will be utilizing a wide range of information documentation technologies including: handwritten and computer generated notes, photographs, voice recordings, photocopies, graphs charts, maps, computer, and video footage.

As a beginning historian, you probably will be wondering about topics and data sources. Suppose you were interested in a local historical research project, your own development as an art teacher, for example. This very personal history could begin with your attic or other storage facility; it could expand to interviews with family members, friends and past art teachers. Each of those sites of learning has a history, which you could research through local libraries, historical societies, and newspapers. Do not be shy about asking for help from the local historical society. Did you take a course at a community center? A question about a community center can lead to question about support for the arts in general in your town or neighborhood or to questions about community arts in general. Were you influenced by artists on TV, in books, or on the radio? History is an expansive thing where local, regional, national, and global conditions conspire to alter our experiences of the world. Constraining your initial interests to the local does not mean your interests will remain there any more than working from a global concern will prevent your research from coming back to your home. Historical research could begin locally from an artwork handed down from within your family, practices in your school or school district, effects of national initiatives on local practices, alumni accomplishments, public art in your area, changing reactions to populations, art festivals and events, zoning effects on your town, collections and collectors, the art supply industry, local manufacturers, local, regional or media-delivered artists and art forms. All these can lead to fascinating and far-reaching conclusions, or to a rich and developed respect for your region, family, neighbors, school, friends, etc.

Historians use the term, *primary* and *secondary resources* to indicate the validity of the reference material. Most often, especially during initial stages of a research project, you will rely upon secondary resources to formulate the scope of the project. Secondary resources on a crime show would be called circumstantial evidence. As in those shows, you will need to make your case by reaching beyond the circumstantial to the smoking gun. These are primary resources that are explicit about some transaction that has taken place.

The most common *secondary sources* are histories written by others. As a researcher you will engage in a critical reading of these texts to glean support and identify gaps in relation to your area of interests. These histories can be found in a wide range of styles: sweeping histories of the field (Efland, 1990a; Green, 1948; Logan, 1955; Stankiewicz, 2001; Wygant, 1993), social histories (Collins & Sandell, 1984; Zimmerman & Stankiewicz, 1982;), personal histories (Bolin et al., 2000; Congdon et al., 2001; Korzenik, 1985); collections of papers (Amburgy, Soucy, Stankiewicz, Wilson, & Wilson, 1992; Anderson & Bolin, 1997; Soucy & Stankiewicz, 1990; Wilson & Hoffa, 1985); biographies (Corwin, 2001; Saunders, 1960); political histories

(Freedman, 1987); technologies (Funk, 1998; Stankiewicz, 1984); cross cultural histories (Chalmers, 2000); institutional histories (Berry & Mayer, 1989; Michael, 1997; Saunders, 1978); and curriculum studies (Efland, 1976). You will find that many research papers, and even textbooks dedicated to non-historical studies and topics, ground their work with a history section.

These authors will cite, in the reference section, those primary sources that support their story. *Primary sources* are original artifacts that have not been interpreted by a second party. Probably you will not possess these materials, so you must study them by going to the sites where they are housed. One of the great pleasures of historical research is reviewing archived materials. Such artifacts can include but are not limited to past publications, curriculum materials, letters, photographs, artworks, professional correspondences, receipts, memos, diaries, interviews, contracts, deeds, taxes, and laws. While many of these are retrievable through online searches, travel to sites, including libraries, historical societies, town records, museums, state archives, family homes, local schools, and university archives, is the best way to move through large quantities of archives. If materials are held in a special collection, research librarians can mail you photocopies if you can specify the exact location and document that you need. Although these sources are evidence, it is important not to ascribe more meaning to them than what they document. They evidence their existence and an exchange but not the contexts or rationales for their development.

Still more gratifying are interviews and personal accounts of individuals associated with your object of study. My work on deLemos led to an acquaintance with his grand-daughter and meaningful encounters with curators, librarians, town folk, architects, art dealers, and collectors, among others. I recall a particular conversation with a resident of a small town in New Mexico, whose story confirmed the existence and conditions of a 1930s trading post at that particular location. The stories told by the man provided this East Coast researcher with some insight into the relations between the Hispanic, Anglo and Native American populations of rural New Mexico. You will need to be cautious, not overstating the truth conditions of witnesses, even when the interviewee is intimately connected to your topic. These events, however, can provide some of the most memorable rewards in your research, as you engage with people that know your subject in intimate ways.

THE STORY

Historical research relies upon getting the facts straight (the past) and telling the story (historiography). If you follow the methods of objectivist historians, your goal would be to remove yourself as much as possible in order to reveal a causal explanation of why we are where we are today (Iggers, 1997). However, most contemporary historians are pragmatists who situate their own perspective within their

work and see the world as a dense and contingently constituted space (Iggers, 1997). Historians of all stripes develop narrative structures to organize the past into a comprehensible study. Collecting, analyzing and narrating the data are not a linear process. Usually, one enters into the process with some story in mind, or infers some causality, or possesses some facts. The historian needs to delay closure on these so that a robust, reliable, and verifiable narrative can emerge. In my history of deLemos, I started with *School Arts Magazine* and images of Native Americans. Those facts, when analyzed, led my recovery of Pedro deLemos, as a force within art education. Subsequently, I developed future questions about his motivations—perhaps a search for legitimacy—and the motivations of the field—perhaps a willful forgetting to advance notions of the creative self. Facts consequently become drama. The same facts, narrated by another historian, would result in a different story. Even historians who work out of discontinuities and gaps utilize narratives that demonstrate the continuity of omission. Some histories develop rich or thick descriptions of the past, where chronology is less important than developing a sense of place or personhood (Burke, 1991). The telling of this story is an essential element of your research.

The narrative that you construct will require you to engage critically with your data. This engagement will include everything from: (1) organizing the data chronologically; (2) reconstructing social, spatial, and temporal relationships; (3) connecting events to larger world forces; (4) interrogating the reliability of data sources; (5) imagining uncomfortable but possible relationships; (6) theorizing underlying motivating forces; (7) confirming and/or resolving conflicting data; (8) acknowledging and revealing unresolved questions and gaps; and (9) applying the results to analogous situations and relationships. To achieve this, you will need to keep a substantial amount of conflicting and often irrelevant information in play.

You may find that your narrative about the past may differ from the stories that others have told about it. During your research, you may form relationships with people, whose lives will be influenced by the things that you say and vice versa. As a historian, you need to be both empathetic and truthful. Here you will have difficult choices to make that will require both accuracy and tact. Your job is to interpret the past in ways that may confront cherished beliefs held by yourself and others. It may seem overwhelming at first to think that you might have a story to tell that has not been told. Start with a part of the story that you feel you can grasp and reveal your knowledge with a sense of assuredness and humility. It might be helpful to keep in mind that the possibilities for meaningful histories are never-ending. You are making a contribution to an evolving account of the relative importance of your subject, the breadth of the field of art education, and your own agency as a researcher.

REFERENCES

Amburgy, P. (1990). Culture for the masses: Art education and progressive education reforms, 1880-1917. In D. Soucy & M. A. Stankiewicz (Eds.), *Framing the past: Essays on art education* (pp. 103-116). Reston, VA: National Art Education Association.

Amburgy, P., Soucy, D., Stankiewicz, M. A., Wilson, B., & Wilson, M. (1992). *The history of art education: Proceedings from the second Penn State conference, 1989.* Reston, VA: National Art Education Association.

Anderson, A., & Bolin, P. (1997). History of art education: Proceedings from the third Penn State International Symposium, Oct 12-15, 1995. University Park: The Pennsylvania State University.

Barzun, J., & Graff, H. (1977). *The Modern researcher* (2nd ed.). New York, NY: Harcourt Brace Jovanovich.

Berry, N., & Mayer, S. (1989). *Museum education: History, theory, and practice.* Reston, VA: National Art Education Association.

Bolin, P. (1990). The Massachusetts Drawing Act of 1870: Industrial Mandate or democratic maneuver? In D. Soucy & M. A. Stankiewicz (Eds.), *Framing the past: Essays on Art Education* (pp. 59-68). Reston, VA: National Art Education Association.

Bolin, P., Blandy, D., & Congdon, K. G. (2000). *Remembering others: Making invisible histories visible.* Reston, VA: National Art Education Association.

Burke, P. (1991). *New perspectives on historical writing.* University Park: The Pennsylvania State University.

Chalmers, F. G. (2000). Art education in "Indian" residential schools in British Columbia. *Canadian Review of Art Education, 27*(1), 21-35.

Collins, G., & Sandell, R. (1984). *Women, art, and education.* Reston, VA: National Art Education Association.

Congdon, K. G., Blandy, D., & Bolin, P. E. (2001). *Histories of community-based art education.* Reston, VA: National Art Education Association.

Corwin, R. (2001). *Exploring the legends: Guideposts to the future.* Reston, VA: National Art Education Association.

Efland, A. (1976). The school art style: A functional analysis. *Studies in Art Education, 17*(2), 37-44.

Efland, A. (1990a). *A History of art education: Intellectual and social currents in teaching the visual arts.* New York, NY: Teachers College Press.

Efland, A. (1990b). Art education in the twentieth century: A history of ideas. In D. Soucy & M. A. Stankiewicz (Eds.), *Framing the past: Essays on art education* (pp. 117-138). Reston, VA: National Art Education Association.

Freedman, K. (1987). Art education and changing political agendas: An analysis of curriculum concerns of the 1940s and 1950s. *Studies in Art Education, 29*(1), 17-29.

Funk, C. (1998). The Art in America Radio Programs, 1934-1935. *Studies in Art Education, 40*(1), 31-45.

Green, H. (1948). *The introduction of art as a general subject in American Schools* (Doctoral dissertation). Palo Alto, CA: Stanford University.

Iggers, G. (1997). Historiography in the twentieth century: From scientific objectivity to postmodern challenge. Hanover, NH: Wesleyan University Press.

Kaestle, C. (1997). Recent methodological developments in the history of American education. In R. Jaeger (Ed.), *Complementary methods of research in education* (pp. 61-80). Washington, DC: American Educational Research Association.

Korzenik, D. (1985). *Drawn to art: A nineteenth century American dream.* Hanover, NH: University Press of New England.

Logan, F. (1955). *Growth of art in American schools.* New York, NY: Harper & Brothers.

MacMillan, M. (2009). *Dangerous games: The uses and abuses of history.* New York, NY: Random House.

Michael, J. (1997). The National Art Education Association: Our history— Celebrating 50 years 1947–1997. Reston, VA: National Art Education Association.

Nochlin, L. (1973). Why have there been no great women artists? In T. Hess & E. Baker (Eds.), *Art and sexual politics.* New York, NY: Collier Books.

Saunders, R. (1960). The contributions of Viktor Lowenfeld to art education: Part I: Early influence on his thought. *Studies in Art Education, 2*(1), 6-15.

Saunders, R. (1978). First steps: The FCAE & the NAAE: A brief history. *Art Education, 31*(7), 18-22.

Soucy, D., & Stankiewicz, M. A. (1990). *Framing the past: Essays on art education.* Reston, VA: National Art Education Association.

Stankiewicz, M. A. (1984). Self expression or teacher influence: The Shaw system of finger painting. *Art Education, 37*(3), 20-24.

Stankiewicz, M. A. (1997). Historical research methods in art education. In S. Lapierre & E. Zimmerman (Eds.) *Research methods and methodologies for art education.* Reston, VA: National Art Education Association.

Stankiewicz, M. A. (2001). *Roots of art education practice.* Worcester, MA: Davis.

White, J. (2001). Imaging (Native) America: Pedro deLemos and the expansion of art education (1919-1940). *Studies in Art Education, 42*(4), 298-317.

Wilson, B., & Hoffa, H. (1985). *The History of Art Education: Proceedings from the Penn State Conference.* University Park: The Pennsylvania State University College of Art and Architecture, School of Visual Arts.

Wygant, F. (1993). *School art in American culture.* Cincinnati, OH: Interwood Press.

Zimmerman, E., & Stankiewicz, M. A. (1982). *Women art educators.* Bloomington: Indiana University Press.

JOHN HOWELL WHITE is Professor of Art Education and Chair of the Department of Art Education and Crafts at Kutztown University. He has served as Director of the Higher Education Division of the National Art Education Association and chairs the NAEA Research Commission. He is a member and past Chair of the Council for Policy Studies in Art Education. Dr. White has published his philosophical and historical research in *Studies in Art Education, The Journal of Art Education, The Handbook of Research and Policy in Art Education, Visual Arts Research, International Journal of Education and the Arts, Translations,* and *School Arts Magazine.* His areas of historical research include: mid-20th century American art education, the California Arts & Crafts Movement, Native American & Spanish Colonial imagery in *School Arts Magazine,* Pedro deLemos, Russell Sage Foundation, Southern Highlands crafts, and the Carnegie Corporation of New York.

18 / Schools and Social Conflict: A Historian's Approach to Understanding Curricula

PATRICIA M. AMBURGY / ASSOCIATE PROFESSOR EMERITA OF ART EDUCATION, PENNSYLVANIA STATE UNIVERSITY

ABSTRACT: *Why is art positioned as a marginal subject rather than a central or basic part of school curricula? In 2002, I published a historical study (Amburgy, 2002) that helped suggest some answers to this question. I approached the study from a standpoint of looking at schools as sites of social conflict, places where different social groups struggle with one another over the nature and purposes of schooling, and resolve their differences through domination, compromise, revisions, and, sometimes, significant change. Using my study as an example, in this chapter I discuss primary and secondary sources in historical research, and the importance of telling meaningful stories about the past.*

Like many art educators, I have often wondered about the status of art in schools. Why is art positioned as a marginal subject rather than a central or basic part of school curricula? Although looking at schools as sites of social conflict is not a common approach among historians of art education, it has long been a perspective adopted by historians of education overall (e.g., McClellan & Reese, 1988; Spring, 2008; Tyack & Cuban, 1995; Violas, 1978). When viewed from a social conflict perspective, historians do not understand curriculum as a reflection of the essential value of subjects; instead, school curriculum is understood as a record of the ways that social conflicts have been resolved over time.

In my study, I examined social conflicts in the spring of 1893 over the status of "special" subjects that were then part of the curriculum in Chicago public schools—drawing, music, German, physical culture, sewing, and manual training. As a historian of art education, I found this time and place to be especially interesting because the public debates over these subjects involved a broad array of social groups. Working class people, business leaders, progressive educators, politicians, and members of the press—all expressed an opinion, one way or the other, about subjects such as drawing and music in the public schools. Whereas supporters referred to them as "special" subjects, opponents called them "fads" and "frills" in the school curriculum. The attacks on subjects such as drawing and music were so forceful that contemporary observers sometimes characterized opponents as waging a "war" against fads (e.g., Clark, 1897; "War on Fads, 1893;" "War on Fads To-Night," 1893). In my study, I examined the way this 1893 "war" against

fads in the curriculum became "a political issue in municipal elections, an assault on immigrants in the city, a question about the role of women in public life, and a conflict between social classes" (Amburgy, 2002, p. 110).

CONTEXTS AND STARTING POINTS: SECONDARY SOURCES

For their research, historians typically draw on two kinds of evidence: primary and secondary sources. Primary sources of information are sources that originated in the time and place being studied. In the case of my study, examples of primary sources include newspaper articles and editorials that were published in 1893 such as those I cite above ("War on Fads, 1893; "War on Fads To-Night," 1893) as well as proceedings of the Chicago Board of Education (Chicago Board of Education, 1893) and the annual report of the board for 1892–93 (Chicago Board of Education, 1894). Secondary sources of information are sources that were created later, often long after the period of time being studied. Examples of secondary sources in my study include histories of public schooling published in the 20th and 21st centuries, such as those I cite previously (McClellan & Reese, 1988; Spring, 2008; Tyack & Cuban, 1995; Violas, 1978), histories of Chicago (Mayer & Wade, 1969; Miller, 1996; Spinney, 2000), and histories of social movements in the United States (Blair, 1994; Ruyter, 1999).

Historians often see primary sources as the most important kind of information because primary sources offer direct evidence about the past; the nature of primary evidence is not as mediated (although it is still mediated to some degree, of course) as interpretations that have been constructed later in different times and places. Nonetheless, secondary sources are still very useful to historians. I find them especially useful for generating topics for historical research, suggesting primary and secondary sources of information that I might use to investigate a topic further, and providing contexts for understanding primary evidence.

The topic for my study of conflicts surrounding special subjects in Chicago public schools in 1893, for example, grew out of a brief historical description of the background of 20th-century debates over vocational education in the city:

> In 1893, the conservative newspapers of the city had mounted an attack on the "fads and frills" of the public school curriculum. For nearly half a year, the issue was a source of controversy in the press, in civic associations, and in public meetings. The *Chicago Tribune* was the most vituperative; in one year it published 30 editorials critical of the waste of public money on frivolous subjects. During the 1893 mayoral election, the *Tribune* interjected the fads as a political issue, criticizing the Democrats and their candidate. (Wrigley, 1982, pp. 54-55)

I wanted to know more. Why did the *Tribune* consider subjects such as drawing and music to be "frivolous"? Whose interests did the newspaper represent? Why did the *Tribune* criticize the Democrats specifically and their candidate for mayor? Did the Democrats support special subjects in 1893? If so, why? Were there other groups that supported special subjects in Chicago's public schools at the time? If so, what were their reasons for supporting subjects such as drawing and music?

In addition to suggesting a topic, Wrigley's (1982) history was also helpful in suggesting sources of information with which I might start to investigate the 1893 "war" against fads further. In the passage that piqued my interest, I could already identify one primary source of information: editorials in the *Chicago Tribune* in 1893. Looking at Wrigley's list of references for the chapter in which the passage appeared, I found several other promising leads: an almost-contemporary study of Chicago public schools (Clark, 1897) and two additional secondary sources, a social and political history of Chicago schools (Herrick, 1971) and a history of newspapers and the schools in Chicago (Beck, 1953).

From Beck's (1953) history, I was able to identify other Chicago newspapers in circulation in 1893, in addition to the *Tribune*, which were also good primary sources of information about the conflicts surrounding special studies in the schools. Additionally, Beck's history was helpful in identifying the political affiliations of various newspapers, thus providing a context for understanding the different editorials and articles that appeared in various papers. Over the course of my study, I found other secondary sources to be helpful as well in providing contexts for understanding the primary evidence related to my topic. For example, from secondary sources, I learned when and why German had been added as a special subject in Chicago public schools, and what percentage of the students who received instruction in German were German American (Herrick, 1971; Mayer & Wade, 1969; Miller, 1996). I determined which immigrant groups were most populous in the city in the 1890s and what political tensions existed between immigrants and nativist Anglo Americans. Additionally, I identified which groups—immigrant or Anglo, Democratic or Republican—supported or opposed subjects such as drawing, physical culture, and music in public schools in the past (Herrick, 1971; Pierce, 1957; Spinney, 2000). I learned how members of the Chicago Board of Education were appointed to 3-year terms by city mayors, who themselves were elected for 2-year terms, thus explaining why, in 1893, the board was a mixture of Democrats and Republicans. I also found out that a Democratic and a Republican mayor, respectively, had appointed the two women who served on the board in 1893, and I ascertained which male members of the board were Democrats or Republicans (Leonard, 1905; Marquis, 1911). When, in the course of examining primary sources, I came across an unfamiliar term for a special subject—*Delsarte*[1]—again, I turned to secondary sources to explain what this term had meant in the 19th century (Blair, 1994; Ruyter, 1999). Throughout my study of the "war" on fads in 1893 in Chicago, I drew extensively on secondary sources to provide contexts for primary evidence. Secondary sources helped me understand the evidence I was looking at in primary sources.

EVIDENCE AND INTERPRETATION: PRIMARY SOURCES

I put it this way—I used secondary sources that "helped me understand the evidence I was looking at in primary sources"—because primary evidence is not self-interpreting. As with art, there is more than meets the eye in primary evidence. Historians of education interpret what they find in primary sources, going beyond what is immediately observable, just as historians of art go beyond what is immediately observable to contextualize and interpret what they see. This does not mean that histories of education or histories of art are entirely subjective, completely made up. History is not fiction. Histories are, however, stories about the past; they are interpretations of factual evidence that make sense of the facts.

The principal sources of primary evidence for my study of the "war" on fads were Chicago newspaper articles and editorials from the spring of 1893, and the proceedings and annual report of the Chicago Board of Education for the school year 1892–1893. Using the board's proceedings and annual report, plus accounts of public meetings and speeches in contemporary newspapers, it was a fairly straightforward procedure to construct a timeline of events—who did what, when, and where. This was an important step in my construction of a story about the 1893 "war," but the bare facts of who, when, and where did not in themselves tell a full story. To tell a fuller story, I needed to go beyond bare facts to explain the *whys*—why some social groups supported special subjects and others did not, and why the Board of Education ended up making its decisions.

Primary evidence for the *whys* came principally from articles and editorials in Chicago newspapers, which not only reported events at the time, but frequently commented on them as well. I did not expect the information in contemporary newspapers to be unbiased, or completely objective. On the contrary, because I was interested in studying conflicts between various social groups on the issue of special subjects in schools, I welcomed the overt partisanship of some newspapers as providing evidence of differing views. I drew evidence for my study from the *Chicago Tribune*, a Republican paper representing the interests of the business community, as well as the *Chicago Times*, a paper owned by Carter Harrison, a popular Democrat who was seeking his party's nomination for mayor in 1893. I examined articles and editorials from the *Chicago Daily News*, a paper that was often critical of fads, as well as articles in the *Inter Ocean*, a paper that tended to be more supportive of special studies in its reporting of events.

Using multiple secondary sources to help me fully understand the primary evidence I collected, I constructed a story about the "war" on fads in 1893 in Chicago that interpreted the event as a conflict of interests between various social groups at the time—Democrats and Republicans, immigrants and nativist Anglo Americans, working class people and businessmen, and women and men. My story was not a fictional account. The story was "true" in the sense that it was based on factual evidence. The social groups in my story were real people, and conflicts over special studies in the public schools actually happened in Chicago in 1893. My history was a "story" in the sense that it was an interpretation of the evidence, a way of putting together information from primary and secondary sources to make sense of an event from the past. Of course, the story I constructed was not the only way to interpret this event—there is never only one right interpretation of historical events—but it was *a* way to construct a story that made meaning of the event.

TELLING MEANINGFUL STORIES ABOUT THE PAST

I did not invent the idea that histories are stories about the past. One of my favorite professors in graduate school, Paul C. Violas, an accomplished historian of education, used to say this all the time. After I graduated and went on to construct my own stories about the past (histories of art education, in my case), I realized there was something else that could be added to the saying. Generically, histories may be stories about the past, but ideally, they are *meaningful* stories about the past.

What counts as meaningful is, of course, a matter of judgment. For me, meaningful stories are not only ones

that explain the *whys* of things in the past and suggest answers about why things may be the way they are today. Meaningful stories about the past are also ones that raise questions about current conditions, challenging us to reconsider old assumptions and to work toward new beliefs and practices.

In my study of social conflicts over special studies in school curricula, for example, I found that opinions were divided along lines of class, ethnicity, and political party in Chicago in 1893. For the most part, opponents of so-called "fads" were businessmen, nativist Anglo Americans, and Republicans. Groups that supported "special" studies were principally working class men and women (as distinct from "business men"), progressive educators, immigrants, and Democrats. The reasons given for opposing or supporting special studies varied. Among the opponents, businessmen saw fads as being frivolous and costly. They believed the public schools should focus on "basic" subjects that would prepare students for practical aspects of life. Nativist Anglo Americans were concerned with issues of social cohesion and creating a common culture. They did not want German or any other foreign language to be taught in public schools because they believed a central purpose of schooling was to Americanize immigrants, not to perpetuate divisive immigrant cultures. Among groups that supported special studies, German Americans held that subjects such as drawing, music, and language instruction were part of a well-rounded education. Progressive educators claimed that special studies made schooling more enjoyable for students. Working class people argued that their children should have the same educational advantages as children of the privileged classes. From the perspective of working class people, special studies were means of social empowerment.

When I discuss this study in courses or at art education conferences, people are often surprised by the position of working class people. I think this may be because we tend to assume that working class people and other average citizens do not value art. But is this actually true? It was not true in Chicago in 1893. Of course, this was a specific time and place, and we would not want to over-generalize its significance. It does raise some provocative questions, though. Do working class people today support subjects such as art in public schools? Instead of being our opponents, might working class people today be one of our allies in promoting the importance of art in schools?

To conclude the discussion of my study, I return to the initial question: Why is art a marginal subject in school curricula today? My story about the social conflict in Chicago in 1893 suggests the reason is not because there is something inherently marginal in the nature of art. Instead, my story suggests that the status of art in schools has to do with political and economic interests, social privilege, and power to determine what is taught in schools. If my story about the past is convincing, then the next question is this: What can we do from this point forward to change the status of art in schools today? Meaningful historical research not only explains why things are the way they are today; it challenges us to change them.

REFERENCES

Amburgy, P. M. (2002). Fads, frills, and basic subjects: Special studies and social conflict in Chicago in 1893. *Studies in Art Education, 43*(2), 109-123.

Beck, J. M. (1953). *Chicago newspapers and the public schools, 1890-1920* (Unpublished doctoral dissertation). University of Chicago, Chicago, IL.

Blair, K. J. (1994). *The torchbearers: Women and their amateur arts associations in America, 1890-1930*. Bloomington: Indiana University Press.

Chicago Board of Education. (1893). *Proceedings of the Board of Education of the City of Chicago, July 6, 1892 to July 5, 1893*. Chicago, IL: Author.

Chicago Board of Education. (1894). *Thirty-ninth annual report for the year ending June 30, 1893*. Chicago, IL: Author.

Clark, H. B. (1897). *The public schools of Chicago: A sociological study*. Chicago, IL: University of Chicago Press.

Herrick, M. J. (1971). *The Chicago schools: A social and political history*. Beverly Hills, CA: Sage.

Leonard, J. W. (Ed.). (1905). *The book of Chicagoans: A biographical dictionary of leading living men of the city of Chicago*. Chicago, IL: A. N. Marquis.

Marquis, A. N. (1911). *The book of Chicagoans: A biographical dictionary of leading living men of the city of Chicago*. Chicago, IL: Author.

Mayer, H. M., & Wade, R. C. (1969). *Chicago: Growth of a metropolis*. Chicago, IL: University of Chicago Press.

McClellan, B. E., & Reese, W. J. (Eds.). (1988). *The social history of American education*. Urbana: University of Illinois Press.

Miller, D. L. (1996). *City of the century: The epic of Chicago and the making of America*. New York, NY: Simon & Schuster.

Pierce, B. L. (1957). *A history of Chicago* (Vol. 3, The rise of a modern city, 1871-1893). New York, NY: Alfred A. Knopf.

Ruyter, N. L. C. (1999). *The cultivation of body and mind in nineteenth-century American Delsartism*. Westport, CT: Greenwood Press.

Spinney, R. G. (2000). *City of big shoulders: A history of Chicago*. DeKalb: Northern Illinois University Press.

Spring, J. (2008). *The American school: From the Puritans to No Child Left Behind* (7th ed.). Boston, MA: McGraw-Hill.

Tyack, D., & Cuban, L. (1995). *Tinkering toward utopia: A century of public school reform*. Cambridge, MA: Harvard University Press.

Violas, P. C. (1978). *The training of the urban working class: A history of twentieth century American education*. Chicago, IL: Rand McNally.

The war on fads [Editorial]. (1893, January 21). *Chicago Tribune*, p. 12.

War on fads to-night. (1893, February 23). *Chicago Daily News*, p. 1.

Wrigley, J. (1982). *Class politics and public schools: Chicago 1900-1950*. New Brunswick, NJ: Rutgers University Press.

ENDNOTE

1   *Delsartism* was a system of dance, expression, and physical training that grew out of the work of François Delsarte in France. In the United States, the Delsarte system was popular in women's clubs and public schools as well as the world of professional dance. For more information see Blair (1994) and Ruyter (1999).

PATRICIA M. AMBURGY is Associate Professor Emerita of Art Education at the Pennsylvania State University. Her research interests include visual culture as well as the history of art education. She is especially interested in histories of art education that focus on past struggles of women, ethnic minorities, and working class people to attain personal and social power through public schooling. In spite of—or perhaps because of—continuous social conflicts over the purpose and content of schooling in the United States, from day one to the present time, she continues to believe in the power of knowledge, art, and education to transform people's lives.

PORTRAITURE RESEARCH

19 / The Art of Portraiture

HEATHER LEAH RYERSON FOUNTAIN / ASSOCIATE PROFESSOR, ART EDUCATION AND CRAFTS, KUTZTOWN UNIVERSITY OF PENNSYLVANIA

ABSTRACT: *This chapter will illuminate the art of portraiture as a form of inquiry and highlight the unique qualities that distinguish this methodology from other narrative research methodologies. The history, purpose, and procedures of using portraiture as a form of inquiry will be explored through the following related constructs: (1) voice; (2) context; (3) building relationships; (4) the lens of goodness; (5) emergent themes; (6) the aesthetic whole. Through this chapter the role of the researcher, often called a portraitist, will be defined and the challenges of this type of research will be examined. In addition, the methods of data collection and analysis used to construct a portrait, as well as ethical considerations related to portraiture, will be explored.*

PORTRAITURE: ORIGIN AND PURPOSE

Portraiture is a qualitative methodology of research with roots firmly embedded in the phenomenological framework. This framework, grounded in experience, honors the perspectives of the subjects as unique even when common experiences may be shared (Patton, 2002). Portraiture also shares common elements with ethnography, case study, and other narrative research methodologies. The methodology of portraiture, first introduced by Harvard University sociologist Sara Lawrence-Lightfoot in her book *The Good High School: Portraits of Character and Culture* (1983), has four key elements that guide the process: Voice, Emergent Themes, Context, and Aesthetic Whole. Lawrence-Lightfoot and co-author Davis (1997) describe portraiture as a, "genre of inquiry and representation that seeks to join science and art… in an effort to capture the complexity, dynamics, and subtlety of human experience and organizational life" (p. xv).

Lawrence-Lightfoot developed this research methodology to allow her, as a researcher, the ability to empirically study, record, and interpret the personal stories of individuals, the culture of schools, and the relationships that existed between schools and the communities she studied. This methodology allowed her to maintain the right to aesthetically represent her subjects through "interpretive description" (Davis, Soep, Maira, Remba, & Putnoi, 1993, p. 2). Portraiture, like a novel, seeks to connect an audience to personal stories through the use of rich description and context that captures and draws the reader into the narrative. Unlike a novel, portraiture does not seek to tell a story for entertainment alone, but as a tool to help the reader understand the nuances of a place, a person or a group of people.

ROLE OF THE RESEARCHER
BUILDING RELATIONSHIPS

In many research methodologies, both quantitative and qualitative, connections with the subject of study are made by the researcher only in-so-far as they establish a site for research or permission to engage in research. A clear line of distance or separation between researcher and subject is generally established to help maintain objectivity. In portraiture, however, the intimacy of relationship is crucial, as is empathy. Portraiture is centered on the researcher's ability to build relationships with the individuals involved and understand things from their point of view. It crosses the often perceived hard, fast line that separates the researcher from the subject and requires that the researcher be invested in the subject; continually building a relationship that evolves over time, navigates intimacy, and builds trust and safety, while ensuring reciprocity, honesty, and authenticity.

Lawrence-Lightfoot (1997b) expounds upon the importance of relationship through the following excerpt:

> Whether the encounters are brief or sustained, then, it is important that portraitists view relationships as potentially meaningful and significant to the lives of the actors… we want actors to feel our full attention, our deep engagement, and our challenge—and we want people to leave the encounters feeling safe and whole. At the center of relationships, portraitists hope to build trust and rapport—first, through the search for goodness; second, through empathetic regard; and third, through the development of symmetry, reciprocity, and boundary negotiation. (p. 141)

The portraitist knows that relationships lead to deep findings that extend beneath the surface (Oakley, 1981). For this reason the portraitist values the unique perspectives offered by the actors and remains vigilant in protecting the trust that has been afforded to them. This display of respect helps to deepen the bond of trust between the researcher and actor leading to a deeper level of shared knowledge.

NEGOTIATING BOUNDARIES

The boundaries between the researcher and the subject can be increasingly difficult to negotiate in portraiture. The subject may be a place or person that you are close to or you may develop a close relationship with those you interact with over the course of your many encounters. The boundaries are blurred with portraiture and must be negotiated and carefully considered on a weekly or daily basis; they will likely evolve or change over time as comfort and ease develop. The one boundary that will need to be immediately established in writing will be the researcher's intentions, focus, and responsibilities to those involved.

All participants in the research must sign a consent form, as required by institutional review boards (IRB), that clearly states how data will be collected, stored, and used. This step is critical in protecting the subject and building integrity in your role as researcher. It will also ensure clarity, from the onset, of the direction the researcher is heading and will help guide the topics or themes of the encounters, keeping all participants on topic. Due to the nature of portraiture, which involves minimal interventions, the process may be expedited.

SARA AND MELANIE: ASSENT AND CONSENT: *If working with children, the researcher should obtain consent forms signed by the parents or guardian of the children, as children under the age of 18 are not of legal age to give consent. In addition to the consent form, some researchers choose to create assent forms. These forms delineate the nature of the research in age-appropriate language for children so that they will understand what the research will be about and what they will be expected to do. This form does not replace the consent form, but it does allow children to gain familiarity with the study and feel like they are making an important contribution.*

Although there are many elements to negotiate within portraiture, the careful consideration of boundaries will help the portraitist to set clear parameters of expectation prior to beginning the study. Understanding the boundaries of the study upfront will help both the researcher and the subject by creating a professional atmosphere of respect and trust. As the relationship with the subject changes over time, the boundaries can be renegotiated, but once trust is broken no amount of work can restore that relationship.

METHODOLOGY
VOICE

One of the unique elements of portraiture is the use of *voice* as a research instrument (Lawrence-Lightfoot, 1997a). The researcher tool of *voice* can be defined as what is said or included in the portrait, how it is said, and what context is chosen to frame it. All these factors are contingent on the portraitist and how s/he chooses to construct the narrative. It is through the eyes, ears, thoughts, and interactions of the researcher that the audience experiences the subject or actor of the portrait. As noted by Jessica Davis (1997a) upon first reading portraiture, "The writer was inside—not outside—the work… and the spirited writing had a rhythmic pace more reflective of works of art than of science" (p. 21). Thus, the researcher's narrative becomes a portrait of the subject under study.

Unlike many other methodologies, portraiture embraces and values the perspectives and experiences of the researcher as relevant elements within the narrative, as long as those perspectives do not overshadow the subject. Portraiture expects, even demands, that the researcher create an aesthetic experience through their telling of the portrait. Such attention to details adds color to the narrative and helps the reader "see" the subject more clearly.

BALANCING VOICE

A portraitist must be aware of voice at all times and ensure that each choice is respectful and mindful of the original storyteller; creating a portrait that honors the person's stories (J. H. Davis, personal communication, February 12, 1997). Each choice of inclusion or exclusion of data shapes the narrative in different ways. Such choices are to be weighed carefully by the researcher as they examine whether the element in question is relevant to the research focus as defined by their research questions. An important consideration is whether each inclusion of self is pertinent to the narrative or a self-indulgent inclusion on the part of the portraitist. This balancing act requires that the portraitist continuously and rigorously examine his or her choices, ensuring that their voice is, "premeditated…, restrained, disciplined and carefully controlled… as to never overshadow the actors' voices (though it sometimes is heard in duet, in harmony and counterpoint)" (Lawrence-Lightfoot, 1997a, p. 85).

SARA AND MELANIE: *Working with IRB and/or school district research personnel, you may decide to use either pseudonyms or ask participants whether they want their real names to be included in the study. While this action of renaming the participants or actors within your research may seem distancing or inauthentic, it may be required for IRB approval. Researchers, using many different methodologies, will often involve the participant in choosing their name to be used throughout the research. This involvement can assist in maintaining closeness and authenticity in voice.*

In the following excerpt of a portrait of a girl named Kaiyah,[1] the voice of the portraitist weaves the story that helps us understand the theme of originality as it relates to Kaiyah's daily behavior. This small vignette is one moment that was observed during a year-long study about creativity where numerous data were collected through observations, interviews, artifact collection, testing, and journaling. Give special attention to how the portraitist uses voice to weave the narrative and reveal what she is wondering, observing, and even how she is situated within this portrait:

> For Kaiyah, simple mundane tasks were opportunities to express her originality. Getting dressed in morning, choosing what foods to pack in her lunch bag, and bringing school supplies to class seem like ordinary activities that require little thought, but not for Kaiyah. An example of this behavior can be seen through her choice of a water bottle. Students were allowed to keep one water bottle at their desks throughout the day and fill it as needed from the bubbler by the sink area in the classroom. The only requirement was that the bottle be able to close when not in use, avoiding spills. Most students had large sports bottles with pop-up tops either of a solid color or a ribbed *Poland Springs* bottle, but not Kaiyah. First of all, most students brought the same bottle every day, but I noticed that her choice of water bottle changed frequently. One particular morning, as she unpacked her bag, laying each item out on her desk carefully, I noticed her take a sip from a small bottle which closely resembled a liquor nip. Concerned at first by what she was drinking, I watched more closely from my desk. She repeatedly took small sips from the three-inch-tall decorative glass bottle replacing its red cap after each drink. Throughout the course of the morning she made several trips to the sink to refill her "water bottle," unconcerned by the inconvenience of its small size, seemingly happy with her unconventional selection. (Fountain, 2007, p. 164)

As seen in the example, the voice of the portraitist helps to tell the story of Kaiyah and is only included when it helps move the narrative along. A true balance of voice ensures that the main subject of the narrative is always the central focus, whereas the researcher is the conduit through which the story is told.

CONTEXT

Context creates a framework that aids the reader in understanding the portrait through rich description of the physical, emotional, cultural, and historical setting in which it takes place. Davis (personal communication, February 27, 1997) describes context as walking from the *outside in*; describing everything from the initial arrival into a setting in a way that allows the reader to "be" there, to see, and experience what you have experienced, themselves. The *outside in* description often begins at the physical location or with the physical person you are writing about. The interpretation of the portrait relies on understanding the context that the subject occupies. Contextual information helps to round out the portrait by seeking to find deeper connections, beyond what is seen at first glance. This deeper understanding of context can be gained through observations, interviews and document analysis. Many portraitists choose to record thoughts, ideas, feelings, and interviews. This method of data collection allows them the freedom to visually attend to the subject and not feel compelled to write everything down immediately.

Many research studies control the setting or context of the study to minimize its effects on the subject. In contrast, portraiture uses the setting to aid in the examination of the subject and as the frame through which interpretation occurs. As with the concept of *voice*, the portraitist must be clear about her presence, biases, intentions, and role within the setting she occupies. She becomes part of the story herself, revealing her perspective, physical location, and thoughts.

The following excerpt from *Lisa Flegle: Portrait of an Art Therapist* (Kenney,[2] 1997) describes my first visit to meet Lisa at the adolescent psychiatric hospital unit where I began collecting data for the portrait. Notice the use of "I" statements, as I paint a portrait of the context that aids in defining Lisa Flegle's character.

> After the click of the lock, Lisa enters through a heavy wooden door and extends her hand to me as I rise from the bench where I have been waiting. Lisa, like her art room, is a combination of vibrant excitement and calm comforting familiarity. Lisa's short brown curly hair and glasses frame her soft glowing face and draw your attention to her expressive eyes which put you at ease instantly. Her eyes seem wiser than her years and greet you with an understanding gaze that assures you that her attention is completely yours. (Kenney, 1997, p. 4)

Context in this example provides the reader enough information to envision themselves in the scene, seeing Lisa and shaking her hand. This is the essential goal of context; to help the reader "be there" in the story. They should be able to see, hear, smell and feel everything the researcher and subject are experiencing.

LENS: SEARCH FOR GOODNESS

Portraiture is not the search for weakness or a search for a solution, but rather a focus on a search for goodness. *Goodness* is defined as seeing the positive in a subject; it is seeking to know more. Portraiture is not a deficit model of research that looks for what is wrong or what is not working in a situation. With a focus on goodness, portraiture seeks to understand the following questions: What's happening here? What is working and why? Who is this person or community of people? What is their perspective? These questions guide the portraitist as she develops her specific research questions. This search for goodness does not denote that a portraitist ignores challenges or contradictions, but rather uses them to inform the understanding of the whole. Searching for goodness also does not mean that the portraitist creates an idealized view of the subject or represents only the positive or happy aspects of the subject; but it does mean that all inquiry values the subject's voice, stories, and experiences as unique and respected, while focusing always on the research questions. In the words of Lawrence-Lightfoot (1997b), "The nuanced search for goodness is really a search for a generous, balanced, probing perspective. It is a search for truth—or for the complex and complete truths that combine to shape an authentic narrative" (p. 146).

The previous quotation reminds me that portraitists, like myself, aspire to create narratives that are neutral in judgment, providing a balance to all aspects of the subject. It is often difficult to remember that everything about the subject is part of the story, whether it could be conceived as negative or positive, it helps provide a deeper, more complex understanding of the subject. As your relationship with the subject grows there is a tendency to want to share only the positive aspects, but similar to a photograph, without the balance of darkness and light the image or portrait would have less impact.

Dialogue and Collaboration in Art Classroom Research

SHERRI POLANIECKI KUSHNER / MEDIA ARTS TEACHER, CHUTE MIDDLE SCHOOL, EVANSTON, ILLINOIS AND **CHING-CHIU LIN** / FACULTY ADVISOR, TEACHER EDUCATION OFFICE, THE UNIVERSITY OF BRITISH COLUMBIA

Here we describe a study conducted by Ching-Chiu, a university researcher, in collaboration with Sherri, a classroom teacher, and describe how this collaborative effort benefited both Sherri's teaching and Ching-Chiu's research. One significant limitation of classroom research is that researchers often can only provide a "snapshot" view of the learning experience from an outsider's standpoint, while teachers often find it hard to objectively assess classroom realities due to their sustained personal involvement. This tension is often exacerbated by the fact that some researchers relate to teachers as distanced research subjects, a circumstance that often inhibits collaborative dialogue and teamwork. By sharing our respective views of what was happening in the classroom, we were able to overcome this tension and take advantage of a unique opportunity to benefit from each other's perspectives while learning more about ourselves.

For Ching-Chiu's research, she interviewed Sherri about her views on media literacy and how this shaped Sherri's students' use of technology in the art classroom. Ching-Chiu used portraiture (Lawrence-Lightfoot & Davis, 1997), a methodology in which the researcher attempts to trace the development of his or her subject's views by forming an ongoing dialogue with the sub-

COLLECTING DATA

Collecting data for a portrait requires that a relationship or rapport of trust is first developed between the researcher and subject. Most data are collected through interviews or encounters which are defined by intense discourse that occurs frequently over time. Each encounter may vary in length, location, or intensity, but does require a consistent effort by the researcher to take on an active role as listener as she listens *to* and *for* a story. Most interviews are taped and transcribed, to ensure that all information is captured. In addition the portraitist takes field notes that help gather context, specific terms used by the subject, and/or the direction she, the researcher, would like to follow as the conversation continues. Although the main tool for collecting data is conversational interviews and observational encounters, artifacts and documents can often add context to further inform the researcher.

Another vital tool for a portraitist is the use of the "impressionistic record" (Lawrence-Lightfoot, 1997c, p.188). At the end of each encounter with either a person or the setting, the portraitist organizes the data and looks for common themes or phrases that arise. The impressionistic record, similar to a researcher's personal journal, is the place where researchers note their questions, wonderings, things they notice, things that puzzle them, and notes about possible anticipated themes or topics that arose during the encounter. The entries in this record help the researcher reflect on the encounter and check for inconsistencies she notices, while helping identify areas that need more attention or clarity during the next encounter.

Portraiture is a type of research that is designed to cover a longer period of time. The process of data collection in portraiture continues until the researcher has explored all interview questions and areas that require clarity. This process could take days or years depending on the size and complexity of the subject being studied. As the researcher starts to see convergence, or multiple pieces of data that relate to each other, she knows that she is close to the end of her data collection. The last step in this process is to check for any inconsistencies or holes in the data and conduct the steps needed to gain as complete a view of the topic as is feasible.

Another factor to consider is the time needed to build a relationship of safety and trust where the subject becomes comfortable with the researcher. This is a process, like any other relationship, that takes time. It is not something that can be achieved in one or two visits. Challenges exist even if the researcher already has an established relationship with the subject. Although this type of relationship can help a researcher gain access to a person or location, it also can hinder the process of data collection. For example, I conducted research in the school where I had taught for many years. This pre-existing

ject. Portraiture emphasizes that the researcher-subject relationship plays a critical role in the success and authenticity of the final "portrait." The write-up is called a portrait because, rather than just reflect back what Sherri already knew about herself and her classroom, Ching-Chiu looked to capture the richness, complexity, and dimensionality of Sherri's and her students' experiences within their social and cultural contexts. In addition to conducting interviews, transcribing them, and putting the information she gathered into a chronological timeline, Ching-Chiu showed her working data to Sherri and, together, they came to new understandings about Sherri's ideas and their influence in the classroom.

We met frequently to discuss the classroom events and exchange our impressions, in the course of which Ching-Chiu realized that Sherri's ideas about media literacy and using technology in the art classroom were constantly evolving as she interacted with her students and with Ching-Chiu. Simultaneously, Sherri became more reflective about her own teaching practices. The personal relationship that Ching-Chiu formed in the course of the study with Sherri and her students enabled her to overcome the limits of her own subjective experience and produce a more nuanced and higher-quality research product. Because of our distinctive roles and research perspectives, our teacher-researcher partnership benefited both of us by allowing each of us to gain deeper insights about ourselves, our work, and each other. ■

REFERENCE

Lawrence-Lightfoot, S., & Davis, J. (1997). *The art and science of portraiture.* San Francisco, CA: Jossey-Bass.

relationship helped me quickly gain access to the research site, but I had challenges establishing myself as a researcher. Although my role had changed from the last time I was part of this community from teacher/colleague to researcher, their view of me had stayed the same. I was still their buddy, their colleague, their dinner companion. They wanted to stop by and visit, but I needed to observe and to take field notes without interruption. It took approximately a month for my return to the site to fade into the background and become a non-issue. Part of this process was allowing people to have the time they needed to catch-up with me and share their news. As an ethical researcher, I prioritized allowing the time to meet the participants' varied needs and put my agenda on hold until their needs were met. This process honored their need to connect, while discussing my new role within the setting. This example highlights the difficulties in creating a specific time frame for research. Like people, each portrait research situation is unique and needs to be negotiated individually.

ANALYZING DATA: SEARCHING FOR PATTERNS AND EMERGENT THEMES

The aesthetic construction of a portrait is woven together through the use of emergent themes organized under one cohesive overarching story. The evolution of emergent themes begins when a portraitist enters her/his research and continues through the final creation of the portrait. Emergent themes are used to structure the aesthetic whole. At the conclusion of each day, the researcher reviews all data, whether written, auditory, or visual, looking for patterns. Researchers may notice these patterns through the appearance of repetitive phrases, words, metaphors, expressions, images or topics that emerged through the course of the encounter. As the patterns revealed themselves, they can be noted and tested against further collected data, to see if the pattern is truly an emergent theme. Initial patterns often can be dismissed as numerous sources of data are collected and convergence, all data pointing to a similar idea, is lacking. Three types of problems of pattern weakness (Lawrence-Lightfoot & Davis, 1997) can occur:

1. **Differing Meanings**: Similar words were used which seemed to form a pattern, but upon further examination had different meanings to the individuals using them; therefore they do not refer to the same topic or idea.
2. **Random Collections**: The items in the pattern were distantly related, but had no strong connection to each other.
3. **Isolated Occurrences**: What appeared to be a pattern at first did not arise again as data collection continued or the pattern existed in only one area of your data and was not corroborated by others.

Only when the pattern has relevance to the whole and can be triangulated from multiple sources of data does it become an emergent theme.

AESTHETIC WHOLE: CREATING THE PORTRAIT

Often three or more emergent themes arise from the data. These themes provide the structural canvas on which the portrait is developed. The following research example is a portrait about a child who had been identified as artistically gifted. As I sifted through and organized my data I began to notice that all information about Dora related to three distinct themes. These themes helped to provide a structure or outline that aided in telling her story. An understanding of how themes form the structure of a portrait can be seen in the following outline (Fountain, 2008).

> *Overarching Story: Dora: Finding Her Voice*
> I.   Introduction
> II. Emergent Theme One: Alternative Form of Communication
>   a.   Supporting Evidence
> III. Emergent Theme Two: Creativity
>   a.   Supporting Evidence
> IV. Emergent Theme Three: Art Battle
>   a.   Supporting Evidence
> V.   Conclusion

The portraitist uses this scaffolding to build the structure of the portrait as she organizes the themes to create an aesthetic sequencing of events. The themes build upon each other; the order of the themes is dependent on what is needed in the beginning, middle, and end to help the narrative gracefully unfold so that the flow of the story is organized in a way that makes sense to the reader.

When considering the aesthetic whole of a portrait, unity is the ultimate goal. It should have a flow that allows the reader to be enveloped within the narrative without getting caught or sidetracked by unnecessary or unrelated things along the way. To ensure this, it is helpful for the portraitist to consider the following questions as they scrutinize the whole (Davis, 1997b):

- Has context informed the portrait by providing a clear frame through which the subject can be understood?
- Has voice been clearly stated and balanced to ensure that it values, not overshadows, the subject's authentic voice?
- Have relationships been respected and trust honored throughout the shaping of the aesthetic whole?
- Have the emergent themes been carefully considered and corroborated through the triangulation of multiple sources of data to ensure that they remain true to the language, culture, and stories of the actors?
- Have all elements of the portrait been weighed in their importance to ensure that unnecessary items have not been included that could disrupt the flow of the narrative?

CONCLUSION

A final portrait is a gift that reveals what is often concealed from the world. It is a chance to explore, preserve, and gain perspective on a subject with such depth that you cannot help but be drawn into it. Like feminist pedagogy, portraiture respects all voices and perspectives through the co-construction of a safe place where meaning is created and all voices and perspectives are equally valued and honored (Lawrence-Lightfoot & Davis, 1997; Patton, 2002). As a teacher, researcher and artist, I have found this aspect of portraiture to be most rewarding. I am grateful to all who have allowed me into their worlds and have helped me see beneath the painted surface as I crafted their portraits.

REFERENCES

Davis, J. H. (1997a). Perspective taking: Discovery and development. In S. Lawrence-Lightfoot & J. H. Davis, *The art and science of portraiture* (pp. 19-38). San Francisco, CA: Jossey-Bass.

Davis, J. H. (1997b). Implementation: Composing the narrative. In S. Lawrence-Lightfoot & J. H. Davis, *The art and science of portraiture* (pp. 261-274). San Francisco, CA: Jossey-Bass.

Davis, J. H., Soep, E., Maira, S., Remba, N., & Putnoi, D. (1993). *Safe havens: Portraits of educational effectiveness in community art centers that focus on education in economically disadvantaged communities.* Cambridge, MA: Harvard Project Zero, Harvard University.

Fountain, H. L. R. (2007). *Using art to differentiate instruction: An analysis of its effects on creativity and the learning environment* (Unpublished doctoral dissertation). Purdue University, West Lafayette, IN.

Fountain, H. L. R. (2008). *Creativity and learning in a classroom that uses art to differentiate instruction: Five portraits.* Unpublished manuscript.

Harding, S. (1987). *Feminism & methodology.* Bloomington: Indiana University Press.

Hesse-Bieber, S. N. (2007). *Handbook of feminist research: Theory and praxis.* Thousand Oaks, CA: Sage.

Lather, P. (1991). *Getting smart: Feminist research and pedagogy within/in the postmodern.* London, England: Routledge.

Kenney, H. L. R. (1997). *Lisa Flegle: Portrait of an art therapist.* Unpublished manuscript.

Lawrence-Lightfoot, S. (1983). *The good high school: Portraits of character and culture.* New York, NY: Basic Books.

Lawrence-Lightfoot, S. (1997a). On voice. In S. Lawrence-Lightfoot & J. H. Davis, *The art and science of portraiture* (pp. 85-130). San Francisco, CA: Jossey-Bass.

Lawrence-Lightfoot, S. (1997b). On relationship. In S. Lawrence-Lightfoot & J. H. Davis, *The art and science of portraiture* (pp. 135-182). San Francisco, CA: Jossey-Bass.

Lawrence-Lightfoot, S. (1997c). On emergent themes. In S. Lawrence-Lightfoot & J. H. Davis, *The art and science of portraiture* (pp. 185-238). San Francisco, CA: Jossey-Bass.

Lawrence-Lightfoot, S., & Davis, J. H. (1997). *The art and science of portraiture.* San Francisco, CA: Jossey-Bass.

Oakley, A. (1981). Interviewing women: A contradiction in terms. In H. Roberts (Ed.), *Doing feminist research* (pp. 30-61). New York, NY: Routledge.

Patton, M. Q. (2002). *Qualitative research and evaluation methods* (3rd ed.). Thousand Oaks, CA: Sage.

ENDNOTES

1   A pseudonym.

2   The author's (Heather Fountain) former last name was Kenney.

HEATHER FOUNTAIN'S research interests include the effects of Differentiated Instruction on learning and creativity in both the general and art education classrooms, preserving voices of arts educators who work in various settings for future generations through portraiture, and the effects of arts integration on learning. She is the author of *Differentiated Instruction in Art* (2013), part of the Best Practice in Art Education series by Davis Publications.

20 / Portraiture, Pottery, and Pedagogy: Examining Portraiture Methodology in the Contexts of Ceramics and Teaching

COURTNEY LEE WEIDA / ASSISTANT PROFESSOR OF ART EDUCATION, ADELPHI UNIVERSITY

ABSTRACT: *This chapter serves as a methodology exemplar, examining portraiture methodology and emphasizing linkages between art teaching and arts research. Specifically, the chapter draws upon a recent study of contemporary female ceramic artists and a range of gender experiences they describe in their field. Portraiture methodology focuses on the nuances of language and speech within the research data, attending to it as the "texture" of the interviews. The interview data of this study suggest that a focus on multiple perspectives and re-envisioning social expectations, allows for fuller and richer understandings of ceramic works and ceramics makers' identities. In this regard, a portraitist's approach can help educators and researchers to avoid overlooking important expressions of artistic, social, and personal growth.*

ENCOUNTERING PORTRAITURE

Researcher Corrine Glesne (2005) has written that "learning to do qualitative research is like learning to paint" in that we study the research of others, apply various methodologies, and adapt our own research approaches (p. 3). Portraiture, as Sara Lawrence-Lightfoot and Jessica Hoffmann Davis (1997) describe it, compares the ways in which artists paint portraits of their subjects to the processes of researchers writing descriptions of their research participants. As one of Jessica Hoffmann Davis' students, I was struck by portraiture research methodology as an approach that uniquely honors the practices of artists. I was immediately drawn to the possibilities of artistry in the descriptions and interpretations of this research approach. At that time, research itself seemed a far-off and lofty goal for me—a text-heavy endeavor of those many years my senior in experience and education. While I enjoyed the occasional literature review assignment, I mainly identified as an art teacher (and on good days, as a ceramic artist).

However, I felt a meaningful connection with Jessica's sensitive and detailed class presentations about research portraits of artists, art-centers, and school art programs. Portraiture offers a rich space to be as careful and thoughtful as possible, and yet it acknowledges the researcher as learner: a person still in the process of describing and interpreting. This balance was new to me as a young researcher, and the sustained dispositions of perception and doubt were crucial to my own investigation of nuances and complexities within ceramic practice. This chapter will draw upon research from my doctoral dissertation (Weida, 2008) and discuss recent scholarship relating to portraiture methodology, emphasizing linkages between art teaching and art research.

PRELUDE TO MY PROCESS: FRAMING INFLUENCES

As a potter who engages with portraiture methodology, my perspective as principal investigator necessarily frames this research (similarly to the frame in a work of art). While I learned about other ceramic artists, I also began to think about and discuss some of my own experiences of gender and how they colored my view of contemporary ceramics. I had experienced several moments of uncertainty and doubt as a female artist and teacher that alternately intrigued, haunted, and daunted me. I wanted, then, to explore the events and stories of others that also contained common threads of gender, and the symbolic, mythic, and socially-constructed connections of women and clay. My main research question was: How do women in this study experience the influence of gender on their artworks and practices?

Within the earliest interviews during my research, I found that the stories of other artists connected, overlapped, and diverged, (with one another, and with my own) but were contextualized by a sense of empathetic community around social constructs that alternately restricted and excluded women. Literature from archaeology, art history, and cultural/gender studies suggests that women were the first makers of clay objects and that females are often associated with nature, earth, and domesticity or the home (all features commonly linked with clay as a material). However, there is also documentation of women's exclusion from glaze and kiln technologies, profit and credit for their own ceramic work, and acknowledgment as leaders of the field of studio ceramics (Poesch, 1984) with reference to the American Art Pottery Movement. Vincentelli (2000) has asserted that there exists a commonly held belief that pottery was historically "an exclusively female activity," so that working with clay becomes a "'naturalized' activity linked to females," yet she argues that "such roles are not dictated by nature but by culture and the result of choices that particular groups have made." (p. 15). Knowles (1997) points out that although hand-building in ceramics was initially an almost entirely female endeavor, men have dominated texts of art history as well as art education history. Within such historical research, I perceived a tension between the ways in which womanhood is linked with ceramics, and yet individual women may be excluded from and within it.

In examining the interviews, I found that the depth and range of these exclusions were varied. They (we) did not share a singular view or experience of being women in the field of ceramics, but rather sensed relationships among the ranges and depths of views and experiences. Once I appreciated some of the experiences and understandings of others, I began to see subtleties in their work and in my own that I wanted to explore further. Discussions with other artists have shaped my thoughts and my research, and created a sort of composite portrait or landscape of my field. They have also nourished me as an artist, a researcher, and a teacher.

Like British potter Elspeth Owen (one of my research participants), I have paradoxically found both a sense of community and individuality within collectives and histories of women artists. The late Jo Spence (2001), a photographer whose writings also inspired me, described her very identity as a "site of contradiction… a dialectical self… in a constant process of change, of working and reworking the past" (p. 355). So, too, I have positioned myself as an investigator of nuance and contradiction, locating and recording re-viewings and identity shifts of women artists in ceramics through my portraits.

RESEARCH SOURCES: A GATHERING OF ARTISTS AND ARTWORKS

Portraiture includes the use of many documents and diverse data sources to tell stories of research. To explore how

gender impacts experiences and artworks, I examined literature addressing the history of female ceramic artists in the United States, gender studies and art history, and a range of related subjects within cultural studies and ceramic archaeology. My study used data in the form of interviews, conversations, and artworks surveyed in studios, coffee shops, publications, and via e-mail. Portraiture methodology focuses on the nuances of language and speech within the research data, attending to it as the "texture" of the interviews. Feminist researcher Mary Maynard (1994) has similarly noted that many women may experience their lives as having a set of "different contours and patterns" than those of men. My research has stemmed from an interest in the textures and patterns of gender experience that manifest through art.

The research participants for this study included 21 women artists who make ceramics. These individuals were self-selected in response to several of my calls for participation among listservs and journals relating to ceramic art. Geographically, my research sample included women from the United States, Canada, England, and France. Emphasizing the communal and personal nature of ceramics practice and teaching, I should also mention that many of the participants were recruited through word-of-mouth and recommendations of other artists. I contacted a few colleagues, as well as ceramicists whose artistic work and research has inspired me as an artist and researcher. In my view, this shows how research and learning can coincide in very direct ways, for I was able to learn directly about some individuals and works I found most intriguing from the beginnings of my career.

I have noted that all of the women in my study are ceramic artists. Additionally, nearly all of these women serve or have served in some teaching role, whether informally or formally. It should also be pointed out that all artists gave permission to use their real names (rather than pseudonyms) in research documents, as they are known as public figures. Additionally, part of my goal as a researcher is to contribute art historical writings through the respectful representation of leading women artists. Women from this study identified

---

SARA AND MELANIE: *Feminist research methodologies can take a variety of forms. A researcher may embrace a critical theory paradigm in her/his approach to research seeking to change the ways gender shapes art experiences, for example. Often many qualitative methodologies like narrative inquiry and portraiture are described as feminist methodologies because of the attention to voice—the voice of the participants and also the voice of the researcher. Additionally, attention to issues of power is typically hallmark in feminist research. For more information, please consider:*

Collins, G., & Sandell, R. (1997). *Feminist research: Themes, issues, and applications in art education.* In S. D. La Pierre and E. Zimmerman (Eds.), Research methods and methodologies for art education. (pp. 193-222). Reston, VA: National Art Education Association.

Harding, S. (1987). *Feminism & methodology.* Bloomington: Indiana University Press.

Hesse-Bieber, S. N. (2007). *Handbook of feminist research: Theory and praxis. Thousand Oaks, CA: Sage.*

Lather, P. (1991). Getting smart: Feminist research and pedagogy within/in the postmodern London, *England: Routledge.*

Wolf, M. (1992). A thrice-told tale: Feminism, postmodernism, and ethnographic responsibility. *Palo Alto, CA: Stanford University Press.*

with a rather diverse range of ages, geographical locations, and artistic identities (ceramic sculptors, functional potters, tile-artists, etc). It should also be noted that while a variety of ethnicities/races/cultures were represented, there were more apparently Caucasian women than women from any other single racial/ethnic group. This should be seen as a limitation of this research, just as a curriculum that is not wholly culturally diverse may be seen as limited in some regard. However, many of these women have noted the influence of non-Western traditions and/or individual artists in their work and processes including art of Africa, Asia, and others.

I conducted interviews in homes, studios, coffee shops, and via e-mail or phone. I continually asked participating ceramicists to contribute to the process of interpreting the interviews, by sending them follow-up questions and transcriptions through ongoing correspondence. This coincides with portraiture practices as well as Maynard's (1994) notion that "the legitimacy of women's own understanding of their experiences is one of the hallmarks of feminism" (p. 23). Andrea Fontana's (2001) emphasis on blurring the boundaries of researcher and subject has also inspired my use of conversation between subjects and within the process of writing the research narrative.

Conversations as [a form of] research data is used here in attempt to allow the voices of participants to dialogue in response to one another directly, and to decentralize myself as the questioner and sole source of the research questions and analysis as much as possible. Although I facilitated the interviews, my inclusion of comments from the artists themselves about their own interviews and those of other artists raised new questions and themes within this research that I had not initially considered. These questions became subsequent topics for additional interviews. From my perspective, this was not unlike constructivist teaching approaches in which the teacher aims to position herself as facilitator as well as learner.

INTERVIEW DESIGN: TALKING GENDER AND CERAMICS

During the interviews, I asked participants to reflect upon their artistic experiences, artworks, and artistic identity as each relates to gender issues. Through a series of open-ended questions, all participants engaged in preliminary interviews. My interview questions were open-ended to allow for what Steiner Kvale (2000) has described as a conversation co-produced by interviewer and subject. Reinharz and Chase (2001) also have proposed the use of open-ended questions to empower women to speak more openly. Using preliminary data within biographical and artistic information available in literature and artist websites, I asked interviewees questions about gender that were carefully tailored to their own work and interests. The

development of these questions was greatly influenced by the personalized conversational style of bell hooks' (1995) interviews with artists in *Art on My Mind: Visual Politics*.

My initial concern as I began the interviews addressed the conversion of research questions into interview questions. Seeking to understand more about the background and experiences of my colleagues in terms of gender issues, I framed the interview with ten open-ended queries. My questions ranged from "ice breaker" inquiries about biographical details, to influential educators/mentors, to experiences concerning perceptions of gender, and the role of gender in one's artworks and art processes. My interview protocol was directly influenced by portraiture methodology, for like Lawrence-Lightfoot and Davis (1997), I incorporated phrases from answers into subsequent questions. For example, as I listened to find out about what my interviewees noticed about perceptions of male and female ceramists, I framed my following question around how those specific perceptions mentioned by the artists might actually influence artwork and practice. My inquiries were conversational in nature and often varied from one artist to the next, as opposed to a rigid questionnaire.

DATA CODING AND ANALYSIS: RE-DEFINING FEMININE, FEMALE, AND FEMINIST

I transcribed both my inquiries and each response from the artists. From the research conversations, I interpreted many complex themes posed by the artists. I coded the data by highlighting words and phrases that formed refrains. Given my focus on issues of gender as anticipatory themes, I reflected on my own biases and experiences as I looked for gender-related words and phrases such as: *women, men, male, female, feminist, feminine, girlie, womanly,* etc. As a potter as well as a ceramic sculptor, I felt the usefulness of Terkel's comparison of the process of carving sculpture to looking at and editing research transcripts (Platt, 2001, p. 43). There was a metaphorical artistry to the process of interpreting words from the interview as research data, given the history of clay as a material often inscribed with words and messages dating back to the time of cuneiform.

I also recognized the ways in which my interpretations of the data served to shape the research itself, for a different researcher would identify different themes and their research document as a sort of work of art would be quite distinctive. The next few sections will outline a few selected refrains, or commonly mentioned issues from these interviews with which I attempted to create a conceptual unity in which the bits of data form a story. Lawrence-Lightfoot and Davis (1997) emphasize attaining unity in the structure of the research narrative as akin to creating a quilt or weaving, with separate but related pieces forming a cohesive whole.

"SERIOUSNESS" AND "HOBBY"IST IN CERAMICS

As a portraitist, I located and described tensions, reversals, and revisions pertaining to gender in the interview transcripts. When I asked artists to address how male artists are perceived versus how female artists are perceived in society, most participants identified the contrasting concepts of women being perceived as "hobbyist" ceramic artists, whereas men are often viewed as more "serious" or professional ceramic artists. Most of the artists interviewed maintained that lack of seriousness was a major perception of female versus male ceramic artists, even though they also asserted that gender does not make a difference in ceramics overall.

Participants described this notion of seriousness versus hobby status as stemming from a variety of sources. Most suggested that men are generally taken more seriously by people (in general), by customers, and/or by other viewers. For many of the women artists in this study with multiple career paths (psychologist-artists, lawyer-artists, mother-artists, etc), tensions between serious artmaking versus hobbyist status of the past overlapped complexly with their senses of pride in the uniqueness and value of having dual careers that inform ceramics making. For example: One research participant, psychologist Joan Hardin, often spoke not only of the aesthetics and making of her ceramic tiles, but also of the interactions and identities of her patrons. Such overlapping interests underscore the challenges and joys of interdisciplinary learning experiences explored by teachers as well. Further, Lawrence-Lightfoot (1995) has noted the importance of "undoing caricatures" (p. 12) in her portraits, and I found that there was a similar potential in undoing stereotypes and perceptions about individual women and the seriousness in their work and processes as part of this research.

"FEMININE" VERSUS FEMALE SUBJECT MATTER

Participating artists Esta Carnahan and Maureen Burns-Bowie described the tension between addressing what they describe as specifically female and feminine issues with creating work that is also universal. I had previously located themes of goddess imagery and emphasis on nature in a review of the literature as major threads of women's ceramic art (including such ceramic works as *Persephone Studies* [1985] by Mary Frank). For many of the interviewees, goddess themes were present symbolically or indirectly. There was much diversity among various "feminine" subject matters and the numerous ways in which these artists utilize them, including interplay of gender with culture, race, religion, artistic style, and many other factors.

For artist-participant Dolores Dunning, "feminine" imagery such as "tulips" was not of interest to her, as she viewed herself as a controversial artist engaging with "images of power, anger, aggression, or war" (Weida, 2008, p. 140). Dunning explained that she felt that creating "feminine" work was a social expectation placed upon her in her earlier works, but she also wondered if her perception was true. This ambivalence about gender, perception, and reality was a thread in the interviews. Comments such as these resulted in a "layering" of description similar to those noted by Haggerson, Bell, Fuller, Lawrence, Vanosdall, and Hunnicutt (2005) in their portraiture study. In my study, definitions "feminine," "female," and/or "feminist" were variously empowering or limiting, but consistently fluid in definition and association.

FEMININE AND FEMALE PROCESSES

I also noticed definitions and associations of gender in artists' descriptions of the processes of making ceramics. Some artists mentioned both acceptances and rejections of domestic, female, and/or feminine qualities within their artistic processes. This included making pots and making food as potentially linked, as well as how ceramic sculptures such as those by Tsehai Johnson critique (though are created within) a context of domesticity. As a researcher participating in conversations with these artists, I found that talking about women's processes as distinctive from those of men seems more empowering and less potentially restrictive than analyzing themes and subject matters unique or more common to women. Perhaps this is because processes may lead to many outcomes, whereas subject matters indicate the finished project of an artistic process and may be readily classified in simplistic terms and dismissed critically as work that is not "serious." This underscores the complexity of conversation and honoring of process in art and teaching.

CONCLUDING REMARKS: RESEARCH AND TEACHING PRACTICES

Many of the observations and interpretations of this research have implications for educators interested in gender and art. This research contributes to an underrepresented area of research by documenting contemporary ceramicists' narratives and artistic work as each relate to issues of gender. Within this research, a discussion of women and an interest in gender equality begins to interrogate, for example, how women artists are seen as major players in the history of ceramics and yet how they are often excluded from the canon of individual ceramicists. Addressing women and gender also allows us to contextualize the nuances of how the women artists in this study identify the lack of importance of discussion of gender, and yet nearly universally claim that women are taken less seriously as artists than men. This research process has been both educational and transformative for myself and (reportedly) for the artists who took part in this study, allowing us to search out persisting social expectations about women's work in ceramics and illuminating the tensions and in-between spaces of women artists' experiences. These artists have identified a great range of symbols and metaphors of women and ceramics (including representations of the body, symbolic uses of goddesses, and negotiations of domesticity), and also provided clarification of the dual sense of historically female clay traditions with conflicting individual artistic recognition of women.

This research has engaged the telling of personal stories as part of its structure and methodology. These shared narratives are resonant with many of my experiences and observations, but they also illuminate perspectives I did not previously understand. The interview data of this study suggest that a focus on multiple perspectives and re-envisioning social expectations, allows for fuller and richer understandings of ceramic works and ceramics makers' identities. In this regard, a portraitist's approach also helps educators and researchers to avoid overlooking important expressions of artistic, social, and personal growth.

I have also found that the voices of these women have provided me with the criticality, creativity, encouragement, anger, humor, and patience that I have come to locate, contemplate, and reprise within my own voice. Throughout subtly gendered situations in art and teaching, I have continuously struggled with my artistic ideas, my research inquiries, and my teaching persona as a woman. I found myself wanting to continue to connect with others who had worked through similar struggles and joys about the constraints and uncertainties of being a female, ceramic artist, and educator. Over the course of my conversations with other artists and the collaborative creation of their portraits, I have gained an increasingly complex and inspiring view into the landscape of my field.

REFERENCES

Fontana, A. (2001). Postmodern trends in interviewing. In J. Gubrium & J. Holstein (Eds.), *Handbook of interview research: Context and method* (pp. 161-175). Thousand Oaks, CA: Sage.

Glesne, C. (2005). *Becoming qualitative researchers: An introduction*. New York, NY: Allyn & Bacon.

Haggerson, N., Bell, G., Fuller, A., Lawrence, R., Vanosdall, R., & Hunnicutt, K. H. (2005). Do "transformative" research approaches make a difference, and if so, how do we know? *International Journal of Humanities & Peace, 21*(1), 19-24.

hooks, b. (1995). *Art on my mind: Visual politics*. New York, NY: New Press.

Knowles, J. (1997). *Out of the hands of orators: Mary Louise McLaughlin, Adelaide Alsop Robineau, the American art pottery movement and the art education of women* (Unpublished doctoral dissertation). Ohio State University, Columbus.

Kvale, S. (2000). *InterViews: An introduction to qualitative research interviewing*. New York, NY: Sage.

Lawrence-Lightfoot, S. (1995). *Balm in Gilead*. New York, NY: Penguin.

Lawrence-Lightfoot, S. & Davis, J. (1997). *The art and science of portraiture*. New York, NY: Jossey-Bass.

Maynard, M. (1994). Methods, practice and epistemology. In M. Maynard & J. Purvis (Eds.), *Researching women's lives from a feminist perspective* (pp. 10-26). London, England: Taylor and Francis.

Platt, J. (2001). The history of the interview. In J. F. Gubrium & J. A. Holstein (Eds.), *The handbook of interview research: Context and methods* (pp. 33-58). London, England: Sage.

Posech, J. (1984). *Newcomb pottery: An enterprise for southern women, 1895-1940*. Eaton, PA: Schiffer.

Reinharz, S., & Chase, S. E. (2001). Interviewing women. In J. F. Gubrium & J. A. Holstein (Eds.), *The handbook of interview research: Context and methods* (pp. 221-238). London, England: Sage.

Spence, J. (2001). Beyond the family album. In H. Robinson (Ed), *Feminist art theory: An anthology 1968-2000* (pp. 352-363). Oxford, England: Blackwell.

Vincentelli, M. (2000). *Women and ceramics: Gendered vessels*. New York, NY: Manchester University Press.

Weida, C. (2008). *Ambivalences of art: Nuance, contradiction, and duality in the words and works of women in contemporary ceramics* (Doctoral dissertation). Columbia University Teachers College, New York, New York.

COURTNEY LEE WEIDA is an Assistant Professor of Art Education at Adelphi University. She has taught pre-K-12 in Boston and New York. She earned licenses in Visual Art, English, and Elementary classroom teaching. She completed her doctorate in Art & Art Education at Columbia University Teachers College. She earned an EdM from Harvard University, specializing in Museum Education. Her BA (Northeastern University) included a double major in Visual Art and English Literature. Her recent publications address ceramic art, studio craft, and gender issues in art education. As a practicing ceramic artist, she possesses a unique background in archaeology museum work that has informed her art and research in ceramics. As a teacher educator, she tries to consider carefully which views and voices are being represented and how students might be invited to have diverse and meaningful encounters with art research.

SECTION IV: MAKING MEANING

Introduction

MELANIE L. BUFFINGTON AND **SARA WILSON MCKAY**

HOW DO WE MAKE MEANING FROM OUR PRACTICES?

MUSINGS AND WONDERINGS FROM THE FIELD

How does awareness of our immersion in contemporary digital visual culture influence what teachers and students do in the art classroom? What shapes assessment in visual arts classes? What does it mean to be a certified teacher when there are some teachers who take the privilege and responsibility of teaching lightly? What impact does the annual PTA Reflections Art contest have on my school community? How does the development of an after school art club based on student interests influence student interest in art? How does (my) art training affect how I teach art?

Another motivation for teachers to conduct research may be a search for meaningfulness in their practice. The methodologies in this section are especially adept at taking up these kinds of questions: Theoretical or Philosophical research; Case Study; and Autobiographical and Narrative Inquiry.

OVERVIEW OF METHODOLOGIES

- Researchers choose to conduct **theoretical research** when they are intrigued to theorize for themselves about a particular topic or phenomenon. Researchers often delve into a particular philosophy or theoretical concept and offer various connections among works of art, educational theories, classroom practices, teachers' beliefs and value systems, and a wide range of critical theories.
- **Case studies**, frequently long-term studies that are quite limited in scope, look in depth at a particular phenomenon or case; researchers tend to spend a considerable amount of time at the research site. Researchers may choose typical cases or exceptional ones, which embody positive or negative extremes of the phenomenon.
- **Autobiographical inquiry** is a form of narrative inquiry that encourages exploration of our practices based on the past with an eye toward how we self-construct our futures.
- **Narrative inquiry**, emphasizing meaningful stories and the contradictions of everyday living, views the interaction of researcher and participants in a holistic manner, and allows for flexible interpretations that may shift over time and vary with each reading.

THEORETICAL
RESEARCH

21 / Obtuse Research: Flights of Excess in Art Education

CHARLES R. GAROIAN / PROFESSOR OF ART EDUCATION, THE PENNSYLVANIA STATE UNIVERSITY AND **YVONNE M. GAUDELIUS** / ASSOCIATE VICE PRESIDENT AND SENIOR ASSOCIATE DEAN OF UNDERGRADUATE EDUCATION AND PROFESSOR OF ART EDUCATION AND WOMEN'S STUDIES, THE PENNSYLVANIA STATE UNIVERSITY

ABSTRACT: *Curiosity, the opening of new questions, and new flights of excess enabled through obtuse meaning represents what in a traditional research framework might be called a hypothesis. However, unlike the if/then binary of hypotheses in the sciences and social sciences where research questions lead to conclusive objective answers that can be reproduced by those who follow predetermined and predictable methodologies, the obtuse meanings discussed here through theoretical research leads to hypothetical possibilities in research that resist and exceed conclusions and synthetic closures.*

> *Research... is an adventure of the signifier, an excess of exchange...*
> —Roland Barthes (1977, p. 198)

Works of art spark our curiosities. We look at images millions of times a day and work to understand what they mean for us. Some we interpret quickly, without even recognizing that we are doing so. Others cause us to puzzle for a moment as we come to terms with levels of meaning contained within an image. Still others cause us to surrender to the image—they open new questions, they bring about transformations, and new flights of excess[1]...

SARA AND MELANIE: *The purpose of theoretical research is to develop and build theories related to a topic of study. This is different from many other forms of research that rely on collecting forms of data from humans in specific settings. In this case, Garoian and Gaudelius use theory and contemporary works of art to expand on the ways that researchers might employ theoretical research to explore new ideas in the field.*

...a hole in his cheek, as if the seven orifices on and around his face were not enough, electronic media artist Matt Kenyon returned from New Orleans with an eighth hole in the middle of his right cheek, a piercing fitted with a stainless steel stud with a shiny ball at each end, one on the inside and the other on the outside. Its curious, obtrusive placement begged questioning. What is that ball on your cheek? What is it for? Why is it in the middle of your cheek? Did the piercer miss his mark? Unlike piercings that are ordinarily studded through the ears, tongue, lips, nostrils, or brow, Kenyon had had the center of his cheek perforated to prepare for a performance (Figure 1).

When we asked, he informed us that the hole would be used as a side entrance, a conduit through which to feed a wire through his cheek, connected at one end to a barcode scanner attached to his belt, a Nielsen Homescan that he acquired by joining the Nielsen Family as an interloper, and at the other end of the wire, a micro-video camera implanted inside the cavity of his mouth—altogether constituting a homemade, electronic self-surveillance[2] device to transmit his consumption of barcode readings from his body, and to hack into the Nielsen Company, a national consumer data bank.

> In a world increasingly defined by global markets, connected consumers and volumes of digital information, The Nielsen Company employs advanced data collection methodologies and measurement science to help businesses turn new and traditional sources of data into customer intelligence to better manage their brands, launch and grow product portfolios, optimize their media mix and establish meaningful customer relationships. (The Nielsen Company, n.d.a)

FIGURE 1. Matt Kenyon, *Consumer Index*, 2009. Performance photo courtesy of the artist.

FIGURE 2. Matt Kenyon, *Consumer Index*, 2009. Performance photo courtesy of the artist.

The stainless steel stud remained in place for close to a year to properly heal the soft thick tissue, the flesh of Kenyon's pierced cheek in order to prevent infection, to keep its hole open for ease of pushing the wire in and out of his mouth when connecting and disconnecting the camera with the scanner-transmitter.

With his body having accepted and acclimated to the piercing, and registered with The Nielsen Company, Kenyon performed *Consumer Index*, a live site-specific artwork, at a local Walmart department store. During this unannounced public performance, he walked into the store, removed the stainless steel stud… then, mashing machine and the meat of his body, he pushed a wire through his cheek, pulled it out through his mouth, connected it to the micro-video, then shoved the assembly back into his mouth cavity, and attached the other end of the wire to the scanner (Figure 2).

Then, walking up and down the aisles of Walmart, Kenyon proceeded "to shop" for grocery items in the store, a sealed package of AA Duracell Batteries, a red can of Great Value Baked Beans, a jar of Polar brand Fuji Apple fruit preserves, and each and every other food stuff and household item on the shelves… opening his mouth to reveal their containers, packaging, and labels to the lens of the camera (Figure 3)… rotating them in hand to expose and transmit their barcodes to the Nielsen Homescan attached to his belt, adjacent to his belly, near his stomach, consuming without consumption, supplying the craving growl of that feckless area of the body with the spectacle of mass mediated food… a feeding to feed the insatiable appetite of the "Nielsen Family," to hack its tracking and measuring consumption, analyzing purchasing trends and behavior, in determining and manufacturing desire (The Nielsen Company, n.d.b) for what millions of Americans eat… a virtual consumption manifested in the body politic as false consciousness, a consumption that begets consumption that Kenyon baits, parodies, and subverts through the Baudrillardian viral phenomenon of *Consumer Index*… the "virtual and the viral go hand in hand," his body ingesting while infecting the marketing and commodity fetishism of consumer capitalism (Baudrillard, 2002, p. 63).

FIGURE 3. Matt Kenyon, *Consumer Index*, 2009. Performance photo courtesy of the artist.

IMAGE/MEANING

In his writings, French theorist Roland Barthes (1977, pp. 52–55) introduces us to the idea that images can carry different forms or levels of meaning: the representational, the symbolic, and the obtuse. While we will focus this chapter on the obtuse, it is useful to first outline the representational and the symbolic, recognizing that it is difficult to separate these forms of meaning from one another.

> **SARA AND MELANIE:** *Meaning is often understood as part of a system involving* **signifiers** *(words, pictures, etc.) and* **signifieds** *(the meanings of the word or picture). How we understand this system, called semiotics (or the science of signs), helps us understand how meaning is made, often differently among a group of people even when the same signifier is under consideration. In the discussion that follows, Garoian and Gaudelius explain the ideas of Roland Barthes to differentiate among several different kinds of meaning.*

REPRESENTATIONAL MEANING

For Barthes, representational meaning can also be referred to as the *denotational* meaning of an image. The denotative context is primarily a self-contained representation, which is composed of a signifier and a signified. These types of representations carry an agreed-upon meaning by members of a cultural group even while the assignment of particular signifiers to signifieds can seem arbitrary. They are easily recognizable, and our descriptions of denotative meanings often draw heavily upon the nouns that we use to describe an image. In the example of Matt Kenyon's performance, *Consumer Index*, we construct the denotative meaning through our naming of the objects of the image: the camera, his cheek, the barcode scanner, his mouth,… at the denotative level, when we look at Kenyon's work we see images of an artist using a camera to record and document the interior of a large American department store, Walmart.

CONNOTATIVE/SYMBOLIC MEANING

Barthes argued that these signifiers and signifieds construct a second level of understanding, that of the connotative or symbolic. The connotative meaning of an image relies upon codes that suggest additional meanings. These are often dependent on tropes such as metaphor or our use of language. For example, our symbolic understanding of Kenyon's work can shift depending on whether we choose to describe Walmart as an example of a large store that provides (primarily) North American consumers with convenient, one-stop shopping at low prices or whether we describe Walmart as an oppressive corporate monolith that has a business model dependent on taking advantage of low-wage employees who are given few, if any, benefits such as health insurance, and that engages in environmentally unsustainable models of production and distribution.

MYTH

Signs and their connotations sustain and are sustained by what Barthes has called myths, shared cultural meanings that can change over time but that serve to naturalize ideological beliefs. In this sense myths are not fairy tales nor do they suggest stories that are somehow false, but rather they are stories that sustain and reinforce specific ideologies at specific points in cultural history. In Kenyon's *Consumer Index*, one such myth revolves around the ideology of capitalism and consumerism and the position of Walmart within this ideology that he exposes, examines and critiques.

KENYON AND BARTHES'S OBTUSE MEANING

Kenyon intentionally directs the viewer's attention away from the representational and symbolic charac-teristics of *Consumer Index*, the familiar and shared meanings and uses of the technologies attached to his body: the physical setting of the Walmart department store; the familiar labels and food stuffs; activities of shopping; and, ideologies of consumer capitalism, which are part of the lives of millions of in the United States. Kenyon's intentional directing away from the familiar corresponds with Barthes's notion of the obtuse meaning in a work of art, that which "seems to extend beyond culture, knowledge, information […] It belongs to the family of puns, jokes, useless exertions; indifferent to moral or aesthetic categories (the trivial, the futile, the artificial, the parodic), it sides with the carnival aspect of things" (Attridge, 2009).

Compared with representational and symbolic meanings, Barthes (1977) characterizes the obtuse meaning in a work of art as "a signifier without a signified, hence the difficulty in naming it… [it] remains suspended between the image and its description, between definition and approximation" (p. 61). Curiosity, the opening of new questions, and new flights of excess enabled through the obtuse meaning represents what in traditional research framework would be called a hypothesis. However, unlike the if/then binary of hypotheses in the sciences and social sciences where research questions lead to conclusive objective answers that can be reproduced by those who follow predetermined and predictable methodol-ogies, the obtuse meaning leads to hypothetical possibilities in research that resist and exceed conclusions and synthetic closures. Here, we are not espousing obtuse meanings at the expense of representational and symbolic meanings. The transgressive and transformative potentiality of the obtuse depends on the connotative and denotative parameters of representational and symbolic meanings. In other words, the obtuse research of art, in dialectical tension with the socially and historically determined assump-tions of representational and symbolic meanings, opens multivalent possibilities for interpretation and understanding.

OBTUSE MEANINGS IN ART/EDUCATION

For us, as art educators, research begins with works of art because of their indeterminate and undecid-able meanings. Art historian Thomas McEvilley (1991) has argued that a work of art accrues meaning over time (p. 79). Similarly, we argue that the obtuse characteristics of a work of art provokes manifold possibilities of research into its meaning over time without achieving synthetic closure. Moreover, as art educators, we find Barthes's notion of the obtuse in works of art a compelling research metaphor for art pedagogy. Indeed, there exist parallels between Barthes's three levels of meaning and critical educator Peter McLaren's (1993) three types of teaching performance: teacher-as-hegemonic overlord, teacher-as-en-tertainer, and teacher-as-liminal-servant (p. 113). The teacher-as-hegemonic overlord is an educator who dominates the classroom, a pedant who expounds knowledge to fill the minds of students as if they are empty vessels. McLaren describes this type as teaching by the book and as "serv[ing] as a conditioned reflex of the culture's consensus ideology" (p. 116). The teacher-as-entertainer, like the overlord, also teaches by the book but introduces anecdotal narratives and activities to make informational learning fun for students. While such teaching introduces disjunctions and ambiguities that are enjoyable, it is nonetheless "intent upon conditioning for sameness, [a homogenous learning that] fails to see the value of unique human experience" (p. 116), namely, the private memories and cultural histories that students bring to class everyday.

McLaren's third type of teaching performance, the teacher-as-liminal-servant, is constituted by exploratory, experimental, and improvisational practices in the threshold spaces of teaching and learning. Academic knowledge is not closed and absolute, but open for examination and critique as teachers and students engage in discourses that allow personal knowledge to challenge the public discourse of schooling. Such an opening constitutes the classroom as a mediated space of curiosity, an in-between, liminal, and contingent space, where immutable, binary representations and understandings of "teacher" and "student" are brought into question and new, alternative ways of learning are continually imagined and negotiated through critical, meaningful exchange and interaction, and where teachers are as much learners as learners are teachers.

Like Barthes's obtuse level of meaning, the teacher-as-liminal-servant demystifies knowledge that is socially and historically determined; to "help students crack the prevailing cultural crust and discover alternative meanings" (McLaren, 1993, p. 117). While McLaren positions teaching as a space of liminality, works of art also open such pedagogical possibilities. By tracking his body's consumption of barcodes and hacking into the Nielsen Family Homescan, the liminality of Kenyon's *Consumer Index* enables viewers' critical interventions within the corporation's hegemonic practices and the disruption of its manufacturing of homogeneous desire. In other words, such spaces of liminality in art practice, like Kenyon's, make possible heterogeneous, alternative imaginings and transformations contrary to those of corporate capitalism. In doing so, they throw representation and symbolic meanings into an obtuse dimension where flights of excess speculations and hypotheses can occur.

Socially and historically agreed upon representational and symbolic meanings in art and teaching are susceptible to intentional fallacies,[3] namely the presumption that such meanings are of primary importance because they serve an intended academic, institutional, and/or corporate purpose. Limiting representational and symbolic meanings to intentionality constitutes a fallacy that presumes that content in works of art and teaching are predetermined, immutable, and serve a moralizing purpose, when in actuality they are prone to slippages of interpretation and understanding and that they accrue over time as they are encountered and experienced through the multifarious contexts of viewers' and students' personal memories and histories. In other words, students' contexts constitute obtuse interventions that create slippages of meaning that contribute to the mutability of accrual. The accrual that occurs over time is not about converging on a particular or "correct" meaning. Instead, theoretical research resists meanings that are specific and opens an excess of divergent speculations and understandings.

A significant means by which to expose, examine, and critique obtuse hypotheses in art and education is to situate them in a contiguous, dialectical relationship with critical theories, other works of art, pedagogies, and other cultural constructs within its space of liminality, which enables an organic theoretical scaffolding to emerge. Our juxtaposition of Kenyon's performance *Consumer Index* with Barthes's theory of the representational, symbolic, and obtuse meanings in works of art, and with McLaren's teacher-as-liminal servant, is a case in point as it enables a conversation to occur between and among scholars, educators and artists. Hence, the liminality of the obtuse hypothesis constitutes an open space where predetermined conclusions are held at bay and where an open exchange of ideas and images are made possible. In doing so, the obtuse hypothesis resists the reinforcement of pre-existing theories and opens speculations that enable readers to create new theoretical perspectives as they bring their own imaginings and understandings to the discourse.

REFERENCES

Attridge, D. (2009). Roland Barthes's obtuse, sharp meaning and the responsibilities of commentary. In J.-M. Rabate (Ed.), *Writing the image after Roland Barthes*. Retrieved from http://books.google.com/books?id=2V_4eBK6klMC&pg=PA77&lpg=PA77&d-q=barthes+obtuse&source=bl&ots=XYwCshgiD&sig=Y9AbtMWF_vnLBw3zY3QEYF8HfIY&hl=en&ei=TyQZS6e-FJJCwlAewwuXtAg&sa=X&oi=book_result&ct=result&resnum=3&ved=0CBAQ6AEwAg#v=onepage&q=barthes%20obtuse&f=false

Bachelard, G. (1969). *The poetics of space* (M. Jolas, Trans.). Boston, MA: Beacon.

Barthes, R. (1977). *Image—music—text* (S. Heath, Trans.). New York, NY: Hill and Wang.

Baudrillard, J. (2002). *The transparency of evil: Essays on extreme phenomena* (J. Benedict, Trans.). London, England: Verso.

Deleuze, G., & Guattari, F. (1987). *A thousand plateaus: Capitalism and schizophrenia* (B. Massumi, Trans.). Minneapolis: University of Minnesota.

Kenyon, M. (2008). SWAMP in conversation with Alessandro Ludovico. *Neural, 31*. Retrieved from http://mic.org.nz/events/exhibitions/twothousandandnine/swamp-fire-sale/swamp-interview/

McEvilley, T. (1991). *Art & discontent: Theory at the millennium*. New York, NY: McPherson.

McLaren, P. (1993). *Schooling as ritual performance: Towards a political economy of educational symbols & gestures*. London, England: Routledge.

The Nielsen Company. (n.d.a) Profile. *Nielson*. Retrieved from http://en-us.nielsen.com/main/about/Profile

The Nielsen Company. (n.d.b) Nielson Homescan. *Nielson*. Retrieved from http://en-us.nielsen.com/tab/product_families/nielsen_homescan

Wimsatt, W. K., Jr., & Beardsley, M. C. (1946). The intentional fallacy. *The Sewanee Review, 54*(3), 468-488. Retrieved from www.jstor.org/stable/27537676

ENDNOTES

1   We derive "flights of excess" from Deleuze and Guattari's (1987, pp. 88-89) concept of "lines of flight," which constitute escape routes from cultural repression and stratification. "Excess," as we are using it in this chapter, is not intended for the sake of extreme, unwarranted interpretations, but to form a dialectical relationship that respects the work of art as a significant partner in critical discourse without limiting it to mere illustration. Hence, our use of "excess" corresponds with philosopher Gaston Bachelard's concept of "immensity," which he describes as "a 'category' of the poetic imagination, and not merely a generality formulated during contemplation of grandiose spectacle [and consumption]" (Bachelard, 1969, pp. 198-199).

2   In a conversation with media critic Alessandro Ludovico, Kenyon describes the enticement of the Nielsen Family Homescan: "Through prize drawings and accumulation of redeemable purchase points, consumers are lured into participating in this marketing system. Throughout their day, they rescan purchases with this special barcode scanner. Every so often Nielsen Family members dock the Homescan device to their computers, and the dates are uploaded to Nielsen where it is analyzed and sold to corporations. These consumers are essentially creating a type of consumer-based panopticon: they willfully brick themselves into a limited and non-competitive panorama to perambulate" (Kenyon, 2008).

3   For a discussion of the intentional fallacy in literary criticism, see Wimsatt and Beardsley (1946, pp. 468-470).

CHARLES R. GAROIAN, Professor of Art Education at The Pennsylvania State University, is the author of *Performing Pedagogy: Toward an Art of Politics* (SUNY, 1999) and *The Prosthetic Pedagogy of Art: Embodied Research and Practice* (SUNY, 2013). Garoian's scholarly articles are featured in journals on art and education, and he has performed and lectured in colleges and universities, galleries and museums nationally and internationally. His current research focus is on the implications of Gilles Deleuze and Félix Guattari's theories for art and teaching practice.

YVONNE M. GAUDELIUS is Associate Vice President and Senior Associate Dean of Undergraduate Education and a Professor of Art Education and Women's Studies at The Pennsylvania State University. Her current research focus is on participatory culture and the impacts of globalization on art practices and pedagogy and her writings include the co-edited book *Contemporary Issues in Art Education* (2002) with Peg Speirs, and scholarly articles in journals such as *Studies in Art Education, Journal of Social Theory in Art Education*, and the *Canadian Review of Art Education*. Her honors and awards include the Mary J. Rouse Award and the June King McFee Award from the Women's Caucus of the National Art Education Association and a College of Arts and Architecture Faculty Teaching Award.

Together, Garoian and Gaudelius have collaborated on a number of research projects for which they have received major grants including from the Rockefeller Foundation, the Ford Foundation, and the Pennsylvania Council of the Arts. In addition to their several collaborative journal articles on art education, they co-authored *Spectacle Pedagogy: Art, Politics, and Visual Culture* (SUNY, 2008).

22 / Post-Representational Approaches to Theoretical Research in the Arts

JASON WALLIN / ASSISTANT PROFESSOR OF MEDIA AND YOUTH CULTURE IN CURRICULUM, UNIVERSITY OF ALBERTA, CANADA

ABSTRACT: *Drawing upon examples from contemporary film, music, and performance art, this chapter offers students of theoretical research an introduction to the philosophical thought of Gilles Deleuze. In this approach, this chapter will raise important questions for a style of theoretical research that aspires to creation, to the production of new forms of thought and ways of living. Offering an alternative approach to the question of how one might theorize, this chapter departs from the familiar question of what art* is, *commencing an analytic inquiry pertaining to what art* **might do**. *Rethinking the purpose of theoretical inquiry, this chapter asks how research might go about liberating life from those contemporary habits of thought and action that unnecessarily restrict the potential forms of subjectivity, collective production, and artistic enunciation emerging today.*

THE CHALLENGES OF ART AGAINST HABIT AND SEDIMENTATION

The purpose of this essay is to offer new researchers a broad approach to the philosophical thought of Gilles Deleuze. I will describe a theoretical study I conducted in order to begin articulating the significance of Deleuzian thinking for education. The study is distinctly creative insofar as it asks us not what a particular phenomenon means, but rather, *what it does* and *what it might do*. Within the work of Deleuze (2000, 2004) this shift marks a general repudiation of *representational thinking*, or rather, the habit of framing difference in terms of what already *is*. Instead, Deleuze encourages us to not simply accept those images and ideas that have come to constitute orthodox ways of thinking about ourselves and our world. As Deleuze (1991) argues, the images we take for ourselves and our world are not *fundamental*. They too have been created, and hence, *might be created differently*.

Contemporary theory must begin to recognize the ways in which life aspires to habit and sedimentation. Put differently, we must become weary of those images and ideas meant to think *on our behalf*. Certainly, to live in a world composed of such *readymade* images and ideas can be comforting. To look into the mirror and know that you have a specific gender, race, nationality, and age might inspire feelings of certainty and comfort. Indeed, within the field of educational theory, we might find that the autobiographical narratives of researchers increasingly rely on such terms in order to articulate their uniqueness. Yet, such terms of reference can constitute a profound danger to life itself. Having become accustomed to accepting those external images and ideas by which we define our own desires, capacities, and subjectivity, we have yet to encounter *radical difference* (Deleuze, 1990). In Nietzschean (1969) terms, we have

become *human-all-too-human*, caught in the *reactive* habit of thinking only in terms of what has *already been thought*.

A PRODUCTIVE FAILURE

In order to live free of the habits that I began to detect in both educational literature and life in schools, I oriented my research toward an analysis of those recurring images and ideas in educational thought itself. Primary amongst these was the image of the curriculum. From the Latin *currere*, meaning *to run the course*, curriculum carries with it the historical image of the Grecian racetrack within which competitors took flight. For me, this conceptual image bore uncanny resemblance to the state of contemporary education, premised on competition, preordained ways of succeeding, governing rules, surveillance, habits of movement, and established points of entry and exit. The uncanny correspondence between these formations suggested to me that new images of pedagogical life were desperately required. Toward this, I aimed to mobilize new images that *productively failed* to fall back upon *prior* categories of thought. It is here that the study of film (Goddard, Haynes), literature (Kafka, Joyce, Carroll), music (Massiaen, Nancarrow), and youth culture (punk, queer, otaku) became crucial recourses insofar as they *already* imagined *a* life not yet anticipated by any prior categories for thinking.

Theoretical research must not simply regurgitate *what already is*, but set into motion new "tools" for thinking, teaching, learning, and—ultimately and above all—living. Instead of aspiring to the all-too-familiar interpretive query: *"what does this mean?"*—a question that most always finds its location in some *a priori* category or image—theoretical research in the arts might be recommended along the ethical question of *"What can art do?"* In my own research, the ethical question of *what art can do* was linked to an analysis of how contemporary art is being employed as a counter-surveilling force (See The Institute for Applied Autonomy), as a way of imaging new relationships between humans/animals/machines, in addition to questioning how emerging art forms are being used to rethink the ownership of social space (graffiti, manhunt, and parkour). In a more theoretical mode, my research analyzed the ways in which film has created new ways of thinking about the movement of time and memory that differ from those typically employed in contemporary forms of autobiographical research and the linearity of developmental discourse. Drawing upon jazz music, I began to rethink the traditional image of education in terms of improvisation, collective production, and the significance of chance in pedagogical encounters. Lastly, my research drew the ethical question of *what art can do* into relationship with the task of theorizing new forms of life no longer equal to those representational categories (gendered, ethnic, national, ageist, etc.) *already available*. In this vein, I aimed to question the emerging significance of transexuality, mutation, human-animal, and human-machine interfaces for opening life to its broader potentials for expression.

RETHINKING THE PURPOSE OF THEORETICAL INQUIRY

In *What is Philosophy?* (1994) Deleuze and Guattari assert that the purpose of philosophical inquiry is located not in its characterization of the world *as it appears*, but rather, in its capacity to *create concepts*. As a researcher, one might reach a critical impasse in which the available theoretical resources fail to adequately address the problem(s) that they study. Although we might attempt to retrofit the subject of our study to the frameworks with which we are most comfortable, this strategy can have consequences. Avoiding a reliance upon what Deleuze refers to as an *automatic interpretation machine* (via which difference is framed within familiar

pre-existing representational patterns), theoretical researchers must begin the task of carefully crafting new concepts, images, and sensations capable of once again *making us think*. In rethinking theoretical research as a "fulcrum for a processural relaunch… between art and life," it becomes necessary that we not simply say what other theorists or philosophers have said, but to do what they did, that is, to *create new tools for the problems they posed* (Alliez, 2006, p. 158). But what does it mean to use a concept like a *tool*? It does not, in my opinion, mean to work *on* something. Rather, it might more adequately be understood in terms of the approach it demands of the researcher.

In my own research for example, I attempt to think through the Deleuzian (1987) concept of the *rhizome* (a concept borrowed and modified from the biological sciences) in order to theorize a *non-hierarchical* and *non-foundational* form of pedagogy. The concept is more than simply a word that one uses, it is a passage for thinking that *affects* what is capable of being thought. Let us take the rhizomatic tendencies of improvisational jazz as an example. In the experimental movement of improvisation, jazz musicians cease to aspire to the representation of a prior musical score. That is, improvisational jazz does not begin with an instrumental image of what will be produced. Instead, as it unfolds through the dynamic dialogue of its musicians, its instruments, and performance space, jazz improvisation might more adequately be thought as a rhizomatic, or non-representational art form. It is further to this point that jazz improvisation overturns the familiar image of a conductor who impels the labor of his players. Rather than reflecting the singular voice of the conductor, jazz improvisation becomes a rhizomatic or heterogenic way of thinking about non-hierarchical forms of creative practice. However, such rethinking is not simply a means to privilege a sovereign individual. Instead, in the process of dynamic

Alternative Educational Methodologies

SUMMERHILL

Founded by Alexander Sutherland Neill (1883-1973) in 1921, the philosophy of Summerhill asserts that the school should be made to suit the desires of the child. Opposed to what Neill characterized as "the school as barracks," Summerhill is organized in the image of radical democracy in which students would hold equal powers to teachers in collective decision-making and matters of student discipline. Overturning the lock-step developmentalism of institutional schooling, classes at Summerhill are optional, attended based on the interest and abilities of individual students. This non-hierarchical and collective co-educational boarding school in Suffolk, England is oriented to freeing students from the anxieties and constant demands of institutional life. ■

FREINETIAN EDUCATION

Célestin Freinet (1896-1966) is perhaps best known for employing an alternative form of educational organization focusing on the role of the printing press as vehicle for the collective delivery of his classes. Rethinking education as a pedagogy of work, Freinet suggested that the classroom should become a space for the production of useful products and services. Yet, opposed to the individualism espoused in institutional educational settings, Freinet linked such productivity to group work and inquiry-based learning related to the curiosities of students themselves. Through these conceptual approaches, Freinet sought to improve the lives of working-class children, instigating a revolution in educational thinking. ■

communication with the other musicians, the improvisational artist becomes less an "individual" than a collective "dividual." Put differently, the rhizome becomes a way of understanding the productive connections that might be made in the formation of new group dynamics and forms of creative organization that are non-instrumental. This is not to say that jazz is a metaphor of the rhizome, but rather, that the practice of improvisation is itself rhizomatic. In this brief example, the analysis of improvisational jazz as both a non-representational and non-hierarchical rhizome advances two particular challenges for educational research. First, through a rhizomatic approach to curriculum we might question both what it means to *do* research without aspiring to represent a model, framework, or readymade image of life. Second, through the rhizomatic composition of non-hierarchical relations, we can begin to think of alternative pedagogical formations requisite on neither an organizing authority (the master-teacher) or the relegation of classroom life to the reproduction of work that has already been produced. In Deleuzian (2003) terms, such a process of thinking might be called the *pedagogy of the image* insofar as it reveals something otherwise inaccessible.

We might begin to think about the strength of theoretical research in terms of the quality and affective potential of the conceptual tools it is able to introduce. Concomitantly, the strength of theoretical research must be linked to the kinds of problems it is able to advance for the future of the field. Such an approach undercuts the common scenario of working on problems that continually come from elsewhere, and further, challenges the researcher to link their problems to the specific milieu of their study. Returning to the image of the Grecian racetrack that informs the meaning of *curriculum*, I attempt to articulate the danger associated with what Aoki (2005) has dubbed *the curriculum as plan*. For Aoki, the *curriculum as plan* is distinctly representational. That is, it seeks to project an image of what the classroom will look like and what will happen within it. In lieu of the instrumental and representational image of the *curriculum as plan*, my own research focuses on the ways in which the curriculum might be performed in a manner particular to the desires of those who enact it. Refocusing the field of art education in this way, we might shift from a transcendent image (an ideal image) to one that is *immanent* (an existing, occurring image) capable of deviating from an already decided image of how life will go. Toward this, research must become resituated in terms of thinking *a* pedagogical life, or rather, an image of pedagogy subtracted from pedagogy *in general*. It is in this vein that my analysis of contemporary education in North America is continually offset by such educational singularities (unique formations) as Summerhill School, Freinetian pedagogy, and the alternative pedagogical organizations advocated by Deleuze's frequent collaborator, Felix Guattari (2000).

RESEARCHING NEW CONCEPTS FOR EDUCATIONAL THOUGHT

As Deleuze and Guattari (1983) suggest, we have yet to fully explore what a body—a course of life—can do. As a means to imagine life particular to the unique times, spaces, and formations in which it might emerge (and is emerging), research must begin to turn away from the implicit presumptions of universality common to the developmental, instrumental, and increasingly standardized contours of contemporary educational thought. In this task, theoretical research might become oriented to the creation of unconventional images of pedagogy, teaching, and learning. More specifically, researchers might begin to mobilize examples from contemporary film, music, and other performative arts as an experimental "plateau" for thinking how a life *might* go—that is, how the time, space, and becoming of *a* life might be thought in ways unhinged from prior images and investments of desire.

Such experimentation is alive today in a litany of dynamic art practices that rethink conventions of knowledge, meaning, and significance. For example, Todd Haynes' (2007) film, *I'm Not There,* develops a unique, anti-biopic style of filmmaking in order to rethink the "overdocumented" life of Bob Dylan. Significantly, the libratory potential of Haynes' work is not to found in an attempt to *represent* Dylan, but rather, in the way he utilizes the filmic apparatus to *create* a complex and non-categorical life. Life is, after all, a practical matter for creation. This insight applies also to teaching and learning. We can orient our students to those *readymade* forms of thinking, or rather, rethink the pedagogical space as one in which to *think again*, to pose new answers for old problems, and create connections not yet foreseen within prepackaged teaching guides (Aoki, 2005).

If difference is primary, constituting something of a foundational *anti-foundation* for thinking, difference does not come *after* stability. As Deleuze (1991) claims via examples of musical, filmic, and literary innovation, society is *already* "leaking." That is, life continually escapes from the attempt to capture it, represent it, or pin it down. It is hence the task of theoretical researchers to draw these leakages (differences, queer formations) into new formations unequal to the image of the world as it is transcendently, morally, or ideally *given*.

Following, theoretical researchers might begin to consider the material ways in which the "arts" have opposed power, affirmed difference, and de-habituated normalized images of life. The question here is: What does education have to learn or use from such practices; or rather, what becomings are available to education if we take such artistic innovations seriously? I argue that such artistic "deterritorializations" (the potentials for difference within the social sphere) offer us a way of thinking unfettered from both instrumentalism (which organizes or colonizes desire) and positivism (which posits a system of ideals and morals insensitive to local conditions and the desires of specific groups) (Deleuze and Guattari, 1987). The purpose of this research relates directly to the contemporary call for an end to experimentation in the social sciences, and concomitantly, an institutional intolerance for the often jarring desires produced via the arts.

NEW RESOURCES FOR THEORETICAL RESEARCH

The emphasis of research should become more intimate to the detection and creation of social *potentials* unanticipated in the correspondence of *possible* and *real*. Today, the coming-together of diverse social groups and their equally diverse art forms (stenciling, graffiti, turntablism, digital design, zines, etc.) in common protest against the increasing governmental constraints being placed on life marks one emerging potential for micropolitical change. In another example, such artistic practices as digital sampling in music and mash-ups in visual culture open spaces for the reconsideration of image copyright, plagiarism, and an emerging commitment to the *fair use* of artistic products.

Deleuze (1991) writes that "The search for a new means of… expression was begun by Nietzsche and must be pursued today in relation to the renewal of other certain arts" (p. xxi). We must today begin the task of creating new forms of expression capable of *stuttering* the sphere of representational art. For theoretical researchers, this means taking seriously those artists and scholars who were dedicated to the creation of new concepts, percepts, and affects. Avoiding the desire to know *too soon*, we must work alongside such creative figures to see what their thinking might *do*, and further, what it might mean for thinking about education today. This necessitates that theoretical researchers become vigilant against an overreliance upon interpretive frameworks, themes, and categorical referents. This is no doubt a difficult challenge, and yet, it is one upon which the difference of the future depends.

In an age dominated by transcendent and instrumental images of life, it is increasingly crucial that *a* life (life as a singularity) be stolen back from the idea of *life in general*. In this task, theoretical research must become *more than critical*. It must itself begin to survey and mobilize creative practices of a different *kind*—practices adequate to an ethical challenge that asserts: *We do not yet know how a life might go!* That is, we do not yet know how a life *might* be composed, with what organisms, images, or machines it might enter

into productive alliance (Colebrook, 2009). We do not yet know what its capacities to affect might become. These are questions for the researcher's careful and deliberate consideration. Such an approach will enable theorists and educators alike to compose their work as an act of creation rather than reproduction, warding off the symptoms of pointlessness and cynicism rampant in institutional life.

REFERENCES

Alliez, E. (2006). Anti-Oedipus–Thirty years on (Between art and politics). In M. Fuglsang & B. M. Sorensen (Eds), *Deleuze and the social* (pp. 151-168). Edinburgh, Scotland: Edinburgh University Press.

Agamben, G. (1999). Absolute immanence. In J. Khalfa (Ed.), *An introduction to the philosophy of Gilles Deleuze* (pp. 151-169). London, England: Continuum.

Aoki, T. (2005). Legitimating lived curriculum: Toward a curricular landscape of multiplicity. In W. Pinar & R. Irwin (Eds.), *Curriculum in a new key: The collected works of Ted T. Aoki* (pp. 199-218). Mahwah, NJ: Lawrence Erlbaum. (Originally published in 1993)

Baudrillard, J. (1990). *Seduction* (B. Singer, Trans.). New York, NY: St. Martin's Press.

Baudrillard, J. (1994). *Simulacra and simulation*. Ann Arbor: University of Michigan.

Bogue, R. (1999). Minority, territory, music. In J. Khalfa (Ed.), *An introduction to the philosophy of Gilles Deleuze* (pp. 114-132). London, England: Continuum.

Colebrook, C. (2002). *Gilles Deleuze*. New York, NY: Routledge.

Colebrook, C. (2009). On the very possibility of queer theory. In C. Nigianni & M. Storr (Eds.), *Deleuze and queer theory* (pp. 11-23). Edinburgh, Scotland: Edinburgh University Press.

Deleuze, G. (1990). *The logic of sense* (M. Lester & C. Stivale, Trans.). New York, NY: Columbia University Press.

Deleuze, G. (1991). *Bergsonism* (H. Tomlinson & B. Habberjam, Trans.). New York, NY: Zone Books.

Deleuze, G. (2000). *Proust & signs* (R. Howard, Trans.). Minneapolis: University of Minnesota Press.

Deleuze, G. (2003). *The time-image* (H. Tomlinson & B. Habberjam, Trans.). Minneapolis: University of Minnesota Press.

Deleuze, G. (2004). *Desert islands and other texts 1953-1974* (D. Lapoujade, Ed.)(M. Taormina, Trans.). Los Angeles, CA: Semiotext(e).

Deleuze, G. & Guattari, F. (1994). *What is philosophy?* (H. Tomlinson & G. Burchell, Trans.). New York, NY: Columbia University Press.

Deleuze, G., & Guattari, F. (1987). *A thousand plateaus* (R. Hurley, M. Seem & H. R. Lane, Trans.). Minneapolis: University of Minnesota Press.

Deleuze, G., & Guattari, F. (1983). *Anti-Oedipus: Capitalism and schizophrenia* (R. Hurley, M. Seem & H. R. Lane, Trans.). Minneapolis: University of Minnesota Press.

Guattari, F. (2000). *The three ecologies* (I. Pindar & P. Patton, Trans.). London, England: Athlone Press.

Haynes, T. (Writer & Director). (2007). *I'm Not There* [Motion Picture]. Toronto, ON: Alliance Films.

Nietzsche, F. (1969). *Thus spoke Zarathustra* (D. Smith, Trans.). Oxford, England: Oxford University Press.

JASON J. WALLIN is Assistant Professor of Media and Youth Culture in Curriculum in the Faculty of Education at the University of Alberta, Canada, where he teaches courses in visual art, media studies, and cultural curriculum theory. He is the author of *A Deleuzian Approach to Curriculum: Essays on a Pedagogical Life* (Palgrave Macmillan), co-author of *Arts-Based Research: A Critique and Proposal* (with jan jagodzinski, Sense Publishers), and co-editor of *Deleuze, Guattari, Politics and Education* (with Matt Carlin, Continuum). Jason is assistant editor for the *Journal of Curriculum and Pedagogy* (Routledge) and reviews editor for *Deleuze Studies* (Edinburgh University Press).

23 / Networked Art Educational Research Practices

ROBERT W. SWEENY / ASSOCIATE PROFESSOR AND COORDINATOR OF ART EDUCATION, INDIANA UNIVERSITY OF PENNSYLVANIA

ABSTRACT: *This chapter outlines three approaches to conceiving of and conducting research through the use of networked digital technologies in art educational spaces. It describes how research might be rethought through the utilization of social media, ubiquitous media, and locative media, suggesting practical applications as well as theoretical extensions of such media forms. Art educators interested in using new technologies for theoretical research should take into consideration the ways in which these media open up forms of participation, incorporating feedback in the creation of dynamic forms of communication. In addition, the chapter highlights the strategies of relevant contemporary artists who use a variety of media, providing suggestions and raising questions for art educators interested in conducting research using networked digital media at a variety of levels and in numerous spaces.*

Currently the use of digital technologies in the art classroom extends beyond the use of the computer as media; educators, students, staff and administrators each access a wide variety of networks throughout the school day, from cellphones and PDAs to laptops and portable videogame players, even infiltrating the world of stuffed animals.[1] While the educational possibilities for digital technologies have been thoroughly discussed in the field of art education (Dunn, 1996; Heise & Grandgenett, 1996; Keifer-Boyd, 1996, 1997; Krug, 2002; Taylor & Carpenter, 2002), few art educators have presented studies of *networked* digital technologies.[2]

Networked digital technologies should be understood as technologies that are able to connect with a wide variety of machines in numerous ways; computers connected through the Internet, wireless devices that use Bluetooth, and an increasing number of previously isolated objects are becoming networked (Gershenfeld, Krikorian, & Cohen, 2004). The ability to share information, collaborate in novel ways, and distribute a variety of products makes networked digital technologies vastly different from those that are disconnected. As Thurber (2004) discussed, networked digital technologies can allow for "communication and collaboration between and among researchers and practitioners" involved with teacher education (p. 513). In a similar manner, Wilson McKay (2006) has described how a technology-infused action research project in art education can connect practitioners and areas of knowledge across isolated work spaces. Both examples point to the need to include students in the process of developing meaningful technological connections, as they are often the ones who quickly develop facility with technologies such as those previously mentioned.

As such, it is incumbent upon art educators to explore possibilities for networked research methodologies, as these networks expand and infiltrate the spaces of art education, allowing for new forms of participation, creation, and visualization. This chapter will present three forms of networked approaches to data collection and analysis based in distinct yet related digital media forms: ubiquitous computing, social media, and locative technologies. Though I address them here as methods, they could be expanded upon to lead to the development of new theoretical or technology-based methodologies. Each of these media forms provide art educators with numerous possibilities for conducting research; not only are they easily accessible, personally engaging, and culturally influential, but they each present the user with radically new ways to see and be seen.

UBIQUITOUS COMPUTING

Ubiquitous computing is a branch of physical computing that addresses the everyday use of digital technologies; as it deals with common activities and accessible technologies, ubiquitous computing may allow art educational researchers to use and discuss those technologies that common today. The June 2009 presidential elections in Iran resulted in a public outcry for justice, which, due to media crackdowns, was broadcast not by mainstream media, but via decentralized online media sources such as Twitter. This so-called "Twitter Revolution" thrust the already-popular technology into a global spotlight, and allowed many to see first hand the marches, protests, and repercussions of civil disobedience in an authoritarian regime. This use of networked digital technologies also resuscitates a well-worn dialectic: technologies are liberatory; technologies are repressive (Morozov, 2009).

Much of the history of technology is rooted in an oppositional model, one that pits determinism against constructivism, and tends to ignore the complexities of actual technological use (Feenberg, 1999). The "Twitter Revolution" has shown at least one thing: Digital technologies are pervasive. However, ubiquitous technologies may not be welcomed in all social settings. In U.S. public schools, cell phones are routinely confiscated; MP3 players are hidden under the clothing, or worn brazenly, as fashion accessories or political statements. When networked technologies are implemented in the classroom, they are often placed under severe restrictions, as in the case of firewall protections that limit even the most banal word search; they have also been used to track students, as in the case of Radio Frequency Identification (RFID) cards in Sutter, CA schools (Zetter, 2005) and iPhones in Tokyo (June, 2009).

While it is necessary for educators to resist the oppressive use of networked technologies in the classroom, it is also important not to paint all technologies with the same broad brush. Art educators may learn to channel the power that decentralization brings, through research methods that incorporate the multiple forms of technology that weave through the classroom and provide greater access to art and visual culture. As Freedman and Stuhr (2004) write: "Newer technologies have enabled encounters with the visual arts to become embedded in all aspects of our daily lives" (p. 819).

In my teaching I have used Twitter to explore possibilities for opening participatory forums in the art classroom. Twitter, which has been called "microblogging," allows the user to post short updates, which can be read by subscribers. It can be accessed by computer or web-enabled cellphone, which expands its ubiquity. Allowing students in class to both "tweet" each other, and post comments to a running "sidebar" in the lecture hall begins to point to openings in the transmission model still found in many educational settings. The sidebar, essentially an additional screen opened up next to the classroom management software, also allows for responses to be catalogued. As this brief example shows, ubiquitous computing can represent a casual form of data collection. Verbal comments that might go unnoticed in the classroom are preserved for future scrutiny through assistance of digital technologies such as Twitter. Art educational researchers who wish to utilize ubiquitous computing as data collection should carefully consider the ramifications of such activities. In Iran, the ability for the cleric-led government to track user activity in social networks has been a real danger to freedom of political speech (Morozov, 2009). While not nearly as serious, similar concerns apply in the use of ubiquitous computing in the art classroom. The art educator should resist the obsessive cataloguing of student data generated by networked digital technologies in the classroom (Sweeny, 2005), as these data tend to represent in a quantitative manner activities that are qualitative in nature.

Ubiquitous technologies raise issues regarding civil liberties and personal responsibilities as individuals use and adapt existing digital media forms. Art educational researchers who wish to use ubiquitous technologies as research tools must use these technologies in an ethical manner. Students should discuss the shifts that take place in digitally mediated discussions, and art educators should not expect that students abide by the same social norms as those reinforced in the non-networked classroom. The use of pseudonyms is a simple way to respect the rights of the users as they enter into networks of communication that are located somewhere between the casual and the formal, the political and the personal, the single and the social.

SOCIAL MEDIA

Social media, also known as Web 2.0, are those digital technologies that allow for interaction and social engagement; Flickr, YouTube, and Facebook are each changing how individuals present themselves in digital environments, creating networked forms of identity (Sweeny, 2009). Social media such as Wikipedia, YouTube, Facebook and MySpace have been analyzed as they relate to economic structures (Benkler, 2006), political interactions (Rutenberg & Nagourney, 2009), and media access (Shachtman, 2009). While generally viewed as representing a positive cultural influence, social media is not without its critics (Keen, 2006; Lanier, 2006).

The MacArthur Foundation has acknowledged the importance of social media in education, funding numerous research ventures through the Digital Media and Learning Competition (www.dmlcompetition.net/about08.php). Art educators have also begun to consider pedagogical applications of social media, with discussions involving social networking, (Buffington, Helms, Johnston & Yoon, 2011) identity formation (Sweeny, 2009) and ethical considerations (Buffington, 2009). For instance, *Art Ed 2.0*, a blog started by Craig Roland in 2006, contains a heavily used message board, allowing members to post comments and join interest groups. McClure (2011) has written specifically about possibilities for young learners and blogging. While this research is important, and continues to expand, there has been little discussion within the field of art education of the possibilities for social media as artmaking, though many artists have been utilizing these networks since their inception. Keith and Mendi Obadike (2001) have explored the possibilities for critiquing race and masculinity through projects such as *Blackness for Sale*. Johnathan Harris and Sep Kamvar (2005) mine the data generated in blog posts in their project *We Feel Fine,* visualizing the massive amounts of information generated in the blogosphere while identifying emotional connections.[3]

These projects point to the opportunities for social media as arts-based research. Blogs are free to establish, easy to maintain, and require very little knowledge of coding procedures or related technical know-how. Of the various social media forms, the blog seems to stand out as one that offers art educators vast potential because they offer users a chance to post thoughts on any topic of her/his choice, with the possibility that it will be read by a wide audience, who has the opportunity to respond. For a researcher, this is an opportunity for data collection and analysis. Research questions can be proposed and adjusted. Once the researcher determines that an audience exists for the blog, readers can respond in a qualitative manner to questions posed. Surveys can be linked to blog posts, and participants can remain anonymous.

> **SARA AND MELANIE:** *In this example, the researcher is analyzing questions posted on a blog. This kind of research requires awareness of IRB policies with regard to theoretically analyzing data through digital networked technologies without the explicit permission of the original author of the blog post as well as those who offer comments on the post.*

As such, social media allows for the formation of "feedback loops": instead of information flowing in one direction (from researcher to participant), participants can influence the direction of the conversation, the research. These digital feedback loops are prevalent in social media forms, in that the media form incorporates the mechanisms for increased participation. Each individual has the opportunity to control the information that he/she generates. As the researcher would no longer be central to the flow of information, but would instead facilitate the flow among participants, the landscape of art educational research could change dramatically with the extended use of social media for research purposes.

To illustrate, I will offer an example from my teaching. I have had the opportunity to incorporate blogs in my University-level courses, typically within predetermined course software packages such as WebCT. Though these are often limiting, depending on the motivation and comfort level on the part of the educator (Sweeny, 2007), they can also incorporate dynamic communication forms rarely found in traditional classroom settings. In the online course ARHI 101: Introduction to Art, which I have taught in both traditional and distance education formats for 5 years, my class was discussing the work of Freewayblogger, a group that places politically provocative signs over freeways in the US and abroad.[4] While the discussion board-based conversation started with perfunctory questions concerning the definition of art and the relationship between propaganda and art, things quickly changed when a student posted an excerpt of the conversation that she had just had with "Scarlet P." of the Freewayblogger site, discussing artistic intent.

This comment led to a discussion of the rules of the online class conversation, with at least one student objecting to the use of the artist's statement in the flow of the discussion. Happening in real time, this dynamic would not have been possible within the boundaries of the traditional classroom, due to limitations of time and space. The students began to reflect upon the nature of education as represented by the class, creating a feedback loop that influenced all taking part. Social media offers similar opportunities for art educators who wish to include the voice of the artist in the classroom; participation is no longer limited to the model of the "visiting artist" when networked digital media allow for synchronous and asynchronous forms of communication and collaboration.

As a model for conducting research, this example demonstrates the power of decentralized media. Though I organized the activity, I could not predict that one student would contact the artist, which altered the structure of the activity, and made students hyperaware of the rules, both implicit and explicit, of a class. Researchers should continually engage with the information being generated, in the model of the participant-observer. Social media can allow for the shared production of knowledge. Such an approach to research changes models of academic authorship as participation, emphasizing that authorial positions remain fluid. Though these types of change are often resisted in academia (Castells, 1996), it is inevitable that the fundamental social shifts that social media represent will come to influence ways in which data is collected and research is pursued.

LOCATIVE MEDIA

Locative technologies provide the user with an indication of his or her place, usually through some type of GPS system, and are increasingly used to synthesize the actual with the virtual. Many contemporary networked technologies allow the user to map locations, move through space, and augment reality. While increasing connectedness and mobility, these technologies also create possibilities for tracking and being tracked, as shown through the ability to easily adapt the Nike + iPod shoe. Intended to monitor mileage and provide supportive feedback, researchers at the University of Washington were able to follow the wearer of such a shoe from a distance (Saponas, Lester, Hartung, & Kohno, 2006).

One variant of the intersection between contemporary new media art and locative media is represented by hybrid reality games (HRG). In HRG, the realities of the digital and the physical are merged, incorporating various forms of gameplay in the process. A HRG that I have been involved with is titled *CitySneak* (Sweeny & Patton, 2009).[5] CitySneak consists of three levels; each can be played independently, or in conjunction with one another (Sweeny & Patton, 2009).

The first level of CitySneak is *mapping:* players walk through a public space, marking where surveillance cameras are located. This information is then uploaded to a Google

Map, which is then imported into a location-based program called MScape. MScape allows the user to indicate "hotspots" on the map, which will send a message to the player when he/she has come into proximity of the camera. Once completed, the map is uploaded to a central site, where players can choose from a variety of mapped locations.

In the second level, *playing,* a chosen map is downloaded to a mobile phone or handheld GPS-equipped device. Once the MScape program is aligned with the GPS satellites, the player has to try to maneuver from a selected start point to a finish point, without coming into contact with the surveillance cameras. If players do get caught by a camera, the device emits a signal and produces an image, and the game is over. If the player reaches the finish, his/her time is recorded, leading to the third stage: *scoring.* In this last stage the player(s) upload scores, in the form of elapsed time, to the central site, where they can be compared and competition can ensue. *Scoring* makes use of the feedback loops discussed earlier with regards to social media, as players compare strategies and potentially influence how the map is maneuvered in the future.

HRG's such as CitySneak allow art educators unique models for conducting research. The process of mapping, playing, and scoring each relate to data collection, as players are actively engaged in the interpretation of his or her environment; in this case, utilizing the playful engagement of games. Educators can easily change the parameters of the game; for instance, by replacing surveillance cameras with green spaces, the conversation shifts from civil liberties and safety to environmental topics and urban planning. Perhaps students, instead of avoiding the hotspots, try to come into contact with these spaces, making field notes that are then shared in a centralized manner.

Research using locative media has the chance to acknowledge the idiosyncratic ways that individuals use digital technologies. As with the previous examples, locative media presents user interaction as complex and multifaceted. In CitySneak, the city acts as a text that inscribes as it is written upon (de Certeau, 1984), shifting the meanings of both player and technology. Locative media as research tool holds the potential to further destabilize the researcher/researched binary while taking into consideration the context of the research (Galloway, 2008). In art educational research, locative media can incorporate performative strategies, critiquing cultural assumptions dealing with technology and the body (Garoian & Gaudelius, 2001).

CONCLUSION

The networked research methods discussed in this chapter are socially relevant, technologically timely and educationally applicable. Ubiquitous technologies can allow researchers to collect and interpret data in a decentralized, self-critical manner, through technological interfaces such as Twitter that are generally easy to find and use. The dynamic qualities of social media can allow for research projects to incorporate feedback through a wide variety of communication models, primary of which is the blog. And finally, locative media can allow for research that is embedded in specific social and cultural contexts, accessing the direct input of participants in potentially playful ways. Each of these three types of digital networked technologies is woven into the fabric of contemporary life (Benkler, 2006). Art education researchers have the opportunity to explore the complexities of these interweavings through networked art educational research strategies.

REFERENCES

Benkler, Y. (2006). *The wealth of networks: How social production transforms markets and freedom.* New Haven, CT: Yale University Press.

Buffington, M., Helms, K., Johnston, J. & Yoon, S. (2011). Web 2.0 and social constructivism. In R. Sweeny (Ed.), *Inter/actions/Inter/sections: Art education in a digital visual culture* (pp. 161-169). Reston, VA: National Art Education Association.

Buffington, M. L. (2009). The myth of Wikipedia. *The Journal of Social Theory and Art Education, 29*(1), 42-55.

Castells, M. (1996). *The rise of the network society.* Malden, MA: Blackwell.

Colman, A. (2004). Net.art and net.pedagogy: Introducing internet art to the digital art curriculum. *Studies in Art Education, 46*(1), 61-73.

de Certeau, M. (1984). *The practices of everyday life.* Berkeley: University of California Press.

Dunn, P. (1996). More power: Integrated interactive technology and art education. *Art Education, 54*(1), 6-11.

Feenberg, A. (1999). *Questioning technology.* New York, NY: Routledge.

Freedman, K., & Stuhr, P. (2004). Curriculum change for the 21st century: Visual culture in art education. In E. Eisner & M. Day (Eds.), *Handbook of research and policy in art education* (pp. 815-828). New York, NY: Lawrence Erlbaum.

Garoian, C., & Gaudelius, Y. (2001). Cyborg pedagogy: Performing resistance in a digital age. *Studies in Art Education, 42*(4), 333-337.

Galloway, A. (2008). A brief history of the future of urban computing and locative media (Unpublished dissertation). Carleton University, Ottawa, Canada.

Gershenfeld, N., Krikorian, R., Cohen, R. (2004) The internet of things. *Scientific American, 291*(44), 76-81.

Harris, J., & Kamvar, S. (2005). *We Feel Fine* (artwork).

Heise, D., & Grangenett, N. (1996). Perspectives on the use of internet in art classrooms. *Art Education, 54*(1), 12-18.

June, L. (2009). Japanese college giving away free iPhones using them to track students. Retrieved from www.engadget.com/2009/05/22/japanese-college-giving-away-free-iphones-using-them-to-track-s/

Keen, A. (2006). *The cult of the amateur: How today's internet is killing our culture.* New York, NY: Broadway Business.

Keifer-Boyd, K. (1996). Interfacing hypermedia and the internet with critical inquiry in the arts: Preservice training. *Art Education, 54*(1), 33-41.

Keifer-Boyd, K. (1997). Interactive hyperdocuments: Implications for art criticism in a postmodern era. In J. Hutchens & M. Suggs (Eds.), *Art education: Content and practice in a postmodern era.* (pp. 122-131). Reston, VA: National Art Education Association.

Krug, D. (2002). Electronic media and everyday aesthetics of simulation. *Visual Arts Research, 28*(2), 27-37.

Lanier, J. (2006). Digital Maoism: The hazards of the new online collectivism. *Edge: The third culture.* Retrieved from www.edge.org/3rd_culture/lanier06/lanier06_index.html

McClure, M. (2011). Digital visual childhood: Preschoolers and the new narratives of digital video in the blogosphere. In R. Sweeny (Ed.) *Inter/actions/Inter/sections: Art education in a digital visual culture* (pp. 20-29). Reston, VA: National Art Education Association.

Morozov, E. (2009). The repercussions of a Twitter revolution. *The Boston Globe.* Retrieved from www.boston.com/bostonglobe/editorial_opinion/oped/articles/2009/06/20/the_repercussions_of_a_twitter_revolution/

Obadike, K., & Obadike, M. (2001). *Blackness for sale* (artwork).

Reason, P., & Bradbury, H. (2008). *The Sage handbook of action research: Participative inquiry and practice.* London, England: Sage.

Rutenberg, J., & Nagourney, A. (2009). Melding Obama's web to a YouTube presidency. *New York Times.* Retrieved from www.nytimes.com/2009/01/26/us/politics/26grassroots.html

Saponas, T., Lester, J., Hartung, C., & Kohno, T. (2006). Devices that tell on you: The Nike+iPod sport kit. Retrieved from www.cs.washington.edu/research/systems/nikeipod/tracker-paper.pdf

Shachtman, N. (2009). Army orders bases to stop blocking Twitter, FaceBook, Flickr. *Wired Online.* Retrieved from www.wired.com/dangerroom/2009/06/army-orders-bases-stop-blocking-twitter-facebook-flickr/

Sweeny, R. (2004). Lines of sight in the 'network society': Simulation, art education, and digital visual culture. *Studies in Art Education, 46*(1), 74-86.

Sweeny, R. (2005). Visual culture of control. *Studies in Art Education, 47*(4), 294-307.

Sweeny, R. (2007). Silence between the nodes of the networked classroom. In S. Worden, L. Green & P. Thomas (Eds.), *Proceedings for the Computers in Art and Design Education Annual Conference.* Perth, Australia: Curtin University of Technology.

Sweeny, R. (2009). There's no "I" in YouTube: Networked identity, social media, and art education. *InSEA Journal, 5*(2/3). London, England: Intellect Press.

Sweeny, R., & Patton, R. (2009). CitySneak: Play, pedagogy, surveillance. In A. de Souza e Silva & D. Sutko (Eds.), *Digital cityscapes: Merging digital and urban playspaces.* (pp. 204-216). New York, NY: Peter Lang.

Taylor, P. G., & Carpenter, S. (2002). Inventively linking: Teaching and learning with computer hypertext. *Art Education, 55*(4), 6-12.

Thurber, F. (2004). Teacher education as a field of study in art education: A comprehensive study of methods and methodologies used in research about art teacher education. In E. Eisner & M. Day (Eds.), *The handbook of research and policy in art education* (pp. 487-522). New York, NY: Lawrence Erlbaum.

Wilson McKay, S. (2006). Living the questions: Technology-infused action research. *Art Education, 59*(6), 47-51.

Zetter, K. (2005). School RFID plan gets an F. *Wired Online.* Retrieved from www.wired.com/news/privacy/0,1848,66554,00.html

ENDNOTES

1 WebKinz,® an online environment, allows children to build a virtual lifeworld around an 'adopted' pet which exists in both domains.

2 See Sweeny (2004) and Colman (2004) for analyses of networked forms of art and art education.

3 Project available at www.wefeelfine.org

4 See www.freewayblogger.com for more information.

5 Documentation can be found at www.boomboxgames.org

ROBERT W. SWEENY is Associate Professor and Coordinator of Art Education at Indiana University of Pennsylvania. His research deals with the topics of digital visual culture, new media art, complexity theory, network culture, and the relationship between surveillance and works of art. He serves on the editorial board for *Studies in Art Education, The Journal for Cultural Studies in Art Education,* and *Surveillance and Society,* and is the editor of the anthology *Inter/actions/Inter/sections: Art Education in a Digital Visual Culture* (2011, NAEA).

24 / Unspoken Lessons: The Semiotics and Visual Culture of K-12 Classrooms

CHRISTINE M. WOYWOD / ASSISTANT PROFESSOR OF ART EDUCATION, UNIVERSITY OF WISCONSIN-MILWAUKEE AND **DEBORAH L. SMITH-SHANK** / PROFESSOR AND CHAIR OF THE DEPARTMENT OF ARTS ADMINISTRATION, EDUCATION, AND POLICY, THE OHIO STATE UNIVERSITY

ABSTRACT: *Human-made environments demonstrate and silently communicate politics, belief systems, stereotypes, and biases. These spaces can provide unspoken lessons or hidden curriculum; they can inform, influence, and expose children to political, personal, and institutional power dynamics. This study is an example of ways to interrogate visual data using semiotic strategies. It was designed to gain insights into the visual codes of three contemporary art education classrooms using observation, photography, and interview data, which were combined to recognize and translate the classrooms' visual discourse. This chapter includes a discussion of semiotic practices that can be used to interrogate the visual culture of art classrooms.*

> *The starting point of these reflections was usually a feeling of impatience at the sight of the 'naturalness' with which newspapers, art and common sense constantly dress up a reality, which, even though it is the one we live in, is undoubtedly determined by history.*
> —Barthes, 1957/1972, p. 11

The placement of desks and tables, bins and bulletin boards, as well as playful objects and signs tacked to the walls of art classrooms give us clues about teacher, school, community, and disciplinary identities and beliefs. These objects and their placements represent ideas and reflect important discourses. This study uses a hybrid methodology (theoretical and case study) to theorize the visual environment of three art classrooms and translate the silent communication of visual artifacts in these spaces. Using semiotic strategies from theoretical research, this case study interrogates the objects of classroom visual cultures to reveal snapshots of art education worldviews (Danesi & Perron, 1999; Lotman, 1990) and implicit cultural meanings in art education policy, practice, and production that might ordinarily go unnoticed (Lotman, 1990).

CONTEXT: THEORETICAL FRAMEWORK

Semiotics has been described as a science (Danesi & Perron, 1999) and a point of view (Deely, 1990). As a method for analyzing how cultural signifiers communicate and produce meaning(s) (Eco, 1976; Smith-Shank, 2004), semiotics assists in interpreting material culture objects as the signs and symbols of culture. Material culture objects always have histories, contexts, and meanings, which should be thoughtfully considered and interpreted to signify information. When taken seriously, all objects can share information.

Though many semiotic scholars interrogate text (Chandler, 2007; Danesi, 2008; van Leeuwen, 2005), it is also important to observe and question objects of visual and material culture to understand their codes, signs, and their interactions, which can be understood as significant components of cultural myths (Smith-Shank, 2004). Roland Barthes (1957/1972) defined myth as "a system of communication" (p. 109) and demonstrated many ways cultures can be deconstructed through considerations of their myths. Like Barthes, Guy Debord (1967/2006) also considered special cultural myths and/or "spectacles" and the ways they represent and signify meanings of that culture. A myth can be understood as any story or tale accepted as history that serves to explain a worldview or particular cultural knowledge.

The spectacle serves, for this chapter, as the focus of attention and the ground of myth. Examining Barthes's and Debord's work together facilitates exploration of the stories of cultures and provides a model for research into material culture and social relationships mediated by visual and material objects. Because art education privileges visual discourse, Barthes's and Debord's work is a good point to begin uncovering the significance of visual culture and to begin to understand some of the myths of art education classrooms (Barthes, 1957/1972; Debord, 1967/2006). As Smith-Shank (2004) argued, "Ordinary objects, places, and events are visually loaded aesthetic signifiers, and they have the power to inform, modify desires, and educate" (p vii).

RESEARCH PROBLEM

Semiotics and art education's foundational tenets combine easily, as do myth and spectacle (Smith-Shank, 1995, 2004; Taylor, 2008; Wilson & Toku, 2004). Combining these ideas to consider classrooms provides a rich and multifaceted way of interrogating the spaces. Classrooms are loaded with aesthetic signifiers, have the power to communicate teachers' beliefs (Hickman, 2001), inform students' expectations (Garoian, 2002; Susi, 1986), and subtly teach layers of hidden curriculum (Jackson, 1968; Susi, 1989). Classrooms can give hints to the significance of subject areas and share evidence of ethical, social, and political values. For several decades, theorists have urged art teachers and students to question the images that permeate our existence (e.g. Chapman, 1978; Lanier, 1982; McFee & Degge, 1980) and acknowledge the multiple narratives, contexts, and motives associated with them (e.g. Darts, 2004; Efland, Freedman, & Stuhr, 1996; Freedman, 2003; Tavin & Anderson, 2003). This study responds to those scholars' suggestions and interrogates art classrooms' visual narratives and cultural myths to understand more clearly how art classrooms influence the negotiation and construction of meaning in that space.

Specifically, this study focuses on the following questions:

- What clues can we use to interpret what the material and visual artifacts of a classroom say about the profession, the pedagogy, and the power of art education mythology?
- What meanings and values are communicated through the visual environments of art classrooms?

RESEARCH DESIGN

The design and visual content of art classrooms is influenced by cultural habits, instructional needs, and fiscal possibilities. Throughout the history of art education the environment of the classroom has been of significant interest to both scholars and practitioners (Baker, Ng-He, Lopez-Bosch, & Nuere, 2008; Broome, 2008; Efland, 1990; Kushins & Brisman, 2005; Susi, 1986, 1989) and discussed as a "third-teacher" (Kushins, 2008; Tarr, 2001; Yu, 2008).

This case study employs a theoretical lens and is informed by the work of these researchers and critical visual methodology (Rose, 2007). It uses semi-structured interviews, observations of classroom spaces (Baker et al., 2008), and analysis of classroom photographs (Kushins & Brisman, 2005) to make sense of what art classrooms are communicating. Semiotic lenses inform each part of this process, including the design of research and interview questions, discussions resulting from the photographs, and analysis to uncover meanings and values. Similar approaches have been used to guide the interrogation of sites such as teenagers' bedrooms (Grauer, 2002), faculty offices (Gasman & Epstein, 2003), and elementary and high school art rooms (Kushins, 2008). This study extends these previous studies by using similar lenses to interrogate layers of meanings that emerge from art classroom environments.

PARTICIPANTS AND LOCATION OF THE RESEARCH

A total of six participants agreed to be part of this study. The researcher selected all participants purposively due to their reputations as excellent art teachers/educators. Three participants were art teachers (one K-5, one middle school, and one 5-12). The art teachers participated in informal semi-structured interviews and the lead researcher took multiple photos of their classrooms. The sites for data collection were the three schools at which these teachers work. In the following sections, the grades 5-12 art room will be described as Site 1, the middle school art room as Site 2, and the grades K-5 art room as Site 3. The three college/university art educators, one tenured faculty, one adjunct faculty, and one full-time doctoral candidate, all with significant classroom experience also participated in the study as interpreters of the photographs. Their "readings" of the photos was juxtaposed with the researcher's readings, for triangulation of data (Denzin, 2006).

DATA COLLECTION

The lead researcher took between 40 and 60 photographs of each of the three K-12 art classroom during individual, informal interviews. She photographed general views of the classrooms, views of each wall, visual displays and arrangements around the classrooms, details of focal points, elements unique to the classroom, and points of pride indicated by the K–12 participants. Notes were handwritten following each interview/photography session.

After printing and organizing the photographs, compiling notes, and scheduling time to meet, the lead researcher presented the college/university participants with the three sets of classroom photographs. Each set was in a binder that contained 40 to 60, color photographs (size 8.5" by 11") of multiple angles and groups of details, objects, and artifacts placed in each of the three classrooms. The photographs presented the room from entry to exit. Each of the college/university participants viewed the three binders in the same order. The binders were not labeled by grade levels. This presentation served as a spectacle, creating a specter of potential meanings for the college/university participants to interpret based on their experiences. The visual documentation of the classrooms relied on the myth that art practices and pedagogy can be understood through objects within educational environments.

The lead researcher observed while the college/university participants individually viewed the binders. She also prompted discussion of the photographs and asked for the participants' thoughts about the meanings of both the sites and the objects in the photos. The discussions about the photographs took from 60 to 120 minutes total for all three settings.

THEORIES THAT INFORM DATA ANALYSIS

For this research project, a classroom is considered both a text and a semiosphere. A semiosphere (Lotman, 1990) is a conceptual and physical space that we inhabit as meaning-making creatures. Estonian semiotician, Yuri Lotman's (1990) notion of the semiosphere suggests that culture is driven by recognition of difference, asymmetry, and contradictions. Lotman (1990) is especially concerned with the tensions between "us" and "them," and "inside" and "outside," which are necessary for creativity and growth. In this cultural semiotic view, development of any culture depends on input from and communication with other cultures and human development depends upon interaction with a community of inquiry. Considered at its most essential level, growth and new knowledge can occur only through tensions and difference, through community and conversation.

In Lotman's (1990) semiosphere, a classroom is an interactive space in which the objects and the participants are inextricably interrelated. They are filled with meanings that oftentimes seem contradictory, so identifying a series of dichotomies was a useful strategy to start recognizing patterns and understanding differences between the rooms. As the researchers toiled through potential ways to (re)search and (re)present, we often revisited Barthes' myths and Debord's spectacles, and finally themes emerged through the open coding of the data (Charmaz, 2006). Certain structures emerged as dichotomies, but there were also more slippery ideas, not so readily organized along a continuum. Some dichotomies surfaced as echoes in the teacher participants' identification of differences between their actual classroom and their ideals. Others became apparent through comparisons that the college/university participants made as they looked through one set of images after another, comparing and contrasting the rooms, the objects in the rooms, and their thoughts about them. While helpful in identifying descriptors, dichotomies did not account for the "storied data," the narratives, the myths and cultural tales of the three art teachers' semiospheres. The stories were more complex than continuums permit. To address these complex ideas, it was important to consider the fertile ground of metaphor (Lakoff & Johnson, 1980; Marshall, 2004; Sacks, 1979).

LAYERS OF DATA AND ANALYSIS

The lead researcher analyzed the data, organized by physical site, using a layering approach. Each analysis started with a thick written description of the classroom and its contents, followed by a summary of the notes made of the teacher's comments while the researcher was photographing. The lead researcher then wrote about the data that gave meaning to various myths (Barthes, 1957/1972) that seemed to be present in the classroom. The next layer of data included a summary of the college/university participants' analyses of the images. The final layer of meaning was a reflection by the lead researcher on her experience, insights, surprises, and clues to the myths of art education that she found in the photographs she took. The juxtaposition of each of these layers added to the richness of the insights.

A semiotic analysis purposefully and thoughtfully considers each single layer of meaning only in relationship with others. While layers were collected individually, they were considered as meaningful only as they related with one another. It is as if they are layered, and then laced so that the meaning(s) can emerge more richly than they could by looking at the individual pieces of data as separate clues. The patterns that emerge from the lacing and weaving become important considerations for semiotic analysis.

LAYER 1: ANALYTICAL DESCRIPTION OF THE THREE CLASSROOMS

Upon entering Site 1, the lead researcher was struck by the large environment, where cool grey walls led up to lofty ceilings, with student-painted artist banners hanging down (See Figure 1). This teacher actively showed the researcher around parts of the room and seemed very interested in being helpful. In Site 2, a colorful, mural-filled hallway indicated the entrance to the room. It felt like an older space, but lively, with posters, paintings, and yards of beautiful tie-dye fabric swooping below the ceiling (See Figure 2). This teacher was especially interested in hearing about how other art teachers arrange and display work in other schools. Lastly, Site 3 was stimulating and colorful, but also felt crowded with large furniture and student work piled all over the room (See Figure 3). This art teacher welcomed the researcher into her classroom and pointed out sections of particular interest. During the visit however, she was distracted and began sorting items at her desk, picking paper and crayons off the floor, rinsing cups at the sink, and offering apologies for the classroom's messiness, as if she were seeing the room through new eyes.

FIGURE 1 (LEFT). Site 1, grades 5-12 art classroom.

FIGURE 2 (TOP RIGHT). Site 2, middle school art classroom.

FIGURE 3 (BOTTOM RIGHT). Site 3, grades K-5 art classroom.

LAYER 2: MYTHS IN THE CLASSROOM

Jodi Kushins (2008) argues that images in art classrooms have the power to communicate philosophy and objectives, which can be considered the foundations of educational myths and systems of beliefs (Freedman, 2003). The classroom sites in this study bear witness to several myths of art education. The myth of "who artists are" emerged through the many visuals representing individual, deceased, white, male artists. The repeated color wheels and elements and principles posters communicate the myth of "impor-tant/objective art knowledge" and the idea that if students acquire knowledge about these tenets, they will be successful student artists. Though there were artworks and other items created by students in each room, the largest works on permanent display directly referenced artists from cannons of art history. The teachers at two sites communicated that they intended the students' contributions to the classrooms to serve as teaching tools but the student work in many cases, were studies of the adult artwork, adding to the myth "adult art is more important than child art" and possibly, "adult ideas are more important to than the ideas of children." Without displays of lesson plans, student artist statements, or images of the processes involved in art creation, the myth that "art just emerges" is inadvertently promoted. The locations of visual placement, size of imagery, and duration of display are significant silent indicators of the importance of the objects to the teachers' informal pedagogy.

LAYER 3: COLLEGE/UNIVERSITY PARTICIPANTS' ANALYSIS

In the contemporary context of critical visual approaches to art education, interrogation of visual phenomena is timely and appropriate (Barthes, 1957/1972; Eco, 1976; Lotman, 1990; Pink, 2007; Rose, 2007; Smith-Shank, 2004). All of the college/university participants offered insights into the research process along with their assigned task of interrogating the photographs. One college/university participant said, "I think this is an awesome exercise… while in the room, you focus on what happens… with this [photographs], you focus on the aesthetics of the room… we don't often notice our environments as much as we should."

Each of the three college/university participants had different thoughts about the quantity of the photographs and the presentation process. One indicated that she would have liked more photographs. Another spent most of her time studying the photographs, and wondered if all three collections of images should be viewed at the same time or if different viewing sessions would be more expedient. At the same time, she noted the desire to be able to compare and contrast each of the rooms in order to "pick up on things." The third college/university participant, like the elementary art teacher, seemed distracted. She focused on the significance of the items and organization of the rooms, but she was a bit rushed with concerns about a meeting that afternoon; she did not give as much time to the interrogation and comparison of the photographs as the others.

Metaphor as a lens of data analysis. Just like any other system of meaning, metaphors function as a semiotic device for finding more thorough understandings of phenomena and for reconsidering habits of belief (Lakoff & Johnson, 1980). An example of ways that metaphors can be used to reconsider beliefs and habits of thought, occurred in a conversation with art educator Ed Check (personal communication, February 2009) about potential research topics. Check pointed out that "there's nothing wrong with looking at your own backyard with new eyes." When classrooms are considered metaphorical backyards, the way we are able to think about them shifts. Like a backyard, an art classroom can be a place for children to play, make discoveries, learn, and grow. In a backyard, we may experience contentment and after a while, cease to notice visual subtleties until we see someone else's yard. In (re)cognizing the differences between the three art classrooms in this study, we realized that metaphors of three types of gardens emerged: a manicured garden, a casual garden, and a garden with irregular maintenance.

Metaphorical findings. Site 1, with an extreme sense of order, neatness, and newness could be described as manicured. The college/university participants found this room to be highly positive and desirable. It was "an attractive room" and "the kind of room teachers dream of." It was "impeccable," "intentionally meticulous," and "regularly tended to" just like a structured formal English garden. However, such a refined garden may not easily accommodate active children. Though lovely, does it welcome serious play, risk taking, and experiments? Can it foster creativity? The boundaries of an impeccable space, perceived through the use of metaphor, presented an interesting contradiction to the college/university participants' positive reaction to images of this room.

There was more of a sense of casual gardening in reflecting upon Site 2 and the discussions related to it. Things are tended to, but also allowed to grow naturally. The teacher turned "tending" into an opportunity to let students work creatively and experience ownership of the space through their creation of well-crafted permanent artworks on cabinets and hallway walls. While the room showed age and layers of history, there was evidence of very organic interaction with the resources and fixtures available to the students and teacher in this room.

A backyard with irregular maintenance metaphorically represents Site 3 in this inquiry. This metaphor suggested an important myth that challenged initial impressions of this room. The room seemed visually busy, with posters crowded up to the ceiling, and messy, with landslides of student work on the counters and dirty supplies piled up in the sink. All of the college/university participants reacted to photographs of this room with negative comments. One said, she personally needs "order" and another "could not handle teaching in there." The garden metaphor in this situation gave us insights into complexities of this classroom that we had initially overlooked because we could not see anything but the messiness. When leaves are not raked or the yard starts to get wild and overgrown, it may not be for lack of care or interest. It could be a symptom of the gardener's attention and time being consumed by other (and possibly more important) things. While a messy art room can signify slovenly practices, it also could mean that a teacher is deeply involved in dealing with the immediate needs of individual students, collaborating with colleagues, advocating for their program, or, as was the case in this instance, teaching at more than one site.

LAYER 4: THE RESEARCHERS' REFLECTIONS

The visual environments of art classrooms are indicators of art education's identity and practice. In these three classrooms, similar to most other classrooms we visited in the U.S. Midwest, there was an abundance of color wheels, masterwork posters, and images initially selected by publication companies for mass production. These artifacts of art education may even be the signifiers that visually say "art education classroom" since they always seem to be present. As Debord (1967/2006) observed, "Everything that was directly lived has receded into a representation" (p. 7). Visuals in art classrooms are always spectacles with lists of the elements and principles of art hung alongside classroom rules and the American flag. It seemed to all viewers of the photos, that adult art artworks and products were privileged over student art and that adult art was spatially treated as most valued of the room displays. The adult masterworks were primarily paintings by dead white male European artists including daVinci, van Gogh, Monet, Dali, and Munch. Although Site 1 had a collection of African tribal masks and Site 2 had images of contemporary 3-D art made out of recycled materials, these were the only instances of 3-D artwork, crafts, design work, or art from a range of cultures. Two sites had student art referencing/mimicking adult art as permanent displays in the room, and the third room included a display of student watercolor paintings, which were copies of the *Mona Lisa*, depicting her holding contemporary objects. Individually, all three of the art teachers discussed the multiple images on their walls, saying that they used images and posted rule signage to teach the students both art content and appropriate art class behavior.

There was a potential conceptual contradiction to socially transformative art education practices in the interviews with the teachers. The disconnection between the postmodern points of view of the teachers as evidenced by analysis of their interviews and their primarily modernist resources led one of the teacher participants to apologize for what she felt was a lack of contemporary multicultural images and representations of diversity. Clearly, a contradiction exists between what is valued in contemporary visual culture art education and the nonverbal visual classroom communication of these classrooms. But this may be the discourse of art education. While the teachers add limited items for their classrooms each year, based on their budget, their classroom visual culture juxtaposes the few new objects with instances of visual artifacts from multiple art education stances and prior art teachers.

CONCLUDING THOUGHTS

The semiosphere of the art classroom is a meaning-producing place where students, teachers, visitors, and the objects relate to the spectacle and embedded myths of art education in multiple and varied ways. Photographs of three classrooms gave observer/readers the opportunity to make sense of the spaces from photographs taken from the researchers' points of view. The researchers' immersion in the spaces added a layer of meaning, and the transcripts of interviewers with three teachers were overlaid on these interpretations, compounding the types of possible responses to the rooms and photographs, and adding to the depth of analysis. This study provided one way of considering the multiple juxtapositions of signifiers of art education content and practices. Taking a theoretical semiotic approach to understanding the interrelations of objects in art classrooms provides metaphoric understanding of the overt and covert pedagogy of art classroom spaces and insights into contemporary practices in art education.

Semiotic research strategies make it possible to question the varied meanings that exist in any environment. In theorizing the visual environment of these art classrooms and considering what artifacts and material culture objects communicate, layers of meaning emerged. The analytic description, apparent myths, college/university participants' analysis, and the researchers' reflections were all necessary to face the challenge of representing multiple possibilities and points of view while describing beliefs and implied meanings about art education that might ordinarily go unnoticed.

USE OF VISUAL DATA

Visual data is central to this inquiry. Photographing individual classrooms facilitated methodical exploration and stimulated a rapport with the three teachers; the K–5 teacher responded to the focus, point, and shoot process of photography with a desire to clean her room and the other two teachers also noticed things they may not otherwise have thought about. The very action of camera movement privileged points of view(ing), which the researchers acknowledge, but it also focused the vision/sight of the person watching the photograph being taken. The photographs served as field notes, leading to a richer thick description than what may have been possible with only written notes and memory.

Finally, the presentation of the visual data had the unexpected result of focusing the college/university participants' commentary on research methodologies. The college/university participants expressed a difference in considering environments while in a room versus experiencing a space through photographs. Remembering her own experiences as an art teacher, one participant explained that this was an opportunity to clearly pause and consider physical environment in a way that might not have been possible in the midst of teaching. Analyzing the images of the classrooms not only caused the college/higher education participants to look carefully, but also made it possible to describe qualities that become evident through the perception of difference.

POTENTIAL FOR FURTHER RESEARCH

This study is a preliminary inquiry for a larger study of nonverbal classroom meanings. Presenting this research and the insights gleaned from it in multiple venues have complicated and expanded the researchers' ideas about methodologies that can be used to study classroom environments and their meanings. Semiotic strategies including the layering of metaphors and myths, through the deconstruction of classroom spectacles, have been useful in looking at art classrooms, and could be used to analyze other educational spaces.

As researchers, we found metaphor particularly useful in framing the discussion and analysis of the three classrooms in this study. The garden metaphors used to analyze the classrooms helped us with the process of data analysis. However, after serious consideration and reflection, we realized that we imposed the garden metaphors and thus, they did not yield significant new insights beyond our autoethnographic, postmodern, and feminist theoretical frameworks. Another way to approach the use of metaphor in this study could have been to have each teacher suggest a metaphor for her classroom and the other classrooms in this study.

Further research could involve photo-elicitation (Rose, 2007) in which art teachers become collaborators in the investigation, photographing their favorite parts of their art classrooms. Giving cameras to students to photograph their own favorite parts of the room and asking them to analyze their own photos could also elicit more voices and points of view. Through the potential spectacles revealed by multiple cameras, the insights into the significance of art classroom culture(s) and the various metaphors of art education could be more varied and provide richer opportunities for analysis.

REFERENCES

Baker, M., Ng-He, C., Lopez-Bosch, M., & Nuere, S. (2008). Reflections on the role of artists: A case study on the hidden visual curriculum of the School of the Art Institute of Chicago. *Teaching Artist Journal, 6*(4), 290–297.

Barthes, R. (1972). *Mythologies* (A. Lavers, Trans.). New York, NY: Hill and Wang. (Original work published 1957)

Broome, J. (2008). Arranging your art room for effective learning. *NAEA Advisory.* Reston, VA: National Art Education Association.

Chandler, D. (2007). *Semiotics: The basics.* New York, NY: Routledge.

Chapman, L. (1978). *Approaches to art in education.* New York, NY: Harcourt Brace Jovanovich.

Charmaz, K. (2006). *Constructing grounded theory: A practical guide through qualitative analysis.* London, England: Sage.

Danesi, M. (2008). *Of cigarettes, high heels, and other interesting things: An introduction to semiotics* (2nd ed.). London, England: Palgrave.

Danesi, M., & Perron, P. (1999). *Analyzing cultures.* Bloomington: Indiana University Press.

Darts, D. (2004). Visual culture jam: Art, pedagogy, and creative resistance. *Studies in Art Education, 45*(4), 313–327.

Debord, G. (2006). *The society of the spectacle* (K. Knabb, Trans.). Oakland, CA: AK Press. (Original work published 1967)

Deely, J. (1990). *Basics of semiotics.* Bloomington: Indiana University Press.

Denzin, N. (2006). *Sociological methods: A sourcebook.* Piscataway, NJ: Aldine Transaction.

Eco, U. (1976). *A theory of semiotics*. Bloomington: Indiana University Press.

Efland, A. (1990). *A history of art education: Intellectual and social currents in teaching the visual arts*. New York, NY: Teachers College Press.

Efland, A., Freedman, K., & Stuhr, P. (1996). *Postmodern art education: An approach to curriculum*. Reston, VA: National Art Education Association.

Freedman, K. (2003). *Teaching visual culture: Curriculum, aesthetics, and the social life of art*. New York, NY: Teachers College Press.

Garoian, C. (2002). Children performing the art of identity. In Y. Gaudelius & P. Speirs (Eds.), *Contemporary issues in art education* (pp. 119-129). Upper Saddle River, NJ: Prentice Hall.

Gasman, M., & Epstein, E. (2003, December 31). Doorways to the academy: Visual self expression among faculty members in academic departments. *International Journal of Education and the Arts, 4*(8). Retrieved from www.ijea.org/v4n8/

Grauer, K. (2002). Teenagers and their bedrooms. *Visual Arts Research, 28*(2), 86-93.

Hickman, R. (2001). Art rooms and art teaching. *Art Education, 54*(1), 7-11.

Jackson, P. (1968). *Life in classrooms*. New York, NY: Holt, Rinehart and Winston.

Kushins, J. (2008). The artroom as teacher. *NAEA Advisory*. Reston, VA: National Art Education Association.

Kushins, J., & Brisman, A. (2005). Learning from our learning spaces: A portrait of 695 Park Avenue. *Art Education, 58*(1), 33-39.

Lakoff, G., & Johnson, M. (1980). *Metaphors we live by*. Chicago, IL: University of Chicago Press.

Lanier, V. (1982). *The arts we see: A simplified introduction to the visual arts*. New York, NY: Teachers College Press.

Lotman, Y. (1990) *The universe of the mind* (A. Shukman, Trans.). Bloomington: Indiana University Press.

Marshall, J. (2004). Metaphor in art, thought, and learning. In D. L. Smith-Shank (Ed.), *Semiotics and visual culture: Sights, signs, and significance* (pp. 63-71). Reston, VA: National Art Education Association.

McFee, J. K., & Degge, R. (1980). *Art, culture, and environment: A catalyst for teaching*. Dubuque, IA: Kendall/ Hunt.

Pink, S. (2007). *Doing visual ethnography* (2nd ed.). Los Angeles, CA: Sage.

Rose, G. (2007). *Visual methodologies: An introduction to the interpretation of visual methodologies*. London, England: Sage.

Sacks, S. (1979). *On metaphor*. Chicago, IL: The University of Chicago Press.

Susi, F. (1986). Physical space and the teaching of art. *Art Education, 39*(2), 6-9.

Susi, F. (1989). The physical environment of art classrooms: A basis for effective discipline. *Art Education, 42*(4), 37-43.

Smith-Shank, D. (1995). Semiotic pedagogy and art education. *Studies in Art Education, 36*(4), 233-241.

Smith-Shank, D. L. (2004). *Semiotics and visual culture: Sights, signs, and significance*. Reston, VA: National Art Education Association.

Tarr, P. (2001). Aesthetic codes in early childhood classrooms: What art educators can learn from Reggio Emilia. *Art Education, 54*(3), 33-39.

Tavin, K., & Anderson, D. (2003). Teaching (popular) visual culture: Deconstructing Disney in the elementary art classroom. *Art Education, 56*(3), 21-23/32-35.

Taylor, P. G. (2008). Editorial. *Art Education, 61*(6), 4-5.

Van Leeuwen, T. (2005). *Introducing social semiotics*. New York, NY: Routledge.

Wilson, B., & Toku, M. (2004). "Boys' Love," yaoi, and art education: Issues of power and pedagogy. In D. L. Smith-Shank (Ed.), *Semiotics and visual culture: Sights, signs, and significance* (pp. 94-103). Reston, VA: National Art Education Association.

Yu, G.S. (2008) Documentation: Ideas and applications from the Reggio Emilia approach. *Teaching Artist Journal, 6*(2), 126-134.

CHRISTINE WOYWOD earned her PhD in Art Education at Northern Illinois University. Through her dissertation, she interrogated the narratives emerging from the material culture of high school art environments, as described by National Board Certified art educators. She has taught art in elementary, high school, and university level, and has presented her research at state, national, and international venues. As a result of her teaching experiences and research, she believes it is important to take issue-based approaches to art instruction, and she is also passionate about collaborating with other educators to create interdisciplinary learning experiences for students. Woywod is an Assistant Professor of Art Education at the University of Wisconsin-Milwaukee.

DEBORAH L. SMITH-SHANK received a PhD from Indiana University and is Professor and Chair of the Department of Arts Administration, Education, and Policy at The Ohio State University. Her research is involved with artifacts of visual culture and social justice examined through semiotic and feminist lenses and has published over 100 journal articles and book chapters, and edited the 2004 book, *Semiotics and Visual Culture: Sights, Signs, and Significance*. Smith-Shank currently serves as elected Vice President of InSEA (www.insea.org) and is co-editor of the *Journal of Visual Culture & Gender*, an international, freely accessed, multimedia juried journal (www.emitto.net/visualculturegender).

SARA AND MELANIE: *The following two contributions relate to uses of discourse analysis, a form of theoretical research, to understand classroom practices. The authors investigate different research questions, but both utilize discourse analysis.*

Power and Resistance: The Relevance of Discourse Analysis to a Classroom

RINA KUNDU /ASSISTANT PROFESSOR, UNIVERSITY OF WISCONSIN-MILWAUKEE

WHAT IS DISCOURSE ANALYSIS?

Discourse is a social process by which meanings are produced. *Discourse analysis* allows researchers to ask why, at any given time, certain things are said or written and others are not. For instance, a school district may have a motto, "art makes us better people." This phrase promotes our field and conveys the fact that art is a process of intellectual, spiritual, and aesthetic development. Who would not want to adopt such a phrase? But as you look around the art classrooms of this particular school district, you discover that the curriculum emphasizes European drawing traditions and artistic practices, that the images posted on walls are of the works of Picasso, Kandinsky, and Michelangelo, and that as you interview teachers, they all discuss the need to study old masters.

As a researcher interested in discourse analysis, you may ask at this point how schooling directs action, who gets to define the terms to enable the "betterment" for our students, and what values, understandings, and ways of knowing are being promoted, circulated, and silenced. Ultimately, what is said and done in the classroom also leads to ways of participating in the world and understanding our relationship to others. In the case of this school district, "betterment" of students may mean to provide them with the best of the collected art European males have produced and the ideas and standards they have created.

In discourse analysis, language is understood as something that shapes our experiences. Try to imagine thinking without using language; we use it to explain ideas and feelings to ourselves and others. Language is not a tool or a medium but social practice, a means by which to do things. Language organized into discourses has the power to shape the ways in which people participate in the world, drawing attention to how the structuring effects of language produce and limit ways of knowing (Burman & Parker, 1993; Fairclough, 1995, 2003; Potter & Wetherall, 1994). Discourses not only condition the meaning of words but also refer to all types of texts, spoken and written, and can be extended to semiotic modalities such as images. Social and cultural fields, such as education, speak about themselves using texts, constituting meanings and practices that people act on and participate in. When discourses become institutionally sanctioned, they have power. For example, statements made about "learning" not only fix ideas about learning—how it is seen and understood, such as learning styles—but also order actions taken—what should be done to those that learn and those that do not, such as classifying people as on-task, successful, or at-risk and learning disabled. Therefore, when a researcher employs discourse analysis, she provides a way to look critically at the function of the discipline of art education. Such analysis requires the researcher to be attentive to discursive structures, working to highlight assumptions framing art education, how it is practiced and understood, and what it claims to do, critiquing practices for its effects on people.

According to Burman and Parker (1993), there are a variety of ways in which discourse analysis research is being done. What seems to be common among these approaches is that they are united by their attention to the structuring effects of language and are associated with interpretive styles of analysis. Discourse analysis is used to comment on social processes that maintain structures of domination and oppression and require the researcher to account for knowledge claims. Discourse analysis can be used by researchers to intervene in the ways in which art education constructs our understandings of art, culture, and difference, among other things. My understanding of discourse grew from my engagement with the work of poststructuralist Michel Foucault (1969/1972, 1976/1990, 1975/1995) and his influence on education (Ball, 1990; Britzman, 2003; Cherryholmes, 1988; Spanos, 1993; Popkewitz & Brennan, 1998). Foucault's investigations reveal that people are products of discourse and producers of discourse.

WHY IS DISCOURSE ANALYSIS RELEVANT TO THE WORK OF TEACHERS?

Art education as a field of practice is made up of schools, museums, community centers, universities, professional organizations, and constituted by relationships between teachers and students, among others. Institutions exercise their authority from their capacity to make statements about a situation, such as teaching or learning, and to regulate communication through their practices. The discourses within the institution of art education position art educators in relation to what can be said and how it can be said, making particular practices possible and others not. For example, curricula are manifestations of the discursive practices of a specific time. For example, discipline-based art education curriculum was supported and promoted throughout the 1980s-1990s. Discourse analysis could be used to understand the social processes that maintain what is made visible and what is not within these formations. Some art educators (Chalmers, 1992; Zeller, 1989) realized that the majority of Discipline-Based Art Education (DBAE) curricula largely reinforced a bias toward European art and male artists and used Western frameworks to understand the works of other cultures. This realization occurred through attentive discourse analysis.

HOW HAVE I USED DISCOURSE ANALYSIS IN A CLASSROOM?

My research project was a discourse analysis of one university art history course undergoing education reform. I was hired as the education consultant to conduct an assessment of the reform. As I interviewed the teachers and students to gather data, I noticed that participants in the class were being pulled in different directions by competing social interests, such as seeing the class as a way to expand their knowledge of what is great art or as a way to construct a better understanding of people and their ways of living and making to promote personal growth and a healthy society. I wanted to know why there were competing social interests and what values, understandings, and ways of knowing were being promoted, circulated, and silenced.

Fairclough (1995, 2003) offers an analytic framework that I used to perform discourse analysis. He relates that each discursive event, that is language in use, has three dimensions: a text, an instance of discourse practice, and a piece of social practice. A text creates a representation of the world by foregrounding information and constitutes identities of speakers and readers and the social relationships between them. I considered the students' and teachers' educational choices as texts. As such, I made a list of keywords and phrases related to art, culture, and people because these words continually emerged in the conversations occurring in the classroom, assignments written by teachers and responded to by students, and in interviews conducted with teachers and students. I searched for these words in all the data collected including my observations of interactions in the classroom, in transcriptions and recordings of interviews, and in documents, such as examinations, handouts, papers, and journal entries students wrote about their learning.

I was also attentive to rupture, breaks, and shifts in how participants were practicing art history and how teachers and students within the survey course talked about art, culture, and people. For example, there were shifts in how culture was talked about; some students discussed it in a hierarchical manner such as the best products that society could produce, others discussed it as a shared belief system among groups, and still others discussed it as a signifying system that constructs meanings and values for objects. These differences helped to identify the specific discourses that enable talk or practice in art historical learning.

The second component of Fairclough's analytic framework examines the instance of discourse practice that involves the production, circulation, and consumption of texts (Fairclough, 1995). Accordingly, I focused on what discourses were included and excluded in class discussions and in assignments in relationship to larger conversations in the fields of art history and education, how they were different from each other, and how discourses shaped people and participation. For example, there were humanistic discourses that emerged, which is a dominant discourse formation in the fields of art history and education. Giroux (1988) connects humanism to education by reflecting on how those in the field institutionalize the processes by which the grand narratives of progress and human development can be passed on to future generations. While seeking to make discourses visible, I also asked what problems were presupposed by the statements made by participants in relationship to fields of study and what solutions are being offered in response. Such questions helped to construct what sense participants were making of their experiences in the classroom.

Lastly, Fairclough (1995) explains that all discursive events have a social practice. I asked what social conditions are constructed by particular discourses—that is, how do they perpetuate and justify the social status quo, and how do they transform the status quo in situations, institutions, and society? The status quo I found consisted of hegemonic practices that normalize power inequities that operate under the guise that they benefit all involved, but really construct a social order. I analyzed the discourses to understand how they socially ordered the field of art history in practice, specifically looking for justifications made by participants who chose to do things this way versus that. It was helpful for me to reverse my thinking about the ways particular discourses structure our talk about art, culture, and people. Instead, I looked at how the discourses create limitations too. For example, many people believe humanism is a progressive social practice that allows people to think about themselves as rational and autonomous; in control of their futures; and having power over self, others, and things to make the world better. But, an uncritical acceptance of humanism can also be limiting because such questions as "Whose reason is most rational?", "Who will control?", "Who will be dominated?", and "Who decides what progress is?" are necessary to consider. Conducting a discourse analysis can bring these issues to the fore.

AN EXAMPLE OF DISCOURSE ANALYSIS IN ACTION

The textbook used for the survey class was Sherman E. Lee's *The History of Far Eastern Art* (2003). The author organized the book chronologically, tracing and interpreting patterns of stylistic development and discussing conceptual, philosophical, and other contextual issues. Because discourse analysis deals with language in use, students can understand this text as a means by which to do things. In other words, this textbook situates the language used in the interaction of the art history classroom, enabling and constraining the teacher and students and their expression of ideas.

Lee's (2003) art history textbook relates to the discourses of the art history survey and Orientalism. The survey class format itself is a discursive practice that shapes art historians and their teaching. What can be said within a set of stable relationships among people and objects regulates the discourse. In survey classes, the teacher structures the content in particular ways. Graham (1995) identifies four notions common to the structure of the art history survey—canonicity, chronology, closure, and subjectivity. Canonicity comes out of the belief that there are cultural artifacts whose study cannot be negotiated. Although Lee (2003) expands the canon of objects to be studied, he situates art historical study within formalism, which limits how the works can be seen and judged. This is equivalent to an additive approach (Sleeter & Grant, 1994) to the study of art, where previously neglected artifacts are added to the list of what is to be studied without challenge to the frameworks themselves. Moreover, chronology acts upon the history of art by sequencing events along a linear timeline that implies that a culture matures over time, but in Lee's book, he stops short of covering the modern. Furthermore, Graham (1995) refers to how the art historical survey denotes closure, and Lee (2003) basically introduces a story about Asian art based on who did what when. Lastly, the teaching of the survey creates subjectivity, an act of normalizing and reproducing what comes to stand as truth. However, as Lee (2003) sheds the idea that Asia is homogeneous, he constructs binary oppositions by using such terms as "oriental," "exotic," and "mysterious." He does not discuss the modern art of these countries because he feels it is part of a worldwide internationalism rather than of the traditions discussed in the book. There is a contradiction inherent here because he says that Asia is not static and changes through a variety of influences, but then he maintains that there is something essentialist to these countries' artistic practices that gets lost in modern times. How many of us, as teachers, do what Lee is doing—using familiar frameworks such as formalism to discuss other people's art, holding cultures still as if they do not change over time, and presenting information about objects as if this knowledge is complete and without scholarly conflict?

WHAT ARE THE CONSEQUENCES OF SUCH TALK?

The textbook is an anti-Eurocentric intervention in art history, making the arts of Asia visible. Formalist analysis helps hold together the complex histories of artist practices, institutions, and aesthetics of these countries. The logic that shapes Lee's (2003) narrative, which is stylistic evolution, set within a chronology, not only maintains a sense of context and history but also a particular ideology for art—that it is timeless and universal. Lee (2003) does not assume that Far Eastern art is self-evidently worthwhile; therefore, he defines it in relationship to the West to create a conceptualization of it as art. Lee privileges style over context to remove these works from an anthropological understanding. He focuses on individual works as art objects instead of their function in people's lives. The aesthetic dimension takes precedence over any site-specific association, emphasizing the object's autonomy.

Art here rises above the local and is considered a shared human experience. It promotes humanistic values for art and culture and the appropriation of difference. Culture here is enculturation, providing one with the best of the collected artworks in societies.

Art curriculum whether in an art history survey class or in a K-12 art education classroom is a discourse that not only orients students to what needs to be known but their capacity to know, making some practices visible and others not. It is important to use discourse analysis to reveal the values, beliefs, and ways of knowing that get circulated and silenced, so that critique of our practices can take place. ■

REFERENCES

Ball, S. (Ed.). (1990). *Foucault and education: Disciplines and knowledge*. New York, NY: Routledge.

Britzman, D. P. (2003). *Practice makes practice: A critical study of learning to Teach* (rev. ed.). Albany: State University of New York Press.

Burman, E., & Parker, I. (1993). Introduction—Discourse analysis: The turn to the text. In E. Burman & I. Parker (Eds.), *Discourse analytic research: Repertoires and readings of texts in action* (pp. 1-16). New York, NY: Routledge.

Cherryholmes, C. H. (1988). *Power and criticism: Poststructural investigations in education*. New York, NY: Teachers College Press.

Chalmers, F. G. (1992). DBAE as multicultural education. *Art Education, 45*(3), 16-24.

Fairclough, N. (1995). *Critical discourse analysis: The critical study of language*. New York, NY: Longman Group.

Fairclough, N. (2003). *Analysing discourse: Textual analysis for social research*. New York, NY: Routledge.

Foucault, M. (1972). *The archaeology of knowledge and the discourse on language* (A. M. Sheridan Smith, Trans.). New York, NY: Pantheon Books. (Original work published 1969)

Foucault, M. (1990). *The history of sexuality: An introduction* (R. Hurley, Trans.). Harmondsworth, England: Penguin Books. (Original work published 1976)

Foucault, M. (1995). *Discipline and punishment: The birth of the prison* (A. Sheridan, Trans.). New York, NY: Vintage Books. (Original work published 1975)

Giroux, H. (1988). Postmodernism and the discourse of educational criticism. *Journal of Education, 179*(3), 5-30.

Graham, M. M. (1995). The future of art history and the undoing of the survey. *Art Journal, 54*(3), 30-34.

Lee, S. E. (2003). *A history of Far Eastern art*. New York, NY: Prentice Hall.

Popkewitz, T. S., & Brennan, M. (1998). Restructuring of social and political theory in Education: Foucault and a social epistemology of school practices. In T. S. Popkewitz & M. Brennan (Eds.), *Foucault's challenge: Discourse, knowledge, and power in education* (pp. 3-38). New York, NY: Columbia University Press.

Potter, J., & Wetherall, M. (1994). Analyzing discourse. In A. Bryman & R. G. Burgess (Eds.), *Analyzing qualitative data* (pp. 47-66). New York, NY: Routledge.

Sleeter, C., & Grant, C. A. (1994). *Making choices for multicultural education : Five approaches to race, class, and gender*. New York, NY: Merrill.

Spanos, W. V. (1993). *The end of education: Toward posthumanism*. Minneapolis: University of Minnesota Press.

Zeller, T. (1989). The role of the humanities in art education. *Art Education, 42*(4), 48-57.

Visual Utterances: Analyzing Children's Communication Through Artmaking

HYUNSU KIM / PHD CANDIDATE, ART EDUCATION, THE PENNSYLVANIA STATE UNIVERSITY

SARA AND MELANIE: *Theoretical research can inform any aspect of a study or it can be the methodology of the entire study. In this case, Kim demonstrates how Bakhtinian theory exploring the linkages between utterances and social groups is a useful tool for employing and interpreting data analysis.*

The process children use when they make art is complicated and dynamic. It involves layers of discourse and visual languages used within a cultural meaning system. Traditionally, children's artmaking has been validated by focusing only on the visible aspects, whereas implicit messages and intents have not been considered (Pearson, 2001). This essay presents an example of how the discourses, communication, and actions that occurred while children were creating visual art were researched and analyzed. To do this, the theories of Mikhail Bakhtin (Holquist, 1990) were applied by valuing particular situated contexts and how utterances functioned in the children's internalization processes.

Discourse analysis is used to comprehend spoken, written, or other communication and languages in use between people. In this study, I used discourse analysis to examine children's communication through art, because it clarifies the context of their discourses and the dynamics of their actions. In the words of James Paul Gee (1999),

Discourse analysis is always a movement from context to language and from language to context. We gain information about a context in which a piece of language has been used and use this information to form hypotheses about what that piece of language means and is doing. (p. 14)

This research was conducted with 5-year-olds in a preschool classroom for 2 months in the U.S. Midwest. Various qualitative research methods were used, such as participant observation, field notes, pictures of the children's visual art, and audio and video recordings of the children's art activities. Video recording was exceptionally helpful in capturing students' interaction patterns because the tension and dynamics of the children's interactions with each other were easy to miss in the moment of artmaking. Video recordings were transcribed to capture the flow of children's conversations related to art making and their interactions surrounding particular events. After the data were examined repeatedly, while focusing on how young children used visual art, the children's communication was coded to trace their visual and verbal utterances.

An utterance was defined as an expression in words of ideas, thoughts, and feelings. The utterance implies a context of responses to dialogues and communication through various forms of language and other cultural tools. Art is also a form of visual discourse that has been formed with specific cultural standards and tastes. Children's art serves as a series of visual utterance that functions in the social context of the art-making process. In addition, children's visual utterances belong to a community; Bakhtin (1974/1986) regarded any utterances as inseparably linked to society.

In the first step of analysis, the children's discourses, actions, and contexts were noted. In the second step of analysis, visual images were interpreted. Special attention was paid to how the children's art served as a series of visual utterance that functioned in the social context of the artmaking process. Below is an excerpt from a transcript illustrating the use of discourse analysis:

Jean: Is this pretty? (holding up her picture to show it to a friend) [Jean's classmate did not pay attention to her.] Is this pretty? (to the teacher, holding the picture up higher and making her voice louder)[The teacher did not say anything for a second, so Jean waved the picture several times. There was no response, so she put it down on the table.]

Jean: Pam (teacher's name), I found something. Look at this. This will be my sprinkles. [She was going to use small, precut shapes to decorate her picture.]

Pam: Those are tiny sprinkles.

Jean: Excuse me. Look at this.

Pam: Wow, look at the tiny ones on yours.

Jean: Yeah, it's tiny. [She was busy decorating her picture with precut patterns and glue.] Excuse me, look at this. [Nobody paid attention to her.] Hey, these are stuck. [Looking at one of her classmates.]

[James stopped by to look at her picture on his way to look at the computer, but did not pay much attention to her. Jean returned to her work and started to decorate it again. She continued to glue patterns on the paper. She seemed to focus on it for a short while, and then she turned to me.]

Jean: Look at this.

Me (researcher): Yeah, that's pretty. [Jean was finally satisfied with my response.]

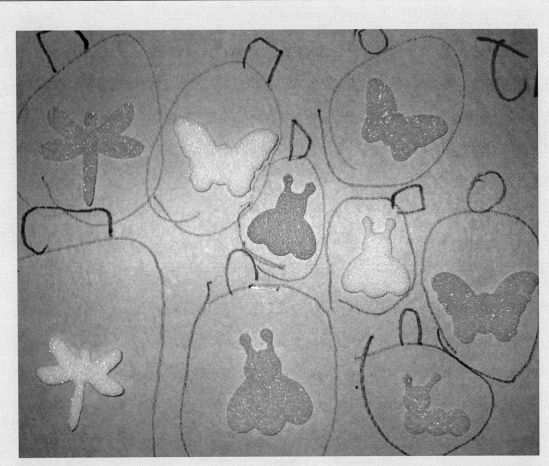

FIGURE 1. *Untitled* by Jean.

Pam: Tell me about your picture, Jean.

Jean: You can (Embedded incomprehensible utterance) name on it [in a very soft, quiet voice].

From this particular scene, we can see how Jean used visual art to gain recognition from others. She paid less attention to the content or the quality but instead kept checking other people's responses and what they thought of her art. From this example, we can infer how children use the arts for social exchange. Especially among children in this young age group, art is frequently used to gain recognition from others (Minam Kim, personal communication, October 20, 2006).

The artmaking process functions as a semiotic process in social practice. Bakhtin (1974/1986) views discourses as always located in sociohistorical venues that are constantly in communication with both prior and upcoming dialogues. From this point of view, forms of discourse, including children's dialogues, actions, and visual language, function as living tools, which are used to live inseparably together. This short transcript shows how a young child used her artmaking process to gain recognition from adults and peers. In interpreting Jean's visual image, it is interesting to see how she continued to check others' responses before making her own images on paper. After decorating her pink paper with other shapes, she drew a handbag shape

around each item. If we fail to consider how she selected those images through negotiation, by eliciting other people's responses, it is easy to misinterpret her intention. Jean valued the perspectives of others as she created her picture. This is a good demonstration of Bakhtin's theory because it highlights the mutuality of children's interaction and communication as they engage in reciprocating the utterances of others.

It is meaningful to look at how children's artmaking is integrated with other social factors, and how children's art functions as both a verbal and visual utterance to communicate with others. Discourse analysis makes unseen visual factors in children's artmaking more visible because attention is paid to the details of and relations among those images and children's actions during their artmaking process. ■

REFERENCES

Bakhtin, M. M. (1986). *Speech genres and other late essays* (2nd ed.) (C. Emerson & M. Colquitt, Eds.) (V. W. McGee, Trans.). Austin: University of Texas Press. (Original work published 1974)

Gee, J. P. (1999). *An introduction to discourse analysis: Theory and method* (2nd ed.). New York, NY: Routledge.

Holquist, M. (1990). *Dialogism: Bakhtin and his world.* London, England: Routledge.

Pearson, P. (2001). Towards a theory of children's drawing as social practice. *Studies in Art Education, 42*(4), 348-365.

CASE STUDY
RESEARCH

25 / Conducting Case Study Research

KARIN TOLLEFSON-HALL / ASSISTANT PROFESSOR AND ART EDUCATION
GRADUATE PROGRAM DIRECTOR, JAMES MADISON UNIVERSITY

ABSTRACT: *This chapter is a description of case study methodology. Case study methodology is used when a researcher is interested in studying a particular case or phenomenon in depth. The topics presented in this chapter include types of case studies, developing research questions for case studies, collecting and analyzing the data, criticisms of case study methodology, and writing up the final report. To illustrate the explanation of case study methodology, examples from case studies conducted in art classes at various school settings are presented.*

INTRODUCTION TO CASE STUDY

What can art education learn from art instruction at private schools? How is art present in a Waldorf curriculum? These are examples of two of the questions I have attempted to answer using case study research. Case study is used as the research methodology when a researcher wants to study a particular "case" in depth. The purpose of the case study is to present a detailed description of the case and the researcher's interpretation of its significance to the field of study. A case can be as small as one child, one family, or a group of students—or as large as one classroom or one school.

> A case study is a detailed study of a single social unit. The social unit is usually located in one physical place, the people making up the social unit being differentiated from others who are not part of it. In short, the unit has clear boundaries which make it easy to identify. (Payne & Payne, 2004, pp. 31-32)

For example, in researching art instruction in nontraditional school settings I have conducted case studies of a home-school family, a preschool, an elementary school, and the art class at three different private schools.

CONTEXT OF THE CASE

In order to present an accurate description of the case under investigation the researcher will most likely have to expand the study to include the history and overall context where the case is situated. At the three private schools I visited my case was the art class, but I also learned about the history of each school, its philosophical background, and the overall organization of the school. This was important as background to the study in order to describe the art classes as they exist within the context of the school and community. Every school environment and community is unique, and private schools can be structured much differently than public schools. Researching the school as a whole helped me to describe the art classes in relation to the environment and community in which they exist.

For example, when I visited a middle school photography class at a Transcendental Meditation school, the class was taking pictures in the school courtyard surrounded by edible landscaping and an organic greenhouse. Sustainability, healthy lifestyles, green technology, and organic agriculture are all part of the mission of the school and the university affiliated with the school. Knowing the philosophy and environment of the school gave me a frame of reference to put the art classes into context and make connections between art activities, meditation, school environment and teacher comments all related to well-being and sustainability.

TYPES OF CASE STUDIES

Robert Stake (2000) identifies three types of case study research: *intrinsic, instrumental,* and *collective.* The purpose of an intrinsic case study is to better understand a specific case. The researcher's reason for the study is to present the case in and of itself. In contrast, an instrumental case study is conducted when the researcher uses a case as an example of a larger topic or issue. For the instrumental case study, the researcher selects the case to use as an example to illuminate the issue or topic of interest. When a researcher conducts and presents several individual case studies simultaneously, it is called a collective case study. My research of Waldorf curriculum began as a single intrinsic case study of a home-school family. As I read about Waldorf and observed the family my curiosity led me to expand the study to include a Waldorf preschool, a conference at a Waldorf elementary school, and a public elementary school using a curriculum with many similarities to Waldorf. The Waldorf study became a collective case study because I needed to expand my original ideas to include other related sites for greater understanding of the context in which Waldorf curricula are presented.

Initiated as a collective case study, I conducted three separate case studies at three different schools in my study of art classes at private schools. The three case studies were presented together in the final writing. In the writing, I presented each school independently in separate chapters and then made connections between the schools in the concluding interpretations and implications of the study. The purpose of my study was not to produce a comparison of the cases, but to provide multiple examples of art instruction in private schools, giving the project a broader scope and greater credibility.[1] Providing multiple cases can allow greater possibilities for readers to make generalizations in response to the research.

RESEARCH QUESTIONS

Like all research, a case study centers on research questions. While there may be one general question encompassing the ideas of the study, the researcher often has a series of sub-questions to help guide the research. A research project can begin with identification of a case, or with the researcher's questions and interests. For example, I had an unexpected opportunity to be an evaluator of a home-school family using a Waldorf curriculum. From that opportunity my curiosity to learn about Waldorf and the inclusion of art in the curriculum led to my research questions and project. I identified the case first, and my research questions arose from the case. In contrast, my study of art classes in private schools began with my interest in discovering nontraditional teaching practices. After identifying my research questions I located three private schools that consented to be in the study.

For a case study, the research questions have to be broad enough to allow for investigation and, at the same time, narrow enough to make the project manageable. For example, I am interested in teaching practices at all grade levels. To conduct a research project of art classes at all grade levels would be a study too large to conduct by myself. The differences between instructional strategies for elementary and secondary education are too diverse to describe in one study. As a result, my study of private schools was limited to high school art classes and my study of Waldorf was limited to elementary-age students. The research questions that guided my study of art classes at private schools included three main questions and five sub-questions.

1. How does the mission and philosophy, or purposes, of the school influence the practices and experiences in the art classroom?
2. What are the practices for the art classroom at each school?
   a. What is the physical environment of the art classroom?
   b. What is the art curriculum?
   c. How does the art teacher teach?
   d. What is the art teacher's philosophy of art education?
   e. What is the art budget or what resources are available to the teacher?
3. In what ways are the purposes and practices of the school and art classroom qualitatively different [from those of] a public school? (Tollefson-Hall, 2009)

Robert Yin (2009) advises using three stages to help focus case study research questions.

1. Use the literature to narrow your interest to one or two key topics.
2. Closely examine a few studies on your topic and identify the research questions used in those studies as well as any concluding questions or suggestions for further research. These questions may lead you to articulating some questions of your own.
3. Review more studies on your topic and determine if they can support your potential questions or suggest ways of sharpening them (p. 27-28).

In all of my research, discussion of research questions and ideas with colleagues and advisors helped me to define and refine my interests into formal research questions.

DATA COLLECTION

The most common sources of data collected for a case study are observations, interviews, and documents. Because a case study researcher's primary goal is to understand the case in depth, the researcher spends the majority of her/his time in the research setting with the study participants. Detailed fieldnotes are essential, along with interviews from key participants. Fieldnotes are the written observations and evidence of what the researcher is witnessing in the field. Fieldnotes include anything that the researcher notes while in the research setting as well as what the notes the researcher writes up after an observation. Case study researchers may also choose to include surveys or focus groups conducted with the participants. Document review includes the study of any printed materials related to the case, such as historical documents, texts, and demographic information. In my experiences studying schools, I utilized books on the history and philosophy of particular schools, student handbooks, and school websites to learn about school policies and organization.

The preferences of the researcher and the research setting determine choices in how to collect the data. When deciding how to collect the data and what role that the researcher takes, it is important for the researcher to act in a manner that will make the participants comfortable with the researcher's presence. No matter what measures the researcher takes, the presence of an outsider in the classroom or setting will be a disruption. It was most comfortable for me and the participants when I began as an observer in the classroom and slowly moved into a role of participant-observer functioning as a teacher's assistant. Being a teacher, it is hard for me to sit in a classroom of students and not want to connect with them and help the teacher. Because I am familiar with the subject matter it is easy to be incorporated into the classroom. I have found that most teachers appreciate the extra help and the students are more comfortable relating to someone who is taking interest in their artwork and class instead of just staring at them from the corner of the room.

In any research setting, the researcher will encounter richer interviews and interactions if they have gained the trust of the participants. When I am strictly observing in a classroom I sit out of the way of the class activities and type fieldnotes directly on my computer. When I am active in the classroom, it is distracting to use a computer so I carry a small note pad for writing quick notes that will serve as reminders of what occurred in the classroom when I write up the fieldnotes immediately after the observation. Some schools I have visited limit the presence of technology in the classroom and therefore, it is less distracting to participants if I only use a notebook. After visiting the research setting and being introduced to the participants, the researcher will have a good sense of what materials should be used to collect data most comfortably. For example, on the first visit to the research setting, the researcher should take note of the size and layout of the classroom, as well as the use or presence of technology. If the classroom is small or if the researcher is going to be moving around within the room it may be difficult to have a computer out without being intrusive in the space. Be attentive to how students and the teacher are reacting to you if you are sitting and typing on the first visit. As the researcher ask yourself the following questions: Are the students hesitant to approach you? Does the teacher seem nervous? How much time is the class distracted by your presence and losing instructional time? Do you as the researcher feel uncomfortable taking notes on paper or on a computer in the classroom? Be aware of the fact that an open laptop can serve as a barrier between the researcher and interaction with the participants.

To obtain accurate documentation of interviews it is best to tape record all interviews and transcribe them exactly. While this is best for the data, the researcher has to remember that it is the participant's decision if they want to be recorded or not. Ethically, a researcher must honor the request of a participant to not be recorded or photographed and to end participation in the study at any time without consequences. For both transcribing interviews and writing up fieldnotes, the notes will be more accurate and include greater detail if they are written as soon as possible after the observation. One benefit I discovered of having to travel 30 minutes or more to a research setting was that the drive home became a time when a lot of ideas, questions, and reflections would come to me. I often left my tape recorder out in the car to record important ideas to add to my fieldnotes when I had access to a computer.

Above all, it is important to capture as many details as possible in the fieldnotes. Details of the physical environment, activities, and behaviors of the participants, and the emotions and responses of the researcher should be noted at each observation. Silverman (2005) recommends including visual data (videos, photographs, visual culture of the setting) in the fieldnotes. Researchers have to be careful with the photographic data they collect. Participants must give consent to be photographed or in any way represented in a recognizable image. At the same time, a researcher cannot know at the beginning of a study which details, no matter how small, will be significant to the final interpretations.

DATA ANALYSIS

Analysis of case study data is continuous and emergent. As the researcher writes fieldnotes and transcribes interviews, the process of analysis is already beginning. While still active in the research setting, the researcher is reviewing his/her notes, reflecting on what is occurring in the setting in relation to the research questions, and most likely finding new questions emerging through the observations. The researcher should be open to modifying the research study as needed during the course of the project. Any changes made to the proposed study, such as the addition of research participants or settings, must be approved by IRB.

There is not a specified amount of time that researchers must spend in the field to conduct a case study. The researcher has to decide how much time will be sufficient to be familiar with the setting and participants, to be able to present an accurate account of the situation, and to answer the research questions. Case studies conducted over very short periods of time, such as a few hours or weeks, may not be seen as valid studies and the researcher's conclusions may be suspect. In addition to answering the research questions, researchers also demonstrate in the final report that they have evidence of spending a sufficient amount of time in the research setting to present an accurate description and interpretation. In my study of private schools, I visited the same art class at each school, every week for one semester. I also spent time outside of the art class interviewing the art teachers and school administrators on several occasions. At the end of the study I had spent 35-40 hours in each school.

At the beginning of a case study I find myself typing pages of fieldnotes, unsure of what, if any, of the information will be pertinent to the final writing. After spending time in the setting and reviewing fieldnotes, recurrent themes in the data often become apparent. For example, in the study of private schools, after my last observation each week I would review my previous notes from each school. Reflecting on what had caught my attention each week, I began to notice patterns or similarities among the schools. Some of the patterns related to my research questions and interview topics such as the art teacher's teaching philosophy, the art curriculum, and the students' artwork. Other topics unexpectedly appeared at each school such as dress code and all three teachers being practicing artists.

As themes or topics for grouping ideas appear it is helpful to begin coding fieldnotes and generating categories of information. Sometimes the categories seem to jump out of the page. But the topics maybe more subtle within the notes and the researcher can begin by using the research questions to help create some broad categories to divide the data. Using the research questions from the study of private schools, I categorized my data in the following groups: curriculum, teaching philosophy, physical environment, teaching style, school history, budget and resources, and school philosophy. Looking at my notes from each school, I listed important passages of data related to each category. Once the data were grouped within each school it was easy to compare the data on the school philosophy among all three schools, for example. Sorting the data into categories also makes it easy for the researcher to see which areas of the study have a lot of supporting examples and data and which areas are lacking or may need further study before writing.

Notes can be color-coded with highlighters, written on notecards, or arranged into separate files by category. The physical data might be on paper that can be sorted and arranged by hand, or in files on the computer if the researcher prefers manipulating multiple digital files. Sorting data into themes or categories will allow the researcher to easily review and include all of the relevant data for each category in the final writing of the study.

WRITING UP THE STUDY

In the process of writing the final study the accuracy of the researcher's information and interpretations of the setting are important. The most common method of checking the accuracy of research is through triangulation. Triangulation can be performed many ways, and in general means that the data have been checked against multiple sources. Reviewing multiple texts, documents and artifacts to check information is one method of triangulation. For observations and transcriptions the researcher can send the participants a copy of the notes or drafts of writing for their review, often called a member check. The participant may accept or reject the researcher's interpretations, and it is up to the researcher to determine what action, if any, will be taken to accommodate the participant's views. For example, a participant may feel that the researcher has misinterpreted a comment in an interview or an activity observed in the classroom and ask the researcher to remove or change the data. The researcher now has to decide how to proceed. The researcher can thank the participant for their opinion and leave the data unchanged since it is the researcher's interpretation of the situation. The researcher could agree with the participant's explanation of the situation and alter the data, or note in the data the difference of opinion and let the reader of the research decide which interpretation is accurate.

The depth of detail captured in the fieldnotes and lengthy interview transcriptions of a case study make the amount of information available for the final writing of the study daunting. When I begin writing up a study, after spending many hours getting to know teachers and students, I find all of the details of the case interesting and important to me, and the details now connect to the participants and setting. As a researcher it is tempting to want to convey every detail of the experience. In the interest of the reader, it is important for the researcher to choose a focus for the writing and determine what details are both interesting and necessary. Going back to the coded notes is a good way to

organize the final writing. By looking at all of the notes for a category, I not only ensure that I will not leave out an interesting or important detail, but I also can see which examples are redundant, which are the best illustrative examples of the point I want to make, and which will be the most interesting for the reader.

The final writing often requires several drafts. When I feel the urge to tell the "whole" story of a school and include every last detail, sometimes I begin by writing it all down and then go back and edit out the examples and observations that are not necessary to the final writing. Do not be afraid to write entire chapters that may not make it to the final draft of the writing. Finding an advisor, colleague, or writing center that can read each chapter as it is completed is helpful to keep the writing focused and give suggestions on how to proceed. The writing of qualitative research can be very creative and take many forms, be sure to find out if there are guidelines or styles set by the department, college, or publisher before starting to write. Knowing the expectations for the form of the final writing will help organize the chapters and determine what to include in each chapter.

An interesting lead in to catch readers' attention and draw them into the research is key to successful writing. Case study research, based on detailed observations and experiences within a specific setting, has data filled with interesting moments from the field. The story of the case may begin with an illustrative anecdote from the setting or by explaining how the researcher became interested in the subject of inquiry.

CRITICISM OF CASE STUDY

One criticism of case study is the presence of researcher bias. The motives of the researcher in selecting the case and the accuracy of the observations and interpretations can come into question. One way of decreasing the presence of researcher bias is for the researcher to honestly and straightforwardly state in the writing, his/her background, beliefs, known biases, and assumptions. A helpful exercise that I performed as a beginning researcher was to write out my assumptions, biases, and stereotypes about my research topic before I began the actual study. Confronting my own presuppositions made me aware of areas that I may be tempted to portray through my bias rather than with true objectivity, and made me more critical of my own interpretations of the research setting. Yin (2009) suggests a test for researcher bias is to determine "the degree to which you are open to contrary findings" (p. 72). If you are willing to accept findings that are contrary to your assumptions than you are less likely to be biased. Yin continues with advice on how to test for bias: "To test your own tolerance for contrary findings, report your preliminary findings… to two or three critical colleagues… if the quest for contrary findings can produce documentable rebuttals, the likelihood of bias will have been reduced" (p. 72).

Stake (1995) recommends including sufficient detail to make a study believable and to demonstrate that the researcher is an objective observer.

> To describe the case, we try to present a substantial body of uncontestable description. We want to tell quite a bit about the case that almost anyone, who had our opportunity to observe it, would have noticed and recorded, much as we did...
>
> We even look for information to report that the reader is likely to know in order to assure the reader that we can see straight and think straight—or deliberately to indicate what sort of a slant on things can be expected from us. (pp. 110-111)

These two suggestions will contribute to building the reliability of the research.

A second criticism to studying one case in depth is that the study is not generalizable. As with many forms of qualitative research the intention of case study is not to present a case as representative of other populations. "Researchers do not usually claim that their findings can automatically be generalized. They have studied an *example* in its own right, and for its unique importance, not a *sample* of one" (Payne & Payne, 2004, p. 32). That is not to say, however, that the researcher cannot use a case study to support existing theories or research, to generate theories based on the case studied, or provide recommendations for practice in more general settings. Readers tend to view collective case studies as more valid in terms of generalizability because they are presenting more than a single case as evidence of the researcher's claims (Yin, 2009). Stake (1995) describes generalizations from case studies as "naturalistic generalizations" (p. 85). Naturalistic generalizations are generalizations the researcher and reader make based on the case presented by connecting with previous experiences and knowledge of related cases. In my studies of art instruction I did not present teaching practices as mandates of how every art teacher should teach, but as suggestions of teaching methods that could be adapted by teachers in public schools who found it relevant to their own classrooms and teaching philosophies.

> In private and personal ways, ideas are structured, highlighted, subordinated, connected, embedded *in* contexts, embedded *with* illustration, laced with favor and doubt. However moved to share ideas, however clever and elaborated their writings, case researchers, like others, pass along to readers some of their personal meanings of events and relationship—and fail to pass along others. They know that the reader, too, will add and subtract, invent and shape—reconstructing the knowledge in ways that leave it differently connected and more likely to be personally useful. (Stake, 2000, pp. 442-443)

Similar to my goal in studying art classes at private schools, Stake describes how researchers transfer knowledge to the reader. The difficult aspect of transfer is that the researcher cannot know all of the past experiences and knowledge of the reader. Researching for specific knowledge transfer would be impossible. Instead, the researcher writes the report and conducts the study in the hope that the descriptions and interpretations of the case will be valuable as each individual reader makes personal connections to the case that build on previous knowledge and experience, and ultimately gain new understandings.

SUMMARY

A researcher uses case study methodology when the researcher wants to study a specific case in depth. The research is highly descriptive and focuses more on the transfer of knowledge by connecting to the readers' previous experiences rather than creating generalizations. Researchers conduct case study methodology typically through observation, participation in the setting, and interviews. The writing of a case study includes rich descriptions from the field set alongside the researcher's interpretations and connections to literature, theory and philosophy within the field of study.

REFERENCES

Grenier, R. S. (2008). Practicing what we preach. *Journal of Interpretation Research, 13*(1), 7-25.

Kiebert-Gruen, C. (2010). *Community arts programs: Cohesion and difference case studies: Henry Street Settlement and El Museo del Barrio* (Doctoral dissertation). Retrieved from ProQuest. (UMI Number: 3367983)

Kirschenbaum, R. J., & Reis, S. M. (1997). Conflicts in creativity: Talented female artists. *Creativity Research Journal, 10*(2-3), 251-263.

Payne, G., & Payne, J. (2004). *Key concepts in social research.* London, England: Sage.

Silverman, D. (2005). *Doing qualitative research.* London, England: Sage.

Stake, R. (1995). *The art of case study research.* Thousand Oaks, CA: Sage.

Stake, R. (2000). Case studies. In N. Denzin & Y. Lincoln (Eds.), *Handbook of qualitative research* (2nd ed.) (pp. 435-454). Thousand Oaks, CA: Sage.

Tollefson-Hall, K. (2009). *Alternativeness in art education: Case studies of art instruction at three private schools* (Unpublished doctoral dissertation). University of Iowa, Iowa City.

Yin, R. (2009). *Case study research* (4th ed.). Thousand Oaks, CA: Sage.

Zimmerman, E. (1992). A comparative study of two painting teachers of talented adolescents. *Studies in Art Education, 33*(3), 174-185.

ENDNOTE

1   For examples of comparative case studies used in art education research, see Grenier (2008), Kiebert-Gruen (2010), Kirschenbaum and Reis (1997), and Zimmerman (1992).

KARIN TOLLEFSON-HALL is Assistant Professor and Art Education Graduate Program Director at James Madison University. A graduate of the doctoral program at the University of Iowa, her teaching and research interests include art instruction in alternative school settings, school reform, and improving teaching practice.

26 / Two Case Studies of Gendered Spaces: Translations of Practice

LINDA HOEPTNER POLING / ASSISTANT PROFESSOR IN ART EDUCATION, KENT STATE UNIVERSITY

ABSTRACT: *As a case study methodology exemplar, the aim of this chapter is to illuminate understanding of what it means to be a feminist art teacher committed to practicing feminist pedagogy. In order to make sense of the many layers embedded in what it means to be a feminist art teacher cognizant of gender issues, I studied two self-proclaimed feminist art teachers. Observations, field notes, and audiotaped interviews were the primary forms of data collection. Within each teacher's practice, I found that safe spaces were created and controversy was dealt with in meaningful ways. Pluralist and separatist teaching approaches were consciously put into practice and both teachers critically reflected on their teaching. I also found evidence of each teacher assuming the role of transformative intellectual and likewise practicing the critical theory notion of radical love.*

There is no lack of discussion about gender and feminism in the field, recently seen in the work of Garber, Sandell, Stankiewicz, and Risner (2007), and Rosenberg and Thurber (2007); but is understanding of feminist practices *transparent* in the classroom? I assert feminist practices remain instead *translucent*, often muddled, overcast with questioning doubt, with little that is predictable or concrete to hold our conceptual gaze. Those concerned with gender issues and feminist pedagogy in art education often talk about what feminist pedagogy *should* be; but rarely do we see *how* it takes form in our practice. Illuminating this translucent understanding of what form feminist pedagogy takes in order to make feminist pedagogy more transparent was the aim of my two case studies of self-proclaimed feminist art teachers. Both teachers are National Art Education Association Women's Caucus Carrie Nordlund Award recipients, an award that recognizes the practice of feminist pedagogy in preK-12 art classrooms.

GENDERED SPACES: FEMINISM/FEMINIST PEDAGOGY

Before describing the findings, a brief examination of feminism and feminist pedagogy is necessary to establish the context in which this research is situated. Feminism, according to Smith-Shank (2000) "involves the beliefs that gender inequities exist within cultures and that reducing these inequities is possible" (p. 68). Having roots in feminism, feminist pedagogy is based on the central tenet that all human experiences are tempered by gender and are therefore not immune to social dictates of cultural expectations. The goals of feminist pedagogy in seeking gender equity include empowerment of students, creating community or communal classroom spaces, and shared leadership. More specifically, Kilmer (2007) asserts that "[f]eminist pedagogy aims for equality in the classroom

and supports cooperative learning, focusing on community in the classroom and continually analyzing ways in which we can best engage students in critical thinking about the topics of inequality, privilege, and power" (p. 57). According to feminist scholars in art education (Garber et al., 2007; Rosenberg & Thurber, 2007) teachers should treat students as individuals, necessarily upholding the feminist tenet of creating equitable (as opposed to equal) conditions for male and female students. This chapter shares two case studies of women art educators who exemplify feminist pedagogy and equitable practice in action.

RESEARCH FRAMEWORK

I conducted the case studies over the course of 3½ months each, in 2007-2008. Through each, I attempted to answer the research question: *How do art teachers conceptualize and negotiate issues of gender related to their practice?* Understanding how gender impacts art teaching and learning can improve how we make sense of our experiences in striving to be more equitable art educators. An equitable art educator acknowledges that inequities exist (whether inequities take form in our curriculum, our interactions with students, or what is said and done in our classrooms) and consciously works to achieve equitable classroom climates. Equitable educators establish a sense of community and collaboration. Empowerment of both boys and girls to reach their full potential, as learners and stakeholders in society are goals toward which equitable educators work. Teachers promote gender awareness and critical thinking within their curricula, with a focus on positions of privilege and power in connection to gender. According to Garber et al. (2007), art teachers need to "increase their knowledge of feminist issues and content in the arts, and develop teaching strategies to address sex equity issues in their classrooms" (p. 359). Ways in which art teachers Christine Gorbach and Caryl Church (names used with permission) created feminist art classrooms are the foci of this chapter.

Stake (1995) claims that researchers choose case study methodology because they want to gain a better understanding of a particular case. Case study methodology emphasizes personal interpretation and thick description (Geertz, 1973) in order to create a holistic experiential understanding for the reader. Researchers attend to what is happening in key episodes (primarily through observations) or testimonies (primarily through interviews). The subjective view as presented in data analysis and interpretation is not, of course, the only view. Readers of case study research are given the opportunity to make their own interpretations alongside the researcher's assertions.

Observations and audiotaped interviews were the primary forms of my data collection. Both sites are public school districts in Northeast Ohio. I observed Christine first in her suburban high school art room from September-December 2007; and later I observed Caryl in her rural elementary art room January-May 2008. I collected data for 2, sometimes 3, days a week at the suburban secondary site and for 1 or 2 days a week at the rural elementary site. Each observation lasted for 3 to 4 hours. Students in classes at both schools were co-ed and had mixed abilities. The majority of students were Caucasian and of lower- to middle-class socio-economic status. Working from my field notes and teacher interviews, I described and analyzed the gender dynamics, focusing particularly on teacher-student conversations, whole class discussions and critiques of both artists' and students' works. Member checking and peer debriefing (Guba & Lincoln, 1983) were important indicators of rigor in my study. Through member checking, both Christine and Caryl verified the accuracy of the interview transcripts and clarified unresolved questions I had following observations. This process of member checking was necessary to ensure my collection and subsequent interpretations of data were error-free. I also utilized peer debriefing throughout the studies. Peer debriefing involves sharing and discussing a researcher's data with trusted individuals familiar with the content and type of research being conducted. In my research, colleagues familiar with both feminist pedagogy and case study research provided necessary "checks" and insights I might otherwise not have considered. From the analysis, themes emerged.

FINDINGS AND DISCUSSION
SAFE SPACES: COURAGE IN THE CONTROVERSIAL

Both Christine and Caryl took, in their minds, *necessary* risks in cultivating a safe classroom climate that confronted—not ignored—the controversial, including incidents related to gender. Concerning controversial art, Christine recalled being asked by a student, "are you sure that you are

supposed to be showing us this kind of art?" For example, Christine showed contemporary versions of Leonardo da Vinci's *Last Supper* (1495-1498) with Jesus Christ and the apostles replaced by the heads of women artists (*Some Living American Women Artists/Last Supper* [1972], by Mary Beth Edelson) and superheroes (Don Wilkinson's *The Last Superhero Supper* [2006]. See Internetlurker [2008, December 15]). In these pieces, Jesus is replaced by Georgia O'Keeffe and Superman; Mary Magdalene by Wonder Woman. Within the context of showing and discussing the gender issues both overt and latent within the images, Christine expressed her realization that she had "fallen into a safe zone": "I felt very comfortable taking important risks within the classroom. I easily made decisions that were in the students' best interest even if it meant taking a bit of flack from fellow teachers, administrators and the community" (personal communication, 2007).

Another example illustrating how Christine creates a safe space within the controversial was during a Drawing/Painting II class critique of in-process works in which students were challenged to re-conceptualize established "masterpieces" (as defined by traditional canons common in Western art history) in the context of current societal issues (chosen by the students). Without hesitation, Christine complimented a student's controversial work and the explanation of it. The piece illustrated the tension of the Iraqi-US war and the student's support for U.S. troops. He expressed that we all need to show support for the troops. Christine responded enthusiastically, "You have really thought this out!" Other students expressed verbally that they liked the work and idea of supporting the U.S. troops, while others argued against the war. Christine allowed the discussion to take place unhindered. Within the same critique, another student presented his work representing an ornate and decorative "border" between the US and Mexico, commenting on the issue of immigration that was prominent in the media at the time. Christine complimented the student for conceptualizing the issue in a unique manner, and saying the work reminded her of Byzantine mosaic art. It was clear to me that the students were comfortable in this type of open sharing, always remaining respectful of one another's opinion. Christine established a safe atmosphere in which inquiry about controversial contemporary issues takes place.

In a sixth-grade lesson, Caryl took a courageous risk in showing and teaching Judy Chicago's controversial feminist piece *The Dinner Party* (1974-1979). She distributed paper plates. On each side was the name of a female artist; on the other, the name of a male artist. She asked the students first, "Who knows the female artist named on your plate?" Two out of 22 students recognized the female artists. Caryl then asked the students to flip their plate over, and said "Raise your hand if you know this male artist." Eleven students now knew the artists. This activity initiated a lively discussion. Caryl posed the question, "Why is it that

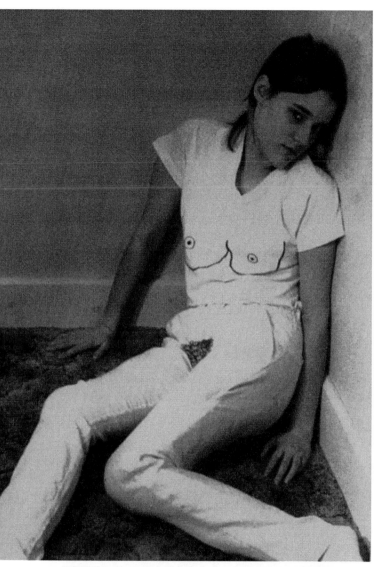

FIGURE 1. Manipulated photo courtesy of Christine Gorbach, by Brittany Del'Aglio, 2006, (shown with the student's permission). Christine provided this image from her former student to illustrate the often controversial art that emerges in her classes.

we know more male artists than female artists?" Students' answers varied, from "Men did more things in history than women;" "We study men more;' "Women didn't have the same rights that men did, so they couldn't do the same things." Caryl followed this discussion with a viewing of *The Dinner Party*, explaining that Chicago's goal was to symbolize and highlight women who have done important things, but have been minimized in, erased from, or omitted altogether from history. They were not given their due credit. After viewing the plates and place settings, students then looked at the *Heritage Floor* of *The Dinner Party*. Caryl followed this up with a studio challenge: to explore the "branches" and "roots" of those who have inspired the students in their lives, resulting in drawings titled "Plant the Seed" to symbolize the inspirational person's impact on students' personal

growth and development. Caryl admitted to not addressing the obvious reference to female genitalia in Chicago's work, and instead focused on the message communicated in the piece. This lesson was a very personal, powerful, and visibly feminist way of connecting art curriculum to gender issues. She, like Christine, does not shy away from showing controversial works or discussing controversial subjects (in this case, the gender imbalance of representation of male and female achievement). Caryl created a safe space in which students were allowed to respectfully express their opinions and understandings of controversial issues.

PLURALIST AND SEPARATIST PRACTICE

In both classroom spaces, I observed the fostering of gender equity through *pluralist* and *separatist* practices with tacit and concrete attention paid to "the contributions of both traditional and feminist educational thought and art content" (Rosenberg & Thurber, 2007, p. 20). Pluralist teachers recognize *diverse* viewpoints and strive toward transformation through "responsive pragmatic action monitored by critique" (Collins & Sandell, 1992, p. 103). The separatist approach is characterized by highlighting gender issues, particularly of women, *separately* and in isolation from existing mainstream (male dominated) art content (Rosenberg & Thurber, 2007).[1] I observed the separatist approach in action particularly in the feminist art criticism both Christine and Caryl conducted as a means to teach feminist principles. Christine's students, for example, were very familiar with the politically charged work of The Guerrilla Girls whose work aims to expose the gender inequity in women artists' visibility in mainstream art venues. Both Christine and Caryl consciously worked toward correcting the gendered notion that women serve as objects—instead of producers—of art and culture through critiques of art and student art. As such, Christine and Caryl confidently shared with students, societal obstacles, constructs, and biases associated with gender identity, particularly in the art world, and ways to overcome them. During my observations of them conducting critiques and introducing lessons, I witnessed a distinct disposition in which Christine and Caryl expressed no hesitancy or tentativeness when discussing issues of gender. For example, Caryl shared a conversation she had with a male student: "I had a student say to me that his mom in his house was his maid; that's what his mom is for. I responded, 'Your mother is more than that, and I don't even know your mother.' I said something like 'Mothers do *this*, and mothers do *that*,' or you know, and I was pretty disgusted with him, and I let him know that; my opinion." Caryl also stated, "I try to project a strong woman, an intelligent woman, an artistic creative woman" (personal communication, 2008). Her way of being and conceptualizing her gender tacitly and concretely communicated to her students that both women and men matter in the world and art world.

Christine told a story of a gendered incident that informed her practice of feminist pedagogy and pluralist practice. She recalls:

> I had a great group of young men, who couldn't wait to take my class. The class was great, except one young lady came in everyday; she was very attractive, dressed very provocative[ly], and we were having a critique one day, and I said "Becky, (named changed) why don't you sit down?" And she said, "I can't sit down because I just went to the suntan salon and I burnt my butt!" The young men in my class, who I know are very good students, dropped their jaws and just stared at her. And I said, "Gentlemen, can— gentlemen? Gentlemen? Hello?" And they look at me and said, "Ms. Gorbach, how can you expect us to focus on our photography after that?" (personal communication, 2007)

Christine then recalled the conversation she had with "Becky" individually, away from the group. She asked the student if she was aware of the charged atmosphere she created as a result of what she said, and the student replied, "I *do* that Ms. Gorbach, because it gives me *power*." Christine told me, "I couldn't have asked her to say anything better! So then we talked about that, and how it wasn't fair for the rest of the class" (personal communication, 2007). She followed up the story with the following statement, indicating her commitment to fostering gender equity:

> All who enter my art room enter with equal importance. For years, I have been creating lessons and developing a culture where each individual student is required to use their own voice when creating art. There are many teaching styles that do not allow women or men to show their voice. Students enter my classroom with all different backgrounds, experiences and skill levels. It is my job as an art teacher to provide an environment in which each student, no matter their gender, can build on their strengths while improving their weak areas. (personal communication, 2007)

One key area identified in both Christine and Caryl's teaching that characterizes their practice as both pluralist and separatist is how both teachers handle disagreement. During critiques of artwork in particular, I observed both teachers capitalizing on and seizing moments of discord as teachable moments, embracing the atmosphere charged by disagreement. They both appeared confident in entertaining conflicting opinions. An example to illustrate this was seen in Christine's classroom. A male student shared his social commentary artwork (contemporary underwear-clad models drawn in a pose similar to the iconic "Three Graces" pose) on the objectification of women as seen in the advertisements of Victoria's Secret models. He felt that women (in particular, as opposed to men) were too critical in their opinions that the models are objectified for the pleasure of men. The male student questioned (rhetorically) why some of the female students believed that models are more than sexual objects to be enjoyed. The male student reported that he enjoyed beautiful women, and their beauty should be celebrated. Christine played a secondary role, allowing the discussion to unfold and take form according to the pace of the students' contributions. She responded respectfully, asking the rest of the class to verbalize what they thought of the issues raised. Few did. I asked why she did not probe the students to answer more fully. She responded, "Because that is where they are developmentally. I give them the space to work it out" (personal communication, 2007).

According to Brookfield (1995), democratic discourse associated with such pluralist (and in this latter case, separatist) approaches to teaching is characterized as the ability to talk, listen, and respond respectfully to those who hold differing views. This ability certainly characterizes Caryl's and Christine's teaching, and feminist pedagogy.

CRITICALLY REFLECTIVE PRACTICE AS PART OF FEMINIST PEDAGOGY

Reflection is not necessarily of a critical nature (Brookfield, 1995). As Brookfield states, "[o]ne of the hardest things teachers have to learn is that the sincerity of their intentions does not guarantee the purity of their practice" (p. 1). When we critically reflect, we confront taken-for-granted beliefs and assumptions and consciously engage with ideas and our resulting actions through reflection (Brookfield, 1995). In my study, it was clear that both Christine and Caryl take a critically reflective stance toward how they teach within the framework of feminist pedagogy. They possess a personally reflective "habit," which, I believe, provided a buffer against the risk of making potentially poor or controversial decisions that could lead to community, parental, or administrative objections to course content.

Christine exemplified critically reflective practice during a critique of student work with a thematic focus on students' personal beliefs about a timely societal issue of their choice. During this critique, she expressed to students her (negative) opinion of Rudolph Giuliani during the 2008 national Republican primary race. She felt comfortable doing this, solid in her commitment to creating a feminist and democratic space in which all voices are valued, including her own. Some students expressed agreement with Giuliani's opinions on the responsibility of artists (recall that Giuliani threatened to cut funding of the Brooklyn Museum of Art due to a controversial exhibit he found offensive [See BBC News, 1993, September 23]) and other students agreed with Christine that artists should have freedom of expression free of censorship. She respectfully allowed and listened to all students' opinions. She critically reflected on the non-neutrality of her opinion and students' possible reactions and defended her actions as good role modeling. Sharing her opinion was indeed controversial. However, when I asked Christine how she defends the sharing of her biased opinion in light of respect for diversity of opinion, she told me that she thought long and hard about what diversity means to her. She asserts that all voices need a platform, and there should be room on the platform for her voice as well. In an interview she said, "You just have to find a way to make sure that their [students'] voices don't exclude everybody else. I often have to gently quiet some students and then remind the class of others' opinion" (personal communication, 2007). I responded,

> I noticed that there were key moments where you would interject your personal opinion about things. And I looked around the room for reactions, and it was clear that it was accepted as, you know, not necessarily the *opinion* was accepted, but it was accepted that everyone could express, including the teacher." (Christine): Including the teacher; oh, yeah. I'm a huge model for the students. (personal communication, 2007)

Successful feminist pedagogy acknowledges and affirms diversity such as that highlighted in the previous example; it also seems that critically reflective practice goes hand-in-hand with successful feminist pedagogy.

What makes Christine's and Caryl's reflection particularly critical is two-fold: reflection as illumination of power, and reflection as an aid in recognizing hegemonic assumptions (Brookfield, 1995). Christine shared power with her students in the previous example, and visibly confronted Giuliani's assumed and perceived position of power in influencing others' opinions. She respectfully presented information, allowing students to formulate their own conclusions while also sharing her own, but not before critically reflecting beforehand on the impact on her students of her words and actions.

During an interview, Caryl recalls, for example,

> It [gender] has always been a theme in my life, like a vein, you know, there's always been like a kind of justice or equality theme in my life, and part of that's gender and all the other things that go along with it… I had a year of teaching between undergrad and grad school to kind of reflect back on. And I started thinking about my practice that first year. And I knew I wasn't happy with my practice that first year. So I mean, I thought it was a successful first year, but I knew that I could do better. But as far as thinking about the roles I was assigning students, especially like clean up, I was being biased. Even though I had all this awareness, you know? And you know, trying to kind of dictate my idea more than giving them a flow which isn't so much gender-related, but it is more I think feminist ideals that you're giving choices, that you're not just saying "do something"… so I think that was kind of eye-opening for my teaching. (personal communication, 2008)

The character of Christine's and Caryl's critical reflection illustrates the recommendation of Garber et al. (2007) for conceptualizing gender equity. Garber et al. recommend that we define goals of feminist teaching practice as something fluid, flexible, and inclusive. Over the course of my study, Christine's and Caryl's reflections were at times shared verbally in broad and sweeping terms; other times, their reflections were more specific and contextually bound, yet connected to a broader social context. One such example shows how Caryl's critical reflection is fueled by her students' individual stories as well as by larger societal conditions. She shared with me during an interview that reading students' dreams as expressed in their written texts interwoven in their visual images through Aborigine Dreamtime-inspired journey drawings moved her. She internalized and critically reflected upon the feelings of powerlessness the students felt in their lives. Her critical reflection on this resulted in a renewed impetus to give students empowered voice, a key feminist principle (Garber et al., 2007).

ART TEACHERS AS TRANSFORMATIVE INTELLECTUALS

Giroux (1988) recommends reconceptualizing the work of teachers as something transformative. Through feminist pedagogy, Christine and Caryl advance and affirm their commitment to issues of equity in the art room. This transformative intellectualism enhances in turn students' critical powers. Both of the teachers in my study treat their students as individual critical agents with voices, ideas, and visions capable of impacting their own lives and the lives of others. In her 2009 Carrie Nordlund Award acceptance speech, Caryl addressed transformation achieved with students: "Our knowledge combined with our students' knowledge is transformative knowledge. If it's shared, connected, linked with others, we are all better for it."

A visible example of transformative intellectualism in action was Caryl's "The Power of an Image: Chief Wahoo" bulletin board. Chief Wahoo is the controversial Cleveland Indians baseball team logo and mascot, well loved by many and hated by others who deem it racist in nature. She encouraged students to post their opinions on the board for all to read. This open invitation to democratically express an opinion is potentially transformative, reinforcing in students that their voice matters among countless other voices. Similarly, imagine the focus of Caryl's lesson for fourth-graders on Maya Lin's Vietnam Memorial; her use of words like "sexism" and "racism" are not typically associated with our knowledge of the memorial, instead focusing on the emotional impact of lives lost in the war. What Caryl did was use the memorial as a transformative vehicle to point out the challenges Lin faced as an Asian-American woman designing a memorial for American soldiers who died in the Vietnam War. Students listened intently and were able to extend how they experienced the memorial as evidenced by student contributions during the critique of Lin's work. Students said, "I had no idea," "I was at the Memorial, and I never knew she got in trouble," "I can't believe people reacted like that—it's wrong!" and "People need to know these things."

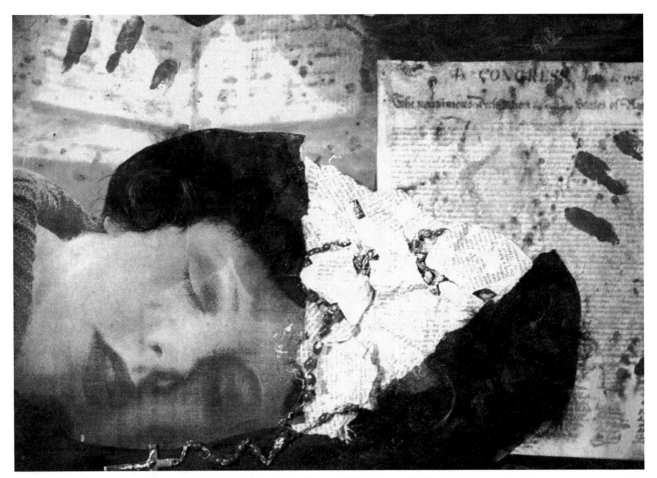

FIGURE 2. Photomontage courtesy of Christine Gorbach, by Amy Young, 2006 (shown with the student's permission).

POSITIONING THROUGH RADICAL LOVE

Also transformative in nature, Christine and Caryl practice the critical pedagogy notion of "radical love," whereby,

> Nothing is impossible when we work in solidarity with love, respect, and justice as our guiding lights… Love is the basis of an education that seeks justice, equality, and genius… Critical pedagogy uses it to increase our capacity to love, to bring power of love to our everyday lives and social institutions, and to rethink reason in a humane and interconnected manner. (Kincheloe, 2004, p. 3)

For example, both Caryl and Christine worked in tacit ways to confront the zeitgeist of the current wars in which the United States is involved, terrorism, and ultra- (American) patriotism. They allowed and encouraged the expression of opinions about the war within student artwork. Both Caryl and Christine teach the visual tools, language, and thinking skills that promote confidence in freely expressing opinions and feelings, often of a very personal nature. I observed numerous student artworks that boldly expressed students' confusion of being children in a time of war, of being confused by the reasons for the war, and of visualizing a time of peace.

Christine and Caryl both believe in a central tenet of critical pedagogy, to create knowledge that works to reduce human suffering (Kincheloe, 2004). Through expressions of radical love, the teachers express to their students a vision of the elimination of gender inequity. Christine in particular reinforced the importance of boys and girls reflecting on gender expectations in society. For example, a girl shared in her critique that girls shouldn't be afraid of wearing clothes with shoulder pads, that shoulder pads make her feel more powerful and physically more equal to men in stature. I reflected in my notes upon hearing this comment,

> Christine has set the tone for independent work and free thinking with her guidance and affirmation in making powerful statements. Empowerment through helping them find their voice; the choices are always there for Christine's students… she's not in charge, she's present with them, providing gentle boundaries…. is this "radical love" in action?

Caryl's response to the student who referred to his mother as a "maid" also echoes the practice of radical love. She guided the student to reconsider how he conceptualized his mother. Students in Christine's class reworked art pieces through drawing to reflect their concepts of beauty. Self-portraits were created that considered both inside and outside identity, including gender identity. The feminist atmosphere of visible attention paid to gender issues

Christine created in her classroom allowed for confident exploration and sense making of gender issues, permitting and encouraging meaningful expression of ideas and beliefs.

IN CONCLUSION: TO BE CONTINUED

Feminist pedagogy and feminist art teaching approaches are complicated. Making sense of the gendered spaces art teachers create in classrooms requires sustained engagement and commitment to attending to gender dynamics with openness to the belief that gender differences exist and do matter. I found through my research on feminist pedagogy that Christine's and Caryl's positions and positioning of their feminist teacher identities were exemplified through equitable, empowering, and transformative teaching in spaces where voice is honored and given both tacit and concrete forms. Each woman revealed translucent intersections of feminist pedagogy in how they created safe spaces and dealt with controversy; made pluralist and separatist teaching approaches visible; reflected critically on her teaching practice; embodied what it means to be a transformative intellectual; and practiced radical love.

Gender issues are translucent in nature, unclear due to layers of implications, whose meanings can only be made clearer through purposeful reflection and analysis that attend to both individual constructions of gender and to broader social indicators. More time, more commitment, more voices are needed to continue this task in art education. Caryl perhaps said it best:

> Isn't this what feminist pedagogy is about? Bridging flexibility, fluidity, collaboration, transformation of knowledge, the valuing of multiple perspectives and voices all can lead to the end of sexism and gender inequity. The responsibility of bridge-building demands consciousness, fairness, and inclusion. No one can do it alone. (personal communication, 2008)

To be continued.

REFERENCES

BBC News. (1999, September 23). Sensation sparks New York storm. *BBC News*. Retrieved from http://news.bbc.co.uk/2/hi/entertainment/455902.stm

Brookfield, S. D. (1995). *Becoming a critically reflective teacher*. San Francisco, CA: Jossey-Bass.

Collins, G. C., & Sandell, R. (1992). The politics of multicultural art education. *Art Education, 45*(6), 98-103.

Edelson, M. B. (2009). Posters. *Some living American women artists/Last supper*. Retrieved from www.marybethedelson.com/content/posters.html

Garber, E., Sandell, R., Stankiewicz, M., & Risner, D. (2007). Gender equity in visual arts and dance education. In S. Klein (Ed.), *Handbook for achieving gender equity through education* (2nd ed.). Mahwah, NJ: Lawrence Erlbaum.

Geertz, C. (1973). Thick description: Toward an interpretive theory of culture. In C. Geertz, *The interpretation of cultures: Selected essays* (pp. 3-30). New York, NY: Basic Books.

Giroux, H. (1988). *Teachers as intellectuals*. New York, NY: Bergin & Garvey.

Guba, E. G., & Lincoln, Y. S. (1983). Epistemology and methodological bases of naturalistic inquiry. In G. F. Madauss, M. Scriven & D. L. Stufflebeam (Eds.), *Evaluation models: Viewpoints on educational and human services evaluation* (pp. 325-329). Boston, MA: Kluwer-Nijhoff.

Internetlurker. (2008, December 15). Re: The last superhero supper [Web log message]. Retrieved from http://lastsuppers.blogspot.com/2008/12/last-superhero-supper.html

Kilmer, J. J. (2007). Reclaim your rights as a liberal educator. *Academe, 93*(4), 56-57.

Kincheloe, J. L. (2004). *Critical pedagogy*. New York, NY: Peter Lang.

Rosenberg, M., & Thurber, F. (2007). *Gender matters in art education*. Worcester, MA: Davis.

Smith-Shank, D. L. (2000). You don't need a penis to be a genius. In D. E. Fehr, K. Fehr & K. Keifer-Boyd (Eds.), *Real-world readings in art education: Things your professors never told you* (pp. 65-71). New York, NY: Falmer Press.

Stake, R. (1995). *The art of case study research*. Thousand Oaks, CA: Sage.

Zimmerman, E. (1990). Issues related to teaching art from a feminist point of view. *Visual Arts Research, 16*(2), 1-9.

ENDNOTE

1   For more detailed explanations of the pluralist and separatist approaches to teaching, see Collins and Sandell, 1992; Rosenberg and Thurber, 2007; and Zimmerman, 1990.

LINDA HOEPTNER POLING has been an art educator since 1989 and currently is Assistant Professor in Art Education at Kent State University in Kent, Ohio. Linda's positions in K-12 teaching provided the foundation for her passion to prepare future art educators. She is particularly interested in promoting awareness and deeper understanding of gender issues in art education. Her research threads include the intersections of gendered identity, narrative inquiry as knowledge construction, and equitable pedagogy at all levels of education.

27 / Understanding and Using Case Study Methodology Informed by Autoethnography

AMY PFEILER-WUNDER / ASSISTANT PROFESSOR AND CO-CHAIR OF GRADUATE STUDIES, KUTZTOWN UNIVERSITY

ABSTRACT: *As a case study exemplar informed by autoethnography this chapter explores the research practices of a doctoral student while she simultaneously engaged in teaching elementary art in a K-6 setting. The chapter intertwines personal story, an important aspect of autoethnography, while using multiple case studies to inform the reader on the intricacies involved in developing research questions, researching, analyzing data and coming to a conclusion on how the research can best serve students and inform reflective practices on the part of the teacher.*

"My momma has 10,000 dollars saved."

"Well, my momma has 20,000 dollars saved."

Many signs and symbols emerged feverishly from the drawings produced by K-6 elementary children in the art class. Among the socioeconomically diverse student population of 300 that I worked with, the use of the dollar sign as a marker of identity stands out as a symbol of power and status. As first-grade students studied a vase of flowers using observational skills, I was drawn to the dollar bill signs floating around the page of one particular student's work. It was evident the flower image was secondary to the more important symbolic representation of money. I had to ask,

"Darion, why do you draw money?"

"I love money."

The paraprofessional working with Darion piped in: He draws money every chance he has. Darion likes to draw money so he can pretend it rains money.

"Yeah, I want it to rain money, so I have lots of it."

Through taking a keen view of the stories that emerged in my classroom around socioeconomic status, I was drawn to my research project (Pfeiler-Wunder, 2010). Long before being introduced to the terms "case study" or "autoethnography" I heeded stories through the subtle workings of my professor and advisor, Steve McGuire at the University of Iowa. Noticing how he captured his audience through detailed stories, I learned to strip away my preconceived notions of what it meant to do "authentic" academic work and discovered that 13 years of experience as K-6 art teacher *did* matter. Doing research "offers the opportunity to answer questions for ourselves" leading to a greater understanding of our students and ourselves as learners (Chiseri-Strater & Sunstein, 2006, pp. xvii-xviii).

Pursuing my own questions, I selected a case study methodology informed by autoethnography. I was just as much as a part of the research as my students. I developed my research study using two methodologies to provide opportunities for interpretation based on my experience grounded by the method of a case "or bounded system" (Creswell, 1998) to illuminate a phenomenon. Creswell explains the use of a bounded system "or case (or multiple cases) over time through detailed, in-depth data collection involving multiple sources of information rich in context" (p. 61).

Often a researcher's personal background and story influence topics s/he selects for a study. Creswell (1998) describes how a case study might begin with a vignette, aligning nicely with "autoethnography" where the author reveals their stream of consciousness while conducting and writing the research: "connecting the personal to the cultural" and "focusing outward on social and cultural aspects of their personal experiences; then they look inward, exposing a vulnerable self" (Patton, 2002, p. 85).

Storytelling became a tool through which I discovered the importance of reflecting on how one's lived life expresses our interests and informs one's research. In my work, beyond what I deemed a "lack" of art education experiences as a child from a working class background, I questioned my own notions of sound art teaching based on my limited exposure and experiences with "fine art" until undergraduate school.

My limited exposure to "great masters" was one element which led to the development of my research focus. Images by Darion and other children sparked my interest in how socioeconomic status impacts a shared curriculum within a district, both in hidden and overt ways. I was curious to examine how art curricula surrounding the stories or narratives produced by children are then interpreted and negotiated by particular school communities. My initial research question was: What does the lens of socioeconomic status reveal about the culture and community of the art room and how is the "child artist" framed within this space?

EXPLORING MY RESEARCH QUESTIONS

In regard to data collection, Lincoln and Guba (1985) describe a general format for conducting a case study. One begins with the problem or phenomenon of interest to study, examines the context and issues using rich description and then concludes with the lesson learned. My study operated under an evaluative case study format, which involves description, explanation, and then judgment (Merriam, 1998).

In order to facilitate the study, I conducted preliminary work before I entered the research sites. I began almost a year prior by developing a research notebook which included notes on case study methodology, my research questions, possible contacts for research sites and participants, my timeline for the study, and plans for dissemination. The first time I made contact with schools, I was unable to secure the sites for various reasons. For example, one school had a new administration and was not open to having research conducted at their school. This put my initial timeline on hold, but I used the time to refine my research questions and clarify my methodology.

Before entering the research sites, I began by contacting the curriculum director within the school district I was planning to conduct research to obtain the correct documentation and paperwork. Once the curriculum director approved my study, I applied for approval from the Institutional Review Board (IRB) at the institution where I was studying as a doctoral student. All research involving human subjects must be approved by an IRB. While I waited for approval, I made initial contacts with the teachers and administrators to ask for permission to conduct the study. It was after IRB approval that I mailed packets of information to the art teacher and the administrator at each of the buildings I wanted to include in this study. The packet included a letter explaining who I was, the general study, the interview questions I would be using with the students, art teachers, and administrators and a formal document by IRB, which explained the study and requested signatures by participants.

Once I had approval, I met with the principals about a month before the study to review if they had any questions before I formally began research and interviews on site. I also collected the art teachers' schedules so I could ensure I was seeing consistent grade levels at each site. Additionally, I worked to develop my class and work schedule around the preferences of the teachers involved.

As I developed specific interview questions, I reflected on how using the lens of socioeconomic status might reveal a particular focus within the culture and community of the art room and how the "child artist" was framed within this space. In the context of my own room, I observed the use of the "almighty" dollar sign as a marker of identity and a symbol of power on children's art. I was curious if symbols of power and wealth emerged on children's artwork in other art classrooms. Further, I was interested in knowing if these symbols were allowed or dismissed in student artwork.

Over the course of one semester, to "bind my case" in context of time and space, I spent one day a week in three different art rooms at three different schools, meeting with the same third/fourth-grade combination class. I selected the three economically diverse schools based on the number of students receiving free and reduced lunch. The schools are located in a midwestern state, with two schools in an urban area and one in a sub-urban setting. The schools ranged in size from 200 students to slightly over 400 students. The location of School One would be considered an urban area, located in the heart of the historical district of the city, with houses ranging in price from $150,000 to $500,000. School Two is located in a suburban area of the adjacent city near a golf course, with homes ranging in the upper $200,000 range to well over a million dollars. School Three is located in an urban area, near subsidized housing with most homes from $80,000 to the low $100,000s.

After collecting data through observations and interviews with the teachers I began to see three common themes or discussion points relevant to my research question. I spent time working one-on-one with my advisor and mentor to clarify my research question and began focusing my attention during subsequent observations on three themes that emerged: identity, class, and curriculum. The revised research questions included:

- What does the lens of socioeconomic status tell us about how children construct identity within different school cultures and similar curriculums?
- What does the lens of socioeconomic status tell us about how children use story to negotiate and explore their understanding of class, status, and power?
- What does the lens of socioeconomic status tell us about how curriculum functions and unfolds within a given school culture?

After I had been in the schools for around 4 weeks, I noticed that my initial idea of collecting story and images from children who had agreed to participate would need to be narrowed. I began focusing the case studies of each school by looking at one child's story within each of the school settings. The nature of this type of research involves not only using one's experience as a tool promoting reflexivity, but also being open to how the stories both illuminate and shadow the initial research questions. Van Manen (1990) reminds the reader that the "three most important skills for the qualitative researcher are tolerance for ambiguity, sensitivity to context and data, and good communication skills" (p. 116). Because I was in ongoing dialogue with the teacher participants and constantly reflected on my initial questions, I was able to create the subquestions listed earlier, which made data collection more manageable.

DATA COLLECTION AND ANALYSIS

To create a sound study, I designed my research to involve multiple forms of data such as using formal and semi-formal interviews with students, teachers, and administrators; field notes; and photographic documentation of artwork. Collecting data from multiple sources is one form of triangulation. Additionally, I analyzed current articles in the local newspaper that addressed the culture and community of neighborhood schools versus schools to which students were bused. These articles often had ties to issues of class and race, which I explored through discourse analysis, examining the "language" of the articles and the voice(s) that were heard or unheard.

Before collecting data from students, I described the study in "child friendly" terminology and sent a formal letter and consent form to the parents of the children introducing myself, the study, and the potential impact of the study to the families. Once the parents/guardians signed the consent form and the child returned it, I was able to begin the study but could only include the children who returned the consent form. When I was not in the building, the art teachers helped by collecting the consent forms. I had to adjust my original visions of this study as the number of consent forms the students returned was relatively small, and the use of the dollar sign in student art and conversations around power and wealth were not as prevalent in these classrooms as they had been in my classroom.

In terms of data collection, I conducted observations, interviews, and document analysis. To track my observations, I kept a divided notebook, one section for each of the three schools in which I was conducting research. Once at the research site, I took notes at the beginning of the class while the teacher was engaged in whole group instruction and then sat next to the students involved in the study to record their conversations in written form or to write detailed observations about their artwork. I also documented the students' artwork to examine the use of symbols pertinent to socioeconomic status or to make references to the type of aesthetics promoted through the teacher's philosophy and interpretation of the curriculum. Because I was also examining the culture and community of the art room, I also photographed the room and work done by other grade levels, posters in the room, mission statements, and teaching philosophies that might be present in the space.

My observation notes recorded direct story and conversation from students in each school. I wrote detailed notes, not just pertaining to the students' conversations, but also notes about the physical space and what students were wearing, and I tried to investigate "what was not said" by listening carefully to their conversations and probing them with further inquiry when a curiosity struck me about their dialogue. For each case I set the stage by describing the physical space of the school and art room. Related to School One, the one in the historical district, I wrote the following:

Walking toward the entryway of School One, the area is teeming with history. There is the historical home of a famous artist, among other structures, which housed local grocery stores, galleries, and a craft guild now turned bakery. Framing the school are old oak and maple trees, cascading shadows on the facade. Gardens surround the school, planted by the school parent association. The school is four stories, red brick and framed by an arched stone entry. It feels comfortable, like a good pair of sneakers, ready to be replaced but so full of stories they can't be discarded.

As I enter the school, I climb the stairs to reach the office where I am welcomed by a bulletin board filled with art. Splotches of watercolor are outlined in neon string where kindergartners created abstract images or highlighted what images emerged from their imaginations. Birds, dragons, bunnies, and fish make their way to the viewer's attention. I wander through the library where framed art from students is on display, return to a set of stairs and then find myself in the art room. Posted on the door are quotes, including:

> Imagination is more important than knowledge. For while knowledge defines all we currently know and understand, imagination points to all we might yet discover and create.
>
> —Albert Einstein

I wrote as much as possible during the class observations, but I also relied on writing notes immediately after the observations. When observing, I made a point to always mingle with the students so that I did not seem "distant" or "strange" to the students. I wanted the students to feel comfortable with me as a person, so they felt open to share their ideas, thoughts and opinions. During the interviews with the principals and teachers, I took careful notes and recorded the interviews to transcribe later. At times, I felt a tension between wanting to write everything down, composing the notes into story form, or trusting my "remembering." Emerson, Fretz, and Shaw (1995) wrote that, "Doing" and "writing" should not be seen as separate and distinct activities, but as dialectically related and interdependent activities" (p. 15). This meant rereading notes, thinking through them, and discussing them with participants and other scholars.

My professor shared with me that I would know I had enough data when the experiences began "repeating" themselves. This "repetition" revealed itself when I started to see commonalities, connections, and at times tensions within the stories from each school. At this point, I analyzed the stories from the children in this study determining themes focused on the ways children identified themselves, understood class and interpreted curriculum through a socioeconomic lens.

FINDINGS AND ISSUES THAT INFORMED MY DATA ANALYSIS

Two important aspects of my research marked my data analysis. First, I was simultaneously a part-time teacher and a researcher in the same district. Second, I used within-case analysis because I was working with multiple cases. As I wrote about each school, I labored to be extremely cognizant of how my perspective showed in my writing (Creswell, 2007). The connection between theory and practice was a constant negotiation in my work as I balanced multiple roles of being a teacher in the district, a teaching assistant at a university, and a graduate student.

In analyzing my data, I ensured that my audience was aware of my relationships with the schools. While doing research, the teachers I worked with were colleagues. Although we did not work in the same buildings, we saw each other at monthly staff meetings. In addition, they were all older than me and had mentored me, leading me to feel like a student, yet I was conducting the study. Ann DiPardo (1993) discusses the challenges associated with a "place" when teachers leave the classroom to pursue graduate studies. It is during this departure from the classroom one's identity changes in the negotiation of a new space.

> ...I found myself re-entering the emotions that had attended my own movement out of teaching and into graduate school-my deep satisfaction in finding new ways to admire the complexities of my work, and my equally deep regrets about suddenly contemplating classroom life from a distance. (DiPardo, 1993, p. 209)

Because of the nature of the case study, I conducted a cross-case analysis where I looked at themes across the whole case (Creswell, 2007, p. 75). I examined the emerging themes as I reviewed field notes and transcribed interviews with teachers and administrators, then created chapters related to my research questions. I categorized and coded the types of images students created along with notes about their conversations, noticing commonalities and differences in stories related to power and wealth, and finally examining the ways the curriculum unfolded within a given school. From this arrangement of chapters, I could return to the initial questions to illuminate how children's construction of identity within different school cultures, yet a common district's curriculum, might be understood through the lens of socioeconomic status (SES). In addition, I noted how children use story to negotiate and explore their understanding of class, status, and power. Finally, I noted how curriculum functions and unfolds within a given school culture.

CONCLUDING THOUGHTS

What I had observed in my research was sometimes a disconnect between the children's lives and the curriculum. In some cases, this in turn allowed for fewer opportunities for students to have autonomy and an identity marking experience in artmaking. Examining these facets of curriculum development should not be exclusive to the lens of socioeconomic status. Using this lens to explore how curriculum functions revealed the importance of making curriculum pertinent to students. Children have a personal history that must be understood in lesson and curriculum development. This was illuminated by listening to the stories from the children in my research project with keen attention to conversations around power and wealth.

The reminder of the importance of students' particular histories in developing curriculum directly correlated to my own experience as a young artist. I had limited exposure to the arts, and the only print I remember viewing was Auguste Renoir's *Girl with a Watering Can*. I remember coming home to quickly tear off my school uniform and wondering what the girl with beautiful blonde hair and pristine crisp blue lace trimmed dress had to do with my life as a farm girl. Art in my experience seemed to be a form of "cultural grooming," instead of centered on my personal history, and this is what I questioned in terms of current school curriculum. Through this case study, I was able to set my story side-by-side with my students' stories and in analyzing them, similarities emerged. This finding gives me pause to consider curriculum reform so students are involved in meaning making processes in the art room.

The use of autoethnography in conducting case study research allowed me to travel the landscape of memory and experience. By being tuned in to the nuances illuminated in the lived culture of the art room through the lens of socioeconomics, I came to deeper understandings of the multifaceted lenses necessary to meet the needs of all learners. As I thought about the ways in which curricula are often centered on teaching elements and principles of design, I was reminded by the students of the importance of using Big Ideas (Walker, 2001) in curriculum. This connected with the ideas of Marilyn Zurmuehlen (1990) where the work of artmaking should manifest idiosyncratic meaning where it is "uniquely bound to a particular person and situation" (p. 25). This is what I saw when Darion was asked to draw a still life in my art room. The lesson happened to be one of the more structured lessons I used in the curriculum. It was evident as he drew a vase and flowers he had done the work of the assignment. More importantly, he felt as an artist, his work was an opportunity to symbolically share his personal history. In this case, his infatuation with money. As a professional, I struggled with following a particular curriculum, while also keeping student voices front and center. Darion's work was a reminder of how the student's personal history should mediate curriculum development.

I believe I was able to come to these conclusions because the use of case study research informed by autoethnography focuses on dialogue and reflection. My findings, centered around a curriculum that focuses on the personal histories and identity of students, align with my belief that the art room offers a unique place for students to engage in experiences related to identity formation. I believe this is significant to the field because of the way in which art education is sometimes viewed as non-essential outside core subject matter such as reading and math. Curriculum reform related to No Child Left Behind (NCLB) has put much more focus on a curriculum aligned with test taking. The art room, in contrast, offers a place for student voice.

At the same time, the art curriculum should be rigorous in content. I had been told once my role of the art teacher was easy. I simply "created pretty pictures" for the walls. Artmaking certainly has an aesthetic component, but when art curricula are viewed from single vantage points, what is absent is the very multi-layered opportunities around problem solving and creativity that art education provides. The use of Big Ideas (Walker, 2001) illustrates to children how artists come to focus on a particular content within their work. By centering the work around human experience, it allows children to create more than "pretty pictures" but meaningful artwork.

I also wanted to use story as a way to make my work accessible and engaging to a large audience. When I entered higher education after 13 years in a public classroom, I remember several art educators coming up to me at a meeting, asking me not to forget teachers' needs. I believe there is something important about being able to communicate in the language of story, to invite a reader in, to create dialogue in a manner by which others would want to read the research. As Chapman (2005) writes in her authoethnography on schooling, empire, class, gender and sexuality, "What is the point of research and theory, if only six other people in the world get it?" (p. 261).

REFERENCES

Chapman, V. (2005). Making a good Victoria sponge cake: Schooling, empire, class, gender and sexuality. *International Journal of Qualitative Studies in Education, 18*(3), 259-284.

Chiseri-Strater, E., & Sunstein, B. S. (2006). *What works? A practical guide for teacher research.* Portsmouth, NH: Heinemann.

Creswell, J. (1998). *Qualitative inquiry and research design: Choosing among five approaches.* London, England: Sage.

Creswell, J. (2007). *Qualitative inquiry and research design: Choosing among five approaches* (2nd ed.). London, England: Sage.

DiPardo, A. (1993). When teachers become graduate students. *English Education, 25*(4), 197-212.

Emerson, R. M., Fretz, R. I., & Shaw, L. L. (1995). *Writing ethnographic fieldnotes.* Chicago, IL: The University of Chicago Press.

Lincoln, Y. S., & Guba, E. G. (1985). *Naturalistic Inquiry.* Beverly Hills, CA: Sage.

Merriam, S. (1998). *Qualitative research and case study applications in education.* San Francisco, CA: Jossey-Bass.

Patton, M.Q. (2002). *Qualitative research and evaluation methods* (3rd ed.). Thousand Oaks, CA: Sage.

Pfeiler-Wunder, A. L. (2010). "It's raining money": Identity, class, and the unfolding curriculum at three schools through the lens of socioeconomic status. (Doctoral dissertation, University of Iowa). Retrieved from http://ir.uiowa.edu/etd/723

Van Manen, M. (1990). *Researching lived experience: Human science for an action sensitive pedagogy.* Ontario, Canada: The University of Western Ontario.

Walker, S. (2001). *Teaching meaning in art making.* Worcester, MA: Davis.

Zurmuehlen, M. (1990). *Studio art: Praxis, symbol and presence.* Reston VA: National Art Education Association.

AMY PFEILER-WUNDER is Assistant Professor and Co-Chair of Graduate Studies at Kutztown University, in Kutztown, Pennsylvania, where she works with undergraduate students and graduate students in the Art Education and Crafts Department. She received her master's and PhD from the University of Iowa in Art Education and completed her undergraduate work at Mount Mercy College in Cedar Rapids, Iowa. While pursuing her master's and PhD she worked with preK-9th grade staudents in various settings for 13 years. In 2006, she was awarded Iowa's Outstanding Elementary Art Teacher and was named the Western Region Elementary Art Educator by the National Art Education Association in 2007. She works as faculty advisor to the student chapter of NAEA at both the university and national levels. Her research examines the various interpretations of curriculum tied to the particular aesthetics promoted in a school culture through the lens of socioeconomic status. She plans to continue her research in urban settings.

NARRATIVE AND AUTOBIOGRAPHICAL RESEARCH

28 / Narrative Inquiry: Revealing Experience

MARY ELIZABETH MEIER / ASSISTANT PROFESSOR OF ART AND PROGRAM DIRECTOR OF ART EDUCATION, MERCYHURST UNIVERSITY

ABSTRACT: *Narrative inquiry is a methodology for research that brings forward specific stories of lived experience. In suggesting how the teacher-researcher might use narrative methods to critically reflect on processes of teaching and learning, I use narrative inquiry to remember and revision experience, and to study the complexities of classroom life from multiple perspectives. This chapter begins with a brief overview of narrative inquiry in educational research as it grows from a Deweyan view of experience. The discussion continues with formulating research questions, methods of data collection, analysis, interpretation, and composing the final research text. As an example, I interweave a narrative fragment from my teaching experience as part of a discussion of writing as inquiry and my critical reflective practice as an art teacher.*

Narrative inquiry is a qualitative research methodology focused on stories of experience. Narrative and autobiographical methods, falling under the broader category of qualitative inquiry (Chase, 2005), are particularly well-suited to uncovering the nuances of human experience through story. "Issues of complexity and human centeredness" are the focus of a narrative inquiry study (Webster & Mertova, 2007, p. 3).

Scholars in art education use narrative inquiry as a method to bring forward the lived experience of artists, art teachers, and students. More specifically, narrative methods are helpful in exploring how artistic and pedagogical discourses overlap (Markello, 2006), the experiences of art teachers and students engaged together in reflective practice (Collins, 2002), and self-explorations of professional practice (Ortiz, 2008; Trevino, 2006). There is also a growing body of research pairing arts-based and narrative inquiry methods (de Mello 2007; Ortiz, 2008; Thomas, 2009; Vaselenak, 2006).

THE NARRATIVE OF EXPERIENCE

While there is no single way of approaching narrative research, Jean Clandinin and Michael Connelly are widely recognized as leading narrative inquirers[1] who are advancing an emerging methodology (Chase, 2005; Clandinin, 2007; Clandinin & Connelly, 1994; Clandinin, Pushor, & Orr, 2007). Their research in teacher knowledge (Connelly & Clandinin, 1990) is part of a body of research focused on constructing meaning through stories of experience (Clandinin & Connelly, 1989; Connelly & Clandinin, 1994). As such, John Dewey's (1938) notion of *continuity* in experience is useful in narrative inquiry in order to recognize and value experiences as they unfold into further experiences on a temporal continuum (Clandinin & Connelly, 2000; Dewey, 1938). Experiences appreciated in "the living present" are those that are in continuity with past and future (Dewey, 1938, p. 23).

In a qualitative inquiry, the researcher makes decisions about how to represent personal experience in relationship to participant experience. Often, the narrative inquirer will situate his or her experience in the form of autobiographical writing, or "personal experiential narratives" (Conle, 2000, p. 189). Working "in the midst" of the research context (Clandinin & Connely, 2000, p. 65), a researcher may use autobiographical writing in various stages of the inquiry— articulating the research problem, framing the inquiry, as field texts, or later in composing a research text.

> **SARA AND MELANIE:** *This section addresses narrative inquiry and autobiographical inquiry. We view autobiographical inquiry as a subset of narrative inquiry in which researchers emphasize understanding their own experiences. Further, there is a range of relationships among many methodologies in this text. For example, Ortiz references a/r/tography in her autobiographical chapter later in this section.*

Personal and social experiences in continuum are central to a narrative inquiry. Clandinin and Connelly (2000) call this experiential continuum the "three-dimensional narrative inquiry space" (p. 60). This space is a metaphor for the constantly shifting forward and backward, inward and outward view of the narrative inquirer. By thinking about inquiry as moving in a three-dimensional space, or "back and forthing" the researcher attunes to the relational and reflexive qualities of the narrative inquiry work (p. 167).

In a narrative inquiry, the researcher attends to the changing complexities of lived experience over time.[2] A narrative inquiry research question is focused on a particular setting, particular people, and the particular stories we tell of our experiences (see Clandinin, 2007, p. 21). Narrative inquirers develop a research question (or questions) to narrow the scope of a study. A well-formed narrative inquiry research question is one that guides inquiry in the phases of searching and re-searching. This process occurs over time as ongoing observation of experience, storytelling, writing, and re-writing/re-storying. "Narrative inquiry carries more of a sense of continual reformulation of an inquiry than it does a sense of problem definition and solution" (Clandinin & Connelly, 2000, p. 124). While the narrative inquirer will likely pose research questions at the outset of a study, it is not uncommon for the phenomena under study to shift. Just as life does not stand still, neither does a "narrative view of experience" (Clandinin & Connelly, 2000, p. 127).

The back-and-forth nature of inquiry as an ever-shifting process is important to consider when designing and proposing narrative inquiry research. I began a narrative inquiry about my teaching by asking: What early experiences in my art teaching do I remember as turning points? How can writing narrative reflections about my experiences as an art teacher help me to articulate shifts in my teaching philosophy? Later in this chapter, I offer a fragment of a narrative inquiry text that I am developing to explore these research questions.

DATA COLLECTION

Early in the inquiry process, the researcher will likely negotiate a role in the field, or the context in which the study takes place. If in a classroom, the researcher may be a participant observer, working alongside students and teacher (Mitton, 2008). The inquirer working through a self-exploration may use artifacts, photographs, or arts-based methods (Ortiz, 2008) to reconstruct memory or as catalysts to engage the telling and interpretation of personal experience. In a narrative study, the researcher and participants are part of a narrative history that is continually shaping before, during, and after the inquiry. The field texts and research text are also part of the inquiry space. During the course of the data collection and data analysis, "plotlines" develop as events unfold in a story, creating possible trajectories for how the inquirer engages in the work of telling stories of experience (Clandinin & Connelly, 2000, p. 60). Plotlines are the various events and descriptions that emerge as part of the narrative inquiry. In the later stages of the research, the narrative inquirer will analyze, organize and retell these stories as part of the research text (see further discussion in the Analysis and Interpretation section of this chapter).

FIELD TEXTS

Field texts are the fundamental data in the inquiry. Data collected in the form of field texts can include observations, notes, interviews, memos, letters, documents, chronicles, poems, photographs, artwork, or other data collected in the field. Nespor (2006) describes fieldnotes as recordings of both detailed experiential observations and the researcher's reflections.

For the researcher who is observing events in the classroom, Frank (1999) distinguishes between descriptive and interpretive fieldnotes. Descriptive fieldnotes are acts of *notetaking* whereas interpretive fieldnotes are acts of *notemaking*. As a notetaker, the researcher records rich descriptions and observations. As a notemaker, the researcher makes memos of reflections, inner thoughts, questions, and emotions as they occur in response to observation.

If the researcher is also acting in the role of teacher, it can be nearly impossible to take detailed notes during busy moments in the classroom. In this case, or if interviewing participants is part of data collection, transcriptions of audio and video recordings in combination with brief notes can also be used to generate field texts. The researcher will make decisions about how to structure an interview so that the participant is the narrator of his or her own story (Chase, 2005). The researcher may choose to pose just one or two open-ended questions to the interviewee in order to spark the recollection of experiences and life events.

SELF-QUESTIONING

A teacher-researcher engaged in the self-study of practice might use self-questioning to generate data. One might use an audio recorder and begin the inquiry like a self-interview. For example, Knowles, Cole and Presswood (1994) suggest leading questions for inquiry into what it means to become a teacher. Some of these questions include: "Who am I as a teacher? What does it mean to be a teacher? Who are the students? What are their needs as learners? How do I come to know them as persons and as learners? How do I teach? What teaching methods are most appropriate?" (p. 67). Responses to these broad and open-ended questions are likely to lead into a story, illustrating an example, and therefore lend themselves well to a narrative inquiry.

In general, data collection methods in narrative inquiry move from processes of constructing field texts as data sources, to the analytic and interpretive writing of interim texts, to the crafting of a public research text. As stated earlier, there is no single approach and many researchers tailor narrative methodologies to address the emerging problem statement of the study by drawing from more than one approach. For example, Riessman (2008) and Bach (2007) offer useful reviews of how researchers are using visual narratives such as photography, collage, film, and video diary; they offer recommendations for using visual and written texts together in analysis and interpretation.

ANALYSIS AND INTERPRETATION

In the process of analysis, the researcher will likely develop keywords and tags as systems for organizing field texts, locating and linking meaning in the data. The researcher who is constructing a retelling of the data as a story may elect to make use of literary elements in analysis. Literary elements like plot, characters, setting, and points-of-view can function as a framework for analysis and as possibilities for re-telling the stories in the research text. Polkinghorne (1995) describes a way the researcher may link together events and descriptions as storied accounts: "The analytic development of a story from the gathered data involves recursive movement from the data to an emerging thematic plot" (Polkinghorne, 1995, p. 16).

Tsai (2007) offers a detailed description of her data analysis methods in her study of Taiwanese kindergarteners' classroom storytelling. Tsai's data analysis began by studying transcripts of the children's narratives collected in her classroom observations. Tsai approached these transcripts as stories to understand rather than as texts to analyze. Using literary terms (e.g. *background, crisis, resolution,* and *complicating actions*), she began analysis by identifying key elements and themes and creating headings for sections of the stories transcriptions. In her analysis, Tsai (2007) attended to how the children constructed the narratives independently or co-constructed them with others, the lengths of each story, the content of the story, how each child presented her/his narrative, and the narrative structure.

Clandinin and Connelly (2000) urge the beginning narrative inquirer to avoid matching data to broad categorical generalizations. Rather, narrative inquiry is better suited to tell particular stories situated in particular contexts. The researcher's task is to represent "storied lives in storied ways, not to represent storied lives as exemplars of formal categories" (2000, p. 141). One approach is to tell a story while creating a dialogue between theories represented in the literature. For example, Thomas (2009) describes her teaching experience in respect to a larger conversation about philosophies of teaching and possibilities for re-visioning education. Thomas (2009) writes, "We recursively move from global to local perspectives, asking ourselves who we are amidst larger theoretical conversations about pedagogy and how our practices are informed by the larger scope" (p. 3). Using a metaphor similar to Richardson and St. Pierre's (2007) *crystallization,* Thomas (2009) describes her experimental process of inquiry as a *prism* refracting, illuminating, and "casting diverse strands of light" (Thomas, 2009, p. 24). Employing this process of analysis makes interim texts important for testing interpretations in narrative inquiry.

Interim texts are beginning interpretations of the field texts, often shared with participants in the research, in order to open a conversation about how to represent researcher and participants' voices. Interim texts are the in-between texts in the inquiry, a step toward the research text. They also can be described as drafts of storied interpretations. Writing an interim text is likely to inform data interpretation or lead to a different strategy of analysis. For example, the researcher might draft an interim text in the form of a letter, describing an event and posing some possible interpretations. The process of writing interim texts in the midst of data collection is likely to fuel the inquiry by helping the researcher to follow-up on questions that arise.

Central to the inquiry process is writing and rewriting, telling and retelling stories of experience. A researcher may go back and forth among texts engaging in the writing and re-writing process as interpretation. Clandinin and Connelly (2000) describe data analysis as a process of asking questions of the field texts: What are the meanings of the poem, the transcript, the daily field notes? What alternative meanings are possible in reading the field texts? (p. 130).

BRAIDING TOGETHER MULTIPLE PERSPECTIVES

The metaphor of braiding is useful in imagining how field texts are woven together into a narrative research text. Threads of personal histories and life experiences are interlaced thoughtfully with theoretical discussion and support from scholarly literature. The researcher is like an artisan in selecting a form of expression for the research text (such as poems, letters, stories, photographs, or a combination).

An exemplar of this "interweaving" is the scholarly work of Hasebe-Ludt, Leggo, and Chambers (2009) who work collaboratively in a multi-vocal research approach. Their scholarly work is based on the conceptual foundation and practice of *méttisage* (from the Latin word *mixtus*), the weaving of *mixed* fibers into cloth (Lionnet, 1989; Zuss, 1997). Literary méttisage is the braiding of stories that give voice to lived experience and self-knowledge. By valuing what is "mixed," the collaborators create space for a range of voices. Multiple forms of narrative (poetry, story, memoir) are braided as méttisage, presented together in the research text to represent three voices, each speaking of the rich and nuanced life of teaching and learning. For example, a text can present multiple viewpoints situated together on the page like a script with multiple actors.

WRITING AS INQUIRY

By living and re-living experience through writing as inquiry, one can initiate a conversation in the *living present* (Dewey, 1938). Way-finding through writing is a process that both uncovers lived experience and constructs living experience. The creative process of writing as inquiry can reveal aspects of experience that reside in the field texts but come to life in the retelling. In that same process of writing and re-writing, new understandings crystallize (Richardson, 2006; Richardson & St. Pierre, 2007). Lionnet (1989) refers to this as a process of *self-reading* and *self-writing.*

In the following section, I share an interim text that emerged from an early teaching experience. It is followed by a brief discussion of how writing as inquiry can be part of a reflective, critical practice.

Though I may be writing about lived experience, my process in re-living through writing allows for re-orientation to living experience. Moreover, in the writing as inquiry process, I write not only to reconstruct memory from the field text but also to deconstruct my assumptions, reflect critically, and consider new meaning. My aim goes beyond reading myself historically in the recalling and retelling of memory; rather, my purpose is a reflexive process of inquiry in which I am writing to understand new things about myself.

...

What is the sensation of knowledge in the making? (Ellsworth, 2005). How can we pay closer attention to the sensations of learning? What does it feel like to achieve a realization, or an understanding? I vividly remember one particular moment in my classroom as a first year elementary art teacher. I was teaching a class of 23 third graders who were all in the final stage of fastening yarn to their art project. I was using a hot glue gun to fasten yarn and raffia under the direction of the student who was among those waiting at the crowded "glue station." The feeling of intensity, the sensory experience of being in a busy room with so many children, is impressed on my memory. Smelling the heat of the glue, hearing the buzz of excited voices in my ear, I followed the instructions of a child who eagerly directed where I should attach the yarn, the final addition to her art project. Another child took a turn directing the application of the yarn and raffia. Bright sunlight flooded in through the huge picture windows that looked out onto the butterfly garden. Long thread-like strands of glue floated in the air as the child skipped back toward her seat to show off her work to classmates. The room became hot with bustling bodies and soon it was well-past time to remind the children to clean up. Their homeroom teacher stood in the doorway ready to take the children back to their classroom. Where did the time go?

I now reflect critically on the procedure that I set up that day in the classroom studio, early in my first year. I placed myself at the front of the room with my glue gun station in order to assist students in a final embellishment of their artwork. What does it mean when students, simultaneously needing yarn and raffia, are in the "final step" in the artmaking process? What are the pedagogical implications of teacher at the center of activity and art students who are working through a series of steps? Alternatively, what would a third grade art classroom look and feel like when students are at the center of activity, sensing "new and previously unthought of or unfelt senses of self, others, and the world *in their process of emergence*?" (Ellsworth, 2005, p. 16). How will I re-envision my classroom as a place of "knowledge in the making" (p. 17) as opposed to a place of step-by-step following directions?

As I gained more experience as an elementary art teacher, I began to explore how my teaching could support students' "process of emergence" (Ellsworth, 2005), and I began to de-emphasize sequential steps as central to the process of art as a thing made. I began to attend to teaching as listening. I listened more closely to students' conversations among each other, hearing their interests, and I worked to facilitate learning with their ideas as central to the artmaking process.

...

In the example just given, I share how I engage with writing as inquiry as part of a desire to critically examine my practice as art teacher. Notes and photographs I collected over years of teaching fasten me to my lived experience as part of an unfolding professional practice. I use these photographs and texts to stimulate recall and work back through my memory of events and emotions (see also Kuhn, 2000; Mitchell & Weber 1999; Radstone, 2000; Suominen Guyas, 2007).

After describing a moment in my remembered classroom life, I placed the description in dialogue with Elizabeth Ellsworth's (2005) theory of knowledge in the making and began to interpret my memory in respect to my shifting philosophy of teaching. By placing narrative experience in dialogue with theory and through writing as inquiry, we can approach the interpretation of narrative data. For example, Thomas (2009) writes about her inquiry as a place new with possibilities. She uses the *poetic dwelling place,* critical reflection in dialogue with philosophy, as her theoretical framework. Writing her dissertation as narrative, searching and re-searching her professional experience, Thomas (2009) reflects: "I sought to honor a more informed and confident voice, to more clearly interpret the felt tensions within my teaching identity and the general ethos of the larger educational landscape" (p. 11). Here, Thomas proclaims a commitment as a narrative researcher to convey her voice of experience in such a way that is relevant to others.

THE RESEARCH TEXT

In this final section, I look ahead to the public research text as it represents the inquiry. It is important for the researcher to consider how the audience, or reader, will access the meaning gleaned from the inquiry.

Connelly and Clandinin (2006) recommend that the researcher continue to think narratively in the writing of the research text, remaining attuned to the "temporal unfolding" of experiences as they happen in both personal and social contexts (p. 485). By experimenting with interim texts, the researcher remains open to literary forms that arise from the inquiry-as-writing process. It is important to remember that the research text is not a final truth, but rather (as is the nature of narrative) a moment in shifting phenomena, the value of which comes when the reader finds meaning in the text. The research text could be written a number of ways and would be different in another time or social context and for another reader. Finally, we as narrative researchers should consider the relevance of the text to multiple audiences and thus, be prepared to discuss the inquiry in terms of its social significance.

The strength of narrative inquiry is to illuminate shades of intensity and varied textures surrounding a complex phenomenon. Narrative inquiry is a flexible qualitative research methodology. Simultaneously it is a process for critically reflecting on narrative as it is used to remember and revision human experience. The narrative form allows for artistry in the final research text. Also, the personal and interpersonal qualities of narrative inquiry create many ways to interpret, understand, and share art education research including the classroom practices of teacher-researchers.

REFERENCES

Bach, H. (2007). Composing a visual narrative inquiry. In D. J. Clandinin (Ed.), *Handbook of narrative inquiry: Mapping a methodology* (pp. 280-309). Thousand Oaks, CA: Sage.

Chase, S. (2005). Narrative Inquiry: Multiple lenses, approaches, voices. In Y. S. Lincoln & N. K. Denzin (Eds.), *The Sage handbook of qualitative research* (pp. 651-678). Thousand Oaks, CA: Sage.

Clandinin, D. J. (2007). *Handbook of narrative inquiry: Mapping a methodology*. Thousand Oaks, CA: Sage.

Clandinin, D. J., & Connelly, M. F. (1989). *Narrative and story in practice and research*. Retrieved from www.eric.ed.gov/ERICWebPortal/contentdelivery/servlet/ERICServlet?accno=ED309681.

Clandinin, D. J., & Connelly, M. F. (1994). Personal experience methods. In N. K. Denzin & Y. S. Lincoln (Eds.), *Handbook of qualitative research* (pp. 413-427). London, England: Sage.

Clandinin, D.J., & Connelly, M. F. (2000). *Narrative inquiry: Experience and story in qualitative research*. San Francisco, CA: Jossey-Bass.

Clandinin, D. J., Pushor, D., & Orr, A. M. (2007). Navigating sites for narrative inquiry. *Journal of Teacher Education, 58*(1), 21-35.

Collins, M. P. (2002). *The dialogue journal-sketchbook in art education: Developing creative abilities in art students through mutually self-reflective dialogues between teacher and student* (Unpublished doctoral dissertation). Concordia University, Montreal, Canada.

Conle, C. (2000). Thesis as narrative or "What is the inquiry in narrative inquiry?" *Curriculum Inquiry, 30*(2), 189-214.

Connelly, M. F., & Clandinin, D. J. (1990). Stories of experience and narrative inquiry. *Educational Researcher, 19*(5), 2-14.

Connelly, M. F., & Clandinin, D. J. (1994). Telling teaching stories. *Teacher Education Quarterly, 21*(1), 145-158.

Connelly, M. F., & Clandinin, D. J. (2006). Narrative inquiry. In J. Green, G. Camilli & P. Elmore (Eds.), *Handbook of complementary methods in education research* (pp. 477-488). New York, NY: Routledge.

de Mello, D. M. (2007). The language of arts in a narrative inquiry landscape. In D. J. Clandinin (Ed.), *Handbook of narrative inquiry: Mapping a methodology* (pp. 203-223). Thousand Oaks, CA: Sage.

Dewey, J. (1938). *Experience and education*. New York, NY: Touchstone.

Ellsworth, E. (2005). *Places of learning: Media, architecture, pedagogy*. New York, NY: Routledge.

Frank, C. (1999). *Ethnographic eyes: A teacher's guide to classroom observation*. Portsmouth, NH: Heinemann.

Hasebe-Ludt, E., Leggo, C., & Chambers, C. (2009). *Life writing and literary méttisage as an ethos for our times*. New York, NY: Peter Lang.

Huber, J., Murphy, M. S., & Clandinin, D. J. (2011). *Places of curriculum making: Narrative inquiries into children's lives in motion*. Bingley, England: Emerald Group.

Knowles, J., Cole, A., & Presswood, C. (1994). *Through preservice teachers' eyes: Exploring field experiences through narrative and inquiry*. New York, NY: Merrill.

Kuhn, A. (2000). A journey through memory. In S. Radstone (Ed.), *Memory and methodology* (pp. 179-196). New York, NY: Berg.

Li, X., Conle, C., & Luwisch, F. E. (2009). *Shifting polarized positions: A narrative approach in teacher education*. New York, NY: Peter Lang.

Lionnet, F. (1989). *Autobiographical voices: Race, gender, self-portraiture*. Ithaca, NY: Cornell University Press.

Markello, C. (2006). *Artist narratives: Artmaking and teaching discourses on the professional landscape* (Unpublished doctoral dissertation). University of Houston, Houston, TX.

Mitchell, C., & Weber, S. (1999). *Reinventing ourselves as teachers: Beyond nostalgia*. London, England: Falmer Press.

Mitton, J. (2008). *A narrative inquiry into the negotiations of children's and families' lives in classroom curriculum making* (Unpublished doctoral dissertation). University of Alberta, Edmonton, Canada.

Nespor, J. (2006). Finding patterns with field notes. In J. Green, G. Camilli & P. Elmore (Eds.), *Handbook of complementary methods in education research* (pp. 297-308). New York, NY: Routledge.

Ortiz, C. (2008). *A self-exploration of the relationship between art teaching and artistic practice* (Unpublished doctoral dissertation). University of Houston, Houston, TX.

Polkinghorne, D. E. (1995). *Narrative configuration in qualitative analysis. International Journal of Qualitative Studies in Education, 8*(1), 12-28. Reprinted in J. A. Hatch & R. Wisniewski (Eds.). (1995). Life history and narrative (pp. 5-23). London, England: Falmer.

Radstone, S. (2000). *Memory and methodology*. Oxford, England: Berg.

Riessman, D. C. K. (2008). *Narrative methods for the human sciences*. Thousand Oaks, CA: Sage.

Richardson, L. (2006) Skirting a pleated text: De-disciplining an academic life. In S. N. Hesse-Biber & P. Leavy (Eds.), *Emergent methods in social research* (pp. 1-12). Thousand Oaks, CA: Sage.

Richardson, L., & St. Pierre, E. A. (2007). Writing: A method of inquiry. In N. K. Denzin & Y. S. Lincoln (Eds.), *Collecting and interpreting qualitative materials* (pp. 473-499). Thousand Oaks, CA: Sage.

Suominen Guyas, A. (2007). Re-constructing self within the family: Re-building the family album. *Visual Culture and Gender, 2*, 16-23. Retrieved from http://vcg.emitto.net/2vol/guyas.pdf

Thomas, S. (2009). *Seeking vision and voice in poetic dwelling* (Unpublished doctoral dissertation). The University of Nebraska at Lincoln, Lincoln, NE.

Trevino, S. (2006). *Self-study: A teacher's narrative inquiry into curriculum making and reflective practice in a residential treatment center context* (Unpublished doctoral dissertation). University of Houston, Houston, TX.

Tsai, M. L. (2007). Understanding young children's personal narratives. In D. J. Clandinin (Ed.), *Handbook of narrative inquiry: Mapping a methodology* (pp. 461-488). Thousand Oaks, CA: Sage.

Vaselenak, L. E. (2006). *The search for creativity: A visual narrative inquiry* (Unpublished doctoral dissertation). University of Alberta, Edmonton, Canada.

Webster, L., & Mertova, P. (2007). *Using narrative inquiry as a research method: An introduction to using critical event narrative analysis in research on learning and teaching*. New York, NY: Routledge.

Zuss, M. (1997). Strategies of representation: Autobiographical méttisage and critical pragmatism. *Educational Theory, 47*(2), 163-180.

ENDNOTES

1 Throughout this chapter, I use the terms *narrative inquirer* and *researcher* interchangeably.

2 Narrative inquiry is a methodology that can help researcher(s) and particiapnts attend to the way experiences unfold over time and in relation to particular contexts. Narrative inquires often extend over a period of years in order to study how ideas and experiences shift or develop (see Li, Conle, & Luwisch, 2009; Huber, Murphy, & Clandinin, 2011). Planning narrative inquiry research in an educational context often means engaging in field research that extends over a semester or school year.

MARY ELIZABETH MEIER taught visual art in Connecticut and Pennsylvania. In 2012, she joined the Mercyhurst University faculty in Erie, Pennsylvania as Assistant Professor of Art and Program Director of Art Education. She earned her PhD in Art Education from The Pennsylvania State University, and MS and BS degrees in Art Education from The Florida State University. The title of Meier's (2012) narrative inquiry dissertation is "Shifts in Thinking" in Arts Teachers' Narratives: Documentation as Inquiry and Artifact. Her research interests include collaborative inquiry, documentation of learning in the arts, reconceptualist curriculum theory, and narrative inquiry methodologies.

29 / A Research Journey: Narrative Inquiry With Three Artist-Teachers

CARRIE MARKELLO / CLINICAL ASSOCIATE PROFESSOR, UNIVERSITY OF HOUSTON

ABSTRACT: *In this narrative inquiry example, I share my experiences researching the relationship among three artist-teachers' verbal and written discourse and their visual arts practice. My journey reveals how and why I used narrative inquiry, a methodology relying on emerging and developing stories among participants in a particular setting. Narrative inquiry provided an avenue for me to collect stories reflecting the lives and practices of the three participants, analyze their narratives, and present research findings for each participant. The research focus on artmaking and art talk revealed a tension between the participants' artist and teacher roles. These connections to teaching ranged from minimal to fully-integrated teaching and artmaking. Each artist demonstrated a different relationship with her artmaking and her teaching, placing her in unique locations on the professional landscape in terms of her past, present, and future. Narrative inquiry provided me an able vehicle to understand the artistic and personal experiences, transformations, contexts, and outlooks of the artist-teacher participants in this study.*

As a self-taught artist, teaching became a means to support my artmaking. Increasingly teaching became as important to me as artmaking, leading me to question my role in the hybrid profession of art education and the role of art *in* education. Once standing at the intersection of these issues, I embarked on an arduous, yet rewarding journey in graduate school in art education. My interests in artmaking and education led me to question the connection of verbal and written discourse surrounding personal artmaking (Markello, 2006). Through the transitions I observed in my own artmaking process, education, and teaching experiences, along with pilot study narratives of an artist-teacher (Markello, 2005), I developed questions regarding the relationships among discourse, artmaking, and teaching practices.

In the following pages, I share my experiences researching these questions with three artist-teacher participants[1]. I reveal how and why I used narrative inquiry, a methodology relying on emerging and developing stories among participants in a particular setting. Based on Dewey's (1934) notion of experience, narrative inquiry addresses personal and social interactions in terms of past, present and future experiences in particular contexts (Clandinin & Connelly, 2000).

FINDING A RESEARCH VEHICLE

SARA AND MELANIE: *This description of the connection between research methodology selection and the purpose of a study relates to the discussion about methodologies in Chapter 5. If we think of research as a journey, aligning the methodology with the intent of your study creates a situation where the parts of the study work well together to carry you where you are hoping to go.*

For any long journey an appropriate vehicle is required. There are many methodologies for researchers to choose to carry her/him from initial questions to research findings. The key for a successful journey means finding a methodology that best bears the load of the intent and depth of the research questions. My journey began with typical graduate level courses surveying quantitative and qualitative research methodologies. Guided by Dr. Cheryl Craig, a colleague's research progress using narrative inquiry ignited my interest, well beyond the extent of my coursework. Through my colleague's experiences, I learned how narrative inquiry was applied to people in authentic settings. As I considered the complexity of the artistic process and its intersection with verbal and written language, I began to think that qualitative research questions regarding artist-teachers could be understood through their stories.

With further investigation, I learned how effectively narrative inquiry methodology can acknowledge participants' "personal practical knowledge," (Connelly & Clandinin, 1988, p. 25), which comes from experience. Connelly and Clandinin (1999) drew from Dewey (1938), Polyani (1967), Johnson (1989) and others in order to "understand teachers as knowers: knowers of themselves, of their situations, of children, of subject matter of teaching, of learning" (p. 1). Metaphor is an important link between language and imagery, and a primary focus of my study. Thus, I also embraced narrative inquiry's philosophical ties with Lakoff and Johnson's (1980) embodied metaphors and Dewey's (1934) concepts regarding experiencing images.

My journey began with my initial questioning of the relationship among three artists' verbal and written discourse and their visual arts practice. This question shaped the main inquiry: How do these artists' verbal and written discourse influence and relate to the artmaking process? This central question gave way to five subsidiary questions:

- What transformations or changes in the artists' artistic practice or artistic outlook take place as they negotiate between visual artmaking and discourse?
- How does the context of the artists' life and work influence their practice?
- How do the artists' personal oral and written discourses or reflective practices regarding their artistic process influence their awareness of social issues?
- What impact does an awareness of social issues have on the artist's artistic practice?
- How might narratives of artistic practice and talking about art influence practices in education?

DOCUMENTING THE JOURNEY: GATHERING FIELD TEXTS

Narrative inquiry provided an avenue for me to collect stories reflecting the lives and practices of three artist-teachers: Kelli, Rebecca, and Katie. Kelli, a photographer, taught elementary art before returning to graduate school to pursue an MFA. She currently teaches photography at the college level. Rebecca, a sculptor, teaches art classes for private schools, museums, art centers and non-profit organizations. She does not hold teacher certification. Katie, also a sculptor, earned teacher certification after receiving her MFA. She taught elementary art for several years and currently is a faculty member and gallery director at a community college. Their narratives revealed their past and present thoughts about their artmaking, their teaching and the social contexts of these endeavors.

I know these artist-teachers through my work as an artist and art educator. Therefore my role as a researcher takes on the ethnographic characteristic of participant/observer. Participant observation takes place through immersion in a culture where lengthy exposure "helps the researcher internalize the basic beliefs, fears, hopes, and expectations of the people under study" (Fetterman, 1998, p. 35). As a participant/observer, I was active in the same community of artists as my participants, attending events including art openings, public lectures, and studio visits. In my role as a participant/observer, I needed to be continually reflective. This reflective behavior involved periodically re-evaluating my experiences before and after talking with the artist-teachers and observing the process and progress of their artmaking as the study progressed. As an artist and teacher, my perspective regarding artmaking and teaching influenced my interactions and conversation with the participants. I did not consider my knowledge of artmaking and teaching to be the same as my participants, but I did expect and experience a sense of mutual understanding because of our related experiences.

I selected the three artist-teachers based on evidence of active artmaking and availability. Thus, the three participants comprised a purposeful sample of convenience. The selection was purposeful because I selected them based on their active roles as artists and teachers. Further, I considered it a sample of convenience because the artist-teachers' availability was also part of the selection process (Gall, Gall, & Borg, 2003).

Over a 4-month period during 2006, the three participants shared narratives with me reflecting past, present, and future goals for their artmaking and teaching. These stories, as I interpreted them, in my role as the researcher, comprised the field texts for the study. The tools for constructing field texts included: transcriptions of recorded structured and semi-structured interviews and conversations through telephone calls and face-to-face meetings, email communications, participant sketchbooks, journal writings, and traditional and digital photographs of the artist-teachers' work and studios. New questions about artmaking and teaching arose from the initial set of questions as a natural response to a conversational flow and as a result of my reflecting on the narratives. I asked additional questions to clarify and establish pertinent background information. For example, I might respond to an answer that needed clarification with one of the following questions: Could you tell me more about…? Can you explain what you mean when you say…? I also collected any publications regarding the artists' work, as well as resumes, selected journal and sketchbook documents, and digital photos of artworks in progress and completed artworks. I analyzed archival materials when pertinent to the research questions.

At the initiation of the study, the participants signed a consent form informing them that they could request access to all information gathered. They were also verbally informed that they could request copies of all notes transcripts, and written documents at any time during the study. Only one of artist-teachers requested transcripts during the study. She read her transcripts with the intent to help articulate her professional goals. I gave the artist-teachers copies of the documents once they evolved from field texts into research texts.[2] None of the three artist-teachers questioned the content of the research texts. All received final copies of the research.

REFLECTING ON THE JOURNEY: INTERPRETING FIELD TEXTS

As a researcher, I viewed the interpretation of field texts as a collaborative negotiation between the participants, myself as a researcher, and the art education audience. I perceived the art education audience as a combination of the authors contributing to art education literature in general and the members of my dissertation committee in particular. I read, re-read and analyzed transcribed telephone and face-to-face conversations for pertinent narrative themes related to the research questions. Additionally, I reviewed each artist's story in terms of how she came to her current role as artist, how she viewed herself professionally, and how her discourses in terms of their particular contexts influenced her work. I gleaned this information from the field texts that I color-coded in terms of eight categories pertinent to the study's intent.

The first four categories provided the basic information characterizing each participant within her own personal historical/social/cultural context. These categories included: (1) the participant's educational and professional backgrounds; (2) philosophies, artistic concepts, and artmaking strategies and intentions; (3) teaching experiences, views, and strategies and or influences on artmaking; and (4) descriptions and/or examples of in-progress and/or completed artworks. The fifth category addressed the primary research question: (5) artistic practices influenced through talking, writing, reading, reflective practices, and/or formal or informal critique. Finally, the setting for each artist-teacher, significant events, and social awareness was identified through the following categories: (6) specifics of each participant's social/cultural/political contexts; (7) significant turning points in artmaking and teaching; and (8) the level and or development of social awareness related to their artist roles.

In order to move from the artist-teachers' narratives as field texts into research texts, I rephrased or repeated some questions to clarify and to affirm each participant's responses. I asked the participants directly to clarify their answers during our conversations and in subsequent discussions as needed. Rephrased and repeated questions resulting in different responses also indicated changes in the artist-teachers' contexts and discourses over time. I cross-checked texts with any published materials available in print and online, journal writings, emails, conversations, and artworks. The transition of the field text to the research texts (findings) provided voice for the multiple participants, the researcher, and audience in the research text (Clandinin & Connelly, 1994, 2000).

SNAPSHOTS FROM THE JOURNEY: RESEARCH FINDINGS

The artistic practices of Kelli, Rebecca, and Katie involved a continual back-and-forth action between their oral and written experiences and artmaking experiences. This is similar to Schön's (1983) notion of reflective back talk. Although the exact nature of this back and forth action between the artists and their artmaking and oral/written discourses is unique for each artist, their narratives reveal transcognitive/transformative processes (Sullivan, 2005). In other words, these artists used thinking strategies to conceive and execute their ideas with their chosen materials in an ongoing interchange of ideas throughout their process. This interchange included at least two of the following reflective processes: reading, writing, looking, and talking in conjunction with their artmaking. Each artist's cycle of reflective activity was particular to her. For example, Rebecca did not rely on reading to inform her practice, but Kelli and Katie both did. The back and forth interaction between oral/ written and artmaking experience was embedded in the participants' studio practice. Studio practice also emerged as embodied action, a unified interaction of both mind and body. While qualitatively different than language, such interaction between mind and body provided rich and deep experiences for the construction of knowledge.

The artist-teachers revealed through their knowledge communities (Craig, 1995) their particular relationship to artmaking and oral/written discourse. Despite varying levels of social interactions, none of these artists worked in total isolation. Furthermore, each artist formed knowledge communities with colleagues, friends, and family as safe arenas for sharing ideas. The way in which each artist integrated her knowledge community with her artmaking was particular to her own practice.

The focus on artmaking and art talk revealed a tension between artist and teacher roles. Kelli's, Rebecca's, and Katie's connections to teaching ranged from minimal to fully integrated teaching and artmaking. Each artist demonstrated a different relationship with her artmaking and her teaching, placing her in unique locations on the professional landscape in terms of her past, present, and future.

Kelli honored teaching as a profession and described herself as "born to teach." She nurtured her artmaking and teaching as compatible, but distinctly separate career paths. She recognized teaching as financially and personally rewarding. However, even with these acknowledgements, Kelli believed that if she were able to support herself only through artmaking, she would drop teaching in favor of the sole pursuit of her artistic practice. Through art talk regarding her artwork, Kelli developed a greater awareness of the social impact of her work. After giving a talk about her artwork at a conference, she was questioned by an audience member about her limited discussion regarding her personal connection to her work. This experience compelled Kelli to re-examine the way she talked about her work. In her next presentation, Kelli revealed more of her personal story and motivation for creating the work. The audience response was overwhelmingly positive, resulting in a significant moment in Kelli's career. Kelli's experience and reflection on her artmaking led her to re-evaluate and change her approach to presenting her work. Kelli's presentation change brought her to a new realization; she became aware that her artwork was "bigger" than she was. As a result of this event, Kelli learned that her work could evoke social awareness in others.

Rebecca's decisions were driven by her intense desire to be recognized in the artworld. Consequently, Rebecca's oral and written discourse focused primarily on her path to achieve this goal. Teaching rarely became part of the conversation, unless I specifically asked. As the only uncertified teacher in this study, Rebecca held teaching in high regard, yet was not interested in pursuing certification or a full time teaching job. However, Rebecca did seek teaching opportunities through museums and art centers to supplement her income. She viewed teaching opportunities as a way to give back to the community.

For Katie, teaching emerged as an integrated part of her artmaking discourse. Katie's conversations with me were embedded with not only artmaking but also teaching, viewing both as mutually compatible professions. She wove artmaking and teaching into the fabric of her life. From

Katie's point of view, one career pursuit is not privileged over the other; instead both nurture and mutually benefit the other. Considering art education as a hybrid term, Katie's stories become exemplars for the integration of both professions.

NARRATIVE INQUIRY PROCESS

As an art educator, learning about the artists' weaving of their artistic processes into their life and work through narrative inquiry was both intriguing and inspiring. The realization that narrative inquiry held potential for each artist to gain from the research process was also rewarding. For example, Kelli mentioned at one point during our weekly conversations how our talking helped her organize her thoughts about her work, better preparing her for upcoming lectures. At another time, Rebecca requested to review her transcripts in order to glean some of her own quotes for a website she was constructing. After spending some time going through the transcripts, she mused that she wished that the story she told me continued, so she could read what happened next. We laughed at the irony of her remark because indeed real life had continued and she did know what happened next. However, that next period of her life was recorded only in her memory not in our field texts.

Rebecca's comment emphasized an important aspect of this study. Talking about present artmaking experiences, projecting future goals and reflecting on talking, reading, writing, and artmaking were valuable and important endeavors for fueling and re-fueling each artist's artistic practice. The act of looking at present experiences, future goals and past actions, events, and relationships allows for gaining understanding of the thoughts, decisions, and experiences surrounding them. The opportunity to access these personal thoughts and endeavors within the three-dimensional inquiry space (Clandinin & Connelly, 2000) constructed by the past, present, and future sequences of time provides an opportunity to view oneself from a different perspective. A new viewpoint of experienced events offered a kind of distance or hindsight that allowed for fresh insights important to present and future productive artmaking.

Professions of practice such as teaching and artmaking can be described as existing in the "swampy lowland" (Schön, 1983 p. 42), an unstable and messy place existing well below loftier practices that embrace technical rigor over messy human issues. As I considered my questions about artmaking, discourse and teaching, I viewed narrative inquiry as a vehicle capable of providing the best ride for my journey exploring complex experiences of the artist-teachers. Narrative inquiry acknowledges the messiness of everyday living, views the interaction of researcher and participants in a holistic manner, and allows for fluid interpretations. Narrative inquiry provided me a vehicle to understand the artistic and personal experiences, transformations, contexts, and outlooks of the artist-teacher participants in this study.

REFERENCES

Clandinin, D. J., & Connelly, F. M. (1994). Personal experience methods. In N. K. Denzin & Y. S. Guba (Eds.), *Handbook of qualitative research* (pp. 413-427). Thousand Oaks, CA: Sage.

Clandinin, D. J., & Connelly, F. M. (2000). *Narrative inquiry: Experience and story in qualitative research.* San Francisco, CA: Jossey-Bass.

Connelly, F. M., & Clandinin, D. J. (1988). *Teachers as curriculum planners.* New York, NY: Teachers College Press.

Connelly, F. M., & Clandinin, D. J. (Eds.) (1999). *Shaping a professional identity.* New York, NY: Teachers College Press.

Craig, C. J. (1995). Safe places on the professional knowledge landscape: Knowledge communities. In D. J. Clandinin & F. M. Connelly (Eds.), *Teachers' professional knowledge landscapes* (pp. 137-141). New York, NY: Teachers College Press.

Dewey, J. (1934). *Art as experience.* New York, NY: Berkley.

Dewey, J. (1938). *Experience and education.* New York, NY: Collier Books.

Fetterman, D. M. (1998). *Ethnography* (2nd ed. Vol. 17). Thousand Oaks, CA: Sage.

Gall, M. D., Gall, J. P., & Borg, W. R. (2003). *Educational research: An introduction.* Boston, MA: Allyn and Bacon.

Johnson, M. (1989). Embodied knowledge. *Curriculum Inquiry, 19*(4), 361-377.

Lakoff, G., & Johnson, M. (1980). *Metaphors we live by.* Chicago, IL: The University of Chicago Press.

Markello, C. G. (2005). *Composing an image: A look through a photographer's lens at the relationship between written and verbal discourse and the art making/viewing process.* Unpublished manuscript, University of Houston, TX.

Markello, C. G. (2006). *Artist narratives: Artmaking and teaching discourses on the professional landscape* (Unpublished doctoral dissertation). University of Houston, TX.

Polyani, M. (1967). *The tacit dimension.* New York, NY: Doubleday.

Schön, D. A. (1983). *The reflective practitioner.* New York, NY: Basic.

Sullivan, G. (2005). *Art practice as research.* Thousand Oaks, CA: Sage.

ENDNOTES

1 The three artist-teacher participants are also referred to as *artist-teachers* or *participants.*

2 Clandinin and Connelly (2000) refer to research texts as a richly textured "narrative soup" (p.155) where all the bits and pieces of the field texts generated by the people, places, and things situated in time and place are mixed together.

CARRIE MARKELLO is Clinical Associate Professor at the University of Houston where she teaches art education classes to preservice generalist teachers and art educators. She is an active member of the Houston art community and founding member of GRASSROOTS: Art in Action, a nonprofit organization encouraging connections between artists and art educators. In addition to her teaching, Markello creates mixed media artworks and holds an extensive exhibition history. Markello's artmaking, teaching, and community involvement foster her research interests. Her primary interest is in artmaking as a way of knowing. Markello's research interests also include historical perspectives and current practices for teacher education and professional development in art education.

30 / The Narrative and the Normative: Pedagogy in the Balance

PAMELA KRAKOWSKI / ART TEACHER, FALK LABORATORY SCHOOL, UNIVERSITY OF PITTSBURGH

ABSTRACT: *This chapter is an exemplar of how I used narrative inquiry as a research method to study my pedagogy. Through collecting, analyzing, and interpreting narrative data of pedagogical moments in my early childhood art classes, I came to see two overarching concepts: the* **narrative** *and the* **normative.** *The narrative referred to the is—what is happening in the children's lives at the moment, and the normative referred to the* **ought—***what I thought* **ought** *to be happening in the classroom. They existed in a dynamic tension and required a delicate balancing act. I represented the results of my study through the metaphor of a mobile. Balancing the children's narrative with my normative agenda required sensibilities similar to an artist relying on her aesthetic sensibilities to balance the shapes of a mobile. To illustrate this, I selected an excerpt from a written portrayal in which I explored the tension between the children's interest in popular culture and my adult notion of appropriate subject matter, examining what it meant to be curious, attuned, and open to children's interests. The implications of my study became the lessons learned in cultivating sensibilities such as these.*

For my graduate research I used a method of narrative inquiry to study my pedagogy within the context of my early childhood art classes (Krakowski, 2004, 2006). Five research questions framed the study: (1) Why is the concept of narrative pedagogy important for early childhood art education? (2) How did I engage in "narrative inquiry" to gain insight into the meanings of narrative pedagogy? (3) What is the portrayal of my narrative pedagogy? (4) What insights did I derive from my portrayal? (5) What are the implications of these insights for other early childhood art educators?

THEORETICAL GROUNDINGS

In conceptualizing my version of narrative inquiry I drew from Connelly and Clandinin (1988, 1990) on teachers' personal practical knowledge, Bruner (1985, 1986) on narrative as a way of knowing, Barone and Eisner (1997) on aesthetic forms of representation, and McMahon (1993, 2006), Richards (1996), and Piantanida and Garman (1999, 2009) on the use of narrative to study one's pedagogy. I clearly delineated between narrative pedagogy as the *phenomenon* under study, and narrative inquiry, the *methodology* used to study that phenomenon. My procedures for engaging in narrative inquiry involved: (1) collecting narrative data of significant classroom events (Hankins, 2003; van Manen, 1991), (2) analyzing and interpreting the data through recollective, introspective, and conceptual reflection (Piantanida & Garman, 1999, 2009), and (3) representing the results of the study through the metaphor of a mobile (Eisner, 1979; Greene, 1997; Stinson, 1991).

DESIGN OF THE STUDY

Over the course of a school year, I kept a teaching journal in which I systematically documented classroom situations that invited me to ask, "Did I do the right thing?"—what van Manen (1991) refers to as "pedagogical moments" (p. 40). Engaging in a storied form of writing (Hankins, 2003; Paley, 1990), I captured the particulars of these moments, including setting, dialogue, and conflict, and attended to the "qualities of experience" (Eisner, 1979, p. 199).

For every account I wrote reflections—"recollections, introspective musings, and evolving insights" (Piantanida & Garman, 2009, p. 64)—an essential process for reconstructing meaning from experience (Dewey, 1916). As I regularly revisited my journal and critiqued my reflections, I came to see two overarching concepts: the narrative and the normative. The narrative referred to the "is"—what is happening in the children's lives at the moment. It included the children's interests, stories, experiences, emotional concerns, ways of coming to know, and ways of being in the world. The normative referred to the "ought"—what I thought ought to be happening in the classroom. It represented my notion of curriculum, my aims, objectives, specific lesson plans, expectations, and values. It stood for what I believed was worth teaching (May, 1995; Schubert, 1986). As I continued to journal, this narrative-normative lens guided my interpretation of my storied events.

Eventually I came to conceptualize narrative pedagogy as a pedagogy that listened to the children's narrative, and welcomed the narrative into the teaching-learning space. Listening to the narrative—what I called responding in a narrative frame of mind—required certain qualities or sensibilities. According to van Manen (1991), these pedagogical sensibilities could not be learned as behavioral principles or techniques; they were embodied knowledge, not a repertoire of teaching methods. Embodied knowledge—a teacher's intuitive, tacit, somatic knowing—manifested itself in such sensibilities as being sensitive to children's emotional concerns and knowing when to respond, being present to the atmosphere of a classroom and knowing when to be flexible, or being attentive to students' interests and knowing when to improvise.

I represented the results of my study through the metaphor of balancing a mobile. I viewed the narrative and normative elements in my art classroom as the shapes of a mobile gently suspended in a state of tension. Balancing the children's narrative with my normative agenda required embodied sensibilities, similar to an artist relying on her sensibilities of intuition, an embodied understanding of materials, a feeling for coherence, a rightness of fit (Eisner, 2002).

Guided by the metaphor of balance, I represented my understandings of the relationship between the narrative and the normative through crafting written portrayals. Piantanida and Garman (1999) state that a portrayal creates "a 'picture' that allows others to experience vicariously the phenomenon under study" within a particular context (p. 133). It brings the reader to the classroom. A descriptive portrayal also makes visible the features that the researcher wants to examine through interpretation.

In my larger project, crafted five separate art classroom portrayals: "Art Classroom as Studio," "Art Classroom as Haven," "Art Classroom as Stage," "Art Classroom as Museum Gallery," and "Art Classroom as Laboratory." I arrived at these groupings after many readings of my journal, highlighting every pedagogical moment that reflected the narrative, normative or some tension between the two, and grouping together similar narrative-normative tensions. Eventually I named these groupings according to what happened in the teaching-learning space of my art classroom. For example, when I listened to and welcomed the children's emotional concerns, the art classroom became a haven. Or when I listened to and welcomed the children's interest in weaving together play, story and art making, the art classroom became a stage.

For each portrayal I wrote two vignettes where I explored the tension between the narrative and normative in that art classroom context, attending to a pedagogical moment. Following each vignette I wrote reflections in which I explored the sensibilities of a narrative frame of mind, connecting my musings to theoretical discourses. I concluded each art classroom portrayal with "Balancing Lessons."

AN EXCERPT FROM THE PORTRAYAL OF "ART CLASSROOM AS STUDIO"

In the portrayal of "Art Classroom as Studio," listening to the narrative meant listening to and respecting the children's choice of subject matter. In one of the vignettes, Whose Art Is It Anyway?, I explored the tension between the children's interest in Pokemon and my adult notion of what subject matter I thought was appropriate for "in class" art projects. I narrated:

It was Michael who first introduced me to Pokemon. His class had been creating puppets of their pets, and now they were designing puppet stages. I noticed that Michael had drawn an elaborate stage for his young age of eight years. He had spent hours carefully rendering columns, an auditorium, curtains, audience seating, ticket counters, dressing rooms, and refreshment stands. I looked forward to seeing how his drawing would evolve during the next class.

When Michael's class came to art the following week, he and a group of boys asked to go outside into the hallway to finish their stages. I believed in collaboration and encouraged them to go ahead. When I went out later to check on their progress, I found them engaged in an animated conversation about their images. I walked over to see why they were so excited. I was horrified. Michael had drawn hundreds of strange, cartoon-like characters all over the front of his beautifully rendered stage. I looked at the other boys' drawings. They, too, had covered their stages with odd-looking cartoon characters. From my not-so-slightly-biased adult aesthetic viewpoint of what children's art should look like, I felt that they had ruined their stages.

"Michael, what are you drawing?" I asked incredulously, unable to conceal my disappointment.

"Oh, we're drawing Pokemon." He then proceeded to tell me about the different characters. He returned to his drawing, totally engaged in his work, oblivious to my disappointment. All of the boys admired Michael's stage. I sensed his pride as the boys asked him to show them how to draw their favorite Pokemon character…

The vignette continues with leaving the boys to draw their Pokemon imagery and choosing to say nothing. However, for the next art project I made sure that I announced at the beginning, "No Pokemon!" Although some children expressed disappointment, I noticed that when they began to illustrate their puppet biographies, they became engaged and excited; no child was at a loss for ideas. I felt a twinge of guilt, however, and questioned if I had done the right thing by censuring Pokemon.

Following the vignette, I reflected on what sensibilities were present or lacking. In the situation with Michael and his friends I saw how much I disliked the Pokemon aesthetic and what little desire I had in understanding what it meant to the children. According to Dewey (1934), I lacked the curiosity that would move me to inquire. Van Manen (1991) reminded me that children need to be listened to by adults without criticism. Teachers need to possess a sensibility he refers to as *nonjudgmental understanding*. He writes: "A nonjudgmental understanding involves a listening that is receptive, open, sympathetic, authentic, and facilitative" (p. 83). In fact, my question to Michael—"What are you doing?"—and my tone of voice may have communicated a judgment on his drawing. Listening to children, Carlina Rinaldi (2001) writes, "requires a deep awareness and at the same time a suspension of our judgments and above all our prejudices; it requires an openness to change" (p. 81). In understanding children and their point of view, William Ayers (1993) reminded me that teachers need to be one part detective, one part researcher, and one part world class puzzle master. I needed to "sift the clues children leave, follow the leads, and diligently uncover the facts in order to fill out and make a credible story of their growth and development" (p. 33). I also realized, as Maxine Greene (1995) states, that I needed to take "a fresh look at the taken for granted" (p. 100), and examine—even challenge—my assumptions. I then immersed myself in contemporary discourses on the image of the child (Dahlberg, Moss, & Pence, 1999), child art (Thompson, 2003), and popular culture (Giroux & Simon, 1989; Kincheloe, Slattery, & Steinberg, 2000) and examined how my developmental and cultural assumptions about children and their art making guided my practice.

IMPLICATIONS OF THE STUDY

In the final chapter of my study, I explicated the aesthetic dimension of the sensibilities of a narrative frame of mind, using the lenses of aesthetic knowing, the art of teaching, the teacher-as-artist, and the art of Alexander Calder (Barrell, 1991; Eisner, 2002; Lipman, 1976; Sullivan, 2000; Zurmuehlen, 1986). I then concluded with implications for art teaching derived from cultivating these sensibilities. I shared four "lessons learned": (1) being willing to honestly examine one's shadows, fears and assumptions as well as one's strengths and potentials (Palmer, 1998); (2) engaging in thoughtful reflection with self and other teachers through sharing classroom stories of struggles, doubts, mistakes, and successes (van Manen, 1994); (3) teaching in close collaboration with other teachers whereby one can internalize new ways of being with children (van Manen, 1991); and (4) making listening to children an impassioned focus of one's teaching and research (Cadwell, 1997; Matthews, 1994; Paley, 1986, 1990; Schultz, 2003).

REFERENCES

Ayers, W. (1993). *To teach: The journey of a teacher*. New York, NY: Teachers College Press.

Barrell, B. (1991). Classroom artistry. *The Educational Forum, 55*(4), 333-342.

Barone, T., & Eisner, E. (1997). Arts-based educational research. In R. M. Jaeger (Ed.), *Complementary methods for research in education* (pp. 71-98). Washington, DC: American Education Research Association.

Bruner, J. (1985). Narrative and paradigmatic modes of thought. In E. Eisner (Ed.), *Learning and teaching the ways of knowing: Part II 84th NSSE yearbook* (pp. 97-115). Chicago, IL: University of Chicago Press.

Bruner, J. (1986). *Actual minds, possible worlds*. Cambridge, MA: Harvard University Press.

Cadwell, L. B. (1997). *Bringing Reggio Emilia home: An innovative approach to early childhood education*. New York, NY: Teachers College Press.

Connelly, F. M., & Clandinin, D. J. (1988). *Teachers as curriculum planners: Narratives of experience*. New York, NY: Teachers College Press.

Connelly, F. M., & Clandinin, D. J. (1990). Stories of experience and narrative inquiry. *Educational Researcher, 19*(5), 2-14.

Dahlberg, G., Moss, P., & Pence, A. (1999). *Beyond quality in early childhood education and care: Postmodern perspectives*. Philadelphia, PA: Falmer Press.

Dewey, J. (1916). *Democracy and education*. New York, NY: Macmillan.

Dewey, J. (1934). *Art as experience*. New York, NY: Putnam.

Eisner, E. (1979). *The educational imagination*. New York, NY: Macmillan.

Eisner, E. (2002). What can education learn from the arts about the practice of education? *Journal of Curriculum and Supervision, 18*(1), 4-16.

Giroux, H. A., & Simon, R. I. (Eds.). (1989). *Popular culture, schooling, and everyday life*. Granby, MA: Bergin & Garvey.

Greene, M. (1995). *Releasing the imagination: Essays on education, the arts, and social change*. San Francisco, CA: Jossey-Bass.

Greene, M. (1997). Metaphors and multiples: Representation, the arts, and history. *Phi Delta Kappan, 78*(5), 387-394.

Hankins, K. H. (2003). *Teaching through the storm: A journey of hope*. New York, NY: Teachers College Press.

Krakowski, P.G. (2004). *Balancing the narrative and the normative: Pedagogical implications for early childhood art education*. UMI ProQuest Digital Dissertation #ATT 3139692.

Krakowski, P. G. (2006). A search for balance: Representing a narrative pedagogy. In N.B. Garman & M. Piantanida (Eds.), *The authority to imagine: The struggle toward representation in dissertation writing* (pp. 67-80). New York, NY: Peter Lang.

Kincheloe, J. L., Slattery, P., & Steinberg, S. (2000). *Contextualizing teaching*. New York, NY: Addison Wesley Longman.

Lipman, J. (1976). *Calder's universe*. Philadelphia, PA: Running Press.

Matthews, G. B. (1994). *The philosophy of childhood*. Cambridge, MA: Harvard University Press.

May, W. T. (1995). Teachers as curriculum developers. In R. W. Neperud (Ed.), *Context, content, and community in art education: Beyond postmodernism* (pp. 53-86). New York, NY: Teachers College Press.

McMahon, P. (1993). *A narrative study of three levels of reflection in a college composition class: Teacher journal, student portfolios, teacher-student discourse*. UMI ProQuest Digital Dissertation #ATT 9329582.

McMahon, P. (2006). Narrative yearnings: Reflecting in time through the art of fictive story. In N. B. Garman & M. Piantanida (Eds.), *The authority to imagine: The struggle toward representation in dissertation writing* (pp.183-199). New York, NY: Peter Lang.

Paley, V. G. (1986). On listening to what children say. *Harvard Educational Review, 56*(2), 122-131.

Paley, V. (1990). *The boy who would be a helicopter: The uses of storytelling in the classroom*. Cambridge, MA: Harvard University Press.

Palmer, P. J. (1998). *The courage to teach*. San Francisco, CA: Jossey-Bass.

Piantanida, M., & Garman, N. B. (1999). *The qualitative dissertation: A guide for students and faculty*. Thousand Oaks, CA: Corwin Press.

Piantanida, M., & Garman, N. B. (2009). *The qualitative dissertation: A guide for students and faculty* (2nd ed.) Thousand Oaks, CA: Corwin Press.

Richards, L. A. (1996). *Pictures in our minds: A narrative study of the incorporation of creative dramatics pedagogy in elementary classroom content areas.* UMI ProQuest Digital Dissertaton #ATT 9637875.

Rinaldi, C. (2001). Documentation and assessment: What is the relationship? In C. Guidici, M. Krechevsky & C. Rinaldi (Eds.), *Making learning visible: Children as individual and group learners* (pp. 78-89). Reggio Emilia, Italy: Reggio Children.

Schubert, W. (1986). *Curriculum: Perspective, paradigm, and possibility.* New York, NY: Macmillan.

Schultz, K. (2003). *Listening: A framework for teaching across differences.* New York, NY: Teachers College Press.

Stinson, S. W. (1991). Dance as curriculum, curriculum as dance. In G. Willis & W. H. Schubert (Eds.), *Reflections from the heart of educational inquiry: Understanding curriculum and teaching through the arts* (pp. 190-196). Albany: State University of New York Press.

Sullivan, A. (2000). Notes from a marine biologist's daughter: On the art and science of attention. *Harvard Educational Review, 70*(2), 211-227.

Thompson, C. M. (2003). Kinderculture in the art classroom: Early childhood art and the mediation of culture. *Studies in Art Education, 44*(2), 135-146.

van Manen, M. (1991). *The tact of teaching: The meaning of pedagogical thoughtfulness.* Albany, NY: State University of New York Press.

van Manen, M. (1994). *Pedagogy, virtue and narrative identity in teaching.* Albany, NY: State University of New York Press.

Zurmuehlen, M. J. (1986). Reflecting on the ordinary: Interpretation as transformation of experiences. *Art Education, 39*(6), 33-36.

PAMELA KRAKOWSKI is the art teacher at the Falk Laboratory School, University of Pittsburgh. She has also taught part-time in the Children's Studio at the Carnegie Museum of Art for the past 25 years. Her research interests include how to create meaningful art experiences for young children and their families in museum settings, how to deepen children's emotional connections to the natural environment through aesthetic ways of knowing, and how to support young children in making their thinking visible through aesthetic forms of representation. She has been exploring the Reggio Emilia approach to early childhood education for the past 15 years and works closely with her school's kindergarten teachers in creating classroom studio environments that cultivate children's coming to know through the arts. Her most passionate interest as a teacher-researcher is listening to and observing children's natural interests in play and exploring the relationship between their play and artmaking.

31 / Re-Searching Alternate Routes/Roots: Art Teachers Reconstructing Practice and Identity Through Autobiographical Inquiry

NADINE M. KALIN / ASSISTANT PROFESSOR OF ART EDUCATION, UNIVERSITY OF NORTH TEXAS

ABSTRACT: *This methodological description chapter outlines the processes and parameters of autobiographical inquiry, a form of narrative research and self-study that invites you to explore how you have arrived at your current destination. Suggestions for research questions, data collection, analysis, and example autobiographies written by art educators are also shared. If you were to survey the antecedents of your priorities as an art teacher, you may find a confluence of your past imprinted on and entangled within your present. As Carl Leggo (2008) states, "Everybody lives autobiographically, all the time," (p. 9) and yet, "many of us do live without the privilege of telling our stories, or the privilege of being heard" (p. 10). Autobiographical inquiry aims to increase understanding of experience through a dialectic relationship among past, present, and future actions. If teaching itself is an "autobiographical act" (Cole & Knowles, 2000, p. 22), then autobiography may provide an entry point to engage in our lived experiences and complex meaning-making as art educators. As we tell our stories and grow in autobiographical consciousness, we may move toward and work through past and present difficulties within our teacher/learner selves that make possible alternative routes for our future practices and perceptions as art educators.*

AUTOBIOGRAPHICAL JOURNEYS

While autobiography has been around since antiquity, it has evolved from a form of simple documentation of life events, to confessional, to celebratory chronicle, toward an inquiring into the "extraordinary in the ordinary" (Leggo, 2008, p. 92). Autobiographical inquiry aims to increase understanding of experience through a dialectic relationship among past, present, and future actions. By revisiting the past from the perspectives of the present we can become more aware of how we have been socially and historically constructed by education, media, memory, discourses, practices, institutions, ideologies, and power relations. For Diamond (1999) autobiography provides "ways for teachers to imagine and represent ever-changing combinations of their present, past, and possible selves, including the teacher "'I am,' 'fear to be,' and 'hope to become'" (p. 191). Autobiographical inquiry requires us to attend to our processes of becoming through texts including writing and the creation of art. As we retrace the roots, we can begin to recognize, unravel, and revise limited ways of seeing and being in the world. Autobiographical inquiry opens us up to the ways we are formed and transformed, in turn helping us to better attend to and empower those in our care (such as students) that are also in the process of self-construction.

Autobiography is a form of the narrative genre of writing. Within this chapter, autobiographical inquiry refers to the methodology of autobiography. As a type of qualitative research, narrative inquiry in education attempts to increase understanding of issues related to teaching and learning through the collection, retelling, and interpretation of individual and collective stories. These stories can take many forms within the typology of narrative approaches including biography and autobiography. What all narratives have in common is a reliance on memory, which is viewed as always partial and selective instead of a resurrection of the one, true past. Like memory, narrative is interpretive, less a reproduction and more a reconstruction. While biography is a narrative record of the events that have shaped an individual's life researched and written by the author/researcher, autobiography is "the first-person interpretive reconstruction of either a life in its entirety or significant portion of it" (Freeman, 2008, pp. 45-46). Both biography and autobiography aim to go beyond the mere recounting of events in a search for greater understanding from previous and current vantage points as well as from the private and the social.

Autobiography is one path to increased self-understanding through the reconstruction and revisiting of experience, which, in turn, increases one's ability to direct the course of subsequent action and understanding. While this seems a worthwhile endeavor for the author, what value does an autobiography hold for readers? As others read and identify with another's story, narrative threads may comingle between reader and author as one gets the sense that our lives are embedded in the lives of others and that we cannot easily disentangle our narrative threads. We can detect echoes in each other's stories as we revisit our shared social, cultural, and historical journeys. Put another way, as a form of narrative research, autobiography strives to understand rather than control or generalize across individuals. The complexity of an individual's storied experience can provide readers with a deeper understanding of the human condition.

LOOKING BACKWARD TO MOVE AHEAD

Residues from the past underpin and define our actions as art educators. In the practice of teaching art we reveal our presuppositions, values, and, undeniably, our histories. Your favorite lesson, pedagogical approach, and chosen artistic exemplars reflect how you conceptualize your art teaching practices and orient yourself as an art teacher through your journey as student and teacher of art. The past shows up in our curricular plans, images we choose to display, the ordering of materials, and assessment criteria. Indeed, both Gude (2007) and Atkinson (2006) maintain that the teaching of art in schools today is a hybrid of historical approaches (some dating back centuries) largely insulated from contemporary practices and priorities found in the art world. A dependence on already established paths restricts possible courses of action, setting up a recurring cycle, and continuity with the past in art curriculum that can impede your potential for self-reform. Coming to a more self-conscious understanding of how we frame the present through an enduring past has the potential to reconstruct our continuity with the past. If you were to survey the antecedents of your priorities as an art teacher, you may find a confluence of your past imprinted on and entangled within your present. Autobiographical inquiry allows for a contextualizing (Gude, 2000) of not only the how and what of your art teaching, but likely the why behind your practices. This individual consciousness, or coming to understand ourselves as historical beings, helps us to better reflect on how the present, future, and past inform one another.

BLAZING TRAILS: LEARNING FROM OTHERS WHO HAVE GONE BEFORE

Autobiographies of the famous are abundantly available. They tell of triumph and chronicle life events. In art education, autobiographies are often shared by our own celebrities in the form of lectures and acceptance speeches. Raunft (2001) published a collection of autobiographical lectures of 28 prominent art educators culled from the Miami University in Oxford series of autobiographical lectures. John Michael established this series in 1972 aiming "to preserve the life histories and narratives of art educators, perceived as historical documents and records that would not only reveal personal experience, but which also could point to certain actions that may affect art education theory, practice and leadership" (Raunft, 2001, p. vii). These lectures honoring our field's leaders are typical

of autobiographies celebrating a life's chronology in first person. They are alluring because they are stories of real people, rooted in actual experience, and specific contexts. Nevertheless, increasingly autobiography is being explored by art educators for reasons other than career celebration (see list of examples at the end of this chapter). Personal accounts in research journals of grief and disease, family albums and class warfare are contextualized within societal, political, artistic, and disciplinary movements that aim to not only make powerful connections with their readers, but also provide our field with alternative ways of conceptualizing art education.

> **SARA AND MELANIE:** *Throughout the remainder of this chapter, Kalin offers the reader many questions for thinking about your practice leading you to your current professional position. While reading this chapter, we recommend writing out reflective answers to these questions as a way to strengthen your understanding of autobiography. Thinking about how personal answers to questions have meaning can be the beginning of a narrative research process.*

FINDING PASSAGE: GENERATING RESEARCH QUESTIONS

Autobiographical inquiry must strive to reach beyond the purely personal by asking questions of compelling significance that will engage readers from the field of art education. The research questions that drive autobiographical inquiries in art education should bridge routes between the personal and the professional as well as the historical and the social. Key questions (adapted from Grumet, 1981) within this methodology might include: How does my present influence my understanding of the past? How does my past blind me to the present? How does the past both limit and enable the future? You can start by examining your daily world and confronting "not only what [you] see but also *why [you] see what [you] see*" (Kincheloe, 2005, p. 161, italics from original). What do your pedagogical practices ignore, omit, or valorize? What are the historical and personal roots of your current priorities? While research questions associated with this form of qualitative inquiry can lead your research, your research activities may raise additional questions along the way that further your inquiry and tighten your focus.

My autobiographical work has often emerged from points of frustration within my art teaching at the K-12 and higher education contexts. Why didn't that art lesson work as I had predicted? What are the disconnections between my expectations and the actual results of an art activity? Why don't some art educators feel comfortable using contemporary art in their teaching? How can I get through all of this content while facilitating a student-centered pedagogy? These were questions I repeatedly asked of myself that acted as starting points for autobiographical inquiry into the roots of my priorities and practices. In each of these instances I turned the question toward myself. How are my methods, content, values, and aesthetic judgments constructed by my earlier educational experiences? What are the bases of my priorities? Where, when, and how did I learn to think and act this way? Contextualizing my own art education within larger discourses and movements within art education inevitably brings about a greater historical and autobiographical consciousness about the roots of current values, while concurrently providing openings for routes forward. How are these approaches not working for me today? What remnants of my past do I no longer believe and want to re-imagine?

SOUVENIRS AND MARKERS ALONG THE WAY: DATA COLLECTION

Data collection, like the generation of questions, involves a re-searching of the past within the present and the personal within the social along your life's journey. Your experiences leave some sort of trace of that activity that you need to access, linger over, and confirm. Pertinent material culture artifacts and memories are carriers of story and markers of time and place. Photographs, art works, textbooks, yearbooks, and report cards can trigger thoughts and connections that assist in the re-telling and interpreting of your autobiography.

Norum (2008) maintains, "Artifacts become data through the questions posed about them and the meanings assigned to them by the researcher" (p. 23). In the analysis of the collected items we "are asking the data to tell us something. An artifact has a story to tell about the person who made it, how it was used, who used it, and the beliefs and values associated with it" (Norum, 2008, p. 23). As you consider artifacts, you are actively moving between the past and present, looking for connections and disconnections from where you have been in relation to the artifact's context and place in history and where you are now. What was happening in society, in education, in a specific location during the use and creation of the artifact? How is it used, valued, or ignored today?

Going beyond your own memories to encompass multiple sources and artifacts helps to minimize the bias of your own memory, thereby adding to the rigor and credibility of your data collection and analysis—it is not simply your account, your interpretation, your history. Solicit the memories of others that shared your experiences through interviews, email correspondence, or conversation. (Be sure to request permission when soliciting and collecting these stories. Transcribe interviews and provide participants with copies to undergo member checks of any of their collected and analyzed data.) Additionally, shared incidents that occurred within particular contexts may be revisited virtually, through memory, physically, and/or recreated through research. Returning to the sites of your history can also reconfigure and ignite memories while confronting how our environment impacts our understanding. Collect any of these data through an active searching of your own archives, public collections, and those of others. Track the meaning these items, places, and events hold for you through

reflective writing and the creation of related narratives. You may wish to keep a journal handy as looking back may mobilize the present in new, possibly unexpected ways.

MAPPING THE JOURNEY: DATA ANALYSIS

Data interpretation naturally occurs throughout the data collection process, but there are some key dispositions you should be aware of as you sift, group, contextualize, and critically reflect on your collected data. In autobiographical inquiry, the collection and writing up of personal memories do not become research until they are "connected through evidence and analysis to the issues and troubles of a time and place" (Bullough & Pinnegar, 2001, p. 15). This seeking of how our life stories are related to "the context and ethos of a time" (Bullough & Pinnegar, 2001, p. 15) marks the transition from solipsism, a theory that all we can ever know is the self, or isolated confessional, toward autobiographical research in dialogue with the social, historical, and cultural discourses and practices that influenced and permitted your journey. There needs to be a balance between the personal and the social/historical in the data collection (from self and other) and writing up of the research, along with how these are analyzed and laid out within the final autobiography. Here again, as you review your past within your present as a learner and teacher of art, you are contextualizing what influences—people, places, art education approaches, curriculum, artistic movements, theories, values, and students, for example—have shaped your priorities and practices.

For example, if there is an aspect in your art teaching you wish to reflect on autobiographically, such as your experiences with drawing, you might collect personal drawings from your own education, locate artists or artworks that inspired you, consider how you were taught to draw, interview your drawing teachers, re-draw something from your memory like an art classroom, draw in a way you used to, find books about drawing from specific periods of your life, ask classmates and family about their memories of your drawing, use old tools (like the oversized, red pencil I had to draw with in elementary school), contrast the drawing curriculum you implement today with the activities you completed as a student, or examine lessons you have taught in the past and interrogate why you discarded those approaches. These items and the groupings of these items will likely trigger memories and questions, which may start your writing of autobiographical narratives. I have found a chronological or thematic mapping of personal artifacts, learning contexts, pivotal moments, and influential people particularly helpful in making connections, recalling events, providing context, and spurring self and other-questioning.

Again in my work, I have been inspired by my own frustrations as an art educator/researcher. As Fowler (2006) quoting Pinar (1981, p. 173) states, "Wherever difficulty exists, there is a story behind it, often 'whole, bright, and deep with understanding'" (p. 15). The difficulties of art teaching and learning are many and these may prove a fertile starting point for your own autobiographical inquiry into the disconnects of what we think we know, based on prior education and experience, and what is yet to be understood in all its complexity. Grumet (1988) encourages us to seek out the gaps, contradictions, leaks, and explosions within our histories and presents as generative places for reinterpreting our historical selves and reimagining our futures. While you revisit critical incidences in your life, honestly search for omissions, prejudices, difficulties, and the underside of the story or that which is not stated. What are the limits of your art education/learning? What resides outside of those parameters? How did you, the field, the institutions of learning, and social/historical norms establish those parameters?

The autobiography cannot contain all the details of one's remembered experience—"it is censored with a purpose that must not be self-serving" (Bullough & Pinnegar, 2001, p. 18). As you select, arrange, and weave pieces together while interpreting data for themes, patterns, and significance, ask yourself why am I telling this story? Why is it important beyond self-documentation? Why do I want others to hear it? Why is it of value to art education?

I advise you to keep notes related to how you are analyzing and constructing your autobiographical narratives. What triggered a memory? How did you verify or triangulate your story? How have you contextualized your memories within art education? Some (i.e., Connelly & Clandinin, 1990; Feldman, 2003) recommend ending an autobiography with a reflective methods chapter or appendix that reconstructs the processes of inquiry—revealing how you created your autobiography, what counted as data, how you collected and analyzed your data, how you attempted to verify your analysis of events, memories, documents, and artifacts.

WRITING THROUGH THE REARVIEW MIRROR

Autobiographical inquiry is more than a story of one's accomplishments or struggles; a crucial element is the analysis of the life events. Within autobiographical inquiry, through reflecting on and writing up accounts of your experience, you are also listening for nuanced complexities, contradictions, limits, and unresolved tensions of art teaching and learning. What were/are you ignoring? What were/are the limits of your understanding? What have you learned as a teacher-in-training that did not transfer easily in practice? Either in the writing up of experience or in subsequent readings of your writing, you are partaking in a "dialectic of self-questioning" (Bullough & Pinnegar, 2001, p. 19).

If you are simply writing up your success stories, you are immersed in what Kincheloe (2005) refers to as a "lapse into a narcissistic enterprise" (p. 156). You need to step back and undertake some further interpretation of events in dialogue with the social, cultural, historical, gendered, institutional, and educational discourses that have influenced your identities, views, habits, choices, and practices through

questioning your memories. What has been left unresolved, glossed over, or now understood differently when re-viewed through contemporary lenses? What does the field of art education value today and how is that at odds with your previous and current practices as an art educator and learner? For me, this remembering, writing, interpreting, reflecting, rewriting, and questioning, has to involve reading of theory, other narratives, and historical viewpoints in order to re-contextualize my remembering and understanding of my past within my present.

Most autobiographies present a series of events organized linearly in chronological order, while others embrace plot lines synonymous with fiction that rearrange events deliberately "so as to reveal their dramatic, thematic, and emotional significance" (Burroway, 1987, p. 13). Experiment with different ways of re-presenting your autobiography. You can move within time periods, weaving the past and present through themes (Connelly & Clandinin, 1990). Like fiction you will also need to carefully lay out settings and develop characters so the reader is able to follow you along through the issues your autobiographical narratives address. Be aware that the reader is continually attempting to find resonance across the critical incidences you outline by seeking connections between the whole and the particular of your story. This is what we do when we read—we relate the particular to our own situation, asking "how do I relate to this?" Consider your intended audience carefully. If it is the field of art education, how might your autobiography offer implications beyond your own art teaching practices? How has your story changed your views as an art educator and why is this significant for others to be made aware of?

U-TURN: REVISITING OUR JOURNEY

Our histories shape our current actions in ways we may or may not be aware. Autobiographical research takes this way of knowing further through articulating, analyzing, contextualizing, critiquing, and transforming historical experience. In this form of qualitative inquiry, "Autobiography becomes the practice, oneself the provocation, and the classroom the site to reconstruct the private and public spheres in curriculum and teaching" (Pinar, 2007, p. 29). As a process, autobiographical inquiry can unsettle and complicate our taken-for-granted art education roots. As we tell our stories and grow in autobiographical consciousness, we may move toward and work through past and present difficulties within our teacher/learner selves that make possible alternative routes for our future practices and perceptions as art educators. This chapter proposed autobiographical inquiry as a way to work "back through the past in order to better understand the present" (Mitchell & Weber, 1999, p. 6). The suggested methodological parameters are not meant to be read as definitive rules for the genre, but as signposts to consider as you re-search your own journey as an art educator.

REFERENCES

Atkinson, D. (2006). School art education: Mourning the past and opening a future. *International Journal of Art and Design Education, 25*(1), 16-27.

Bullough, R. V., & Pinnegar, S. (2001). Guidelines for quality in auto-biographical forms of self-study. *Educational Researcher, 30*(3), 13-22.

Burroway, J. (1987). *Writing fiction: A guide to narrative craft* (2nd ed.). Boston, MA: Little, Brown, and Company.

Cole, A. L., & Knowles, J. G. (2000). *Researching teaching: Exploring teacher development through reflexive inquiry.* Boston, MA: Allyn & Bacon.

Connelly, F. M., & Clandinin, D. J. (1990). Stories of experience and narrative inquiry. *Educational Researcher, 19*(5), 2-14.

Diamond, C. T. P. (1999). Reciting and reviewing the educator self: An exhibition of five self-works. In C. T. P. Diamond & C. A. Mullen (Eds.), *The postmodern educator: Arts-based inquiries and teacher development* (pp. 191-221). New York, NY: Peter Lang.

Feldman, A. (2003). Validity and quality in self-study. *Educational Researcher, 32*(3), 26-28.

Fowler, L. C. (2006). *A curriculum of difficulty: Narrative research in education and the practice of teaching.* New York, NY: Peter Lang.

Freeman, M. P. (2008). Autobiography. In L. M. Given (Ed.), *The SAGE Encyclopedia of Qualitative Research Methods* (Vol. 2, pp. 45-48). Thousand Oaks, CA: Sage.

Grumet, M. R. (1981). Restitution and reconstruction of educational experience: An autobiographical method for curriculum theory. In M. Lawn & L. Barton (Eds.), *Rethinking curriculum studies: A radical approach* (pp. 115-130). London, England: Croom Helm.

Grumet, M. R. (1988). *Bitter milk: Women and teaching.* Amherst: University of Massachusetts Press.

Gude, O. (2000). Investigating the culture of curriculum. In E. D. Fehr, K. Fehr & K. Keifer-Boyd (Eds.), *Real world readings in art education* (pp. 75-81). New York, NY: Falmer.

Gude, O. (2007). Principles of possibility. *Art Education, 60*(1), 6-17.

Kincheloe, J. L. (2005). Auto/biography and critical ontology: Being a teacher, developing a reflective persona. In W. M. Roth (Ed.), *Auto-biography and auto-ethnography* (pp. 155-174). Rotterdam, The Netherlands: Sense.

Leggo, C. (2008). Autobiography: Researching our lives and living our research. In S. Springgay, R. L. Irwin, C. Leggo & P. Gouzouasis (Eds.), *Being with a/r/tography* (pp. 3-23). Rotterdam, The Netherlands: Sense.

Mitchell, C., & Weber, S. (1999). *Reinventing ourselves as teachers: Beyond nostalgia.* London, England: Falmer Press.

Norum, K. E. (2008). Artifact analysis. In L. M. Given (Ed.), *The SAGE Encyclopedia of Qualitative Research Methods* (Vol. 2, pp. 23-24). Thousand Oaks, CA: Sage.

Pinar, W. F. (1981). "Whole, bright, deep with understanding": Issues in autobiographical method and qualitative research. *Journal of Curriculum Studies, 13*(3), 173-188.

Pinar, W. F. (2007). *Intellectual advancement through disciplinarity: Verticality and horizontality in curriculum studies.* Rotterdam, The Netherlands: Sense.

Raunft, R. (2001). The autobiographical lectures of some prominent art educators: Introduction. In R. Raunft (Ed.), *The autobiographical lectures of some prominent art educators* (pp. vii-xxviii). Reston, VA: National Art Education Association.

EXAMPLES OF ART EDUCATOR AUTOBIOGRAPHIES

Baker, A. (1998). Painting and poetry as autobiography and grief-work. In E. J. Saccá & E. Zimmerman (Eds.), *Women art educators IV: Herstories, ourstories, future stories* (pp. 87-99). Boucherville, Quebec, Canada: Canadian Society for Education Through Art.

Barrett, T. (2004). Learning from histories of art education: An overview of research and issues. In E. W. Eisner & M. D. Day (Eds.), *Handbook of research and policy in art education* (pp. 11-31). Mahwah, NJ: Lawrence Erlbaum Associates.

Barrett, T., Smith-Shank, D. L., & Stuhr, P. (2008). Three art educators in cancerworld. *Journal of Cultural Research in Art Education, 26*, 3-23.

Check, E. (2000). Caught between control and creativity: Boredom strikes the art room. In D. E. Fehr, K. Fehr & K. Keifer-Boyd (Eds.), *Real-world readings in art education: Things your professors never told you* (pp. 137-145). New York, NY: Routledge.

Check, E. (2005). (Un)Becoming working class? Living across the lines. *The Journal of Social Theory in Art Education, 25*, 45-68.

Check, E. (2006). My working-class roots in an academic war zone: Creating space to grieve and honor. *Journal of Cultural Research in Art Education, 24*, 23-35.

Jaksch, M. (2003). Troubling histories: Schooled identities & autobiographical explorations. In K. Grauer, R. L. Irwin & E. Zimmerman (Eds.), *Women art educators V: Conversations across time. Remembering revisioning reconsidering* (pp. 144-149). Reston, VA: National Art Education Association.

Kind, S. (2006). *Of stones and silences: Storying the trace of the other in the autobiographical and textile text of art/teaching* (Unpublished doctoral dissertation). University of British Columbia, Vancouver, Canada.

La Pierre, S. D. (1998). An autobiographical account: The development and understanding of artistic expressiveness as a woman artist. In E. J. Saccá & E. Zimmerman (Eds.), *Women art educators IV: Herstories, ourstories, future stories* (pp. 112-118). Boucherville, Quebec, Canada: Canadian Society for Education Through Art.

Rahn, J. (1998). Autobiography as a tool in a teaching environment and studio practice. In E. J. Saccá & E. Zimmerman (Eds.), *Women art educators IV: Herstories, ourstories, future stories* (pp. 128-137). Boucherville, Quebec, Canada: Canadian Society for Education Through Art.

Suominen Guyas, A. (2007). Re-constructing self within the family: Re-building the family album. *Visual Culture & Gender, 2*, 14-23.

Suominen Guyas, A. (2008). Water: Moving stillness. In S. Springgay, R. L. Irwin, C. Leggo & P. Gouzouasis (Eds.), *Being with a/r/tography* (pp. 25-32). Rotterdam, The Netherlands: Sense.

Wilson, B. (1994). Reflections on the relationships among art, life, and research. *Studies in Art Education, 35*(4), 197-208.

NADINE KALIN is Assistant Professor of Art Education at the University of North Texas in Denton, Texas. She earned her PhD at the University of British Columbia. She teaches courses in the areas of art museum education, preservice teacher preparation, and the theories and methods of art education research. She is also involved in mentoring students in the master's and doctoral degree programs, the art museum education certificate, and the K-12 art teaching certification program. Her accomplishments include presentations at numerous national and international conferences, published papers in conferences proceedings, chapters in books, and articles in peer-reviewed journals including *Visual Arts Research, Art Education, International Journal of Art and Design Education,* as well as *Arts and Learning Research.* Her research interests include mentorship, arts-based educational research, teacher and museum education in art, as well as qualitative research pedagogy.

32 / A Self-Exploration of the Relationship Between Art Teaching and Artistic Practice

CHRISTY ORTIZ / PROFESSOR, SAVANNAH COLLEGE OF ART AND DESIGN

ABSTRACT: *Through my lived experiences as a high school art teacher, I relied on myself as the teacher, learner, and investigator to uncover underlying strengths and weaknesses of my practice. Uncovering these elements prompted me to utilize self-study inquiry to explore my art teaching and artistic practice. The purpose of this autobiographical study was to examine my professional practices as a teacher and an artist and how these experiences affected my actions as a high school art teacher. By using critical reflective practices, I gathered artifacts and compared them with other elements in my teaching portfolio, journal writings and responses from a survey that was posted to two art education listservs. Additionally, the concept of a/r/tography helped me understand how I could work within my teacher and artist identities, and accept them on equal terms. Ultimately, this study helped me to understand my dual identity in the art education profession and supported my continued critical reflection upon my practice as a teacher and an artist.*

During my career as an art teacher, I continuously explored the strengths and challenges in my teacher practice. Despite an established community of three other art teachers in my school and myself, there was an element of independence in my work environment. This was especially true when I stepped into my classroom. Whereas this may be conceived of as isolation, I utilized this independence as a vehicle for strengthening my teaching.

SARA AND MELANIE: *Note how Ortiz took her professional reality and turned it into a powerful position. She viewed this situation as one of independence, which is power-giving and full of possibilities, instead of viewing it as power-stripping isolation.*

In general, I enjoyed managing my classroom and the students without others questioning my teaching methods. My independence not only affected the manner in which I conducted my classroom but how I proceeded to strengthen it. I relied on myself as the teacher, learner, and investigator to uncover underlying strengths and weaknesses of my practice. As a result, I utilized self-study inquiry to explore my art teaching and artistic practice.

The purpose of this self-study was to explore my professional practices as a teacher and as an artist and how these experiences affected my actions as a high school art teacher. The main question that guided the direction of the inquiry was "What is the relationship between my teacher identity and artist identity as a high school art teacher?"

OVERVIEW OF SELF-STUDY

Self-study, or autobiographical research, draws on one's life experiences and gives particular thought to connections from those experiences to one's teaching practice. Some qualities of self-study include that it is self-initiated, improvement-aimed, and involves multiple qualitative methods. Hamilton and Pinnegar (2004) proposed that self-study draws on more than the elements of one's life. "Self-study also involves a thoughtful look at texts read, experiences had, people known, and ideas considered. These are investigated for their connections with and relationships to practice as a teacher educator" (p. 236). I conducted an autobiographical study centered on my practice both within the confines of my classroom environment and outside those classroom walls.

As I considered my development as a teacher, conducting a self-study allowed me to look at all aspects of my practice along with what I learned in the process. The investigation of my teaching and artistic practice also led me to explore aspects of my teacher and artistic identity. Cohen-Evron (2002) conducted a study that specifically focused on art instructors, employing Britzman's (1992) framework for defining teacher identities as "constructed through an ongoing process of becoming and making sense of who they are, who they are not, and who they wish to become" (p. 80). For the purpose of this self-study, I considered artist identity as a changeable trait in myself "and [could] be best characterized as an ongoing process, a process of interpreting oneself as a certain kind of person"(Beijaard,

Meijer, & Verloop, 2004, p. 108). Overall, self-study provided me a means of following the story of my ever-changing dual identities and exploring the relationship between my teaching practice and my artistic practice.

DATA COLLECTION AND ANALYSIS METHODS

Part of the process in self-study research is to make public what is normally private. I used critical reflective practices, such as journal entries, personal artworks, and autobiographical narratives, to gather information. I used journaling as a means of documenting my personal stories regarding my teacher and studio practice. I included photographs from my teaching portfolio, which documented my personal artworks, travels overseas, exhibiting experiences. I also included pamphlets of lectures and exhibitions that I attended. In gathering these artifacts and stories, I made multiple comparisons between the elements in my teaching portfolio, my journal writings and responses from a survey that I posted to two art education listservs.

Because my portfolio was based upon my teaching and artistic practice, grouping the artifacts in a portfolio format allowed me to look past their initial purposes and helped me make sense of my practices. I compared the written and visual information that was included in the portfolio, and found a consistency in my attendance to lectures and art exhibits and an increase in exhibiting and oversea travels to view original artworks. During the research period, I wrote in my journal about changes I wanted to make in my curriculum, changes that I made in my curriculum, and the results of those changes.

I also wrote reflections on each experience that was included in my teaching portfolio and continued to reflect upon them through my journaling. The writings in my portfolio represented my initial responses toward these experiences. I placed each document in a plastic sleeve that fit into a notebook, with both pieces facing out and visible to whoever viewed it. The teaching portfolio and journal were elements of my teaching and studio practice that I shared with colleagues, within different educational settings. My coworkers and I ate lunch together every workday and, on Fridays, met after school to have coffee. I used these opportunities to discuss and share my journal and teaching portfolio with them. They were always willing to discuss topics I presented and provided me new ways in which to perceive my original ideas.

At the time, my teaching portfolio helped me put into perspective aspects of my teaching practice that I believed to be significant. Some of these elements included the continued pursuit of my studio practice and viewing original artworks in context. By reflecting on my teaching portfolio, I realized that providing myself time to indulge my artistic self through these kinds of experiences helped me to strengthen my teaching practice as well as encourage me to make modifications to my curriculum.

In addition to compiling a teaching portfolio, I gathered data through a 10-question survey I created and posted online. Collecting these survey responses allowed me to unite multiple viewpoints, and further my understanding of my research topic. The questions were directed to all levels of art teachers, accessed via listservs, and touched on topics relating to their practice as art teachers and as artists. Some questions included: Do you prioritize your work as an art teacher over making art or are they of equal importance? As an art teacher how often do you make art? What kind of support would be necessary to encourage art teachers to pursue their studio practices?

In order to make teachers aware of the posted survey, I sent e-mails through two listservs, VisArtsNet and Grassroots Art in Action. VisArtsNet is a New Zealand based email group and is provided for art educators, as well as other interested educators. Grassroots Art in Action is based in Houston, Texas and is also open to those interested in the visual arts. I chose these listservs as a means of reaching out to two diverse groups of educators. One group seemed to represent a region in which I was familiar (Houston, Texas), and the second one connected to art educators on an international level. I received 20 responses in total.

Upon reading the survey responses, I wrote down key words and phrases beside each response. Next to these key phrases I read through my journal and selected a group of entries that related to the survey questions. From each of these entries, I wrote down key phrases and ideas from those writings. I then compared the phrases selected from the surveys to ones from my journal entries, as well as comparing the survey responses to each other. I found many similarities among my writings and the survey responses. Some of these included that time and energy were two reasons why art teachers did not pursue their studio practice. Another similarity included that the continued practice of one's artmaking could enhance one's teaching practice. Although these ideas may seem contradictory, they were reiterated in multiple survey responses, as well as my journal entries.

FINDINGS AND ISSUES

Through the investigation of my practice, I became more aware of the manner in which I treated my teacher and artist identities. When I read of a new arts-based research methodology named "A/r/tography," which refers to the various roles held by the artist, researcher, and teacher (Beer, Bickel, Grauer, Irwin, Springgay, & Xiong, 2006), it provided me the freedom to investigate my dual practices as a teacher and artist through self-study inquiry, on equal levels.

Although I was aware that I prioritized my teaching practice over my work as an artist, it was not until I came upon the concept of a/r/tography that I fully understood how I could work within both identities. A/r/tography helped me to accept them on equal terms, changing my attitude toward teaching and making time to create art. These changes became apparent when I reflected upon periods in my teaching career of producing and not producing artworks. I found that when I was at my greatest artistic production, I had the least amount of time because I was simultaneously a full-time teacher and a doctoral student. These conclusions led me to believe that if I used my time at work wisely, I could take at least 15 minutes every day to express myself creatively. This proved to be valuable resulting in a continued pursuit of my artmaking and a more relaxed yet confident attitude when I taught. Overall, the major findings of my study included the growing awareness in my identities and that I was most productive as an artist when I was busiest. I grew as a teacher over a 5-year time frame, and I came to see my teacher and artist identities as equals.

CONCLUSION

Currently, I teach preservice art educators at an art college. I continue to share my stories and new knowledge, acquired from this study, with my students and art educators. I talk about how strengthening one's teaching practice can come from building lessons as well as creating personal artworks. Art teachers should not forget the passion that brought them into the field of art education. They should view their artist and teacher identities with equal importance. In the future I would like to continue to explore the relationship between my art teaching and artistic practice as a teacher educator, through a collaborative self-study with other art educators.

REFERENCES

Beer, R., Bickel, B., Grauer, K., Irwin, R. L., Springgay, S., & Xiong, G. (2006). The rhizomatic relations of a/r/tography. *Studies in Art Education, 48*(1), 70-88.

Beijaard, D., Meijer, P. C., & Verloop, N. (2004). Reconsidering research on teachers' professional identity. *Teaching and Teacher Education, 20*(2), 107-128.

Britzman, D. P. (1992). The terrible problem of knowing thyself: Toward a poststructural account of teachers' identity. *The Journal of Curriculum Theorizing, 9*(3), 23-46.

Cohen-Evron, N. (2002). Why do good art teachers find it hard to stay in the public school system? *Studies in Art Education, 44*(1), 79-94.

Hamilton, M. L., & Pinnegar, S. (2004). Conclusion: The value and the promise of self-study. In J. J. Loughran, M. L. Hamilton, V. K. LaBoskey & T. Russell (Eds.), *International handbook of self-study of teaching and teacher education practices* (pp. 235-246). Boston, MA: Kluwer Academic.

CHRISTY ORTIZ joined the faculty of the Savannah College of Art and Design in 2008 as professor in the Department of Professional Education. Some of her research interests include: teacher practice-artistic practice, arts teacher education, and arts-based research methods. In her future research plans, she would like to continue to explore the relationship between her art teaching and artistic practice as a teacher educator, through a collaborative self-study with other art educators. In other research plans, she is interested in exploring how art educators view themselves in the role as curriculum makers, and the relationship between their understanding of the term "art teacher" and their teaching practice.

SECTION V: CHANGING OUR PRACTICES

Introduction

MELANIE L. BUFFINGTON AND **SARA WILSON MCKAY**

HOW DO WE MAKE CHANGE IN THE WORLD THROUGH OUR PRACTICES?

MUSINGS AND WONDERINGS FROM THE FIELD

I know there are many strategies for behavior management but how do I know what will work in my situation? The girls in my class rarely speak during critique. Is there something the students and I can do together to change the format of critique to increase their participation? The lessons I taught in my old school don't seem to be working in my new school where I am not the same race as my students. What can I do about this?

This section shows what happens when teachers engage in research intended to bring about a change, large or small. When the intent of research is focused on topics or phenomenon that would benefit from some change, teachers who conduct the research maximize their power in the classroom. Broader reaches of teachers' research beyond their own classrooms may involve the community, museums, city-wide issues, under-served or over-looked populations and so on. This section, structured differently from the others, includes additional material that not only introduces two methodologies, but also offers tips and considerations for research and example research studies. Through change-oriented research, teachers can grow the power in their daily practice.

OVERVIEW OF METHODOLOGIES

- **Action Research** is a spiral process of research where the researcher observes a situation, identifies a problem, designs an intervention or new strategy, implements the new action, reflects on the intervention, and then observes again beginning the cycle anew. In ongoing efforts to improve their professional practice, health care workers, social workers, teachers, among others, often find this methodology useful. Because it mirrors typical practice, but brings focus to one aspect of your practice at a time in order to take action and improve practice it can result in meaningful professional growth.
- **Participatory Action Research**, like action research, is the same spiral process of observe, plan, act, and reflect though in this methodology, the participants are actively involved with the researcher in each step of the process.

I make hundreds of decisions each day; I don't have time to think carefully through every decision that I make as a teacher. How will I ever find time and support to conduct research while I'm teaching? How can conducting and reading research positively impact what I do everyday? Could the special program I already have in place in which students partner with students with special needs be a starting point for a research project?

- **Tips and Considerations** offers readers perspectives from other teachers who have developed successful systems and explored important factors that impact their effectiveness as teacher/researchers. This section is intended to share experiences in ways that help you identify your own necessary factors for success in research.

How does "culturally relevant pedagogy" compare to how I teach in my classroom? How could I collaborate with community members to improve a museum experience? Is anyone really interested in what I think and do?

- **Example Research Studies** offers you the opportunity to see how a study can be presented when it is fully developed. Reading other research in journals like *Art Education, Studies in Art Education, Visual Arts Research, The Journal of Social Theory in Art Education,* and *Journal for Cultural Research in Art Education* can often spur your thoughts about your own classroom practice as well as inspire you to pursue your own meaningful research process.

ACTION
RESEARCH

33 / Critical Action Research Activism: Social Structure and Human Agency

KAREN KEIFER-BOYD / PROFESSOR, THE PENNSYLVANIA STATE UNIVERSITY

ABSTRACT: *This chapter introduces critical action research methodology. Critical action research involves exposing, questioning, and changing embodied values as they emerge in educational practice. Moreover, the keystone of critical action research methodology in art education is a well-informed critical ACTION developed from reflective and iterative inquiry processes. Its purpose is to create and improve socially responsible and culturally responsive teaching and learning environments and practices for equitable and inclusive art classrooms. The focus in this chapter is to guide art teachers to conceptualize, implement, and critique a well-informed critical action from study of teaching and learning social structures and practices for human agency in the K-12 art classroom. This chapter focuses on the connection between social structure and human agency— i.e., how lived experiences are both shaped by social forces and re-visioned through human action.*

Action research in art education involves an art educator, team of educators, or art teacher with students systematically studying art education practice. Action researchers use what they learn to better understand or improve art education practice or to solve a particular problem in an authentic setting (May, 1993; Noffke & Somekh, 2009). A hallmark of various forms of action research is the four-step ongoing spiral of planning, acting, observing, and reflecting (McNiff & Whitehead, 2006). Researchers alternately refer to action research as "practitioner inquiry" (Dana & Yendol-Hoppey, 2008, p. xi), "practitioner research, teacher research, and practice-based research" (Nolen & Putten, 2007, p. 406). Action research, thus, is a reflective and iterative inquiry process with the aim of improving strategies, practices, and knowledge of the environments within which one teaches (Schoen, 2007). This chapter provides guidance on how to conduct research that develops, leads to, implements, and assesses a genuinely well-informed action in the midst of an emerging teaching and learning landscape.

Action research is a relatively recent methodology introduced by Kurt Lewin's (1951) field theory, which focused on empowerment and change in Germany and the United States after WWII. The methodology became well known in the field of education as critical or emancipatory action research through the participatory action research work of Paolo Freire (1972). Since the 1970s, action research has entered educational research as a critical problem-posing and solving methodology that uses "multiple perspectives of knowing, [and] triangulation of appropriate methods and theories" (Zuber-Skerrit & Fletcher, 2007, p. 417). There are many texts on conducting action research in education (e.g., Holly, Arhar, & Kasten, 2009; McNiff & Whitehead, 2002,

2006; Meyers & Rust, 2003; Mills, 2003; Stringer, McFadyen Christensen, & Baldwin, 2010) and an increasing number of published art education action research studies (e.g., Burnaford, 2007; Erler, 2006; Gamwell, 2005; Gardner, 2008; Hutzel, 2007; Kalin, 2007; Kratochvil, 2009; Lovett, 2008; Matthews, 2008; Veltman, 2007).

CRITICAL ACTION RESEARCH

While the spiral of observing, planning, acting, and reflecting is a constant within action research, there are multiple ways to conduct an action research project. This chapter largely assumes a critical stance with regard to action research because action research can be considered a powerful space of social action. To this end, critical action research activism emphasizes a "commitment to social transformation, challenging power relations, showing solidarity, recognizing and using emotions, being the change you want to see, and building spaces for critical dialogue" (Chatterton, Fuller, & Routledge, 2007, p. 222). Attention to how race, class, gender, and sexuality intersect to *legitimize* privilege, directs activism to disrupt oppressive social constructs that limit *difference*. Purposes of critical action research include creating and improving socially responsible and culturally responsive teaching and learning environments and practices for equitable and inclusive art classrooms.

Inherent to action research are concepts such as *situated learning* in *socioconstructivist art classrooms* (Pitri, 2006), *reflective practitioners* (Suter, 2006), *community of practice* (Wenger, McDermitt, & Synder, 2002), and *change agents* (Nolan & Putten, 2007). These practices share the premise that learning is a social process of generating knowledge from critical reflection. However, these concepts reflect that there are multiple ways to conduct a study. This chapter primarily addresses action research conducted from a critical stance, though it is important to remember that other researchers present other points of view (Brennan & Noffke, 2009; Carr & Kemmis, 2009; Griffiths, 2009).

RESEARCHER ROLES (SITUATING LOCATIONS): POWER RELATIONS—AGENCY/SUBJECTIVITY

The role that a researcher assumes informs how s/he investigates an experience. A researcher's role in action research is commonly that of *participant* or *participant-observer* who inquires into and plans an action to change a teaching situation, and shares critical insights from those experiences, reflections, and actions. A *participant* researcher is fully involved in the activity under study and critically reflects for a self-study. A *participant-observer* involves recording and reflecting on observations and interactions in which the participant-observer's role is frequently a part of the situation.

However, variations and other roles convey different power structures within a study's design. For example, an *observer-participant* researcher creates a role for the sole purpose of collecting data. An *interviewer* learns about others' perceptions of an experience. In critical action research, transcript analysis often identifies unequal social positions and self-labels used by the interviewee, such as referring to her teacher-self as a *gardener* or *not-a-mother*. Identifications, commitments, and values inform what is seen, known, and experienced. Each researcher role leads to different questions and insights from different power relationships in a situation (Lal, 1999).

Further, the researcher should reflect on the power relations (e.g., hierarchical, consensual, transformative[1]) within the particular research situation. These reflections need to inform what and how data is collected, the triangulation of different perspectives, analysis, and what is made visible in presenting the research. For example, a first-year teacher felt belittled in front of her students when the principal observed her teaching and interrupted each moment that students' eyes lost contact with the teacher's eyes. The strategy of *all eyes on the teacher* that she was expected to enforce did not align with the new teacher's pedagogical theory she was attempting to enact. She was looking for student engagement in which signs of motivation included comments by students to each other regarding how artworks they created or studied were meaningful to their lives. She explained to the school principal the action plan she was implementing, which involved student dialogue in small groups about artworks with emphasis on cultural identity and local and global injustices. Also, she shared with the principal her documented observation that enthusiasm for art seemed to wane with the time taken to make sure every eye was on her. She asked for 2 months to try her action plan to see if she could create a classroom climate that would draw in those seeking attention with wandering eyes

to engagement if she emphasized the importance of their art learning for their lives. In short, knowing your theoretical framework is imperative in action research, and critical action research involves attention to voice, agency, identity, injustice, dialogue, critical reflection, problem-solving, collaboration, self-disclosure, and power (Agnello, 2007).

ETHICAL CONSIDERATIONS FOR HUMAN PARTICIPANT RESEARCH

When teachers' typical cycle of planning, teaching, observing, and reflecting becomes a systematic cycle of intentional inquiry, then they must consider ethical principles for the protection of human subjects. In submitting Institutional Review Board (IRB) proposals to institutions, the researcher must specify the recruitment process and data collection methods, which can run a gamut of possibilities. For socially responsible ethical action, researchers must anticipate and address the needs and potential sensitivities of the many facets of a study's participants (Eikeland, 2006). The researcher must consider the importance of wording in introducing a study, the need for consent forms and alternative consent forms for minors, reciprocity, rapport, allowing participants to turn off the recorder, and care in writing up and presenting action research.[2]

PLANNING
DEVELOPING A PROBLEM STATEMENT

The desire to research one's teaching practice should come from questions that arise from immersion in teaching. Questions can arise throughout one's career and they may change as a teacher's understanding of students, curriculum, school structures, and power change. For instance, in the first year of teaching, a teacher's philosophy of teaching may change due to the realities of an institution; or after years of teaching, questions may form about students, curricula, content, knowledge, pedagogy, beliefs, practices, identity, social justice, and context.[3]

One of the most difficult aspects of all research, and particularly the "messiness and uncertainty in action research," is focusing data collection, analysis, and presentation with a statement of a problem and specific research question (Goodnough, 2008, p. 449). A problem statement is more specific than a topic because it communicates the importance of the problem, limits the scope of data collection by placing the problem in a context, and alludes to a theoretical concept that serves as a framework for directing analyses and reporting findings. Additionally, there are several strategies that can help to locate a topic and develop a meaningful research question suitable for an action research project. Work with others to brainstorm reflective questions about your teaching.[4] Expose that which often goes unnoticed in your teaching (e.g., patriarchal, White male artist, heterosexual). Re-envision how you frame what you teach (e.g., feminist, Black women artists, talented). Look for what is absent (e.g., attention to social class), and critique the prevalent cultural stories that underlie the metaphors, analogies, and examples in your teaching context. Use concept and cultural mapping to make connections and open the inquiry terrain before focusing on one phenomenon to investigate.[5]

LOCATING AND REVIEWING LITERATURE

Throughout your developing research process, search for published research to help formulate a critical question, plan an action, and inform your reflections.[6] Locate published studies by other art educators about how they utilized action research in their settings. These types of studies may help you plan your study and build the basis for the use of the methodology. Pay specific attention to how they conducted their studies and analyzed their data; they may have strategies that you can adapt and use for your study. Additionally, be sure to notice the references cited in the studies. When you find multiple authors mentioning the same source, it is a signal to you to read it, seek critiques of the source, and consider its relevance to your developing action plan. The hermeneutic circle of citations has been biased against women and people of color, and sometimes continues to privilege White male heterosexual authors (Habermas, 1990; Haraway, 1991; Harding, 1991; Hoy, 1991; Ricoeur, 1981). Therefore, skepticism, critical reading, and a search for scholarship overlooked are important too.

ACTING

An example of an action researcher working with students as research participants to develop an action plan with emancipatory strategies begins with the teacher and/or students recognizing a problem. For example, the art teacher notices that the more affluent students, who have access to broadband and computers in their homes, tend to monopolize the limited time on the one computer in the art classroom. Other students seem uninterested in using the computer. The art teacher decides to share with her seventh-grade students the National Education Technology Standards (NETS) and asks the students, in carefully selected pairs of those enthusiastic and those less enthusiastic about the creative potential of the Internet as an art medium, to work together at the computer to develop ideas of how to meet these standards in art activities. The National Education Technology Standards (NETS)[7] include:

- Facilitating and inspiring student learning and creativity
- Designing and developing digital-age learning experiences and assessments
- Modeling digital-age work and learning
- Promoting and modeling digital citizenship and responsibility
- Engaging in professional growth and leadership

The students create blogs to record their ideas each time they are at the computer over a period of several weeks and prepare to present their favorite idea to the class. From the students' ideas the teacher facilitates art projects incorporating all the students' ideas.

OBSERVING
DATA COLLECTION: INTERVIEWS, OBSERVATIONS, JOURNALS, STUDENT WORK

Often in action research projects, the enactment of a carefully designed plan and the data collection process are simultaneous. An action researcher collects data to ascertain if the planned action produces the desired effects. Data collection in action research can take many forms and often focuses on collecting qualitative data including interviews, observations, journals, other texts, and student work. Collecting data in an action research study should be a "change-enhancing, reciprocal educative encounter" (Lather, 1991, p. 72) that focuses on "the social process that produced the data and how the data are used" not on the information at face value (McMillian & Schumacher, 1997, p. 455). Wilson McKay (2006) proposes "digital data gathering and collaborative inquiry and interpretation to attempt a cumulative notion of research" (p. 49). Types of data collection that action researchers use include student and teacher visual journals, blogs, artworks, video-recordings, and programs such as VoiceThread,® which archives students' critiques from their speaking into a computer microphone. Participant-observation processes include "anecdotal records, rating scales, running records, checklist forms, category recording, event recording, duration recording, [and] interval recording" (Schoen, 2007, p. 213).

Critical self-aware strategies of data collection seek to understand worldviews of participants in a "dialogic research design where the respondents are actively involved in the construction and validation of meaning" (Lather, 1991, p. 63). Discuss with the participants if and how their involvement with the action research study altered their understanding of the research problem. Show the participants the transcriptions of your interviews and the write-ups of your observations to see if what you recorded is also what they remembered. This practice is commonly called a *member check*. Include the researcher's words in transcriptions and the researcher's actions in observation notes of nonverbal exchanges, as well as reflections about the dialogue by all involved in the dialogue.

REFLECTING
LAYERED DATA ANALYSIS: ASSEMBLE, DISASSEMBLE, REASSEMBLE

Action research is "politically committed research" (Chatterton et al., 2007, p. 217), conducted in a spiral that involves framing critical questions, collecting relevant data, planning and taking specific actions. The process of data analysis, which is ongoing throughout the study, occurs by assembling data, reflectively disassembling assumptions through planned action, and reassembling it to share findings.

In a critical action research model, reflection involves seeing from multiple social justice positionalities and revealing differential power and privilege relationships. Chatterton, Fuller, and Routledge (2007) refer to the global justice activist phrase "be the change you want to see" to emphasize the need for a "relational and ethical approach, which accepts that everyone can participate in building change every day" (p. 221). This research spiral of planning, implementing, and reflecting on change can confront social inequalities and seek transformative social change toward global ecological visions of peace and well-being. This is the ultimate goal for critical action research in art education.

CODING, SORTING, AND PATTERN-SEEKING

Data analysis should be layered with many revisits to the data collected. Visually coding data with colors or symbols avoids the limits of the hierarchical system of coding with numbers and lengthy textual codes. Layered analysis in an action research project can be conducted as follows.

- *Layer 1: Code to disassemble and reassemble.* Code—and maintain an interpretive key for the codes created—everything (metaphors, phrases, and actions) that relates to the research question and theoretical lens. Use scale and color changes and symbols to subdivide areas that are too broad, and rearrange codes to form various groups. Highlight what seems important to theorize. Code to expose ideology and to reveal power dynamics. Look for patterns, relationships, permutations, uncertainties, and variations, and identify what you notice using your codes.
- *Layer 2: Inquiry prose.* Write about the patterns you notice while reflecting on the research question. This discovery of patterns articulated as prose can be organized with the data in separate columns, or as footnotes, or merged in paragraph form. Discovery through writing is part of qualitative data analysis processes (Holly, 2009; Pushor & Clandinin, 2009). Refer to data to support discoveries. This writing can take the form of a research journal or memos logged on your computer throughout the research process.
- *Layer 3: Reflexivity and action.* Action researchers build and support interpretation with theory and data, which may be shared through story, poetry, performances, exhibitions, or various literary forms. Use the research question to focus explanations and the action plan. Enact the plan and work through the layers again with new data from the action. Reflexivity involves continuously questioning theoretical frames from analyses of data.

Prioritize goals from analysis of data. Plan one new action, rather than several changes too quickly. For example, if a goal is for students to create artwork meaningful to them, do their responses about their work indicate this goal is met? Or, does a plan need to be developed to change teaching approaches to achieve this goal? Plan time after teaching each day to write about the results of that day's teaching, for gradual implementation of a plan, and for further documentation and reflection during the process of implementation. Observation, data gathering, and analysis point toward specific needs for developing an action plan in the research spiral of planning, acting, observing, and reflecting. Develop a plan from analysis of data (i.e., from better understanding your teaching style with its strengths and shortfalls) that involves professional development that might include attending conferences, workshops, in-services, and reading art education studies. For example, if bullying is common among the students you teach, or there is a clear demarcation of gifted, or other behaviors that diminish student potential, research the impact of approaches to change this, such as peer teaching in which carefully formed teams seek to learn from and teach each other. Another idea is to observe specific actions in the art classroom. For example, over several weeks on an art project, is the care of the art tools manifested in the increasing skillful use of the tools and in the students' pride expressed regarding the finished artwork? Student reflective textual, audio, and visual blogs and journals expected at each class session are helpful to gain insight into problems and change.

BUILDING CREDIBILITY AND VALIDITY

Keep a journal throughout your research process concerning your decisions, and why you made them, in terms of epistemology (the nature of knowledge or truth-claims you make), ontology (what is perceived as reality and what it means to be human), and axiology (what is valued). Being clear on these are ways to frame the study theoretically and provide context-bound validity.

Validity in action research is produced collaboratively in enacting an action plan, and results through reflexivity and triangulation of data sources, methods, theoretical schemes, and by seeking counter-patterns, i.e., "intersectional analysis that takes difference into account" (Cahill, 2007, p. 181). *Catalytic Validity* "represents the degree to which the research process re-orients, focuses and energizes participants toward knowing reality in order to transform it" (Lather, 1991, p. 68). Such validity can come from multiple interviews using a dialogic process with the same group for planning an action. *Construct Validity* is based in theory, yet the researcher seeks counter-patterns and alternative explanations from the emergent categories in data gathered in regards to how a specific theory is lived or experienced (Lather, 1991). *Face Validity* is "operationalized by recycling description, emerging analysis, and conclusions back through at least a sub sample of respondents" (Lather, 1991, p. 67). For example, a researcher can provide a coded transcript of a class discussion or observations, and ask for students' and/or teachers' layered analysis.[8]

SARA AND MELANIE: *Validity is an issue in all types of research; factors that increase a study's validity vary depending upon the methodology. The examples in this section on validity relate to a range of qualitative methodologies and are not limited to action research.*

PRESENTING AND PUBLISHING ACTION RESEARCH

Presenting action research involves researcher self-disclosure through exposing critical self-aware strategies and the uncertainties of action plans. In the presentation of your research—which could be publications, performances, artworks, installations, exhibitions, websites, videos, workshops, or other forms of sharing—it is important to disclose connections between the researcher and what was researched, as well as how others participated.[9] Through the process of sharing your research in a presentation or a journal article, you can make connections with other people that will help you build a network of engaged teacher researchers.

CONCLUSION

"The fresh insights that are gleaned through a process of questioning, assessing, investigating, collaborating, analyzing, and refining instruction empower educators in their daily practice" (Schoen, 2007, p. 215) to "produce critical interpretations and readings of the world, which are accessible, understandable to all those involved, and actionable" (Chatterton et al., 2007, p. 218). Further, critical action research, as noted at the beginning of this chapter, is activism when the study is a process for transformative change relating to social justice issues, and differs from other forms of action research that are intended for production of knowledge or solving individual problems. Thus, this chapter describes critical action research as compared to other emphases in action research. New researchers might begin with study of one aspect of art teaching that the teacher researcher would like to change. Later, they may move toward critical action research in which the plan for change takes into account an inclusive view of how the change benefits a broad constituency of difference, and how the change is in response to social justice concerns of equity, potentiality, and respect for difference.

REFERENCES

Agnello, M. F. (2007). Public understanding to political voice: Action research and generative curricular practices in issues and reform. *The Social Studies, 98*(5), 217-224.

Brennan, M., & Noffke, S. E. (2009). Social-political theory in working with teachers for social justice schooling. *The Sage handbook of educational action research* (pp. 432-441). Thousand Oaks, CA: Sage.

Brydon-Miller, M., & Greenwood, D. (2006). A re-examination of the relationship between action research and human subjects review processes. *Action Research, 4*(1), 117-128.

Burnaford, G. E. (2007). Moving toward a culture of evidence: Documentation and action research in the practice of arts partnerships. *Arts Education Policy Review, 108*(3), 35-41.

Cahill, C. (2007). Participatory data analysis. In S. Kindon, R. Pain & M. Kesby (Eds.), *Participatory action research approaches and methods: Connecting people, participation and place* (pp. 181-187). New York, NY: Routledge.

Carr, W., & Kemmis, S. (2009). Educational action research: A critical approach. *The Sage handbook of educational action research* (pp. 74-84). Thousand Oaks, CA: Sage.

Chatterton, P., Fuller, D., & Routledge, P. (2007). Relating action to activism: Theoretical and methodological reflections. In S. Kindon, R. Pain & M. Kesby (Eds.), *Participatory action research approaches and methods: Connecting people, participation and place* (pp. 216-222). New York, NY: Routledge.

Dana, N. F., & Yendol-Hoppey, D. (2009). *The reflective educator's guide to classroom research: Learning to teach and teaching to learn through practitioner inquiry* (2nd ed.). Thousand Oaks, CA: Corwin Press.

Dana, N. F., & Yendol-Hoppey, D. (2008). *The reflective educator's guide to classroom research: Learning to teach and teaching to learn through practitioner inquiry.* Thousand Oaks, CA: Corwin Press.

Dick, B. (2005). *Making process accessible: Robust processes for learning, change and action research.* DLitt thesis, International Management Centres Association. Retrieved from www.bobdick.com.au/DLitt/

Erler, C. R. (2006). *Learning from the Beehive Collective: A participatory action research study of image-based education in an experimental community* (Unpublished doctoral dissertation). The Florida State University, Tallahassee, FL.

Eikeland, O. (2006). Condescending ethics and action research. *Action Research, 4*(1), 37-47.

Fisher, K., & Phelps, R. (2006). Recipe or performing art? Challenging conventions for writing action research theses. *Action Research, 4*(2), 143-164.

Freire, P. (1972). *Pedagogy of the oppressed.* Harmondsworth, England: Penguin.

Gamwell, P. (2005). Intermediate students' experiences with an arts-based unit: An action research. *Canadian Journal of Education, 28*(3), 359-383.

Gardner, L. C. (2008). *Preservice art education: Art making, reflecting, learning, art teaching* [Dissertation AAT 3325521]. Union Institute and University.

Goodnough, K. (2008). Dealing with messiness and uncertainty in practitioner research: The nature of participatory action research. *Canadian Journal of Education, 31*(2), 431-458.

Griffiths, M. (2009). Action research for/as/mindful of social justice. *The Sage handbook of educational action research* (pp. 85-98). Thousand Oaks, CA: Sage.

Habermas, J. (1990). The hermeneutic claim to universality. In Gayle Ormiston & Alan Schrift (Eds.), The hermeneutic tradition: From Ast to Ricouer (pp. 245-272). New York: State University of New York Press.

Haraway, D. J. (1991). *Simians, cyborgs, and women: The reinvention of nature.* Ithaca, NY: Cornell University Press.

Harding, S. (1991). Whose science? Whose knowledge? Thinking from women's lives. Ithaca, NY: Cornell University Press.

Holly, M. L. (2009). Writing to learn: A process for the curious. *The Sage handbook of educational action research* (pp. 267-277). Thousand Oaks, CA: Sage.

Holly, M. L., Arhar, J. M., & Kasten, W. C. (2009). *Action research for teachers: Traveling the yellow brick road.* Boston, MA: Allyn & Bacon/Pearson.

Hoy, D. (1991). Is hermeneutics ethnocentric? In D. Hiley, J. Bohman & R. Shusterman (Eds.), *The interpretive turn: Philosophy, science, culture* (pp. 155-175). Ithaca, NY: Cornell University Press.

Hutzel, K. (2007). Reconstructing a community, reclaiming a playground: A participatory action research study. *Studies in Art Education, 48*(3), 299-315.

ISTE (2008). The ISTE National Educational Technology Standards (NETS•T) and Performance Indicators for Teachers. Retrieved from www.iste.org/Content/NavigationMenu/NETS/ForTeachers/2008Standards/NETS_T_Standards_Final.pdf

Kalin, N. (2007). *Conversations on teaching and learning drawing: Drawn toward transformation* [Dissertation AAT NR31794]. The University of British Columbia, Vancouver, Canada.

Keifer-Boyd, K. (2008). Mentoring graduate students in conducting qualitative research. *ORP (Office for Research Protections) Newsletter, 19,* 1-3. The Pennsylvania State University. Retrieved from http://cyberhouse.arted.psu.edu/ORP_issue19_2008_Keifer-Boyd.pdf

Keifer-Boyd, K., & Maitland-Gholson, J. (2007). *Engaging visual culture.* Worcester, MA: Davis.

Kratochvil, K. R. (2009). *The survival of arts education in the NCLB era: A case study of one K-8th grade arts-focused charter school in a California program improvement school district* [Dissertation AAT 3367731]. University of California, Santa Cruz, CA.

Lal, J. (1999). Situating locations: The politics of self, identity, & other in living and writing the text. In S. Hesse-Biber, C. Gilmartin & R. Lydenberg (Eds.), *Feminist approaches to theory and methodology: An interdisciplinary reader* (pp. 100-137). New York, NY: Oxford University Press.

Lather, P. (1991). *Getting smart: Feminist research and pedagogy with/in the postmodern.* New York, NY: Routledge.

Lewin, K. (1951). *Field theory in social science: Selected theoretical papers.* New York, NY: Harper & Row.

Lovett, M. K. (2008). *Creative intervention through video action research and pedagogy* [Dissertation AAT 3314841]. University of Illinois at Urbana-Champaign, Urbana-Champaign, IL.

Matthews, M. (2008). How can we create the conditions for students' freedom of speech within studies in art? *International Journal of Art & Design Education, 27*(2), 133-143.

May, W. T. (1993). Teachers-as-researchers or action research: What good is it, and what good is it for art education. *Studies in Art Education, 34*(2), 114-126.

McMillian, J., & Schumacher, S. (1997). *Research in education: A conceptual introduction* (4th ed.). New York, NY: HarpersCollins College.

McNiff, J., & Whitehead, J. (2002). *Action research: Principles and practice* (2nd ed.). London, England: Routledge.

McNiff, J., & Whitehead, J. (2006). *Doing action research in education.* London, England: Sage.

Meyers, E., & Rust, F. O. (Eds.). (2003). *Taking action with teacher research.* Portsmouth, NH: Heinemann.

Mills, G. E. (2003). *Action research: A guide for the teacher researcher* (2nd ed.). Upper Saddle River, NJ: Merrill Prentice Hall.

Noffke, S., & Somekh, B. (Eds.). (2009). *The Sage handbook of educational action research.* Thousand Oaks, CA: Sage.

Nolan, A. L., & Putten, J. V. (2007). Action research in education: Addressing gaps in ethical principles and practices. *Educational Researcher, 36*(7), 401-407.

Pitri, E. (2006). Teacher researcher in the socioconstructivist art classroom. *Art Education, 59*(5), 40-45.

Pushor, D., & Clandinin, D. J. (2009). The interconnections between narrative inquiry and action research. *The Sage handbook of educational action research* (pp. 290-300). Thousand Oaks, CA: Sage.

Ricoeur, Paul. (1981). *Hermeneutics and human science: Essays on language, action and interpretation* (John Thompson, Trans.). London, England: Cambridge University Press.

Rogers, D., Bolick, C. M., Anderson, A., Gordon, E., Manfra, M. M., & Yow, J. (2007). *"It's about the kids": Transforming teacher-student relationships through action research.* Washington, DC: Heldref.

Schoen, S. (2007). Action research: A developmental model of professional socialization. *Clearing House: A Journal of Educational Strategies, Issues and Ideas, 80*(5), 211-216.

Stringer, E. T., McFadyen Christensen, L. M., & Baldwin, S. C. (2010). *Integrating teaching, learning, and action research: Enhancing instruction in the K-12 classroom.* Thousand Oaks, CA: Sage.

Suter, W. N. (2006). *Introduction to educational research: A critical thinking approach.* Thousand Oaks, CA: Sage.

Veltman, H. M. (2007). *Girls and their body image: Sociopolitical issues in art education* [Dissertation AAT NR30148]. Concordia University, Montreal, Canada.

Wenger, E., McDermott, R., & Synder, W. (2002). *Cultivating communities of practice: A guide to managing knowledge.* Boston, MA: Harvard Business School Press.

Wilson McKay, S. (2006). Living the questions: Technology-infused action research in art education. *Art Education, 59*(6), 47-51.

Zuber-Skeritt, O., & Fletcher, M. (2007). The quality of action research thesis in the social sciences. *Quality Assurance in Education, 15*(4), 413-436.

ENDNOTES

1   See Chapter 6 of Keifer-Boyd and Maitland-Gholson (2007) for more on power.

2   For real-life ethical encounters art educator researchers have experienced see Keifer-Boyd (2008). Also see Brydon-Miller and Greenwood (2006) and Eikeland (2006).

3   To learn how to develop research questions about your teaching practice see what Nancy Fichtman Dana and Diana Yendol-Hoppey (2009) refer to as the eight passions (especially Chapter 2 of their book). Also, Dick (2005) is a helpful online resource on the process of action research.

4   Dana and Yendol-Hoppey (2009) suggest a series of exercises in their Chapter 3 on why it is so important to collaborate in teacher inquiry in "schools that are often structured in ways that promote teacher isolation" (p. 65).

5   Schoen (2007) provides eight helpful guidelines for "framing critical questions and collecting relevant data" (p. 214).

6   Inspiration may come from reading the *Action Research Journal.*

7   For more specifics about NETS see ISTE (2008).

8   See also Rogers, Bolick, Anderson, Gordon, Manfra, and Yow (2007).

9   For a helpful article on writing an action research thesis see Fisher and Phelps' (2006) article in the journal *Action Research.*

KAREN KEIFER-BOYD, PhD, Professor of Art Education and Women's Studies at The Pennsylvania State University, co-authored *Including Difference: Communitarian Approach to Art Education in the Least Restrictive Environment* (NAEA, 2013), *InCITE, InSIGHT, InSITE* (NAEA, 2008), *Engaging Visual Culture* (Davis, 2007), co-edited *Real-World Readings in Art Education: Things Your Professors Never Told You* (Falmer, 2000), and served as editor of the *Journal of Social Theory in Art Education* and guest editor for *Visual Arts Research.* In 2005, she co-founded the journal, *Visual Culture & Gender.* Her research on feminist pedagogy, visual culture, and cyberactivism is published in more than 45 peer-reviewed research publications and translated into several languages. Keifer-Boyd has been honored with several teaching, arts administration, and research awards.

34 / Student Engagement: Toward a Democratic Classroom

BETSY MURPHY / ART INSTRUCTOR AND ART DEPARTMENT CHAIR, CEDAR PARK HIGH SCHOOL

ABSTRACT: *The purpose of the action research plan described in this chapter was to determine what kinds of art activities might lead to higher levels of authentic learner engagement. The action research cycle of observing, reflecting, planning, and action are described through practical application. Of particular interest are strategies for building trust, studio art research, and new approaches to class critiques that resulted in a more democratic classroom and promoted authentic engagement.*

On the surface, my high school art classroom appeared ideal; my classes were well managed, full of seemingly compliant students. The artwork lining the halls received compliments, and students did well in competitions. Everything at my large suburban high school appeared first-rate; nevertheless, I was uncertain. Questions lingered in the back of my mind about why students had difficulty getting started or finishing, why they seemed reluctant to take risks, and about the lack of variety in student artwork.

OBSERVING

My teaching schedule included four introductory art classes and two sections of painting; however, I limited my focus to the mixed level painting classes. I began informal inquiry by observing my mostly White middle class painting students. It appeared that many of them were going through the motions—their artwork lacked enthusiasm. I noticed that some rarely completed their work. Critiques seemed

Reflective Practice as Classroom Research

KATHLEEN UNRATH /ASSISTANT PROFESSOR OF ART EDUCATION, UNIVERSITY OF MISSOURI AND **MELISSA MUDD** /ART TEACHER, ROCK BRIDGE HIGH SCHOOL, COLUMBIA, MISSOURI, DOCTORAL STUDENT, UNIVERSITY OF MISSOURI

During university coursework preservice art teachers learn about the importance of developing a classroom that encourages creative development, empowers an artistic voice, and supports a dynamic interchange of ideas. The ideals of reflective practice are often modeled and the ethic of intellectual analysis of the decision rich environment of the classroom is often reviewed through journaling and case studies. Pedagogy courses provide an intellectual space for students to theorize about the art of teaching art. However it is when art teachers take charge of their own learning practice that the pragmatic lessons of teaching are learned, often through trial and error. By drawing on the action research methodology of thinking, acting, and reflecting (Carr & Kemmis, 1983; Kolb, 1984; Stringer, 1999), teachers are able to work through many attempts and failures, transforming frustration into illumination.

The concept of reflective practice (Dewey 1933; Schön, 1983, 1987; Unrath & Nordlund, 2006; Zeicher & Liston, 1996) is illuminated through the eyes of a beginning teacher working with her university professor in a graduate program that emphasizes action research as a form of personal and professional inquiry into practice. In what follows, the teacher defines a problem and then seeks a solution utilizing action research as a methodology, the outcome of which eventually evolved into a rich and powerful catalyst for creative production in her classroom.

AN ART TEACHER'S STORY ABOUT JOURNALING

I'd always envisioned the benefits that artful experiences with journals could bring to my students because an ethic of reflective practice was a strong component of my teacher preparation at the University of Missouri. Philosophically, I also felt that it was forced and uncomfortable. The biggest red flag was the number of paintings left behind. Apparently students did not value their work enough to take it with them. This concerned me because I attended workshops, read art education publications, collaborated with peers, and planned what I thought were interesting lessons. Despite my best efforts, many of my painting students were not authentically engaged; their assignments seemed irrelevant. Authentic engagement occurs when "the task, activity, or work the student is assigned or encouraged to undertake is associated with a result or outcome that has clear meaning and relatively immediate value to the student" (Schlechty, 2002, p. 3).

REFLECTING

The heart of action research is a desire to change teaching practice (Kincheloe, 2003; Waters-Adams, 2006). Understanding my own professional actions helped me plan instruction designed to improve student engagement. Guided by my values, intentions, and beliefs within the context of my teaching practice, I reflected on subtle clues about what might be meaningful to my students (Waters-Adams, 2006). Writing about what I saw helped to jumpstart my planning, I wrote primarily about my fear of change and loss of control. Though my students craved freedom, I was concerned about balancing open-ended work while providing necessary guidance in painting skills and techniques (Zemelman, Daniels, & Hyde, 1998). Assessment of varied work was a complicated issue, as were diverse student attitudes toward quality and effort. I was faced with much ambiguity, but through regular journaling, guided by desire to inspire my students, I attained clarity and planned my first course of action.

PLANNING

The purpose of my action research study was to increase authentic engagement within my painting classes. To begin, I developed an anonymous questionnaire designed to collect data about what students perceived as motivating and to measure their current levels of engagement (Schlechty, 2002). Although unsure if my plan would remedy the situation, it was time to act. Planning must be for "strategic action," keeping the ultimate goal in mind. This action becomes part of the research process (Waters-Adams, 2006). By seeking student input and implementing their learning preferences I showed my students that I was sincere about understanding and honoring them (Check, 2002; Combes Malcom, 2008).

---

essential to develop a community of learners who were reciprocal partners in the studio process. I strongly believed that the implementation of journals would result in meaningful opportunities for students to engage in the construction of their own learning though thoughtful written and visual dialogue. Despite my informed intentions I was disheartened to find that student results resembled little more than a teacher-required notebook. What was I doing wrong?

Thinking: Defining the Problem

I soon realized that before I could remedy this instructional ailment I first had to understand the symptoms. As I reflected upon the experiences and discussions I had regarding sketchbook journaling from my art education classes I kept returning to the idea that effective journals should *make thinking visible*. In contrast, my students' entries were minimal, rarely showcased engagement beyond the requirements of the assignment, and showed little evidence of artistic thinking. For the experience to be valuable, students would have to be invested in the process, but how?

Acting: Implementing Changes

Taking the idea of student investment into consideration I began to toy around with potential remedies. I began testing issues I felt might be inhibiting students from becoming invested by changing the format of the journal (binder versus sketchbook) and providing more focused use of the journals during class time. Unfortunately, these changes yielded disappointing results. By the time winter recess rolled around my outlook on the fate of journals in my classroom was particularly dismal. Fortunately, rejuvenated by the holiday break and some encouraging discussions with my university mentor, I began a new plan of action.

Re-Thinking and Re-Acting

I began by asking myself: What does a reflective journal look like? By beginning with this end in mind, I sat down to visualize what a successful journal and journaling process would look like. Through this reflective process, I decided that three main components exemplified quality journaling practices:

1. *Reflection*: Students should display thought-provoking responses in their journal. Discussion of these responses should ignite inquiry and dialogue from other students as well.
2. *Exploration*: The journals should be an avenue in which students take creative and artistic risks, both visually and verbally.
3. *Engagement*: The journals shouldn't seem like busy work, students should feel strongly connected and committed to the journaling process as a form of artistic thinking.

(continued)

ACTION

In an effort to address lagging student engagement, I administered the questionnaire, which contained seven questions concerning assignments that students responded to, using a Likert scale. I formulated questions after analyzing variable and non-negotiable components of typical art assignments. It remained imperative for students to meet state curriculum standards and district assessment mandates. Areas open for negotiation included content and subject matter, media and materials, critique format, and responsibility for choosing the direction of their work. My own experience told me that many students need some structure in order to work productively. Of the 40 students who participated in the survey, 35 agreed that they would like to choose the content, media, and direction of assignments, and 36 preferred a wide variety of painting experiences. Thirty-six wanted clear expectations, and 25 worried about being unsuccessful when attempting an unfamiliar assignment. Only 7 of 40 believed that the traditional class critique was a good use of time. Additionally, 19 rated themselves as authentically engaged. Sixteen believed they were ritually engaged, meaning they did what they were asked to do; they did the task well, but were not motivated by the task itself. Five students considered themselves to be either passively compliant or retreatists. None of the students rated themselves as rebellious (Schlechty, 2002).

REPEATING THE CYCLE

Data analysis and reflection should occur as soon as possible so that the teacher researcher can begin planning the next action (Waters-Adams, 2006). I was apprehensive about the results of the questionnaire and how I would accept my students' honesty. At times it was difficult to be both teacher and researcher; personal feelings aside, I recorded and analyzed the data without becoming defensive.

I evaluated the results of the questionnaire and planned changes; the results verified my original suspicions that many of my painting students lacked interest and enthusiasm, in order to transform their attitudes I had to transform my own. It was necessary for me to look at painting practice through their eyes, to reframe the image of art teaching that had been my viewpoint for too long. Much of what they considered important had been right in front of me all along. Through informal conversations students began to share with me the novels they were reading, the pictures on their cell phones, the music they listened to, the ups and downs of their relationships, part-time jobs, plans for the future, the list went on and on. I was striving to understand the needs of my students in the context of their world, to motivate and inspire them, to present a dynamic curriculum that could help them make real world connections in a

I realized that motivation seemed to be the thread that wove all of the components together. Students could not be authentically engaged without being motivated. The passion to explore and take risks could not be ignited without the sparks of curiosity. New questions emerged as I put myself in the shoes of my students: What kinds of experiences or exploration might excite me? What motivates me to use my journal as a vessel for my ideas in process?

Acting: Putting a Plan Into Motion

It became clear that I had left out a key element in my earlier journaling attempts: *choice*. As choice is particularly powerful for adolescents I predicted that students would invest ownership in their journals when empowered by options. Instead of dictating one assignment for all students to respond to, I constructed a list of creative prompts for journal entries that included a wide range of design problems and provocative aesthetic questions. The prompts encompassed under-represented art disciplines such as fashion and game design, areas that several students passionately connected to. When I acted on these decisions the journal assignments transformed from perfunctory exercises to meaningful personal experiences for the students.

Reflecting

The changes that I made were immediately empowering for both my students and myself. I watched in awe as the learning climate of my classroom transformed. Choice became a powerful motivator. Through their choices students assumed the role of expert researcher of their own particular design interests. Our journal share days, once dreaded awkward critiques became causes for celebration as students looked forward to sharing their newest discoveries with their peers. Journal entries became catalysts for student-led discussions and investigations that trounced perceived curricular restraints. The thinking processes facilitated through the journals led to increased understanding of design and visual culture through meaningful collaborative and meta-cognitive experiences. From the university to my classroom the reciprocity of ideas has come full circle, as students not only teach one another, but their teacher as well.

CONCLUSION

This art teacher's story models the value of reflective practice as she joined together with her students to focus on artistic thinking, problem solving and decision making. The journals themselves became the vessels for creative research—providing opportuni-

more democratic classroom (Kincheloe, 2003). My students were bored with authoritarian education; they knew how to play the game. Likewise, I was exhausted from my role as the authoritarian teacher Ayers (2004) refers to as "…the Big Noise: thinking, acting, telling, directing, planning, choosing, controlling, managing, disciplining" (pp. 6-7).

I mapped our new direction, planning backward. Work would be based on clear objectives that were important to art learning and knowledge creation, and activities would have clear evidences of that learning (Tomlinson & McTighe, 2006). Through their responses, my students had made it clear that covering art elements and design principles in a variety of media and hitting the highlights of art history with a critique thrown in at the end was not motivating. I needed to design instruction that blended highly differentiated activities with significant art themes and skills, in order to increase authentic student engagement. Consequently, I planned for classes to tackle broad themes like the transitional nature of our environment and inspirational qualities of music and literature, while honing compositional skills and a variety of painting techniques.

Students indicated, via the survey, that they were particularly interested in choosing the content and media for their own paintings. As much as they longed for freedom of choice, many still wanted guidance regarding techniques and broad themes. As I planned the next phase of my research—the action—I realized that since my students are digital natives, the use of technology could be a motivator. I reserved a mobile lap top lab to be used for Internet research. Anderson and Milbrandt (2005) propose that students can construct knowledge through art research, not to replicate the artworks of others, but rather to analyze and reflect; to advance student understandings of artists' ideas, thoughts, forms, style, and inspirations to stimulate their own creativity. It seemed natural to begin my students' quest for their own inspiration with a study of what inspires and motivates other artists; to discover not only images of their work, but to locate artists' statements, biographies, and influences that are easily accessed on the Internet. Together these elements could model the complex decisions artists make and how their experiences and environments impact their studio practice.

BUILDING TRUST

Though I had expressed my desire to change class dynamics and students looked forward to more freedom, I wanted to gain their trust since we would be partners in this action research project. I presented images of paintings that inspired me, followed by images of my paintings, along with two

ties for students to share their thinking processes and encourage a dialogue among all the participants, as students became teacher to their peers. This learner-centered approach promotes deep reflection and deep personal engagement. What has come into being is a more dynamic studio atmosphere where students take ownership of their work; feel responsible for their own emerging artist identity and to the group as a democratic community (Dewey, 1916; Noddings, 2003). For the teacher this experience has reinforced the practitioner research paradigm, as journals became the evidence that demonstrated the reflective processes of both student and teacher.

Connelly and Clandinin (1988) remind us that what a teacher contemplates will show up in the teacher's actions. With the aim of improving our practice, it is worthwhile for us to systematically think about our teaching actions–our doings. Thus, through continued mentorship with a university professor, a new teacher/graduate student found answers by taking action that focused on change and improvement and in doing so emerged from the experience as reflective practitioner (Schön, 1983, 1987). ∎

REFERENCES

Carr, W., & Kemmis, S. (1983). *Becoming critical: Knowing through action research*. Geelong, Australia: Deakin University Press.

Connelly, F. M., & Clandinin, J. (1988). *Teachers as curriculum planners: Narratives of experience*. Toronto, Canada: OISE Press.

Dewey, J. (1916). *Democracy and Education*. New York, NY: Macmillan.

Dewey, J. (1933). *How we think: A restatement of the relation of reflective thinking to the educative process*. Boston, MA: DC Heath.

Kolb, D. A. (1984). *Experiential learning: Experience as the source of learning and Development*. Englewood Cliffs, NJ: Prentice-Hall.

Noddings, N. (2003). *Caring: A feminine approach to ethics & moral education*. Berkeley: University of California Press.

Schön, D. A. (1983). *The reflective practitioner: How professionals think in action*. San Francisco, CA: Jossey-Bass.

Schön, D. A. (1987). *Educating the reflective practitioner: Toward a design for teaching and learning in the professions*. San Francisco, CA: Jossey-Bass.

Stringer, E.T. (1999). *Action research*. Thousand Oaks, CA: Sage.

Unrath, K., & Nordlund, C. (2006). Teaching art as reflective craft. *Translations: Theory to practice*. Reston, VA: The National Art Education Association.

Zeicher, K. M., & Liston, D. P. (1996). *Reflective teaching: An introduction*. Mahwah, NJ: Lawrence Erlbaum Associates.

originals and encouraged closer examination. Students eagerly made connections. By sharing my vision and my art making process I made myself vulnerable. By modeling my expectations, I established a deeper level of trust with my students (Hauboldt & Humphries, 2007).

DEMOCRATIC ACTION

Students conducted research on a painter of their choice, documented biographical information, medium, style, and philosophy, along with four images of the artist's work, then saved the file (see Figure 1). Some students had an artist in mind immediately; others discovered painters by searching subject matter, style, technique, or culture. They chose a painter whose work they found inspirational. Students used sketch-books to plan their paintings; considering prior knowledge of art elements and design principles. Each demonstrated their painter's influence on their own work through content, media, technique, or style. Options were wide open with regard to size, materials, and content; they were in control.

ARTIST'S CHOICE PAINTING PROJECT OBJECTIVES & ASSESSMENT CRITERIA

1. Research a painter of your choice and document important facts.
   Collect the following information and save it to a Word document on your server account:
   - Artist's first & last name
   - Nationality
   - Dates of birth & death
   - Philosophy
   - Artistic style or subject matter (realism, fantasy, portraiture, landscape, abstract, non-objective, etc.)
   - Affiliation with an art movement (Impressionism, Pop Art, etc.)
   - Primary medium (acrylic, oil, mixed media, etc.)
   - 3 or 4 images that represent the art work that interest you (when inserting images make sure that all will fit on one page)

   AFTER SAVING, PRINT ONE COPY TO GIVE ME

2. Execute an original painting in your choice of content/subject matter and media
   In your sketchbook begin planning a painting. You choose what and how.
   Media includes:
   - Acrylic on canvas
   - Oil on canvas
   - Mixed media on canvas or paper
   - Watercolor on paper
   - Pastels on paper

   When planning make a list of things such as supplies, other resources, color scheme, emotional impact, mood of the painting, symbolism, etc.

3. Finished painting must be clearly influenced by chosen artist in regard to at least one of the following:
   - Style
   - Technique
   - Media
   - Content

4. Consider the art E & P, composition, visual path, focal point, use of space, etc.

5. Participate in a short presentation of your painting and artist research
   More about this later.

FIGURE 1. Artist's choice painting project objectives and assessment criteria.

Managing varied activities was challenging; while some learners completed research, others began painting, and still others needed help stretching and priming canvas. I learned to expect the unexpected; things didn't always go as planned. I became more flexible. Soon students painted independently, allowing me to return to spend more time observing them at work and taking note of their conversations. The roles of teacher and researcher are not mutually exclusive; I found that while teaching I was able to informally gather data and began to formulate future actions. This is something most teachers do naturally, not done especially for research. However, there were times that I felt inclined to step back and observe, focusing my attention on how my students were adjusting to the changes that were underway.

REFLECTIVE JOURNALING

Triangulation of data collection methods assures accuracy (Hesse-Biber & Leavy, 2006). I used reflective journaling to record observations. Throughout the study I clarified cause-and-effect relationships and defined what students deemed important, then planned changes. Descriptors like *chaos* and *unexpected* emerged from my journal entries and indicated that I was still viewing my classes through the authoritarian lens. But my journal also illustrated authentic engagement as evidenced by my entry:

Some kids were doing photo transfers, painting with crushed-up plastic wrap, crumpled paper towels, splattering, masking tape lines, cutting stencils, etc. Others experimented with oil pastels, watercolor, as well as traditional uses of acrylics and oils.

I recorded and later transcribed conversations with students. It was important for me to hear and understand my students in the context of their experiences (Kincheloe, 2003). All students enjoyed freedom to choose content and media, yet some struggled with the open-ended nature of the assignment. Kate felt "lost"; she did not know "how to make the project work." We discussed scaffolding provided on the criteria sheet and she discovered her own solution (Hart, 1994). Eric concluded that "freedom helps us to find our own artistic voice." The energy level changed, periods of silence when students worked intently were followed by heated debates as students considered the directions of their paintings. By giving students choices in how they developed their work, they had become problem solvers and decision makers (Tomlinson, 1995).

My journaling recorded discourse about student perspectives for future assignments. Would they find my introduction of new techniques and art media in future projects restrictive? During their discussions they all agreed that they enjoyed learning to use materials like plaster and experimenting with monoprint and photo-transfer techniques. Hollis believed that constantly using the same material was restricting. Others concurred and Stephen elaborated, "It's good to experiment with different materials, but it is hard to do when you have no interest in the subject matter." Across the board, students confirmed that they want control of content and direction, yet they enjoy experimenting with new materials; they have a need for novelty (Dissanayake, 1988). A national survey (1999) of instructional practices by secondary art teachers in the U.S. indicated that 92% of respondents believed that working with a wide variety of media and processes was very to moderately effective in motivating and inspiring students (Burton, 2001b).

A Student in My Own Classroom: Understanding Teacher Practice

KAREN L. CUMMINGS / ASSISTANT PROFESSOR OF ART EDUCATION, UNIVERSITY OF MISSOURI–ST. LOUIS

What began as my desire to change students' behaviors in the art classroom led to an evaluation of my teaching and the teacher's role in students' learning experiences. I became a student in my own classroom, learning about the nature and value of art, and learning how to be a better teacher. As I engaged in inquiry, reflection, discovery, and change, I came to a new understanding of the influences of curriculum and socialization on students' learning and classroom behaviors.

I was teaching art in a public high school and observed a decline in my students' academic performance and an increase in their negativity toward learning. Responses of "so what, "who cares," and "whatever" had become routine rather than rare. I recognized a need for change and embarked on a journey to im-prove my students' levels of engagement in art class. Responding to my students' interests in popular culture, I developed and implemented a visual culture art curriculum[1] offering students opportunities to study and decode the visual language found in contemporary imagery.[2] My research brought to light the implications of the classroom environment and the influences of the teacher on students' behaviors. In the process of studying my classroom, I came to a new understanding of my self as a teacher, as an artist, and as an individual.

Action research (Kemmis & McTaggert, 2000; McNiff, 2002) guided changes to my teaching.[3] As my students engaged in the critical inquiry of visual culture imagery, I observed and evaluated the changes in their attitudes and behaviors. I analyzed discussion and critique transcriptions, teacher and student

(continued)

A DIFFERENT KIND OF CRITIQUE

The first questionnaire indicated the majority of students had negative perceptions of traditional class critiques. On written reflections completed at the conclusion of the Artist's Choice Painting assignment, students described them as "embarrassing," "boring," and "too long." Evaluation and reflection in the context of a culminating exhibition activity are fundamentals and students need opportunities to demonstrate their accomplishments and gain constructive feedback from peers (Baron & Boschee, 1995; Guay, 2002). Burton (2001a) affirmed, "Listening perceptively to another person can often be more important than expressing an opinion or providing information, and it can lay the foundation for understanding the art itself" (p. 45). I restructured critiques to give students two product options: A poster with information and images about the artist they researched or a digital presentation including talking points. Both required explanations of artist influence on their original work. Students had saved the artist information and images during the Internet research activity, and this was easily retrieved for use in either product option.

The length of the critique was cut in half. Organized more like a gallery opening, paintings were displayed with posters nearby. Students interacted as they would in a gallery; they moved around the classroom, posed questions and discussed artistic influences. The students who chose to make digital presentations spoke about how artist research influenced their own paintings, answered questions, and accepted feedback.

TRIANGULATION

After the critique, I distributed reflective questionnaires, seeking rich descriptive data about student perceptions. All six questions required elaboration. The first question directed individuals to describe their thoughts about the creative process at the beginning, middle, and end. They were also asked to discuss their feelings about the finished painting and any successes or problems. Next, students were instructed to rate their level of success when compared to previous assignments. I requested that they explain their perceptions about the use of artist research in directing the development of their paintings. They were asked to share their opinions on the open-ended nature of the assignment. Finally, they were to compare the gallery style critique with the traditional format. Not only did students give me highly textured information to guide my next action, but through self-reflection they were able to recognize their capabilities and accept personal responsibility for growth (Covey, 1998; Tomlinson & McTighe, 2006).

journal entries, and classroom artifacts to guide me in developing lessons responding to the students' interests and, at the same time, inform my understanding of the learning experience. I sought students' input on topics of inquiry, studio activities, and assessment criteria, and I designed curriculum activities fostering divergent thinking, encouraging collaboration and cooperation, and emphasizing personal experiences. By year's end, my students exhibited increased enthusiasm and interest in curricular activities. They approached lessons in a deep and meaningful manner, thinking seriously and sincerely about issues of personal importance. Analysis of the data collected revealed it was the relationships and interactions occurring in the classroom that were of utmost significance in altering the adolescents' behaviors in the art classroom (Cummings, 2007).

I developed curricular and classroom changes in an attempt to engage my students in their learning; through studying the subsequent students' behaviors I came to a new understanding of the learning experience. The action research model of planning, acting, observing, reflecting, and revising allowed me to demystify actual occurrences in the classroom as opposed to what I hoped or assumed was happening. I transitioned from the teacher as expert in control of learning to facilitator and partner in the educational process becoming a student in my own class-

room, learning about the nature and value of art, and learning how to be a better teacher. In teacher research there is the need to be both insider and outsider simultaneously. As the teacher, I was an insider in my classroom; my decisions and actions in the classroom were always made in effort to further the educational experiences of my students. As a researcher, I tried to be an outsider and view the classroom and myself as a stranger would; classroom decisions, actions, and outcomes became conscious choices to know and understand the students' learning experiences more fully.

My students' willingness to participate, interests in the subject, and honesty encouraged me to become critical of my practice and recognize the influences on students' learning experiences. Noddings (2004) suggests, "When we listen to them, we learn what they are going through, and this knowledge can be used to shape what we do in teaching" (p. 154). By creating a classroom atmosphere conducive to a continuous exchange of ideas, mutual respect, and tolerance of differences, I encouraged change in my students' behaviors. I became more student-centered and responsive to my students' needs. I supported and encouraged their personal growth and advanced their questioning of self-understanding and individuality. It is because of my research that I now work with a new attitude in my teaching, routinely

Coding and analyzing the data was more complicated than on previous questionnaires. As I read over each student's responses to the six questions, I kept a tally of positive or negative reactions, and then I listed descriptive words and phrases for each. Overall students had positive responses. They described feeling excited, eager, and challenged, some felt nervous and unsure about where to start. Many wrote that they worked harder and put more time, effort, and thought into this painting because they cared about it. Several expressed a sense of responsibility for the results. A few mentioned possible improvement or regretted not trying harder. With a few exceptions, artist research provided guidance for their paintings. Most needed structured freedom. Using artist research as a springboard, students discovered inspiring ideas, interesting materials, and unique approaches. Everyone embraced choices. Alex wrote, "In school you have no freedom, you're constantly told what your assignment is and it gets real boring... but this painting let me be free with what I wanted and my ideas." The gallery critique was a big hit. Only 2 students out of 39 preferred the traditional style of critique. One student was unable to respond due to an extended absence. In general, students' writing indicated that their exchanges were more honest and personal, they felt less pressure, and they enjoyed seeing a variety of work up close. Aimee explained that the gallery critique allowed her to "understand why each student did their painting the way they did." Suggested improvements included written feedback cards and refreshments, both implemented in later critiques.

CONCLUSIONS

The cycle of observing, reflecting, planning, and action spiraled on. Each phase overlapped the next. I observed my students as they worked to create meaningful art. Reflective teacher journaling became a mainstay. When planning, I took into account student ideas, opinions, and feedback. Their input, coupled with my own beliefs about important art learning presented new directions for art instruction and paths for more democratic actions; we shared decision making. I sustained student trust by sharing my own paintings and listening to my students. Students continued self-reflection, gallery critiques, and, most importantly, freedom of choice in content. We experimented with unfamiliar materials, techniques, and non-Western aesthetics. Classes wrote about and discussed contemporary painters as diverse as West African artist Angu Walters and Australian native Steve Dix, while students discovered that artists draw inspiration from diverse themes like nature, emotion, music, poetry, science, fantasy, and the human form.

By implementing a more democratic approach to teaching art based on collaborative decisions, my students came to value their work and learning. When an individual teacher makes a commitment questioning, discovering, and changing in a continuous spiral of self-understanding in effort to improve my teaching and my students' learning experiences. My students allowed me into their lives and because of them I became a better teacher. It was through their eyes that I came to a new understanding of adolescents' learning and the influences of interactions on the classroom experiences. ∎

REFERENCES

Anderson, G., Herr, K., & Nihlen, A. (1994). *Studying your own school: An educator's guide to qualitative practitioner research.* Thousand Oaks, CA: Corwin Press.

Cochran-Smith, M., & Lytle, S. (1993). *Inside/outside: Teacher research and knowledge.* New York, NY: Teachers College Press.

Cummings, K. (2007). Webs, windows, and reflections: Experiences in a secondary art classroom (Doctoral dissertation). Retrieved from Dissertations & Theses: A&I (Publication No. AAT 3290213.)

Dadds, M., Hart, S., with Crotty, T., Ferguson, L., Frost, R., Geraci, J., et al. (2001). *Doing practitioner research differently.* New York, NY: Routledge Falmer.

Duncum, P. (2002). Visual culture art education: Why, what and how. *Journal of Art and Design Education, 21*(1), 14-23.

Duncum, P. (Ed.). (2006). *Visual culture in the art class: Case studies.* Reston, VA: National Art Education Association.

Freedman, K. (2003). *Teaching visual culture: Curriculum, aesthetics, and the social life of art.* New York, NY: Teachers College Press.

Gude, O. (2007). Principles of possibility: Considerations for a 21st-century art & culture curriculum. *Art Education, 60*(1), 6-17.

Kemmis, S., & McTaggart, R. (2000). Participatory action research. In N. Denzin & Y. Lincoln (Eds.), *Handbook of qualitative research* (pp. 567-605). Thousand Oaks, CA: Sage.

McNiff, J. (2002). *Action research for professional development: Concise advice for new action researchers.* Retrieved from www.jeanmcniff.com/booklet1.html

Noddings, N. (2004). Learning from our students. *Kappa Delta Pi Record, 40,* 154-159.

Noffke, S. (1999). What's a nice theory like yours doing in a practice like this? And other impertinent questions about practitioner research. *Change: Transformations in Education, 2*(1), 25-35.

ENDNOTES

1 Curriculum objectives, outline, and lessons available in Cummings (2007).

2 See Duncum (2002, 2006), Freedman (2003), Gude (2007) for further reading on Visual Culture in Art Education.

3 See also Anderson, Herr, and Nihlen (1994); Cochran-Smith and Lytle (1993); Dadds Hart, Crotty, Ferguson, Frost, and Geraci (2001); Noffke (1999).

to change it can have a powerful effect on student achievement (Marzano, Pickering, & Pollock, 2001). Conducting an action research project within the context of my own teaching practice solidified my commitment to change. I constructed new teaching strategies designed to motivate and inspire my high school students, allowing them to direct their own learning. Students initiated second paintings when finished early, completion rates grew; they eagerly took their paintings home. On a final Likert scale, about two-thirds of my students rated themselves as authentically engaged, as compared with one-half in the beginning. The remaining one-third believed they were ritually engaged, as compared to about one-half. Two students were passively compliant. None rated themselves as retreatists or rebellious.

During a final group interview, students were relaxed and made comments as they felt inclined. Their remarks assured me that not only had we had accomplished my objective to enhance authentic engagement, but that they had become partners toward this goal. A junior shared her interest in painting about societal issues. One boy mentioned his desire for "skill builder" activities. A graduating senior added, "By being able to pursue our interests we were able to be more productive and motivated." Clearly, these high school students were involved and felt comfortable suggesting activities that resulted in work that they found meaningful and valuable. They were sharing responsibility for their own learning, constructing their own knowledge, working toward a democratic classroom.

REFERENCES

Anderson, T., & Milbrandt, M. K. (2005). *Art for life.* New York, NY: McGraw-Hill.

Ayers, W. (2004). *Teaching toward freedom.* Boston, MA: Beacon Press.

Baron, M. A., & Boschee, F. (1995). *Authentic assessment: The key to unlocking student success.* Lancaster, PA: Technomic.

Burton, D. (2001a). Social dynamics in exhibiting art: Rethinking the practices of art education. *Art Education, 54*(1), 41–46.

Burton, D. (2001b). How do we teach? Results of a national survey of instruction in secondary education. *Studies in Art Education, 42*(2), 131–145.

Check, E. (2002). In the trenches. In Y. Gaudelius & P. Spears (Eds.), *Contemporary issues in art education* (pp. 51–58). Upper Saddle River, NJ: Pearson Education.

Combes Malcom, L. A. (2008). Achievement beyond expectations: Results of positive student/teacher relationships in the classroom. *Trends: The Journal of the Texas Art Education Association,* 2008, 9–15.

Covey, S. (1998). *The 7 habits of highly effective teens.* New York, NY: Fireside.

Dissanayake, E. (1988). *What is art for?* Seattle: University of Washington Press.

Guay, D. M. (2002). The dynamic project, contemporary issues, and integrative learning. In Y. Gaudelius & P. Speirs (Eds.), *Contemporary issues in art education* (pp. 302–315). Upper Saddle River, NJ: Pearson Education.

Hauboldt, J., & Humphries, H. (2007). Facing life's challenges. *Trends: The Journal of the Texas Art Education Association,* 2006 & 2007, 7–16.

Hart, D. (1994). *Authentic assessment: A handbook for educators.* Menlo Park, CA: Addison-Wesley.

Hesse-Biber, S. N., & Leavy, P. (2006). *The practice of qualitative research.* Thousand Oaks, CA: Sage.

Kincheloe, J. L. (2003). *Teachers as researchers: Qualitative inquiry as a path to empowerment.* London, England: Routledge.

Marzano, R. J., Pickering, D. J., & Pollock, J. E. (2001). *Classroom instruction that works: Research-based strategies for increasing student achievement.* Alexandria, VA: Association for Supervision and Curriculum Development.

Schlechty, P. C. (2002). *Working on the work.* San Francisco, CA: Jossey-Bass.

Tomlinson, C. A. (1995). *How to differentiate instruction in mixed-ability classrooms.* Alexandria, VA: Association for Supervision and Curriculum Development.

Tomlinson, C. A., & McTighe, J. (2006). *Integrating differentiated instruction and understanding by design.* Alexandria, VA: Association for Supervision and Curriculum Development.

Waters-Adams, S. (2006). *Action research in education.* Retrieved from University of Plymouth website: www.edu.plymouth.ac.uk/resined/actionresearch/arhome.htm

Zemelman, S., Daniels, H., & Hyde, A. (1998). *Best practice: New standards for teaching and learning in America's schools.* Portsmouth, NH: Heinemann.

BETSY MURPHY is an art instructor and Art Department Chair at Cedar Park High School near Austin, Texas. She received her BFA in Art Education from the University of Texas and her Master's of Art Education from Texas Tech University. She began her career as a public school art educator in 1984 and taught elementary art for 16 years and middle school art for 7 years before moving to the high school level. Her areas of research include cultural diversity and social justice in public school art, as well as the prehistoric rock art of Texas and New Mexico. She has published in *Trends: The Journal of the Texas Art Education Association, School Arts, Arts & Activities, Duke University Voices Magazine,* and *The Austin American Statesman.* She is a regular presenter at state and local conferences. Most importantly, she continues art research in her painting studio where she loses track of time and rekindles her artistic passion.

35 / Acts of Engagement

ELIZABETH M. DELACRUZ / ADJUNCT ASSISTANT PROFESSOR,
UNIVERSITY OF FLORIDA

ABSTRACT: *This chapter sets forth a notion of art education as a form of public engagement, and describes how action research informs this approach through a description of a course titled Museums in Action: Engaging the Community. I use this description to set forth a vision of art education as professional activity deeply connected to notions of directly engaging diverse communities both within and outside of our classrooms, and with the lofty aims of making a difference in the world. In this framework, I envision art educators' professional activities, pK-20, as acts of engagement. My thesis here is that critically informed, civic engagement with diverse people in real world settings is not only facilitated by action research, the kind of professional engagement advocated here necessitates a reflexive, collaborative action research approach.*

ACTS OF ENGAGEMENT

Recently, I co-developed and co-taught a course titled "Museums in Action: Engaging the Community" with my colleague Anne Sautman, the Director of Education at the Krannert Art Museum at the University of Illinois in Urbana-Champaign. Now offered every semester, the purpose of the course is to extend the reach of the Krannert Art Museum to a broader community in East Central Illinois and to involve university students in the museum's public engagement activities. In this chapter I share how action research informs both this course and other courses I teach. I use this description to set forth a notion of art education as professional activity directly engaging diverse communities both within and outside of our classrooms, and with the lofty aims of making a difference in the world. In this framework, I envision art educators' professional activities, pK-20, as *acts of engagement*.

ART EDUCATION AS *ACTS OF ENGAGEMENT*

Teaching art, for me, has always had a strong community-oriented component. While teaching in K-12 schools my professional work involved art exhibitions in public places; presentations by my students and myself in varied community settings; field trips to local sites; creating art, posters, or visual materials for other school programs, newspapers, yearbooks, events, plays, and banquets. All of these professional activities embraced the communities in which my students lived. Since coming to the university, I have focused some of my teaching and research outside the confines of my university classrooms. This work included off-campus teaching and collaborations (Delacruz, 2004), engaging my on-campus students in local service learning activities (Delacruz, 2009a), and Internet-based information sharing, networking and planning. I have given presentations, workshops, and consultations to teacher institutes, museums,

community organizations, governmental agencies, and professional associations.

My work with preservice teachers, non-art majors, teachers, museum educators, and colleagues has dealt with educational reform and practical problems we faced together as educators.[1] My professional activities embraced the question: *How are my teaching acts relevant to real lives and needs of the children, families, and communities I serve?* Now I refer to these teaching activities, collectively, as *Engaged Teaching*. *Engaged Teaching* is a hybrid of scholarship, teaching, and public engagement. *Engaged Teaching* reaches out beyond the classroom walls—through knowledgeable and responsive teaching acts—to develop meaningful connections to local individuals, places, and communities of practice.

I have recently integrated into my professional work findings from my ongoing research resulting from a 2007 Faculty Fellowship with my university's Center on Democracy in a Multiracial Society. This research is a community ethnography in a culturally diverse town located north of Urbana-Champaign, Illinois. My project utilizes oral histories and arts-based research to inquire about the multicultural identities, creative expressions, and intercultural community activities of the residents of this town. Because of my *engagement* orientation, the study quickly morphed, and I am now advising two local community organizations, have written grants, helped plan festivals, and (in collaboration with Anne Sautman) linked the local high school art program in this town with the Krannert Art Museum for an ongoing partnership (Delacruz, 2009a). I now characterize my research as *Engaged Scholarship*. *Engaged Scholarship* is a hybrid of community-oriented arts-based public engagement, social activism, and action-research oriented inquiry. My own version of *engaged scholarship* investigates ways that contemporary forms of art education changes and enriches people's lives. This expereince has inspired me to involve my own students more directly in community-oriented work (Delacruz, 2009a).

ACTS OF ENGAGEMENT AND ACTION RESEARCH

I find a perfect fit between *Engaged Scholarship and Teaching* and action research. But more than *fit*, my thesis here is that *acts of engagement* with diverse people in real world settings necessitates an action research approach. Action research allows us to examine our varied professional decisions and activities, to ask the much-needed questions: *Is it working?* and *What is the moral relevance of this professional activity to the larger educational goals and social agendas with which we find ourselves aligned?* The remainder of this chapter describes how action research informs the course "Museums in Action," a brief synopsis about how action research supports my other teaching activities, and some thoughts about art education as public engagement.

Action research is mixed method, qualitative research conducted in social settings with intact groups of people, often carried out by the professional practitioner responsible for the development or delivery of services to these groups (Elden & Chisholm, 1993; Newton & Burgess, 2008). Action research is based on the belief that professional practitioners may, through self-initiated systematic investigations, develop deeper understandings about the value and efficacy of their practices while at the same time bringing about desired changes in concrete situations (Carson, 1990; McCutcheon & Jung, 1990). Action researchers utilize a variety of approaches, blending informal and formal methods that include keeping a research journal, systematic reflective writing, document collection and analysis, participant observation, questionnaires, surveys, photo and video documentation, interviews, focus groups, and case studies (May, 1993; O'Brien, 1998). The aims of critical action research include: (1) gaining a deeper understanding of aspects of the practice along with the social systems in which the practice is embedded, (2) clarifying professional aims, needs, and strategies, (3) assessing outcomes, (4) determining the success of practices, and revealing aspects of practice needing improvement, (5) considering social, political, and economic issues embedded in social situations in which power relations between interacting individuals, groups, and institutions are unequal and unjust, and (6) suggesting specific actions and improvements (Noffke, 1997; Reason, 2006). Due to its emphasis on practical problems, action research is typically conducted in the setting where the problem is encountered, and the focus is usually on a person, unit, or intact group, (Small, 1995).

HOW DOES ACTION RESEARCH INFORM *ENGAGED PRACTICE*?

Action research has helped me work with my colleague Anne to improve "Museums in Action" with the idea that many of our strategies may be adapted to other kinds of teaching. Students in "Museums in Action" read about museum education, conduct art historical research on

selected museum objects, create and deliver museum programming and educational materials, and conduct audience surveys and museum event evaluations. Student artifacts and programming produced in this course include museum object guides, interactive school tours, studio explorations used in conjunction with tours, family-festivals, a night in the museum for college students, and a student-created podcast. Action research is a fundamental aspect of "Museums in Action," shaping and informing the course. Action research strategies are *embedded in* the assignments and projects that comprise the course. That is, evaluations take place throughout the course as it unfolds.

OUR ACTION RESEARCH STRATEGIES

Utilization of students' personal interest statements and experiential writings that were assigned as prompted responses to scholarly readings. Reading these responses has helped us get to know students individually and as a group. We also used these writings to initiate in-class discussions.

Conducting group discussions with students both prior to and after implementation of student-designed museum events. Discussions included planning sessions for upcoming events, and evaluative discussions following events. Occurring both during and at the end of the semester, discussions were also prompted by their audience surveys and onsite observations of the museum events they designed. We used information gathered from these group discussions to shape future museum events, and to refine and improve course aims and strategies. These discussions also helped us create a sense of shared responsibility and cohesiveness with students.

Evaluation of student work-in-progress. Student research and drafts of material to be shared with museum audiences were reviewed and annotated with instructor and museum curatorial feedback, revised by students, and final drafts then accepted and graded. Exemplary student work has been archived for later use and possible wider dissemination beyond the class, with permission from the students.

Weekly staff briefings. Focused on immediate course and student needs, brief staff meetings attended to specific pending assignments and preparations for coming class sessions and museum events. We also deliberated about whether student work was of sufficient quality to be disseminated publicly by the museum and what we needed to do to facilitate high quality student work.

Photographs and videos taken at museum events to document the nature, look, feel, and quality of the event and the audience. These informal documentary photographs have been used to create an archive of student museum events, and shared with museum staff, future students, and fellow museum educators in conference presentations.

Dated notations on instructor created course materials; dated instructor notes written directly on photocopies of student artifacts and writings; and annotations to our grading records. Annotations were used to determine the flow, feasibility, quality, clarity, and appropriateness of course requirements as well as for grading purposes. Made and utilized both during and at the end of the semester to make adjustments to assignments or scheduling, these notations commented on the clarity of the instructional materials and the quality of student artifacts in relation to course objectives. Grading record annotations sometimes noted the quality of individual student work, participation, and professionalism.

Gathering information and subjecting it to closer scrutiny throughout the semester facilitated our understanding of how this course functioned; informed our deliberations about what changes needed to occur; and brought clarity to issues that needed to be addressed. Some of the data gathering was actually part of the course assignments. Student audience studies conducted on site at museum events (with prior IRB approval) informed the students about the audience reactions to their specific programming ideas, and informed the instructors and the museum more generally about the value of this kind of programming. Taken together, the abundance of evaluation data gathered, analyzed, and shared with students has provided a rich context for developing revisions to our "Museums in Action" syllabus, assignments, schedule, grading strategies, and communications about the course.

In summary, in "Museums in Action" teaching, research, museum program development, and action research evaluation were intermixed in the real-world arena of museum public programming. Action research strategies served to ensure that the museum practices represented both the values and aspirations of the museum. Action research activities also facilitated our efforts to clarify and challenge some of our own beliefs underlying the course.

SOME THOUGHTS ABOUT ACTION RESEARCH AND *ENGAGED SCHOLARSHIP AND TEACHING*

- For me, action research is real-world research, conducted with people I know and is aimed at things that are important to us. Although the example provided here focused on a single course, I have long utilized action research strategies, before I knew there was an academic name for the research methodology, as a means of improving my practices in my other courses, both in my K-12 teaching and now at the University of Illinois. It seems to me that exemplary K-12 art teachers also already do many of the things one might legitimately call action research. My own action research strategies on other classes have included:
- keeping the diverse array of materials from my courses organized and archived into course binders (portfolio keeping);
- making extensive dated evaluative comments, insights, and notations on these course materials and student artifacts (document analysis and field notation);

- photographing exemplary student studio work and archiving student written work;
- incorporating on all of my student self-assessment instruments a question asking them to suggest how the project could be made better or more relevant to their needs and interests (responsive feedback);
- hosting round table discussions with students at the end of each semester, soliciting informations about their experiences of and recommendations for the course (focus groups);
- soliciting anonymous student feedback (surveys and questionaires);
- annotating my grading records with personal and professional observations, insights, and concerns; and
- talking to students about things they want to talk about, taking the time to listen to them, and thinking about what they have to say.

Between semesters, I review collected materials and notes, and make adjustments to my courses, deleting and updating projects and classroom activities based on information gathered each semester. In some cases my action research methods are intensive and time consuming. Sometimes they involve collaborators. But in most cases, my action research is my own—private, informal, less systematic, and more sporadic. Regardless of intensity or formality, themes of responsive, socially just engagement with diverse people and communities pervade both my action research strategies and my vision of *engaged scholarship and teaching*.

Following Harry C. Boyte's (2002) ideas, I view these *acts of engagement* as a form of democratic, critically informed public work, work that brings individuals together across cultural divisions to work on community projects of lasting impact.[2] In closing, I am compelled to add a caveat to this chapter. Over the years, I have frequently found myself justifying and explaining *engaged scholarship and teaching* to administrators and colleagues who sometimes seem ill-informed about art education.[3] Sometimes frustrated but nevertheless undaunted by these limitations, I have found great satisfaction in this kind of work. I do not think my approach is particularly unique or bold, and there are many art educators doing much more than I could ever hope to accomplish. Their work inspires me, but most of all, I am motivated by the ways in which simple acts of engagement bring their own internal rewards. Finally, I conceptualize *engaged scholarship and teaching* and *action research*—these interrelated *acts of engagement*—as *shared* and I envision myself as a collaborator and co-learner with my students, fellow educators, community friends, consultants, and peers, who with greatest patience and generosity, tell me when I have got it right, and when I am off the mark. For the engaged scholar/educator wanting to make a difference in the world, this kind of information is most useful.

REFERENCES

Boyte, H. C. (2002). *A different kind of politics: John Dewey and the meaning of citizenship in the 21st Century.* Retrieved from www.cpn.org/crm/contemporary/different.html

Campus Compact. (n.d.). *Educating citizens: Building communities.* Retrieved from www.compact.org

Carnegie Foundation for the Advancement of Teaching. (2009). *Community engagement elective classification.* Retrieved from www.carnegiefoundation.org/classifications/index.asp?key=1213#

Carson, T. (1990). What kind of knowing is critical action research? *Theory into Practice, 29*(3), 167-173.

Delacruz, E. M. (1992). Reconceptualizing art education: The movement toward multiculturalism." In A. Johnson (Ed.), *Art education: Elementary* (pp. 55-77). Reston, VA: National Art Education Association.

Delacruz, E. M. (1995a). Multiculturalism and the tender years: Big and little questions. In C. M. Thompson (Ed.), *The visual arts and early childhood learning* (pp. 101-106). Reston VA: National Art Education Association.

Delacruz, E. M. (1995b). Multiculturalism: Myths, misconceptions, and misdirections. *Art Education, 48*(3), 57-61.

Delacruz, E. M. (1996) Multiculturalism in art education: "Business as usual." *Journal of Aesthetic Education, 3*(1), 29-41.

Delacruz, E. M. (1997). *Design for inquiry: Instructional theory, research, and practice in art education.* Reston, VA: National Art Education Association.

Delacruz, E. M. (2000). Making a difference. In K. Keifer-Boyd, K. Fehr & D. Fehr (Eds.), *Real-world readings: Things your professor never told you about art education* (pp. 11-20). New York, NY: Falmer Press.

Delacruz, E. M. (2004). Teachers' technology working conditions and the unmet promise of technology. *Studies in Art Education, 46*(1), 6-19.

Delacruz, E. M. (2009a). *Change agency and faculty entrepreneurship: Merging community based education, research, social justice, and public engagement within a feminist framework.* Invited lecture to the Women's Caucus on the occasion of receiving the 2009 June King McFee Award for contributions to the profession. 47th Annual Convention of the National Art Education Association. Minneapolis, MN, 2009. Available at http://naeawc.net/awards

Delacruz, E. M. (2009b). Art education in the age of new media: Toward global civil society. *Art Education, 62*(5), 13-18.

Elden, M., & Chisholm, R. F. (1993). Emerging varieties of action research: Introduction to the special issue. *Human Relations, 46*(2), 121-142.

Imagining America. (n.d.) Imagining America: Artists and scholars in public life. *Imagining America.* Retrieved from www.imaginingamerica.org

May, W. (1993). "Teachers-as-researchers" or action research: What is it, and what good is it for art education? *Studies in Art Education, 34*(2), 114-126.

McCutcheon, G., & Jung, B. (1990). Alternative perspectives on action research. *Theory into Practice, 29*(3), 144-151.

Newton, P., & Burgess, D. (2008). Exploring types of educational action research: Implications for research validity. *International Journal of Qualitative Methods, 7*(4), 18-30.

Noffke, S. (1997). Professional, personal, and political dimensions of action research. *Review of Research in Education, 22*, 305-343.

O'Brien, R. (1998). An overview of the methodological approach of action research. In R. Richardson (Ed.), *Theory and practice of action research.* João Pessoa, Brazil: Universidade Federal da Paraíba. Retrieved from www.web.net/%7Erobrien/papers/arfinal.html#_Toc26184651

Reason, P. (2006). Choice and quality in action research practice, *Journal of Management Inquiry, 15*(2), 187-203.

Small, S. (1995). Action-oriented research: Models and methods. *Journal of Marriage and the Family, 57*(4), 941-955.

ENDNOTES

1. My research deals with several main topics: contemporary art practices (Delacruz, 2009a), multicultural education (Delacruz, 1992, 1995a, 1995b, 1996), new technologies (Delacruz, 2004, 2009b), and teachers' practices and concerns (Delacruz, 1997, 2000).

2. Although it has not always been the case, my sense is that my university, a Carnegie Foundation RU/VH: Research Universities (very high research activity) institution (a classification formerly called "Research 1"), is gradually moving in the direction of embracing faculty professional work that is public engagement oriented in the manner I describe in this chapter—as evidenced by our alignment with nationwide community engagement initiatives including *Imagining America* (n.d.), Campus Compact (n.d.), and our recently acquired Carnegie Foundation for the Advancement of Teaching Community Engagement Elective Classification (2009).

3. After almost 30 years of teaching art, I have not been able to determine if their lack of information about art education is benign neglect or willful ignorance, but explain I must, regardless of where I happen to be teaching. While teaching in K-12 schools, I had to explain why art is important to people I thought should already know why. At the university, I now have to explain why K-12 education or community-based work is important to people I think should already know why.

ELIZABETH DELACRUZ is Adjunct Assistant Professor at the University of Florida online master's program in Art Education, Editor of *Visual Arts Research* journal, Education Associate at the Krannert Art Museum, Faculty Fellow at the University of Illinois Center on Democracy in a Multiracial Society, and Professor Emerita and former Chair of Art Education at the University of Illinois. She is recipient of the NAEA Higher Education Division Art Educator of the Year, the NAEA Women's Caucus June King McFee Award, the United States Society for Education through Art National Edwin Ziegfeld Award, the University of Illinois Vice Chancellor's Teaching Scholar's Award, and the UI College of Fine and Applied Arts Teaching Excellence Award. Delacruz has authored over 60 scholarly essays and chapters, two books, and has presented her research all over the world. Her research fuses scholarship and teaching with public engagement, and considers the nature and value of culturally diverse artistic expressions, from folk art to new digital media, and the role of visual arts education in promoting civil society.

PARTICIPATORY ACTION RESEARCH

36 / Participatory Action Research in Art Education: Possibilities for Social Change Through Collaborative Visual Inquiry

KAREN HUTZEL / ASSOCIATE PROFESSOR OF ART EDUCATION, THE OHIO STATE UNIVERSITY

ABSTRACT: *This chapter describes Participatory Action Research (PAR) as a research methodology that seeks transformation and social change through collaboration and community-building. Specifically, the chapter suggests strategies for art educators to engage in PAR work for the potential of collaborative inquiry practices to promote liberating opportunities among students, teachers, school administrators, and communities, specifically through visual inquiry and collaborative artmaking to address pressing social concerns and inequalities. The chapter highlights key elements defining PAR methodology, the potential for PAR to address social issues within schools, strategies for implementing PAR in a school, with an emphasis on arts-based and qualitative research methods, and approaches to facilitating PAR by engaging students, teachers, and administrators in collaboratively exploring issues and taking action to promote change. Finally, collaborative artmaking is offered as a specific strategy to PAR in art education whereby the collaborative artwork represents communicating the research results.*

Action research (AR) represents a broad field of inquiry based loosely around common ideals for social justice and theoretical notions of pragmatism claiming theories are only useful insomuch as they work in the real world (James, 1907). Action research goals usually include social change and transformation through co-learning opportunities. Participatory action research (PAR) provides a specific understanding of action research that emphasizes the collaborative nature of co-learning through qualitative inquiry with the ultimate goal to create social change by addressing power dynamics through collaborative activism.

In this chapter, I present PAR in art education for the potential of collaborative inquiry practices to promote liberating opportunities among students, teachers, school administrators, and communities, specifically through visual inquiry and collaborative artmaking to address pressing social concerns and inequalities. Despite my PAR work outside of school sites (Hutzel, 2006, 2007), and the potential to address issues of power and oppression in such community spaces, I focus this chapter predominately on school locations. I begin by offering components of PAR as an area of Action Research (AR) practice, highlighting key elements defining PAR methodology, or as Reason and Bradbury (2006) describe it better not "as a *methodology* but as an *orientation toward* inquiry" (p. xxi). I then propose the potential for PAR to address social issues within schools, as a space where power and inequality are prevalent, mirroring similar issues present in larger society. Schools are ultimately smaller sites where power and inequality feed problems such as behavior issues and disproportionate opportunities based on social factors including race, class, and gender. I then provide strategies for implementing PAR in a school, with an emphasis on arts-based and qualitative research methods, despite the argument that PAR can also include quantitative methods of data collection (Greenwood & Levin, 2007). As PAR is grounded in the participatory practice of researching local issues, I offer approaches to facilitating PAR by engaging students, teachers, and administrators in collaboratively exploring issues and taking action to promote change. Finally, I suggest utilizing collaborative artmaking as a specific strategy to PAR in art education.

DEFINING AND EXPLORING PARTICIPATORY ACTION RESEARCH

Participatory action research is a form of action research that, at its core, emphasizes democracy through participatory forms of inquiry focused on local issues and solutions that seek social justice and collaborative learning. The following descriptions constitute components of PAR:

1. Collaboration, participation and community building is inherent in a systematic and democratic process (Reason & Bradbury, 2006; Stringer, 2007);
2. Specific issues are defined, analyzed, and addressed locally in an effort to promote social justice by "seeking to improve the participants' situation" (Greenwood & Levin, 2007, p. 3);
3. The research process is concerned with "developing practical knowing in the pursuit of worthwhile human purposes" (Reason & Bradbury, 2006, p. 1);
4. Theory and practice as well as action and reflection constitute the research (Reason & Bradbury, 2006); and
5. Similar to "constructivist approaches to pedagogy" (Stringer, 2004, p. 2), learning through collaborative inquiry is significant to the research process.

Due to ambiguities in defining AR and the particular approach PAR offers within the larger field, it may be necessary to contrast PAR with various approaches to AR. For instance, in many cases AR in classroom settings is applied in less emancipatory, less participatory ways than PAR, focused more on the teacher conducting individual research on her or his teaching practice with the goal to improve that practice (Reason & Bradbury, 2006). I do not disagree with this practice; in fact, I encourage it in my own students as they work toward becoming art teachers who are reflective practitioners. However, a necessary variable toward defining PAR is in the collaborative component. It is in this regard that I define the essence of PAR's methodology as *collaboration*. Reason and Bradbury (2006), building on the work of Paulo Freire, offer that "action research is research *with*, rather than *on* practitioners, who in many instances become co-researchers themselves…" (p. xxv). This is how I present PAR for art educators in this chapter.

In school settings, PAR practices extend AR approaches by emphasizing the political nature of knowledge production and the pursuit of social justice and human liberation (Brydon-Miller, 2001). PAR has traditionally focused on populations and communities considered exploited or oppressed in addressing causes of oppression toward positive social change (Brydon-Miller, 2001). Robin McTaggart suggested the aim of PAR is "to change practices, social structures, and social media which maintain irrationality, injustice, and unsatisfying forms of existence" (in Reason & Bradbury, 2006, p. 1). This could play out in varying ways in a school setting which, due to PAR's social activist stance, is sometimes not fully welcomed by teachers and administrators. While I do not have the space within this chapter to adequately address purposes and procedures of schools, challenges of power and injustice in the United States' public school system are prevalent, causing oppression and exploitation within schools and school systems that PAR practices might address.

Inequality is inherent in schools, both within individual schools and across the entire educational system of the United States (Kozol, 1991, 2005). Pressing social issues plague many schools to the point that students feel unsafe in their own school. In response to these issues, through PAR practices teachers can engage each other and students in a process of inquiry and social action to address social issues and inequalities present in their schools. As a research process and a learning opportunity, PAR is a means by which teachers can engage each other and their students in exploring local issues and seeking practical solutions together. The process should build community, a key element of PAR practice (Stringer, 2007), and subsequently can provide a useful outcome for schools with conflicts among cultural or other groups. Art teachers stand in an ideal position for implementing PAR in schools due to art education's emphasis on culture and social critique and art teachers' connections with many teachers and most students in their schools.

STRATEGIES FOR IMPLEMENTING PAR

Generally, PAR research methods do not vary much from other research methods. What does vary, however, includes identification of a problem and collaboration with co-participants. Ideally, PAR methods, from the generation of research questions to the analysis of data, involve collaboration. In practice, however, collaboration does not necessarily happen at every phase in the research process, although it should be the goal of PAR studies. In this section, I will suggest collaborative strategies for each stage of the research process of PAR, emphasizing qualitative methods.

Issue identification and question formulation. Research begins with identifying an issue and generating a research question. In a collaborative process, the PAR facilitator will engage fellow teachers, school administrators, and/or students in a brainstorming process to identify an issue or problem in the school. Oftentimes, participants come together because of casual conversations about a particular problem, such as bullying. In this case, the facilitator should encourage co-researchers to consider all the ways someone might bully another person in an effort to expand the concept to include other issues, such as sociocultural dynamics, social cliques, and even war. The co-researchers might also explore media imagery for visuals that depict social stereotypes, degradation of women, or masculinity. After a thorough investigation of art and visual culture, which serves to broaden co-researchers' perspectives of their identified local issue, the facilitator should bring the topic back to the local school site and ask students to discuss their views on the topic: What do we want to know about this school issue? What data do we need to collect to know more about this school issue? Who should be involved in the process and how do we include them? What is our investigative question to focus our exploration? Through these, and more questions, the facilitator should use consensus methods to lead the group toward identifying one question to direct the research. The research question should be open, not leading, and focused on the local. In terms of bullying, the guiding research question might become: How is bullying impacting our students and what can we do to prevent it?

Data collection. Once a research question is developed, participants will decide how to collect data. There are many methods to choose from, including questionnaires, interviews, focus groups, surveys, photography, and observations. The facilitator should guide the group in selecting a limited number of data collection methods that most directly answer the guiding research question. In the case of bullying, the co-researchers might decide to interview a variety of students, teachers, and administrators about how bullying affects them in the school. Alternatively, they might hold a series of focus groups to ask the same questions. Focus groups should be grouped according to similar positions, such as a group of sixth graders, a group of eighth graders, a group of teachers, and a group of staff/administration. Another method might be to hand out questionnaires across the entire school with a series of questions about the personal impact of bullying. Photography is another option for sharing personal stories. Lykes' (2006) use of "Photo Voice" contributed to the telling of war and post-war stories in Guatemala toward improving quality of life. "Photo Voice" formalizes a photography activity as storytelling by providing co-researchers with cameras

Considering the Tensions: Beginning Researchers and Participatory Action Research

LESLIE GATES / ASSISTANT PROFESSOR OF ART AND DESIGN, MILLERSVILLE UNIVERSITY AND **CONNIE NORTH** / PSYCHOTHERAPIST, MADISON, WISCONSIN

According to long-time participatory action researcher Patricia Maguire (1993), participatory research (PAR) is "a process of collective, community-based investigation, education, and action for structural and personal transformation" (p. 157). In other words, PAR ideally poses questions that emerge from the participants' lived experiences. Graduate students attempting to conduct PAR may find it difficult to use this methodology of *collaborative* inquiry and still satisfy the expectations of universities, given their traditional expectation that students *individually* conduct all aspects of their research. In particular, the community-based formation of research questions esteemed in an ideal PAR model contrasts with the lone researcher model used by many graduate programs. Reflecting on

her own experience as a graduate student conducting PAR, Maguire (1993) asked, "How could I write a dissertation proposal with its problem statement unless I did it unilaterally—the antithesis of participatory research?" (1993, p. 162).

Maguire's question points to the tensions inherent in PAR, wherein the researcher shares control of the inquiry process with the participants. PAR demands that the researcher relinquish power to others and, in so doing, engage in an uncertain, dynamic research process. Moreover, an important intention of PAR is to advance positive social change. Such transformation often evokes resistance from those invested in the status quo, including ourselves. Therefore, beginning researchers will benefit from honestly reflecting on their commitments to this methodology before attempting

in order to capture significant images. When presenting these images to the group, each photographer tells the story of the image and why it was personally significant. Whatever data collection methods are identified and planned, the research group should divide up the task of collecting the data and prepare to come together again to co-analyze what is collected.

Co-analysis of the data. After collecting data on the topic, the co-researchers will analyze the results. This could be done in a number of ways. Co-researchers might divide into smaller groups and focus on one set of data to analyze. One group might analyze interviews while another might analyze questionnaires. Alternatively, the facilitator might lead the entire team in a dialogue toward identifying themes in the data. In either case, the team should come back together as a whole to discuss the results. What themes have co-researchers seen in the data? What seems most pressing about the issue? Are particular groups of people most affected by the problem? Are others causing the problem? As the team discusses the results, many will become ready to discuss solutions. It is important to capture ideas for solutions when they are presented, but not to move too quickly to the solution stage. The facilitator might post a large sheet of paper on the wall to "bank" comments, ideas, and solutions to the problem for later use.

In concluding co-analysis of the data, it is important to return to the original research question in an attempt to answer it. In this case, the research question was: How is bullying impacting our students and what can we do to prevent it? Co-analysis of data should have answered the first part of this two-part question. The facilitator will want to have the results listed in the front of the room while clarifying that the team has agreed to the results of the analysis. At this point, it is time to move on to the second part of the research question and the solution stage of the PAR study.

Acting on the results. The next stage of the research process involves identifying solutions or actions toward addressing the school issue. Again as a group, the facilitator should lead co-researchers in a discussion of potential solutions, including artmaking activities and awareness campaigns. This discussion could identify actions such as a collaborative mural, a recycling project, or performance-based art. The circular process of PAR transcends the linearity of traditional research approaches, instead suggesting the process as spiraling to include look, think, and act components (Stringer, 2007). In essence, co-researchers may decide it is necessary to identify the problem differently, create a new research question, or collect additional data about the problem based on their desires to act. For instance, the team might take the issue even further than the art piece, pushing for policy changes in the school or programs to continue addressing the identified problem.

to enact it. The literature supporting PAR can help a beginning researcher unearth and work through their commitments to and rationale for undertaking a collaborative, action-oriented study (see our References for works that we found particularly helpful).

In our experience, obstacles to PAR in a university setting often result from a faculty member's lack of information about PAR rather than conscious, intentional resistance to it. For example, PAR aims to produce knowledge grounded in local contexts that is useful to local participants (Herr & Anderson, 2005). However, universities often encourage knowledge production that fills gaps in scholarly literature and, in the process, demonstrates a researcher's intellectual competence. The goals and intended outcomes of PAR therefore challenge the model with which many faculty members are familiar. For this reason, knowing the language of PAR scholarship can help us both justify and explain our reasons for using this methodology.

Nevertheless, expectations prevail in many institutions that graduate students will take a more university-centered approach to research (Herr & Anderson, 2005). Researchers likely will have to accommodate some demands made by universities and/or funding agencies that differ from those of the community members involved in the research. As Maguire (1993) notes, ideal versions of PAR, with their demand for community-driven research projects, may not be realizable in university settings. However, researchers with a commitment to PAR can resist being colonized by these external expectations. We can decide "to learn and grow from doing, and to celebrate the doing, no matter how flawed, small-scale, or less than ideal" (Maguire, 1993, p. 176). Viewing participatory methodologies as "release points," or openings, can promote a fluid and reflexive methodology that, in addition to meeting institutional requirements, allows us to honor participants as co-constructors of knowledge and "re-vision what could be." (McClelland & Fine, 2008, p. 254). ∎

REFERENCES

Herr, K., & Anderson, G. L. (2005). *The action research dissertation: A guide for students and faculty.* Thousand Oaks, CA: Sage.

Maguire, P. (1993). Challenges, contradictions, and celebrations: Attempting participatory research as a doctoral student. In P. Park, M. Brydon-Miller, B. Hall & T. Jackson (Eds.), *Voices of change: Participatory research in the United States and Canada* (pp. 157-176). Westport, CT: Bergin & Garvey.

McClelland, S. I., & Fine, M. (2008). Writing on cellophane: Studying teen women's sexual desires, inventing methodological release points. In K. Gallagher (Ed.), *The methodological dilemma: Creative, critical and collaborative approaches to qualitative research* (pp. 232-260). New York, NY: Routledge.

It is important that the teacher remain focused on positive solutions, suggesting activities that could change the direction away from the identified problem. In the case of bullying, for instance, instead of an anti-bullying visual message, it is important to focus on the positive characteristics of the school community that can contribute to greater change. The result could be a collaborative art piece such as a quilt to celebrate the school's diversity or some other artwork visualizing positive solutions and outcomes for the community. Students might locate media imagery that is somehow degrading to groups of people and alter the meaning of the images, hanging their altered images around the school with messages of change. In essence, positive messages and responses, based on an asset-based approach to community development, go further in a school climate than do protests and attacks (see Kretzmann & McKnight, 1993).

COLLABORATIVE ARTMAKING AS PAR

An important possibility of the role of art in PAR is in the opportunity to re-tell stories through visual imagery. The collaborative component of PAR can contribute to a collaborative artmaking process by engaging a community, in this case a school or classroom community, in negotiating meaning toward addressing a shared problem.

Collaborative artmaking shares common ideals with PAR due to its emphasis on collaboration, social critique, activism, and social justice. The outcome of a collaborative artmaking experience might be a public mural or sculpture, such as in the *Art in the Market* program in Cincinnati, Ohio (Bastos & Hutzel, 2004), or indoor collaborative artworks such as quilts, mosaics, exhibits, poster campaigns, or digital imagery. In my own work, I have utilized photography and murals the purpose of addressing social issues while re-telling community stories through collaborative negotiation of meaning and outcomes. In this process, children and adults work collaboratively to develop a displayable, finished art piece to represent the co-learning experience. In one case, neighborhood children collaborated with college students shooting photographs of both the college campus and with the children's community in discovering similarities and differences. Using the computer as an artmaking tool, each pair of college student and youth created an image to represent the selected theme. Recently, the group selected the theme "bridging the gap" to represent their collaborative work. Each artwork was then printed and connected together into one final piece and was hung in a community space. In this way, the co-learning was shared visually while the story of college life and community realities was re-told.

CONCLUSION

In this chapter I offered PAR as a research process intended to create positive social change through collaborative co-learning and inquiry experiences. Key to utilizing PAR in a school is the teacher's role as the facilitator of an inquiry-based process that bring together students, teachers, and/or administrators toward finding solutions to pressing local and school issues. Art education offers a particular role in PAR due to its emphasis on social and cultural analysis and critique. Through PAR processes, art serves as a useful tool for re-telling community stories, bringing awareness to an issue, offering hope, and bringing together individuals who share a space to work toward social change. PAR is intended to address issues of power and oppression through knowledge production that is political and potentially liberating, with the ultimate goal of social justice.

REFERENCES

Bastos, F. M. C., & Hutzel, K. (2004). "Art in the Market" project: Addressing racial issues through community art. *Journal of Cultural Research in Art Education, 22,* 86-98.

Brydon-Miller, M. (2001). Education, research, and action: Theory and methods of participatory action research. In D. L. Tolman & M. Brydon-Miller (Eds.), *From subjects to subjectivities: A handbook of interpretive and participatory methods* (pp. 76-94). New York: New York University Press.

Greenwood, D. J., & Levin, M. (2007). *Introduction to action research: Social research for social change.* (2nd ed.). Thousand Oaks, CA: Sage.

Hutzel, K. (2006). Challenging our students' place through collaborative art: A service-learning approach. *Journal of Higher Education Outreach and Engagement, 11*(4), 125-134.

Hutzel, K. (2007). Reconstructing a community, reclaiming a playground: A participatory action research study. *Studies in Art Education, 48*(3), 299-320.

James, W. (1907). *Pragmatism: A new name for some old ways of thinking.* New York, NY: Longmans Green.

Kozol, J. (1991). *Savage inequalities: Children in America's schools.* New York, NY: Harper Perennial.

Kozol, J. (2005). *The shame of the nation: Restoration of apartheid schooling in America.* New York, NY: Three Rivers Press.

Kretzmann, J. P., & McKnight, J. L. (1993). *Building communities from the inside out: A path toward finding and mobilizing a community's assets.* Chicago, IL: ACTA.

Lykes, M. B. (2006). Creative arts and photography in participatory action research in Guatemala. In P. Reason & H. Bradbury (Eds.), *Handbook of action research* (pp. 269-278). Los Angeles, CA: Sage.

Reason, P., & Bradbury, H. (2006). *Handbook of action research.* Los Angeles, CA: Sage.

Stringer, E. T. (2004). *Action research in education.* Columbus, OH: Pearson.

Stringer, E. T. (2007). *Action research* (3rd ed.). Los Angeles, CA: Sage.

KAREN HUTZEL is an Associate Professor of Art Education at The Ohio State University where she teaches courses on Computer Art, Multicultural Art Education, and Research. She utilizes asset-based service-learning strategies to build community learning environments and approaches research through a collaborative artmaking process founded on participatory action research. Her scholarship has included exploring social reconstruction in art education and urban community development through action research methodologies. She co-edited the anthology, *Transforming City Schools Through Art: Approaches to Meaningful K-12 Teaching* (2012), has published on the topics of community arts and service-learning—including articles in *Studies in Art Education*, the *Journal of Cultural Research in Art Education*, *Art Education*, and the *Journal of Higher Education Outreach and Engagement*—and has recently had two articles reprinted on the prominent website, www.communityarts.net. She is currently pursuing research on urban education and educational equality through critical race theory. Dr. Hutzel has presented at local, national, and international forums through both invitation and peer review.

37 / A Cultural Interface: New Media Research in Art Education

MICHELLE TILLANDER / ASSISTANT PROFESSOR OF ART EDUCATION, THE UNIVERSITY OF FLORIDA

ABSTRACT: *As technology interfaces develop beyond traditional screen-based frameworks and become intertwined in our everyday work and leisure spaces, art educators can consider the intersections between cultural, human, and digital forms of expression. From a teaching perspective as well as a research perspective, how do we engage students in thoughtful conversations about technology and art? This participatory action research (PAR) exemplar examines the cultural processes of technology, rather than the tools of technology as a way to further understand art and technology practice in art education. Specifically, the study explores the possibilities and limitations of shifting from* **how to use** *digital technology to* **how students and art educators** *use digital technology within a cultural context. Three art educators, along with their students, and I served as co-researchers at three independent sites, exploring through reflection on daily teaching practice, curriculum, art, and inquiry into how the cultural conversation of technology and art are negotiated within our practices.*

I must try... to have the people dialogically involved as... researchers with me... Through this process of investigation, examination, criticism and reinvestigation, the level of critical thinking is raised among all those involved.
—Freire, 1988, p. 292

This article describes a Participatory Action Research (PAR) study that took place in three public high-school art classes. The focus of the study, entitled *Cultural Interface as an Approach to New Media Art Education* (Tillander, 2008), was to recognize the many influences technology has on learning—with a heightened awareness on the cultural aspects. This intersection is called a cultural interface (Johnson, 1997; Manovich, 2001), and I used a PAR study to examine this topic in depth.

RESEARCH QUESTION

The central question for this PAR study is: *In what ways have the discourses, activities, and inquiry processes of a cultural interface approach altered participants' perceptions, interactions, and interpretations of art, art education, and new media technology?* The cultural interactions between technology and learning implicate all participants in the study—teacher, student, and researcher—and all are recognized as active contributors in the PAR process.

THEORETICAL FRAMEWORK: CULTURAL INTERFACE APPROACH

Participatory Action Research was chosen for this study because PAR and a cultural interface theory approach both focus on the negotiations between their respective entities. PAR involves direct participation in a dynamic research process between participants and organizational structures and endorses multiple ways of knowing that are continually translated and negotiated. Similarly, cultural interface theory

involving technology explores the interactions that are being negotiated between knowledge systems inclusive of all actants (e.g., participants and technologies).

RESEARCHER'S FRAMEWORK

Cultural interface theory (Johnson, 1997; Manovich, 2001) is the theoretical framework on which this study rests. This theory views technology not as merely a tool but as an active element in shaping cultural practices and understandings among people. Through my engagement with visual arts high-school students and art educators, as well as with new media technologies over the course of my teaching career, I recognize that technology influences learning in many ways. The teachers and students who participated in this research, like digital new media artists, critically, playfully, and imaginatively remix the processes of art and technology.

METHODOLOGY

The researcher selected Participatory Action Research (PAR) for this study because the cycle of PAR involves sharing the visions of all participants, making decisions relative to resources available, collaboratively developing and validating plans, implementing plans, monitoring the results, and negotiating and revising the plans (McTaggart, 1991, 1997; Reason & Bradbury, 2006; Reason & Torbert, 2001). As part of the collaboration of this project, the participants—art educators, students, and I—continually negotiated the classroom activities and experiences related to the research question. As participants engaged in the classroom, we observed and obtained feedback from each other and negotiated and revised plans that revolved exploring technology more through a sociocultural approach (i.e., cultural interface theory) embedded in institutional contexts then a tool based approach.

This PAR study examines these influences and encourages a cultural dialogue shifting from *how to use* digital technology to *how students and art educators use* digital technology. In considering this shift, digital media are [re] positioned by considering that "…we are no longer interfacing to a computer but to culture encoded in digital form" (Manovich, 2001, p. 70).

PARTICIPANTS IN THE STUDY

Through conference presentations and several workshops in public schools, I met several teachers with an interest in pursuing digital technology issues within art education. As a result, I began collaborating with them about technology in art education. The collaboration grew from e-mails and face-to-face conversations eventually resulting in a research collaboration at three sites. Three art educators Chris, Michelle, and Betsy, along with their students, participated in the research at three independent sites.

DESCRIPTION OF THREE SITES AND PARTICIPANTS

Site 1 is unique in this study because Chris was developing a program/curriculum around the school's newly developed mission statement. The mission statement pertaining to the visual arts states that "…the visual arts strand is to empower students with life-long learning and a passion for the arts through educational experiences that promote creative expression and reflection, individual and global aesthetic awareness, and knowledge of the roles of the play in culture." The Arts Academy is an Eastern Mid-Atlantic urban school that has visual arts, theater, music, and dance as its core components. In Site 1, Chris's classes were driven by a structured, skill-based approach. The classes were part of a special workshop, titled *Digital Art*, that was piloted with 16 sophomores and juniors.

Michelle's school, research Site 2, is a high school situated in a small town outside a very large New England metropolitan area. The school serves about 700 students, and the school's mission statement includes a commitment to "develop and enhance creativity and an appreciation for the arts." The books on Michelle's desk provide insight into her enthusiasm and commitment to young people and quality educational technology experiences. Michelle recognized the importance of technological skills and the ubiquitous nature of technology. Two sections of the Computer Art and Design class participated, each had 20 and 21 students respectively, and involved a mixture of freshman, sophomores, and juniors.

Site 3, where Betsy teaches, serves more than 2,200 students in an Eastern mid-Atlantic area. The school, the oldest secondary school in the district, is a large high school complex with several wings serving distinct student populations. In Site 3, Betsy conducted her class with a classical arts foundation and minimal use of technology in terms of access. The class that participated in the study was an Advanced Placement (AP) Studio, and included a total of 11 high school juniors and senior students.

RESEARCH CYCLE AT EACH SITE

At Site 1, I met with Chris and his technology support staff at the school and discussed the technology resources available for the workshop. We collaborated and developed several possible activities—including a smooth transition from the previous lesson (i.e., use of digital cameras and portrait lighting activity)—and set a schedule of class activities to implement the plans. As we made observations each day, we negotiated any revisions after the class.

At Site 2, Michelle and I communicated by e-mail for about 3 months discussing the resources available and the best approach to transition to her course objectives. We collaboratively developed an initial set of plans and handouts, negotiated class examples, and then finalized the content on my first day at this site. On the second day of my stay, we began implementing our plans with students and monitoring the results, and then negotiating and revising our plans throughout the remainder of the study.

At Site 3, Betsy and I met with her school technology specialist 3 months prior to implementing the project, and discussed the existing technology resources, and the potential teaching objectives. Over the next 3 months, we collaborated by e-mail and occasionally on site to finalize the lessons. Just prior to the end of her current curriculum unit, I met with Betsy and her students to explore the students' artwork and explain the forthcoming research—helping everyone transition into this project. Throughout this study Betsy's schedule required us to meet prior to the AP Studio class to discuss results. This allowed us time to negotiate and revise our plans.

DECISION-MAKING

The PAR process, through a "participatory worldview, places human persons and communities as part of their world—both human and more-than-human—embodied in their world, co-creating their world" (Reason & Bradbury, 2006, p. 7). In this study, the participants—Chris, Michelle, Betsy, their students, and I—offer a variety of perspectives that inform individual and community-identified needs.

NEGOTIATING THE PARAMETERS

The PAR research cycle and the inquiry process involve a series of stages. The first step for this research collaboration involved establishing mutual benefits and initiating roles and responsibilities for the school-based art educators and me. The research process included coming to consensus around:

- developing strategies for the site as a research space, including what my presence and role as the co-learner would be;
- establishing meaningful actions to benefit all participants;
- agreeing about collecting and using data;
- gathering feedback from participants for analysis concerning this research; and
- sharing information for the benefit of all participants.

IMPORTANT CONSIDERATIONS

As a researcher/facilitator, I acted as both a resource and a catalyst affecting the elements of the study. I regularly communicated with each of the three art educators in person, by e-mail, and by phone. We collaborated on definitions in relation to educational objectives and cultural environments (i.e. the level of technology available or the degree to which technology is integrated into artmaking/ meaning). These definitions included research, culture, art, new media, and technology. One goal was to make visible the underlying assumptions and values (subjectivity and activist stances) about art education and technology specific to each site. It took considerable energy to negotiate reciprocity and symmetry of relations and agendas, as I was cognizant of the competing views and institutional forces at play. For example at all three sites, all levels of participants (student, educator, and administrator) had to extend their rule-based approach to technology—to a more comprehensive understanding of technology. Because some participants considered technology as a separate discourse from art, they treated technology in an isolated manner and did not fit it into the conventional art curriculum (i.e., painting, drawing, and sculpture).

THE ROLE OF THE RESEARCH FACILITATOR

One of my initial roles as facilitator was to develop a resource list of potential digital media artists to use as a point of discussion with the teachers and students. After considering many possibilities, each art educator and I reached a consensus about which artists were appropriate for their students, curriculum, and resources available; and which would offer opportunities to consider the research questions.

CLASSROOM INVOLVEMENT

Next, the teachers introduced the students to the intent of the research, asking them to make artwork about the topic of technology in art and their everyday lives. For example, in Site 1 Chris wanted the art lesson to engage students in critically examining shifting forms and meanings in digital advertisement. I recommended showing artists such as Moriko Mori and Nancy Burson, as well as analyzing several contemporary ads in their use of technology for image creation. In Site 2, rather than specific artists, Michelle used a homework reading reflection, titled *Project Earth: Image Ready Animation,* which focused on Internet mapping services. Along with the animations created by her students, Michelle used the prompt "closing the gap between the real world and the computer" to begin a discussion with her students around two short newspaper articles (Vascellaro, 2006a, 2006b) relating to their recent exploration of Google Earth®. In Site 3, Betsy wanted me to give a presentation on new media artists. The presentation served as a catalyst to focus an area of art and technology exploration. From brainstorming sessions involving this class, the final question, "How does technology impact your life?" emerged and provided a juncture for students to reflect on their experiences and provoke potential technology conversations through art making. This process of negotiation encouraged the exploration of personal voice, creative opportunities, and cultural inquiry. In terms of the action research spiral, the process of negotiation through brainstorming discussions served as an "action turn" (Reason & Torbert, 2001, p. 2) to revise our views on art and technology in a high school art classroom and provide the focal point for the creation of artwork.

GATHERING DATA

Since the three sites are not located in the same geographic region, each art educator worked with me to collect data for her or his site. The data collection started with initial e-mail exchanges between the art educators and me, and included summaries of phone conversations. The art educators collected student reflections, conversations, and artwork. When I was on site we shared daily observations through meetings before and/or after class when possible, and then further reflection via e-mails.

The duration of on-site field study at each school varied. The Site 1 Digital Art class consisted of 2-hour sessions each week for 6 weeks; the Site 2 Computer Art and Design class consisted of two classes for 1-hour sessions every day for one week; and the Site 3 AP Studio met once a week for 2 hours for 6 weeks. Throughout the entire collaboration process at each site the art educators, students, and I identified issues of concern about technology in art and our lives, analyzed current conditions, discussed impacts, identified points of change, and analyzed how the change happens. The art educators and I began creating our own knowledge bases (recorded in e-mails and field notes) of the experiences (planning, implementing, and evaluating the lessons). A continual cycle of observations and reflections was collected through e-mails, planning meetings, and written notes of observations and conversations with students about their artworks and ideas about technology in art and art education.

INTERVIEWS

At the end of the research cycle at each site, I conducted audio interviews with the three art educators and several students who volunteered to participate. During each interview I asked the same questions, with a focus on their experiences and this study's research questions. I digitally recorded and later transcribed all of the interviews and field notes, collected and organized all e-mails, and digitally photographed non-digital artwork and archived copies of digital art files to document the artwork. Following the interviews, the three teachers and interested students who participated received electronic copies of the transcriptions to comment on or to modify.

DATA CO-ANALYSIS

As part of the overall study, the data analysis phase was described to the teachers and students, who were encouraged to participate in co-analysis. The analysis of the study was collaborative throughout the study (i.e., making decisions relative to resources, developing and implementing plans, monitoring the results, and negotiating and revising the teaching strategies) and included both teachers and students. The art educators were very involved in the daily reflections on observations, actions, and planning; and less interested in looking at the entire collection of data that I archived over the entire process for their respective sites. Similarly, the student participants were most interested in their analysis on their artistic insight.

In each site, throughout the field experience, the daily discussions often focused on the research question. The discussions centered on exploring the cultural processes of technology, rather than the tools of technology. From a teaching perspective, how do we engage students in conversations about technology in art? The dialogues and reflections challenged our perceptions and biases of student engagement with new media outside of the art class. From a student perspective, how do we engage new media in our artworks? Many of the students gained a heightened awareness the possibilities of using technology as an expressive medium with unique issues different from those of traditional art.

At the conclusion of the last field experience, I consolidated the data from all the sites for a comprehensive analysis. Due to logistics and time constraints, there was limited participation from teachers and students during the comprehensive analysis. The interview transcripts were provided to the teachers and participating students through e-mail; transcript revisions and comments were then sent back to me and combined into the final summary. During the "analytical coding" process (Richards, 2005, p. 94) I used a word processor's editing features to identify and extract ideas, and to find repeated concepts to form categories across all three sites. I then, repeatedly reviewed the text collected from all the data sources, and coded the ideas with the word processor's commenting and highlighting features. When a passage articulated the participants' point of view and clearly connected to the research questions, I highlighted it and labeled it with a conceptual phrase using the Microsoft Word® comment function. At this point, repeated concepts were grouped into categories that revealed patterns and themes, given names and color-coded. I repeated these steps several times until ideas or categories were saturated (i.e., the concepts form naturally, rather than being forced).

ACTOR-NETWORK THEORY

During the analysis, I used Actor-Network Theory (ANT) (Latour, 1987) to include technology as an agent of change in a network of interacting entities (i.e., human participants, cultural interfaces, technology infrastructure, educational definitions of technology, and educational interpretation of technology integration). Using ANT as a lens to analyze data, all members of the network play a role, thus uncovering new relationships among participants. In this study, the agents in the network consist of researcher, classroom art educator, students, institutions, technology, new media art, art education, and colleagues in a community of practice. For instance, through discussions I had with art educator Michelle (Site 2) we each acknowledged our own definitions of technology. She acknowledged her adoption of the NAEA definition of new media that frames technology as a tool, and I acknowledged my more conceptual cultural approach. For me, the cultural interface approach as articulated by Manovich (2001) invites thinking about cultural expression of digital interfaces by linking content and process, as well as critically exploring knowledge, culture, and everyday experiences of creating and communicating through contemporary technology. In terms of pedagogy, this affords an opportunity to develop art and technology curricula that revolves around meaningful conversation about contemporary digital visual culture. ANT allows the analysis to include the various elements of a cultural interface, including the participants' (e.g., students, teachers) interaction and preconceptions as agents of the network. Namely, we discussed the underlying values and assumptions of technology at the personal and institutional level that are implicitly influencing our practices in the classroom.

Through the use of ANT, a researcher is able to see what emerges from analyzing data, to find issues that may be absent. For example, Betsy (Site 3) and I discussed the themes generated by students for their artworks: old technologies as a precursor to new; issues of public and private spaces in regard to surveillance technology; the idea of losing clarity while gaining immediacy; being a fish out of water without technology; and technology's role in creating ideal beauty. These themes metaphorically link agents of change in a network—and see technology as more than just a tool. ANT emphasizes that participants "at some point in

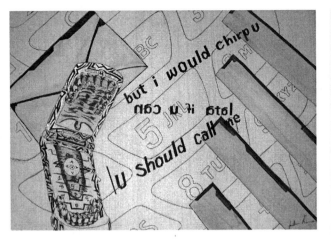

FIGURE 1. *Untitled*. Colored pencil drawing, 18″ x 24″. From Site 3 in response to the prompt, "How does technology impact your life?"

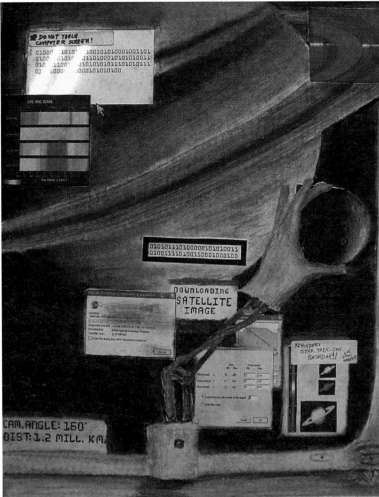

FIGURE 2. *Art Makes What Was Old, New*. 14″ x 24″. From Site 3 in response to the prompt, "How does technology impact your life?"

the network can transform the network, extend its nodes, multiply relationships between the nodes, cut out nodes, and sever the connections between nodes" (Fox, 2005, p. 85).

More specifically, one student's artwork (see Figure 1) about cell phones, text messaging, and cultural hybrids of communicating, and his ideas behind the work, related to local cultural practices and identities.

This artwork was an exploration of the idea of *text messaging and cultural hybrids of communicating, like "chirping."* Specifically, his artwork explored communication with text messaging (icons) as a cultural activity, and his perceptions of meaning with text messaging. I found his insights for this artwork to be more personal and expressive than reflected in his AP portfolio artwork. I found his insights and expressions of his engagement with technology illuminating on how individuals and group communication/identity circulates across the interface.

CROSS-SITE ANALYSIS

Additionally, along with the shared analysis at each site I conducted a cross-site analysis of the artifacts from all three sites until recurring themes emerged from the documents. I continued the analysis using memos about emerging topics such as *real world* or *personal connection* that were written and saved as comments representing intersecting and overarching themes. This process allows interconnecting themes to be traced down to specific passages, which can be analyzed for common conditions, consequences, strategies, and interactions concerning the research questions across all three sites. The process is complete when new themes stop emerging from the data.

FINDINGS

A cultural interface approach revealed that technology is not a singular concept, but is continually reinterpreted and practiced differently, making curriculum more complex and

dynamic. This research also wrestled with extending the object world of technology (tool) into the world of culture, inherently provoking a contextual understanding of technology in our everyday lives.

STUDENT ATTITUDES ABOUT THE RELATIONSHIP OF TECHNOLOGY TO ART

This study revealed that expanding the definition of technology in relationship to art education, often resulted in bringing teachers' and students' lived experiences in relation to technology into the class dynamic. Several students were observed critically wrestling with their attitudes and beliefs about technology and "technology and art." Rene, a student from Site 3, used a playful approach in her artwork to challenge the relationship between the screen images we see and the way we reflect on the world around us.

Art Makes What Was Old, New is a color mixed-media drawing of a robotic arm and a computer screen on a table. The robotic arm, sitting outside the screen space is adding a planet into the existing computer screen image. Rene's interests speak to blurred boundaries of the computer screen

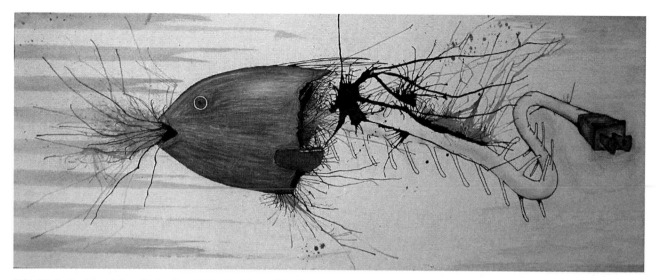

FIGURE 3. *Unplugged from Technology*. Ink, colored pencil, and watercolor, 14″ x 24″. From Site 3 in response to the prompt, "How does technology impact your life?"

and our physical spaces. Additionally, she had computer printouts collaged on the surface of the artwork and a string of binary code in the middle of the image. The binary code which translates to the title, *Art Makes What Was Old, New*, serves as additional layer of meaning making. Betsy (Site 3) stated that her participation in this PAR study would lead her to consider technology conversations throughout her traditional art units (e.g., drawing and painting) with her intermediate students. She thought that it would be an interesting approach to engage students critically in discussions similar to the conversations we had with students who participated with us in this study (Betsy, personal communication, June 23, 2006).

As part of the research process and collaboration, Chris (Site 1) drafted a set of questions to use with students in tandem with their artwork. Once we reviewed these questions and modified as needed, we had participating students provide their insights. For example, one student from Site 1, Andrew, reflected on a question asked by Chris, "How do artists organize their knowledge and skills in the field?" Andrew shared his response, "Artists gain their knowledge and ideas through life itself… and mainly school teaches you how to use technology (i.e. tool) and inspiration [for artists] comes from life (i.e. culture)" (Andrew, response in final refection, May 15, 2006). These questions engaged Andrew and the other participating students into articulating their insights on how they saw technology positioned around them.

UNDERSTANDINGS OF TECHNOLOGY

The research question analyzed the effects of introducing a cultural interface approach (e.g., shifting new media art education from tool to an emphasis on cultural content) as an educational alternative. As examples of negotiation and change, I shared several definitions of technology such

as a tool or machine, as rules such as software processes, as systems, and as a cultural or sociological interface. This began our conversations about how we each defined technology. In Site 1, Chris was comfortable with technology, but only as a tool. He saw the need for its use from a cultural perspective, but struggled when coming to terms with how this would work in her classroom. Like Chris, I saw the value of considering technology as a tool, but favored the cultural perspective as a way to include critical thinking. In Site 2, Michelle recognized technology both as a tool and as a cultural influence, but searched for additional ways to incorporate cultural aspects of technology to engage students. In Site 3, Betsy grounded her teaching in traditional art foundations, which did not include technology as either a [art] tool or as a cultural conversation.

CLASSROOM IMPLICATIONS

Each participant considered new media technology differently and, through the collaboration, applied a variety of strategies in adapting a cultural interface approach. In Site 1, Chris's strategies moved from a focus strictly on skills to one emphasizing interpretations or embodied experiences through identity and metaphors. Michelle, in Site 2, focused on expanding her teaching by bringing students' lived experiences with technology and cultural understanding into the classroom. Betsy's class, Site 3, went from minimal conversations on technology to a collaboration in which participants considered the culture of technology through a variety of art media.

This study shows that both reflection on, and flexibility in, the exploration of alternative approaches to technology in the art classroom is necessary. For example, Betsy, the educator in Site 3, detoured from the class and reflected upon the students' negotiations with art and new media technology. As a result of her reflection, Betsy reconsidered her teaching strategies and course content within the curriculum. This research does not claim that participants experienced any shifts in their approaches to learning, teaching, or technology. Rather, this study shows that participants acquired insight by thinking about culture and technology, and in some cases, expressed a desire to expand their teaching practices.

The discourses, activities, and inquiry processes of a cultural interface approach facilitated the research participants' negotiations of their ideologies in the context of technology, art, and art education practice along with their lived experiences. This was a temporary expansion, not abandonment, of older ideas for new. Bringing participants' lived experiences in relation to technology into the classroom through social and cultural contexts offers possibilities of an integrated approach to consider formal and informal learning environments. Art and cultural discourses explore the value of art through physical and social space, consumption and production, actions, institution, and concepts—a space where the natural, social, and discursive collide. Additionally, the research supports previous research on technology in that teachers, students, and institutional context all embody beliefs, values, and assumptions about technology that influence approaches to teaching and learning (Hemmerla, 2000; Orr, 2003).

FINAL REFLECTION

PAR involving researchers, teachers, and students acknowledges that, "A major task of educational research is to generate knowledge about how educational knowledge is produced within and through relationships" (McNiff & Whitehead, 2002, p. xi). My relationships and situational differences required me to promote a participatory research practice by encouraging art educators to take part in all aspects of a research cycle. The collaborative nature of PAR "differs from solo work because it is accomplished, not first in one person's mind, and then in the other's, but on the loom between them, in the centre of their joint spaces" (Donaldson & Sanderson, 1996, p. 44). As Chris, Michelle, and Betsy, their students, and I wove our local knowledge and joint understandings together, the translations became a rich source of meaning making. Specifically, each participant's unique perception offers an opportunity to empower

art educators' and students' engagement with technology in art education.

I express my deepest thanks to Chris, Michelle, and Betsy and their respective students for their time, energy, and experience. I thank the three participating school systems, including the administration and principals for allowing me the opportunity to work within their community.

REFERENCES

Donaldson, G. A., & Sanderson, D. A. (1996). *Working together in schools: A guide for educators.* Thousand Oaks, CA: Corwin Press.

Fox, S. (2005). An actor-network critique of community in higher education: Implications for networked learning. *Studies in Higher Education, 30*(1), 95-110.

Freire, P. (1988). Creating alternative research methods: Learning to do it by doing it. In S. Kemmis & R. McTaggart (Eds.), *The action research reader* (3rd ed.) (pp. 291-313). Greelong, Victoria, Australia: Deakin University Press.

Hemmerla, P. S. (2000). *Factors related to the level of instructional use of computer-based technology by Missouri secondary art teachers* (Unpublished doctoral dissertation). University of Missouri, Columbia, MO.

Johnson, S. (1997). *Interface culture: How new technology transforms the way we create and communicate.* New York, NY: Basic Books.

Latour, B. (1987). *Science in action: How to follow scientists and engineers through society.* Boston, MA: Harvard University Press.

Manovich, L. (2001). *The language of new media.* Cambridge, MA: MIT Press.

McNiff, J., & Whitehead, J. (2002). *Action research: Principles and practice.* New York, NY: Routledge.

McTaggart, R. (1991). Principles of participatory action research. *Adult Education Quarterly, 41*(30), 170.

McTaggart, R. (1997). *Participatory action research: International contexts and consequences.* Albany: State University of New York Press.

Orr, P. (2003). *A hollow god: Technology's effects on paradigms and practices in secondary art education* (Unpublished doctoral dissertation). Purdue University, West Lafayette, IN.

Reason, P., & Bradbury, H. (2006). Introduction: Inquiry and participation in search of a world worthy of human aspiration. In P. Reason & H. Bradbury (Eds.), *Handbook of action research* (pp. 1-14). Thousand Oaks, CA: Sage.

Reason, P., & Torbert, W. (2001). Toward a transformational science: A further look at the scientific merits of action research. *Concepts and Transformation, 6*(1), 1-37.

Richards, L. (2005). *Handling qualitative data: A practical guide.* Thousand Oaks, CA: Sage.

Tillander, M. (2008). *Cultural interfaces as an approach to new media art education* (Unpublished doctoral dissertation). The Pennsylvania State University, University Park, PA.

Vascellaro, J. E. (2006a, April 5). The race to dazzle: Map sites pile on features. *Wall Street Journal,* p. D1.

Vascellaro, J. E. (2006b, April 7). Discovery's streaming video comes to GoogleEarth.® *Wall Street Journal (Eastern Edition),* p. B2.

MICHELLE TILLANDER is Assistant Professor of Art Education at The University of Florida. Her research explores digital media technologies and contemporary learning. Her research in the area of digital media, including the exploration of digital media's potential impacts and limitations to pedagogy, acknowledges the emerging vernacular of today's youth who are ubiquitously engaged with digital media through the writing, thinking, and visual processes of the digital age and engages art education, technology, and culture as integrated processes critical for continual demands on contemporary learners engaged in technological environments. She began her career with assisting in the development of Virginia's first Governor's School for the Arts, serving as Chair of the Visual Arts Department from 1998 to 2002. She co-developed and implemented an online MA in Art Education at the University of Florida. She currently serves on NAEA's Professional Materials Committee and chairs the Higher Education Division of the FAEA.

TIPS AND CONSIDERATIONS

38 / Tips and Considerations for Meaningful Research

MELANIE L. BUFFINGTON AND SARA WILSON MCKAY

This section includes several short contributions written by a variety of authors who have successfully balanced the dual roles of teacher and researcher. The authors offer practical advice as well as their own experiences related to two topics: negotiating the research process and social justice and empathy in research.

NEGOTIATING THE RESEARCH PROCESS
- Lori Kent—Transforming Research Into Manageable Phases
- Camilla McComb—Teacher Researcher: You Can Manage It
- Michaelann Kelley, Donna J. Reid, Paul D. Gray Jr., and Cheryl J. Craig—The Political Dimension of a Teacher Research Group

SOCIAL JUSTICE AND EMPATHY IN RESEARCH
- Cindy Maguire and Terry Lenihan—Social Justice in Art Education: Fostering the Capabilities of Individuals and Enhancing Collective Solidarities
- Avital Benshalom—Social Justice Education and Art Programs for Seniors
- Mary Stockrocki—What is the Relationship Between Research and Empathy?

Transforming Research Into Manageable Phases

LORI KENT / FULBRIGHT FELLOW (2009-2010) DEPARTMENT OF THEORY AND HISTORY OF ART, JAN MATEJKO ACADEMY OF FINE ARTS, KRAKOW

The process of research can be manageable or even joyful if you organize the research task into phases. At the very beginning, you may not be able to imagine yourself as an expert in a topic or qualified to conduct research. But, developing and implementing a research project can be a transformative experience yielding confidence and skills that improve your professional practice.

Begin with seeing the parts within a whole. One of the secrets of successful research is breaking down your very large task into smaller components. This is what architects do as they delineate interior space within exterior shells. Four phases that can guide your research process are (1) *inventory*, (2) *inter/net/work*, (3) *assemblage*, and (4) *refinement*.

The initial phase of **inventory** draws on your reflection skills. Embrace all of the ambiguities of your project as you give consideration to your topic, goals, resources, timeline, motivations, and personal support systems. What are your questions about conducting research? To whom are you accountable? Agree upon the scope of the work with your advisor. Find a support network. Who will listen when you need a confidant or a late night sandwich? Write your thoughts in a journal or realize them in sketches.

Inter/net/work, the second phase, is the label for multiple connections to be created. The Internet is your portal to social networks, scholarly literature, and current art education research. Networks include your fellow students, administrators, and coworkers; your advisors and readers; and your cyber communities. Networking provides support and knowledge larger than your personal experiences. Despite a need for connection, however, you should consider art education research as relatively independent, entrepreneurial work.

Assemblage is the stage in which, regardless of your aptitudes, the written word becomes your primary medium. Grammar, voice, and content should be developed. An advantage you have as a teacher is that you communicate for a living! Focus what you know about engaging and informing an audience toward your research. Other assemblages include perfecting your prescribed format (APA) from the first mark on paper and gathering an ambitious reference list. Also, look for models. When you read research reports, essays, or other non-fiction, take note of how writers solve structural problems, engage the reader, clarify, or weave a narrative. The archive of papers produced in your program can give you a sense of what is most appropriate.

After most of your work has unfolded, then comes **refinement**. Bracket out incubation time so that you can see your draft with fresh eyes. Be resourceful and engage editors; you may ask the Language Arts teacher at your school for help or you may hire a professional editor. Use your time with your adviser for conceptual discussions. It is your responsibility to give your adviser drafts that are free of grammatical and structural errors. Another valuable refinement tool is your table of contents. This outline reveals the scope and sequence of your research writing.

Over and over, I have witnessed art educators transform from fearful and tentative novices to confident researchers. Success often comes from the ability to see small, sequenced, significant tasks within the larger process. Know as much as you can about art education research culture and what is expected from you. Awareness helps to demystify, simplify, and guide. Although there are many research contexts and methodologies, a reflective beginning coupled with clear procedures propels you toward the joy of accomplishment. ∎

Teacher/Researcher: You Can Manage It

CAMILLA MCCOMB / NBCT ART/EMC, SOUTH-WESTERN CITY SCHOOLS, GROVE CITY, OHIO

Trying to teach and do research at the same time is challenging. Have faith, however; it is possible to conduct high-quality research while teaching if you consider a few management tips.

Talk about your research to anyone who will listen. Parents, teachers, and students care about you and they will genuinely be interested in what you are researching. Their questions and comments, coupled with your replies, will help to shape what you come to know about your study. Each informal attempt to tell someone what you are doing becomes a mirror as you see yourself and your own study through the responses of others.

Really listen to your students. As a teacher/researcher it is easy to get so focused on your teaching and research schedules that you can forget to slow down and really notice how students are responding to research as a creative endeavor. Students love to solve problems. By being receptive to your students as problems arise you just may find them leading you to a "wonderful idea" (Duckworth, 2006, p. 7). Listen to what your students say, knowing that each day provides you the opportunity to learn something from them.

Make your thoughts visible. Students will be intrigued by knowing that you are as inquisitive as they are. Talk about the study in front of them, and use language they can understand. Section off a part of the classroom board before class so that while you are leading a classroom discussion you can scrawl down quick thoughts that come to mind while you are working with students. This makes your inquiry visible to students. As class is cleaning up for dismissal, take a photograph of your notes. It is much easier to take a photo than to try to remember anything when 50 students are simultaneously exiting and entering the art room.

Keep a small research journal handy. Creative thoughts come at the most unexpected times, often, as psychologist Mihaly Csikszentmihalyi (1996) explained, when you are engaged in a "semiautomatic activity," that does not require your full attention (p. 138). For some people, this semiautomatic activity may be showering, for others, it may be stirring a pot of spaghetti sauce, for others, it may be mowing the lawn or pulling weeds. These acts can stimulate creative thinking, allowing you to make connections previously unrecognized. By keeping a small journal handy, you can write important thoughts down whenever and wherever they occur to you.

Post your thoughts. Put Post-it® notes in your pocket, in the car, beside your bed, on your desk, and in your purse, briefcase, or wallet. You will have random thoughts that at the time seem trivial. You will catch yourself wondering whether a thought is relevant enough to include in the research journal, so take the guesswork out of the equation. Put those random, roving thoughts onto Post-it® notes and place them in your journal. More often than not, a thought that seemed random at the moment turns out to be more significant than expected. By posting (and dating) the thought you have it documented.

Plan when to do your most productive writing. Perhaps you will get up early and write before school; stay after school and write at your desk; find a favorite library or coffee shop; or write after dark when your family is in bed. Where you write is not as critical as *when* you write. You will feel less stressed if you write on a regular basis. By setting a reasonable writing schedule ahead of time, you balance time and attention needed for your teaching, for students and for the study you are conducting. Weekends and holidays will prove excellent opportunities for extended writing and reflection.

These six strategies helped me in becoming a teacher/researcher: one able to generate, provide, and interpret reliable data as evidence to a classroom-based question. The benefit of conducting classroom-based research is that I gained another lens through which to see my practice and now speak about it with a greater sense of confidence. I now view my art room as a place dedicated to the exploration of ideas, reactions, and processes—a place where students work in collaboration knowing that their thoughts have the power to positively shape classroom instruction. The visual arts are the subject of meaningful research and are vital and relevant to the education community. As you become a teacher/researcher, I hope that you will also find new ways to view and understand your teaching practice. ∎

REFERENCES

Csikszentmihalyi, M. (1996). *Creativity.* New York, NY: Harper Collins.

Duckworth, E. (2006). *The having of wonderful ideas and other essays on teaching and learning* (3rd ed.). New York, NY: Teachers College Press.

The Political Dimension of a Teacher Research Group

MICHAELANN KELLEY /FINE ARTS DEPARTMENT CHAIR, EISENHOWER HIGH
SCHOOL **DONNA J. REID** / EDUCATION CONSULTANT **PAUL D. GRAY, JR.** / UNIVERSITY
OF TEXAS AT AUSTIN AND **CHERYL J. CRAIG** / PROFESSOR, DEPARTMENT OF
CURRICULUM AND INSTRUCTION, UNIVERSITY OF HOUSTON

What happens when teachers get together to talk about their work? A teacher inquiry group at Eagle High School,[1] an urban majority minority school, provides a practical lens through which to examine this question. Teachers come to this group from a variety of racial and ethnic backgrounds, multiple subject areas, a wide variety of teaching experience and even different careers prior to their move to teaching. Though this particular inquiry group has been in existence for over 11 years, the teacher members of this group have moved in and out of the formal group, mirroring the ebb and flow occurring within most urban school landscapes.

Here we portray a brief, reflective conversation that occurred during an end-of-year meeting among the teacher researchers in the inquiry group and a representative of the external funding agency that has supported the teachers' work for the past 2 years. During this 28-minute conversation, three themes of the political dimensions of the teachers' work emerged: building community, balancing needs, and generating new knowledge.

BUILDING COMMUNITY

Through Craig's (1995, 2007) lens of knowledge communities, the teachers in Eagle's inquiry group have come to value their relationships. Chris, a special education mathematics teacher cherished the support in "having a unit available to me where I can sound off, where I can share ideas, where I can receive ideas, and even observe the teaching." For her, the group was "a resource that helps me do it better."[2]

BALANCING NEEDS

The teachers also struggled with tensions between meeting their own needs and responding to the claims of the group and the expectations of the larger Eagle community. Negotiating which need gets met, and in which order, is a political act. For example, after describing many obstacles the group encountered while forming a cohesive community this year, Bettylu, a visual arts teacher serving as the group's facilitator since its inception, explained, "We had to re-norm ourselves. We had to re-envision a non-common common interest. We had to realize that we all were looking at curriculum differently."

Arthur, an experienced science teacher who came to teaching with a background in biomedical research, revealed some of his internal tensions as he sought to balance his prior research experiences with the very different methodology chosen by his inquiry group. Arthur talked about how he'd "bring graphs into these kinds of meetings and try to quantify everything and go, 'Look, here's the problem,' and that approach didn't work in this milieu." Arthur realized that in order to better inform his practice, he had to release his sole reliance on numbers and weave the narratives behind the numbers into his own personal practical knowledge (Clandinin & Connelly, 1988).

GENERATING NEW KNOWLEDGE

The third theme, generating new knowledge, comes from the ways in which the group bumps into the boundaries of what Clandinin and Connelly (2000) call a *grand narrative*—that the generation of knowledge and theory should take place only in the high ground of academia, and not the swampy lowlands (Schön, 1983) of practice. The No Child Left Behind Act reinforces this notion as it demands the exclusive use of "scientific research" to inform instructional decisions in schools. Rejecting these notions, practitioners in the teacher inquiry group embrace images of themselves as teacher researchers and curriculum makers (Clandinin & Connelly, 1992). Chris describes how engaging in research was a hopeful activity that made her "contemplate what I can do outside of the classroom that will be bigger and have a greater impact on more students." Similarly, Keenan, a beginning science teacher, remains hopeful about his ability to improve while reflecting about the tensions between his personal educational philosophies and the realities of his classroom:

> Being a first-year teacher, I had my ideas and I had the way I wanted things to go, and I had the way I wanted my classroom to run, and I had all of these expectations for how I wanted my first year to be, and it was nothing like that. Nothing at all. But I've gotten a lot of ideas... from my colleagues as to how to ensure that next year is just a little bit closer to my ideal.

What the members of this group seem to value most from each other is the encouragement to be a great teacher—the power to define and grow that teacher self, rather than playing a predetermined role in a group, on campus, or in the larger educational landscape. Teachers' personal practical knowledge is grounded in their own teaching and enriched by the learning experiences that they share. Keenan muses:

> The content [of our conversations] definitely feeds off our relationships because it is in the dynamics of our relationships that we get the content. So without our relationships, without

(continued)

the inquiry group, I don't know if we would have the content to build on because we wouldn't be having these conversations.

As Keenan acknowledges, his group's rich conversation reflects how teacher researchers can harness their own knowledge with the capacity to transform their practice and influence others' practice. ■

REFERENCES

Clandinin, D. J., & Connelly, F. M. (1988). *Teachers' professional knowledge landscapes.* New York, NY: Teachers College Press.

Clandinin, D. J., & Connelly, F. M. (1992). Teacher as curriculum maker. In P. W. Jackson (Ed.), *Handbook of research on curriculum: A project of the American Educational Research Association* (pp. 363-461). New York, NY: Macmillan.

Clandinin, D. J., & Connelly, F. M. (2000). *Narrative inquiry: Experience and story in qualitative research.* San Francisco, CA: Jossey-Bass.

Craig, C. J. (1995). Knowledge communities: A way of making sense of how beginning teachers come to know in their professional knowledge contexts. *Curriculum Inquiry, 25*(2), 152-175.

Craig, C. J. (2007). Illuminating qualities of knowledge communities in a portfolio-making context. *Teachers and teaching: Theory and practice, 13*(6), 617-636.

Schön, D. A. (1983). *The reflective practitioner: How professionals think in action.* New York, NY: Basic Books.

ENDNOTES

[1] Eagle High School and the names of the teachers are all pseudonyms.
[2] All quotes in this section are from personal communications on April 16, 2009.

Social Justice in Art Education: Fostering the Capabilities of Individuals and Enhancing Collective Solidarities

CINDY MAGUIRE / ASSISTANT PROFESSOR OF ART EDUCATION, ADELPHI UNIVERSITY AND **TERRY LENIHAN** / ASSOCIATE PROFESSOR OF ART EDUCATION, LOYOLA MARYMOUNT UNIVERSITY

Social justice, in its broadest sense, is about equal rights and opportunities for all people in every part of society. "A central aim," according to Watts and Guessous (2006), "is to articulate the relationship between the collective [struggle] against social ills and the advancement of personal well-being" (p. 60). But how do we know what is just? What constitutes opportunities for advancement of personal well-being? Perceptions of rights and opportunities vary widely, depending upon how we are situated socially, politically, economically, and culturally. In education, social justice is not simply the absence of injustice but the need to recognize and enact teaching that promotes a deeper understanding of ourselves and our students in relation to the broader social and cultural landscape (Maguire, 2009).

Teaching and research inspired by principles of social justice is referred to by a variety of teaching approaches, including *social reconstructionism/critical theory* (Brameld, 1956; Freire, 1993), *culturally relevant teaching* (Ladson-Billings, 1994), *culturally responsive teaching* (Gay, 2000), *teaching against the grain* (Cochran-Smith, 1991), *teaching for diversity,* (Sadker & Sadker, 1992), and *multicultural education* (Banks, 1993; Nieto, 1999; Sleeter & Grant, 2007). A meta-analysis of research on teacher education illustrates, however, that—in spite of the teaching approaches just listed—preservice teachers are still not equipped to teach in increasingly diverse educational settings, (Cochran-Smith, 2003). Given the growing diversity in our classrooms, we believe it is imperative for current and future teachers to find ways of embodying, implementing, and assessing social justice practices in art classrooms.

In 2008, using case study and action research methods, we developed, taught, and evaluated a social justice-based art education course with a service-learning component for undergraduate art education students. The course was designed to help preservice teachers adopt and put into practice a critical social justice lens for their own artmaking and teaching practices. In this course, students engaged in activities to explore identity. It we then moved outward to address broader social justice issues. The capstone project was a collaborative community art experience with K-8 students (see Figure 1). This service-learning component provided opportunities to put into practice the pedagogy and curriculum learned in the course.

In the study, one discovery was that the capabilities students brought to the classroom directly influenced ways they engaged with and put into practice the social justice course

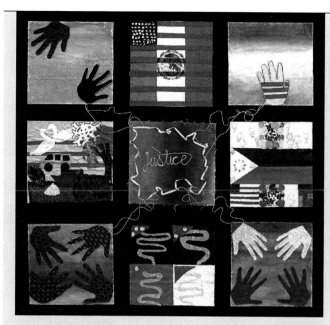

FIGURE 1 (LEFT). Students from Loyola Marymount University collaborated with eighth graders to create a 25-foot-long Family History Quilt. The eighth graders shared family stories through written, oral, and creative storytelling. The result was a visual narrative quilt expressing how issues of social justice have touched the students' lives.

FIGURE 2 (ABOVE). The arts can function as a space to reflect and create responses to new learning—ideal spaces which foster an array of capabilities that address issues of social justice, capabilities often ignored or bypassed in education today.

material. This information, gleaned through a series of ongoing assessments including pre- and post-questionnaires, observations, formal and informal interviews, and students' written and visual stories regarding their experiences, was used to modify instruction. What became clear was the importance of comparing and contrasting students' comments with their actions. During in-class critiques, for example, we found students were often not aware of stereotypes reinforced in their own visual imagery, artwork subsequently used as exemplars with the K-8 students. We modified the critiques to emphasize content and intention, addressing overt as well as covert stereotypical text and imagery (see Figure 2). Targeted readings, critical written reflections, and group discussions were added to address these issues. We found that when we purposefully engaged students in critical reflection, dialogue, and action regarding social justice teaching and learning, we provided ideal spaces to foster their individual and collective flourishing as well as the enhancement of their own teaching practices.

A result of this research, we believe educators at all levels need to cultivate a deeper understanding of prior knowledge and experiences that both our students and we bring into the classroom. These factors have a direct bearing on our preferences and choices in the classroom and in our lives. Using a social justice lens when conducting research attempts to capture these narratives and assess from them whether or not we, as educators, are coming closer to achieving social justice in our classrooms. We ask ourselves: Do all our students have equal access to the curriculum? Are certain voices dominating classroom space? How can we recognize, address, and move through resistance to change? What are some of the ways we can integrate rigorous artmaking experiences with culturally relevant and engaging curriculum? Teachers concerned with social justice need to strategize a curriculum that allows for multiple voices and learning styles to create a teaching and learning environment that is enriching and

equitable for all. Such support helps to create self-directed and empowered students who participate in determining their current actions and responsibilities as well as to establish the direction of their future education. ■

REFERENCES

Banks, J. (1993). Multicultural education as an academic discipline. *Multicultural Education, 39,* 8-11.

Brameld, T. (1956). *Toward a reconstructed philosophy of education.* New York, NY: Dryden Press.

Cochran-Smith, M. (1991). Learning to teach against the grain. *Harvard Educational Review, 61*(3), 279-310.

Cochran-Smith, M. (2003). The multiple meanings of multicultural teacher education: A conceptual framework. *Teacher Education Quarterly, 30*(2), 7-118.

Freire, P. (1993). *Pedagogy of the oppressed* (New rev. 20th anniversary ed.). New York, NY: Continuum.

Gay, G. (2000). *Culturally responsive teaching: Theory, research, & practice.* New York, NY: Teachers College Press.

Ladson-Billings, G. (1994). *The dreamkeepers: Successful teachers of African American children.* San Francisco, CA: Jossey-Bass.

Maguire, C. (2009). Fostering capabilities: The practice of peace and social justice in contemporary art education. In E. Ndura-Ouedraogo & R. Amster (Eds.), *Building cultures of peace: Transdisciplinary voices of hope and action* (pp. 28-43). Cambridge, England: Cambridge Scholars.

Nieto, S. (1999). *The light in their eyes: Creating multicultural learning communities.* New York, NY: Teachers College Press.

Sadker, M., & Sadker, D. (1992). Ensuring equitable participation in college classes. *New Directions for Teaching and Learning, 49,* 49-56.

Sleeter, C. E., & Grant, C. A. (2007). *Making choices for multicultural education: Five approaches to race, class, and gender.* New York, NY: John Wiley & Sons.

Watts, R. J., & Guessous, O. (2006). Sociopolitical development: The missing link in research and policy on adolescents. In S. Ginwright, P. Noguera & J. Cammarota (Eds.), *Beyond resistance: Youth activism and community change.* New York, NY: Routledge.

Social Justice Education and Art Programs for Seniors

AVITAL BENSHALOM / MASTER OF ARTS IN ART EDUCATION, SCHOOL OF THE ART INSTITUTE OF CHICAGO

My study researches the development and implementation of art programs for seniors using a framework of Social Justice Education. Social Justice Education develops awareness of issues of equality and multiculturalism and encourages individual expression and participation. As a social group, seniors, 65 years of age and older, are the poorest and fastest-growing segment of American society (U.S. Department of Health and Human Services, 2006), and more importantly for this research, they are the most under-served and least studied group in terms of art education. Most of the research of art programs for the senior population originates in the field of Art Therapy (Perlstein, 2002). Instead of taking this path, I followed principles of social justice art education demonstrated in a "big ideas" approach. This approach emphasizes that broad ideas (such as equality, freedom, independence, or social responsibility) are the basis of artmaking rather than technical skill development (Gude, 1997). This approach offers new possibilities for engaging a diverse population of seniors in creative dialogues regarding the aging experience, the relationship between seniors and modern society, and seniors' unique contribution and needs.

As part of my research, I conducted an Emancipatory Action Research project to analyze two programs that I led in two senior-centers in Chicago. My research question was, "What is the role of art in the experience of growing older under contemporary social conditions?" I focused on the group dynamics that emerged during the programs, the relationship between seniors and staff, and the social hierarchy among the seniors.

My research was based on theories of developmental aging, art education, art therapy, and critical gerontology. This interdisciplinary background allowed me to re-contextualize seniors' art programs as a meaningful, process-based experience as well as a stimulus for progressive social change. The methodology of Action Research allowed me to conduct and research the programs—to form close relations with the participants, and, at the same time, to review the process critically. The goals of Action Research are to address practical problems, generate new knowledge, and facilitate change.

My research offers a new concept of "Social Therapy" as a central guideline in art programs for seniors. Social Therapy stands for the collective aspects of artmaking that encourage the participants to reflect and analyze their life circumstances and aging experience. Throughout the research I applied the concept of Social Therapy in two distinct ways. First, I designed curricula that encouraged the participants to review their autobiographical visual memories such as photographs and family albums. The "Critical Scrapbooking Curriculum" created a space for seniors to link be-

FIGURE 1. River Senior Center, Chicago, IL. Source: Private (2008). The image incorporates a photograph of two children isolated in a painted jungle, as an expression of the hardship and sorrow that characterized this memory.

FIGURE 2. Canaries Senior Center, Chicago, IL. Source: Private (2008). This quilt is a collaboration made by all the seniors. Its beauty exemplifies the power of group creativity.

tween their private experiences and social developments. For example, a collage made by a senior participant in an art workshop incorporates a 60-year old picture of her sons (see Figure 1). She described the background of the image made with acrylic painting over the picture as a visualization of the difficult social conditions of raising children at the time. Through a collective artmaking process, the participants were able to re-visit, share, reflect, and reinterpret their memories with a group of seniors.

The second way I employed a concept of Social Therapy involved working with a group of older seniors (age 75 and above) and their caregivers. Offering art activities that encourage collaboration among seniors and their caregivers, allowed seniors to demonstrate their unique abilities as well as their rich life experiences as a powerful contribution to their communities. By highlighting seniors' experiences, art programs can reduce phenomena such as seniors' dependency and the "infantalization of seniors" (translating seniors' physical and emotional difficulties to intellectual disabilities). For example, a collective quilt made by a group of 12 seniors and their caregivers, is an example of an art project that utilizes seniors' motor and sensory abilities, offering seniors an opportunity to engage in collective artmaking (see Figure 2). This collaborative art activity balanced between two important aspects of process simplicity and satisfaction from an aesthetic product. The project triggered a lively discussion about collective artmaking such as the *AIDS Quilt*.

Examining seniors' art programs through a Social Justice Education framework allowed me to understand the complexity of aging as a socially constructed experience. The results of my research suggest that art education can and should play a central role in shaping and transforming the aging experience, and in promoting awareness of intergenerational social justice. ■

REFERENCES

Gude, O. (1997). *Investigating the culture of curriculum.* Retrieved from: www.uic.edu/classes/ad/ad382/sites/AEA/AEA_01/AAE-A01b.html

Perlstein, S. (2002). *Arts and creative aging across America. Community Arts. Networks.* Retrieved from www.communityarts.net/readingroom/archivefiles/2002/10/arts_and_creati.php

U.S. Department of Health and Human Service. (2006). 65+ in the United States: 2005. Retrieved from: www.census.gov/prod/2006pubs/p23-209.pdf

What is the Relationship Between Research and Empathy?

MARY STOKROCKI / PROFESSOR OF ART, ARIZONA STATE UNIVERSITY, INSTITUTE OF DESIGN AND THE ARTS

I n their new theory of empathetic education, Laura and Cotton (1999) argue that "The survival of the species depends upon finding new ways of connecting with nature" (p. 137) and other people and not separating ourselves. Connecting implies understanding others, not just existing side-by-side. To understand others is to interact and to question them. Simply put, research is a questioning strategy, a systematic search of some phenomenon or event to uncover information or develop an action plan. Traditionally, researchers aimed for objectivity in their research findings and empathy with subjects was considered nonscientific. However, no research is totally objective, and according to the philosopher Nietzsche, there are no facts, only interpretations (Allison, 1977).

Thus, I ask: how can researchers show empathy and care through their work? Newer forms of research, including autoethnography and narrative inquiry, involve writing the results of the data analysis as in a narrative format. These forms of inquiry are now respected research, and art teachers often choose to conduct research because they have vested interests in knowing more about the subject and the children they are teaching. One form of this involves teachers writing stories about their own artmaking experience or about their school day or even about the lives of students—based upon their data analysis (Stokrocki, 1995). These stories, both real and fictional, are based on real life events. When a teacher studies her/his teaching, the mentoring relationship of teacher and student may become more significant than the art concepts transmitted (Kelehear & Held, 2002).

Empathetic learning in research has become a salient feature to study. Noddings (2002) refers to such learning as "multi-relational, a kind of moral learning based on a teacher's caring willingness to assist students and for students to care for each other" (p. 69). Research practices utilizing empathy can in-

(continued)

clude documenting a local community event, such as altar making and/or a procession to commemorate the victims of violence (Stokrocki, 2000). Thus, students and teachers can photograph commemorative memorials, analyze their functional reasons, write about those for whom they care deeply, and how they honored them. Such studies can be preventive strategies to combat bullying and other forms of violence in schools or in communities (Congdon, 2009). Furthermore, by using oral history interviews and photomontage analysis, teachers can stimulate empathy, bear witness to ways of life, and learn about diverse cultures with their students as secondary witnesses to daily injustices in their community (Bootwala & Desai, 2009). Empathy then becomes a collective community process.

Another example of empathy in a research project is a recent study (Stokrocki, Flatt, & York, 2010) of the importance of teaching ecology in art education, empowering middle school students to write, illustrate, and judge their ecological narratives using the predator/prey theme, a different exploration of violence. In this particular study, the researchers focused on teaching about the Sonoran Desert. The Sonoran Desert is an ecologically fragile area, dissected by a border fence that impedes the north-south migration routes of several animals in the attempt to stop human migration and drug traffic. Many of the resulting student stories and drawings portrayed physical or moral conflicts indicating empathy, the capacity to identify with other creatures' concerns, as in the emerging theme "most heartfelt." These findings beg the question about why art teachers should care about teaching ecology through writing and illustrating. Because some students lack first-hand experience with their local creatures, teachers could invite local speakers (illustrators, museum personnel, or environmental resource management personnel) to motivate students about how to care for animals and the environment.

We need to develop critical interdisciplinary content knowledge about what students might end up learning; in this case, life cycles in the desert, essential issues such as survival, their place in the preservation of this delicate and quickly disappearing wilderness In so doing, art teachers need to reflect on contrasting opinions (e.g., pro-development and pro-preservation).

I encourage art teachers to write their own stories about the morals of everyday life, do research with students about something they care about in their own community, and offer insights to better the world in which we live through art because our lives depend on developing artistic perception and moral consciousness. No magic procedure exists for promoting care in research. Certainly, it is important to consider the meaning of the concept of "care," and the ethics of being careful in how one writes. At the same time, it is of paramount importance to write about WHAT ONE CARES ABOUT—the students and/or subject matter. ■

REFERENCES

Allison, D. (Ed.) (1977). *The new Nieztsche: Contemporary styles of interpretation*. New York, NY: Dell.

Bootwala, M., & Desai, D. (2009). Memoryscapes: Witnessing the crisis of internal refugees through visual practice. *Journal of Cultural Research in Art Education, 27*, 94-106.

Congdon, K. (2009). Special issue art and cultural violence. *Journal of Cultural Research in Art Education, 27*.

Kelehear, Z., & Held, K. (2002). Mentoring in the art classroom. *Studies in Art Education, 44*(1), 67-78.

Laura, R. S., & Cotton, M. C. (1999). Empathetic education: An ecological perspective on educational knowledge. London, England: Farmer Press. Retrieved from http://books.google.com/books?id=I9c9AAAAIAAJ&pg=PA137&dq=empathy++and+education

Noddings, N. (2002). *Educating moral people: A caring alternative to character education*. New York, NY: Teachers College Press.

Stokrocki, M. (1995). A school day in the life of a young Navajo girl: A case study in ethnographic storytelling. *Art Education, 47*(4), 61-68.

Stokrocki, M. (2000). Celebrate the memory of the victims of violence through the arts: A photo essay. *Art Education, 53*(2), 53-54.

Stokrocki, M. with Flatt, B., & York E. (2010). A constructivist study of middle school students' narratives and ecological illustrations. *Journal for Learning through the Arts: A Research Journal on Arts Integration in Schools and Communities, 6*(1), 1-16. Retrieved from http://escholarship.org/uc/item/6nv291vz

EXAMPLE RESEARCH STUDIES

39 / Toward a Framework of Culturally Relevant Pedagogy in Art Education: Using CRP to Explicate Teachers' Relationships With Self, Students, Knowledge, and Community

APARNA RAE / ARTIST

ABSTRACT: *The potential for an art class be grounds for social change becomes a reality, when teachers are able to reflect the students' culture, values, ideas, and beliefs in and through the pedagogy and curriculum. Building on Gloria Ladson-Billings work on culturally relevant pedagogy (CRP), this study takes place in the nexus of collaborative and reflexive research, to propose a framework for culturally relevant pedagogy in secondary art education. The study explores ways in which three exemplary secondary art teachers with parallel educational philosophies and dissimilar teaching environments enact a curriculum and pedagogy with an overt stance on cultural relevancy. Through conversations and collaboration with the teachers, within the context of the schools and communities they teach in, this study explores the pedagogical and curricular choices teachers make to address students' needs, through understanding ways in which teachers negotiated relationships with students, communities of practice, knowledge, and themselves.*

In the midst of discussions about the role of multi-cultural art education, diversity, and visual culture in teacher education, few researchers have made peda-gogy a key area of investigation. This research attempts to challenge existing ideas of the intersections of diversity and teaching. by building on previous work articulating a *culturally relevant pedagogy* (CRP) for art education through a postcolonial lens. CRP asks teachers to help raise students' awareness of inequities while fostering an ability to react to and constructively cope with these negative social realities (Ladson-Billings, 1995a). Postcolonial theory works to dest-abilize Western ways of thinking by producing an alternative dialogue, through creating spaces for the 'other' to speak.

By raising questions about the social location of the researcher and participants, this study attempts to define a framework that grounds research through collaboration and reflexivity. My lived experiences as a teacher and community-based artist, as well as my interest in diverse urban youth, led to the study of pedagogical practices of three exemplary secondary art teachers in Vancouver, Canada. This study was the basis for my graduate thesis. Through a series of interviews and classroom observations, this study builds an understanding of ways in which these secondary art teachers arrive at a stance of culturally relevant teaching. In particular, this research explores ways in which three secondary art teachers with parallel educational philosophies and dissimilar

teaching environments enact a curriculum and pedagogy with an overt stance on cultural relevancy.

THEORETICAL FRAMEWORK

The research relies on CRP, multiculturalism in art educa-tion, and postcolonial theory. Ladson-Billings' (1994) grounded theory of CRP serves as the framework for this research. Multiculturalism in art education aims to raise socio-political awareness and enhance the students' ability to understand his or her location in society (Stuhr & Petrovich-Mwaniki, 1992). In art education, multicultur-alism has evolved over the past two decades to address the changing population in North America (Chalmers, 2002) and serves as a vehicle for art educators to become cultur-ally relevant pedagogues. The study also recognizes the affect of coloniality[1] and the complex relationships among art, education, and the spread of colonialism. Smith (1999) writes that the globalization of knowledge and Western culture continues to reaffirm the "West's view of itself as the center of legitimate knowledge, the arbiter of what counts as knowledge and the source of 'civilized' knowledge" (p. 64). Schools impart imperial views of culture and play an important role in the dissemination of the "domesticated versions" of 'universal' knowledges, produced by and at the center, for "uncritical consumption" (p. 65). In art education, this happens when Western art, particularly 'The Masters', is used as the basis for curriculum and pedagogy, instead of student culture and contemporary multicultural artists.

PURPOSE

Cultural relevancy can be described as how well an idea, or the presentation of such an idea speaks to a certain group. This research explores *tensions* teachers negotiate such as the availability of resources, reallocation of teaching time, visible and hidden agenda of parents, administration, and peers in order to arrive at a stance of cultural relevancy. Through conversations with teachers, within the context of the schools they teach in, we can begin to explore the conditions for CRP. Ladson-Billings (1995a) acknowledges a need for collaboration between teachers and researchers to propose alternate models of pedagogy. Hope (2004) calls for models of research and inquiry that strengthen the field by building on the work of other professionals instead of being an "attempt to correct failures caused by professionals" (p. 99). This study built upon research across disciplines, recognizing the importance of interdisciplinary research. The following research questions serve to guide the study.

- What are the *tensions* that secondary art teachers negotiate when developing the curriculum and pedagogy?
- How do secondary art teachers approach the art curriculum, their teaching and learning, in relation to a framework of cultural relevancy?

LITERATURE REVIEW

This review discusses the theory of CRP, multiculturalism in art education, and postcolonial theory. Ladson-Billings' (1994) work on expounding a framework of CRP, one "that empowers students intellectually, socially, emotionally, and politically by using cultural referents to impart knowledge, skills, and attitudes" (p. 18), serves as the backbone for this study. In *Personal and Cultural Narratives as Inspiration*, Staikidis (2006) explores the chasm between the tendencies of higher education to impart a Eurocentric skill-based curriculum that does not take into account "culturally diverse pedagogical practices" (p. 120), limiting the "development and potential of students to know their world in new ways" (p.120). Although Staikidis does not use the term culturally relevant, she writes explicitly about the need of art curricula and pedagogical practices to become culturally relevant. CRP allows for an emphasis on student culture to minimize the negative effects of dominant culture to create a multicultural art classroom. The study also relies on the work of Canadian multicultural theorists—Ghosh (1996); Bannerji (2000); Irwin, Rogers, and Farrell (1997); Chalmers (2002); and others—to ground this research within the Canadian context[2] as the study is situated in British Columbia, Canada. The final section of the review explores coloniality. Finally, it is important to acknowledge the paradigmatic shifts and inconsistencies in the literature. The literature reviewed falls largely into the critical (emancipatory) and deconstructivist paradigms. Lather (2006) argues for paradigm proliferation as an ontological and historical claim, advocating education research in a way that allows researchers, "[to] develop an ability to locate themselves in the tensions that characterize fields of knowledge" (p. 47). This research and the review attempt to bring together literature from across paradigms in an attempt to locate the tensions experienced and negotiated by secondary art teachers.

CULTURALLY RELEVANT PEDAGOGY (CRP)

CRP, as conceived by Ladson-Billings (1992, 1994, 1995a, 1995b) draws on cultural knowledge, prior experiences, frames of reference and learning styles of ethnically diverse students and is a pedagogy that empowers students to become critical learners. CRP helps students to question the role of education in creating a multicultural society. Teachers in Ladson-Billings' study showed a commitment to becoming a part of the school community, group learning and group success over individual achievement, and saw student culture and experience as knowledge. Through helping students recognize, understand, and critique social inequities, teachers empower students rather than impart an uncritical acceptance of the values of dominant culture.

Teachers in Ladson-Billings' study were primarily elementary teachers who taught a variety of subjects and were selected following recommendations by parents, community elders and school administrators. Through her analysis of data, Ladson-Billings' provides three themes relating to the link between pedagogical practices and student achievement. (1) *Conceptions of Self and others*: Teachers in Ladson-Billings' study believed that all their students were capable of academic success, saw their pedagogy as an art, were active members of the community and saw teaching as giving back to the community. (2) *Social Relations:* The teachers in Ladson-Billings' study created opportunities for social interactions that helped students achieve academic success, cultural competency and critical consciousness. (3) *Conceptions of Knowledge:* The teachers in Ladson-Billings' study believed that knowledge is not static, that it must be viewed critically and that all teachers have to be passionate about knowledge and learning.

MULTICULTURAL EDUCATION

The multicultural education movement has its roots in the civil rights and early feminist movements in the 1960s and 1970s in the United States, and to some extent, Canada (Ghosh, 1996). Initially, multicultural education was concerned with prejudice reduction in schools and providing equal opportunities for all students, particularly, students of color (Ladson-Billings, 1994). In the Canadian context, a federal multiculturalism policy was adopted in

1971 to ensure equality for all individuals, regardless of language, ethnicity, culture, race, or religious affiliations (Ghosh, 1996). Although the implementation of multicultural practices differs widely, many definitions and forms of multicultural education exist in both Canadian and U.S. classrooms. Banks (2003) defines multicultural education through three criteria; an idea or concept, an educational reform, and a process. In art education, Desai (2000) and Chalmers (1992, 1996) trouble the canon of 'art,' and conceptualize the role of multicultural art education as preparing 'all' students to live in an "increasingly pluralistic society" (p. 5). Desai (2000) holds that the primary concern for multicultural art educators is, "to provide accurate and authentic representations of the art of racially and ethnically marginalized groups in the United States and of subordinate cultures around the world" (p. 114).

Kader (2005) challenges art teachers' knowledge of historical and contextual resources to present multiculturalism in a meaningful way, suggesting that art educators struggle with ineffective content in an attempt to present culturally diverse content to satisfy state and provincial requirements. To address these issues, Chalmers (1992) calls for multicultural art educators "who will develop culturally appropriate curricula materials to supplement those whose treatment of different cultural groups is limited or biased" (p. 142). Chalmers (1992) writes, "We need art teachers who provide a classroom atmosphere in which students' cultures are recognized, shared, and respected" (p. 142). However, Chalmers (1992), Stuhr and Petrovich-Mwaniki (1992), and more recently Desai (2005), while addressing social inequities, neglect to address hybridization of identities of students. Ladson-Billings (2004) urges scholars writing on multicultural education to respond to, "the postcolonial and multiple discourses that worldwide change demands. Their work will have to incorporate heterogeneity, hybridity, and multiplicity and be more tentative in its assertions" (p. 63).

INDIGENOUS AND ABORIGINAL CONTEXT

Because my research is located in British Columbia on contested land,[3] it is important to honor the Indigenous narrative and history of the land. Based on dialogues with Aboriginal artists, Irwin, Rogers, and Farrell (1999) argue that, "a purely multicultural system would deny aboriginal peoples the depth of expression necessary to sustain their cultures" (p. 57). Aboriginal people's understanding of art and artmaking varies significantly from that of other contemporary artists working within the Eurocentric traditions (Irwin, Rogers, & Farrell, 1999). Through working closely with Aboriginal artists, acknowledging difference, and creating a space for dialogue, art educators can begin to understand Aboriginal narratives. For art educators, understanding Indigenous or Aboriginal narratives is necessary in order to impart both ideologies and visual content to their students.

POSTCOLONIAL THEORY

Postcolonial theory is a postmodern intellectual discourse that holds together theories from various disciplines including political science, geography and literature. These theories are reactions to the cultural legacy and hegemony of colonialism. The following sections draw on the intersectionality between art, education and impact of a colonial legacy.

Scholars across disciplines attest that education and art have been used as a form of colonialist control (Ashcroft, Griffiths, & Tiffin, 1995; Bhabha, 2004; Said, 1978/79). Battiste, Bell, and Findlay[4] (2002) and Smith[5] (1999) build upon previous scholarship in postcolonial studies, reflecting on issues of identity and representation, and the colonial nature of education, calling for decolonizing education as a way to animate non-Western identities. Bhabha (2004) insists that cultural identities emerge in the contradictory and ambivalent third space of hybridity, writing further that all cultural identity is essentially hybrid. Hybridity becomes a site of conflict, interaction, and assimilation involving all encounters—those between people, nations, histories—forcing individuals to understand the traits of the other as those that comprise the self. This discussion helps situate art, teaching and learning within a larger inherently complex social framework.

METHODOLOGY

Although the 4-month time span of this study does not allow it to be considered true ethnography, it can be characterized as a small-scale ethnographic inquiry. This qualitative research methodology allowed for the observation of (1) discernible elements that influence the development of arts curricula and pedagogy at the secondary level, (2) the relationship between teachers' ideologies and teacher practice, (3) development of culturally relevant curriculum and instruction, and (4) the impact of the educational context.

PARTICIPANTS

This study included three secondary art teachers[6] in the Vancouver Metro area who teach in a range of art programs with a highly diverse student population that mirrors the city demographics; with students from a variety of socio-economic, cultural, gender and ethnic diversity. Vancouver, British Columbia, has a rich ethno-cultural diversity resulting from the original Aborginal presence, British occupation, and a history of migration from China, East India, Korea, and Japan. While many people perceive culture as being a static condition, culture is in flux, and cultural variegation in schools can become a resource in obtaining multiple perspectives (Isar, 2006). The heterogeneity of the research environment enables the construction of a narrative, through conversations and observations, that speaks to multiple worldviews. A university faculty member who works closely with secondary art teachers in the Vancouver area helped me identify the participants.

RESEARCH SITE

McClain and Cobb (2004) assert that an institutional context both constrains and enables the roles teachers and school leaders perform. The researcher conducted the study at two secondary schools in Vancouver, British Columbia. Tree Hill Secondary is a humanities and arts-focused secondary school, requiring admission by application, with a population of 150 students. The school has a strong academic focus, providing a liberal arts education supported by visual and performing arts. West Side Secondary, on the other hand, is a large comprehensive high school with a population exceeding 1,600 students. West Side Secondary school is noted for several district programs including French Immersion, on-site pre-employment and Advanced Placement. In addition to a distinguished academic record, the school is also known for the sports program.

METHODS OF DATA COLLECTION
OBSERVATION

I observed three secondary art teachers' classrooms for 3-7 non-consecutive days; one teacher at Tree Hill Secondary and two teachers at West Side Secondary.[7] Qualitative research methods rely on observing not only the verbal (language) or physical actions (behavior), but also patterns that are not visible directly (Creswell, 1998). These include curriculum choices, emotional space/tensions between a teacher and students and layout of the classroom. Spatial configuration, bulletin boards, division of class time, formality/informality of events, such as critiques, speak to the values that are important to teachers. Ladson-Billings' framework for CRP (1992, 1994, 1995a, 1995b) and Smith's (1999) *Decolonialzing Methodologies* text served as the initial framework for observations. I recorded data into a field notebook and also verbally onto a voice recorder.

INTERVIEWING

Kvale (2006) sees qualitative research interviews as a method for understanding and getting to know private lives and making them public through dialogue. While interviews have helped researchers to see the world from the interviewee point of view, I heed Kvale's (2006) cautions in giving voice to *many and everyone,* illustrating the potential of researcher dominance through interviews and the interviewer's ability to manipulate interviews to gain the goal. Acknowledging that while the relationship between the participants and me is not one that is equal, I align myself professionally with the teachers, and carry the privilege of representing their thoughts and ideas.

DATA ANALYSIS

Coffey and Atkinson (1996) describe data analysis as a process that involves an ongoing, continuous engagement that begins at the moment the first data is collected. Embracing the process, I transcribed the interview tapes using Transcriva.[8]

I relied on two theoretical frameworks to assist with the process of data analysis: CRP and postcolonial theory. Ladson-Billings' theory of a CRP is situated in the critical paradigm, and relies on critical race theory and critical pedagogy to articulate a framework that addresses student achievement and cultural competency. Further, I used postcolonial theory to identify and further deconstruct teaching practices that perpetuate colonial ideologies and address their relevance to the field of art education.

The data analysis include coding transcripts from observations and interviews, and through 'member checks,' where participants had an opportunity to critically reflect on the coding and analysis performed by the researcher. I coded the data in three stages—open, axial, and selective. During open coding, I coded over a hundred categories, which were grouped during axial coding and further refined during the process of selective coding (Strauss & Corbin, 1990). Selective coding gives way to the development of a core category or 'story line' that relies on sub-categories to capture the essence of the research study. At the outset, this research aimed at understanding ways in which teachers negotiated various tensions to arrive at the curriculum in-use, as well as a stance on pedagogy or the ways in which teachers delivered the curriculum. Tensions teachers negotiate range from constraints on time, budgets, opinions of parents and school administration, and personal motivations to teach a particular curriculum.

FINDINGS

Throughout the research, teachers identified with the tensions but located their struggle in negotiating a culturally relevant curriculum and pedagogy through various *relationships.* Following postcolonial reasoning, relationships allow this research to become complex and interconnected. Therefore, the findings of the study are presented in terms of relationships with self, students, knowledge, and communities. The relationships teachers engage in are interconnected and woven together, and the process of analyzing data showed the complexity of the relationships, while developing a closer understanding of each of the four relationships.

Relationships—self. The most important relationship in the study is that of the participants with themselves. All three participants identify as heterosexual women and acknowledge their racially privileged and dominant class backgrounds. Asking these teachers about the way their gender plays into their larger social positionality resulted in anecdotes on their life history, encompassing education, career, marriage, child rearing and also teaching practices. All teachers saw themselves performing multiple roles, assuming various identities of teacher, artist, researcher, student, mother/guardian and mentor to their students.

Relationships—students. Assuming multiple identities, relationships with students revealed many culturally relevant and postcolonial pedagogical choices teachers made daily. Teachers were also very aware of students' needs. Joanne asserted, "I do think about what each individual kid wants and needs and I can kinda keep that as a, as a plateau at the back of my mind and I can" (Interview, February, 2009). Teachers saw students as artists and their teaching practice focused around the development of each student as an artist. By employing independent, self-directed projects, they compelled students to explore issues of culture and identity that interested students most. In both secondary schools, working in outdoor spaces was an indication of trust between the teacher and the student, since students often worked at a distance from the teacher. The teachers also developed a self-guided museum tour for students in the upper grade levels. I believe these practices suggest an epistemological and ontological openness of accepting multiple ways of knowing and learning.

Relationships—knowledge. These teachers believed that knowledge is fluid and changing, and asserted a need for professionals to familiarize themselves with developments in the field. During conversations in-class and in interviews, participants in the study showed a preference towards postcolonial and contemporary art and artists. Karen, in particular, spoke about ways in which contemporary artists working across media, allow her to investigate a range of social issues with her students. Teachers also brought in local artists with a social justice and an activist stance into the classroom. While knowledge brought into the classroom affected the students in profound ways, teachers honored students' lived experiences as knowledge and created spaces for students to share their own knowledge. For example, Joanne explained that culture was rarely an explicit aspect of her teaching, and instead stated, "I give them questions and they bring me their answer with their art piece… a lot of them will look for their own cultures to look for the response for that" (Interview, February 2009). These assignments led students to trouble, question and negotiate their histories and communities.

Relationships—communities. The participants too, engaged in a process of identifying and negotiating their identities through community involvement. Broadening notions of 'the other' was an important aspect of the teachers' work and relationships in the community. Throughout the discussion, all participants spoke about the importance of being a "part of the community," through involvement in student organizations, connections with

parents, awareness of the interests of the community and living in "the neighborhood."

The data analysis suggested that two of the teachers' relationships with their communities of practice (Wenger, 2007) were challenging. Karen, spoke about colleagues who have set notions of art and artmaking; "a lot of my colleagues that think that, art kinda ended with Gordon Smith[9] or that if you're not teaching about Impressionism then you're not teaching them anything about art." (Interview, May, 2009). To strengthen their community of practice, Joanne and Karen rely on regional conferences and university connections to introduce new ideas.

CONDITIONS

The data point to four conditions that enable teachers to become culturally relevant educators: (1) self conception as artists and teachers, (2) belonging to a community, (3) self-reflexivity, and (4) the institutional context.

Self-conception as artists and teacher/ belonging to a community. Teachers' primary identity as an artist created conflict within their teaching-related communities of practice, however, the participants were visibly invested strengthening the various communities they belong to and value. Not only were the participants active in the community, but they also asked students to be active. Karen's projects often encouraged students to broaden their perspectives and use their community as a resource. Joanne's community involvement included teaching textiles and teacher education courses at the university, as well as working with researchers. Since Sharon taught part-time, while attending graduate school, her direct involvement with the communities of practice were minimized.

Self-reflexivity. The teachers' pedagogical and curricular choices emerge from self-reflexivity. Reflexivity refers to a cyclical relationship between cause and effect. Self-reflexivity is visible in all relationships and is the common thread in all relationships. Teachers in the study are not only self-reflexive, they ask students to become reflexive. This critical exploration and creative problem solving skills, as expressed by the participants, is a result of graduate education and engagement with the commitment toward life-long learning.

Institutional context. The final condition for the presence/absence of CRP is the institutional context. At Tree Hill Secondary, there are no administrators or principals in the building; upon entering the building, you find there is simply an office, which is open periodically, and six or seven classrooms. This setting provides teachers with full autonomy over curricular choices. Joanne spoke frequently about the claustrophobic nature of large high schools, and the lack of creativity in some art programs. At West Side

Secondary, all students are required to take art. Divided among four teachers, including Karen and Sharon, teachers find the student-teacher ratio overwhelming. Teaching in this environment does not allow every student the time, space, materials, or one-on-one attention from the teacher to focus on developing an art practice. An important consideration for art educators is to develop strong communities of practice to support teachers that work in such environments. Collaboration between researchers/university and teaching communities can be particularly helpful for practicing teachers and teacher educators.

RECOMMENDATIONS

Drawing from the findings of this study, I offer the following recommendations for teachers and teacher educators to build the practice of CRP:

- **Art practice**: Stress development of secondary art teachers as artists, and make visible the importance of ongoing studio-based inquiry. A studio practice continuously challenges a teacher's skills and creativity and may enhance overall instructional practices. Scholars cited in this study maintain the importance of ongoing personal and professional development. Although teachers in the study maintained close ties with their teaching-community of practice, they had significant investment in the contemporary arts, community of local artists and their studio practice. Participants' studio practices include photography, sculpture, textiles, and experimental drawing.

- **Research and knowledge**: Engage with social theory research to develop ways to collaborate with researchers. An emphasis on research gives way to a relationship with knowledge that is evolving. Teachers in Ladson-Billings' (1994) study recognized knowledge as metamorphosing, rather than static. Teachers in this study echoed Ladson-Billings work, and saw collaborations with researchers as moving their practice and institutional knowledge forward.

- **Interdisciplinarity, transgressing discipline boundaries**: While relationships evolve and differ, interdisciplinarity allows teachers and researchers to move away from disciplinary limitations to develop modes of inquiry that are inclusive. Following Bhabha (2004), interdisciplinarity gives way to expression of hybrid identities and hybrid knowledges. When exploring tensions and the causality, this mode of inquiry equips teachers to cross disciplinary boundaries to create a curriculum and pedagogy that is culturally relevant to their students.

CONCLUSIONS

This study began with intentions to understanding tensions teachers negotiate. While the original research questions seek to explore tensions that teachers negotiate, when developing the curriculum and pedagogy, and ways in which they approach this through a framework of cultural relevancy, the research process altered the course of the study. Over a period of 4–5 months, through observing, interviewing, and negotiating relationships with the participants, the research moved into the direction of explicating a culturally relevant pedagogy for secondary art educators through a postcolonial lens. This chapter presented ways in which culturally relevant teaching in art education can allow for a decolonizing practice through an emphasis on reflexivity, relationships with knowledge, engagement with artmaking, and awareness of the community. My analysis of data through a postcolonial lens, caused my understanding of Ladson-Billings' (1994) culturally relevant pedagogy through the tenets of conceptions of self and other, social relations, and conceptions of knowledge, to evolve and to address concerns specific to art education.

Unlike teachers in Ladson-Billings' (1994) study, participants in this study saw hybridity as an important element of urban teaching, furthering the necessity of academics to speak to multiethnic concerns. Issues of hybridity lay in juxtaposition to the dominant discourse that forces individuals to compartmentalize their [cultural] identities, forcing binaries and dualisms. And although the study does not answer the original research questions, it shows a progression of ideas that came about during the study through a process of collaborative research and articulates a new direction for inquiry.

REFERENCES

Ashcroft, B., Griffiths, G., & Tiffin, H. (1995). *The post-colonial studies reader.* New York, NY: Routledge.

Bhabha, H. K. (2004). *The location of culture.* London, England: Routledge.

Banks, J. A., & McGee-Banks, C. A. (2003). *Multicultural education: Issues and perspectives.* New York, NY: Wiley.

Bannerji, H. (2000). *The dark side of the nation: Essays on multiculturalism, nationalism and gender.* Toronto, ON: Canadian Scholars' Press.

Battiste, M., Bell, L., & Findlay, L. M. (2002). Decolonizing education in Canadian universities: An interdisciplinary, international, indigenous research project *Canadian Journal of Native Education, 26*(2), 82-95.

Chalmers, F. G. (1992). The origins of racism in the public school art curriculum. *Studies in Art Education, 33*(3), 134-143.

Chalmers, F. G. (2002). "Celebrating pluralism" six years later: Visual transculture/s, education, and critical multiculturalism. *Studies in Art Education, 43*(4), 293-306.

Chalmers, V. (1996). White out: Multicultural performances in a progressive school. In M. Wong (Ed.), *Off-white: Readings on race, power and society* (pp. 66-77). New York, NY: Routledge.

Coffey, A., & Atkinson, P. (1996). *Making sense of qualitative data: Complementary research strategies.* Thousand Oaks, CA: Sage.

Creswell, J. W. (1998). *Qualitative inquiry and research design: Choosing among five traditions.* Thousand Oaks, CA: Sage.

Desai, D. (2000). Imaging difference: The politics of representation in multicultural art education. *Studies in Art Education, 41*(2), 114-129.

Desai, D. (2005). Places to go: Challenges to multicultural art education in a global economy. *Studies in Art Education, 46*(4), 293-308.

Desai, D., & Chalmers, G. (2007). Notes for a dialogue on art education in critical times. *Art Education, 60*(5), 6-12.

Ghosh, R. (1996). *Redefining multicultural education.* Toronto, ON: Harcourt Canada.

Hope, S. (2004). Art education in a world of cross-purposes. In E. W. Eisner & M. Day (Eds.), *Handbook of research and policy in art education* (pp. 93-114). Mahwah, NJ: Lawrence Erlbaum.

Irwin, R. L., Rogers, T., & Farrell, R. (1997). The irrelevance of multiculturalism. *Kaurna Higher Education Journal, 6*, 43-48.

Irwin, R. L., Rogers, T., & Farrell, R. (1999). Multiculturalism denies the realities of aboriginal art and culture. In D. Boughton & R. Mason (Eds.), *Beyond multicultural art education: International perspectives* (Vol. 87, pp. 49-65). New York, NY: Waxmann Munster.

Isar, Y. R. (2006). Tropes of the "intercultural": Multiple perspectives. In N. Aalto & E. Reuter (Eds.), *Aspects of intercultural dialogue. Theory. Research. Applications.* Cologne: SAXA Verlad.

Kader, T. (2005). SchoolArts: DBAE and multicultural art education in the United States of America. *International Journal of Education through Arts, 1*(1), 65-84.

Kvale, S. (2006). Dominance through interviews and dialogues. *Qualitative Inquiry, 12*(3), 480-500.

Ladson-Billings, G. (1992). Culturally relevant teaching: The key to making multicultural education work In C. A. Grant (Ed.), *Research and multicultural education: From the margins to the mainstream.* Washington, DC: The Falmer Press.

Ladson-Billings, G. (1994). The dreamkeepers: Successful teachers of African America children. San Francisco, CA: Jossey-Bass.

Ladson-Billings, G. (1995a). Towards a theory of culturally relevant pedagogy. *American Educational Research Journal, 32*(3), 465-491.

Ladson-Billings, G. (1995b). But that's just good teaching! The case for culturally relevant pedagogy. *Theory into Practice, 34*(3), 159-165.

Ladson-Billings, G. (2004). New directions in multicultural education. In J. A. Banks (Ed.), *The Routledge Falmer Reader in Multicultural Education* (pp. 50-65). London, England: RoutledgeFalmer.

Lather, P. (2006). Paradigm proliferation as a good thing to think with: Teaching research in education as a wild profusion. *International Journal of Qualitative Studies in Education (QSE), 19*(1), 35-57.

McClain, K., & Cobb, P. (2004). *The critical role of institutional context in teacher development* Paper presented at the Conference of the International Group for the Psychology of Mathematics Education, Melbourne, Australia.

Said, E. (1978/79). *Orientalism.* New York, NY: Random House.

Smith, L. T. (1999). *Decolonizing methodologies: Research and indigenous peoples.* London, England & New York, NY: Zed Books.

Staikidis, K. (2006). Personal and cultural narrative as inspiration: A painting and pedagogical collaboration with Mayan artists. *Studies in Art Education, 47*(2), 118-138.

Strauss, A., & Corbin, J. (1990). *Basics of qualitative research: Grounded theory procedures and techniques.* Newbury Park, CA: Sage.

Stuhr, P. L., Petrovich-Mwaniki, L., & Wasson, R. (1992). Curriculum guidelines for the multicultural art classroom. *Art Education, 45*(1), 16-24.

Wenger, E. (2007). Communities of practice: A brief introduction [Electronic Version]. Retrieved from www.ewenger.com/theory

ENDNOTES

1 "Coloniality" is a word that is different from "colonialism"—as used in work by postcolonial scholars. My understanding is that "colonialism" implies that colonization is a thing of the past, while "coloniality" reflects its continuing form through cognitive imperialism etc.

2 The histories and politics driving Canadian multicultural policies and practices differ significantly from the United States, and it is critical to examine the differences since they affect the results/findings of the study.

3 Much of the province currently known as "British Columbia" is land that was taken from the First Nations people and was not formally ceded to the Canadian government. Thus, the ownership of this land is the subject of ongoing legal disputes about the land itself, the natural resources, etc. For more information, see www.firstnations.de/indian_land.htm

4 Battiste writes within the context of Canadian education, animating Aboriginal concerns and proposing a "decolonization" of the larger education system that devalues "the other." Her focus is helping maintain aboriginal languages, identity and culture in the modern society.

5 L. T. Smith has written on Maori identities (in New Zealand) and continues to propose decolonizing methodologies.

6 Participants' names have not been changed. Teachers in the study agreed to the use of their first names.

7 Names of both schools have been changed to keep anonymity.

8 Transcriva is a transcription software that embeds a time-stamp within the transcript, allowing the user to return to a audio or video clip with ease.

9 Gordon Smith is prominent Canadian painter, printmaker, sculptor, and teacher living in Vancouver, British Columbia.

APARNA RAE is an artist with an MA in Curriculum and Pedagogy from The University of British Columbia, Vancouver, BC. Her MA thesis explored culturally relevant pedagogy as a framework for decolonizing practices in secondary art education, as well as a means to further explicate teachers' relationships with self, students, knowledge, and community. She worked as Program Manager with urban youth in Seattle, Washington, and created museum education materials for teacher candidates in collaboration with the Faculty of Education and the Helen & Morris Belkin Gallery at The University of British Columbia. She is currently focusing on developing workforce training programs for immigrant and refugee cooks to enter the food industry, earn living wage jobs, and be financially sustainable.

40 / Making Visible Race, Power, and Injustice in Museum and Middle School Art Curriculum: Collaborative Research to Understand Cultural Issues Surrounding Mimbres Pottery

JAMES W. BEQUETTE / ASSISTANT PROFESSOR OF ART EDUCATION, UNIVERSITY OF MINNESOTA AND **JUDI WARRICK PETKAU** / SENIOR EDUCATOR, UNIVERSITY OF MINNESOTA

ABSTRACT: *This chapter brings together three perspectives—that of a suburban art teacher, an art museum educator and a university professor of education—to investigate the practice of teaching seventh-grade art students about ancient indigenous Mimbres pottery. Race and culture are salient features in this work. All of the researchers and most of the students are White and not culturally marginalized. Starting from the classroom teacher's desire to more deeply address the contentious and unexplored cultural histories that surround the Mimbres ceramics, each of the researchers' roles began to shift as they all reflected and worked together, introducing a mindfully critical teaching practice into the art unit. Methods of critical discourse analysis were used to better understand recorded interactions among students and all three teaching researchers and to reveal moments that challenged or reified dominant cultural assumptions of art, knowledge, power and race. Through this analysis, the assumptions carried by students and the teacher-researchers were made visible, providing insight into the complexity of enacting critical pedagogy in the art room.*

A MULTILAYERED RESEARCH STUDY

This interpretive study represents a multilayered qualitative research project, part of an ongoing collaborative relationship formed to promote professional inquiry that bridges institutions, in this case a suburban middle school, an art museum, and a large urban university in the upper Midwest. Together three teachers—a middle school art teacher, a university art museum educator, and a university art education professor—look at how art teachers might shift their classroom practice to reveal and challenge dominant Western assumptions about art and cultural understanding. The population of the middle school under study is predominantly affluent and White. The suburban district in which this school resides is one of the most racially homogenous in the state, very different from the racial diversity found in the urban center, and also much more homogeneous than other neighboring suburban districts. This research setting was conducive to the enactment of critical art pedagogy and student investigation of Indigenous American objects.

Although we each came to this work with different expectations and purposes, increasing students' critical responses to art and cultures in art classrooms was important to all of us. As university researchers, we authored this chapter and include the key perspective of Lockie Chapman, our middle school colleague, engaging her in comment and critique of this analysis. As the classroom specialist, Lockie's reflections and experiences are central to our questions of teacher practice and professional support.

FORMING A RESEARCH PARTNERSHIP
THE RESEARCH TEAM

We became research collaborators over time. Judi coordinates youth programs at the Weisman Art Museum and met Lockie, a mid-career art teacher, while leading a summer 2007 class on writing in the museum that stressed a collegial relationship between museum and school educators. Lockie reconnected with Judi as the following school year began, wanting classroom resources specific to teaching about the Weisman's extensive collection of Mimbres pottery. Judi had taken those classroom materials out of circulation, finding them problematic because they did not address deeply important cultural aspects of this pottery as grave goods. Lockie agreed to use the museum's classroom resources "as is" in her suburban art room and to reflect and share her experiences and ideas with Judi. The goal was improving the museum's Mimbres teaching materials.

After Lockie taught the Indigenous pottery unit twice during that school year, Judi, who is also a PhD student in art education, asked Jim, whose research interests includes critical cultural issues surrounding American Indian art education, to join the discussion about the Mimbres content. Specifically, they wanted to improve ways of teaching the Mimbres content in the middle school art room to address the troubling histories of the artifacts. Jim is a former K-12 art teacher who worked in schools with mostly Native populations and currently is a faculty member in the art education program from which Lockie earned a master's degree and completed initial licensure requirements 8 years earlier. Although Lockie's Mimbres unit addressed ancient objects unearthed in what today is New Mexico, Jim wondered whether contemporary Native art and artists could be included in the unit to better inform students that the Pueblo cultures thought to have indirect Mimbres ancestry are not static.

We were highly supportive of Lockie's desire to understand and make visible to her students the potentially contentious cultural issues of race, power, and injustice surrounding the collection, display, and study of a museum "collection" of Indigenous Mimbres pottery. As art educators, we knew topics like this are often not only excluded from museum presentation but also from art classroom inquiry (Bequette, 2005, 2009; Hooper-Greenhill, 2000). As Lockie's university partners, we also knew that observing first-hand how she problematized teaching about non-Western Mimbres material culture (Bolin, 1995; Bolin & Blandy, 2003) could yield the type of critical pedagogical knowledge our field needs. That said, Judi and Jim proposed conducting qualitative research that would chronicle Lockie's reflective reaction to teaching about Mimbres pottery, including how her students responded to those lessons. We argued that findings from our research could be shared with other teachers who struggled with critically teaching about culture in art classrooms. Lockie agreed. When we suggested she conduct action research simultaneous to our qualitative research study, Lockie wholeheartedly embraced this form of practitioner inquiry as a means for improving the 2-week ceramics unit.

TEACHER ACTION RESEARCH

Lockie's action research project studied the strengths and constraints of teaching a unit on Indigenous pottery differently to two groups of middle school art students. The study was a byproduct of the reflective community of practice, a group of engaged teachers willing to share information and experiences (Lave & Wenger, 1991), that we formed. We agreed that our community of practice (CoP), should focus broadly on researching the travails of educators teaching about cultures other than their own. This joint work was seen as a possible model for a larger CoP of art teachers

organized with support from the university and educators from area museums and/or arts organizations.

The opportunity for us to see what the Mimbres pottery lesson looked like before, during, and after Lockie conducted action research in her seventh-grade art classes provided a comprehensive picture of her teaching practices. After thinking through the effectiveness of her past practice, Lockie asked us to help her revise the Mimbres pottery lesson for a different group of students. That decision broadened the scope of her lesson study, added another layer to our research agenda, and changed all three of our roles in the project over time.

A WILLINGNESS TO CONSIDER HOW THEORY MIGHT IMPROVE PRACTICE

It was Lockie's keen interest in wrestling with critical cultural questions and narratives that reveal the troubling histories of the 1,000-year-old Mimbres pottery—pillaged burial goods (Brody, 1997; Brody & Swentzell, 1996) of lost context, commerce, and colonial domination, the work of humans we do not and can never truly know—that led her to reimagine better ways of teaching the seventh-grade ceramics lesson. The struggle that accompanies adopting a more critical stance when teaching often poses disturbing challenges for art educators committed to conceptions of critical pedagogy (Ellsworth, 1989; Fecho, 2001; Karp & Lavine, 1991; Tavin & Hausman, 2004). For Lockie, the decision to design and implement an inquiry-based project for her seventh graders would not only necessitate deviating from the teacher-centered didactic presentation of American Indian content she previously used, it would relegate mimetic studio tasks like creating Mimbres-style pots to a minor role in the redesigned lesson. Instead of focusing on ceramics, students worked in groups and were challenged to use Movie Maker and/or iMovie software to produce podcasts, short digital essays focused on the exploration of critical questions surrounding the Mimbres objects. This was a difficult decision. In written evaluations of Lockie's earlier unit, students ranked the making of pottery as the most enjoyable activity. She worried that the revised unit challenged the boundaries of art disciplinary content, moving her curriculum into the realm of social studies.

THEORETICAL FRAMEWORK

Conceptions of teacher action research (Kemmis, 1999; Zeichner, 1995), critical discourse analysis (Gee, 1999; Lewis, Enciso, & Moje, 2007), and sociocultural theories (Freire, 1998; Giroux, 1995; Grande, 2004; hooks, 1995) ground our research and professional partnerships. We frame learning as a "collaborative conversation and association between students and educators" (Congdon & Blandy, 2001, p. 274), and suggest that attention to shifting identities and power relations within a learning activity offers a better way to find moments of agency and student learning (Lewis et al., 2007). To aid our investigation of these complex relationships, we consider how they construct genres of discourse (Fairclough, 2001; Gee, 1999) that are used within the specific activity of interpreting meanings from and about objects of ancient Mimbres pottery. Attending to discourse reveals power relationships. As a critical theoretical lens, this shaped our research focus. As a method for analyzing data, critical discourse analysis revealed negotiation and struggle with the Mimbres content issues, and offered insight into the subtle ways power relations moved and changed within our research partnership.

RESEARCH PROCESS
MULTIPLE LAYERS OF RESEARCH
Technically, three research protocols were at play within the larger inquiry project we describe in our chapter: The first layer of research was that overarching look at Lockie's reflexive practice and self-initiated action research process, what methodologically was *case study research* of a single teacher's practice. This inquiry was "an exploration of a 'bounded system' or a case…over time through detailed, in-depth data collection involving multiple sources of information rich in contest" (Creswell, 1998, p. 61). In short, our qualitative case was bounded by time—the 16 days we observed Lockie teaching—and place—the two seventh-grade art classes in her 600-student middle school. The focus of this case study was the Mimbres pottery lesson we saw Lockie teach twice. We collected multiple sources of data rich in context, including written observations or field notes, recorded interviews with Lockie, audio and video files of her teaching episodes, and samples of student artwork (ceramic pots and critical podcasts).

Secondly, Lockie was conducting *action research* that examined her own teaching practice. In this instance, action research was an empowering activity that challenged her values and beliefs about multicultural teaching and learning. Lockie and her principal perceived this inquiry as a form of professional development aimed at improving her reflective practice. On another plane, action research enhanced Lockie's understanding of traditional teacher-centered versus discovery teaching methods. She learned about the potential of discovery teaching methods in art education and how they might assist in modifying students' value systems and challenge the domination and distorting influences of Western ideals.

The third layer of our research can be characterized as an alternative paradigm of critical education research that we call *participatory research*. This research protocol came into play when our simple case study of a single teacher's practice morphed into hands-on participation as co-teachers with Lockie. Our transition was from silent observers to mentors to collaborators in the action research project. This

change in roles began when Judi added museum-based contextual instruction about the funerary uses of pottery in Mimbres cultures for the third- and fourth-quarter classes. That participation continued when Jim taught a history lesson in Lockie's classroom as part of the fourth-quarter unit. Jim focused on the conduct of the archeology professor who unearthed nearly 500 pieces of Mimbres pottery from a burial site in southwestern New Mexico, from 1929 to 1931. Through this approach, Jim encouraged students to trouble the ethical issues surrounding the excavating practices of 20th century social scientists. That conversation also considered pothunters who, to this day, ransack and desecrate Indigenous graves for profit or for museums to display.

RESEARCH QUESTIONS
This work explores three central themes: (1) How educators from an urban research university's art museum and preservice teacher education program can collaborate as reflective colleagues to investigate and support classroom practice; (2) The impact of Lockie's action research investigation of the (re)enactment of a Mimbres pottery unit designed to better connect North American Indian material culture and societies past and present; and (3) How two groups of seventh-grade art students' critical response to Lockie's pottery lessons was mediated by viewing Mimbres bowls in a museum and/or their experience shaping clay mimetically into pots of similar style.

DATA SOURCES
Reflecting on her own practice, Lockie engaged in systematic action research around her existing Mimbres lesson's strengths. She collected and analyzed a range of data to inform changes to the Mimbres pottery unit. Data sources included Lockie's reflective journal, video and audio tapes of her teaching the daily lessons (later, also including teaching episodes led by Judi and Jim), student evaluations of each activity of the unit, student artwork (including bowls and digitally produced critical podcasts), and audio files of daily debriefing conversations with us. After Lockie spent 2 weeks considering the data collected while teaching the Mimbres unit to third-quarter seventh graders, we met as a group to discuss her self-assessment of this process. Only when asked for our reactions did we provide constructive feedback on her teaching that led to a discussion of possible unit revisions. Aware of, and hoping to circumvent, the practice-theory disconnect among teachers in the field and university faculty, our conversation with Lockie was as non-prescriptive as possible. In other words each of us honored the experiences and insights we as art educators collectively brought to the task.

When Lockie asked for more than just suggestions for reimagining the Mimbres unit, we became participatory researchers. This participation included collaboratively planning and teaching particular lessons. Later, Lockie again took the lead teacher role and we moved to reclaim our earlier roles as passive observers, watching the newly tweaked lesson reach fruition with a studio experience making and decorating pots and a showing and critique of each group's critical podcast of edited audio and video files.

THE MIMBRES POTTERY UNIT(S)

After receiving the Weisman Art Museum's classroom materials and adapting them to her teaching style, Lockie implemented a 2-week unit for her students in the fall of 2007. She stayed in contact with Judi at the museum and shared images of her students' work—black and white patterned ceramic bowls. She reported making minor changes to her pedagogy before we observed her teaching and before we actively collected tangible data—observation fieldnotes, and voice recordings of Lockie's daily debriefings in early spring 2008. The one significant change experienced by third-quarter students was an end-of-unit fieldtrip to the Weisman Art Museum for a private showing of Mimbres pottery. While in the museum, Lockie helped manage the movement of students, but Judi assumed the role of teacher.

Students went "behind the scenes" to see eight Mimbres pots pulled from museum storage, and this investigation was used as an opportunity to present information and raise questions regarding the contested histories of these objects. The selection included some pots previously seen in large photographs shown in the classroom (from the museum's classroom materials), and other pieces that varied in form not previously seen by the students. Lockie's seventh graders were not permitted to handle the pots, but they could get within inches of these very fragile artifacts and point out cracks and technical imperfections or details in the figurative designs not revealed in the photographs. These art students could, as one girl commented, even "smell" how old this pottery was.

After the fieldtrip, and at Lockie's request, we became her onsite curriculum consultants and eventually her co-teachers. Jim assisted her in the art classroom, trying to connect the Mimbres civilization to later Indigenous American societies. Judi helped redesign the museum visit experiences that occured midway through the unit and used the fieldtrip to launch an inquiry-based learning project. Lockie veered dramatically from her initial interpretation of the museum's Mimbres curriculum to better contextualize questions surrounding the making, collecting, and museum exhibition of these Indigenous ceramics. Through our collaborative process, the Mimbres unit morphed into an opportunity for the fourth group of seventh graders to conduct critical inquiry in small "design teams." Each of the three- or four-student groups received a salient, researchable question to center their investigations. Judi posed questions to the seventh graders during their trip to the Weisman

Art Museum that included "Whose voices and perspectives have shaped the museum exhibition? How do these bowls relate to present-day American Indians? Or do they?" and "Why and how were these bowls collected? Are there any historic issues with that?" Although the students' research began in the museum, it culminated in their school's media lab where the Internet and other collected print resources helped them script and add images to their final digital productions. Short video podcast slide shows thus became the medium through which the students made public their responses to the critical issues surrounding the Mimbres pottery. Interestingly, the fourth-quarter students who lacked an embodied experience making clay bowls before the art museum visit were less enamored of the technical details and physicality of the actual Indigenous pottery than the third quarter students. Instead, the fourth quarter students had opportunities to explore the breadth of museum resources and museum-based teaching to support their critical classroom inquiry of Mimbres artifacts.

DATA ANALYSIS AND FINDINGS

Judi transcribed and analyzed recorded interactions between students, teacher, and researchers from both the first and second group of students, using Gee's (1999) methods of critical discourse analysis to reveal hidden and underlying assumptions of power, legitimacy, and knowledge, constructed within learning situations in the school and museum. Within the transcriptions of conversations, complex interactions were coded as potential moments serving to reinforce or reify particular dominant Discourses—those of Western art, of scientific archeology, of Western schooling, and American Indian historicization. Continuing to draw on Gee's methods, Judi also analyzed the museum-produced print and Web texts used as partial sources of information for the teacher and students. Then, she further examined the students' video products, looking for the potential production or reproduction of dominant Discourse and seeking evidence of critical awareness in practice. As Judi, Jim, and Lockie each featured in the student discussions and instructional exchanges, these findings were revealing, serving to challenge teaching practice and had a strong impact on our critical reflection. This analysis of institutional texts and student production did reveal brief moments of critical shift, of addressing the contentious nature of the artifacts. But what it revealed more clearly was the difficulty in directly challenging and significantly changing the dominant Discourse around these objects, even when mindfully trying to do so.

Overall, students created videos that did not challenge the art museum's claim of ownership, or the situation of these objects as legitimate property of the dominant culture. In more than one instance, and in spite of directed instruction, the exact text of the museum's website served as unquestioned "official" or "expert" resource for student work. However, we did find a few moments of critical shift, of addressing the contentious nature of the artifacts though the posing of questions and the student use of contingent language such as "might" and "could" rather than settling for one fixed and untroubled perspective. Within our own teaching practices, the recorded conversations revealed instances when we reinforced a positivist, dominant art historical lineage, falling back on tropes of timelines, treasure hunts, and masterworks which served to fix these cultural objects rather than open them to question. This experience revealed how challenging and dynamic such critical cultural work is within situated traditional teaching practice.

We brought three reflective perspectives to Lockie's classroom practice: that of art teacher, museum resource and support, and teacher educator. Each of us had unique and overlapping research interests upon entering into this professional partnership. Lockie was highly motivated to pursue professional development opportunities, because, like many art teachers, she works in isolation. As a midcareer professional she had a demonstrated appetite for weaving more cultural content into her art lessons and struggled finding relevant curriculum resources and the time to do so in a school program that valued art production. Lockie often asked if deeper conversations about culture, race, and social justice were perhaps better aligned with social studies curricula. As individuals we embody and represent dominant White culture and dominant institutions—school, museum, university. Those roles and the authorities they afforded in classroom and museum interactions bounded the critical possibilities of our interactions with students. Issues of representation and the limitation of voice troubled us all. Through reflection on our practice we realized the extent to which we lacked texts, recordings, live and legitimate representation of these alternative perspectives. The research assignment itself cast the Mimbres as a knowable object of study.

Judi felt that her work with Lockie was action research specific to her practice as a museum educator and curriculum designer. The valuable opportunity to observe a "field test" of the Mimbres materials developed by her museum confirmed Judi's suspicion that this curriculum lacked components that might give teachers (and their students) guidance for ways to wrestle with the contested nature of this pottery. She wondered if the critical examination of the ethical and cultural issues surrounding Mimbres ceramics would prove interesting to students in middle school and wanted to try to design resources and activities that would support this kind of work in the art room. The data revealed the limits of the original and revised resource texts available from the museum and suggested the power of recorded statements (in lieu of live visitation) to represent alternative and contesting perspectives on the Mimbres objects.

For Jim, Lockie's school district's upper middle class demographic provided a good setting in which to investigate whether studying Mimbres pottery could engage privileged White students to better understand contemporary American Indian cultures and postcolonial thinking that inspires many Native artists today. This interaction seemed like a logical way to invite many of these seventh graders to rethink monolithic, stereotypic views of American Indians and their material culture. Critical discourse analysis of episodes of classroom conversations from two different Mimbres units, and the student-produced video essays provided data to analyze student understandings and to study complex processes of critical pedagogy in action. Recognizing the significance of Lockie's action research and using the data she collected to challenge teachers' trepidation of teaching about a culture other than their own and assumptions about art and culture resulted in a shift in one teacher's practice that could inform the pedagogy of other art teachers. In keeping with that proposition, other art teachers may benefit from Lockie's decision to infuse cultural research into art activities and develop relevant but non-mimetic studio assignments that are less likely to stereotype or simplify the culture(s) being studied.

Finally, our relationship with Lockie offered an opportunity to support her reflective practice by introducing her to action research methods and the theoretical literature that supports this scholarship of teaching and learning (Shulman, 2000). Lockie's initiative and professionally reflective stance made her a likely candidate to help build an emerging CoP. Such a network can support inservice teachers to improve their pedagogy, counter their disciplinary isolation in schools, and potentially increase teacher retention for early- and mid-career professionals (Lieberman & Miller, 2007). For educators working in museums or universities, it offers a way to bridge institutional boundaries, counter distances that may exist between practice and theory, and gain understanding of real and relevant classroom challenges.

SIGNIFICANCE FOR ART TEACHERS

By her own choice, Lockie is not an author of this chapter. She remains supportive of making findings from this joint work accessible to others in art education, and we continue to discuss ways to carry on our investigations and CoP. For Lockie, empirical evidence of the seventh graders' cooperative work ethic, level of engagement, and technical achievement as video artists confirmed why the revised Mimbres unit added opportunities for student critical inquiry and deeper understanding. Weaving more "cultural pieces" into her art teaching, balancing studio and cultural aspects of the curriculum, and better tapping the multidisciplinary potential of existing "multicultural" projects were all outcomes of Lockie's action research project. The reflexive use of student evaluations, a variety of student work, and class videos as data to help her think through her classroom changes—what she called "a paradigm shift"—is expanding her idea of important art content.

Analysis of Lockie's teaching reveals significant change in how she structured these lessons. Her first Mimbres unit included classroom discussion of the formal qualities of the bowls, setting the stage for students' mimetic studio work with clay. Persistent student questions about the obvious and curious holes found in the pots (what contemporary Pueblo artists call "breath holes") were not explored. In the revised unit, the significance of the holes became a central discussion related to the excavation of the pots from gravesites and the ethical issues this history raised. It became a feature at least mentioned in all of the student video podcasts; for Lockie, this was evidence of deeper student engagement in the critical cultural questions surrounding the objects. Critical discourse analysis of Lockie's presentation of the revised unit revealed a shift in how the museum resource was presented, based on her own deeper knowledge of the Mimbres issues.

The first time she taught the Mimbres unit, Lockie presented all the cultural information as one legitimate perspective—"the experts say…."That shifted to the more specific perspectives of "art historians say… the archeologists believe… [and] some Native people feel…." Representation of multiple perspectives and discourses around the Mimbres pots marks a significant shift in Lockie's intentional teaching of this content, though still unconsciously privileging the art historical perspective. Analysis shows the new unit did not result in dramatically altered discourse. In the seventh graders' video productions, we found evidence of a beginning understanding of the contested nature of the Mimbres objects.

Judi's primary findings supported her initial concern that the Mimbres resources provided by the museum were problematic and limited. The curriculum did not support or encourage teachers to present the contested cultural issues that surround the Mimbres objects. Critical discourse analysis of the texts presented as the museum's resources revealed a prevalent reification of the museum's ownership claim in the name of the "public good."The pots were mainly presented as primitive works of art, using the dominant discourse of

Western art history. Most revealing in Judi's action research was the analysis of her conversations with students. When looking at the pottery in the museum with students she sought to explain diverse positions and turned to methods of storytelling and analogy, attempting to give voice to both the ancient and unknown makers and contemporary Native descendents. Upon reflection these exchanges were very problematic, and another form of cultural mimicry. Our analysis of these interactions leads us to believe that museum resources that support critical investigations into diverse cultural positions should provide video or live representation of or interaction with contested perspectives. Issues of voice and representation became paramount in the (re)envisioning of the museum's Mimbres materials.

Our collaboration with Lockie and her school district provided a clearer picture of how "hands on" outreach and participatory research can empower and serve constituencies our university programs may have ignored in the past. In short, we were all teachers and also teacher researchers, seeing the power of collaborative inquiry through the lens of our individual practice. Underpinning all these efforts are the racial and cultural issues surrounding the objects, the institutions, and the people involved.

Lockie's voice was valued and central throughout this research collaboration and should be evident in this text. To confirm our interpretative analysis of the data, we member checked our findings with Lockie. More often than not, her perspective was similar to ours. When it was contradictory we reanalyzed the data to include Lockie's perspective. One such insight Lockie provided involved the influences that shaped the scope and sequence of her art curriculum. The expectations of students and parents were much more influential than we realized and heightened our respect for Lockie's willingness to try new and perhaps controversial activities that pushed school understandings of the discipline of art. She also regularly provided a reality check on the time, labor, and resources needed as she worked to serve each of her seventh graders. These professional discussions deepened our research relationships and strengthened our data analysis. Doing so was helpful, ethical, and a fundamental precept of conducting inquiry in our research partnership.

REFERENCES

Bequette, J. W. (2005). Renegotiating boundaries between authenticity and relevance when choosing content for an American Indian multicultural arts program. *Journal of Cultural Research in Art Education, 23*(1), 64-74.

Bequette, J. W. (2009). Tapping a postcolonial community's cultural capital: Empowering Native artist to engage more fully with traditional culture and their children's art education. *Visual Arts Research, 35*(1), 78-92.

Bolin, P. E. (1995). Investigating artifacts: Material culture studies and art education. *NAEA Advisory.* Reston, VA: National Art Education Association.

Bolin, P. E., & Blandy, D. (2003). Beyond visual culture: Seven statements of support for material culture studies in art education. *Studies in Art Education, 44*(3), 246-263.

Brody, J. J. (1997). *Mimbres painted pottery.* Santa Fe, NM: School of American Research.

Brody, J. J., & Swentzell, R. (1996). *To touch the past: The painted pottery of the Mimbres people.* New York, NY: Hudson Hill Press.

Congdon, K. G., & Blandy, D. (2001). Approaching the real and the fake: Living life in the fifth world. *Studies in Art Education, 42*(3), 266-278.

Creswell, J. (1998). *Qualitative inquiry and research design: Choosing among five traditions.* Thousand Oaks, CA: Sage.

Ellsworth, E. (1989). Why doesn't this feel empowering? Working through the repressive myths of critical pedagogy. *Harvard Educational Review 59*(3), 297-324.

Fairclough, N. (2001). *Language and power* (2nd ed.). Essex, England: Pearson Education.

Fecho, B. (2001). "Why are you doing this?" Acknowledging and transcending threat in a critical inquiry classroom. *Research in the Teaching of English, 35*(1), 9-37.

Freire, P. (1998). *Pedagogy of freedom: Ethics, democracy, and civic courage.* Lanham, MD: Rowman & Littlefield.

Gee, J. P. (1999). *An introduction to discourse analysis theory and method.* New York, NY: Routledge.

Giroux, H. (1995). Radical pedagogy as cultural politics: Beyond the discourse of critique and anti-utopianism. In P. McLaren (Ed.), *Critical pedagogy and predatory culture* (pp. 29-57). New York, NY: Routledge.

Grande, S. (2004). *Red pedagogy: Native American social and political thought.* Lanham, MD: Rowman & Littlefield.

hooks, b. (1995). *Art on my mind: Visual politics.* New York, NY: The New Press.

Hooper-Greenhill, E. (2000). *Museums and the interpretation of visual culture.* London, England: Routledge.

Karp, I., & Lavine, S. (1991). *Exhibiting cultures: The poetics and politics of museum display.* Washington, DC: Smithsonian Institution Press.

Kemmis, S. (1999). Action research. In J. P. Keeves & G. Lakomski (Eds.), *Issues in educational research* (pp. 150-160). Oxford, England: Elsevier Science.

Lave, J., & Wenger, E. (1991). *Situated learning: Legitimate peripheral participation.* Cambridge, England: Cambridge University Press.

Lewis, C., Enciso, P., & Moje, E. B. (2007). *Reframing sociocultural research on literacy: Identity, agency, and power.* Mahwah, NJ: Lawrence Erlbaum.

Lieberman, A., & Miller, L. (2007). Transforming professional development: Understanding and developing learning communities. In W. Hawley (Ed.), *Effective schools: Educational reform as continuous improvement* (2nd ed.) (pp. 99-116). Thousand Oaks, CA: Corwin Press.

Shulman, L. (2000). From Minsk to Pinsk: Why a scholarship of teaching and learning? *Journal of Scholarship of Teaching and Learning, 1*(1), 48-53.

Tavin, K., & Hausman, J. (2004). Art education and visual culture in the age of globalization. *Art Education, 57*(5), 47-52.

Zeichner, K. (1995). Beyond the divide of teacher research and academic research. *Teaching and Teachers, 1*(2), 153-172.

JAMES W. BEQUETTE is Assistant Professor of Art Education in the Department of Curriculum & Instruction at the University of Minnesota. His current work with Minnesota Native populations to improve American Indian school success and all students' understanding of colonization's impact on Native material culture was inspired by 15 years teaching art in K-12 schools with mostly American Indian students. With colleagues he currently studies how non-Western arts and culture knowledge can intentionally target integrated learning in mathematics, language arts, and science. He also researches contentious state-level policy questions regarding media arts education standards and art teacher licensure.

JUDI WARRICK PETKAU was Senior Educator at the Weisman Art Museum at the University of Minnesota prior to completing her graduate work. Her PhD research investigates pedagogic discourse and student meaning-making processes in relation to aesthetic objects and spaces. Currently, she is a program officer with the Margaret A. Cargill Foundation focusing on support for teacher professional development in arts teaching and learning.

CONCLUSION
Facilitating the Research Process and Contributing to the Field of Art Education

MELANIE L. BUFFINGTON AND **SARA WILSON MCKAY**

SARA: *As we embarked upon this book project, we also both decided to train for and run our first 10K in Richmond, Virginia. Neither of us perceived ourselves to be runners previously, but we decided to run in an annual race held each March with 35,000 people. In thinking about the process of research, our commitment to running may be a useful analogy for new researchers. I viewed this event as a challenge both physical and mental. The first step was committing to the process, as I never thought I could run or wanted to run even a mile before. Then I had to determine how to get my body and my mind ready to do this run. I researched online for advice and a training schedule recommended for first time 10K runners. I was grateful for a timeline and a guide for the physical activities daily. I also found that a motivating music playlist and a way of tracking progress (a calendar hanging on my refrigerator) helped me stay motivated. On days I did not feel mentally ready for the next step, I would talk to runner friends of mine for advice about how to get to the next level. Hearing from them that the first two miles are just hard, or that it helps to have a mantra to just keep going, really helped me realize this is difficult, but achievable. Over time, running became something I looked forward to and craved. I felt more powerful and more capable after each successful run. Melanie and I would often share tales of training, doubts and questions, when we were feeling strong, and when we were feeling unsure. We did not train together, but we shared the process and tips we learned along the way. On the day of the event, we had our hesitations, but we brought determination and commitment and each of us finished strong. I have gone on to run more 10Ks and continue to work toward incorporating more frequent physical activity into my life.*

The work of research is not unlike the process of training for a running race. In this chapter, we will discuss some ways to facilitate the research process including useful steps and important tools. Some of these tools include contemporary digital tools and software, which will continue to evolve over time. We recap the scope of this text and offer an assessment of where we think research in art education may be heading. This chapter ends with some questions about why teachers engage in research and how art education will benefit from strong focus on research by teacher researchers.

HELPFUL HINTS FOR A FIRST RESEARCH STUDY: WHERE CAN YOU GO FROM HERE? WHAT ARE LIKELY NEXT STEPS?

As in the running example above, we suggest some ideas that may be helpful in designing and implementing a research study.

FORM A SUPPORT GROUP

Identifying others who are engaged with a similar process can be one of the most valuable things to do to increase the likelihood for success. Knowing who to reach out to can offer needed support to help a research project proceed and succeed. As with our running efforts, we each identified who could offer both moral support and advice along the way. This applies to the research process as well. Often, fellow graduate students or teachers can be the best support as they are experiencing similar issues and may be able to offer feedback, suggestions, and encouragement. Depending upon the research topic, friends, family, fellow teachers, or administrators may be able to offer assistance as well. Additionally, electronic groups like the art education Ning site (http://arted20.ning.com) or various listservs (teacherartexchange@lists.pub.getty.edu) have members who can offer knowledge and support.

Some researchers find it helpful to develop a formal or informal mentoring relationship with an experienced researcher. As Carpenter, Sullivan, and Zimmerman (2009) note, it is important to carefully choose a mentor for a research project. For more details about mentoring graduate students, see the special issue of *Visual Arts Research* (edited by Elizabeth Delacruz and Steve McGuire), on this topic (Volume 35, Number 2, Issue 69, Winter 2009).

CRAFT A RESEARCH PROJECT WITH A REASONABLE SCOPE

In our work with students, we frequently see beginning researchers wanting to take on large sweeping projects that might take years to thoroughly study. Though we certainly encourage graduate students to set high standards and impressive goals, we also want students to be successful. Thus, we suggest that a first research project be of limited scope with a relatively straightforward research design. As researchers gain experience through additional research projects, they learn ways to navigate the IRB process, to work with local teachers and students, and to collect and analyze data. Experienced researchers can then take on additional and more complex research studies. Before settling on an idea for a study, we suggest that all graduate students meet with their advisors to make sure they think the scope and topic of the proposed study are reasonable.

MAKE A TIMELINE AND STICK TO IT

It is very important to be able to break the large research process into manageable steps, and putting these smaller tasks on a calendar helps. We suggest that new researchers make an appointment with their advisor to discuss the topic and timeline. Next make a calendar and mark due dates, especially considering any required deadlines of a graduate program. It is crucial to have the advisor's approval for the timeline. A good recommendation is to set several small manageable and measurable goals for each month. Writing down these goals, telling people when they are accomplished, and crossing the goals off the master list are good ways to stay on track.

TECHNOLOGY TOOLS FOR RESEARCHERS

Though the process of research may seem daunting, there are many available technological tools that can assist researchers in their work. Some of these tools are free and simple to utilize, while others are costly and will take some time to learn. As researchers develop their research plan, it is useful to pilot test all aspects of the research design including the tools intended for data collection and analysis. Not only will this help the researcher work out any technological problems, but it will also help the researcher in developing a system to use throughout the research process. This simple step can save time by helping a researcher identify and troubleshoot procedural, methodological, or technological difficulties.

EARLY STAGES OF THE RESEARCH: SOCIAL BOOKMARKING

As a researcher is narrowing her or his topic, we suggest looking into various social bookmarking sites. Names of some sites include Delicious, Digg, and reddit. Through these sites, users can "bookmark" websites using multiple, meaningful tags. These tags could relate to different aspects of a research project. For instance, if a possible topic is multicultural education, the researcher might tag with terms including "art multicultural education" "multicultural elementary," "multicultural secondary," or other related terms. When the researcher is ready to work on that section of the study, all the websites that s/he previously located will be available through the social bookmarking site. Because they are Web-based rather than based on the user's computer, the user's marked sites can be accessed from any computer with Internet access. This may be particularly useful for a researcher who has one computer at work and another one at home.

MELANIE: *I find Delicious particularly helpful with long-term projects. Before I started using Delicious, I frequently spent a fair amount of time looking for sites that I located before that seemed like they would be useful. Inevitably, it seemed that I was only able to find the best sites again after spending quite some time looking. Now that I use my Delicious account regularly, I tag all the sites that I locate with meaningful terms and whenever or wherever I need the information (as long as I have Internet access), I can easily locate them. It has literally changed the way that I work and helped me become more efficient.*

DATA COLLECTION AND ANALYSIS: ELECTRONIC SURVEYS, RESEARCH SOFTWARE, AND OTHER TOOLS

Depending upon the methodology of a study, different techniques may assist a researcher in collecting data. If a researcher is conducting a survey, electronic surveys, such as SurveyMonkey or Zoomerang, are free or relatively inexpensive means to collect data. Because they are often simple to set up and eliminate many of the expenses associated with mail surveys, electronic surveys can help the researcher reach a wide audience. Further, because they reduce the time necessary for a mail survey to reach intended participants, researchers may be able to amass a large amount of data relatively quickly. However, electronic surveys are not without their drawbacks as the response rate is typically lower than other types of surveys and the participants may be limited demographically to those who have Internet access (Adler & Clark, 2008; de Leeuw, 2008; de Leeuw, Hox, & Dillman, 2008; Lynn, 2008).

Regardless of the intended data collection method, it is useful to test a survey on people outside the population in a study before beginning the research process. For instance, a researcher could create a short survey through SurveyMonkey for friends and family members related to their thoughts about a simple topic different from the research topic. This will allow a researcher to learn to use the SurveyMonkey tools, and provide some "data" to use for practicing analysis techniques. Though SurveyMonkey and other online survey tools have analysis capabilities built in, a researcher might choose to hand code or otherwise analyze the data.

In addition to online tools, there are many other technology tools that researchers may find helpful for collecting and analyzing data. For instance, when conducting interviews or focus groups, most researchers make an audio or video recording of the session. Though some researchers prefer to use an audiotape system, others prefer to make digital recordings. Regardless of the recording device, an external microphone is usually necessary to pick up high quality audio during an interview or focus group. There are microphones that can plug directly into MP3 players that allow a researcher to use that device to record conversations. Further, there are high-quality microphone apps that researchers can download directly to a smart phone. Any microphone and recording system should be tested several times in similar situations before the research begins. For instance, if a researcher is planning to run a focus group, she or he should gather a group of people who are not part of the research and engage them in a conversation. The researcher should test the recording equipment in this group scenario to ensure that it picks up all the voices of the various speakers.

To transcribe recordings, a researcher can use a foot pedal that plugs into a computer and works for digital recordings to control the speed that the recording is playing, rewind it, or fast-forward it. As it typically takes quite a long time to transcribe a recording, foot pedals can significantly speed up the process. Another option is to use voice recognition software and upload the digital voice recordings. However, high-quality voice recognition software is expensive and there are issues with the need to "train" the computer to recognize all the voices present in the recordings. There are also people who will transcribe recordings for a fee if the researcher so chooses; however, this choice requires a researcher to read through the transcripts with the audio playing, annotating, correcting, and making additional notes, in order to make sure that she or he agrees with many decisions that are made in the transcription process.

Two widely used data analysis software packages are NVivo and Statistical Package for the Social Sciences (SPSS). NVivo is used to analyze qualitative data and helps a researcher to classify, sort, and arrange non-numerical data. The software allows researchers to investigate what may be complex relationships in the data. Researchers use SPSS for statistical analyses making it very useful for quantitative research, though SPSS also offers ways to conduct mixed methods analysis by converting qualitative text into quantitative data. Both of these programs are expensive and will likely require a researcher spend some time learning the intricacies of how to utilize their analysis capabilities effectively.

Two simple and widely available programs for data analysis include Microsoft Word (or any other word processing software) and Microsoft Excel (or similar spreadsheet software). For instance, if analyzing the transcript of an interview, a researcher has many options in Microsoft Word. A researcher can use the Find function to identify and color-code text segments with specific relevant words, add comments or notes via track changes or other means, and split text into columns to have the participant's words on one side of the page and the researcher's comments or codes on the other side of the page. Further, Word allows for either line-by-line coding or larger holistic codes. Excel (or a similar spreadsheet program) can be used in some of the same ways with a researcher developing simple formulas for various calculations. Data can be easily categorized and placed in appropriate columns and then a researcher can analyze segments of text-based data side-by-side or can easily rearrange them to find new meanings. The graphing features of a spreadsheet program may also be useful.

Regardless of the tools, technological or otherwise, a thorough researcher plans and tests the data collection and analysis methods before collecting the actual data for the study. Not doing so can lead to significant difficulties and delays in the research process.

FILE MANAGEMENT AND WRITING THE RESULTS OF A STUDY

While conducting research and writing the results of the study, researchers likely have many versions of important files, and it is imperative to develop a system for tracking files. We suggest developing a naming convention for files that includes the date in the file name to assist in easily identifying the most recent version. Also, some researchers may find the use of online tools such as Google Drive or Drop Box helpful because they allow access to files from any computer with Internet access. Google Drive can be an especially helpful tool when collaborating with someone else on the same document.

Some Thoughts About Research

F. ROBERT SABOL / PURDUE UNIVERSITY, NAEA PRESIDENT 2011-2013

When making the decision to conduct research of any kind, it is important to consider the purposes for which the research may be used and the methods that will be employed in conducting it. In some cases research may be conducted to understand a situation or phenomenon, something like taking a snapshot of what exists. In other circumstances, research may be conducted to provide new ways of thinking about a problem or set of variables or to argue for a new or unique way of thinking or understanding. Many other purposes can be considered and it is important to select a research methodology that will provide the kinds of answers to questions being asked by the researcher. Various research methodologies produce differing kinds of findings that can have a variety of applications. Findings from empirical research can be used to help legislators, superintendents, or parents make up their minds about a decision, but qualitative research measures can put a face or context on a problem that statistical findings may not be able to achieve. Framing research questions in a manner that are stated in a neutral stance and that allows for the unexpected is of critical importance. It is of equal importance to consider the audience who may be interested in the research. In some cases researchers study things simply because they need to know about a thing and there are few implications for the uses of their findings by others. They simply need to inform themselves. On another scale decision makers from parents to superintendents and policy makers from the local, national, or international levels are influenced by research and use it to inform their thinking and decisions. Often researchers have no indications of the impact or real importance their research may have when they begin their research. From researching something as seemingly mundane as deciding what kind of paper to purchase for an art program to conducting research that will provide findings that can assist elected officials in crafting legislation, research can have varied and multifaceted purposes and be of value to a variety of audiences with widely different needs. It is personally gratifying to a researcher when others respond to a particular piece of research in positive or useful ways to influence outcomes or decisions. Beginning researchers need to be open to all of these possibilities and be bold in learning how to use research in its many and varied applications. ∎

STATE OF RESEARCH IN ART EDUCATION

In response to our initial call seeking examples of methodologies and studies in art education, we received a significant number of proposed contributions related to arts-based inquiry and narrative-based methodologies. We also noticed that action research continues to be a strong avenue of research for teachers, and we received many submissions that utilized participatory and socially conscious approaches to research.

Our initial organizational structure evolved over the course of this book project as we worked to respond to the submissions we received and as our thinking changed over time. By considering seriously the continuum of formal to informal research, we imagine a time when they are not separate entities that are practiced by different individuals with power relationships inherently privileging certain ways of knowing. Thus, we conclude with a series of questions relating to our hopes for the future of inquiry in art education.

- What if multiple aspects of teaching and learning were valued as much as test scores?
- What if the federal government regularly commissioned a series of case studies of high-performing teachers and included art teachers?
- What if mandates for advanced degrees for teachers also required time for participation in research groups?
- What if teachers were invited to present their classroom research and participate in decision-making for their schools and communities as a regular course of action?
- What if art education researchers worked to build connections among various methodologies?
- What if art educators at various levels conducted large-scale and small-scale studies using different methodologies to understand the same problem?
- What if art educators shared more of their data and analyzed this data in various ways?
- What if art education researchers could access and analyze the data that NAEA or other professional organizations have?

Underscoring how vital teacher researchers are in bringing these possibilities into reality, we chose to structure this book around the reasons art teachers might conduct research: to know our practices, to understand people, to make meaning, to make changes in our practices. We encourage teachers to recognize the power that exists in opportunities for conducting inquiry in their own classrooms. Additionally, we hope that research, whether it is at the formal or informal end of the continuum, becomes a meaningful way of life in the classroom. As we envision the ultimate results of this book, we want readers to see their practice as full of possibility and power and to be educators who create change and are not passive in the face of change. Further, we encourage the readers of this book to think through the reasons behind what they do in their practice, the theories they hold, and how they might use inquiry to vary their practice and work from a more powerful position.

REFERENCES

Adler, E. S., & Clark, R. (2008). *How it's done: An invitation to social research.* Belmont, CA: Thompson Wadsworth.

Carpenter, S., Sullivan, G., & Zimmerman, E. (2009). Mentoring graduate research; A Conversation with B. Stephen Carpenter II, Graeme Sullivan, and Enid Zimmerman. *Visual Arts Research, 35*(2), 127-136.

de Leeuw, E. D. (2008). Choosing the method of data collection. In E. D. de Leeuw, J. J. Hox & D. A. Dillman (Eds.), *International handbook of survey methodology* (pp. 113-135). New York, NY: Taylor & Francis.

de Leeuw, E. D., Hox, J. J., & Dillman, D. A. (2008). The cornerstones of survey research. In E. D. de Leeuw, J. J. Hox & D. A. Dillman (Eds.), *International handbook of survey methodology* (pp. 1-17). New York, NY: Taylor & Francis.

Lynn, P. (2008). The problem of nonresponse. In E. D. de Leeuw, J. J. Hox & D. A. Dillman (Eds.), *International handbook of survey methodology* (pp. 35-55). New York, NY: Taylor & Francis.

About the Editors

SARA WILSON MCKAY, PhD, is Chair and Associate Professor of Art Education at Virginia Commonwealth University. She teaches undergraduate and graduate students, including the senior art education practicum course and a study abroad course in Comalapa, Guatemala. She was recently selected as a service-learning Faculty Fellow for the new ASPiRE living and learning community focusing on Youth Engagement and the Arts. Wilson McKay is co-Principal Investigator of an interdisciplinary research team developing VCU Art of Nursing. This novel art-based teaching-learning initiative brings together art education graduate students, beginning nursing students, and clinical faculty in a rich interprofessional relationship addressing ways to enhance clinical reasoning at the bedside through rich art experiences in a museum setting. More generally, her research on the politics of vision explores the ways that works of art create new seeing, how looking can be a dialogic process, and the possibilities of seeing more of the educational process in and through art. In her publications in the leading journals of art education including *Studies in Art Education*, *Art Education*, and *Journal of Social Theory*, Wilson McKay examines how the arts encourage democratic participation toward social action. She lives in Richmond, Virginia, with her partner Steven, two daughters Avery and Ainsley, and their dog Becca.

MELANIE L. BUFFINGTON, PhD, is currently an Associate Professor of Art Education and Graduate Studies Director at Virginia Commonwealth University where she teaches undergraduate and graduate courses. She earned her PhD and MA at The Ohio State University and her BS at The Pennsylvania State University. Previously she taught middle school art in Maryland and has worked with numerous art museums. Buffington recently received a grant to work with a graduate student to develop and evaluate an arts-based service-learning program for youth living in a food desert. Working with several local non-profits, this year-long study will evaluate the program and its effects on the youth participants. Her current research interests include: museum education, technology in art/museum education, social media, multicultural education, contemporary art, and preservice teacher preparation. Buffington has published articles and chapters in several publications in the field. Currently, she is the Associate Editor for the *Journal of Social Theory of Art Education*, serves on the review board for the *Journal of Cultural Research in Art Education*, and has been an invited reviewer for the *International Journal of Education and the Arts*.